AF076727

Corporate Business Principles

Corporate Business Principles

A Guide to the Jamaica Companies Act

Suzanne Ffolkes Goldson

The Caribbean Law Publishing Company
Kingston

First published in Jamaica, 2020 by
The Caribbean Law Publishing Company
An imprint of Ian Randle Publishers
16 Herb McKenley Drive
Box 686
Kingston 6
www.ianrandlepublishers.com

© 2020 Suzanne Ffolkes Goldson

ISBN 978-976-8167-88-0

National Library of Jamaica Cataloguing-In-Publication Data

Names: Ffolkes Goldson, Suzanne, author.
Title: Corporate business principles : a guide to the Jamaica Companies Act / Suzanne Ffolkes Goldson.
Description: Kingston : Caribbean Law Publishing Company, 2020. | Includes index.
Identifiers: ISBN 9789768167880 (pbk) | ISBN 9789769628328 (hbk)
Subjects: LCSH: Corporation law – Jamaica. | Corporate governance – Law and legislation.
Classification: DDC 346.0667292 -- dc 23.

All rights reserved. No part of this publication may be reproduced, stored in a retrieval system or transmitted in any form or by any means electronic, photocopying, recording or otherwise, without the prior permission of the publisher and author.

The Companies Act included is extracted from the revised Laws of Jamaica and is being used with the permission of the Government of Jamaica as copyright owner.

Cover and Book Design by The Caribbean Law Publishing Company
Printed and Bound in the United States of America

CONTENTS

TABLE OF STATUTES	*ix*
TABLE OF CASES	*xix*
FOREWORD	*xxvii*
ACKNOWLEDGEMENTS	*xxxi*
INTRODUCTION	*1*
1. Incorporation	*7*
2. Corporate Finance	*7*
3. Corporate Management	*7*
4. Complainants' Remedies	*8*
5. Winding Up	*8*
1. INCORPORATION	*10*
Corporate Capacity and Powers	*12*
Mode and Requirements	*14*
Articles of Incorporation	*14*
Classification of Corporations	*16*
Reservation of Company Name	*17*
Registration	*17*
Articles of Incorporation	*18*
Companies Limited by Guarantee	*19*
Definition of Member	*19*
Private Companies	*21*
Pre-Incorporation Transactions	*22*
Collective Investment Scheme Companies	*24*
Companies Incorporated Outside of the Island Carrying on Business Within the Island	*25*
2. CORPORATE FINANCE	*27*
Shares and Classes of Shares	*27*
Share Capital and Stated Capital Accounts	*30*
Par Value and No-Par Value Shares	*32*
Consideration for the Issue of Shares	*34*

Prospectus 37
Redeemable Shares 40
Power of Companies to Purchase their Own Shares 41
Pre-emptive Rights 44
Redeemable Preference Shares 45
Miscellaneous Provisions as to Share Capital 45
Reduction of Share Capital 46
Transfer of Shares 47
Debentures 49
Registration of Charges 50
Prohibition of Financial Assistance by Companies 53

3. CORPORATE MANAGEMENT 54
Definition of Directors 54
Definition and Qualifications of Company Secretaries 58
Election, Tenure, Remuneration, and Removal of Directors 59
Duties and Liabilities 60
The Duty to Avoid a Conflict of Interest and Duty 66
Conflict of Interest: Directors' Interests in Contracts and Disclosure 68
Disqualification of Directors 70
Relief from Liability 71
Offences of Officers Antecedent to or in Course of Winding Up 74
General Offences by Officers of Companies in Liquidation 74
Accessories 74
Falsification of Books 75
Fraud by Officers of Companies Which Have Gone into Liquidation 75
Failure to Keep Proper Accounts 75
Fraudulent Trading 75
Damages Against Delinquent Directors 76
Prosecution of Delinquent Officers and Members of the Company 76

4. COMPLAINANTS' REMEDIES 77
The Statutory Derivative Action 78
The Oppression Remedy 81

5. WINDING UP 88
Arrangements and Reconstructions 89
Winding Up and Liquidation 91
Modes of Winding Up 92
Contributories 92

Winding Up By The Court *93*

Default in Delivering the Statutory Report or in Holding the Statutory Meeting *93*

Just and Equitable Winding Up *94*

Application for Winding Up by the Court *95*

Commencement of Winding Up by the Court *96*

Consequences of Winding Up Order *97*

Trustee in Bankruptcy *97*

Trustee *98*

Committees of Inspection *102*

General Powers of the Court in Case of Winding Up by the Court *102*

Voluntary Winding Up *104*

Members' Voluntary Winding Up *106*

Provisions Applicable to every Voluntary Winding Up *107*

Winding Up Subject to the Supervision of the Court *108*

Provisions Applicable to Every Mode of Winding Up *108*

Proof and Ranking of Claims *108*

Effect of Winding Up on Antecedent and Other Transactions *108*

Fraudulent Preference *108*

Onerous Property *109*

Receivers and Managers *110*

General and Definition *110*

Receivers and Managers Appointed Out of Court *111*

Court Appointed Receivers and Managers *112*

Winding Up of Unregistered Companies *112*

BIBLIOGRAPHY *115*

INDEX *117*

THE COMPANIES ACT *119*

AMENDMENTS NO. 40 – 2013 *569*

AMENDMENTS NO. 11 – 2017 *605*

Table of Statutes

Australia

Corporations Act 2001

s 124 12
s 131 24

Barbados

Companies Act 1982 Cap 308

s 4 14
s 5 15
s 5(1)(b) 16, 30
s 16 22
s 17 12
s 20 13
s 30 .... 31, 34
s 31 35
s 34(2)(b) 44
s 39 42
s 40 42
s 41 40
s 58 58
s 61 .... 12, 15
s 89 68
s 89(5) 68, 70
s 90 68
s 91 68
s 95 (1) 60
s 95(2) 64
s 95(3) 64
s 97 71
s 98 71
s 99 .... 71, 73
s 100 74
s 101 73
s 197(1)(d) 45
s 197(1)(f) 45
s 225 79
s 228 81
s 237 50
s 238 52
s 245 52
s 288 37
s 289 37
s 290 37
s 291 37
s 292 37
s 293 37
s 294 37
s 295 37
s 296 37
s 297 37
s 298 37
s 299 37
s 300 37
s 356.1 25
s 356.2 25
s 356.3 25
s 415 17
s 448(o) 40

Canada

Alberta Business Corporations Act Revised Statutes of Alberta 2000

cl 34(3) 43

British Columbia Business Corporations Act 2002 Cap 57

ss 52–54 33

(Canada Business Corporations Act 1975) 1

Canada Business Corporations Act 1985

s 6 15
s 6(1)(c) 16, 30
s 6(2) 15
s 11 17
s 17 13
s 25 34

s 25(3) 31
s 26 35
s 28(2)(b) 44
s 35 43
s 36 40
s 38 47
s 120 68
s 120(5) 69
s 122(1) 60
s 123(4) 63
s 124 71
s 124(2) 74
s 124(5) 73
s 124(6) 74
s 124(7) 73
s 238 79
s 241 81

(Canada Corporations Act 1970) 1

Ontario Business Corporations Act 1990
s 134(1) 66

Jamaica

Arbitration Act 1900 106
Building Societies Act 1897 35
Companies Act 1965 .... 7, 9
s 3 .... 14, 16
s 4(4) 30
s 11 15
s 13 15
s 22 18
s 37(4)(a) 33
s 37(5) 33
s 39 37
s 40 37
s 41 37
s 42 37
s 43 37
s 44 37
s 45 37
s 46 37
s 54 53
s 56 .... 33, 36, 45
s 57 .... 33, 45
s 57(1)(d) 33, 40
s 58 33
s 59 45
s 61(2) 30
s 64 .... 33, 45
s 65(f) 46
s 65A 46
s 66 33
s 67 33
s 68 33
s 69 33
s 70 46
s 84 49
s 85 49
s 86 49
s 87 49
s 88 49
s 89 49
s 90 49
s 91 49
s 92 49
s 99 50
s 187 70
s 191 .... 71, 72
s 196(1)(a) 78
s 201(f) 78
ss 201-203 .... 71, 72
s 223(2) 87
s 372(1) 71
s 372(2) 71

First Schedule, Table A art 11 33

First Schedule, Table A arts 15–21 33

Companies Act 2004
s 2 .... 27, 33
s 3 16
s 4 .... 12, 15
s 4(1) 12
s 4(2) 12

s 4(3) 12
s 4(4) 12
s 5 13
s 6 13
s 7 13
s 8(1) 14
s 8(1)(c) 28, 30
s 8(2)(a) 15
s 8(2)(b) 15
s 8(2)(c) 15
s 8(2)(d) 15
s 8(7) 16, 30
s 8(4) 28
s 8(8) 28
s 19 18
s 20 19
s 23 19
s 24 19
s 25 21
s 27A 24
s 27A (3) 25
s 27A (4) 25
s 29 22
s 34 .... 25, 31, 32
s 34(1) 32
s 35 .... 25, 32
s 37 .... 32, 33
s 37(2) 33
s 37(3) 33
s 37(4)(a) 33
s 37(5) 33
s 38 .... 25, 34, 44
s 38(1) 25, 34
s 38(2) 25, 34
s 38(3) 25, 35
s 38(4) 25, 35
s 38(6) 25, 35
s 38(7) 25, 35
s 38(8) 25, 35
s 39 .... 25, 35
s 39(2) 35, 36, 37
s 39(3) 36
s 39(4) 36
s 39(5) 36
s 39(6) 36
s 39(6)(b) 34
s 39(7) 37
s 40 .... 25, 37, 38
s 41 .... 25, 37
s 42 .... 25, 37, 39
s 43 .... 25, 37, 39
s 44 .... 25, 37, 39
s 45 .... 25, 37, 39
s 46 .... 25, 37, 39
s 47 .... 25, 37
s 56 .... 25, 40
s 56(2) 25, 40
s 56(3) 25, 40
s 56(4) 25, 40
s 56(5) 25, 41
s 57 .... 25, 40, 42, 43
s 57(1) 25, 41, 43
s 57(2) 25, 41
s 58 .... 25, 41, 42, 43
s 58(2) 25, 42
s 58(3) 25, 42
s 58(4) 25, 42
s 58(5) 25, 42
s 59 .... 25, 41, 42, 43
s 59(3) 25, 43
s 59(6) 25, 43
s 60 .... 25, 41, 43
s 61 44
s 62 .... 25, 45
s 63 45
s 64 45
s 65 45
s 65(1) 30
s 65(2) 45
s 66 45
s 67 .... 25, 46
s 68 46
s 69 46
s 70 46
s 71 .... 36, 43, 47
s 71(1) 47

s 71(3) 47
s 71(4) 47
s 71(5) 47
s 71(6) 47
s 71(7) 47
s 72 36
s 72(1) 47
s 72(2) 47
s 72(3) 47
s 73(4) 29
s 74 47
s 78 48
s 79 25
s 84(4) 49
s 84(5) 49
s 84(6) 49
s 86 49
s 93 .... 52, 50
s 93(1) 50
s 93(2)(b) 50
s 93(3) 7, 50
s 95(3) 52
s 97 52
s 98 52
s 99 52
s 102 52
s 112 25
s 113 25
s 120 25
s 161 95
s 165(4) 95
s 172 .... 54, 58
s 172(3) 58
s 173 59
s 174 60
s 174A 67
s 174(1)(a) 66
s 174(1)(b) 66
s 174(2) 63
s 174(3) 63
s 174(4) 64
s 174(5) 64, 66
s 175 59
s 176 59
s 180 .... 70, 71
s 182 .... 70, 71
s 183 58
s 183 (3) 57
s 183 (3A) 57
s 183(8) 57
s 184 53
s 187 70
s 189 68
s 190 68
s 192 68
s 193 68
s 193(2) 68, 69
s 193(6) 69, 70
s 193(8) 68
s 194 58
s 194(4)(a) 57
s 196 70
s 197 58
s 197(5) 57
s 201 71
s 202 71
s 203 71
s 204 74
s 205 73
s 205A 89
s 206 .... 89, 90
s 206(1) 89
s 206(2) 89
s 206(3) 89
s 206(4) 90
s 207 90
s 208 .... 90, 91
s 209 91
s 212 .... 18, 29, 78, 80, 81, 87
s 212(2) 80
s 212(3) 78
s 213 .... 85, 87, 95
s 213A 18, 29, 81, 86, 87
s 213A(3)(1) 87

s 213B..91
s 213(4)..85
s 214..91, 92
s 215..92
s 215(2)..92
s 216..93
s 218..93
s 219..93
s 220..91
s 220(e)..86
s 222(1)(a)..93
s 222(d)..95
s 223(1)..96
s 223(1)(a)..95
s 223(2)..94
s 223(3)..94
s 224..96
s 225..96
s 226..96
s 227..96
s 228..97
s 229..97
s 230..97
s 231..97
s 232(1)..98
s 232(2)..98
s 232(3)..98
s 232(4)..98
s 232(6)..98
s 232(7)..98
s 233..98
s 233(2)..98
s 234..98, 108
s 235..98, 99
s 236..96, 98, 99
s 236(1)(a)..98, 99
s 237..98, 99
s 238..98, 99
s 238(5)..98, 99
s 239..96, 98, 99
s 240..98
s 241..96, 98, 102
s 241(1)..96, 100
s 241(1)(b)..105
s 241(3)..98, 100
s 242(1)..98, 101, 102
s 243..98, 101
s 244..98, 101
s 245..98, 101
s 246..98, 101
s 247..98, 102
s 248..98, 102
s 249..102
s 250..98, 102
s 251..102
s 252..102
s 253..103
s 254..103
s 255..103
s 256..103
s 258..103
s 259..103
s 260..103
s 261..103
s 262..103
s 263..103
s 264..103
s 265..98
s 266..98, 104
s 268..104
s 269..104
s 272..91, 104
s 273..91,105
s 274..105
s 275..105
s 276..105
s 277..104, 106
s 277(2)..105
s 277(3)..106
s 279..106
s 280..106
s 281..106
s 281(3)..106
s 282..104, 106

s 377 25
Part X 25
First Schedule 69
First Schedule Table A 69
First Schedule Table A
art 90 (1) 69
First Schedule Table A
art 90 (2) 69
Third Schedule 38
Twelfth Schedule 21

Companies (Amendment) Act 2013
s 3 14
s 13 17
s 93(3) 50
Sixteenth Schedule 14

Companies (Amendment) Act 2017
s 109 (1) (ab) 20
s 109 (1) (b) 20
s 109 (1) (c) 20
s 109 (1) (d) 20
s 116(5) 21
s 174A 66
s 174A(1) 66
s 174A(2)(a) 66
s 174A(2)(b) 67
s 174A(10) 67
s 174(4) 67
s 174(5) 67
s 213A 6
s 363A 26
s 383A 48
s 383A(3) 48
s 396 48

Companies (Winding Up)
Rules 1949 rule 33 86

Employees Share Ownership
Plan Act 1995 46

Financial Institutions Act 1992 35

Insolvency Act 2014
s 3 .... 6, 88
s 202 97
s 311 .... 91, 93, 95, 97, 98, 99, 103, 107
s 355 91

Registration of Titles
Act 1889 s 59 46

Securities Act 1993
s 67B 19

Securities (Amendment)
Act 2013 s 17A (2) 24

Security Interests in
Personal Property Act 2013
s 48 (6), s 47 51

Stamp Duty Act 1937
s 3, s21 30

Schedule 30

Saint Christopher and Nevis

Companies Act No 22 of 1996
s 4 14
s 18 12
s 19 13
s 21 22
s 25 19
s 29 37
s 30 37
s 31 37
s 32 37
s 33 37
s 34 31
s 55 40
s 56 40
s 57 42
s 74(1) 60

United Kingdom

Companies Act 1948............................8
s 7 17
s 206 89
Companies Act 1985
s 159 40
s 160 41
s 162 42
s 324 70
s 459 86
s 741(2)..55

Companies Act 2006 Cap 46
s 8 15
s 39 60
s 40 60
s 63 46
s 65(2)...46
s 171(b)..62
s 172 64
s 232 74
s 233 74
s 239 61
s 273 58
s 688 41
s 689 45

Company Directors
Disqualification Act 1986..............8, 70

Financial Services
and Markets Act 2000....................... 37

Table of Cases

A

Aberdeen Rly Co v Blaikie Bros (1854) 1 Macq 461 61
AG v Antigua Times [1975] 3 All ER 81, 1975 3 WLR 232 10
American Wollastonite Mining Corp v Scott (2003) 44 BLR (3d) 1, 2003 BCCA 627 34
Arawak Woodworking Establishment Ltd v Jamaica Development Bank (1987) 24 JLR 15 111
Ashbury Railway Carriage and Iron Co Ltd v Riche (1875) LR 7 HL 653 13

B

Balestreri v Robert (1985) 30 BLR 283 72
Banco Ambrosiano Hoblings S.A. et al. v Colvi et al. B5 1987 SC 97 12
Banco Nacional de Cuba v Cosmos Trading Corp [2000] BCC 910 114
Bank of Gibraltar and Malta, Re (1865) 1 Ch App 69 108
Barclays Bank v Clarke BS 1998 SC 126 12
BCE Inc v 1976 Debentureholders 2008 SCC 69 .... 65, 84
Bennett v Bennett Environmental Inc (2009) 53 BLR (4th) 100, 308 DLR (4th) 530 72
Benkley Northover v Eric Northover and Rohan Northover and Godfrey Dixon and Winston G. Northover Associates Limited [2014] JMCC Comm. 14 [46] [56] [69] 44, 62, 85
Birch v Cropper [1889] 14 App Cas 25 Eng. (HL) 28
Bishopsgate Investment Management Ltd. v Maxwell (No. 2) (1993) BCLC 814 61
Blair v Consolidated Enfield Corp [1995] 4 SCR 5, 24 BLR (2d) 161 .... 63, 72
Boffo Family Holdings Ltd v Mountain View Developments Ltd 2010 Carswell BC 990, 2010 BCSC 560 72
Bridgewater Navigation Co, Re [1891] 2 Ch. 317 Eng. (CA) 27
British American Nickel Corporation Limited and Others v M.J. O'Brien Ltd (1927) AC 369 (PC) 90
Browne v La Trinidad (1888) LR 37 Ch D 1 18
Bruneau v Irwin Industries (1978) Ltd 2002 BCSC 757 87
Burnett v Tsang (1985) 29 BLR 196 82

C

Canadian Aero Services Ltd v O'Malley [1973] 40 DLR (3rd) 37 67
Canwest International Inc et al. v Atlantic TV Limited BB 1994 CA 27 .... 79, 82
Caribbean Paper Recycling Company Limited, Re JM 2006 SC 83 .... 79, 81, 86
Catalyst Fund General Partner I Inc v Hollinger Inc (2006) 15 BLR (4th) 171, 266 DLR (4th) 228 72
Chancery Lane Partners Ltd v Dell 1986, BB 1986 CA 12 83
Chesterfield Catering Co Ltd, Re (1977) Ch 373 95

Chin v Chin [2007] UKPC 57 44
Chromex Nickel Mines Ltd v British Columbia (Securities Commission) (1991) 4 BLR (2d) 189 .... 72, 73
City Equitable Fire Insurance Co, Re [1925] 1Ch 407 (CA) 428 .... 62, 63
CJ's Rent A Car Limited v Premium Finance Limited JM 1996 CA 49) 95
A Company, Re [1985] BCLC 33 11
Constitution Insurance Co. of Canada v Kosmopoulos [1987] 1 SCR 2 11
Cotronic (UK) Ltd v Dezonie (t/a Wendaland Builders Ltd) [1991] BCC 200 22
Cox v Roberts BB 2007 HC 8 .... 82, 83
Cullen v Investments Limited and Others v Brown and Others [2017] EWHC 2793 67
Cumana Ltd, Re (1986) BCLC 430 61
Cumbrian Newspaper Group Ltd. v Cumberland and Westmoreland Herald Ltd. [1987] Ch. 1 Eng. Ch. D 27
CVC/Opportunity Equity Partners Ltd v Demarco [2002] UKPC 16, (2002) 60 WIR 70 .... 86, 93, 94
CW Shareholdings Inc v WIC Western International Communications Ltd (1998) 160 DLR (4th) 131, 38 BLR (2d) 196 63

D

Dallas Corp., Thomas Baker v Alnando Corporation et al. CV2011-04466 High Court, Trinidad and Tobago, May 24, 2017 84
Debbian Dewar v Ervin Moo Young et al. [2015] JMCC Comm 23 80
Demerara Holdings Limited v Demerara Life Assurance Company of Trinidad and Tobago Limited HCA No. 3015 OF 2000/CV2006-00099 High Court, Trinidad and Tobago, April 1, 2011 .... 84, 86
Devaux v Du Boulay Holdings Ltd Civ App No 32 of 2003 Court of Appeal, St Lucia, February 28, 2005, LC 2005 CA 3 83
Diligenti v RWMD Operations Kelowna Ltd (1976) 1 BCLR 36 83
Donovan Crawford v FIS SCCA Nos. 64 & 88 of 1999, delivered July 31, 2001(unreported) 10, 61
Dorman Long and Co Ltd, Re [1934] Ch 635 90

E

Ebrahimi v Westbourne Galleries Ltd [1973] AC 360 .... 78, 86, 94
Eclairs Group Ltd. (Appellant) v JKX Oil & Gas plc [2015] UKSC 71 62
Edgington v Fitzmaurice (1885) 29 Ch D 459 39
Edwards v Halliwell [1950] 2 All ER 1064 77
Edwards v Standard Rolling Stock Syndicate [1893] 1 Ch 574 110

F

F De Jong Ltd., Re [1946] Ch. 211 Eng. (CA) 28
Federated Strategic Income Fund v Mechala Group Jamaica Limited JM 2000 CA 49 90
Financial Institution Services Ltd v CNB Holdings Ltd JM 1999 SC 20 61
Financial Services Commission v Dyoll Insurance Company Limited JM 2005 SC 60 99
First Choice Capital Fund Ltd v First Canadian Capital Corp 1997 Carswell Sask 435, [1997] SJ No 390 85

First Edmonton Place Ltd v 315888 Alberta Ltd (1988) 40 BLR 28 79
Five Star Medical and Ambulance Services Limited v Telecommunications Services of Trinidad and Tobago Limited TT 2002 HC 64 .... 79, 81, 82
Foss v Harbottle (1943) 67 ER 189 .... 77, 78, 79, 80
Furry Creek Timber Corp v Laad Ventures Ltd (1992) 75 BCLR (2d) 246 .... .87

G
Gencor ACP ltd v Dalby [2000] 2 BCLC 734 67
German Date Coffee Co, Re (1882) 20 Ch D 169 94
Golden Pheasant Holding Corp v Synergy Corporate Management 2011 BCSC 173 94
Goodfellow v Nelson Line (Liverpool) Ltd [1912] 2 Ch 324 90
Gopal v Burke 2007 BCSC 1930 87
Graham v Edge (1888) LR 20 QBD 683 (CA) 100
Great Eastern Electric Co Ltd, Re [1941] Ch 241 100
Greenhalgh v Arderne Cinemas Ltd. [1946] 1 AER 12 .... .29
Grenada General Insurance Company Limited v Grenada Insurance Services Limited GD 2000 CA 1 .... 79, 84, 85
Guidezone Ltd, Re [2001] BCC 692 86

H
Halcyon Heights Limited, Re BB 1981 HC 6 95
Hamilton v Sartorio [1991] 3 WWR 670 83
Hellenic & General Trust Ltd, Re [1975] 3 All ER 382, [1976] 1 WLR 123 90
Hickman v Romney Marsh Sheepbreeders Assoc. [1915] 1 Ch. 881 Eng. Ch.D 18
HMRC v Holland [2010] 1 WLR 2793 54
Hogg v Cramphorn [1967] Ch. 254 61
House of Fraser, Re plc [1987] BCLC 293 29
Howard Smith v Ampol Petroleum Ltd. [1974] AC 821 PC 61
Howell v Bryan JM 1990 CA 61 95
Hydrodam (Corby) Ltd, Re (1994) 2 BCLC 180 56

I
Island Export Finance Ltd v Umunna [1986] BCLC 460 67
Isle of Thanet Electric Co., Re [1950] Ch. 161 28
The Inertia Partnership LLP, Re [2007] BCC 656 [51] 93
Independent Asset Management Company Ltd. v Swiss Forfaiting Ltd. 2017 ECSC BVI, BVIHCMAPP 206/0034 62
Industrial Development Consultants v Cooley [1972] 2 All ER 162 67
International Hotels (Jamaica) Limited v Proprietors Strata Plan [2013] JMCA Civ 45 11

J
JCA BTA Bank v Ablyazov and others [2014] EWHC 455 11
John Reid and Sons Ltd, Re [1900] 2 QB 634 99
Jon Beauforte (London) Ltd, Re [1953] Ch 131 13
JSC Mezhdunaroniy Promyshlenny Bank [2016] EWHC 248 Ch 11

K

Keech v Sandford (1726) SelCasCh61, (1726) 25 ER 223 61
Kelner v Baxter (1866) LR 2 CP 174 22
Khemlani v Public Supermarket Ltd JM 2008 CA 26 95
Kinsela v Russell Kinsela Pty Ltd (in liquidation) [1986] 4 NSW L Rep 722 .... .65
Knox v Deane BB 2006 HC 17 .... 82, 83
Kosmopoulos v Constitution Insurance Company of Canada (1983) 149 DLR (3d) 77, 22 BLR 111 11
Kuwait Asia Bank v National Mutual Life Nominees Ltd [1991] 1 AC 187, [1990] 3 All ER 404 (PC) 56

L

Lakatamia Shipping Co. Ltd. v Su and others [2014] EWCA Civ 636 11
Lalla v Trinidad Cement Limited TT 1998 HC 172 .... 82, 83
Lo-Line Electric Motors Ltd, Re [1988] Ch 477 71
Loch v John Blackwood Ltd [1924] AC 783 (PC) .... .94
London and Mediterranean Banking Co, Re (1866) 15 WR 33 108
Lopez v Telecommunications Services of Trinidad and Tobago Ltd TT 2004 HC 84 ... 79, 82

M

Manchester and Milford Ry Co Ex parte Cambrian Ry Co, Re (1880) LR 14 Ch D 645 110
Manitoba (Securities Commission) v Crocus Investment Fund (2006) 14 BLR (4th) 229 73
MCAL (Barbados) Ltd. v Banks Holdings Ltd. and SLU Beverages Ltd. Civil Appeal No. 21 of 2015 84
McClurg v Minister of National Revenue [1990] 3 SCR 1020 SCC 28
McMahon v North Kent Ironworks Company [1891] 2 Ch 148 110
Mora Ven Holdings Ltd v Krishna Persad & Associates TT 2005 HC 32 79
Moss Steamship Co Ltd v Whinney [1912] AC 254 (HL) 112
M v H 1993 Carswell Ont 365 (Ct J (Gen Div) 85

N

Naneff v Con-Crete Holdings Limited [1995] 23 OR (3rd) 481 81
Nelson v Rentown Enterprises Inc (1992) 96 DLR (4th) 586, 7 BLR (2d) 319 .... .53
New Zealand Gold Extraction Co (Newbery-Vautin Process) v Peacock [1894] 1 QB 622 (CA) 93
Newborne v Sensolid (Great Britain) Ltd [1953] 1 All ER 708, 1 QB 45 .... .22
Newdigate Colliery Ltd, Re [1912] 1 Ch 468 110
Newhart Developments Ltd v Co-operative Commercial Bank Ltd [1978] 1 QB 814 (CA) 111
Newhart Ltd v Co-op Commercial Bank [1978] QB 814 112
Newman and Howard Ltd, Re (1962) Ch 257 95
Nicholson v Permakraft [1985] 1 NZL Rep 242 (CA), 249 65
Norcan Oils Ltd v Fogler [1965] SCR 36 90

Noren Investments Ltd v Brownie's Franchises Ltd 37 DLR (4th) 1 53
North Wales Gunpowder Company, Re [1892] 2 QB 220.. 99
North-West Transportation v Beatty (1887) LR 12 App Cas 589...................................... 61

O
OJSC Ank Yugraneft v Sibir Energy Plc, Re [2010] BCC 475 114
O'Neil v Phillips [1999] 1 WLR 1092.. 84, 86
Ontario Inc v Harold E Ballard Ltd [1991] 3 BLR (2d) 113... 87
1394918 Ontario Ltd v 1310210 Ontario Inc (2002) 57 O.R. (3d) 607 (CA) .... .23

P
Palmieri v AC Paving Co Ltd (1999) 48 BLR (2d) 130 (BCSC).................................... 94
Pasnak v Chura 2004 BCCA 221 87
Paulson v Dogwood Holdings Ltd [1990] BCJ No 2281 (SC)... 94
Paycheck Services 3 Ltd., Revenue and Customs Commissioners v Holland, Re (2010) UKSC 5 54
PCL Industrial Constructors Inc. v CLR Construction Labour Relations Association of Saskatchewan Inc. (1995) QBG No 1651, 2000 SKCA 15 (CA) 82, 83
Pender v Lushington [1877] 6 Ch. 70 Eng. Ch.D... 18
People's Department Stores Ltd. (1992) Inc, Re [2004] 3 S.C.R. 461; 244 D.L.R. (4th) 564... 63, 65, 66
Peso Silver Mines Ltd v Copper (1966) 58 DLR (2nd) 1 .... .67
Peveril Gold Mines Ltd, Re [1898] 1 Ch 122 (CA) 105
Philip Towers v Premier Waste Management Limited [2011] EWCA Civ 923 [51] 67
Prest v Petrodel [2013] 4 All ER 673 11
Private Trust v Grupo Torras BS 1997 CA 1... 12

Q
Queensland Mines Ltd v Hudson (1978) 52 ALJR 399.. 67
Quin & Axtens Ltd v Salmon [1909] 1 Ch 311 18

R
Rayfield v Hands [1960] Ch.1 Eng. Ch.D... 18
Real Estate Development Co, Re [1991] BCLC 210.. 114
Red Rock Gold Mining Co Ltd, Re (1889)61 LT 785 94
Regal (Hastings) Ltd v Gulliver [1942] 1 All ER 378 (HL) 61
Regent's Canal Ironworks Co Ex parte Grissell, Re (1876) LR 3 Ch D 411 (CA)........... 100
Royal British Bank v Turquand (1856) 6 E&B 327.. ..60
Rubber and Produce Investment Trust, Re [1915] 1 Ch 382 .... .102

S
Salomon v Salomon [1897] AC 22 Eng. HL, 31 .... 10, 14
Sally Ann Fulton v Chas E Ramson Ltd [2006] JMSC Comm 14................................. 80
Schnake v Trincan Oil Ltd TT 2008 HC 222... 79, 86
Scottish Co-operative Wholesale Society Ltd v Meyer [1959] AC 324.............................. 82

Scottish Insurance Corporation v Wilson & Clyde Coal Co [1949] AC 512 Sc (HL) 28
Secretary of State for Trade and Industry v Aviss [2006] EWHC 1846 (Ch), [2007] BCC 288 .... 55, 58
Secretary of State for Trade and Industry v Baker (No 4) (1999) 1 WLR 1985 71
Secretary of State for Trade and Industry v Deverell [2000] BCC 1057 .... 55, 56
Secretary of State v Jones [1999] BCC 336 55
Selangor United Rubber Estates Ltd v Craddock (No 3) [1968] 1 WLR 1555, 2 All ER 1073 53
Sevenoaks Stationers (Retail) Ltd, Re [1991] 3 All ER 578 71
Sharp v Jackson [1899] AC 4 109
Sherwood Designs Services Inc v 872935 Ontario Ltd (1998) 39 OR (3d) 576, 158 DLR (4th) 440, 38 B.L.R. (2d) 157 23
Smith and Fawcett Ltd, Re (1942) Ch. 304 61
Smith v Henniker-Major & Co [2003] Ch 182 60
Smithton Limited v Naggar [2013] EWHC 1961 Ch 54, 56
Soper v The Queen [1997] 149 DLR (4th) 297 63
South Barrule Slate Quarry Co, Re (1869) LR 8 Eq 688 102
St. George v Hayward BS 2008 SC 113 82
Stanton Ltd v Drayton Commercial Investment Co Ltd [1983] 1 AC 501 (HL) 34
Stech v Davies (1987) 53 Alta LR (2d) 373 83
Strait Line Contractors Ltd (Receiver of) v Rainbow Oilfield Maintenance Ltd (1991) 79 Alta LR (2d) 169, (1991) Carswell Alta 47 53
Szecket v Huang (1998) 168 DLR (4th) 402, 42 BLR (2d) 1 23

T

Tavarone Mining Co, Re (1872-3) LR 8 Ch App 956 18
Telecommunications of Jamaica Limited v Hector Bernard JM 1991 CA 64 .... 70, 78
Tilt Cove Copper Co Ltd, Re [1913] 2 Ch 588 110
Trade Board v CRG Lee Corporation [2013] JMSC Civil 158 50
Trevor v Whitworth (1887) 12 App Cas 409 41

U

UDC v Jacitar [2017] JMCA Civ. 1 11
UKLI Ltd. Secretary of State for Business, Innovation and Skills v Chohan and others, Re [2013] EWHC 680 Ch 54
Unisoft Group Ltd (No 3), Re [1994] BCC 766 56
Unisource Canada Inc v Hongkong Bank of Canada (1998) 43 BLR (2d) 226 46
United Provident Assurance Co Ltd, Re [1910] 2 Ch 477 90

V

Victoria Steamboats Co, Re [1897] 1 Ch 158 110
Vivendi SA and another v Richards and another [2013] EWHC 3006 CH 58
Vivian v Firth 2012 BCSC 517 94

W
Walter L Jacob and Co Ltd, Re (1989) 5 BCC 244 (CA) .93
Ward v Rum Refinery of Mount Gay Ltd BB 1990 HC 64 86
Webb v Earle [1875] LR 20 Eq 556 28
Welton v Saffery [1897] AC 299 105
Westcom Radio Group Ltd v MacIsaac (1989) 70 OR (2d) 591, 63 DLR (4th) 433 ..23
Westfair Foods Ltd v Watt (1991) 5 BLR (2d) 160 82
West Mercia Safetywear Ltd (in liquidation) v Dodd (1988) Butterworths Co L Cases 250 (CA) 252-3 65
White v Bristol Aeroplane Co. Ltd (1953) Ch. 65 29
Will v United Lankat Co. Ltd (1914) AC 11 Eng. (HL) 28
Wood v Odessa Waterworks Co (1889) LR 42 Ch D 636 ..18
Wragg, Re [1897] 1 Ch 796 34

Y
Yaiguaje v Chevron Corporation, [2018] ONCA 472 11
Yukong v Rendsburg Investments Corporation (No2) [1998] 1 WLR 294 58

Z
Zysko v Thorarinson (2003) 42 BLR (3d) 75 68

Foreword

The corporate structure has shown great resilience over many years as the preferred vehicle of organisation for doing business, whether large or small. In Britain, in a White Paper on Company Law Reform presented to Parliament in March 2005 (in the run-up to the enactment of the Companies Act 2006), the Department of Trade and Industry emphasised the central importance of an effective framework of company law and corporate governance to a modern economy:

> A genuinely modern and effective framework can promote enterprise, enhance competitiveness and stimulate investment. Conversely, an ineffective or outmoded framework can inhibit productivity and growth and undermine investor confidence.

This statement reflected the growing consensus around the idea that the actual content of company law, which was long regarded, as Professor Paul Davies observed (in Introduction to Company Law, 2nd edn, 2), as 'a vast catalogue of unrelated and tedious rules', has a significance that goes beyond the interests of shareholders, directors and their lawyers. It is in fact a key component in the ongoing struggle throughout the world to promote improved economic performance by countries and their citizens.

Efforts to modernise companies legislation in the Commonwealth Caribbean, though still not yielding results as widespread as may have been hoped for in the heady days following the Caribbean Law Institute's draft uniform bill in 1991, have seen significant forward steps in the last 35 years. Notably, there have been thoroughly revised Companies Acts in Barbados (1985), Trinidad & Tobago (1995), Saint Christopher & Nevis (1996) and Jamaica (2004). In the case of Jamaica, Suzanne Ffolkes Goldson's illuminating exposition, the first of its kind, of the core features of the Companies Act 2004 provides the added benefit of very helpful cross-referencing to statutory provisions and judicial decisions from the other regional jurisdictions. Equally helpfully, this study is set against the backdrop of the 1985 Canada Business Corporations Act, to which, as Ffolkes Goldson explains, the modern regional efforts all owe debts of origin, albeit to varying degrees.

The book's main areas of focus are the mode and consequences of incorporation, corporate finance, corporate management, complainants' remedies, and winding up, both solvent and insolvent. Appreciable departures from longstanding orthodoxies are noted and discussed in depth in relation to the first three of these areas. First, as regards incorporation, there are the formation of one person companies; the simplification of incorporation procedures; the bringing of the rules governing pre-incorporation transactions more closely in line with modern business realities; the farewell to the long outmoded doctrine of *ultra vires*; and the abolition of the doctrine of constructive notice. Next, in the area of corporate finance, there are the introduction of no par value shares; the issue of redeemable shares; the provision for company buy-back of shares; the reduction of share capital; the registration of charges; and the relaxation of the rules relating to the provision of financial assistance by a company for the purchase of its own shares ('the "notorious" section 54'). And then, and hardly least, there are the modernisation and strengthening of corporate governance mechanisms (in particular with regard to the duties and liabilities of directors); the new statutory derivative action and the quietus of the rule in *Foss v Harbottle*; and a remedy for complainants of oppressive or unfairly prejudicial conduct.

Notably, in relation to winding up, Ffolkes Goldson discusses in some detail the provisions of the still relatively new Insolvency Act 2014, which seek to achieve the fair balance which modern company law demands between the rehabilitation and preservation of debtors in appropriate cases and the interests of creditors and others. As Ffolkes Goldson notes, however, the provisions of the Companies Act 2004 continue to govern the winding up of solvent companies.

The most recent legislative development which Ffolkes Goldson discusses is The Companies (Amendment) Act 2017. As she explains, the principal aim of that measure was –

> ... to amend the Companies Act to a) ensure its provisions conform with international obligations in relation of transparency, accountability and good governance and b) to accord with accepted international standards for tax transparency and compliance, the detection of financial crimes and for a governance regime conducive to foreign investment.

The requirement for information in relation to beneficial ownership and ownership information for foreign companies with central management in Jamaica is a clear reminder of the continued tension between traditional company law tenets and the modern impetus towards greater openness in all areas of commercial activity.

Written in a clear and accessible style, *Corporate Business Principles* provides a resource that will be of tremendous benefit to lawyers, both academic and practising, students, company directors and all persons involved in any way in the formation, operation and governance of companies. Looking ahead, I fully expect Suzanne Ffolkes Goldson's complete grasp of all aspects of the subject matter, and her insightful analyses, to inform the renewed impetus to further reform of company law that is bound to come before too long, in Jamaica and elsewhere in the region. It is true that, in times past, the 15 years which have gone by since the Companies Act 2004 came into force would have been regarded as but a brief moment in the leisurely world of company law reform. But I strongly doubt whether the accelerated pace of change in the world around us will provide indefinite support to the luxury of complacency in such an important area of national life.

I have been greatly honoured by Mrs Ffolkes Goldson's invitation to prepare the foreword to what is by any measure an outstanding achievement. For this pathbreaking contribution to the existing literature on the subject of company law in the Commonwealth Caribbean, we are all greatly obliged to her.

C. Dennis Morrison
President, Court of Appeal, Jamaica
May 2019

Acknowledgements

This publication began as a commentary on the Companies Act 2004, which came into effect in January 2005. At the time, the Act was a radical departure from the company law regime we had known for over 40 years, and my intention was to create a guide for the judiciary, legal profession, business community and academia to navigate the changes, especially since I was acquainted with the Canadian model, through my participation on the CARICOM Committee on the Reform of Company Law in the Commonwealth Caraibbean, and then the Joint Select Committee of Parliament in Jamaica. As fate would have it, a number of further amendments were made due to the development of the jurisprudence locally, regionally and internationally, and the demands of external agencies for greater transparency and accountability. As a result, publication was delayed twice, in order to facilitate the re-writing of some of the chapters. Amendments have been made as late as April 1, 2019.

It is against this backdrop that I wish to thank the publishers for their enduring patience, as the weeks have rolled into months and then into years.

I am grateful for the work of my research assistants over the years, many of whom started out as students and are now highly accomplished legal professionals: Kathryn Denbow, Alicia Dixon Stone and Lanasia Nicholas. I also wish to acknowledge Nadelle Clarke, for the invaluable clerical help I received on an early draft and more recently, my niece Abigail Ffolkes.

I would also wish to thank my Writing Action Group (WAG), Tracy Robinson and Janeille Matthews, without whom I would have abandoned the project a long time ago.

I cannot express enough, how grateful I am for my husband, Peter, who has literally stood with me for better and for worse, in sickness and in health; his input was invaluable. To my sons James (Alex), Peter-John and David, you all complete me. It is to you all I dedicate this work.

Foremost I wish to thank God for every good thing, who is indeed a great and merciful Father. I give Him all the praise.

Finally, I hope this guide will be a useful tool, as I have made every effort to be accurate and up to date. I am committed to a new edition, as the law develops, but in the meantime, as former Chairman and CEO of Grace Kennedy, Douglas Orane once advised me, 'don't make it perfect.... make it Tuesday'. So here we are.

Blessings

Suzanne Ffolkes Goldson

Introduction

Company law in the Commonwealth Caribbean was originally adopted from a series of United Kingdom (UK) Companies Acts dating from 1844–1948.[1] The 1864 Jamaica Companies Act was based on the English 1862 Companies Act and the 1965 Jamaica Companies Act was based on the 1948 English Companies Act. This was the natural result of colonialism and, in particular, the control of the economic activities of the colonies before and immediately after independence. The Commonwealth Caribbean started its quest for a new company law regime as far back as the late 1970s at the same time as most of Britain's former colonies.[2] By the early 1970s it was recognized that the UK company law model was out of step with modern approaches to business. Many provisions of the old UK Companies Acts have been variously characterized as 'obsolete', 'anachronistic' and 'trivially arcane'. Canada led the way to reform of Company Law, for a number of Commonwealth countries, with the introduction of the Canada Business Corporations Act (CBCA) in 1975. The precepts which were kept in mind by the authors of the CBCA[3] were those stated by HW Ballantine:[4]

> The primary purpose of corporation laws is not regulatory. They are enabling acts, to authorize businessmen to organize and to operate their business, large or small, with the advantages of the corporate mechanism, they are drawn with a view to facilitate efficient management of business and adjustment to the needs of change. They provide the legal frame and financial structure of the intricate corporate device by which business can be carried out and in which the combined energies and the capital of the managers and of many investors may work together. They deal with the internal affairs of the organization, the content of the articles of incorporation, the rights of the shareholders, the powers and liabilities of directors, the authorized finance, such as the withdrawal of funds by way of dividends, and share purchases, the corporate records, the authorization of organic changes such as amendments, sale of entire assets, merger and consolidation, and dissolution and winding up. Some of these provisions are regulatory, seeking to prevent abuses of management and also the majority and to protect minority shareholders and creditors.

---

1. Andrew Burgess, *Commonwealth Caribbean Company Law* (New York: Routledge 2013), 1–9.
2. Canada introduced the Canada Corporations Act 1970 and later the Canada Business Corporations Act 1975. South Africa introduced its Companies Act in 1973. Other territories introduced companies legislation prior to 1970, including Ghana in 1963 and Singapore in 1967.
3. RWV Dickerson, JL Howard, L Getz, *Proposals for a New Business Corporations Law for Canada* Vol 1, Commentary (Ottawa: Information Canada, Ottawa, 1971) [8] [9].
4. HW Ballantine, *Ballantine on Corporations* (Callaghan and Company 1946) 41–42.

The goal of reform committees in the Commonwealth Caribbean, not least, the Working Party on the Harmonization of Company Law in the Caribbean Community (1979), was to introduce new corporate legislation which would simplify and codify the law. A Bill was introduced by the Working Party in 1979 and the Caribbean Law Institute introduced another Bill in 1991, reflecting the ideals of modernization and harmonization of Commonwealth Caribbean company law. In 1990 the Jamaican government established a committee whose terms of reference was to:

> Review the existing state of company law in Jamaica and to make recommendations as to the changes which are necessary or desirable for the modernization of the law, taking into account the harmonization of Company Law in the Commonwealth Caribbean.[5]

The Committee's objectives were:[6]

1. To provide greater simplification of company formation and operations.
2. To stimulate corporate investment.
3. To achieve a greater measure of corporate democracy and corporate accountability.
4. To provide a vehicle through which employees may secure a stake in the corporate enterprise.
5. To provide greater safeguards for the protection of all interests (shareholders, creditors, employees, consumers and the public at large).

In 1998 Special Select Committees of Parliament and the Senate were appointed to consider and report on a Bill entitled 'An Act to Repeal and Replace the Companies Act'. After several years of debate, the Companies Bill, 2004 was finally passed with the following Memorandum of Objects and Reasons:

a. simplification of company formation by incorporation by a single document and recognition of the 'sole member' company;
b. minimum capitalization of companies having a share capital;
c. shares to be issued without a par value attaching thereto, and in this regard where non-cash consideration is tendered in exchange for shares issued, independent experts should be required to verify that the consideration is at least equal to the value of the shares;
d. the operation of stated capital accounts by companies, stated capital being defined as including—
    i. the total issue price (including non-cash consideration) of all classes of shares;

5. 'Report of the Company Law Reform Committee 1990' (Government of Jamaica, 1990) [1].
6. 'Report of the Company Law Reform Committee 1990' (Government of Jamaica, 1990) [1.12].

   ii. the full value of transfers to capital by the company from profits or revenue reserves, including the total issue price of bonus shares issued upon a capitalization of profits or revenue reserves;
   iii. the full value of transfers to capital from profits or revenue reserves;

e. liquidity/solvency tests to be followed for payment or dividends and the redemption of redeemable shares and the purchase by a company of its own shares;
f. the adoption of pre-incorporation contracts made on a company's behalf by the company after incorporation;
g. the abolition of the ultra vires doctrine and the doctrine of constructive notice of a company's constituent documents and the vesting of the company with the capacity, rights, powers, and privileges of a natural person;
h. empowering directors to take account of the interests of employees and the community as legitimate objects in their own right on the corporate agenda;
i. duties of directors and the standard of care and skill required of directors and in this regard—
   i. a more rigorous standard is prescribed for managing/executive directors;
   ii. the court is empowered to disqualify a director on the ground of unfitness for a maximum limit of 5 years, upon application for such an order is made by the Registrar of Companies, members of a company's board and members and creditors of a company;
j. permitting companies to conclude contracts with their directors if full disclosure of the nature and extent of such contracts is made to the board;
k. prohibiting the making, by public companies of loans or other forms of financial assistance to directors, shareholders or officers of companies or associates of such persons, subject to certain exceptions;
l. providing criminal sanctions for insider trading and prescribing civil remedies in respect of such activity;
m. permitting individual members to bring derivative actions in the company's name with the leave of the court;
n. registration of charges and dealings in securities (excluding charges on land) and in this regard—
   i. the law confirms the established principle that a prior mortgagee/chargee with knowledge of a later charge cannot thereafter up stamp a security to the prejudice of the later chargee;

   ii. the Registrar is empowered to note on the register the fact of out of time lodgments of documents for registration of a mortgage;
   iii. provision is made whereby registration of particulars of a mortgage at the Companies Registry constitutes notice to the world of the existence of the document and its contents;

o. the court is empowered, upon application, to appoint an administrator of a company facing impending insolvency who will assume management of the company so as to ensure, among other things, its survival as a going concern or a more beneficial realization of its assets than would result on a winding up;

p. the court is empowered—
   iv. to disqualify directors of insolvent companies on the ground of wrongful or fraudulent trading or unfitness to act;
   v. to disqualify, for a specific period, company directors from their office or any office of company management, for persistent breaches of companies legislation requiring the submission of returns, notices or other documents to the Registrar;

q. the exemption of certain professionals such as accountants and attorneys-at-law as well as other prescribed groups of professionals, from the restrictions regarding the maximum number of persons in a partnership.

The Bill also made provisions for extensive rules with regard to the preparation of balance sheets and profit and loss accounts and setting out the required formats in relation thereto.

The Bill also expressly provided that redundancy payments owed to company employees on a winding up constitute preferential debts, regardless of whether the payment falls due before or after the appointment of a receiver.

Although much of the modern company law of the Commonwealth Caribbean has been adopted from the later 1985 Canada Business Corporations Act,[7] the Jamaica Companies Act 2004 (Companies Act 2004) has adopted some of the Canadian provisions, retained some of the 1948 UK provisions found in the 1965 Jamaica Companies Act and, in addition, created new provisions. The Companies Act 2004 may, therefore, be seen as a hybrid, and as such, reliance will still be placed on UK cases in addition to Canadian cases, and regional and local cases which will interpret the provisions unique to the Act.

A number of newer provisions have been introduced to the Companies Act 2004, since its enactment, as well as new legislation which has had a significant impact requiring further changes to the Companies Act 2004 in the form of amendments. These include:

7. RSC, 1985, c C- 44.

i. The Companies (Amendment) Act 2013
ii. The Security Interests in Personal Property Act 2013
iii. The Insolvency Act 2014
iv. The Companies (Amendment) Act 2017

i. The Companies (Amendment) Act, 2013:

> … creates a 'one-stop shop' at the Companies Office of Jamaica, which will give registrants of companies and business names the option of making, by means of a single business registration form, applications for registration under relevant laws…this Bill seeks to amend the Companies Act to authorize the use of the business registration form in order to improve the ease with which business enterprises can be registered under the relevant laws to conduct business in Jamaica. Compliance with these requirements is expected to improve the business environment in Jamaica and the competitiveness of Jamaica as a business destination.[8]

The changes relate inter alia to:

a. company incorporation;
b. standardization of the notification of any change of registered office, company secretary and directors to within fourteen days of the change;
c. implementation of the Business Registration form to replace many other forms for several agencies.

ii. The Security Interests in Personal Property Act, 2013 (SIPPA) was introduced:

> …to facilitate the creation of security interests in personal property, to provide for a simple registration process for the recognition of such interests, and to stipulate the rules which will govern the priority in which such interests are enforceable.[9]

Amendments to the Companies Act 2004, due to the introduction of the SIPPA, relate to the registration of charges, including the removal of the distinction between floating and fixed charges and the requirement for registration through the electronic Securities Registry.

8. Companies (Amendment) Act, 2013, Memorandum of Objects and Reasons.
9. The Security Interests in Personal Property Act, 2013, Memorandum of Objects and Reasons.

iii. The Insolvency Act 2014:

> ...seeks to create an environment which aids in (a) the rehabilitation of debtors and the preservation of viable companies, having due regard to the rights of creditors and other stakeholders; and (b) fair allocation of the costs of insolvencies with the overriding interest of strengthening and protecting Jamaica's economic and financial system and the availability and flow of credit within the economy.[10]

The provisions in the Companies Act 2004 which apply to winding up of companies, no longer apply to companies that are insolvent.

iv. The Companies (Amendment) Act 2017:

> The Act seeks to amend the Companies Act to a) ensure its provisions conform with international obligations in relation of transparency, accountability and good governance and b) to accord with accepted international standards for tax transparency and compliance, the detection of financial crimes and for a governance regime conducive to foreign investment.

In particular, the Companies (Amendment) Act 2017, introduces the requirements for information in relation to beneficial ownership, ownership information for foreign companies with central management in Jamaica, the prohibition on the issuance of share warrants and a retention period for records of the company.[11]

The provisions appear to have been fast-tracked to avoid blacklisting by both the Global Forum on Transparency and the Exchange of Information for Tax Purposes (OECD) and the European Union.[12]

Additionally, the Act introduces a duty for directors and officers to avoid a conflict of duty and interest[13] and adds the grounds on which a complainant may bring an action under the 'Oppression Remedy' to include acts done which unfairly disregard the interests of a member of the victim class.[14]

The chapters are divided into the themes reflected in the reform initiatives rather than in order of the sections of the Act.

---

10. The Insolvency Act 2014, s 3.
11. Companies (Amendment) Act 2017, Memorandum of Objects and Reasons, 73.
12. OECD.org and ec.europa.eu.
13. Companies (Amendment) Act 2017, s 174A.
14. Companies (Amendment) Act 2017, s 213A.

1. *Incorporation*

The mechanisms for incorporation are outlined with particular emphasis on the reforms related to the introduction of incorporation by a single document, one-man companies, and pre-incorporation contracts.

The single document required for incorporation is the Articles of Incorporation, however, a number of other documents are required to be registered.

The provisions relating to pre-incorporation contracts appear to settle the anomalies created by the common law as to liability and entitlement to benefits flowing from the agreement. The provisions also relate to both oral and written agreements and recognize adoption of the agreement by a company after incorporation.

2. *Corporate Finance*

The provisions relating to equity finance include, the expansion of classes of shares, rules relating to share capital, the abolition of par value shares, the retention of the rules relating to prospectuses, permitting redeemable shares and a company to purchase its own shares, pre-emptive rights, rules relating to the reduction of capital and the transfer of shares.

Debt financing is addressed by the provisions relating to debentures, which are substantially retained from the repealed Companies Act 1965, and the registration of charges, which settles the common law issues related to the effective date of registration, constructive notice of the charge (although not necessarily its contents), and the effect of registration of a subsequent charge in respect of the same property or undertaking. The Security Interests in Personal Property Act (SIPPA), 2013 amends the Companies Act 2004, by providing inter alia, that only charges over land or interests in land which contain charges over land may be registered at the Companies Office of Jamaica.[15]

3. *Corporate Management*

The Companies Act 2004 reflects the increased duties and responsibilities of directors and officers of the company. The common law fiduciary duty is codified and encapsulates the duty not to make a secret profit, not to have a conflict of interest and to act in the best interest of the company and not for an improper purpose. A conflict of interest, however, may be cured by disclosure in accordance with the provisions of the Act.

While introducing an objective standard to the duty of care, diligence and skill at common law by providing that directors must exercise the care, diligence, and skill that a prudent person would exercise in comparable circumstances, subjectivity is retained by the introduction of a wide due diligence defence.

15. Companies Act 2004, s 93(3).

The concept of the 'shadow director', which was adopted from the UK Companies Act 1985, is introduced, and a 'shadow director', as defined by the Act, appears to be fixed with the same duties and responsibilities as duly appointed directors.

The provisions relating to the disqualification of directors are derived from the UK Company Directors Disqualification Act 1986, and grounds for disqualification include being 'unfit' to be concerned in the management of a company and for persistent breaches of the Act.

Directors and officers may find relief from liability through a variety of defences, and in the broad indemnity provisions and/or through directors and officers liability insurance which the Act permits companies to purchase on behalf of their directors and officers for liability other than for fraud.

4. *Complainants' Remedies*

The Act introduces a category of persons defined as 'complainants' who can sue on behalf of the company for wrongs done to the company (the derivative action), and sue where actions are oppressive, unfairly prejudicial or unfairly disregard the interests of a member of the victim class (the oppression remedy). A derivative action may only be brought where the directors have reasonable notice, the complainant is acting in good faith, and it appears to be in the best interest of the company or its subsidiary.

The provisions reflect the modern stakeholder theory of corporate law, where the interests of a broad group of stakeholders, other than those of shareholders, are protected.

5. *Winding Up*

When the Companies Act 2004 was first introduced, it reflected the 1948 UK provisions on corporate rescue, insolvency and winding up, which were old and ill-suited for modern commerce. Corporate rescue was limited to arrangements and reconstructions, which were expensive and time-consuming, requiring a meeting of creditors, getting the required majority vote and court sanction of the scheme of arrangement. The only alternative for a company in the vicinity of insolvency was receivership, liquidation and winding up, which all contemplate the death of the company.

The introduction of the Insolvency Act 2014 has resulted in the repeal of provisions relating to insolvency and corporate rescue in the Companies Act, and now governs the winding up of insolvent companies.

The Report of the Insolvency Review Committee of the Private Sector Organisation of Jamaica (2012) outlined recommendations for a new insolvency regime in Jamaica to create an environment which, inter alia, 'aids in the rehabilitation of debtors and the preservation of viable companies having due regard to the protection of creditors and other stakeholders'.[16]

Changes in the law under the Insolvency Act 2014, include an increase in the minimum debt for a creditor's petition, the introduction of Proposals to creditors for short term relief from claims with attendant automatic stays of proceedings, the introduction of debtor in possession financing and a change in creditor preference.

This publication is limited to the Companies Act of Jamaica 2004 and the developments in specific areas since the enactment of the law. Attention is therefore placed on the provisions where the jurisprudence is developing as opposed to provisions surviving the repealed Jamaica Companies Act 1965.

16. 'Report on the Reform of Insolvency Law in Jamaica' (Jamaica, April 10, 2012) [2.12].

1. Incorporation

A fundamental principle of company law is that of the separate legal entity doctrine. The doctrine states that on incorporation, a company is a separate (albeit fictitious) legal person, separate from its members. The doctrine was established in the seminal case of *Salomon v Salomon,*[1] which was a case of a de facto one-man company, as Mr Salomon held 20,001 of the 20,007 shares issued, and the remaining 6 shares were held by his wife and five children as nominees for Salomon.[2] Mr Salomon had operated a successful business for over thirty years, and the purchase price was secured by a debenture to him. The company became insolvent less than a year after incorporation, and Mr Salomon wished to enforce his debenture ahead of the unsecured creditors. The liquidator counterclaimed that Salomon was personally liable for the debts of the company, as the incorporation and subsequent debenture was a fraud on the unsecured creditors, and that in effect, the company was his agent or nominee. The House of Lords, in overturning the decision of the Court of Appeal, which had found in favour of the Liquidator, confirmed that the company was a separate legal entity:

> The company is at law a different person altogether from the subscribers...and though it may be that after the incorporation the business is precisely the same as it was before, and the same hands receive the profits, the company is not in law the agent of the subscribers or trustee for them. Nor are the subscribers, as members liable, in any shape or form, except to the extent and in the manner provided by the Act.[3]

The Privy Council confirmed in *AG v Antigua Times,*[4] that a company is a legal person, even for purposes of the constitution where the term 'person' includes a body corporate.

Since the decision in *Salomon*, the case law has been littered with attempts to variously 'lift', 'peek behind' or 'pierce' the 'veil' of incorporation where the corporate form has been used as an instrument of fraud or as a cloak or sham, and to find that the company and the member are one and the same.[5] There have also been instances where the veil has been lifted based on agency, trust, tax, statute, or where the company is part of a group which is a single economic unit. It is arguable, that some of these cases reveal instances where the doctrine simply does not apply, and in others, that

---

1. [1897] AC 22 Eng. HL.
2. The UK Companies Act 1862 required a company to have a minimum of seven members.
3. [1897] AC 22 Eng. HL. 31.
4. [1975] 3 All ER 81, [1975] 3 WLR 232.
5. *Donovan Crawford v FIS* SCCA Nos. 64 & 88 of 1999, delivered July 31, 2001 (unreported).

there has been no consistent principle for ignoring the separate legal entity doctrine. More recently, after much judicial and academic criticism, the courts have displayed a reluctance to ignore the separate legal entity doctrine and will lift the veil only in exceptional circumstances. The Supreme Court of Canada in *Constitution Insurance Co. of Canada v Kosmopoulos*[6] refused to lift the veil of a one-man company in order to avail the sole member of the insurance from damage to the company's property, which was in his name. The Supreme Court of Canada did, however, find that he could benefit from the insurance as he had an insurable interest in the property. The UK Supreme Court case of *Prest v Petrodel,*[7] without overruling the many cases that had lifted the veil, confirmed the doctrine as espoused in *Salomon* and refused to lift the veil where there was no evidence that incorporation of the companies was for a fraudulent purpose.

> ...The corporate veil may be pierced only to prevent the abuse of corporate legal personality. It may be an abuse of the separate legal personality of a company to use it to evade the law or to frustrate its enforcement. It is not an abuse to cause a legal liability to be incurred by the company in the first place. It is not an abuse to rely upon the fact (if it is a fact) that a liability is not the controller's because it is the company's. On the contrary, that is what incorporation is all about.[8]

The Jamaican Court of Appeal embraced *Prest* in *International Hotels (Jamaica) Limited v Proprietors Strata Plan No 461*[9] where it was held that a subsidiary could, and did, acquire an interest against its parent company by adverse possession. In *UDC v Jacitar,*[10] the Court of Appeal arrived at a similar conclusion regarding parent and subsidiary companies, where the parent company, UDC was sued by Jacitar, to whom it had leased commercial premises and provided 24 hour security as part of the lease agreement for damages and/or negligence when the premises was burgled. However, Urban Maintenance Ltd, a subsidiary of UDC, was the company which contracted with the security company. It was therefore held, that having regard to the principle of separate legal entity, the security guards were contracted to Urban Maintenance Ltd and not UDC. Although the court did not cite *Prest* or *International Hotels*, the *Salomon* principle was confirmed.

Since *Prest,* however, there appears to be a retreat from *Salomon/Prest* whereby Courts in the UK[11] have lifted the veil on grounds reminiscent of the words of Cumming-Bruce LJ in *Re A Company* where he stated, 'the court will use its powers

6. [1987] 1 SCR 2.
7. [2013] 4 All ER 673.
8. [2013] UKSC 34 [34]. See also *Yaiguaje v Chevron Corporation* [2018] ONCA 472 where the Ontario Court of Appeal affirmed *Prest v Petrodel.*
9. [2008] SCCA 135, delivered December 4, 2013 (unreported).
10. [2017] JMCA Civ. 1, delivered January 27, 2017 (unreported).
11. *JCA BTA Bank v Ablyazov and others* [2014] EWHC 455; *Lakatamia Shipping Co. Ltd. v Su and others* [2014] EWCA Civ 636; *JSC Mezhdunaroniy Promyshlenny Bank* [2016] EWHC 248 Ch.

to pierce the corporate veil if it is necessary to achieve justice irrespective of the legal efficacy of the corporate structure under consideration.'[12] It has been argued that these cases focus on 'practical realities'. It remains to be seen whether Jamaica will follow suit.

Corporate Capacity and Powers

Section 4(1) states that a company has the capacity and, subject to the Act, rights, powers and privileges of an individual. Section 4(2) gives a company the capacity to carry on its business, conduct its affairs and exercise its powers in any jurisdiction outside Jamaica subject to the laws of Jamaica and of that jurisdiction.[13] The United Kingdom Companies Act 2006 frames the provision differently by providing that 'the validity of an act done by a company shall not be called into question on the ground of lack of capacity by reason of anything in the company's constitution'. This has the same effect as the provisions in the Companies Acts of Barbados, Trinidad and Tobago and Canada.[14]

Section 4(3) states that there is no need for a by-law to be passed to confer any particular power on a company or its directors. Section 4(4) makes it clear that the section does not authorize any company to carry on any business or activity in breach of any enactment prohibiting or restricting the carrying on of the business or activity or any provision requiring any permission or license for the carrying on of the business activity.

The effect of section 4 is to change the previous law in order to allow a company to do anything which it chooses to do, once it is permitted by the laws of the land, or in accordance with the laws of the land.

Section 4(3) removes the requirement under the repealed law for conferring powers on the company or its directors under the Articles of Association. Curiously, there is no reference to by-laws anywhere else in the Act, although by-laws are a feature of the Canadian and reformed Commonwealth Caribbean Companies legislation.[15]

There is also no definition of 'by-law' in section 2.[16] This suggests that the legislators did not intend to include by-laws in the registration of companies. Although by-laws are desirable, it remains to be seen whether the Act will be amended to include by-laws. In the meantime, section 4(3) is inapplicable.

---

12. [1985] BCLC 33. See also Bahamian cases: *Banco Ambrosiano Hoblings S.A. et al. v Colvi et al.* B5 1987 SC 97; *Private Trust v Grupo Torras* BS 1997 CA 1; *Barclays Bank v Clarke* BS 1998 SC 126.
13. See also Barbados Companies Act 1982, s 17; Trinidad and Tobago Companies Act 1995, s 21; cf St. Christopher and Nevis Companies Act 1996, s 18.
14. cf Australia Corporations Act 2001, s 124.
15. See Trinidad and Tobago Companies Act 1995, ss 4 and 66.
16. cf Barbados Companies Act 1982, s 61; Trinidad and Tobago Companies Act Companies Act 1995, s 66, schs 2 and 3.

Section 5 states that a company shall not carry on any business or exercise any power that is restricted by its Articles from carrying on or exercising, nor shall a company exercise any of its powers in a manner contrary to its Articles.

This then means that a company may opt to restrict its business or powers by so stipulating in the Articles. Without such stipulation, a company may do whatever it wishes in accordance with the laws of the land.

Section 6 goes further to abolish the ultra vires doctrine by stating that, 'for the avoidance of doubt', an act of a company that is contrary to its Articles shall not be invalid by reason only that the act is contrary to its Articles. The ultra vires doctrine states that where a company is a party to a contract which goes outside of its objects as stated in its Memorandum of Association, the contract is void. There are further complications that relate to the difference between actions ultra vires the company and actions ultra vires the powers of the directors. As a result of this doctrine, coupled with the 'constructive notice' doctrine, a third party could suffer if the contract was rendered void. In effect, the doctrine 'punished' unsuspecting parties instead of the company. Efforts were made therefore to evade or circumvent the doctrine by drafting wide and varied objects.[17] The doctrine has been abolished in other Commonwealth Caribbean territories.

Section 6, however, begs the question as to what would be the result of an act of a company that is contrary to its Articles, if not to invalidate the act of the company. It is arguable that a derivative action may be brought against the directors for a breach of fiduciary duty or duty of care, diligence, and skill.

Section 7 effectively abolishes the 'constructive notice' doctrine by stating that no person shall be affected by, or presumed to have notice or knowledge of, the contents of a document concerning a company by reason only that the document has been filed with the Registrar or is available for inspection at any office of the company.[18] The constructive notice doctrine had added insult to the injury of the ultra vires doctrine, by stating that all persons are deemed to have notice or knowledge of the contents of the documents relating to a company by reason only that the document has been filed with the Registrar of Companies.[19]

The current provision is derived from the Canadian legislation. Interestingly, the Dickerson Report, from which the Canadian legislation was developed, suggests that this section leaves it open to the court, in an appropriate case, to apply the doctrine of constructive notice if there is good reason for so doing.[20] The doctrine may not, therefore, be extinct, but rather may have been relegated to an exception rather than a rule.

17. See *Ashbury Railway Carriage and Iron Co Ltd v Riche* (1875) LR 7 HL 653.
18. See also Barbados Companies Act 1982, s 20; CBCA 1985, s 17, Trinidad and Tobago Companies Act 1995, s 24; cf St. Christopher and Nevis Companies Act 1996, s 19.
19. *Jon Beauforte (London) Ltd, Re* [1953] Ch. 131.
20. RWV Dickerson, JL Howard and L Getz, *Proposals for a New Business Corporations Law for Canada* (Vol. 1, Commentary, Information Canada 1971) [84].

Mode and Requirements

Section 3 provides that one or more persons may form a company by signing and sending Articles of Incorporation to the Registrar and an application in the form set out in the Sixteenth Schedule and otherwise complying with the requirements of the Act in respect of registration.[21]

The Companies (Amendment) Act 2013 amended the former section 3 to introduce a Business Registration Form in the Sixteenth Schedule to facilitate a 'one stop shop' at the Companies Office for the registration of companies and business names for various purposes, such as the Tax Administration of Jamaica, Ministry of Labour and Social Security, National Housing Trust, and the Human Employment and Resource Training Trust/National Training Agency, required by law.[22]

There are three significant features of this provision:

i. A company may be incorporated with only one person. The one-man company is a feature of all the reformed territories in the Commonwealth Caribbean.[23] In Canada, the introduction of the one-man company initially raised concern about the impact on the separate legal entity doctrine and the opening of the possibility of lifting the corporate veil more readily for such companies. The debate, however, met its quietus in the Supreme Court of Canada, where it was decided that the separate legal entity doctrine remains sacrosanct even in the light of one-man companies.[24] Indeed, the seminal case of *Salomon v Salomon*, oft-cited as the locus classicus confirming the separate legal entity doctrine, involved a de facto one-man company.

ii. A company may incorporate with a single document named the Articles of Incorporation (along with an application in the prescribed form), as opposed to the two previously required documents: the Memorandum of Association and the Articles of Association.

iii. The provision also applies to companies limited by guarantee and companies with unlimited liability which were required to have at least seven subscribing members under the old regime.[25]

Articles of Incorporation

Although the company may include provisions with respect to other matters, Articles of Incorporation ('Articles') as prescribed under section 8(1) shall set out the following:

---

21. Companies (Amendment) Act 2013.
22. Memorandum of Objects and Reasons, Companies (Amendment) Act 2013.
23. Barbados Companies Act Cap 308, s 4; Trinidad and Tobago Companies Act Cap 81:01, s 8; cf St. Christopher and Nevis Companies Act No 22 of 1996, s 4.
24. *Kosmopoulos v Constitution Insurance Company of Canada* (1983) 149 DLR (3d) 77, 22 BLR 111.
25. Jamaica Companies Act 1965, s 3.

i. the name of the company with 'limited' as the last word of the name of the company where the company is limited by shares or by guarantee;

ii. that the registered office is to be situated in Jamaica;

iii. the classes of shares, if any, in the case of a company having a share capital, and the maximum number of shares, if any, that the company is authorized to issue;

iv. whether the transfer of shares in the company is to be restricted, the restriction and the nature of that restriction;

v. the number of directors, or the maximum or minimum number of directors;

vi. restrictions on the business, if any, that the company may carry on;

vii. a statement, in the case of companies limited by shares or guarantee, that the liability of its members is limited.

These requirements differ from those found in the repealed Jamaica Companies Act 1965 in that they are more extensive, and include some of the provisions formerly required to be inserted in the Articles of Association. The repealed Jamaica Companies Act did not require that the Memorandum include provisions set out at (iii), (iv) and (v) above.[26]

The requirement in section 8(2)(a) that the Articles be printed, typewritten or be in some legible form or other form acceptable to the Registrar is found in the repealed Jamaica Companies Act only in respect of the Articles of Association and was not expressly required for the Memorandum of Association.[27] The section, therefore, does not expressly contemplate electronic filing, although this may be captured under 'other form acceptable to the Registrar'. Other Commonwealth territories have simply stated that the Articles be in a 'prescribed form'[28] or 'the form that the Director fixes'.[29] Section 8(2)(b) states that the Articles shall be divided into paragraphs numbered consecutively and section 8(2)(c) provides that Articles shall bear the same stamp duty as if they were contained in a deed.[30] Section 8(2)(d) provides that the Articles be signed by each subscriber of the Articles in the presence of at least one witness who must attest the signature.

The Act does not provide for by-laws, although referred to in section 4. It appears, therefore, that the internal regulation of the company is governed by the Articles of Incorporation. By-laws are a feature of the 'reformed territories'[31] and should be contemplated for Jamaica, even if in the form of model rules.

---

26. Jamaica Companies Act 1965, s 13 and First Schedule.
27. Jamaica Companies Act 1965, s 11.
28. See United Kingdom Companies Act 2006, s 8; Barbados Companies Act 1982, s 5; Trinidad and Tobago Companies Act 1995, s 9.
29. Canada Business Corporations Act 1985 (CBCA 1985), s 6.
30. Stamp Duty Act 1937, s 3 and Schedule.
31. Barbados Companies Act 1982, ss 5, 61; CBCA 1985, s 6(2); Trinidad and Tobago Companies Act 1995, ss 9, 66.

An additional requirement of the Act under section 8 (7) is that companies having a share capital shall, where applicable, file a document with the Registrar setting out:

i. the rights, privileges, restrictions, and conditions attaching to each class of shares where two or more classes of shares are issued;

ii. the authority given to the directors to fix the number of shares in, and to determine the designation of, and the rights, privileges, restrictions, and conditions attaching to the shares of each series where the class of shares may be issued in a series.[32]

This section should be contrasted with provisions found in the 'reformed territories' which provide that, where a company has only one class of shares, the rights of the holders are equal in all respects and include:

a. the right to vote at any meetings of shareholders;

b. the right to receive any dividend declared by the company;

c. the right to receive the remaining property of the company on dissolution.

The requirements where the Articles of a company provide for more than one class of shares are that:

a. the rights, privileges, restrictions, and conditions attaching to the shares of each class must be set out in the Articles; and

b. the rights set out for companies which have only one class of shares, must be attached to at least one class of shares, but all of those rights need not be attached to the same class of shares.[33]

Classification of Corporations

The three types of companies identified in section 3 of the Companies Act 2004 are identical to those provided for in section 3 of the repealed Jamaica Companies Act 1965. These are companies limited by shares, companies limited by guarantee and unlimited companies.

Companies limited by shares are companies which have the liability of its members limited by the Articles to the amount if any, unpaid on the shares respectively held by them.

Companies limited by guarantee have the liability of its members limited by the Articles to such amount as the members may respectively thereby undertake to contribute to the assets of the company in the event of its being wound up, whether or not such a company has a share capital.

An unlimited company is a company not having any limit on the liability of its members.

---

32. See chapter 2 on Corporate Finance.
33. See also Barbados Companies Act 1982, s 5(1)(b); CBCA 1985, s 6(1)(c); Trinidad and Tobago Companies Act 1995, s 9(1)(c).

Section 9 of the Act, however, states the following regulations for unlimited companies and companies limited by guarantee:

i. unlimited companies and companies limited by guarantee must state the number of members and the amount of share capital, if any, with which the company proposes to be registered;

ii. unlimited companies and companies limited by guarantee shall give the Registrar notice of any increase in the number of members beyond the registered number, within fifteen days after the increase was resolved or took place;

iii. the company and every officer of the company who is in default of compliance with (ii) shall be liable to a fine not exceeding fifty thousand dollars.

This provision is derived from section 9 of the repealed Jamaica Companies Act 1965 and does not appear to have an equivalent in Canada or in the reformed territories of the Commonwealth Caribbean. It has its genesis from section 7 of the United Kingdom Companies Act 1948. Its purpose is to provide a basis for payment of fees on registration for these types of companies.[34]

Section 10 allows a company, by special resolution, to alter or add to its Articles. It is assumed that the altered Articles are to be filed with the Registrar, although this is not specified by the section.

Reservation of Company Name

Another feature of the Act is found in section 18,[35] which enables the Registrar to reserve a name for an intended company or for a company about to change its name for ninety (90) days.

A request must be made to the Registrar along with the prescribed fee. The Registrar retains a discretion as to whether or not to reserve a name.

Registration

Section 13 of the Companies (Amendment) Act 2013, repeals and replaces section 13 of the principal Act and states that a certificate of incorporation given by the Registrar in respect of any company shall be conclusive evidence that all the requirements of the Act in respect of registration and of matters precedent and incidental thereto have been complied with, and that the company is authorized to be registered and has been duly registered under the Act. There is therefore no longer a requirement of a statutory declaration, which may have been accepted as evidence of compliance.

---

34. S Magnus and M Estrin, *Companies Law and Practice* 4th edn. (London: Butterworths, 1968), 21.
35. CBCA 1985, s 11; Barbados Companies Act 1982, s 415; Trinidad and Tobago Companies Act 1995, s 492.

Section 14 states that a company registered as unlimited may register as limited, or a company already registered as limited, may re-register. This section should, however, be amended to set out clearly the process for re-registration of a company, which will include the re-registration of a company limited by shares as a company limited by guarantee and vice versa.

Articles of Incorporation

Section 19 is identical to the section 22 contractarian model found in the repealed Companies Act 1965. The section provides that, subject to the provision of the Act, the Articles shall, when registered, bind the company and the members thereof to the same extent as if they respectively had been signed and sealed by each member and contained covenants on the part of each member to observe all the provisions of the Articles. The section in the repealed Act referred to the Articles of Association, however, under the current Act, it can only be interpreted as referring to the Articles of Incorporation.

The Articles of Association as described in section 22 of the repealed Act, was interpreted, according to UK case law, as creating a contract between the members and the company, the company and the members and the members inter se.[36] Much of the case law, therefore, involved the enforcement of this contract.[37]

The contractarian model, however, has not survived modern Commonwealth corporate statutes, which are based on a regulatory model. It appears, therefore, that there may be some disharmony with other sections of the Companies Act which have included the regulatory model such as the section 212 derivative action and the section 213A oppression remedy which entitle claimants, which include shareholders and some outsiders, to make a claim for various remedies under the Act. The question now arises, as to whether the cases, which informed enforcement of the contract between the company and the members, the members and the company and the members inter se should apply. The better view seems to be that the availability of remedies under the Companies Act 2004 renders any discussions on the section 19 contract otiose.[38] It remains to be seen whether section 19 will need to be repealed.[39]

---

36. See *Wood v Odessa Waterworks Co* (1889) Ch. D 636; *Quin & Axtens Ltd v Salmon* [1909] 1 Ch. 311.
37. *Rayfield v Hands* [1960] Ch.1 Eng. Ch.D.; *Hickman v Romney Marsh Sheepbreeders Assoc.* [1915] 1 Ch. 881 Eng. Ch.D.; *Pender v Lushington* (1877) 6 Ch. 70 Eng. Ch.D.
38. Andrew Burgess, *Commonwealth Caribbean Company Law*, (London: Routledge, Taylor and Francis, 2013), 63.
39. See *Browne v La Trinidad* (1887) 37 Ch. D 1; *Tavarone Mining Co, Re* (1873) LR 8 Ch. App 956.

Companies Limited by Guarantee

Section 20 outlines the requirements for Articles of companies limited by guarantee and not having a share capital and prohibits such companies from giving any person a right to participate in the divisible profits of the company otherwise than as a member. It further provides that every provision in the Articles or any resolution of a company limited by guarantee which purports to divide the undertaking of the company into shares or interests shall be treated as a provision for a share capital, notwithstanding that the number of shares or interests is not specified thereby.

Definition of Member

Section 23[40] of the Act defines 'member' as:

a. persons who subscribe to the company's Articles whose names shall, on the registration of the company, be entered in the company's register;

b. the personal representatives of a deceased member and the trustee in bankruptcy of a bankrupt member;

c. persons named as principal account holder or subsidiary account holder, as the case may be, during any period in respect of which eligible securities carrying voting rights are entered against their names in the register of the licensed central securities depository for that company's shares;

d. any other person who agrees to become a member of a company and whose name is entered in its register of members.

The following definitions apply to subsection (1)(c):

'Licensed central security depository' is defined as a company licensed under section 67B of the Securities Act to operate a central securities depository;

'Principal account holder' is a person who maintains an account with a licensed depository holder;

'Subsidiary account holder' is a person in whose name a subsidiary account is opened and maintained by the principal account holder.

This section recognizes the rights of shareholders who hold their shares in listed companies through the Jamaica Central Securities Depository, but requires that the company have the account holder entered on its register and does not include non-voting shares. These requirements are not found in the Securities Act 1993.

Section 24 provides that a body corporate cannot be a member of a company which is its holding company. Any allotment or transfer of shares in a company to its subsidiary shall be void. The section however does not apply where the subsidiary is concerned as personal representative, or where it is concerned as trustee unless the

40. Cf. St. Christopher and Nevis Companies Act 1996, s 25.

holding company or a subsidiary thereof, is beneficially interested under the trust, and is not so interested only by way of security for the purposes of a transaction entered into by it in the ordinary course of a business, which includes the lending of money.

Section 109 of the Companies Act 2004 has been amended by the Companies (Amendment) Act 2017 to facilitate greater transparency in the Register of Members. Section 109 now provides that the company shall keep in one or more documents a register of its members and enter therein:

a. the names, nationalities, addresses, and occupations of

   i. the members; and

   ii. the beneficial owners

(aa) in the case of a company having a share capital, a statement of the shares held by each member and the beneficial owner of the shares, if any, distinguishing each share by its number, and the amount paid or agreed to be considered as paid on the shares of each member.

In respect of beneficial ownership, the entry relating to the relevant member shall include an entry specifying that the ownership of the member is on behalf of a beneficial owner, the name of the beneficial owner, and such cross-reference, index or information as is necessary for convenient inspection of the particulars of the beneficial owner.[41]

The company shall also enter the date at which each person was entered in the register as a member or as a beneficial owner if applicable, the date at which any person ceased to be a member or beneficial owner if applicable, provided that where the shares have been converted into stock and notice is given accordingly, the register shall show the amount of stock held by each member and each beneficial owner, if any.[42]

Section 116 of the Companies Act 2004 has been deleted and replaced by a requirement that where a company has notice of any trust affecting the membership of the company, the company shall enter the particulars of the beneficial owner in the register.

Members holding property in or of a company on behalf of or at the direction of another individual shall notify the company of the name and particulars of the beneficial owner of the property for inclusion in the register and subsequent change in relation to the legal or beneficial ownership of the property within the prescribed period. The beneficial owner shall submit in writing, the particulars required under the Act, to the member for notification to the company or directly to the company.

The company shall, at least once per year, request its members in writing to advise whether they hold property in the company on behalf of a beneficial owner and supply the particulars of any beneficial owner for inclusion in the register under section 109,

41. Companies (Amendment) Act 2017 s 109(1) (ab).
42. Ibid., s 109(1)(b), (c), (d).

whether notified or not, of beneficial ownership or of any change in the particulars of any such beneficial ownership.[43]

Private Companies

Section 25 provides that a private company is a company which by its Articles:

i. restricts the right to transfer its shares; and

ii. limits the number of its members to twenty, not including persons who are in the employment of the company and persons who, having formerly in the employment of the company, were, while in that employment, and have continued after the determination of that employment to be, members of the company; and

iii. prohibits any invitation to the public to subscribe for any shares or debentures of the company; and

iv. prohibits any invitation to the public to deposit money for fixed periods or payable on call whether bearing or not bearing interest; and

v. subject to the exceptions provided for in the Twelfth Schedule, prohibits any person other than the holder from having any interest in any of the company's shares.

Joint holders of shares are treated as a single member for the purposes of the Act and private companies are not obliged to file accounts except where any of its shares are held by a body corporate.

A key feature of private companies is the restriction on the right to transfer its shares, which may be effected through the inclusion of pre-emptive rights in the Articles. Section 61 of the Companies Act provides:

1. If the Articles so provide, no shares or class of shares may be issued unless the shares have first been offered to the shareholders of the company holding shares of that class.
2. The shareholders...have a pre-emptive right to acquire the offered shares in proportion to their holding at such price and on such terms as those shares are to be offered to others.
3. No pre-emptive right exists where they are to be issued for consideration other than cash or pursuant to an exercise of conversion rights privileges, options or rights previously granted by the company.

In addition to compliance with the definition of 'private company', restrictions may be used to prevent intrusion of undesirable business associates; to preserve the relative interests of the owners; to resolve deadlock (or as a control device); to ensure continuity of the business and/or to provide a market at an acceptable price for shares.

---

43. Ibid., s 116(5).

Pre-Incorporation Transactions

The old common law rule states that any person who purports to contract on behalf of an unincorporated company is bound by the contract and that a company cannot ratify or adopt the contract when it comes into existence.[44] Further, where a person, purports to enter into a contract in the name of an unincorporated company, there is no contract with the person who purported to enter into the contract or with the company when it comes into existence.[45]

Section 29 remedies the anomaly created by the common law in respect of pre-incorporation contracts by stating that:

i. a person who enters into an oral or written agreement or contract in the name of or on behalf of a company before it comes into existence or who purports to enter into such an agreement or contract is personally bound by the agreement or entitled to the benefits of the agreement or contract;

ii. a company may, by any action or conduct signifying its intention to be bound thereby, adopt an oral or written agreement to contract referred to in (i);

iii. when a company adopts the agreement or contract referred to in (i), the person referred to in (i) ceases to be bound or entitled to the benefits of the contract and the company is bound or entitled to the benefits of the contract as if the company had been in existence at the date of the contract and had been a party to it;

iv. whether or not an agreement or contract referred to in (i) is adopted by the company, a party to the agreement or contract may apply to the court for an order fixing obligations under the contract as joint or joint and several or apportioning liability between or among the company and a person who purported to act in the name of the company or on its behalf. The court may make any order it thinks fit.

v. an express exemption clause in the agreement or contract referred to in (i) will exempt a person from being bound by or entitled to the benefits of the agreement or contract.

The Jamaican legislature has gone beyond its Commonwealth Caribbean counterparts Barbados and Trinidad and Tobago[46] by extending the provision to 'oral' contracts and by clearly including 'agreements' as well as 'contracts'. However, it stops short of 'transactions', (as is the case in St. Christopher and Nevis,[47] even though it

44. See *Kelner v Baxter* (1866) LR 2 CP 174.
45. See *Newborne v Sensolid (Great Britain) Ltd* [1954] 1 QB 45; *Cotronic (UK) Ltd v Dezonie (t/a Wendaland Builders Ltd)* [1991] BCLC 721.
46. Barbados Companies Act 1982, s 16; Trinidad and Tobago Companies Act Cap 1995, s 20.
47. St. Christopher and Nevis Companies Act 1996, s 21.

does not specify written or oral and does not include the equivalent of (iii), (iv) and (v) of the Jamaica Companies Act 2004), although 'transactions' are arguably included in the word 'agreements'.

The reformed position found in Canadian legislation did away with the semantic quibble at common law and the unsatisfactory results pertaining thereto. However, this has not been free from difficulty.[48]

The problems that have arisen, or are still being debated so far include:

1. Whether the agreements are 'contracts' at all and if not, whether the statutory provision would therefore apply.[49] The unfortunate decision of *Westcom Radio Group Ltd v MacIsaac* has been discredited and arguably effectively overruled by *Szecket v Huang*.[50] The position now appears to be, that the word 'contract' in the Canadian provision is used in a colloquial sense and therefore the statutory provision relates to pre-incorporation agreements or transactions.

2. What amounts to adoption. In *Sherwood Designs Services Inc. v 872935 Ontario Ltd*[51] the Ontario Court of Appeal decided that an attorney's letter to the plaintiffs which informed them that a shelf corporation number had been assigned to the other party to the pre-incorporation contract was sufficient to amount to adoption by an unsuspecting company which was later assigned that shelf corporation number. This is an alarming decision if sustained and therefore attorneys should be careful when using shelf companies for the purpose of pre-incorporation contracts.

3. When it is a reasonable time for adoption. In *1394918 Ontario, Ltd v 1310210 Ontario Inc.*[52] the Ontario Court of Appeal explained that the

48. See *Westcom Radio Group Ltd v MacIsaac* (1989) 70 OR (2d) 591, 63 DLR (4th) 433; *Sherwood Design Services Inc. v 872935 Ontario Ltd* (1998) 39 OR (3d) 576, 158 DLR (4th) 440; *Szecket v Huang* (1998) 168 DLR (4th) 402, 42 BLR (2d) 1; MA Maloney, 'Pre-Incorporation Transactions: A Statutory Solution?' (1985) *Canadian Business Law Journal* 10: 409; AJ Easson, and DA Soberman, 'Pre-Incorporation Contracts: Common Law Confusion and Statutory Complexity' (1992) *Queens Law Journal* 17: 414; JS Ziegel, 'Promoter's Liability and Pre-incorporation Contracts: *Westcom Radio Group Ltd v MacIsaac*' (1990) *Canadian Business Law Journal* 16: 341; WM Estey, 'Pre-Incorporation Contracts: The Fog is Finally Lifting' (2000) *Canadian Business Law Journal* 33: 3; B Welling, *Corporate Law in Canada: The Governing Principles* (2nd edn, Oxford: Butterworths, 1991), 285–96·
49. See JS Ziegel, 'Promoter's Liability and Pre-incorporation Contracts: *Westcom Radio Group Ltd v MacIsaac*' (1990) *Canadian Business Law Journal* 16: 341; WM. Estey, WM. 'Pre-Incorporation Contracts: The Fog is Finally Lifting' (2000) *Canadian Business Law Journal* 33: 3.
50. *Szecket v Huang* (1998) 168 DLR (4th) 402, 42 BLR (2d) 1. See also *Westcom Radio Group Ltd v MacIsaac* (1989) 70 OR (2d) 591, 63 DLR (4th) 433.
51. *Sherwood Design Services Inc. v 872935 Ontario Ltd* (1998) 39 OR (3d) 576, 158 DLR (4th) 440.
52. 2002 Carswell Ont 8, 154 OAC 137, 47 RPR (3d) 10.

legislation requires adoption by the company 'within a reasonable time after it comes into existence' rather than a reasonable time after execution of the agreement. It is difficult to see a rationale for this provision but protection can presumably be provided by a suitably worded condition in an agreement.

4. Difficulties with respect to the terms of 'oral' contracts. The Dickerson Committee has recommended that a corporation should be able to validly adopt only written contracts because 'this seems the only way of ensuring full disclosure of the terms of the contract, which is an essential protection for the corporation'.[53]

Collective Investment Scheme Companies

Collective Investment Schemes (CIS) are governed by the Financial Services Commission (FSC), which oversees the securities industry, the insurance industry, and the pensions industry. The CIS Regulations were passed on December 30, 2013, in the Securities (Amendment) Act, 2013. Regulation 17A(2) provides that a

> 'collective investment scheme' includes any scheme in whatever form, whether in Jamaica or elsewhere, whereby members of the public are invited or permitted to invest money or any other property –
>
> a. into a portfolio of assets managed as a whole by or on behalf of the operator of the scheme; and
>
> b. on terms on which those investors, being two or more in number, hold a participating interest in, receive profits or income arising out of, or share in the risks and benefits of the scheme. [54]

Section 27A provides for collective investments scheme companies defined as a company which:

1. has a share capital;
2. is incorporated for the purpose of investing the moneys of its members for their mutual benefit;
3. states in its Articles that it is a collective investment scheme;
4. has the power to redeem or purchase for cancellation its shares without reducing its authorized share capital; and
5. is registered as a collective investment scheme as provided by the Securities Act.

53. P Puri, 'The Promise of Certainty in the Law of Pre-Incorporation Contracts' 2002 *Canadian Bar Review.* 80: 1051, 1055–56; cf Australia Corporations Act 2001 s 131.
54. Companies Act 2004, s 27A(3).

Section 27A(4) provides, inter alia, that the redemption or purchase of investors' shares, (as defined by section 27A(3)), by a CIS company shall not be taken as increasing or reducing the company's authorized share capital. CIS are also exempt from provisions of the Companies Act which are considered onerous in the context of CIS. These provisions include provisions relating to minimum share capital and authorized minimum (sections 34 and 35); consideration and stated capital accounts (sections 38 and 39); prospectuses (sections 40–47 inclusive); some provisions on allotment (sections 48–49); return as to allotments (section 52); redeemable shares (sections 52, 56–60, 62); notice of increase of share capital (section 67); duties of company with respect to issue of certificates (section 79); register of members (section 109); inspection of register of members and index of names and consequences of failure to comply with requirements as to register owing to agent's default (sections 112–13); provisions as to branch register of companies incorporated abroad kept in the island (section 120); duty to deliver annual returns and annual returns to be made by a company having a share capital (sections 121, 122 and 124); provisions relating to accounts and audit (sections 144–53 inclusive); dividends (section 158) and restrictions on sale of shares and offers of shares for sale (sections 372–77 inclusive).

Companies Incorporated Outside of the Island Carrying on Business Within the Island[55]

Part X of the Companies Act makes provisions for the registration of companies incorporated outside of the island carrying on business within the island. The provision is the same as under the repealed Companies Act save for the amendments to sections 363, 365, 366 and 370 by the Companies (Amendment) Act 2017.

Section 363 provides that:

a. a certified copy of instruments constituting or defining the constitution and containing the name of the company;

b. a list of the directors and their particulars, as required to be registered in accordance with the Act;

c. a list of members and any beneficial owners, containing such particulars as are required by the Act to be entered in the register of members of a company;[56] and

d. the names and addresses of some one or more persons resident in the Island and authorized to accept on behalf of the company service of process and any notices required to be served on the company

55. See Companies Act 2004 Pt X, ss 362–371; cf Barbados Companies Act 1982, ss 356.1–356.3. See also Trinidad and Tobago Companies Act, 1995 ss 317–37; cf St. Christopher and Nevis Companies Act 1996, s 195.
56. Companies (Amendment) Act 2017 provides for inclusion of beneficial owners for the purpose of transparency.

shall be delivered to the Registrar within one month (or longer not exceeding four months as the Minister may allow) from the establishment of the place of business.

The Companies (Amendment) Act 2017 introduces section 363A which requires a register of members to be kept by companies incorporated outside Jamaica, which establish a place of business in Jamaica. The register is to be referred to as the 'overseas branch register'. Provisions in the Act which relate to the Register of Members (sections 109–17) shall apply to this section.

Section 365 requires that where there is any alteration made to the documents and information required by section 363 to be delivered to the Registrar, by a company incorporated outside of the Island which is carrying on business within the Island, that company shall deliver to the Registrar for registration, within 28 days after the date on which the alteration was made. a return containing the prescribed particulars of the alteration and a certified copy of the alteration made. Certified means certified to be a true copy by not less than two directors, or a director and the secretary, or a notary public.[57]

Section 366 provides for companies carrying on business in the Island to deliver to the Registrar, for registration, within 18 months of the registration of the company and thereafter in every calendar year,[58] a balance sheet and profit and loss account, and if the company is a holding company, group accounts in such form and containing such particulars and including such documents, as under the provisions of the Act, it would if it had been a company incorporated under the Act and lay before the company in general meeting. In lieu of this, a company carrying on business in Jamaica may within eighteen months and thereafter in every calendar year,[59] deliver to the Registrar, for registration, a copy of its balance sheet and profit and loss account or, if the company is a subsidiary company, a copy of the balance sheet of its holding company, prepared in the form required under the law of the place of incorporation along with other documents stipulated in the section.

57. Companies (Amendment) Act 2017.
58. Ibid.
59. Ibid.

2. Corporate Finance

One of the main incentives for incorporation is to raise capital through either equity or debt financing. The Companies Act 2004, reflects the modern approach to facilitate financing through the relaxation of the old rules relating to types of shares, permitting a company to purchase its own shares or the giving of financial assistance for the purchase of its own shares, and the abolition of par value shares. The amendments to the provisions on the registration of charges under the Companies (Amendment) Act 2013, in order to provide for security interests in personal property, and the repeal of the sections relating to the winding up of insolvent companies to introduce the Insolvency Act 2013, have also facilitated financing of companies, the former to allow for the creation, registration, and enforcement of security interests of most non-land property under the Security Interests in Personal Property Act, and the latter, to facilitate debtor in possession financing under the Insolvency Act 2013. The relaxation of the old rules is balanced by provisions for the protection of shareholders and creditors.

Shares and Classes of Shares

Shares are defined as a share in the share capital of a company and include stock except where a distinction between stock and shares is expressed or implied.[1] The basic rights of shareholders include rights to vote in general meeting, income in the form of dividends when declared, and a return of capital on a winding up.

At common law, rights carried by shares, rank pari passu.[2] The presumption at common law of equality of shares may be rendered inapplicable under the Companies Act, which permits classes of shares, with varying rights, privileges, restrictions and conditions.[3] A class of shares is established where the shares have the same rights, privileges, restrictions, and conditions afforded to a group of shareholders. Section 8(1)(c) of the Companies Act requires the Articles of Incorporation to set out the classes of shares if any, and the maximum number of shares, if any, that the company is authorized to issue.

Section 8(8) provides that a company having a share capital shall file a document with the Registrar setting out the following:

---

1. Companies Act 2004, s 2.
2. *Re Bridgewater Navigation Co.* [1891] 2 Ch. 317 Eng. CA; *Cumbrian Newspaper Group Ltd. v Cumberland and Westmoreland Herald Ltd.* [1987] Ch. 1 Eng. Ch. D.
3. Companies Act 2004, s 8(8).

a. If two or more classes of shares are issued, the rights, privileges, restrictions, and conditions attaching to each class of shares; and

b. if a class of shares is issued in a series, outlining the authority given to the directors to fix the number of shares in, and to determine the designation of, and the rights, privileges, restrictions, and conditions attaching to the shares of each series.[4]

The most common classes of shares are ordinary shares and preference shares. There must always be a class of ordinary shares, to which all basic rights will attach (voting, income where dividends declared and the return of capital on winding up), even though there is no right to a fixed income or return on capital. This may be contrasted with the rights that attach to preference shares, which may have restricted voting rights, a fixed income and return on capital in priority to the ordinary shareholders. It appears that the requirement that a company file a document outlining the rights, privileges, restrictions, and conditions attaching to each class of shares under section 8(8) puts paid to the question, which has loomed large at common law,[5] as to whether the rights set out in the Articles are exhaustive. It appears that preference shareholders may only participate, after satisfaction of their entitlements as to fixed income, with ordinary shareholders in surplus assets or further distribution of profits if outlined in the Articles[6] or the document required to be filed with the Registrar in section 8(8). It appears that this provision also applies to cumulative dividends and that the common law presumption that preference dividends are presumed to be cumulative, no longer obtains.[7] The Companies Act is silent, however, on the payment of arrears of dividends. In the absence of a provision on payment of arrears of dividends on liquidation, the common law provides that there is a presumption that they may not be paid on liquidation unless rebutted by a provision in the Articles to the contrary. The courts have placed a generous interpretation on provisions in Articles with reference to payment of arrears on a winding up.[8]

The Act provides for the protection of shareholders, where the share capital is divided into different classes of shares, in the event of the variation of their class rights. Section 73(1) provides that a company may vary class rights where provision is made in the Articles, otherwise known as a variation of rights clause. The variation is subject to:

i. the consent of any specified proportion of the holders of the issued shares of that class; or

4. *McClurg v Minister of National Revenue* [1990] 3 SCR 1020 SCC.
5. *Birch v Cropper* (1889) 14 App Cas 25 Eng. HL; *Will v United Lankat Co. Ltd.* [1914] AC 11 Eng. HL; *Scottish Insurance Corporation v Wilson & Clyde Coal Co.* [1949] AC 512 Sc HL; and *Re Isle of Thanet Electric Co.* [1950] Ch. 161.
6. Companies Act 2004 s 8(1)(c) and 8(4).
7. *Webb v Earle* (1875) LR 20 Eq 556.
8. *Re F De Jong Ltd.* [1946] Ch. 211 Eng. CA.

ii. the sanction of a resolution passed at a separate meeting of the holders of those shares.

Note that Articles may also be altered to provide for a variation of rights clause, and as such, should be done in accordance with section 10 which provides that: 'Subject to this Act, a company may by special resolution alter or add to its Articles.'

Section 73(1)(b) provides that where the company varies the rights attached to any class of shares in accordance with 73(1)(a):

i. the holders of not less in the aggregate than fifteen per centum of the issued shares of that class, being persons who did not consent to or vote in favour of the resolution for the variation, may apply to the Court to have the variation cancelled and,

ii. where any such application is made, the variation shall not have effect unless and until it is confirmed by the Court.

The Court may disallow the variation if it is satisfied that the variation would unfairly prejudice the shareholders of that class, having regard to all the circumstances of the case.[9]

At common law, there was an artificial distinction made between a variation of class rights and the enjoyment of those rights.[10] Section 73(7), however, appears to clear up that distinction by providing that a 'variation' includes (therefore not limited to):

i. abrogation, or

ii. any resolution of a company the implementation of which would have the effect of diminishing the proportion of the total votes exercisable at a general meeting of the company by the holders of the existing shares of a class, or

iii. any resolution of a company the implementation which would have the effect of reducing the proportion of the dividends or distributions payable at any time to the holders of the existing shares of a class.

Where the Articles of Incorporation of a company does not have a variation of rights clause, but the company purports to vary the rights attached to the shares of a class, the shareholders of those class of shares would have no recourse under section 73. The shareholders may, however, bring an action as complainants, under section 213A, for the exercise of the director's powers, (inter alia), in a manner which is unfairly prejudicial to their interests.[11] They may also arguably bring a derivative action against the directors, for breach of their fiduciary duty, on behalf of the company for a wrong

---

9. Companies Act 2004 s 73(4).
10. *Greenhalgh v Arderne Cinemas Ltd.* [1946] 1 AER s12 cf.; *Cumbrian Newspapers Group Ltd. v Cumberland & Westmorland Herald Newspapers & Printing Co. Ltd.* [1986] 2 AER 816. [1986] 3 WLR 26; *White v Bristol Aeroplane Co. Ltd.* [1953] Ch. 65; *Re House of Fraser plc* [1987] BCLC 293.
11. Companies Act 2004, s 212 and 213A.

done to the company, where the directors acted outside of the provisions of the Articles of Incorporation.

Share Capital and Stated Capital Accounts

Section 8(1)(c) of the Act requires that a company with a share capital shall set out in its Articles of Incorporation the classes of shares if any, and the maximum number of shares, if any, that the company is authorized to issue.[12]

The old law had required that there be stated a specific number of shares of a certain par value in the Memorandum of Association. Section 4(4) of the repealed Jamaica Companies Act 1965 stated that the Memorandum of Association must state the amount of share capital with which the company proposes to be registered, and the division thereof into shares of a fixed amount unless the company is an unlimited company.

If a company does not initially have classes of shares, section 10(1) requires the passing of a special resolution to alter its Articles of Incorporation. Section 65(1) treats any alteration of its share capital as an alteration of the Articles of Incorporation. This is a change in the old law as section 61(2) of the repealed Jamaica Companies Act 1965 only required an ordinary resolution for the alteration of its share capital as this was not seen as an alteration of the Articles of Association. The change in the law may be due to an increased concern for capital maintenance and the avoidance of abuse.

Section 8(2)(c) requires that the Articles are to bear 'the same stamp duty as if they were contained in a deed'. Deeds attract a fixed nominal rate of stamp duty.[13] Prior to April 1, 2019, an issue arose as to whether section 21 of the Stamp Duty Act 1937, which refers to 'nominal share capital' and provides that the document stating the share capital of the company must be stamped on an ad valorem basis (1% of the authorized capital), would be applicable even though the concept of 'nominal share capital' no longer exists. The Provisional Collection of Tax (Stamp Duty) Order, 2019, now provides for a fixed nominal rate of tax ranging between $100.00 and $5,000.00 depending on the amount of capital.

The Stamp Duty Act does not at present refer to 'Articles of Incorporation' and the 'authorized share capital'. If the Articles of Incorporation was to be stamped on an ad valorem basis, the cost of stamping would increase dramatically, given the no-par value system. It had been argued that this would be undesirable as there would be a disincentive for companies to capitalize with equity rather than debt.[14]

---

12. See also Barbados Companies Act 1982, s 5(1)(b); CBCA 1985, s 6(1)(c).
13. Stamp Duty Act 1937, s 3 and Schedule.
14. Mark Golding, 'A Review of the Major Changes to Jamaican Company Law Introduced by the Companies Act 2004', Paper presented to the Private Sector Organisation of Jamaica on March 25, 2004.

Section 8(7) requires that companies with more than one class of shares, or having one class issued in a series, file a separate document.[15] With respect to companies with more than one share, the document must state the privileges, restrictions, and conditions attaching to each class of shares. In the case of companies with a class of shares issued in a series, the document must set out the authority given to the directors to fix the number of shares in and to determine the designation of, and the rights, privileges, restrictions, and conditions attaching to the shares of each series

Under section 34, public companies having a share capital on its original incorporation are not allowed to do business or exercise borrowing powers unless a certificate has been issued by the Registrar. Section 34 requires that a statutory declaration be delivered to the Registrar setting out the following:

i. that the value of the company's 'allotted share capital' is not less than its authorized share capital;

ii. specify the amount paid up at the time of the application on the company's allotted share capital;

iii. specify the amount or estimated amount of the company's preliminary expenses and the persons by whom any of those expenses have been paid or are payable; and

iv. specify the amount or benefit paid or given, or intended to be paid or given, to any promoter of the company, and the consideration for the payment or benefit.

As it relates to specifying the amount paid at the time of the application of the company's allotted share capital, it appears that the Act contemplates partly paid shares, although it is clearly an undesirable feature. Under the Canadian Business Corporations Act 1985 and the reformed Commonwealth Caribbean Companies legislation, partly paid shares are prohibited.[16]

The Registrar shall deliver the requisite certificate for a public company to do business if:

i. the company applies for the certificate in the prescribed form;

ii. the Registrar is satisfied that the value of the company's allotted share capital is not less than the authorized minimum. 'Authorized minimum' means $500,000.00 or such other sum as may be prescribed by the Minister;[17] and

iii. the statutory declaration is delivered to the Registrar.

---

15. See also Barbados Companies Act Cap 308, s 5(1)(b).
16. See CBCA, s 25(3). See also Barbados Companies Act Cap 308, s 30; Trinidad and Tobago Companies Act Cap 81:01, s 34; cf St. Christopher and Nevis Companies Act No 22 of 1996, s 34. See also Companies Act 2004, s 127.
17. Companies Act 2004, s 35.

The intention appears to be, to ensure that public companies are adequately capitalized. However, questions may arise as to whether to ensure that the allotted share capital is not less than the authorized minimum is enough, since there is no need to properly take into account the amount of paid-up capital but merely only to have it stated in the statutory declaration.

Section 34 states that the section applies to public companies but does not state that it applies to private companies that convert to public companies. It is assumed that the section would apply to the latter instance as well.

Section 34 is limited to 'allotted share capital' and therefore does not contemplate both total issue price and the full value of shares. There is also no provision for sanctions or penalties for non-compliance with the section.

Additionally, section 35 states that the 'authorised minimum' means $500,000.00 or such other sum as the Minister may, by order prescribe. It does not include a penalty for a public company that does business and exercises borrowing powers in contravention of section 34(1). It also does not clearly address the rights of individuals who unknowingly deal with companies who contravene the section wilfully or otherwise by preserving the validity of the transaction notwithstanding the breach. It is proposed that these issues be addressed by imposing appropriate penalties and dealing with redress for unaware individuals. The suggested approach to remedy these issues is to insert the following subsections:

> (4) If any company does business or exercises borrowing powers in contravention of this section, the company and every officer who is in default is liable to a fine.
>
> (5) Nothing in this section affects the validity of any transaction entered into by a company; but if a company enters into a transaction in contravention of this section and fails to comply with its obligations in that connection within fifteen days of being called upon to do so, the directors of the company are jointly and severally liable to indemnify the other party to the transaction in respect of any loss or damage suffered by him by reason of the company's failure to comply with those obligations.

Par Value and No-Par Value Shares

Section 37 changed the old system of par value shares (par value is the nominal value of shares of a specific dollar amount) to that of no par value shares. It had been recognized that the par value system is misleading and does not reflect the true value of shares. Par value shares could be misleading to the purchaser who might be led to believe that the par value is an indication of the value of his investment. The investor should realize that a share merely represents a proportionate interest in the net worth of the business and should not be confused by any arbitrary money denomination attributed to that investment. The removal of the par value concept allows greater flexibility to the corporation in arranging and rearranging its capital structure. The removal of the par value concept also does away with the accounting and disclosure problems relating to transactions in par value shares.[18] Bruce Welling explains:

> Par value was an arbitrary minimum issue price prescribed in the corporate constitution. Such a provision could be disadvantageous to a high-risk investor who financed a corporation through its development into a thriving enterprise, only to see low-risk investors reap the benefit of the gamble by purchasing expansionary issues of shares...Most Canadian statutes now forbid the issue of par-value shares. The rationale is that par value misleads unsophisticated investors and complicates the accounting process.[19]

Notwithstanding the introduction of no par value shares, a company may elect, by ordinary resolution under section 37, to retain its existing shares with a nominal or par value and may continue to issue shares with a nominal or par value within six months of the appointed day[20] for a maximum period of 18 months. This means that Jamaica had a dual system in operation for a maximum of 24 months (2 years) in the worst-case scenario. Welling again explains that '[t]he possibilities of issuing both no par and par-value shares in a corporation with limited authorized capital creates unnecessary accounting complexities...[t]he federal reform of 1975 applied the sword of Damocles to these complexities'.[21] Section 37(3) provides that the company which elects to retain nominal or par value shares should serve the Registrar with notice of the resolution to this effect. Section 37(2) provides that if a company does not elect to retain the nominal or par value system, the company, at the end of the six-month period from the appointed day, will be deemed to have converted its existing shares to no par and any shares issued thereafter shall be issued without a nominal or par value. Section 37(4)(a) and section 37(5) state that the provisions of the repealed Jamaica Companies Act 1965 which are relevant to shares with nominal or par value shall apply to companies which elect to retain the nominal or par value system.[22] At the end of 18 months from the date a company elects to retain nominal or par value shares, all shares will be deemed to be without nominal or par value and any shares issued thereafter shall be shares issued without a nominal or par value.[23]

---

18. RWV Dickerson, JL Howard, and L Getz, *'Proposals for a New Business Corporations Law for Canada'* 1971 Vol 1, Commentary, Information Canada [97]–[101].
19. Bruce Welling, *Corporate Law in Canada: The Governing Principles* (3rd edn, Mudgeeraba: Scribblers Publishing, 2006), 600–602.
20. Jamaica Companies Act 2004, s 2 defines the 'appointed day' as the date of the commencement of the Companies Act 2004.
21. Welling, *Corporate Law in Canada.*
22. The relevant sections of the repealed Jamaica Companies Act 1965 are ss 56–58, 64, 66–69, Table A paras 11, 15–21.
23. See also British Columbia Business Corporations Act 2002 Cap 57, ss 52–54 where the dual par value system was retained.

As a result of the introduction of no-par value shares, the following may be observed:

i. there is no longer an arbitrary sum prescribed to shares;

ii. the real value of shares will be reflected;

iii. the problem of redeeming 'preference' shares at par or a nominal value is avoided;

iv. there is no longer a need for a 'share premium account'; and

v. there is no longer the concern of issuing shares at a discount. This is coupled with the strict rules prescribed in Companies Act 2004 s 38 for issuing shares for consideration other than cash.

The price of the shares will be determined by the directors in the best interest of the corporation. The value would depend on the market value of the company.[24]

Consideration for the Issue of Shares

Section 38 takes a very strict approach towards the payment for shares, thus ensuring the maintenance of capital.[25] This is a radical departure from the old law which held that there was to be no enquiry into the actual value of non-cash consideration received by a private company in exchange for shares as long as the exchange was done honestly and not colourably.[26] There is a clear emphasis on transparency and fairness embodied in the various subsections as follows:

i. section 38(1) provides that shares may be paid for in money or in property or past service rendered for value that is the fair equivalent of the money that the company would have received if the share had been issued for money.

Although section 38 appears to alter the old law, which provided that a company could, if so stipulated in its Articles, arrange for different amounts to be paid on shares by omitting to refer to partial payment and only referring to paid shares, other provisions of the Act seem to assume the possibility of partly paid shares.[27]

ii. section 38(2) makes it abundantly clear that the fair equivalent of money consideration is to be assessed by the directors, who may take into account

---

24. JH Farrar, N Furey, BM Hannigan, *Farrar's Company Law* (3rd edn, Oxford: Butterworths, 1991), 160.
25. See also Barbados Companies Act Cap 308, s 30; CBCA 1985, s 25. The Jamaican Act has a varied definition of 'property' and it sets out conditions for an allotment.
26. See *Wragg, Re* [1897] 1 Ch 796; *Stanton Ltd v Drayton Commercial Investment Co Ltd* [1983] 1 AC 501 (HL); *American Wollastonite Mining Corp v Scott* (2003) 44 BLR (3d) 1, 2003 BCCA 627.
27. See Companies Act 2004, s 39(6)(b) which relates to where a company issues shares in exchange for shares of a body corporate. See also Jamaica Companies Act 2004, s 34 which relates to the statutory declaration required to be delivered to the Registrar by public companies.

reasonable charges and expenses of organization and reorganization, payments for property and past services reasonably expected to benefit the company.

iii. Section 38(3) prohibits the use of a debt security as 'property' save the debt security of a company as part of a merger, acquisition, amalgamation or scheme of arrangement, reorganization or reconstruction or promises to pay that are comprised of government securities or debt instruments that are guaranteed by a financial institution. 'Financial Institution' is defined in section 38(8) as a company licensed under the Banking Act, the Financial Institutions Act or the Securities Act or incorporated under the Building Societies Act; 'Government Securities' includes securities by a body corporate that is owned or controlled by the Government.

iv. Section 38(4) states that no allotment by a company of shares for a consideration other than cash shall be made unless the directors of the company have passed a resolution that the allotment be made and state the nature of the consideration, its value and the extent to which the shares to be issued in respect of it will be credited as paid up by virtue of it.

v. Before passing the resolution in iv) above, where it relates to services, the directors of the company shall have a qualified accountant estimate the value of the services to the company in money terms or in other case have the consideration valued by a qualified accountant, valuer or surveyor.

vi. The accountant or valuer or surveyor must report, not more than 120 days before the allotment of the shares, that in his opinion the value of the services to the company in money terms or the value of the other consideration in question is worth at least as much as the amount which will be credited as paid up on the shares to be allocated.[28]

vii. The nature and value of the consideration other than cash for any allotment should be stated in the company's Articles and the allotment should be approved by a general meeting of the company where the allotment is made pursuant to a pre-incorporation arrangement.[29]

Section 39 requires that a company maintains a 'stated capital account' for each class and series of shares issued by it.[30] This provision changes the old law in that the repealed law had only required a single share capital account to which all share capital was credited. The following rules relating to the 'stated capital account' are embodied in section 39:

---

28. Companies Act 2004, s 38(6).
29. Companies Act 2004, s 38(7). For other rules relating to pre-incorporation transactions, see chapter 1 – Pre-Incorporation Transactions.
30. See also Barbados Companies Act 1982, s 31; CBCA 1985, s 26.

i. Section 39(2) states that a company shall add the full amount of the consideration received by it for any share issued by the company to the appropriate stated capital account.

This reflects a change in the law where there was a separation of share capital and share premium under section 56 of the repealed Jamaica Companies Act 1965 where the share premium account was treated anomalously, in that the share premium account reflected paid-up capital and on the other hand was treated as distributable surplus. Under the Companies Act 2004, all share premiums will be included in the appropriate stated capital account. This acknowledges that all money paid for shares should be treated as capital by the company. This, therefore, means that as a general rule, if any part of such money is later returned to the shareholders, it would only occur through redemption or reduction of capital.

ii. Section 39(3) states that a company shall not reduce its stated capital or any stated capital account except in the manner provided by the Act;[31]

iii. Section 39(4) states that a company shall not add to a stated capital account an amount greater than the amount of the consideration received by the company for the share in respect of a share issued by it.

iv. Section 39(5) provides that when a company proposes to add an amount to a stated capital account maintained by it in respect of a class or series of shares, that addition to the stated capital account shall be approved by special resolution if bonus shares are not being apportioned rateably among all shareholders and the effect of the bonus issue on voting rights is such that the holders of one class of shares assume control of the company or are able to pass a resolution which, prior to the bonus issue, they did not have sufficient voting rights to carry if the other shareholders were against it.

Notwithstanding the rules in relation to the consideration for shares under section 38 and the rule under section 39(2) regarding the addition to the appropriate stated capital account of the full amount of the consideration received by it for any shares issued by the company, section 39(6) states the following:

i. When in exchange for property, a company issues shares to a body corporate that was an affiliate of the company immediately before the exchange, or to a person who controlled the company immediately before the exchange, the company may add to the stated capital accounts that are maintained for the shares of the classes or series issued, the amount agreed by the company and the body corporate or person, to be the consideration for the shares so exchanged, subject to section 39(4) which provides that a company shall not, in respect of a share issued by it, add to a stated capital account, an amount greater than the amount of the consideration received by the company for the share.

31. See also Companies Act 2004, ss 71, 72.

ii. When a company issues shares in exchange for shares of a body corporate that was an affiliate of the company immediately before the exchange, the company may add to the stated capital accounts maintained for the shares of the classes or series issued, the whole or any part of the consideration it received in exchange, subject to the provision that a company shall not add to a stated capital account an amount greater than the amount of the consideration received by the company for the share.

iii. When a company issues shares in exchange for shares of a body corporate that becomes the company's affiliate before the exchange, the company may add to the stated capital accounts that are maintained for the classes or series issued the whole or any part of the consideration it received in exchange, subject to the provision that a company shall not add to a stated capital account an amount greater than the amount of the consideration received by the company for the share.

Section 39(7) provides that companies incorporated before the appointed day (and which continue in existence after that date) shall not be required to add to a stated capital account any consideration received by it before that date unless those shares in respect of which the consideration is received are issued after that date. This provision stands notwithstanding the provision embodied in section 39(2) which states that a company shall add to the appropriate stated capital account the full amount of the consideration received by it for any shares issued by the company.

Prospectus

The Jamaica Companies Act 2004 sections 40 to 47 deal with prospectuses.[32] These provisions have been carried over from the repealed Companies Act 1965.[33] The inclusion of the provisions in the companies legislation fails to follow the modern trend in other jurisdictions of placing prospectus provisions in securities and financial markets regulation legislation, such as the United Kingdom, where prospectus provisions are found in the Financial Services and Markets Act 2000. Also, in Canada, Bill S-11, 2001 completely removes the requirement of filing prospectus information with the federal government.

Section 40 sets out the general conditions for registration of prospectuses and the circumstances in which the Registrar may refuse registration of prospectuses. A copy of a dated prospectus must first be submitted to the Registrar for registration. This copy must be signed by every person named as a director or proposed director. Where the Registrar registers the prospectus, the company or proposer is informed in writing

32. See also Barbados Companies Act 1982, ss 288–300; Trinidad and Tobago Securities Industry Act Cap 83:02, ss 68–78, 128–29 and 141; cf St. Christopher and Nevis Companies Act 1996, ss 29–33.
33. See Jamaica Companies Act 1965, ss 39–46.

of the fact of registration and its date. Upon registration, each prospectus issued by the company must have the fact of registration stated on its face. The issuance of a prospectus without its being registered is a criminal offence which exposes the company and every person who knowingly was a party to the issue liable to a fine of a maximum of $5,000.00 for every day from the issue of the prospectus until it is withdrawn.

Section 40 restricts the Registrar to the basis for refusing to register a prospectus. The Registrar must form the view that the prospectus is misleading in order to refuse its registration. This finding may be made in one of two ways: (i) by finding that the prospectus is misleading on its face or (ii) by conducting an investigation. In both cases, the Registrar must notify the proposer of the prospectus, in writing, of this opinion within 14 days of the delivery of the prospectus. A written notice must set out the reasons for the Registrar's contention that the prospectus is misleading. In the former case, the reasons form part of the notice. In the latter case, the written reasons for such a finding must be provided within six weeks of the prospectus being delivered to the Registrar.

In the event that the Registrar refuses to register a prospectus, the aggrieved company or proposer may apply to the Court for an order to register the prospectus.

Section 41 sets out the specific requirements of the particulars of the prospectus which are set out in the Third Schedule to the Act. The particulars focus on the following details:

a. proprietorship of the company;
b. management of the company;
c. capital requirements which must be met by the subscription;
d. terms and conditions of the offer for subscription and allotment;
e. material contracts to which the company is a party;
f. interests of directors; and
g. auditors' and accountants' reports.

The section creates a criminal offence if shares or debentures in a company are issued pursuant to a form of prospectus which fails to comply with the Act. It sets out the circumstances in which a director or person responsible for the prospectus may have a defence to this contravention. A person has a defence if he proves that:

a. he was unaware of any improperly undisclosed matter;
b. the contravention arose from an honest mistake of fact on his part; or
c. the contravention was in respect of matters which were immaterial or which could reasonably be excused.

No person shall incur liability for the failure to include in a prospectus a statement with respect to the matters that the auditor is required to report, unless it is proved that such person had knowledge of the omitted matters. The section very explicitly states that the section does not operate as a limitation of the common law; therefore, the common law civil liability continues to exist for the tort of deceit and misrepresentation where statements in the prospectus are untrue.[34]

Section 42 requires that where an expert makes a statement in a prospectus, that prospectus should not be issued unless the expert has given unequivocal written consent. The section defines 'expert' as including an engineer, valuer, accountant and any other person whose profession gives authority to the statement made.

Section 43 prescribes that no variation may be made to contracts referred to in the prospectus except with the approval of the statutory meeting. This applies where the prospectus is in respect of a company which has not already held its statutory meeting.

Section 44 affixes statutory civil liability for misstatements in the prospectus. The persons who may be liable for such misstatements are:

a. the directors at the issue of the prospectus;
b. every person who has authorized himself to be named in the prospectus as a director;
c. every person who is a promoter of the company;
d. every person who authorized the issue of the prospectus.

The section exempts experts under section 42 from liability where the misstatement was not made by him.

The section further excludes liability in the following broadly drawn circumstances:

a. where the prospectus was issued without a person's knowledge or consent;
b. where, between the issue of the prospectus and the allotment, a person becomes aware of an untrue statement therein and withdrew his consent and gave reasonable public notice of the withdrawal; or
c. where the person had reasonable grounds to believe up to the time of allotment that the statement was true.

The term 'promoter' means a party to the preparation of the prospectus containing the untrue statement but does not include a person acting in a professional capacity in organizing the formation of the company. This excludes the liability of an attorney-at-law engaged exclusively in his professional capacity.

Section 45 prescribes the criminal penalties for untrue statements in the prospectus. The maximum custodial sentence is 2 years and the fine is $100,000.00. There are 2 statutory defences: (i) that the statement was immaterial and (ii) that the relevant person had reasonable grounds to believe up to the time of the issue of the prospectus that the statement was true.

Section 46 is a deeming section. It classifies any document which offers the allotment of shares or debentures to the public as a prospectus which must conform with the statutory requirements of prospectuses. Section 46 is also a deeming provision.

34. *Edgington v Fitzmaurice* (1885) 29 Ch D 459.

It deems all statements included in a prospectus as untrue if it is misleading in the form and context in which it is used and if it is contained in any report or memorandum which is incorporated or issued with the prospectus.

Redeemable Shares

Historically, the redemption of shares by a company was prohibited. As such, companies were precluded from issuing redeemable shares. However, in the United Kingdom in the 1980s, the government sought to attract equity investment into small businesses by introducing redeemable shares. Redeemable shares facilitated capital injection into small businesses but allowed the owners of such businesses to maintain control of the company by giving the company the option of redeeming the shares.[35]

Section 56, which has its source in section 159 of the United Kingdom Companies Act 1985, allows a company to issue shares which:

i. by the terms of the issue will be redeemed; or

ii. at the option of the company, may be redeemed.

Other Caribbean jurisdictions acknowledge that a company may issue redeemable shares. The sole condition for redemption of the shares is that such redemption does not compromise the solvency position of the company.[36] Also, modern companies legislation in other jurisdictions provide that the power to issue redeemable shares are subject to the Articles.[37]

The rules relating to the redemption of shares are embodied in sections 56 and 57 and are as follows:

i. section 56(2) provides that no redeemable shares may be issued at a time when there are no issued shares of the company which are not redeemable;

ii. section 56(3) provides that redeemable shares may not be redeemed unless they are fully paid and the terms of the redemption must provide for payment on redemption. There is no longer a requirement of a capital redemption reserve fund;[38]

iii. section 56(4) provides that the redemption of shares and the minimum premium, if any, payable on redemption must be out of profits or revenue reserves which would otherwise be available for the payment of dividends or out of a fresh issue of shares made for the purpose of the redemption;

---

35. Farrar et al. *Farrar's Company Law*, 179.
36. See Barbados Companies Act 1982, s 41, 448(o); Trinidad and Tobago Companies Act 1995, ss 4, 45; cf St. Christopher and Nevis Companies Act 1996, ss 55–56 which is in very similar language to the Jamaican provisions.
37. See Barbados Companies Act 1982, CBCA 1985, s 36, s 41; Trinidad and Tobago Companies Act 1995, s 45.
38. See also Jamaica Companies Act 1965, s 57(1)(d).

iv. section 56(5) imposes on the company and every officer who knowingly authorized the breach liability to a fine of $50,000.00;

v. section 57(1) allows for the redemption of shares to be effected on such terms and in such manner as provided by the company's Articles, subject to the Act;

vi. section 57(2) stipulates that where shares are redeemed, the voting rights attaching to those shares shall be suspended and the amount of the company's issued share capital shall be diminished by the value attributed to those shares in the stated capital account accordingly but the redemption of shares by a company is not to be taken as reducing the company's authorized number of shares. There seems to be some confusion as to whether the shares are cancelled as the section does not make it clear that this is so. The current United Kingdom Companies Act 2006 s 688 makes it abundantly clear that the shares are cancelled.[39] The use of the word 'suspension' in relation to the voting rights attaching to the redeemed shares adds to the confusion. It is arguable that the intention of Parliament must have been to cancel the shares, in the absence of any provision for the use of those shares again.

vii. where a company is about to redeem shares, it has the power to issue shares up to the value of the shares to be redeemed as if those shares had never been issued.

Power of Companies to Purchase their Own Shares

The old law has been altered radically by sections 58, 59 and 60 from the rule in *Trevor* v *Whitworth*[40] that a company could not purchase its own shares even if so provided in the Memorandum of Association. The underlying concern was that of capital maintenance. However, it has long been recognized that companies may wish to have the option to purchase their own shares to:

i. permit remaining members to maintain control of the company;

ii. utilize surplus capital and, thereby, return surplus resources to shareholders where that makes more sense than the company investing it;

iii. facilitate the investments in shares where investors can take shares with a put option back to the company;

iv. buy out shareholders who may be dissident, disinterested or deceased;

v. facilitate Employees Share Ownership Plans (ESOPs);

vi. create an additional means of disposing of shares thereby making investment in private companies more attractive; or

39. See also UK Companies Act 1985, s 160.
40. (1887) 12 AC 409.

vii. market support for the price.[41]

Section 58[42] was adopted from section 162 of the United Kingdom Companies Act 1985.

The rules relating to a company buy-back of its shares are as follows:

i. section 58(2) states that the provisions of section 57 as it relates to the redemption of a company's redeemable shares shall apply save for the requirement that the Articles of Incorporation need not determine the terms of the manner of purchase;

ii. section 58(3) provides that a company shall not purchase its own shares if, as a result, there would no longer be any member of the company holding shares other than redeemable shares;

iii. section 58(4) requires that a statutory declaration should be made by not less than 75% of the company's directors[43] and lodged with the Registrar of Companies to the effect that they have no reasonable grounds to believe that the solvency test prescribed by the Act has not been satisfied. The solvency test in section 58(4) requires that the company is or would after the payment be able to pay its liabilities as they become due *or* the realizable value of the company's assets would, after payment, be less than the aggregate of its liabilities and stated capital;

iv. section 58(5) states that the statutory declaration must be based on the company's audited accounts made up no more than 12 months before, the company's unaudited accounts made up no more than 45 days before the date of the statutory declaration and any other relevant facts of which the directors are aware. Section 58(5) does not apply to a purchase or acquisition to settle or compromise a debt or claim asserted by or against the company to eliminate fractional shares or to fulfill the terms of a non-assignable agreement under which the company has an option or is obliged to purchase shares owned by an officer or an employee of the company;

v. section 59 allows a company to purchase or otherwise acquire shares issued by it , if permitted by its Articles, to settle or compromise a debt or claim asserted by or against the company to eliminate fractional shares or to fulfill the terms of a non-assignable agreement under which the company has an option or is obliged to purchase shares owned by an officer or an employee of the company under the same conditions as applies to the redemption

41. M Ladd. 'Companies Act 2004 – Corporate Finance Highlights'. Paper presented to Myers Fletcher and Gordon on April 27, 2004.
42. See also Barbados Companies Act 1982, ss 39–40; Trinidad and Tobago Companies Act 1995, ss 43–44; cf St. Christopher and Nevis Companies Act 1996, s 57.
43. Companies (Amendment) Act 2017 amending Companies Act 2004 to replace 'by the company's directors' with 'by not less than seventy-five percent of the company's directors'.

of redeemable shares under section 57, save that the terms and manner of purchase or other acquisition need not be determined by the Articles as required by section 57(1);[44]

vi. a company purchasing or otherwise acquiring shares issued by it under section 59 must fulfill the same requirements for the making and lodging of a statutory declaration as is required under section 58 where a company purchases or otherwise acquires shares issued by it. It must be noted that it is proposed that subsection (4) be amended to state that the statutory declaration should be signed by a majority of the company's directors;

vii. section 59(3) provides that a company may acquire its shares to comply with a court order made under section 213 which relates to derivative actions and the oppression remedy;

viii. the liability of directors for declarations which are false in any material particular, done willfully or recklessly, is the same as that for false declarations in any material particular under section 58;

ix. section 59(6) provides that a company may accept from any shareholder a share in the company surrendered to it as a gift but may not extinguish or reduce a liability in respect of an amount unpaid on any such share, except in accordance with section 71 which stipulates the manner in which a company may reduce its share capital;

x. section 60 provides that the company must, within 30 days of the purchase or other acquisition,[45] notify its shareholders and the Registrar[46] of the number of shares purchased, the names of the shareholders from whom it has purchased, the price paid for the shares, the nature of any non-cash consideration and the value attributed to it and any balance, if any, remaining due to the shareholders or those shareholders from whom it purchased the shares.[47]

The provisions of section 57 apply to transactions under section 58. Although there are detailed rules concerning the steps which a company must take in advance of the purchase of its own shares, the legislation fails to address the issue of how the shares are treated once purchased. There is no guidance as to whether the shares should be placed in a special account or any clear indication of the impact that the repurchase has on voting rights. Territories with a similar provision also include a provision for the filing of the Statutory Declaration with the Registrar in the prescribed form.

44. See also CBCA 1985, s 35.
45. Companies (Amendment) Act 2017 amending the Companies Act 2004 to add the words 'or other acquisition'.
46. Companies (Amendment) Act 2017 amending the Companies Act 2004 to add the words 'and the Registrar'.
47. See also Alberta Business Corporations Act Revised Statutes of Alberta 2000, cl 34(3).

Pre-emptive Rights

Section 61 provides that a pre-emptive right arises where the Articles of Incorporation allow for a certain class of shares of a company to be offered shares to be issued in that class before anyone else. The pre-emptive right is in proportion to the shareholder's holding at such price and on such terms as those shares are to be offered to anyone else.

The provision adds nothing to the old law, which permitted pre-emptive rights once embodied in the Articles of Association. The statutory provision, however, states that no pre-emptive right exists in respect of shares to be issued for consideration other than cash or pursuant to the exercise of conversion privileges, options or rights previously granted by the company. These situations are clearly inappropriate for the granting of a pre-emptive right. It is significant that section 61 does not explicitly prohibit a pre-emptive right in respect of share dividends as is done in Canada and the reformed Commonwealth territories.[48]

Edwards J in the Jamaican case of *Benkley Northover v Eric Northover and Rohan Northover and Godfrey Dixon and Winston G. Northover Associates Limited* stated the following:

> This allows the balance of control between the respective shareholders to be maintained. The right also prevents the diminution in value of existing shares, which will happen if new shares are issued, especially if issued at a price below their true value...Breach of pre-emption rights provisions however, do not invalidate the new issue but those for whom the right exist are entitled to be compensated under a separate compensation claim.[49]

The case involved, inter alia, the issue of new shares from the authorized share capital, to which, it was held, rights of pre-emption applied in accordance with the Articles of the company. The allotment of the new shares to the claimant and another person was therefore invalidly made. The learned judge found that one of the Defendants had a pre-emptive right to new shares issued by the company which could only be defeated if section 61(3)(a) and (b) applied, and in any event, the company would need to comply with the procedure for the allotment of new shares for a consideration other than cash, as provided in section 38 of the Companies Act. The learned judge also stated that, even where the directors and shareholders are the same people, the procedure must be followed.[50]

---

48. See Barbados Companies Act 1982, s 34 (2) (b); CBCA 1985, s 28(2)(b); Trinidad and Tobago Companies Act 1995, s 38.
49. [2014] JMCC Comm. 14 [46].
50. *Benkley Northover v Eric Northover and Rohan Northover and Godfrey Dixon and Winston G. Northover Associates Limited* [2014] JMCC Comm. 14 [56]; *Chin v Chin* [2007] UKPC 57.

Redeemable Preference Shares

Section 62 provides that a company limited by shares may, if so authorized by its Articles, issue preference shares which are, or at the option of the company are to be liable to be redeemed.

This section appears to be an anomaly as it is reproduced from the repealed Companies Act 1965[51] and relates to concepts which no longer hold in the context of the new regime, such as the 'capital redemption reserve fund'. There are also a number of rules for the redemption of these shares which are now covered under sections 56 and 57. The provision is, therefore, unnecessary and confusing.

Miscellaneous Provisions as to Share Capital

Sections 63 to 70 substantially reproduce sections 59 to 65A of the repealed Companies Act 1965, save for a stipulation of a fine for default where none existed or an increase in fines for default in compliance.

Section 63 relates to the power of a company to arrange for different amounts being paid on shares thereby confirming the retention of partly paid shares.

Section 64 allows a limited company to pass a special resolution to determine that any portion of its share capital which has not been already called up shall not be capable of being called up, except in the event and for the purposes of the company being wound up.

Section 65 allows a company limited by shares or limited by guarantee and having a share capital to alter its share capital if so authorized by the Articles of the company. Section 65(2) states that the powers conferred by the section must be exercised by the company in general meeting. This presumably should be interpreted as meaning by way of ordinary resolution.

The section does not provide for new classes of shares or for the change from one class of shares to another. This does not accord with the reformed position of most territories.[52]

Section 66 states that a company must give notice to the Registrar of the consolidation, division, conversion, subdivision, redemption, cancellation or re-conversion of stock, as the case might be, within one month after so doing. Liability of the company and every officer of the company for default is set at a fine not exceeding $50,000.00.

Curiously, the section only requires notice to the Registrar for the redemption of preference shares. Arguably the section should refer to all types of shares as all types of shares may be redeemed.[53]

---

51. See Jamaica Companies Act 1965, s 57.
52. See Barbados Companies Act 1982, s 197(1)(d), (f); Trinidad and Tobago Companies Act 1995, s 214(1)(d), (f).
53. See UK Companies Act 2006, s 689.

Section 67 requires notice to the Registrar of an increase in share capital and default attracts a fine not exceeding $50,000.00 to the company and every officer of the company. The default fine under the repealed Companies Act 1965[54] was not stated.

Section 68 gives unlimited companies having a share capital, by its resolution for registration as a limited company, the power to increase the amount of its share capital by increasing the amount of its shares (subject to the condition that no part of the increased capital shall be capable of being called up except in the event and for the purposes of the company being wound up), and/or provide that a specified portion of its uncalled share capital shall not be capable of being called up, except in the event and for the purposes of the company being wound up.

Section 69 grants companies the power to pay interest out of capital in certain cases and default attracts liability to a fine not exceeding $50,000.00, up from $100.00 under the repealed Companies Act 1965.[55] The provision in the repealed Companies Act 1965 which stated that 'the payment of the interest shall not operate as a reduction of the amount paid up on the shares in respect of which it is paid',[56] is now deleted. The implications of the deletion of this section of the repealed Act remain to be seen.

Section 70 provides for the redemption or cancellation of shares under the Employees Share Ownership Plan Act (ESOP).[57] This section states that where a company, in the operation of an employee share ownership plan approved under the ESOP Act, purchases its shares and such shares are thereupon either cancelled or transferred to the trustees of the plan or otherwise cancels its shares in the exercise of the company's rights or obligations under that Act or any plan thereunder, such purchase or cancellation of its shares by the company shall not be deemed to be a reduction of the company's capital.[58]

The purchase of shares in accordance with section 70 shall not be taken as reducing the amount of the company's stated capital. It is recommended that a new subsection (4) be inserted to make it clear that section 59 of the Registration of Titles Act will not apply to a purchase of shares under the section.

Reduction of Share Capital

Provisions concerning the reduction of share capital are primarily designed to prevent a company from removing or disposing of its assets in prejudice to its creditors.[59] The provisions relating to the reduction of share capital have been substantially altered in that it is no longer necessary to obtain a court order to approve a reduction of share

54. See also UK Companies Act 2006, s 63.
55. See also UK Companies Act 2006, s 65(2).
56. See Jamaica Companies Act 1965, s 65(f).
57. See also Jamaica Companies Act 1965, s 65A.
58. See also Jamaica Companies Act 1965, s 70.
59. See *Unisource Canada Inc v Hongkong Bank of Canada* (1998) 43 BLR (2d) 226 [80].

capital. Section 71(1) provides that a company may extinguish or reduce liability in respect of an amount unpaid on any shares, reduce its stated capital by an amount that is not represented by realizable assets or return to its shareholders any of its assets which are in excess of the wants of the company by special resolution.[60]

The concern of capital maintenance is met by section 71(3) which provides that a company shall not reduce its stated capital or return assets unless a statutory declaration is made by the directors to satisfy the stated solvency and liquidity tests.

Section 71(4) provides that the declaration shall be based on the company's audited accounts made up no more than 12 months before the date of the statutory declaration, the company's unaudited accounts made up no more than 45 days before the date of the statutory declaration and any other relevant facts of which the directors are aware.

Section 71(5) stipulates that a company shall at 2 intervals, at least 7 days apart, give notice in a daily newspaper circulating in the Island of any reduction of its stated capital reducing its stated capital by an amount that is not represented by realizable assets or any intention to reduce it stated capital to extinguish or reduce a liability in respect of an amount unpaid on any shares or to return to its shareholders any of its assets which are in excess of the wants of the company.

Section 71(6) prohibits a return of assets to shareholders which are in excess of the wants of the company until the expiration of 180 days after the publication of the second notice required.

Section 71(7) requires that directors who wilfully or recklessly make declarations which are false in a material particular to be liable to a fine not exceeding $1,000,000.00 and/or to imprisonment for a term not exceeding two years.

Section 72(1) states that no redemption, purchase, acquisition or forfeiture by a company of its shares or the cancellation of those shares operates to reduce the authorized number of shares of the company. Section 72(2) provides that the stated capital of a company shall be reduced by the amount by which a redemption of redeemable shares is made out of a fresh issue of shares made for the purpose of the redemption not more than 12 months before the date of the redemption. Section 72(3) states that subject to section 72, the general rule is that a company may not reduce its stated capital except as provided by section 71. Section 72(3) states that the provisions of section 71 (reduction of stated capital by special resolution) shall not apply to a redemption, purchase acquisition or forfeiture.

Transfer of Shares

Section 74 states that each share in a company shall be personal estate and not of the nature of real estate. Each share shall also be distinguished by its appropriate number. The latter stipulation has been the subject of a recommendation suggesting

60. See also CBCA 1985, s 38.

that the requirement be removed from the section as most jurisdictions have removed that requirement from their companies legislation as it has proven to be a nuisance to share transactions. However, it has been observed that in those jurisdictions where shares are not numbered, there are no partly paid shares. So, if it is not intended to abolish partly paid shares, then this section should not be amended.

Section 78 declares that the certification by a company of any instrument of transfer of shares in the company shall be taken as a representation by the company to any person acting on the faith of the certification that there have been produced to the company such documents as on the face of them show a prima facie title to the shares in the transferor named in the instrument of transfer, but not as a representation that the transferor has any title to the shares or debentures.

The section also says that where any person acts on the faith of a false certification by a company made negligently, the company shall be under the same liability to him as if the certification had not been made fraudulently. Presumably, Parliament's intention was to equate the liability for negligent certifications with that of fraudulent certifications.

Section 82 of the Jamaica Companies Act 2004, which authorized the issue of bearer shares, is repealed.[61] Bearer shares/bearer warrants differ from normal registered instruments, in that no records are kept of who owns the underlying property, or of the transactions involving a transfer of ownership. Bearer shares are useful to investors and corporate officers who wish to retain anonymity. The abolition of bearer shares is in compliance with the standards published by the Global Forum on Transparency and Exchange of Information about Tax Purposes of the Organization for Economic Co-operation and Redevelopment (OECD), of which Jamaica is a member. The applicable standards published by the Global Forum is as follows:

> Jurisdictions should ensure that information is available to their competent authorities that identifies the owners of companies and any bodies corporate... Where jurisdictions permit the issuance of bearer shares they should have appropriate mechanisms in place that allow the owners of such shares to be identified.

Section 383A of the Companies (Amendment) Act 2017 provides that no company shall issue, or have entered on its register of members, a share warrant. A 'share warrant' is defined as a warrant issued under the company's common seal, stating that the bearer of the warrant is entitled to the shares therein specified, and may provide by coupons or otherwise, for the payment of dividends on the shares included in the warrant.[62] The liability of the company and every officer who knowingly caused the non-compliance is a fine of up to $3,000,000.00. Section 396 of the Companies (Amendment) Act 2017 provides transitional arrangements for current share warrants

61. Companies (Amendment) Act 2017.
62. Ibid., s 383A (3).

by converting the bearer of a share warrant to the owner of the shares, and a member of the company and the share warrant, after 18 months, shall be incapable of effecting the transfer of ownership of the shares specified in the share warrant from the bearer thereof to any other person, and deemed null and void except for the purposes of converting the bearer of the share warrant to the owner. Note that 18 months after the specified date, every company which has issued a share warrant to a bearer before the specified date shall:

i. withdraw the share warrant;

ii. if the bearer of the share warrant presents the share warrant to the company, shall cause the name of the bearer of the share warrant to be entered as a member in the register and issue one or more certificates in respect of that person's ownership; and

iii. amend its Articles, to remove any authorization to issue share warrants or to prohibit share warrants.

Other OECD countries, have taken steps to immobilize or abolish bearer shares in order to comply with the Global Forum's call for the disclosure of company ownership.

Debentures

The provisions relating to debentures embodied in sections 84 to 92 are substantially the same as the provisions relating to debentures under the repealed Companies Act 1965,[63] save for the increase in the fines for default of the provisions relating to debentures as well as an increase in the cost of inspecting and receiving copies of documents relating to debentures.

Section 84(4) provides that the company and every officer of the company shall be liable to a fine not exceeding $50,000.00 where the register of debenture holders is not kept in accordance with the section.

Section 86 provides that a debenture holder or shareholder may inspect the register of holders of debentures of the company for a maximum fee of $50.00 and a copy of the register of holders of debentures of the company, or any part thereof, or a copy of any trust deed or other document securing any issue of debentures on payment of $20.00 for every page required to be copied.

Section 84(5) states that the company and every officer of the company may be liable to a fine not exceeding $50,000.00 for refusal of inspection or refusal of a copy of documents relating to the register of holders of debentures to debenture holders or shareholders who so request. Section 84(6) permits the Court to order immediate inspection of the register or delivery of copies of the register where there is a default.

---

63. See Jamaica Companies Act 1965, ss 84–92.

Registration of Charges

Section 93(1)[64] states that a charge will be valid against the liquidator or other creditor of the company, provided that the charge is filed and delivered to the Registrar prior to the winding up of the company. Default of section 93(1) will result in liability to a fine of not more than $50,000.00 for the company and every officer of the company.

Section 93 provides for the registration of a charge within 21 days of the creation of the charge; however, unlike under the repealed Companies Act 1965,[65] there is no need for Court approval where an extension of time is needed to register the charge. Instead of Court approval, section 93(2)(b) states that a charge, which is created and is not registered until after 21 days of its creation, shall for all purposes of priority and subject to any agreement altering priorities, be deemed to have been created on the date of registration. This eliminates the issue of what the effective date of registration of a charge is. That issue was the source of judicial consideration in *Trade Board v CRG Lee Corporation*.[66]

The Companies (Amendment) Act 2013 introduced section 93(3) which provides that the section relating to the registration of charges in the Companies Act 2004 applies to a charge on land (wherever situated) or any interest therein, but not to a charge for any rent or other periodical sum issuing out of land. The Security Interests in Personal Property Act 2013 provides for charges over interests other than land.

The Memorandum of Objects and Reasons of the Security Interests in Personal Property Act (SIPPA) 2013 states:

> A decision was taken to enact legislation to facilitate the creation of security interests in personal property, to provide for a simple registration process for the recognition of such interests, and to stipulate the rules which will govern the priority in which such interests are enforceable.

The introduction of SIPPA, therefore, has impacted on a number of the provisions in the Companies Act which relate to the registration of charges which then required amendments.

Section 93(3) of the Companies Act, which had formally listed all the registrable charges, was amended following the introduction of SIPPA to:

> remove the requirement to register there all other charges save for "charges on land and any interest therein but not to a charge for any rent or other periodical

64. cf Barbados Companies Act 1982, s 237; Trinidad and Tobago Companies Act 1995, s 251. There does not appear to be any requirement to register charges under the Companies Act in St. Christopher and Nevis.
65. See Jamaica Companies Act 1965, s 99.
66. No E703 of 2002 Supreme Court, Jamaica, delivered November 29, 2004.

> sum issuing out of land and deletes the subsections (6), (7) and (8) dealing with negotiable instruments and debentures.[67]

The effect of this is to remove the distinction between floating and fixed charges in relation to a company. This was done in order to simplify the process requiring registration to a central location, which is the electronic Security Interests Registry.[68]

Section 94 of the Companies Act, 2004, which had provided that:

Where a charge requiring registration under this Act is created then—

(a) the registration of that charge in accordance with this Act shall constitute notice to the world of the existence of that charge;

(b) where a subsequent charge is registered in accordance with this Act in respect of the same property or undertaking and written notice thereof is given to the prior chargee, the amount secured by the prior charge shall not be increased to the prejudice of the later charge notwithstanding any provision to the contrary contained in the document creating the earlier charge.

(2) Where the amount secured by a charge is increased after the charge is registered, the particulars of the increase shall be sent to the Registrar for registration in the prescribed manner.

is now repealed. This is significant as there is now consistency with section 48(6) of SIPPA, which provides that 'Registration of a notice in the registry is not constructive notice or knowledge of its existence or contents to any person.'

This provision in SIPPA, therefore, means that a subsequent chargee cannot be deemed to have notice of any prohibition clauses contained in the charge based simply on the fact the clauses were contained in a charge registered under the Act or even of the fact that a prior charge existed as registration is not constructive notice of the existence of the fact that a registered notice in relation to the asset already exists.

> In fact, SIPPA makes no provision for a copy of the charge to be registered. The only information to be provided is the identity of the debtor the secured creditor and the secured property. It does not even require disclosure of the amount secured. It would seem, however, that this could have the potential of lengthening the time required to finalize loans as the lenders who bother to carry out searches, will need to make contact with prior chargees in order to complete their due diligence and cannot simply rely on information available at a public register.[69]

There have been a number of recommendations on how to improve this section.

67. P Goldson, D Walker, J Thompson-James. 'The Security Interests in Person Property Act'. Presented by the Commercial Law Committee of the Bar Association, Jamaica Bar Association Conference, Montego Bay, Jamaica, November 16, 2013.
68. SIPPA, 2013 s 47.
69. Goldson et al., 'The Security Interests in Person Property Act'.

The Report of the Joint Select Committee on the Bill Shortly Entitled the Companies Act 1998 recommends that charges on land be exempted from the requirement of registering charges under section 93. However, this has not been effected and it would, therefore, be prudent to register charges on land at both the Office of Titles and the Office of the Registrar of Companies.[70]

Section 97 states that the Registrar is to keep a register of charges. Although not stated in the section, a description of the charge should be included to avoid confusion where several charges are filed at the same time for the same company.[71]

Section 95(3) of the Companies Act, 2004 was also amended in order to be consistent with SIPPA, 2013. The provision now states:

> If any company makes default in sending to the Registrar for registration the particulars of any charge created by the company, then, unless the registration has been effected on the application of some other person, the company and every officer of the company who is in default shall be liable to a default fine not exceeding fifty thousand dollars.

The words 'or of the issues of debentures of a series requiring registration as aforesaid' which followed after the 'of any charge created by the company' are now deleted.

Section 97 is amended to require the Registrar to keep a register of '...all the charges to which section 93 applies' (as opposed to the previous wording which 'all the charges requiring registration under this Part...'). Endorsement of the certificate of registration on debentures is no longer necessary and therefore the former section 98 is repealed and section 99, which relates to entries of satisfaction and release of property from charge, no longer includes undertakings.

Section 102(1) was also amended by deleting the proviso and now provides that:

> Every company shall cause a copy of every instrument creating any charge requiring registration under this Part to be certified in the prescribed manner and kept at the registered office of the company.

Another important amendment is found in section 123, which relates to Annual Returns to be made by a company not having a share capital to take into account the advent of SIPPA. Section 123(2) now provides that:

> There shall be annexed to the return a statement containing particulars of the total indebtedness of the company in respect of all mortgages and which are required to be registered under this Act and all security interests registered under the Security Interests in Personal Property Act.

70. Joint Committee on the Bill Shortly Entitled The Companies Act 1998, 'Report on the Joint Select Committee on the Bill Shortly Entitled The Companies Act 1998'(Jamaica) 6, Appendix I, 15.
71. See also Barbados Companies Act 1982, ss 238 and 245; Trinidad and Tobago Companies Act 1995, ss 252 and 259.

Prohibition of Financial Assistance by Companies

Section 184 replaces the 'notorious' section 54 of the repealed Companies Act 1965 by prohibiting a company from giving financial assistance, whether directly or indirectly, to a shareholder, director, officer or employee of the company or affiliated company, or to an associate of any such person for any purpose or to any person for the purpose of, or in connection with, a purchase of a share issued or to be issued by the company or a company with which it is affiliated where circumstances prejudicial to the company exist. LCB Gower states that the former section was notorious 'because it has penalize[d] innocent transactions while failing to deter guilty ones'.[72]

Circumstances prejudicial to the company exist where there are reasonable grounds for believing that the company is unable to pay its liabilities as they become due or would be so unable if the financial assistance is provided by the company or the realizable value of the company's assets (excluding the amount of the financial assistance in the form of a loan or assets encumbered to secure a guarantee) would, after the financial assistance is given, be less than the aggregate of the company's liabilities and stated capital.[73]

The section avoids the 'trap' of section 54 of the repealed Companies Act 1965[74] by stating that a contract made by a company or by a person giving financial assistance in contravention of the section shall not by reason only of that contravention, be rendered void, or unenforceable by the company or person giving financial assistance.

The penalty for liability on summary conviction before a Resident Magistrate for an officer of the company who contravenes section 184 is a fine not exceeding $1,000,000.00 or imprisonment for a term not exceeding two years or both fine and imprisonment. The judge may also order that officer to restore to the company an amount equal to the value of the financial assistance given in contravention of section 184.

72. LCB Gower, *Gower's Principles of Modern Company Law* 5th edn. (London: Sweet & Maxwell, 1992) 227.
73. Although the equivalent Canadian provision was repealed, there were cases decided on how this provision was to be applied. See *Noren Investments Ltd v Brownie's Franchises Ltd* 37 DLR (4th) 1; *Strait Line Contractors Ltd (Receiver of) v Rainbow Oilfield Maintenance Ltd* (1991) 79 Alta LR (2d) 169, (1991) CarswellAlta 47; *Nelson v Rentown Enterprises Inc* (1992) 96 DLR (4th) 586, 7 BLR (2d) 319.
74. See *Selangor United Rubber Estates Ltd v Craddock (No 3)* [1968] 2 All ER 1073.

3. Corporate Management

The worldwide emphasis on corporate governance has been largely due to the various financial scandals, in most cases, involving the abuse of power by directors and officers of companies. There is no doubt that good corporate governance builds investment confidence and ultimately inures to the benefit of the society in which companies operate. Corporate Governance principles have been introduced throughout the Commonwealth through Corporate Governance Codes (soft law), case law and legislation. Provisions relating to the duties, responsibilities and liabilities of directors and officers of the company under the Companies Act 2004 reflect some of the developments in corporate governance by setting high standards relating to fiduciary duties, duties of care, diligence and skill and accountability through disclosure and recognition of the interests of shareholders and other stakeholders. Most of the provisions are adopted from Canada (e.g. directors' fiduciary duties and duties of care, diligence and skill) while others are adopted from the UK (e.g. shadow directors, director disqualification), and still others are a creation of the Jamaican Parliament (e.g. duty of care, diligence, and skill, due diligence defence). In addition to guidance from the Canadian and UK courts, the local courts, therefore, have an opportunity to develop the local jurisprudence.

Definition of Directors

Section 172 provides that a private company shall have at least one director but a public company shall have at least three directors, at least two of whom are not employees of the company or any of its affiliates. Section 2 provides that 'director' includes any person occupying the position of director by whatever name called. A director may, therefore, be de jure or de facto. A de jure director is one who has been properly appointed as a director of the company, however, a de facto director has not been properly appointed but inter alia, holds himself out to be a director and is held out to be a director, by the other directors.

In *Smithton Limited v Naggar*,[1] Hobart, a subsidiary of DDI, brought an action against Naggar, a director of DDI, to recoup losses of the subsidiary on the basis that Naggar was a de facto or shadow director of Hobart. In finding that Naggar was neither

1. [2013] EWHC 1961 (Ch.) [35-44] see also *HMRC v Holland* [2010] 1 WLR 2793; see also *Re Paycheck Services 3 Ltd., Revenue and Customs Commissioners v Holland* [2010] UKSC 5. *Re UKLI Ltd. Secretary of State for Business, Innovation and Skills v Chohan and others* [2013] EWHC 680 Ch.

a de facto director nor a shadow director, Arden LJ, outlined some factors which may be taken into account in determining whether a person is a de facto director:

1. A person may be *de facto* director even if there was no invalid appointment. The question is whether he has assumed responsibility to act as a director.
2. To answer that question, the court may have to determine in what capacity the director was acting.
3. The court will in general also have to determine the corporate governance structure of the company so as to decide in relation to the company's business whether the defendant›s acts were directorial in nature.
4. The court is required to look at what the director actually did and not any job title actually given to him.
5. A defendant does not avoid liability if he shows that he in good faith thought he was not acting as a director. The question of whether or not he acted as a director is to be determined objectively and irrespective of the defendant's motivation or belief.
6. The court must look at the cumulative effect of the activities relied on. The court should look at all the circumstances 'in the round' (per Jonathan Parker J in *Secretary of State v Jones*[2]).
7. It is also important to look at the acts in their context. A single act might lead to liability in an exceptional case.
8. Relevant factors include:
   i. whether the company considered him to be a director and held him out as such;
   ii. whether third parties considered that he was a director;
9. The fact that a person is consulted about directorial decisions or his approval does not in general, make him a director because he is not making the decision.
10. Acts outside the period when he is said to have been a *de facto* director may throw light on whether he was a *de facto* director in the relevant period.

A 'shadow director' is defined by section 2 of the Act as a person in accordance with whose directions or instructions the directors of the company are accustomed to act. The concept of shadow director was known to the law in the repealed Jamaica Companies Act 1965 in the context of insolvency, but has now been given a title and included in other sections of the Companies Act 2004 following the United Kingdom Companies Act 1985 s 741(2).[3] However, the concept of 'shadow director' is not

2. [1999] BCC 336.
3. See *Secretary of State for Trade and Industry v Deverell* [2000] BCC 1057; *Secretary of State for Trade and Industry v Aviss* [2006] EWHC 1846 (Ch.), [2007] BCC 288.

included in other Commonwealth Caribbean territories with similar Companies Acts, mainly because the Canadian legislation, on which they are based, does not include 'shadow directors'.

If the directions or instructions are given in a professional capacity, this is not sufficient to deem a person a shadow director.

Modern case law posits that the concepts of shadow director and de facto director are not exclusive and may overlap[4] although, it is hard to envisage holding oneself out to be a director (de facto director) while hiding in the shadows (shadow director).

This has far-reaching implications for unsuspecting shadow directors which may include a parent company, directors of a parent company, and directors of a partnership service company.

The definition, however, speaks to a company being 'accustomed' to acting in accordance with the directions or instructions of the person in question and this will therefore preclude 'one-off' directions.[5] Note also that the control of a single director or minority of directors will not suffice to include an individual in the definition of a shadow director. The definition clearly states that the 'directors' are the ones to be controlled and this has been interpreted in the UK as the whole board.[6]

The following guidelines for establishing shadow directors were stated by the UK Court of Appeal in *Secretary of State for Trade v Deverell and another*:[7]

1. give effect to parliamentary intention (mischief rule);
2. identify those having real influence of corporate affairs and not necessarily over the whole field of its corporate activities;
3. words or conduct must be construed in light of the whole conduct;
4. concepts of 'direction' and 'instruction' do not exclude the concept of 'advice';
5. it is not necessary that the properly appointed directors cast themselves in a subservient role.

In respect of a register of directors, section 183 was amended by the Companies (Amendment) Act, 2013 to provide that a company shall keep a register of its directors or managers and secretary at the registered office. The following particulars should be contained with respect to each of them:

1. In the case of individuals
    a. Christian name;
    b. Surname;

---

4. *Smithton Limited v Naggar* [2013] EWHC 1961 (Ch.).
5. See *Unisoft Group Ltd (No 3), Re* [1994] BCC 766, 775 (Harman J); *Hydrodam (Corby) Ltd, Re* [1994] 2 BCLC 180, 183 (Millett J).
6. See *Kuwait Asia Bank v National Mutual Life Nominees Ltd* [1991] 1 AC 187, [1990] 3 All ER 404 (PC); *Unisoft Group Ltd (No 3), Re* [1994] BCC 766.
7. *Secretary of State for Trade and Industry v Deverell* [2000] BCC 1057.

c. Usual address;

d. Nationality, and if that nationality is not the nationality of origin, the nationality of origin;

e. Business occupation if any, or, if no business occupation but holds any other directorships, particulars of that directorship or of some one of those directorships.

2. In the case of a corporation, its corporate name, and registered or principal office.

The section also provides that 'a company shall, within 14 days of any change in the appointment of a director, give notice to the Registrar of the change in the prescribed form'. The duty imposed by the section is not satisfied by inclusion of a statement of the names of the company's directors in the annual return.[8]

A shadow director is referred to for purposes of liability in the following sections:

i. Section 183(8) requires that there be a register of directors and specifically states that a shadow director is included in the definition of director for the purposes of the section.

ii. Section 194(4)(a) states that a shadow director is to be included for the purposes of particulars with respect to directors in trade catalogues, circulars, etc.

iii. Section 197(5) states that the register of interests notified under section 196 (disclosure of shareholdings in the director's own company) includes shadow directors.

iv. Section 318 retains the provision in the repealed Jamaica Companies Act 1965[9] which includes shadow directors, although not so named but so described, which imposes personal liability of directors in relation to offences antecedent to or in the course of winding up.

It is arguable that since these provisions provide for shadow directors, the other provisions relating to directors may not apply to shadow directors.

> In clause 2 the definition of "director" includes "shadow director". Your committee felt that this was not appropriate, as the role of shadow director was not general but was restricted to specific situations and sections of the Act. It was therefore felt to be more appropriate to exclude "shadow director" from the definition and to maintain a separate definition for "shadow director." An amendment has been recommended to effect this.[10]

8. Sections 183(3) and (3A).
9. See Jamaica Companies Act 1965, s 301(1).
10. Report of the Joint Select Committee on the Bill Shortly Entitled the Companies Act 1998.

However, by introducing the concept of shadow directors, the intention of parliament must have been to expose persons, hiding in the shadows for purposes of accountability and liability as if they were appointed directors and therefore, all provisions relating to directors should apply to shadow directors. This has been found to be the case in the UK, from where the concept of shadow director was adopted.[11] Therefore, notwithstanding the specific reference to shadow directors in sections 183, 194, 197, 318, it appears that shadow directors may be equally liable for offences for which all other directors may be liable.[12]

Definition and Qualifications of Company Secretaries

Section 172 also provides that every company shall have a secretary. Section 2 of the Act states that an 'officer', in relation to a body corporate, includes a director, manager or secretary. Provisions relating to 'officer' therefore include the 'secretary'.

Section 172(3) prohibits a sole director of a company from also being its secretary and further prohibits a company from having as secretary, a corporation the sole director of which, is secretary to the company. A corporation cannot be secretary to a company if that corporation is the sole director of both companies and there is also a prohibition on a corporation being the sole director of a company where the corporation's sole director is secretary to the company.

Although the Act does not state qualifications for a company secretary, the section imposes a duty on directors of a public company to take all reasonable steps to ensure that the secretary or each joint secretary of the company is a person who appears to them to have the requisite knowledge and experience to discharge the functions of secretary of the company. This differs from the approaches taken in other Commonwealth territories which provide that the secretary should possess one or more of a number of additional qualifications including:

a. that he has held the office of secretary of a public company for at least three of the five years immediately preceding his appointment assecretary;

b. that he is a member of the Institute of Chartered Accountants, Institute of Chartered Secretaries and Administrators, or the Chartered Institute of Public Finance and Accountancy;

c. that he is an attorney-at-law;

d. that he is a person who, by virtue of his holding or having held any other position or his being a member of any other body appears to the directors to be capable of discharging the functions of secretary of the company.[13]

---

11. *Vivendi SA and another v Richards and another* [2013] EWHC 3006 (CH.).
12. See *Yukong v Rendsburg Investments Corporation (No2)* [1998] 1 WLR 294; *Secretary of State for Trade and Industry v Aviss* [2006] EWHC 1846 (Ch.), [2007] BCC 288.
13. See United Kingdom Companies Act 2006 (UK Companies Act 2006), s 273; Barbados Companies Act Cap 308, s 58; Trinidad and Tobago Companies Act Cap 81:01, s 63.

Notice of the appointment of a secretary to a company must be given to the Registrar in the prescribed form within 14 days after the date of the appointment.[14]

Section 173 provides that acts done by a person in the dual capacity as director and secretary will not satisfy provisions requiring or authorizing a thing to be done by or to a director and the secretary and as, or in place of, the secretary.

Election, Tenure, Remuneration, and Removal of Directors

Section 175 provides that a person is not capable of being appointed a director of a company by the Articles and shall not be named as a director or proposed director of a company or intended company in a prospectus or in a statement in lieu of prospectus unless before the registration of the Articles or the publication of the prospectus or the delivery of the statement in lieu of prospectus, the director or proposed director has by himself or by his agent authorized in writing a consent in writing to act as such director which is signed and delivered to the Registrar for registration and either:

i. signed the Articles for a number of shares not less than his qualification if any; or

ii. taken from the company and paid or agreed to pay for his qualification shares if any; or

iii. signed and delivered to the Registrar for registration an undertaking in writing to take from the company and pay for his qualification shares if any; or

iv. made and delivered to the Registrar for registration a statutory declaration to the effect that number of shares, not less than his qualification, if any, are registered in his name.

A list of the persons who have consented to be directors of the company shall be delivered to the Registrar on the application for registration of the Articles of a company. If this list contains the name of any person who has not so consented, the applicant shall be liable to a fine not exceeding one hundred thousand dollars.

Section 175 does not apply to a company not having a share capital or a private company or a company which was a private company before becoming a public company or a prospectus issued by or on behalf of a company after the expiration of one year from the date on which the company was entitled to commence business.

Section 176 states that the acts of a director or manager shall be valid notwithstanding any defect that may afterward be discovered in his appointment or qualification. The provision appears to be more limited than the 'indoor management rule' or rule in *Turquand's* case, which states that an outsider dealing with the company is entitled to assume the internal procedures of the company have been complied

14. Section 172(6) was amended by the Companies (Amendment) Act, 2013 to change the notice period from 15 days to 14 days.

with.[15] The rule in *Turquand's* case does not enable a party to hold the company to an unauthorised transaction entered into by a director, and the third party relying on the rule must first establish that the director had authority, actual or apparent, in the first place. Insiders cannot rely on the rule as they would be in a position to know that the internal procedures have not been complied with.

The rule in *Turquand's* case was introduced to ameliorate the harsh effects of the constructive notice doctrine. It is arguable that the rule in *Turquand's* case is now irrelevant since the constructive notice doctrine has been abolished by section 7 of the Act.

The better view is that notwithstanding the limited nature of section 176, the common law rule in *Turquand's* case might survive, in the context of non-compliance of internal procedures which extend beyond the 'appointment or qualification' of the director or manager. The United Kingdom, Trinidad and Tobago and St. Vincent have introduced comprehensive sections on the indoor management rule which arguably replace the rule in *Turquand's* case.[16]

The question as to whether the rule in *Turquand's* case is limited to substantive irregularities or whether it includes procedural ones was addressed by the UK Court of Appeal which accepted that it includes procedural irregularities, but appears to have so accepted this on the peculiar facts of that case.[17]

Duties and Liabilities

Fiduciary Duties and Duty of Care, Diligence, and Skill

Section 174 provides that every director and officer of a company in exercising his powers and discharging his duties shall (a) act honestly and in good faith with a view to the best interest of the company and (b) exercise the care, diligence and skill that a prudent person would exercise in comparable circumstances, including, but not limited to the knowledge, skill and experience of the director or officer.[18]

The provision to act honestly and in good faith with a view to the best interest of the company is basically a codification of the fiduciary duty imposed on directors and officers of the company by the common law which includes:

i. a duty not to have a conflict of duty and interest;

ii. a duty not to make a secret profit;

---

15. See *Royal British Bank v Turquand* (1856) 6 E & B 327.
16. UK Companies Act 2006, ss 39 and 40; Trinidad and Tobago Companies Act, s 25; St. Vincent Companies Act, s 21.
17. See *Smith v Henniker-Major & Co* [2003] Ch 182.
18. See also Canada Business Corporations Act 1985 (CBCA 1985), s 122(1); Barbados Companies Act Cap 308, s 95(1); Trinidad and Tobago Companies Act Cap 81:01, s 99(1); St. Christopher and Nevis Companies Act No 22 of 1996 (St. Christopher and Nevis Companies Act 1996), s 74(1).

iii. a duty to act bona fide in the interest of the company and not for an improper purpose.[19]

The rule is that there may be no conflict of interest and duty, and that a breach of the duty may result in the rescission of any contract involving the conflict, or where a profit is made by virtue of a breach of that duty, the directors or officers may be required to account to the company for any profit so made.[20] However, where there is a conflict, it may be cured by disclosure in accordance with the Companies Act.[21]

All three fiduciary duties at common law were confirmed by Wolfe CJ in *Financial Institution Services Ltd v CNB Holdings Ltd, Century National Development Ltd, Donovan Crawford et al.*[22] and are embodied in section 174(1)(a) to act honestly and in good faith with a view to the best interest of the company.

The question as to whether the common law rule that a conflict of duty and interest and subsequent profit could be ratified in general meeting has survived the legislation, is yet to be established.[23] In the absence of clear words in the Companies Act, both in Jamaica and in Canada, ratification of a conflict of duty and interest by the shareholders in general meeting is not possible, as the wrong can only be ratified by the company to whom the wrong was done.[24]

Another question relating to the statutory fiduciary duty is whether the common law 'proper purpose' test has survived the legislation. The proper purpose test is the test as to whether, a director has acted for a proper purpose and not for any collateral purpose when exercising his powers, in order to test whether he acted bona fide in the interest of the company.[25] The question is especially relevant, where the director may have mixed motives, in which case, it was established at common law, that the primary purpose would determine whether the director has breached the duty to act in good faith and not for an improper purpose.[26]

There has been academic argument, that the proper purpose doctrine is no longer relevant, however, UK and Jamaican case law still rely on the doctrine when determining whether a director has breached the statutory fiduciary duty. The UK Companies Act 2006, however, has explicitly retained the proper purpose doctrine by stating that directors must exercise their powers (whether conferred under the company's

19. *Regal (Hastings) Ltd v Gulliver* [1942] 1 All ER 378 (HL) applied the strict trust rule illustrated in the ancient trust case of *Keech v Sandford* (1726) Sel Cas Ch 61.
20. *Aberdeen Rly Co v Blaikie Bros* (1854) 1 Macq 461.
21. Suzanne Ffolkes Goldson, 'The Reform of the Law Relating to the Duties of Directors in the Commonwealth Caribbean' (2003) 24 (12) *Co Lawyer* 378, 379.
22. No CL C050 of 1997 Supreme Court, Jamaica, May 25, 1999 (JM 1999 SC 20).
23. *North-West Transportation v Beatty* (1887) LR 12 App Cas 589.
24. Bruce Welling, *Corporate Law in Canada: The Governing Principles* (3rd edn, Scribblers Publishing 2006) 421; *cf* UK Companies Act 2006 Cap 46 s 239.
25. *Re Cumana Ltd.* [1986] BCLC 430; *Re Smith and Fawcett Ltd.* [1942] Ch. 304; *Bishopsgate Investment Management Ltd. v Maxwell* (No. 2) [1993] BCLC 814.
26. *Hogg v Cramphorn* [1967] Ch. 254; *Howard Smith v Ampol Petroleum Ltd.* [1974] AC 821 PC.

constitution or under statute) only for the purposes for which they are conferred.[27] The Jamaican Commercial Court held in *Benkley Northover v Eric Northover et al.*, that shares should be returned to the company as part of its authorized unsubscribed share capital as the allotment of shares was found to be for an improper purpose.

> If the substantial purpose is proper, the exercise of the power will not be invalidated by the presence of some other improper, but insubstantial purpose. However, if the director's opinion is bona fide and shows good managerial judgment the court may conclude that the exercise of the power to allot was, broadly speaking, proper in all the circumstances. The court will consider whether it was for the benefit of the company as a whole as distinct from maintaining control of the company in the hands of the directors themselves or their friends or a few select family members.[28]

The second limb of the section refers to the care, diligence, and skill required of directors and officers of the company and has the desired effect of expanding the common law principle of *Re City Equitable Fire Insurance Co*[29] which has long been regarded as too low a standard to be applied to the modern corporation.

The old common law principle states that a director:

1. need not exhibit a greater degree of skill than is reasonably expected from a person of his knowledge and experience;
2. is not liable for errors in business judgment as his primary function is to use his own particular talents in advocating corporate risk-taking;
3. is not bound to give continuous attention to the affairs of the corporation, in the absence of grounds for suspicion, as he is fully justified in trusting corporate officials, to be honest.

The test at common law is highly, if not solely, subjective, and, therefore, a director is free to plead ignorance or stupidity as a defence to a charge of breach of duty of care, diligence, and skill.

Section 174(1)(b) is consistent with provisions found in some of the Canadian legislation and that of the reformed Commonwealth Caribbean territories in that, the test is based on a prudent person exercising care, skill, and diligence in comparable circumstances. The latter phrase was introduced at a late stage in some Canadian legislation in order to ameliorate the otherwise harsh effect of a purely objective test. This approach was adopted in most of the Commonwealth Caribbean territories. The

27. Section 171(b); *Eclairs Group Ltd. (Appellant) v JKX Oil & Gas plc* [2015] UKSC 71. Similarly, see also *Independent Asset Management Company Ltd. v Swiss Forfaiting Ltd.* [2017] ECSC BVI, BVIHCMAPP 206/0034 where it was held that the directors' resolution, substantially reducing the appellant's voting power, had been passed for an improper purpose within the meaning of s 121 of the BVI Companies Act which provides that directors must exercise their power for a proper purpose, and in a manner that does not contravene the Memorandum or Articles of the company.

28. *Benkley Northover v Eric Northover and Rohan Northover and Godfrey Dixon and Winston G. Northover Associates Limited* [2014] JMCC Comm. 14 [69].

29. [1925] 1 Ch 407 (CA) 428.

legislature in Jamaica, however, introduced additional words, out of an abundance of caution, possibly based on the debate that reigned for some time in Canada as to whether the phrase provided for an objective test or an objective/subjective one.[30] The last word from the Canadian Supreme Court suggests that it is an objective test.[31] The Companies Act 2004 includes the phrase 'but not limited to the general knowledge, skill and experience of the director or officer'. The effect of this unprecedented move has yet to be realized but the addition of this phrase appears to confirm that the intention of Parliament is to preserve the subjective test, an intention evinced by agreement, after much debate, by the Joint Selection Committee on Companies Act.[32]

Sections 174(2) and 174(3) further dilute the responsibilities of directors and officers by introducing a due diligence defence. The safe harbour introduced by section 174(2), unique to the Jamaican legislation, states that a director or officer will have discharged his duty of care, diligence and skill if he in fact exercised due care, diligence and skill in the performance of that duty or believed in the existence of facts that, if true, would render the director's or officer's conduct reasonably prudent. This provision is reminiscent of one of the common law principles found in *Re City Equitable Fire Insurance Co.*[33] Codification, however, cements the defence and clarifies what will amount to documents on which directors and officers can rely.

Section 174(3) is also unique to Jamaica in that it provides that a director or officer shall be deemed to have acted with due care, diligence and skill where, in the absence of fraud or bad faith, the director or officer reasonably relied in good faith on documents relating to the company's affairs, including financial statements, reports of experts or on information presented by other directors or, where appropriate, other officers and professionals.[34]

These provisions are based on reform initiatives recently made in Canada and are the only provisions of their kind in the Commonwealth Caribbean reformed legislation. The Canadian Act creates a defence of reasonable diligence that is now available to directors under section 123(4) of the Canada Business Corporations Act 1985 ('CBCA'). However, it does not go as far as the Companies Act 2004.[35] This protection ensures that a director will only be liable for the mistakes of other advisors of the company in the following circumstances:

i. where the director is also personally negligent; or

---

30. See *Soper v The Queen* [1997] 149 DLR(4th) 297; S Ffolkes Goldson, 'The Corporate Director's Duty of Care, Diligence and Skill: *Soper v The Queen*' (1997) *CaribLB* 2(2) 53.
31. See *People's Department Stores Ltd (1992) Inc, Re* [2004] 3 SCR 461 244 DLR (4th) 564.
32. 'Minutes of the Meeting of the Joint Select Committee on the Companies Act' (Jamaica) June 17, 1999.
33. *City Equitable Fire Insurance Co, Re* [1925] 1 Ch 407 (CA) 428.
34. Ibid.
35. Canadian authorities applying this principle are *Blair v Consolidated Enfield Corp* [1995] 4 SCR 5, 24 BLR (2d) 161; *CW Shareholdings Inc v WIC Western International Communications Ltd* (1998) 160 DLR (4th) 131, 38 BLR (2d) 196; *People's Department Stores Ltd (1992) Inc, Re* [2004] 3 SCR 461244 DLR (4th) 564.

ii. where the director's reliance on the advisor's opinion is unreasonable because there were conditions which brought into question the advisor's honesty or competence.

Section 174(4) attempts to include the interests of the company's shareholders and employees and the community in which the company operates in what directors and officers may take into account in considering the best interests of the company. The Report of the Company Law Review Committee 1993[36] recommended that directors should be empowered to take account of the interests of employees and the community as legitimate objects in their own right on the corporate agenda. It was thought that a modern commercial environment demanded that directors should where necessary, be responsive to a wider net of interests than those of company members. Other Commonwealth Caribbean companies legislation state that directors and officers 'shall' or 'must' take into account the various abovementioned interests.[37]

The Companies Act 2004 section 174(5) states that the duties in subsection (1) which includes both the fiduciary duty and duty of care, diligence and skill, are owed to the company alone. This is a restatement of the common law principle that the duties imposed by law on the directors of a company are owed to the company alone. Interestingly, most of the Companies Acts of the Commonwealth Caribbean territories state that only the fiduciary duty is owed to the company alone. This means that the duty of care, diligence and skill may be owed to the other stakeholders identified in the relevant subsection. Directors and officers in those territories may, therefore, be open to direct lawsuits by a wide range of stakeholders, for breach of the duty of care, diligence, and skill. This may put those directors and officers in the invidious position of defending an alleged breach of either duty to the company, where they were taking into account the interests of other groups. It would appear that directors and officers of a company would constantly be involved in a delicate balancing act. The Jamaican legislation avoids this difficulty by using the word 'may' in section 174(4), although it is arguable that where they have opted to take the interests of other groups into account, they would now have to defend themselves if challenged on a breach of section 174(5).[38]

The UK Companies Act 2006 outlines an even wider range of stakeholders, the interests of which, directors and officers must take into account, in corporate decision-making.[39]

Although, the CBCA does not specify that directors and officers shall take into

36. ('Report of the Company Law Review Committee 1993' (Jamaica) 48 [9.05]). There is a similar provision in Barbados Companies Act Cap 308 s 95(2).
37. See Barbados Companies Act Cap 308 s 95(2). The Jamaican provision says 'may'; the Barbadian provision says 'must'.
38. cf Barbados Companies Act Cap 308, s 95(3); Trinidad and Tobago Companies Act Cap 81:01, s 99(3); St. Christopher and Nevis Companies Act 1996, s 74(3).
39. UK Companies Act 2006, s 172.

account the interests of stakeholders other than the company, the Supreme Court of Canada has confirmed that the interests of a wide range of stakeholders ought to be taken into account in corporate decision-making, even though the fiduciary duty owed by directors and officers is to the company alone.[40] In *Peoples v Wise,*[41] the Supreme Court of Canada relied on the provision of the CBCA, which states that the fiduciary duty is owed to the company alone, and therefore confirmed that the duty of care, diligence and skill may be owed to other stakeholders, and in that case, creditors.[42] *Peoples,* therefore, confirmed that the appropriate remedy for stakeholders, where there is a breach of fiduciary duty, is found in the oppression remedy, where a complainant may bring an action against directors and officers of the company who acted in a manner that was oppressive or unfairly prejudicial or unfairly disregarded the interests of specific stakeholders. The Ontario Business Corporations Act has since been amended to state that both the duties (fiduciary duty, and duty of care, diligence, and skill) are owed to the company alone, even though the interests of a wide range of stakeholders must be taken into account based on the decision in *Peoples.* Where there are competing interests, the interests of the company trump all other interests.[43]

Since the duties owed by directors in Jamaica are to the company alone, and the directors may take into account other interests, the appropriate remedy for stakeholders, is found in the oppression remedy[44] (discussed in chapter 4).

Questions arise as to whether directors owe a duty to creditors where the company is insolvent, near insolvent or of doubtful solvency. Some Commonwealth territories have held at common law, that a duty may be owed to creditors when a company is in the vicinity of insolvency.

> In a solvent company the proprietary interests of the shareholders entitle them as a general body to be regarded as the Company when questions of the duty of directors arise. If so, as a general body, they authorize or ratify a particular action of the directors, there can be no challenge to the validity of what the directors have done. But where a company is insolvent the interest of the creditors intrudes.[45]

The Supreme Court of Canada in *Peoples* has, however, stated that the fiduciary

40. See *People's Department Stores Ltd (1992) Inc.* [2004] SCC 68 [42], [66] (Major and Deschamps JJ).
41. Ibid.
42. Ibid., [42].
43. See *People's Department Stores Ltd (1992) Inc.* [2004] SCC 68 [43] [47]; *BCE Inc. v* 1976 Debentureholders, [2008] SCC 69 [66]. See also OBCA S.134 (1).
44. See *People's Department Stores Ltd (1992) Inc.* [2004] SCC 68 [51]; *BCE Inc. v* 1976 Debentureholders, [2008] SCC 69 [66].
45. Street J in *Kinsela v Russell Kinsela Pty Ltd (in liquidation)* [1986] 4 NSW L Rep 722, 730. See also *Nicholson v Permakraft* [1985] 1 NZ L Rep 242 (CA), 249; *West Mercia Safetywear Ltd. (in liquidation) v Dodd* [1988] Butterworths Co. L Cases 250 (CA) 252-3; PL Davies, *Gower and Davies' Principles of Modern Company Law* (7th edn, London: Sweet and Maxwell, 2003) 372.

duty of directors does not extend to creditors even in the vicinity of insolvency[46] as the CBCA states that the fiduciary duty imposed by the section is owed to the company alone and that any recourse for creditors may be found in the oppression remedy as potential members of the complainant and victim classes. *Peoples,* however, left open the possibility of directors' duty of care, diligence, and skill to creditors, based on the wording of the CBCA.[47] Since the Companies Act 2004 states that the duties in section 174 (1)(a) and (b) are owed to the company alone,[48] (both the fiduciary duty and duty of care, diligence, and skill) creditors would need to rely on the oppression remedy as a member of the victim class. The complainant class, however, does not extend to creditors under the Companies Act 2004. It may be argued, therefore, that given the limitations on access to the oppression remedy by creditors, the common law should be adopted, in acknowledging a duty to creditors on or in the vicinity of insolvency.[49]

The Duty to Avoid a Conflict of Interest and Duty

The Companies (Amendment) Act 2017 introduced a new provision and arguably an additional duty for directors to avoid a conflict of interest and duty, consistent with the purpose of the amendment, which is, to increase transparency and accountability. It has been suggested that this duty exists at common law,[50] however, the legislation puts the issue beyond doubt.

> ...it shall be the duty of the director of a company to avoid circumstance which, whether directly or indirectly, constitute a conflict of interest or may result in a conflict of interest with the interests of the company.[51]

The provision only applies to directors and does not include officers of the company and the provision does not apply where the company has only one director and only one shareholder, who is the same individual.[52] The provision requires disclosure and non-participation in deliberations at a meeting of directors.[53] At common law, a director can be found in breach of his fiduciary duty not to have a conflict of duty and

46. *People's Department Stores Ltd (1992) Inc*[2004] SCC 68 [43].
47. Ibid., [1]. In Companies Acts in the Commonwealth Caribbean eg. Barbados Companies Act Cap 308 s 95(3); Trinidad and Tobago Companies Act Cap 81:01 s 99(3) the duty to the company is limited to the fiduciary duty.
48. Companies Act 2004, s 174 (5). Section 134 (1) of The Ontario Business Corporations Act was amended to state both the fiduciary duty and the duty of care, diligence and skill is owed to the company alone.
49. S Ffolkes Goldson, 'Directors' Duties to Creditors On or Near Insolvency and Duty of Care in the Commonwealth Caribbean: Should the Peoples Decision be Adopted?' (2006) Vol. 6 No. 1 *OUCLJ* 61.
50. *People's Department Stores Ltd (1992) Inc*[2004] SCC 68[35].
51. Companies (Amendment) Act 2017, s 174A (1).
52. Ibid., s 174A (10).
53. Ibid., s 174A (2) (a) and (b).

interest where he exploits any property, information or opportunity that belongs to the company except where the company does not/refuses, or could not take advantage of the property, information or opportunity.[54] Section 174A, however, states that it is immaterial whether the company could take advantage of the property, information or opportunity, and it remains to be seen whether this also applies to situations where the company does not/ refuses to take advantage of the property, information or opportunity even though it could.[55]

There is no infringement of subsection (1) if:

i. the circumstances cannot reasonably be regarded as likely to give rise to a conflict of interest, or

ii. the matter giving rise to the circumstances has been approved by the directors where, in a private company, nothing in the Articles invalidates such approval or in the case of a public company, the Articles enable the directors to approve the matter.[56]

Subsection (7) provides that a director may not accept a benefit from a third-party conferred by reason of his being a director or his doing or not doing an act as a director unless the acceptance of the benefit cannot reasonably be regarded as likely to give rise to a conflict of interest. "Third party" means a person other than the company, its holding company or subsidiary company or any person acting on behalf of the company, its holding company or subsidiary company. The provision appears to go beyond avoidance of a conflict of interest to avoidance of bribery.

i. In *Philip Towers v Premier Waste Management Limited*, the UK Court of Appeal held, on a similarly worded provision, that the appellant/director could not rely on the absence of evidence that the Company would have taken the opportunity, or the company had in fact suffered any loss, or

ii. that the appellant/director or the third party/customer had any corrupt motive, or

iii. that, if there had been no free loan, the appellant/director would have hired that sort of equipment in the market, or

iv. the fact that the value of the benefit to the appellant/director was small and that the third party/customer received no benefit from it

to avoid the breach of fiduciary duty to not have a conflict of duty and interest.[57]

---

54. *Industrial Development Consultants v Cooley* [1972] 2 All ER 162; *Canadian Aero Services Ltd v O'Malley* [1973] 40 DLR (3rd) 371; *Island Export Finance Ltd v Umunna* [1986] BCLC 460; *Queensland Mines Ltd v Hudson* [1978] 52 ALJR 399; *Gencor ACP ltd v Dalby* [2000] 2 BCLC 734; *Peso Silver Mines Ltd v Copper (1966)* 58 DLR (2nd)1.
55. *Cullen v Investments Limited and Others v Brown and Others* [2017] EWHC 2793 seems to suggest that the distinction may still apply.
56. Companies (Amendment) Act 2017, s 174 (4) and (5).
57. [2011] EWCA Civ 923 [51] see also *Cullen Investments Limited and Others v Brown and others* [2017] EWHC 2793.

Conflict of Interest: Directors' Interests in Contracts and Disclosure

Section 192 of the Companies Act imposes a general duty on directors to give notice to the company of any matters relating to him as may be necessary for the purposes of sections 189 and 190, except so far as it relates to loans made by the company or by any person under a guarantee from or on a security provided by the company to an officer thereof.[58]

Written notice is required in the case of section 189 involving the particulars in account of directors' salaries, pensions, and compensation for loss of office. Default attracts a liability of a fine not exceeding $50,000.00.[59]

Directors' interests in contracts is covered by section 193[60] and refers to a director or officer of a company who is a party to a contract or proposed contract or a director or officer of anybody or has an interest in anybody that is a party to a contract or proposed contract with the company.

Section 193(8) provides:

> Where a director or officer of a company fails to disclose in accordance with this section, his interest in a material contract made by the company, the Court may, upon the application of the company, set aside the contract on such terms as the Court thinks fit.

'Material' is not defined by the Act. In Canada, it has been left to the courts to define 'material'. *Zysko v Thorarinson*[61] indicates that the term 'material' is a question of fact and that a good standard to use is that there should be disclosure whenever the director or officer's involvement might be relevant to the company's decision-making process. The better view would be that when in doubt, directors and officers should disclose.

The requirements for disclosure under section 193 are:

1. that it be done in writing to the company or be requested to be entered in the minutes of meetings of directors; and
2. that the notification must include the nature and extent of the interest.

The contract shall be subject to the approval of the board of directors and the shareholders must be notified of the existence of the contract.

If the director becomes interested in a contract after it is made, the director must disclose at the first meeting after he becomes interested and if the director was not then a director of the company, at the first meeting after he becomes a director.

Section 193(2) not only provides that the contract be subject to the approval

58. See also CBCA 1985, s 120.
59. See Companies Act 2004, s 192.
60. See also CBCA 1985, s 120; Barbados Companies Act Cap 308, ss 89–91; Trinidad and Tobago Companies Act Cap 81:01, ss 93–96; cf St. Christopher and Nevis Companies Act 1996, s 75.
61. (2003) 42 BLR (3d) 75.

of the board of directors but also, subject to the *First Schedule*, that the director concerned shall not be present during any proceedings of the board in connection with that approval.

The *First Schedule* provides that:

A director or officer is not allowed to vote on such a contract save where:

i. any arrangement for giving any director any security or indemnity in respect of money lent by him to or obligations undertaken by him for the benefit of the company;

ii. any arrangement for the giving by the company of any security to a third party in respect of a debt or obligation of the company for which the director himself has assumed responsibility in whole or in part under a guarantee or indemnity or by the deposit of a security;

iii. any contract by a director to subscribe or underwrite shares or debentures of the company; or

iv. any contract or arrangement with any other company in which he is interested only as an officer of the company or as holder or shares of other securities.[62]

The prohibition against attending and voting at the meeting may at any time be suspended or relaxed to any extent either generally or in respect of any particular contract, arrangement or transaction by the company in general meeting.

Interestingly, the recent amendment to section 120(5) of the CBCA deletes the exception of 'any arrangement by way of security for money lent to or obligations undertaken by him for the benefit of the corporation or an affiliate' on the basis that it is 'difficult to understand both as to rationale and intent'.[63] The CBCA also omits the requirement that a director shall not be present at any proceeding of the board in connection with the approval of the contract in which he has an interest.

There is a marked absence of another exception found in some Commonwealth Caribbean territories. In Barbados, in relation to certain circumstances, the required approval in general meeting is that of not less than two-thirds of the votes of the shareholders of the company to whom notice of the nature and extent of the director's interest in the contract is declared.[64]

Section 193(6), however, states that a general notice to the directors of the company by a director or officer of the company, declaring that he is a director or officer of another body, and is regarded as having an interest in any contract with that body, is sufficient declaration of interest.

62. Companies Act 2004 *First Schedule* Table A Part 1 art 90(2).
63. Wayne Gray, *The Annotated Canada Business Corporations Act* (2nd edn, Toronto: Carswell 2009).
64. See Barbados Companies Act Cap 308, s 89(5).

Section 196,[65] which requires disclosure of directors' shareholdings and debenture holdings of a company, at the time that the person becomes a director of the company, also requires that it be expressly stated in the disclosure that the disclosure is given in fulfilment of the section.

The changes from the common law, that have been made by the Companies Act 2004, in terms of disclosure of interests in contracts, are as follows:

1. the Act includes officers of the company whereas the previous law only referred to directors;
2. the disclosure must be in writing to the company (where there is no request to have the interest entered in the minutes of the meeting of directors) whereas, generally, under section 187 of the repealed Act there is no stipulation for the disclosure to be in writing;
3. a director cannot vote on a contract in which he is interested unless he satisfies the exceptions whereas, there is no such stipulation under the older legislation. However, one could assume, by way of dicta found in case law, that a director could not vote on contracts in which he is interested.[66]
4. where a director breaches the provisions for disclosure, the relevant contract may be set aside at the instance of the Court on an application of the company or a shareholder of the company on such terms as the Court thinks fit, whereas under the old law, the director would only pay a nominal fine and the contract would be voidable, not void.

Disqualification of Directors

Directors may be disqualified from acting as directors of the company for up to 5 years by sections 180 and 182 of the Act. These provisions are based on the United Kingdom Company Directors Disqualification Act 1986 which has produced a litter of cases involving disqualification of directors since its enactment.

Section180 provides that shareholders, directors, creditors, or the Trustee in Bankruptcy may complain, in writing, to the Registrar that a person is unfit to be concerned in the management of a company, by stating the grounds on which such complaint is made. The Registrar may initiate the action based on her own assessment.

The Registrar, on receipt of such complaint, is required to investigate the matter and to hear the complainants and, if satisfied that there are sufficient grounds for a hearing of the matter by the Court, issue a certificate to that effect, which will give the complainant a right to make an application to the court on the matter.

Where a Court is satisfied that a person is unfit to be concerned in the management of a company, the Court may make an order that the person may not be a director of

65. This provision was derived from United Kingdom Companies Act 1985, s 324.
66. *Telecommunications of Jamaica Limited v Hector Bernard* SCCA No 88 of 1990 Court of Appeal, Jamaica, May 20, 1991 (JM 1991 CA 64).

the company, or in any way, directly or indirectly, be concerned with the management of the company for such period as may be specified in the order, not exceeding five years.[67] The Complainant has the right to appeal to the Master in Chambers where he is aggrieved by a refusal of the Registrar to issue a certificate.

Section 182 provides that a director may be disqualified for persistent breaches of the Act. Breaches may include such 'minor' offences as failing to fulfill the requirements of filing, delivering or sending of any return, account or other document or the giving of notice of any matter to be given to the Registrar.

The Act does not specify who may bring an action in the case of persistent breaches of the Act. It may be assumed that the same persons entitled to bring an action through the Registrar under section 180 will be entitled to bring an action under section 182. This uncertainty, however, may be the basis for an amendment to the Act.

Relief from Liability

Sections 201–203[68] broaden the indemnity provisions previously found in the repealed Jamaica Companies Act 1965.

Under section 191 of the repealed Jamaica Companies Act 1965, a company was prohibited, whether by contract or the Articles of Association, from indemnifying any director or officer of the company or any person employed by the company as an auditor against any liability,

> ...which by virtue of any rule of law would otherwise attach to him in respect of any negligence, default, breach of duty or breach of trust of which he may be guilty in relation to the company'. Any such Article or contract would be rendered void. A company, however, was permitted, by way of discretion, to indemnify any such director or officer or auditor against any liability incurred by him in defending criminal or civil proceedings, once he was successful in the action.

Also, under section 372(1) of the repealed Jamaica Companies Act 1965, the Court could relieve a director, officer or auditor from negligence, default, breach of duty or breach of trust once he had acted honestly and reasonably, and that having regard to all the circumstances of the case, he ought fairly to be relieved. The Court could relieve the director, officer or auditor, either in whole or in part on such terms as it thought fit. A director, officer or auditor could also apply to the Court for relief under this section, where he had reason to apprehend that any claim would or might be made against him in respect of negligence, default or breach of trust.[69]

---

67. See *Sevenoaks Stationers (Retail) Ltd, Re* [1991] 3 All ER 578; *Lo-Line Electric Motors Ltd, Re* [1988] Ch. 477; *Secretary of State for Trade and Industry v Baker (No 4)* [1999] 1 WLR 1985.
68. See also CBCA 1985, s 124 (omitting sub-s (2)); Barbados Companies Act Cap 308, ss 97– 99; Trinidad and Tobago Companies Act Cap 81:01, ss 101–103; cf St. Christopher and Nevis Companies Act 1996, s 77.
69. See Companies Act 1965, s 372(2).

The indemnity provisions under sections 201–203 have the following features:

1. A company may indemnify a director or officer of the company or any person employed by the company as an auditor, a former director, officer or auditor of the company, or person who acts or acted at the company's request as a director or officer of a body corporate of which the company is or was a shareholder or creditor, and his legal representatives, against all costs, charges and expenses (including an amount paid to settle an action or satisfy a judgment) reasonably incurred by him[70] in respect of any civil, criminal or administrative action or proceeding to which he is made a party[71] by reason of being, or having been, a director or officer of that company or body corporate or any person employed by that company or body corporate as an auditor.

The section, therefore, now includes administrative actions and extends to:

i. former directors, former officers, and former auditors;
ii. directors or officers of a company of which the company is or was a shareholder or creditor; and
iii. legal representatives.

The section is also wider than section 191 of the repealed Jamaica Companies Act 1965 in that those persons authorized to be indemnified by the company may be indemnified by virtue of being made a party by reason of being or having been a director or officer of that company or body corporate.

2. Indemnification under section 201 is only possible where the director, officer or auditor employed by the company to be so indemnified:
   i. acted in good faith with a view to the best interests of the company;[72] and
   ii. had reasonable grounds for believing that his conduct was lawful in a criminal or administrative action or proceeding that is enforced by a monetary penalty.[73]

---

70. Consider *Chromex Nickel Mines Ltd v British Columbia (Securities Commission)* (1991) 4 BLR (2d) 189; *Blair v Consolidated Enfield Corp* [1995] 4 SCR 5, 24 BLR (2d) 161; *Boffo Family Holdings Ltd v Mountain View Developments Ltd* 2010 Carswell BC 990, 2010 BCSC 560.
71. Consider *Balestreri v Robert* (1985) 30 BLR 283.
72. The Supreme Court of Canada permitted indemnification of a former director by the company on the basis that persons are assumed to act in good faith unless proven otherwise. See *Blair v Consolidated Enfield Corp* [1995] 4 SCR 5, 24 BLR (2d) 161.
73. Consider *Catalyst Fund General Partner I Inc. v Hollinger Inc.* (2006) 15 BLR (4th) 171, 266 DLR (4th) 228; *Bennett v Bennett Environmental Inc.* (2009) 53 BLR (4th) 100, 308 DLR (4th) 530. The Ontario Court of Appeal in *Bennett v Bennett Environmental Inc.* stated that the corporation also bears the burden of showing that the director did not have reasonable grounds for his or her belief that the conduct was lawful consistent with the principle in *Blair v Consolidated Enfield Corp* [1995] 4 SCR 5, 24 BLR (2d) 161.

This provision provides a check on the otherwise more liberal approach to indemnification taken by the Act.

3. A person is also entitled as of right to indemnity under section 203[74] from the company in respect of all costs, charges and expenses reasonably incurred by him in connection with the defence of any civil, criminal or administrative action or proceeding to which he is made party by reason of being, or having been a director or officer of the company or body corporate, if the person seeking indemnity:
   a. was substantially successful on the merits in his defence of the action or proceeding;
   b. qualified under sections 201and 202; and
   c. is fairly and reasonably entitled to indemnity.

This means that 'substantial' success and being fairly and reasonably entitled to indemnity takes away the discretionary factor and gives a person who seeks indemnity by the company a right to it. [75]

4. A company or person referred to in section 201 may apply to the Court pursuant to section 205[76] for an order approving an indemnity in respect of an action by or on behalf of the company or body corporate to obtain a judgment in its favour and to which he is made a party by reason of being or having been a director or an officer of the company or body corporate.[77] The applicant must give notice of the application to the Registrar and in the case of a public company, notice must also be given to the Financial Services Commission.

The provision on indemnity does not provide for the advancement of defence costs. The provision for advancement is a feature of the CBCA.[78] This is unfortunate as many persons entitled to indemnity could be faced with onerous financial demands to defend themselves by virtue only of having been a director or officer of the company. A written undertaking signed by the person requesting indemnity should protect the company from the risk that the person could lose.

---

74. See also Barbados Companies Act Cap 308, s 99; Trinidad and Tobago Companies Act Cap 81:01, s 103; CBCA 1985, s 124 (5); cf St. Christopher and Nevis Companies Act 1996, s 77.
75. Consider *Chromex Nickel Mines Ltd v British Columbia (Securities Commission)* (1991) 4 BLR (2d) 189.
76. See also Barbados Companies Act Cap 308, s 101; Trinidad and Tobago Companies Act Cap 81:01, s 105; CBCA 1985, s 124 (7).
77. Consider *Manitoba (Securities Commission) v Crocus Investment Fund* (2006) 14 BLR (4th) 229; *Chromex Nickel Mines Ltd v British Columbia (Securities Commission)* (1991) 4 BLR (2d) 189.
78. See CBCA 1985, s 124(2).

Section 204[79] authorizes companies to insure any person who could obtain indemnity in his capacity as a director or officer of the company against any liability incurred by him other than liability for fraud.

Other than the provision of an indemnity, insurance policies are one method by which managerial risk may be shifted or minimized. The 'prohibition' with regard to a company purchasing insurance on behalf of directors for a breach of duty which existed before was a vexed issue which has now finally been resolved in favour of directors. The vexed issue was expressly acknowledged by RWV Dickerson where he stated that:

> Some writers have severely censured these provisions, arguing that they not only conflict with but derogate seriously from the statutory standards. Until experience shows that this broad power to obtain indemnity insurance from commercial carriers has been abused by directors and officers, there appears to be no reason to limit the insurance coverage that may be obtained.[80]

In the United Kingdom Companies Act 2006 sections 232–33 the company is prohibited from exempting directors from liability. However, the legislation permits the company to purchase insurance to cover director liability.

Offences of Officers Antecedent to or in Course of Winding Up

Officers of the company, convicted of offences antecedent to or in the course of winding up will be subject to a fine or imprisonment or both.

'Officer' for the purpose of offences antecedent to or in the course of winding up include 'shadow directors'.[81]

i. General Offences by Officers of Companies in Liquidation

Any past or present officer of a company in liquidation is liable for a range of offences if he had an intention to defraud or an intention to conceal the state of affairs of the company or to defeat the law if the offences were committed at the time the company is being wound up.[82]

ii. Accessories

Persons knowingly receiving property pawned, pledged or disposed of pursuant to the offences outlined in section 318(1)(o) will also be guilty of an offence.[83]

---

79. See also Barbados Companies Act Cap 308, s 100; Trinidad and Tobago Companies Act Cap 81:01, s 104; cf CBCA 1985, s 124(6).
80. RWV Dickerson, JL Howard, L Getz, *Proposals for a New Business Corporations Law for Canada* (vol 1, Commentary, Information Canada 1971) [249]–[250].
81. Companies Act 2004, s 318(5).
82. Ibid., s 318(1).
83. Ibid., s 318(1)(o).

iii. Falsification of Books

Any officer or contributory of any company being wound up is guilty of an offence if he destroys, mutilates, alters or falsifies any books, papers or securities or make or is privy to the making of any false or fraudulent entry in any register, book of account or document belonging to the company with intent to defraud or deceive any person.[84]

iv. Fraud by Officers of Companies Which Have Gone into Liquidation

Any person who was an officer of a company, which is subsequently ordered to be wound up by the Court or subsequently passes a resolution for the voluntary winding up of a company, who was an officer, at the time of the commission of the alleged offence, shall be guilty of an offence if he:

a. fraudulently induced any person to give credit to the company;
b. made or caused to be made any gift or transfer of or charge on or caused or connived at the levying of any execution against the property of the company with intent to defraud the creditors of the company;
c. concealed or removed any part of the property of the company since or within two months before the date of any unsatisfied judgment or order for payment of money obtained against the company.

v. Failure to Keep Proper Accounts

Every officer who knowingly connived not to keep proper accounts may be liable for an offence unless he shows that he acted honestly and that, in the circumstances in which the business of the company was carried on, the default was excusable.[85]

vi. Fraudulent Trading

Any persons who were knowingly parties to the carrying on of the business of the company with intent to defraud creditors of the company, creditors of any other person or for any fraudulent purpose shall be personally responsible without any limitation of liability for all or any of the debts or other liabilities of the company as the Court may direct. The Trustee or any creditor or contributory of the company may apply to the Court for a declaration.[86]

---

84. Ibid., s 319.
85. Ibid., s 321.
86. Ibid., s 322.

vii. Damages Against Delinquent Directors

If any promoter, past or present officer or Trustee of the company has:

a. misapplied or retained or become liable or accountable for any money or property of a company; or

b. been guilty of any misfeasance or breach of trust in relation to the company,

c. the Court may, on the application of the Trustee, any creditor or contributory, examine into the conduct of any of those persons and compel him to repay or restore the money or property or any part thereof respectively with interest or to contribute such sum to the assets of the company by way of compensation in respect of the misapplication, retainer, misfeasance or breach of trust. The offender may also be criminally liable.[87]

viii. Prosecution of Delinquent Officers and Members of the Company

The Court may, of its own motion or on application of any person interested in the winding up of the company, direct the Trustee to refer any matter to the Director of Public Prosecutions if it appears to the Court, in the course of winding up or subject to the supervision of the Court that any past or present officer or any member of the company has been guilty of any offence in relation to the company for which he is criminally liable.[88]

87. Ibid., s 323.
88. Ibid., s 324.

4. Complainants' Remedies

For far too long, protection for minority shareholders was limited at common law, and practically non-existent for other stakeholders, in the wake of corporate misdeeds that affected their interests. The case law is replete with instances where the infringement of minority shareholders' rights, or where the duties owed to the company by directors and officers were breached, went unpunished, due to limitations on the ability for actions to be brought.

The main offender was the Rule in *Foss v Harbottle*,[1] which limited the ability of a minority shareholder to bring an action on behalf of the company for wrongs done to the company.

The Rule is two-fold and states:

1. the company is the proper plaintiff where a wrong is done against the company; and
2. the courts will not ordinarily interfere in the internal matters of a company where the company is competent to settle it itself, or in the case of an irregularity, to ratify.

The purpose of the rule was to prevent shareholders from bringing actions which are frivolous or vexatious against directors or officers or other persons in control of the company and to ensure that the actions are brought on behalf of the company and not its shareholders.

The only recourse was where a shareholder could fit into an exception to bring a derivative action. Jenkins LJ in *Edwards v Halliwell*[2] stated that:

> The cases falling within the general ambit of the rule are subject to certain exceptions... in cases where the act complained of is wholly ultra vires the company or association the rule has no application because there is no question of the transaction being confirmed by any majority... [W]here what has been done amounts to what is generally called in these cases a fraud on the minority and the wrongdoers are themselves in control of the company, the rule is relaxed in favour of the aggrieved minority who are allowed to bring what is known as a Minority Shareholders' action on behalf of themselves and all others... [T]he rule did not prevent an individual member from suing if the matter in respect of which he was suing was one which could validly be done or sanctioned, not by a simple majority of the members of the company or association, but only by some special majority, as, for instance, in the case of a limited company under the Companies Act, a special resolution duly passed as such.

---

1. (1943) 67 ER 189.
2. [1950] 2 All ER 1064, 1065–67.

Unless a shareholder could come within these exceptions, the derivative action would usually be blocked by the board of directors or those in control, from the start.[3]

An Oppression Remedy has also been introduced in modern Commonwealth companies legislation. In the past, only shareholders could bring an action by way of petition for an order based on oppressive conduct, where it affected some part of the members (including himself)[4] or petition to have the company wound up on 'just and equitable' grounds.[5] In the latter case, the petitioner would also need to prove oppression. No winding up order would be made where the court is of the opinion that some other remedy is available to petitioners of the company and that they are acting unreasonably in seeking to have the company wound up instead of pursuing the other remedy.

The introduction of an oppression remedy which, permits a 'complainant' as defined by the Companies Act, to bring an action for oppression, unfair prejudice or unfair disregard of the interests of a specified class of stakeholders, acknowledges the change from an agency model to a stakeholder model and underscores the wide protection of stakeholders.

The Statutory Derivative Action

Section 212 of the Companies Act abolishes the rule in *Foss v Harbottle* ('the Rule'), by allowing a 'complainant' to bring an action on behalf of the company for wrongs done to the company which has been called the derivative action. Section 212 has enabled easier access for a wider range of individuals (beyond shareholders) to the courts to bring a statutory derivative action.

Section 212 enables a complainant to apply to the Court for leave to bring a derivative action in the name and on behalf of the company or any of its subsidiaries, or intervene in an action to which any such company or any of its subsidiaries is a party for the purpose of prosecuting, defending or discontinuing an action on behalf of a company.

The individuals entitled to bring the derivative action are 'complainants' and these persons are defined in section 212(3) as:

---

3. *Telecommunications of Jamaica Limited v Hector Bernard* SCCA No 88/90 Court of Appeal, Jamaica, May 20, 1991.
4. Jamaica Companies Act 1965 s 196(1)(a).
5. Jamaica Companies Act 1965 s 201(f); *Ebrahimi v Westbourne Galleries Ltd.* [1973] AC 360 HL; S Ffolkes Goldson, 'The Use and Misuse of the Oppression Remedy in the Commonwealth Caribbean' (2014) 35 *The Company Lawyer*, Issue 7 Thomson Reuters.

i. a member or former member[6] of the company or an affiliated company;[7]

ii. a debenture holder or former debenture holder of the company or an affiliated company;

iii. a director or officer or former director or officer of a company or an affiliated company.

Although widening the category of persons who can bring a derivative action beyond shareholders at common law, the Act stops short of including creditors and former creditors and 'any other person the Court thinks fit' as is found in Canada and the Commonwealth Caribbean territories who have reformed their companies legislation.[8]

Perhaps the obvious exclusion of the 'any other person the Court thinks fit' category of 'complainant' is due to the fact that it has been interpreted widely in Canada[9] and in Barbados to include a party to a pre-incorporation contract[10] and in Trinidad and Tobago[11] where Ventour J expressed the view that the discretion was 'very wide'.

The provision is, however, faithful to the underlying philosophy of the rule in *Foss v Harbottle*[12] by requiring that the Court be satisfied that certain standards are met before granting leave to a complainant to bring a derivative action.

These requirements are that:

i. the complainant gives reasonable notice to the directors of the company or its subsidiary of his/her intention to apply to the court to bring the derivative action;

ii. the complainant is acting in good faith;

---

6. 'shareholder' changed to 'member' by Companies (Amendment) Act 2017.
7. *Caribbean Paper Recycling Company Ltd, Re* HCV 01705 of 2005 Supreme Court, Jamaica, September 7, 2006, (JM 2006 SC 83); *Grenada General Insurance Co Ltd v Grenada Insurance Services Ltd* Civ App No 12 of 1999 Court of Appeal, Grenada, January 24, 2000 (GD 2000 CA 1); *Schnake v Trincan Oil Ltd* HCA 1245 of 2006 High Court, Trinidad and Tobago, July 30, 2008 (TT 2008 HC 222); *St George v Hayward* Suit No 223A of 2006 Supreme Court, The Bahamas, November 10, 2008 (BS 2008 SC 113).
8. See Canada Business Corporations Act 1985 (CBCA 1985), s 238; Barbados Companies Act Cap 308, s 225; Trinidad and Tobago Companies Act Cap 81:01, s 239.
9. See *First Edmonton Place Ltd v 315888 Alberta Ltd* (1988) 40 BLR 28, 62.
10. See *Canwest International Inc. v Atlantic TV Limited* Civil Appeal No 2 of 1994 Court of Appeal, Barbados, June 8, 1994 (BB 1994 CA 27).
11. *Five Star Medical and Ambulance Services Ltd v Telecommunications Services of Trinidad and Tobago Ltd* HCA No 1593 of 2001, High Court, Trinidad and Tobago, May 28, 2002 (TT 2002 HC 64). See also *Lopez v Telecommunications Services of Trinidad and Tobago Ltd* HCA CV No 1997 of 2003 High Court, Trinidad and Tobago, October 13, 2004 (TT 2004 HC 84); *Mora Ven Holdings Ltd v Krishna Persad & Associates* HCA 2839 of 2002 High Court, Trinidad and Tobago, April 27, 2005 (TT 2005 HC 32).
12. *Foss v Harbottle* (1943) 67 ER 189.

iii. it appears to be in the interests of the company or its subsidiary.[13]

It appears from the wording of subsection (2), that the complainant must first attempt to have the directors of the company or its subsidiary, bring the derivative action. Further, the complainant must then obtain the leave of the Court to commence proceedings and then must maintain the action in the name of the company. Canadian writers have suggested that this is a 'shareholder's Bleak House' due to the judicial and administrative hurdles involved.[14]

Indeed, some commentators have argued that the provisions do not abolish the rule in *Foss v Harbottle:*[15]

> ...but instead seek to provide a statutory derivative action to obviate some of the 'Byzantine complexity' that has traditionally attended shareholder actions at common law. In particular, the statutory provisions preserve the core principle that the company is the proper plaintiff in respect of wrongs allegedly done to the company, but provide a statutory mechanism for 'complainants' to seek leave to bring an action 'in the name and on behalf of the company.[16]

The better view, however, is that the Rule in *Foss v Harbottle* has been abolished by Section 212 of the Companies Act 2004.

In *Debbian Dewar v Ervin Moo Young et al.*,[17] the Commercial Court refused the claimant leave to bring a derivative action, where two of the three preconditions required by the Act were not satisfied (notice and best interests of the company). It was also held, that where the claimant alleged that the defendants sought to remove her as Managing Director because she refused to sanction the payment of significant sums of money to the chairman, the appropriate action should be under the Oppression Remedy.

> ...despite serious allegations of spending significant sums of money without proper authorization the remedies are not seeking to recover any money from the allegedly miscreant directors. The court cannot therefore see how it is in the best interest to permit a derivative action when the final remedy sought although beneficial to the company can be granted without the derivative action.[18]

In *Sally Ann Fulton v Chas E Ramson Ltd.*,[19] the Commercial Court granted leave to the claimant to bring a derivative action where she alleged that the personal use of company property by a director, was not in the best interest of the company. The court

13. Companies Act 2004, s 212(2).
14. W Kaplan and B Elwood, 'The Derivative Action: A Shareholder's 'Bleak House' (2003) 36 *UBCL Rev* 443.
15. *Foss v Harbottle* (1943) 67 ER 189.
16. CD Morrison, 'The Companies Act 2004 – Complainants' Remedies'. (Faculty of Law Companies Act 2004 Symposium, Kingston, April 2004) 5, 6; Kaplan and Elwood, 'The Derivative Action.'
17. [2015] JMCC Comm 23.
18. *Debbian Dewar v Ervin Moo Young et al.* [2015] JMCC Comm 23 [82].
19. [2016] JMSC Comm 14.

confirmed that the same circumstance may give rise to both an oppression action and a derivative action. In deciding whether a claimant may bring a derivative action or an oppression action, the court is to focus on the nature of the complaint.

The Oppression Remedy

Section 213A[20] introduces a remedy for a complainant where conduct is oppressive or unfairly prejudicial or unfairly disregards the interests of any member, debenture holder, creditor, director or officer of the company. Unlike the derivative action, a complainant need not apply for leave to bring an action under section 213A.

Section 213A does not specify the method of application, however, it has been accepted that the appropriate method is by way of petition on the basis that the relevant oppression section of the repealed Act had so stipulated.[21]

Canadian and Caribbean case law have confirmed that the oppressive conduct must affect the interest of the victims in their capacity as shareholder (qua shareholder), debenture holder (qua debenture holder), creditor (qua creditor), director (qua director) or officer (qua officer) of the company.[22]

The section broadens the scope of those persons who may be the victim of oppression or unfair prejudice, beyond that of the complainant, to include creditors. The Act does not include a creditor or former creditor in the definition of 'complainant' in section 212. Whether the inclusion of creditor and former creditor in the victim class in section 213A is a legislative oversight is not clear, but it appears that the intention of Parliament could not have been to have a victim class which is wider than the complainant class.[23]

In most of the Commonwealth Caribbean territories, the complainant class is wider than the victim class as the complainant class, in addition to the complainant class under section 212 of the Act, includes the Registrar and 'any other person, who in the discretion of the Court, is a proper person to make an application'. The victim class, however, does not include the Registrar or 'any other person who in the discretion of the court is a proper person'. Some Commonwealth Caribbean cases have not limited the victims to the victim class such as *Five Star Medical and Ambulance*

---

20. See also CBCA, s 241; Barbados Companies Act Cap 308, s 228; Trinidad and Tobago Companies Act Cap 81:01, s 242; cf St. Christopher and Nevis Companies Act No 22 of 1996 (St. Christopher and Nevis Companies Act 1996), ss141–143.
21. See Jamaica Companies Act 1967, s 196; *Caribbean Paper Recycling Company Limited, Re* HCV 01705 of 2005 Supreme Court, Jamaica, September 7, 2006, (JM 2006 SC 83).
22. See *Naneff v Con-Crete Holdings Limited* [1995] 23 OR (3rd) 481; *St. George v Hayward* Suit No 223A of 2006 Supreme Court, The Bahamas, November 10, 2008 (BS 2008 SC 113).
23. Ffolkes Goldson, 'The Use and Misuse of the Canadian Corporate Oppression Remedy in the Commonwealth Caribbean'.

Services Limited v Telecommunications Services of Trinidad and Tobago Limited,[24] where a party to a contract with the Defendant was considered a complainant as a proper person in the discretion of the court to bring an action and entitled to a remedy, although not a member of the victim class. In *Canwest International Inc. et al. v Atlantic TV Limited*[25] a party to a pre-incorporation contract was considered a 'proper person' to bring an action and entitled to relief, even though not falling within the victim class. Also, in *Demerara Holdings Ltd. v Demerara Life Assurance Co. of Trinidad and Tobago Ltd.*[26] it was held that a merger agreement would be unfairly prejudicial to and unfairly disregard the interests of the policyholders of Demerara Life within the meaning of the Trinidad and Tobago Companies Act, although not a member of the victim class. However, recent Commonwealth Caribbean cases are taking a restrictive approach to the oppression section and limiting remedies only to the victim class.[27] This differs from the approach taken in Canada in *PCL Industrial Constructors Inc. v CLR Construction Labour Relations Association of Saskatchewan Inc.*[28] where the court viewed the difference between the complainant class and the victim class as a legislative oversight. The Saskatchewan Court of Appeal took a purposive rather than a literal approach and filled the legislative gap by expanding the victim class to include the complainant class.[29]

'Oppression' at common law is defined as 'burdensome, harsh or wrongful'[30] and has retained this meaning in recent Canadian and Commonwealth Caribbean territories.[31] It has also included in its meaning, departure from standards of fair

24. *Five Star Medical and Ambulance Services Ltd v Telecommunications Services of Trinidad and Tobago Ltd* HCA No 1593 of 2001, High Court, Trinidad and Tobago, May 28, 2002 (TT 2002 HC 64).
25. *Canwest International Inc. v Atlantic TV Ltd* Civil Appeal No 2 of 1994 Court of Appeal, Barbados, June 8, 1994 (BB 1994 CA 27).
26. HCA No. 3015 of 2000.
27. See *Lopez v Telecommunications Services of Trinidad and Tobago Ltd* HCA CV No 1997 of 2003 High Court, Trinidad and Tobago, October 13, 2004 (TT 2004 HC 84); *St. George v Hayward* which differs from the liberal approach taken previously in *Five Star Medical and Canwest International Inc.*
28. (1995) QBG No 1651, 2000 SKCA 15 (CA).
29. Ffolkes Goldson, 'The Use and Misuse of the Canadian Corporate Oppression Remedy in the Commonwealth Caribbean'.
30. *Scottish Co-operative Wholesale Society Ltd v Meyer* [1959] AC 324, 342.
31. See *Burnett v Tsang* (1985) 29 BLR 196; *Westfair Foods Ltd v Watt* (1991) 5 BLR (2d) 160; *Lalla v Trinidad Cement Ltd* HCA No CV S-852 of 1998 High Court, Trinidad and Tobago, November 30, 1998, 9–10 (TT 1998 HC 172); *Knox v Deane* Civil Suit No 1379 of 2006 High Court, Barbados, November 27, 2006 (BB 2006 HC 17); *Cox v Roberts* Civil Suit No 1948 of 2003 High Court, Barbados, March 29, 2007 (BB 2007 HC 8).

dealing,[32] and abuse of power leading to an impairment of confidence in the probity with which the company's affairs are being conducted. [33]

'Unfairly prejudicial' has been interpreted to mean acts that are 'unjustly or inequitably detrimental'.[34] It has also been defined in England to be a 'visible departure from the standards of fair dealings and a violation of the conditions of fair play on which every shareholder who entrusts his money to a company is entitled to rely.'[35] The Companies (Amendment) Act 2017 amends section 213A to include conduct which 'unfairly disregards' any of those persons named, which already exists in legislation found in Canada and the Commonwealth Caribbean.[36] Canada and some Commonwealth Caribbean territories have interpreted 'unfair disregard' to mean 'unjustly or without cause pay no attention to, ignore or treat as of no importance the interests of security holders, creditors, directors or officers'.[37]

Commonwealth Caribbean cases have acknowledged oppression where a plaintiff director alleged wrongful termination in *Lalla v Trinidad Cement Limited*.[38]

> If the third Defendant acted out of spite or malice, and used his position as Chairman to influence the directors to suspend and terminate the plaintiff's directorship, then the exercise of such power.... may be Oppression as contemplated by section 242 of the Companies Act. Also, if the basis for the plaintiff's suspension and termination as CEO was a loss of confidence in him as such, then such a conclusion ought to be bona fide. That is, it ought to be justifiable. If it is not justifiable it may be unfair, and if it is unfair it may be Oppression.[39]

The concept of 'unfair' has been enlarged beyond the traditional view to include 'legitimate expectation'. Legitimate expectation arises where 'the decision-making body, by action or inaction, has led a citizen to the belief that a benefit that he or she enjoys will continue to be enjoyed or at any rate will not be taken away without

32. See *Chancery Lane Partners Ltd v Dell* Civil Appeal No 1 of 1986 Court of Appeal, Barbados, December 19, 1986 (BB 1986 CA 12).
33. See *Devaux v Du Boulay Holdings Ltd* Civ App No 32 of 2003 Court of Appeal, St Lucia, February 28, 2005 (LC 2005 CA 3).
34. See *Diligenti v RWMD Operations Kelowna Ltd* (1976) 1 BCLR 36, 45; *Lalla v Trinidad Cement Ltd* HCA No CV S-852 of 1998 High Court, Trinidad and Tobago, November 30, 1998 (TT 1998 HC 172).
35. Jenkins Committee in the Report of the Company Law Committee Cmnd 1749 [1962].
36. *PCL Industrial Constructors Inc. v CLR Construction Labour Relations Association of Saskatchewan Inc.* (1995) QBG No 1651, 2000 SKCA 15 (CA).
37. See *Stech v Davies* (1987) 53 Alta LR (2d) 373; *Hamilton v Sartorio* [1991] 3 WWR 670, 676–77; *Lalla v Trinidad Cement Ltd* HCA No CV S-852 of 1998 High Court, Trinidad and Tobago, November 30, 1998 (TT 1998 HC 172); *Knox v Deane* Civil Suit No 1379 of 2006 High Court, Barbados, November 27, 2006 (BB 2006 HC 17); *Cox v Roberts* Civil Suit No 1948 of 2003 High Court, Barbados, March 29, 2007 (BB 2007 HC 8).
38. *Lalla v Trinidad Cement Ltd* HCA No CV S-852 of 1998 High Court, Trinidad and Tobago, November 30, 1998 (TT 1998 HC 172).
39. Jamadar J, *Lalla v Trinidad Cement Ltd* HCA No CV S-852 of 1998 High Court, Trinidad and Tobago at 28.

him or her having an opportunity to make representations'.[40] However, Hoffman LJ in *O'Neill v Phillips*[41] warns that, '...the concept of legitimate expectation should not be allowed to lead a life of its own....'[42] The Supreme Court of Canada in *BCE Inc. v 1976 Debentureholders*[43] introduced a two-pronged test which requires firstly, that the complainant establish a breach of a reasonable expectation and secondly, that the conduct complained of amounts to unfairness to the complainant. This test was applied in the Trinidad and Tobago case of *Demerara Holdings Limited; Bertrand Doyle; Harold Russell and Gervais de Matas v Demerara Life Assurance Company of Trinidad and Tobago Limited; Mega Insurance Company Limited; Wilber Winchester; Peter Gilette and Cyril Gyll*[44] where a merger agreement between two insurance companies was set aside on the grounds that the business or affairs of the First and Second Defendants as affiliated companies had been, and were being carried on or conducted and were destined to be carried on or conducted, and the powers of the Fourth and Fifth Defendants as directors of both companies had been exercised in a manner that was oppressive or unfairly prejudicial to or unfairly disregarded the interest of the First Plaintiff as a former shareholder of the First Defendant and a shareholder of the Second Defendant, and the interests of the holders of life policies issued by the First Defendant for whom the First Plaintiff acted as Trustee. The reasonable expectation test was also applied in *Dallas Corp., Thomas Baker v Alnando Corporation et al.*[45] where it was held that the failure to issue shares, failure to give access to financial records, not allowing the claimants to share in controlling the business of the companies, the failure to allow the first claimant to be represented on the boards of the companies, the exclusion of the claimants from the business operations and the failure to identify other company officers who could provide information, breached the reasonable expectations of the claimant.

The reasonable expectation test was also applied by the Barbados Court of Appeal in *Ansa MCAL (Barbados) Ltd. v Banks Holdings Ltd. and SLU Beverages Ltd.*[46]

> There can be little doubt that the 'interests' sought to be protected in the oppression provisions must be interpreted in light of the purpose of the oppression remedy itself. The purpose of this remedy is to give relief for thwarted expectations of persons in the protected category. Thus, determination of the 'interests' of the

---

40. CD Morrison, 'The Citizen and the Law – Perspectives Old and New' (Grace Kennedy Foundation Lecture 2004, Kingston, March 2004) 17.
41. [1999] 1 WLR 1092. See also *Caribbean Paper Recycling Company Ltd* HCV 01705 of 2005 Supreme Court, Jamaica, September 7, 2006 (JM 2006 SC 83).
42. cf *Grenada General Insurance Co Ltd v Grenada Insurance Services Ltd* Civ App No 12 of 1999 Court of Appeal, Grenada, January 24, 2000 (GD 2000 CA 1).
43. 2008 SCC 69.
44. HCA No. 3015 OF 2000/CV2006-00099 High Court, Trinidad and Tobago, April 1, 2011.
45. CV2011-04466 High Court, Trinidad and Tobago, May 24, 2017.
46. Civil Appeal No. 21 of 2015.

protected category is essentially a determination of the reasonable expectations of the persons in the protected category.[47]

The Jamaican Commercial Court applied the reasonable expectation and legitimate expectation tests in order to determine whether there was oppression or unfair prejudice in the case of, inter alia, an unlawful allotment of shares, a lack of a properly convened general meeting, and a lack of a resolution for the variation of voting rights and rights to dividends.[48]

Unfair Prejudice and unfair disregard were found in *Grenada General Insurance Company Limited et al. v Grenada Insurance Services Limited*[49] where the respondent was denied his legitimate expectation to contribute equally with the second appellant in the decision-making process of the first appellant.

Section 213 also gives the Court the power to make any interim or final order it thinks fit including:

a. restraining the conduct complained of;[50]

b. appointing a receiver or receiver manager;

c. regulating a company's affairs by amending its Articles or by-laws, or creating or amending a unanimous shareholder agreement;

d. directing an issue or exchange of shares or debentures;

e. appointing directors in place of, or in addition to, all or any of the directors then in office;

f. directing a company, subject to subsection (4), or any other person to purchase the shares or debentures of a holder thereof;[51]

g. directing a company, subject to a solvency test, or any other person to pay to a shareholder or debenture holder any part of the monies paid by him for his shares or debentures;

---

47. Andrew Burgess, *Commonwealth Caribbean Company Law*, (Routledge 2013) 332.
48. *Benkley Northover v Eric Northover and Rohan Northover and Godfrey Dixon and Winston G. Northover Associates Limited* [2014] JMCC Comm. 14.
49. *Grenada General Insurance Co Ltd v Grenada Insurance Services Ltd* Civ App No 12 of 1999 Court of Appeal, Grenada, January, 24, 2000 (GD 2000 CA 1).
50. The Canadian courts are still developing a threshold test for the grant of mareva injunctions in oppression cases. One school of thought is that interim relief should be based on the strict standards for interlocutory injunctions (*M v H* 1993 Carswell Ont 365 (Ct J (Gen Div))). Other cases suggest a more relaxed standard (*First Choice Capital Fund Ltd v First Canadian Capital Corp* 1997 CarswellSask 435; [1997] SJ No 390).
51. See *Caribbean Paper Recycling Company Limited* HCV 01705 of 2005 Supreme Court, Jamaica, September 7, 2006 (JM 2006 SC 83).

h. varying or setting aside a transaction or contract to which a company is a party, and compensating the company or any other party to the transaction or contract;[52]

i. requiring a company, within the time specified by the Court, to produce to the Court or an interested person, financial statements or an accounting in such forms as the Court may determine;

j. compensating an aggrieved person;[53]

k. directing rectification of the registers or other records of the company;

l. liquidating and dissolving the company;

m. directing an investigation to be made; or

n. requiring the trial of any issue.

Where the Court orders the winding up of a company, the question arises whether the same criteria of 'just and equitable', under the repealed Jamaica Companies Act 1965, would be necessary.[54]

The better view, as stated in *O'Neill v Phillips*[55] and approved in *Re Guidezone Ltd*,[56] is that 'unfairness' is the criterion and not 'just and equitable' as the 'just and equitable' grounds for winding up are restricted to circumstances of section 459 of the United Kingdom Companies Act 1985 which is the equivalent of the Jamaica Companies Act 2004 section 220(e).

In the Jamaican case of *Caribbean Paper Recycling Company Limited, Re*[57] it was held that although the shareholder could avail himself of the oppression remedy under section 213A, despite the fact that he had not yet paid for his shares, it was inappropriate to grant him the remedy of a just and equitable winding up as he had not first complied with the provisions of rule 33 of the Companies (Winding Up) Rules 1949. Rule 33 provides that a petitioner is required to attend upon the Registrar of the Supreme Court and satisfy the Registrar that the petitioner has complied with the provisions of the Rules with respect to petitions prior to the hearing of the application. It was further held that the appropriate remedy under the circumstances, which was

52. See *Demerara Holdings Limited; Bertrand Doyle; Harold Russell and Gervais de Matas v Demerara Life Assurance Company of Trinidad and Tobago Limited; Mega Insurance Company Limited; Wilber Winchester; Peter Gilette and Cyril Gyll* HCA No. 3015 OF 2000/CV2006-00099 High Court, Trinidad and Tobago, April 1, 2011.

53. See *Schnake v Trincan Oil Ltd* HCA 1245 of 2006 High Court, Trinidad and Tobago, July 30, 2008 (TT 2008 HC 222).

54. See *Ebrahimi v Westbourne Galleries Ltd* [1973] AC 360, 379.

55. *O'Neil v Phillip* [1999] 1 WLR 1092.

56. [2001] BCC 692; see also *CVC/ Opportunity Equity Partners Ltd v Demarco* [2002] UKPC 16, (2002) 60 WIR 70; *Ward v Rum Refinery of Mount Gay Ltd* No 357 of 1990 High Court, Barbados, October 25, 1990 (BB 1990 HC 64).

57. *Caribbean Paper Recycling Company Limited* HCV 01705 of 2005 Supreme Court, Jamaica, September 7, 2006 (JM 2006 SC 83).

found to be oppressive conduct in what appeared to be a quasi-partnership, was an order that the defendants purchase the shares of the petitioner.

It is further established that the orders under section 213 should not be made in excess of the specific wrong but to rectify the matter complained of.[58]

A complainant who initiates a derivative action under section 212 is not precluded from pursuing an action for oppression under section 213A provided that there is evidence of oppression or unfair prejudice which causes direct harm to any member of the victim class.[59] On the other hand, the derivative action may only be brought by a complainant on behalf of the company for a wrong done to the company. There may, therefore, be instances where there is both harm done to the company and direct harm done to a member of the victim class. Indirect harm to a member of the victim class will not suffice for an action under section 213A.[60]

It appears that the Canadian courts are more willing to find direct harm to shareholders of closely-held companies or quasi-partnerships where the directors who are shareholders or controlling shareholders are involved in self-dealing. In *Gopal v Burke*,[61] the Supreme Court of British Columbia found that where a corporate opportunity had been diverted to a majority shareholder, both a derivative action for a wrong done to the company and an oppression action for a wrong done to the minority shareholder were justified.

The Companies Act has retained the provision for winding up on 'just and equitable' grounds from the Companies Act 1965.[62] This, however, may have been an oversight, as arguably the oppression remedy provides for just and equitable winding up where there is oppressive conduct as the Court may make any order as it thinks fit including 'liquidating and dissolving the company.'[63]

58. See *Ontario Inc v Harold E. Ballard Ltd* [1991] 3 BLR (2d) 113.
59. See *Furry Creek Timber Corp v Laad Ventures Ltd* (1992) 75 BCLR (2d) 246.
60. See *Bruneau v Irwin Industries* (1978) Ltd 2002 BCSC 757; *Pasnak v Chura* 2004 BCCA 221.
61. 2007 BCSC 1930.
62. s 223(2).
63. Companies Act 2004, s 213A(3)(l); Ffolkes Goldson, 'The Use and Misuse of the Oppression Remedy in the Commonwealth Caribbean', 196–97.

5. Winding Up

When the Companies Act 2004 was enacted, a decision was made not to amend the provisions relating to corporate rescue, insolvency and winding up until the advent of an Insolvency Act.[1] The provisions relating to the winding up of insolvent companies in the 1965 Companies Act, therefore, survived the new Companies Act 2004, until the enactment of the Insolvency Act 2014, which has as its objects:

1. the rehabilitation of debtors and the preservation of viable companies, having due regard to the protection of the rights of creditors and other stakeholders; and
2. fair allocation of the costs of insolvencies with the overriding interest of strengthening and protecting Jamaica's economic and financial system and the availability and flow of credit within the economy.[2]

The old insolvency regime was time-consuming and costly, created stigma, created little or no provision for rescue and rehabilitation of the business and affairs of the debtor, and consisted of very few specialists. Oftentimes, other remedies were used for addressing insolvency, including informal agreements, compromises, constructive and remedial trusts, Mareva injunctions or freezing orders, and the oppression remedy. Any of these remedies, however, could put the debtor at further risk. Prior to the Insolvency Act, the Companies Act contemplated rescue through Schemes of Arrangement, otherwise, death of the company was the only other option either by receiverships or liquidation and winding up. There were no provisions for voluntary out-of-court arrangements for moratoria or temporary stays of execution.[3]

A number of provisions of the Companies Act 2004 have now been repealed or amended to reflect the Insolvency Act 2014. An insolvent company cannot now be wound up under the Companies Act. The Insolvency Act provides, inter alia, for the filing of a Proposal or an 'Intention to Make a Proposal' to creditors by a company which is insolvent, or facing imminent insolvency, in order to provide short-term relief from their claims. There is an automatic stay of proceedings upon the filing of a notice of intention to make a Proposal or when a Proposal is filed,[4] and special provision is made for securing financing during the stay of proceedings (Debtor in Possession

---

1. Report of the Joint Select Committee on the Bill Shortly Entitled The Companies Act 1998 dates January, 2001.
2. Insolvency Act 2014, s 3.
3. S Ffolkes Goldson, 'The Reform of Jamaica's Insolvency Law: Balancing the Interests of Creditors and Debtors' 37 (2) *West Indian Law Journal* 171.
4. Insolvency Act 2014, s 4 and 5.

Financing).[5] The concept of the Proposal, therefore, facilitates the preservation of the insolvents' assets for the benefit of their creditors, and also the rehabilitation of the insolvents.

The old provisions on winding up of solvent companies, however, are retained in the Companies Act 2004 which still largely reflect the position under the repealed Companies Act 1965.

A. Arrangements and Reconstructions

Section 205A, which is a new section, states that sections 206–211 of the Companies Act,

> ...may be applied in conjunction or together with Part III of the Insolvency Act, but where a notice of intention to make a proposal or a proposal is filed under the Insolvency Act in respect of a company, any compromise or arrangement between a company and its creditors, or with any class of them, shall be effected only in accordance with the Insolvency Act.[6]

Sections 206–211 are substantially the same as sections on arrangements and reconstructions in the repealed Companies Act 1965. The old UK position is therefore retained.[7]

Section 206 defines 'arrangement' for the purposes of sections 206 and 207 as including a reorganization of the share capital of the company by the consolidation of shares of different classes or by division of shares of different classes or by both those methods. 'Company' for the purposes of section 206 and 207 means any company liable to be wound up under the Companies Act.

Section 206(1) provides that a company, any creditor or member of the company, or the trustee (where a company is in the course of being wound up), may make a summary application to the Court to order a meeting of the creditors, or class of creditors, or of the members of the company, or class of members in order to sanction any compromise or arrangement that is proposed between them.

Section 206(2) provides that any compromise or arrangement agreed by a majority in number representing three-fourths in value of the creditors or class of creditors or members or class of members as the case may be, present and voting either in person or by proxy, shall be binding on all those persons concerned and also on the company or the trustee and contributories of the company (where a company is in the course of being wound up), if sanctioned by the Court.

Section 206(3) provides that the order must be delivered to the Registrar for registration and a copy of every such order shall be annexed to every copy of the Articles of the company issued after the order has been made before it has legal effect.

---

5. Insolvency Act 2014, s 55.
6. Ibid., s 311 amending Companies Act 2004.
7. UK Companies Act 1948, s 206.

A stay of delivery of an order to the Registrar sanctioning a scheme of arrangement must be obtained before an appeal against the grant of an order sanctioning a scheme of arrangement can be heard.[8]

Section 206(4) provides for sanctions against the company and every officer of the company who is in default of subsection (3).

Section 207 provides that information as to compromises with creditors and members should accompany every notice summoning the meeting ordered under section 206. The necessary information includes:

1. a statement explaining the effect of the compromise or arrangement which should include any material interests of the directors of the company whether as directors or as members or as creditors of the company or otherwise, and the effect thereon of the compromise or arrangement in so far as it is different from the effect on the like interests of other persons; or
2. alternatively, a notification of the place at which and the manner in which creditors or members entitled to attend the meeting may obtain copies of such a statement, free of charge if the notice is by advertisement.

Where the compromise or arrangement affects the rights of debenture holders of the company, the statement shall give the like explanation as respects the trustees of any deed for securing the issue of the debentures, as it is required to give, as respects the company's directors.

UK case law has outlined the duties of the court where there is an application for the court's approval of a compromise or scheme of arrangement:

i. To see that the statutory prerequisites must be complied with before the Court has jurisdiction to confirm the scheme. The class of creditors or members who will be asked to separately vote for or against the scheme must be properly constituted.[9] They ought not to be treated as one class if they have differing interests.
ii. A discretionary power to see whether the scheme is fair.[10] This means that not only should section 206 be complied with but the proposal is such that an intelligent and honest man, who is a member of the class concerned and acting alone in respect of his interest might reasonably approve.[11]

Section 208 outlines the provisions for facilitating reconstruction and amalgamation of companies in the context of a proposal for a compromise or

---

8. *Federated Strategic Income Fund v Mechala Group Jamaica Limited et al.* SCCA No 47 of 2000 Court of Appeal, Jamaica, December 20, 2000 (JM 2000 CA 49); *Norcan Oils Ltd v Fogler* [1965] SCR 36 in the context of an amalgamation.
9. *United Provident Assurance Co Ltd, Re* [1910] 2 Ch. 477; *British American Nickel Corporation Limited and Others v MJ O'Brien Ltd* (1927) AC 369 (PC); *Goodfellow v Nelson Line (Liverpool) Ltd* [1912] 2 Ch. 324; *Hellenic & General Trust Ltd, Re* [1975] 3 All ER 382, [1976] 1 WLR 123.
10. *Dorman Long and Co Ltd, Re* [1934] Ch. 635.
11. Ibid.

arrangement which will result in the whole or any part of the undertaking or the property of the transferor company to be transferred to the transferee company. The Court may by any order sanctioning the compromise or arrangement, or by any subsequent order, make provision for all or any number of matters.

Creditors for the Blaise Financial entities and the Century National entities initiated successful schemes of arrangements which resulted in the transfer of all their assets to the Financial Institution Services Limited. As a result, the depositors of these entities were substantially, if not entirely, paid out. National Commercial Bank had a successful member/shareholder-initiated scheme of arrangement.[12]

Section 209 provides that where a scheme or contract involves the transfer of shares or any class of shares in a transferor company to a transferee company, the transferee company may have the power to acquire the shares of the shareholders dissenting from the scheme or contract approved by the majority. The majority required for approval is, the holders of not less than nine-tenths in value of the shares whose transfer is involved.

The requirements are as follows:

i. The offer involving the transfer of the shares, or any class of shares in the transferor company to the transferee company, must be approved within four months by the holders of not less than nine-tenths in value of the shares, whose transfer is involved.

ii. The transferee company may, at any time within two months after the expiration of the four months, give notice in the prescribed manner to any dissenting shareholder whose shares it desires to acquire.

iii. The transferee company shall be entitled and bound to acquire those shares on the terms outlined in the scheme of arrangement, unless a dissenting shareholder has made a successful application to the Court for an order otherwise, within one month from the date on which the notice was given.

B. *Winding Up and Liquidation*

Section 213B is an amendment to the Companies Act and states that:

> Except for sections 214 to 220 and sections 272 and 273, the provisions of this Act with respect winding-up, including Part IX shall not apply in respect of a company or unregistered company within the meaning of section 355 that is an insolvent person within the meaning of the Insolvency Act.[13]

Sections 214–220 of the Companies Act, deal with the winding up of companies.

---

12. E Greenaway and S Ffolkes Goldson, 'Booms Need Busts Improving the Legal Framework for Insolvency' (2012) Caribbean Policy Research Institute CaPRI Policy Brief B121. See also S Minott-Phillips, 'Schemes of Arrangement Under the Companies Act, 2004: Lessons for Jamaica' (2005) WILJ Vol 30 (1) & (2), 81.
13. Insolvency Act 2014, s 311 amending the Companies Act 2004.

These provisions are a carbon copy of the provisions on winding up under the repealed Companies Act.

I. Modes of Winding Up

Section 214 outlines the 3 modes of winding up:

1. Winding up by the Court.
2. Voluntary Winding Up.
3. Winding Up Subject to the Supervision of the Court.

II. Contributories

Sections 215–219 deal with the liability of contributories, the definition of contributories, the nature of the liability of a contributory and contributories in the cases of death or bankruptcy of members.

Section 215 provides that in the event of a winding up every present and past member shall be liable to contribute to:

i. the assets of the company to an amount sufficient for payment of its debts and liabilities;

ii. costs, charges, and expenses of the winding up;

iii. the adjustment of the rights of the contributories among themselves.

A past member shall not be liable to contribute if that member has ceased to be a member for one year or upwards before the commencement of the winding up, in respect of any debt or liability of the company contracted after he ceased to be a member, or unless it appears to the Court, that the existing members are unable to satisfy the contributions required to be made by them in pursuance of the Companies Act.

Members of companies limited by shares shall not be required to contribute an amount exceeding the amount, if any, unpaid on the shares in respect of which he is liable as a present or past member.

Members of companies limited by guarantee shall not be required to contribute an amount exceeding the amount undertaken to be contributed by him to the assets of the company in the event of its being wound up, except as provided in section 215(2) in the case of a member of a company limited by guarantee which has a share capital, to contribute to the extent of any sums unpaid on any shares held by him.

Provisions in any policy of insurance or other contract restricting the liability of individual members or making the funds of the company alone liable in respect of the policy or contract is not invalidated by the Companies Act.

Sums due to any member of a company qua member by way of dividends, profits or otherwise shall not be deemed a debt of the company but may be taken into account for the purpose of the final adjustment of the rights of the contributories among themselves.

The liability of a contributory shall create a debt in the nature of a specialty accruing due from him at the time when his liability commenced, but payable at the times when calls are made for enforcing the liability.

Section 216 defines 'contributory' as every person liable to contribute to the assets of a company in the event of it being wound up, and for the purposes of all proceedings for determining and all proceedings prior to the final determination of, the persons who are to be deemed contributories include any person alleged to be a contributory.

Sections 218 and 219 provide for contributories in the case of death of a member or bankruptcy of a member respectively. In the case of death of a contributory, the personal representatives shall be contributories. In the case of bankruptcy, the Trustee of his estate shall be a contributory and shall represent him for all the purposes of winding up.[14] Where there is death of a contributory, it does not mean that the deceased member or his estate is no longer a member of the company, where his name remains on the register and the company has no notice of the death.[15]

1. *Winding Up By The Court*

Section 220 outlines the circumstances in which companies may be wound up by the Court:

i. The company has by special resolution resolved that the company be wound up by the Court;
ii. Default is made in delivering the statutory report to the Registrar or in holding the statutory meeting;
iii. The company does not commence its business within a year from its incorporation, or suspends its business for a whole year;
iv. The Court is of the opinion that it is just and equitable that the company should be wound up.[16]

I. Default in Delivering the Statutory Report or in Holding the Statutory Meeting

Where default is made in delivering the statutory report or holding a statutory meeting, section 222(1)(a) provides that a winding up application shall not be presented by any person except a member, nor before the expiration of fourteen days after the last day on which the meeting ought to have been held.

14. Insolvency Act 2014, s 311 amending the Companies Act 2004.
15. *New Zealand Gold Extraction Co (Newbery-Vautin Process) v Peacock* [1894] 1 QB 622 (CA).
16. *CVC/Opportunity Equity Partners Ltd. Demarco* [2002] UKPC 16, (2002) 60 WIR 70 [31]; *The Inertia Partnership LLP, Re* [2007] BCC 656 [51]; *Walter L. Jacob and Co Ltd. Re* (1989) 5 BCC 244 (CA).

Section 223(3) provides that the Court may make a winding up order or direct that the statutory report be delivered or that a meeting be held and order the costs to be paid by any persons who, in the opinion of the Court, are responsible for the default.

II. Just and Equitable Winding Up

Section 223(2) provides that the Court shall make an order to wind up the company, where an application is presented by members of the company as contributories on the ground that it is just and equitable that the company be wound up where:

i. the Court is of the opinion that the applicants are entitled to relief either by the winding up of the company or by some other means; and

ii. that in the absence of any other remedy it would be just and equitable that the company should be wound up.

The relief sought is equitable in nature and therefore legal rights are subject to equitable considerations.[17]

In the leading House of Lords case of *Ebrahimi v Westbourne Galleries Ltd and Others (On Appeal from In Re Westbourne Galleries Ltd)*[18] it was held that the appropriate remedy was a just and equitable winding up of the company where the relationship between the parties resembled a partnership. Section 223(2), however, states that the remedy is only to be applied in the absence of any other remedy. Recent Canadian cases have recognised grounds which have historically been relied upon to invoke the provision.[19] These grounds are:

a. loss of substratum;[20]

b. lack of confidence among the members;[21]

c. deadlock;[22] and

d. quasi-partnership.[23]

In the Caymanian case of *CVC/Opportunity Equity Partners Limited, Opportunity Invest II Limited v Luis Roberto Demarco Almeida*,[24] the Privy Council confirmed that a company cannot restrain a shareholder from petitioning a winding up of the company

---

17. *Ebrahimi v Westbourne Galleries Ltd* [1973] AC 360.
18. [1973] AC 360.
19. *Vivian v Firth* 2012 BCSC 517.
20. *German Date Coffee Co, Re* (1882) 20 Ch. D 169; *Red Rock Gold Mining Co Ltd, Re* (1889) 61 LT 785.
21. *Loch v John Blackwood Ltd* [1924] AC 783 (PC).
22. *Palmieri v AC Paving Co Ltd* (1999) 48 BLR (2d) 130 (BCSC).
23. *Golden Pheasant Holding Corp v Synergy Corporate Management* 2011 BCSC 173; *Paulson v Dogwood Holdings Ltd* [1990] BCJ No 2281 (SC); *Ebrahimi v Westbourne Galleries Ltd* [1973] AC 360, 500.
24. [2002] UKPC 16, [2002] 2 BCLC 108.

where the company has offered to purchase the shares of the shareholder at a valuation which falls far short of a fair offer and fails to remedy his complaint. In that case, there was no other suitable remedy available to the shareholder. The Privy Council, however, emphasized that the Court will not allow the minority shareholder to use the threat of winding up proceedings in order to bring pressure on the majority in order to yield to the demands of the minority shareholder.[25]

The Jamaican case of *Howell v Bryan*[26] illustrates the necessity to aver that the company is solvent in a winding up application. There are, however, exceptions to this rule.[27]

III. Application for Winding Up by the Court

Section 222 states that an application for the winding up of the company by the court is by way of application[28] and may be presented by:

i. the company;

ii. any creditor or creditors (including contingent or prospective creditors);

iii. any contributory or contributories;[29]

iv. by all or any of the above together or separately.

Section 222(d) provides that a winding up application may be presented by the Minister under section 165(4) which provides for the Minister to present an application for a company to be wound up if the Court thinks it just and equitable that it should be wound up or an application for an order under section 213 or both unless the company is already being wound up by the Court. The Minister may present the application in circumstances if from a report of inspectors to investigate the affairs of a company under section 161, it appears to the Minister that there are circumstances suggesting:

a. that its business is being conducted with intent to defraud its creditors or the creditors of any other person or otherwise for a fraudulent or unlawful

---

25. *Khemlani v Public Supermarket Ltd* Civil Appeal 107 of 2006 Court of Appeal, Jamaica, April 24, 2008 (JM 2008 CA 26); *CJ's Rent A Car Limited v Premium Finance Limited* No 67 of 1996 Court of Appeal, Jamaica, December 20, 1996 (JM 1996 CA 49). See also the Barbadian case of *Halcyon Heights Limited, Re* No 721 of 1979 High Court, Barbados, February 6, 1981 (BB 1981 HC 6).
26. No 11 of 1990 Court of Appeal, Jamaica, July 16, 1990 (JM 1990 CA 61).
27. *Newman and Howard Ltd, Re* (1962) Ch. 257 where the Petitioner's lack of locus standi is due to the company's own default in providing him with information to which he is entitled as a member. See *Chesterfield Catering Co Ltd, Re* (1977) Ch. 373, 379.
28. Insolvency Act 2014, s 311 amending the Companies Act 2014.
29. The shares must have been originally allotted to the contributory or have been held by and registered in the name of the contributory for at least six months during the eighteen months before the commencement of the winding up or have devolved on the contributory through the death of a former holder. Companies Act 2004, s 222(1)(a).

purpose or in a manner oppressive of any part of its members or that it was formed for any fraudulent or unlawful purpose; or

b. that persons concerned with its formation or the management of its affairs have in connection therewith been guilty of fraud, misfeasance or other misconduct towards it or towards its members.

On hearing a winding up application, section 223(1) provides that the Court may dismiss it, or adjourn the hearing conditionally, or make any interim order, or any other order that it thinks fit.

The Court shall not refuse to make a winding up order on the ground only that the assets of the company have been mortgaged to an amount equal to or in excess of those assets, or that the company has no assets.[30]

The Court has the power under section 224 to stay or restrain proceedings against the company at any time after the presentation of a winding up application and before a winding up order has been made on the application of the company or any creditor or contributory.

Unless the Court otherwise orders, any disposition of the property of the company and any transfer of shares, or alteration in the status of the member of the company made after the commencement of the winding up, shall be void.[31] Any attachment, sequestration, distress or execution put in force against the estate or effects of the company are also void after the commencement of the winding up.[32]

IV. Commencement of Winding Up by the Court

The winding up of a company by the Court shall be deemed to commence at the time of the presentation of the application to the Court, however, if a resolution has been passed by the company for voluntary winding up before the presentation of an application for the winding up of a company by the Court, the winding up of the company shall be deemed to have commenced at the time of the resolution.[33]

The date of commencement of winding up is important in order to determine inter alia whether:

a. the Trustee becomes the provisional trustee;[34]

b. transactions such as dispositions of property, attachment, sequestration, distress or executions are void;[35]

c. the company is no longer a going concern;[36]

30. Companies Act 2004, s 223(1).
31. Ibid., s 225.
32. Ibid., s 226.
33. Companies Act 2004, s 227.
34. Ibid., ss 236, 239, 241.
35. Ibid., ss 225–226.
36. Ibid., s 241(1).

d. there is a fraudulent preference;[37]

e. a creditor has a preferential claim;[38]

f. onerous property can be disclaimed by the trustee'[39]

g. there is a restriction on the rights of creditors as to execution or attachment;[40]

h. further proceedings are to be stayed unless otherwise directed by the Court.[41]

V. Consequences of Winding Up Order

A copy of the winding up order must be delivered to the Registrar and every officer of the company or other person who knowingly and willfully authorizes or permits default in forwarding a copy of the winding up order to the Registrar is liable to a fine.[42]

No action or proceeding shall be proceeded with or commenced against the company when a winding up order has been made or a provisional trustee has been appointed, except with the leave of the Court.[43]

A winding up order operates in favour of all creditors and all contributories of the company as if made on a joint application.[44]

VI. Trustee in Bankruptcy

The Government Trustee ('Trustee') means the person appointed as such under the Insolvency Act and the Supervisor means the person designated under the Insolvency Act as the Supervisor of Insolvency.[45]

A statement of the company's affairs must be submitted to the Trustee (unless otherwise ordered by the Court) in the prescribed form, verified by affidavit and showing:

a. the particulars of its assets, debts and liabilities;

b. the names, residences and occupations of its creditors;

c. the securities held by the creditors respectively;

d. the dates when the securities were respectively given;

---

37. Ibid., s 312.
38. Ibid., s 311. Amended by the Insolvency Act, s 311: In every winding up of a company, section 202 of the Insolvency Act (which relates to the ranking of claims for payment from the proceeds of a debtor's property) shall apply.
39. Companies Act 2004, s 315.
40. Ibid., s 316.
41. Ibid., s 229.
42. Companies Act 2004, s 228.
43. Ibid., s 229.
44. Ibid., s 230.
45. Insolvency Act 2014 amending Companies Act, s 231.

e. any such other information as may be prescribed or as the Trustee may require.[46]

The statement is an accounting document the purpose of which is to show the assets and liabilities and whether there is a deficiency, and if so, the extent of the deficiency.[47]

This statement must be submitted and verified by one or more persons who are at the relevant date, (date of the winding up order or date of the appointment of the trustee), the directors and by the person who is at the date the secretary, or other chief officer of the company or by another person the Trustee may require, to submit and verify the statement. The statement must be submitted within 14 days of the effective date, but may be extended by the Trustee or the Court. Reasonable costs and expenses incurred in and about the preparation and making of the statement and affidavit may be recovered. Persons stating themselves in writing to be a creditor or contributory of the company are entitled to inspect the statement submitted at all reasonable times. Any person untruthfully stating himself to be a creditor or contributory shall be guilty of a contempt of court. The Trustee is required to make a report as soon as practicable after receipt of the statement, however, if the Court orders that no statement shall be submitted, the report is to be made as soon as practicable after the date of the order.[48]

Section 233 provides that the preliminary Trustee report shall contain the following:

a. the amount of capital issued, subscribed, and paid up, and the estimated amount of assets and liabilities;

b. if the company has failed, as to the causes of the failure; and

c. whether in his opinion further inquiry is desirable.

The Trustee may make a further report or reports stating the manner in which the company was formed and whether, in his opinion, any fraud has been committed.[49] Where the Trustee asserts fraud, the Court has further powers under sections 265 (powers of examination) and section 266 (powers to cause the arrest of an absconding contributory).

VII. Trustee[50]

The Court may appoint a trustee or trustees for the purpose of conducting the proceedings and performing such duties as the Court may impose in winding up a company. The Trustee or any other fit person may be appointed provisionally. The

46. Companies Act 2004, s 232(1).
47. SW Magnus and M Estrin, *Companies: Law and Practice* (4th edn, Butterworths 1968) 239.
48. Companies Act 2004, ss 232(2), (3), (4), (6), (7), 233.
49. Ibid., s 233(2).
50. Insolvency Act 2014, s 311 amending the Companies Act 2004 ss 234–250.

Trustee shall by virtue of his office become the provisional trustee until he or another person becomes trustee. To determine whether or not an application is to be made to the Court appointing a trustee in place of the Trustee, the Trustee must call separate meetings of the creditors and contributories. The Court must make an order in accordance with the decisions at the meetings, however, if there is a difference between the determinations of the meetings, the Court shall decide the difference and make such order as it thinks fit. The Trustee shall be the trustee if no trustee is appointed by the Court or during any vacancy (e.g. resignation, removal or death). The Trustee shall be described, where a person other than the Government Trustee is trustee, by the style of 'the Trustee', and, where the Government Trustee is trustee, by the style of 'the Government Trustee and Trustee', of the particular company in respect of which he is appointed, and not by his individual name.[51] In *Financial Services Commission v Dyoll Insurance Company Ltd*,[52] it was held that upon a winding up order being made, section 236(1)(a) precludes the appointment of any person other than the Trustee as the provisional liquidator (now trustee) of the company.

A person appointed as trustee, other than the Trustee, must notify his appointment to the Registrar and give security in such manner as the Court may direct. The trustee is also required to give the Trustee access to facilities for inspection of the books and documents and such aid as may be required for enabling the Trustee to perform his duties. Failure to provide the requisite access and aid subjects the trustee to a fine.[53] He shall receive such salary or remuneration as the Court directs and if there is more than one trustee appointed, in such proportions as the Court may direct. A trustee appointed by the Court may resign or, on cause shown, be removed by the Court and any vacancy in the office of a trustee shall be filled by the Court.[54] The acts of a trustee shall be valid notwithstanding any defects that may afterwards be discovered in his appointment or qualification,[55] except where a body corporate is appointed, since a body corporate is not qualified for appointment as trustee.[56]

The trustee or provisional trustee shall take into his custody or under his control all the property and things in action to which the company is or appears to be entitled.[57] The trustee may apply to the Court for an order directing that all or any part of the property belonging to the company vest in the trustee in his official name and, as a consequence, the trustee may bring or defend any action or other legal

51. Insolvency Act 2014, s 311 amending the Companies Act 2004 ss 235, 236.
52. HCV 1267 of 2005 Supreme Court, Jamaica, June 3, 2005 (JM 2005 SC 60). See also *North Wales Gunpowder Company, Re* [1892] 2 QB 220; *John Reid and Sons Ltd, Re* [1900] 2 QB 634.
53. Companies Act 2004, s 237.
54. Ibid., s 238.
55. Ibid., s 238(5).
56. Ibid., s 325.
57. Ibid., s 239.

proceeding which relates to that property or for the purpose of effectually winding up the company and recovering its property.[58]

The exercise of the powers of the trustee is in all cases subject to the control of the Court and any creditor or contributory may apply to the Court with respect to any exercise or proposed exercise of any of those powers.[59]

There are some situations, however, that require the sanction of the Court or the committee of inspection such as:[60]

a. to bring or defend any action or other legal proceeding in the name of or on behalf of the company;

b. to carry on the business of the company so far as may be necessary for the beneficial winding up thereof;[61]

c. to appoint an attorney at law or other agent to assist him in the performance of his duties;

d. to pay any classes of creditors in full;

e. to make any compromise or arrangement with creditors or persons claiming to be creditors inter alia;

f. to compromise all calls and liabilities to calls, debts, and liabilities capable of resulting in debts, inter alia.[62]

The trustee does not require the sanction of the Court to:

a. sell the real and personal property and things in action of the company;

b. do all acts and to execute, in the name and on behalf of the company, all deeds, receipts, and other documents;

c. prove and rank, and claim in the bankruptcy, insolvency, or sequestration of any contributory, for any balance against his estate and to receive dividends in respect of that balance;

d. draw, accept make and indorse any bill of exchange or promissory note in the name and on behalf of the company;

e. raise money on the security of the assets of the company;[63]

---

58. Ibid., s 240. The trustee (formerly liquidator) is not liable for burdens on the property as the property is vested in his official name and not in his personal name. See *Graham v Edge* (1888) LR 20 QBD 683 (CA); SW Magnus and M Estrin, *Companies: Law and Practice* (4th edn, Butterworths 1968) 244.
59. Companies Act 2004, s 241(3).
60. Ibid., s 241(1).
61. The trustee (formerly liquidator) must have been of a bona fide and reasonable opinion that the carrying of the business was beneficial to the winding up of the company. See *Great Eastern Electric Co Ltd, Re* [1941] Ch.241; Magnus and Estrin, *Companies,* 246.
62. Companies Act 2004, s 241 (1).
63. The debenture-holders, however, cannot be prejudiced. See *Regent's Canal Ironworks Co, ex parte Grissell, Re* (1876) LR 3 Ch. D 411(CA); Magnus and Estrin, *Companies,* 246.

f. take out letters of administration in his official name to any deceased contributory and to any other act necessary for obtaining payment of any money due from a contributory or his estate which cannot be conveniently done in the name of the company;

g. appoint an agent to do any business which the trustee is unable to do himself;

h. do all such things as may be necessary for winding up the affairs of the company.

The creditors, contributories or the committee of inspection may control the trustee's powers; however, the creditors and contributories may overrule the committee of inspection.[64]

The trustee may summon general meetings of the creditors and contributories to ascertain their wishes or shall summon meetings at the direction by resolution or request in writing by one-tenth of the creditors or contributories. Any person aggrieved by any act or decision of the trustee may apply to the Court which shall make such order as it thinks fit. On the other hand, the trustee may apply to the Court in the prescribed manner for directions to any particular manner arising on the winding up and, subject to the provisions of the Act, the trustee has a discretion in the management of the estate and its distribution among creditors.

Trustees are mandated to keep proper books in the prescribed manner and to pay money received by him into such bank as the Court may direct. Trustees are also required to send the Registrar an account of his receipts and profit at the prescribed times, verified by an affidavit or a statutory declaration, which the Registrar shall cause to be audited. Contravention of the provisions relating to the keeping of books and the payment of money into the bank by the trustee and submission of accounts shall result in liability of a fine.[65]

The Registrar has control over trustees and shall inquire into any matter and take such action thereon as he may think expedient, where the trustee does not faithfully perform his duties and duly observe all the requirements imposed on him by statute, rules, or otherwise with respect to the performance of his duties, or if any complaint is made to the Registrar by any creditor or contributory in regard thereto.[66]

The Registrar may grant the release of a trustee once:

a. the trustee has realized all the property of the company, or so much thereof as can, in his opinion, be realized without needlessly protracting the liquidation, and the trustee has distributed a final dividend if any, to the creditors and adjusted the rights of the contributories or has resigned or has been removed from his office;

64. Companies Act 2004, s 242(1).
65. Ibid., ss 243, 244, 245.
66. Ibid., s 246.

b. a report on the trustee's accounts is prepared, and the trustee has complied with all the requirements of the Registrar.[67]

The Registrar shall, subject to an appeal to the Court, take into account the report and any objection which may be urged by any creditor or contributory or person interested against the release of the trustee when deciding whether to grant or withhold the release of the trustee.[68]

VIII. Committees of Inspection

A committee of inspection consists of creditors and contributories of the company or persons holding general powers of attorney from creditors or contributories in such proportions as may be agreed on by the meetings of creditors and contributories or as, in case of difference, may be determined by the Court. The determination as to whether there is to be an application to the Court for a committee of inspection and who are to be the members is made at the meeting of creditors and contributories summoned for the purpose of determining whether or not an application should be made to the Court for appointing a trustee in place of the Trustee.[69] Where there is no committee of inspection, the Minister may, on the application of the trustee, do any act or thing or give any direction or permission as could be done by the committee of inspection.[70]

As previously mentioned, certain powers of the trustee are subject to the sanction of the Court or the trustee and the exercise and control of the trustee's powers may be subject to the directions of the committee of inspection.[71] There is no statutory power to remove a committee of inspection.[72]

IX. General Powers of the Court in Case of Winding Up by the Court

The Court has the following powers:

a. to stay a winding up on the application either of the trustee, or the Trustee, or any creditor or contributory;[73]

b. to settle a list of contributories and application of assets;[74]

---

67. Ibid., s 247.
68. Ibid., s 247.
69. Ibid., ss 248 and 249.
70. Ibid., s 250.
71. Ibid., s 241. However, the directions of the creditor and contributories in any general meeting override the directions of the committee of inspection where there is conflict. See also Companies Act 2004, s 242 (1).
72. *Rubber and Produce Investment Trust, Re* [1915] 1 Ch. 382; Magnus and Estrin, *Companies.*
73. Companies Act 2004, ss 251, 301. See also *South Barrule Slate Quarry Co, Re* (1869) LR 8 Eq 688 with regard to voluntary winding up and voluntary supervision.
74. Companies Act 2004, s 252.

c. to require a contributory, trustee, receiver, banker, agent or officer of the company to deliver property to the trustee;[75]

d. to make an order on any contributory to pay debts due to the company;[76]

e. to make calls on all or any of the contributories to the extent of their liability for payment of any money which the Court considers necessary to satisfy the debts and liabilities of the company and the costs, charges and expenses of winding up and for the adjustment of the rights of the contributories among themselves;[77]

f. to make an order for any contributory, purchaser or other person from whom money is due to the company to pay the amount due into a bank to the account of the trustee instead of to the trustee.[78]

g. to appoint a special manager on the application of the Trustee who becomes the trustee or provisional trustee;[79]

h. to exclude creditors not proving their debts or claims in the time or times fixed by the Court;[80]

i. to adjust the rights of the contributories;[81]

j. to make an order for inspection of books and papers of the company by creditors and contributories as the Court thinks just;[82]

k. to make an order, in the event of the assets being insufficient to satisfy the liabilities, that the trustee shall, forthwith apply to the Supervisor for an assignment in accordance with the Insolvency Act and thereafter proceed in accordance with the provisions of the Insolvency Act;[83]

l. to summon persons suspected of having company property;[84]

m. to order public examination of promoters, directors or other officers where the Trustee has made a further report that in his opinion a fraud has been committed by any person in the promotion or formation of the company or by any director or other officer of the company;[85]

n. may cause a contributory, who is believed on proof of probable cause, to be about to abscond or to remove or conceal any of his property for the

75. Ibid., s 253.
76. Ibid., s 254.
77. Ibid., s 255.
78. Ibid., s 256.
79. Ibid., s 258.
80. Ibid., s 259.
81. Ibid., s 260.
82. Ibid., s 261.
83. Ibid., s 311 amending s 262 of the Companies Act 2004.
84. Ibid., s 263.
85. Ibid., s 264.

purpose of evading payment of calls or of avoiding examination respecting the affairs of the company,[86]

o. to make an order that the company be dissolved from the date of the order on the application of the trustee when the affairs of a company have been completely wound up.[87]

Section 268 provides that the Court may, by rules for enabling or requiring all or any of the powers and duties conferred and imposed on the Court, delegate the following powers to the trustee subject to the control of the Court:

a. the holding and conducting of meetings to ascertain the wishes of creditors and contributories;
b. the settling of lists of contributories, and with special leave of the Court, the rectifying of the register of members where required, and the collecting and applying of the assets;
c. the paying, delivering, conveyance, surrender or transfer of money, property, books or papers to the trustee;
d. the making of calls with either the special leave of the Court or the sanction of the committee of inspection;
e. the fixing of a time within which debts and claims must be proved.

2. *Voluntary Winding Up*

The circumstances in which a company (other than an unregistered company and an overseas company incorporated outside Jamaica) may be voluntarily wound up are:

i. when the period fixed for the duration of the company by the Articles expires or the event if any occurs on the occurrence of which the Articles provide that the company is to be dissolved, and the company in general meeting has passed a resolution requiring the company to be voluntarily wound up;
ii. if the company resolves by special resolution that the company be voluntarily wound up.[88]

Resolutions for the voluntary winding up of a company apply to both members' voluntary winding up[89] and creditors' winding up.[90] In a members' winding up the winding up is conducted by the company itself and in a creditors' winding up the

86. Ibid., s 266.
87. Ibid., s 269.
88. Insolvency Act 2014, s 311 amending the Companies Act 2004, s 272.
89. Companies Act 2004, ss 278–285; however, the Insolvency Act 2014, s 311 amends s 282 to provide that where the trustee is at any time of opinion that the company will not be able to pay its debts in full within the period stated in the declaration under section 277, he shall forthwith apply to the Supervisor for an assignment in accordance with the Insolvency Act and thereafter proceed in accordance with the provisions of the Insolvency Act.
90. Companies Act 2004, ss 286–94.

winding up is conducted by the creditors and the members.[91] The Court, however, has the power to intervene in either form of voluntary winding up.[92] The Articles cannot exclude the power to wind up voluntarily.[93]

It is rare for the Articles to provide for a fixed expiration for the duration of a company or for the occurrence of an event for dissolution of a company, but, in any event, the resolution required would be an ordinary resolution.[94]

A voluntary winding up is deemed to commence at the time of the passing of the resolution for voluntary winding up.[95] Within 14 days after the passing of the resolution, the company must give notice of the resolution by advertisement in the Gazette and in writing to the Registrar, failure of which will result in the company and every officer (which includes the trustee) liable to a fine.[96]

At the commencement of the voluntary winding up, the company must cease to carry on its business, except as may be necessary for the beneficial winding up provided that the corporate state and powers of the company shall continue until it is dissolved.[97] This provision is analogous to the provision found in section 241(1)(b) as it relates to a compulsory winding up and the power of the trustee to carry on the business of the company, so far as may be necessary for the beneficial winding up of the company.

Any transfer of shares or alteration in the status of the members of the company made after the commencement of a voluntary winding up is void unless, in the case of the transfer of shares, it is made to or with the sanction of the trustee.[98]

The majority of the directors may, at a meeting of directors, make a statutory declaration to the effect, that on a full inquiry into the affairs of the company, they are of the opinion that the company will be able to pay its debts in full within 12 months from the commencement of the winding up. In order to avoid a declaration being made without a liquidation taking place and in order to avoid declarations being made in a reckless manner,[99] section 277(2) provides that the declaration should be:

a. made within five weeks immediately preceding the date of the passing of the resolution for winding up the company and be delivered to the Registrar before that date;

b. and the declaration must embody a statement of the company's assets and liabilities as at the latest practicable date before the making of the declaration.

91. Ibid., ss 304, 308.
92. Ibid.
93. *Peveril Gold Mines Ltd, Re* [1898] 1 Ch. 122 (CA); *Welton v Saffery* [1897] AC 299.
94. Magnus and Estrin, *Companies,* 265.
95. Companies Act 2004, s 274.
96. Ibid., ss 273–274.
97. Ibid., s 275.
98. Ibid., s 276.
99. Magnus and Estrin, *Companies,* 86.

If a company is insolvent at the end of the period specified in the statutory declaration, there is a presumption that any director making the statutory declaration did not have reasonable grounds that the company is solvent. Any director making a declaration without having reasonable grounds for the opinion that the company will be able to pay its debts in full within the period specified in the declaration may be liable to imprisonment with or without hard labour or to a fine or to both.[100]

I. Members' Voluntary Winding Up

Sections 279 provides for the company in general meeting to appoint and fix the remuneration of one or more trustees for the purpose of winding up the affairs and distributing the assets of the company. The appointment of the trustee is usually made at the time that the resolution is passed to wind up the company. On the appointment of the trustee, all the powers of the directors cease except so far as the company in general meeting or the trustee sanctions the continuance thereof. The company in general meeting has the power to fill a vacancy in the office of the trustee but this is subject to any arrangement with its creditors. The meeting to fill a vacancy in the office of trustee may be convened by any contributory or trustee or continuing trustees and shall be held in the manner provided by the Act or by the Articles or in such manner as may, as determined by the Court, on application by any contributory or by the continuing trustees.[101]

The trustee has the power to accept shares, policies or other like interests as consideration for the transfer or sale of the whole or part of its business or property. Section 281 requires the sanction of a special resolution; however, any member who dissented, in writing, addressed to the trustee and left at the registered office of the company within seven days after the passing of the resolution, may require the trustee either to abstain from carrying the resolution into effect or to purchase his interest at a price to be determined by agreement or by arbitration in manner provided by the Arbitration Act.[102]

The trustee is required to do the following:

a. Call a creditors' meeting if at any time he is of the opinion that the company is unable to pay its debts in full within the period stated in the declaration under section 277. Failure to comply with this section exposes the trustee to liability to a fine and/or imprisonment.[103]

b. Call a general meeting at the end of the first year or at the first convenient date within three months (or such longer period as the Minister may allow) from the end of the year, if the winding up continues for more than one year, and shall lay before the meeting an account of his acts and dealings

100. Companies Act 2004, s 277(3).
101. Ibid., s 280.
102. Ibid., s 281(3).
103. Ibid., s 282.

and of the conduct of the winding up during the preceding year. The trustee is liable to a fine for failure to comply with this section.[104]

c. Call a general meeting of the company as soon as the affairs of the company are fully wound up for the purpose of laying before it an account of the winding up showing how the winding up has been conducted and the property of the company has been disposed. A trustee who fails to call the general meeting shall be liable to a fine.[105]

d. Send a copy of the account and a return of the holding of the general meeting and its date to the Registrar within one week after the meeting, and if the trustee fails so to do, he shall be liable to a fine for every day during which the default continues. On receiving the account and return, the Registrar shall forthwith register them, and on the expiration of three months from the registration of the return, the company shall be deemed to be dissolved, except where the Court makes an order deferring the date, on the application of the trustee or of any other person who appears to the Court to be interested.[106]

II. Provisions Applicable to Every Voluntary Winding Up

Section 296 provides that subject to the provisions of the Insolvency Act[107] as to preferential payments, the company's property must be distributed in satisfaction of liabilities pari passu. Property includes the ordinary property of the company, members' contributions and misappropriated assets which a creditor has a right to be recognized. The rights of secured creditors and certain other creditors rank in priority to all claims of members.

The powers and duties of the trustee in a members' or creditors' voluntary winding up include some of those powers and duties under a winding up by the Court subject to the sanction of an extraordinary resolution of the company or the sanction of either the Court or the committee of inspection as the case may be. The trustees also have the power to exercise the power of the Court to settle a list of contributories, make calls and summon general meetings of the company. The trustee is also required to pay the debts of the company and to adjust the rights of the contributories among themselves.[108]

The Court has the power to appoint and remove a trustee in a voluntary winding up and the trustee must publish and deliver to the Registrar for registration a notice of his appointment in the prescribed form, failure of which exposes him to a fine.[109] The

104. Companies Act 2004, s 283.
105. Ibid., s 284.
106. Ibid.
107. Insolvency Act 2014, s 311 amending the Companies Act 2004, s 296.
108. Companies Act 2004, s 297.
109. Ibid., s 299.

Court has the power to appoint more than one trustee.[110] The trustee has the power to apply to the Court to have questions determined or powers exercised.[111]

All costs, charges, and expenses, including the remuneration of the trustee, are payable out of the assets of the company in priority to all other claims.[112]

A creditor or contributory may apply to the Court for an order that the company be wound up by the Court instead of voluntarily however, a contributory must satisfy the Court that the rights of the contributories would be prejudiced by a voluntary winding up.[113]

3. *Winding Up Subject to the Supervision of the Court*

The Court may make an order that a voluntary winding up may continue subject to the supervision of the Court and shall be deemed to be a winding up by the Court.[114] An application by a contributory or creditor for an order for a winding up subject to the supervision of the Court must be based on a case of fraud, impropriety, corruption or misapplication of assets.[115] The Court may appoint an additional trustee with the same powers and obligations as if appointed under a voluntary winding up.[116]

I. Provisions Applicable to Every Mode of Winding Up

Proof and Ranking of Claims

Section 309 provides that in every winding up of a company, debts of all description are to be proved, however, section 202 of the Insolvency Act 2014 (which relates to the ranking of claims for payment from the proceeds of a debtor's property) shall apply.[117]

II. Effect of Winding Up on Antecedent and Other Transactions

Fraudulent Preference

A fraudulent preference is where a debtor company, in bankruptcy, intentionally prefers one or particular creditors.[118] The dominant or substantial purpose of the

110. Ibid., s 234.
111. Ibid., s 301.
112. Ibid., s 302.
113. Ibid., s 303.
114. Ibid., ss 304–306.
115. *Bank of Gibraltar and Malta, Re* (1865) 1 Ch. App 69; *London and Mediterranean Banking Co, Re* (1866) 15 WR 33.
116. Companies Act 2004, s 307.
117. Ibid., ss 309 and 311.
118. Ibid., s 312.

debtor company must be to prefer one or particular creditors.[119] On winding up, a fraudulent preference of creditors or a fraudulent conveyance, assignment, transfer, sale or disposition is deemed to be invalid.[120] Where there is a fraudulent preference of a person interested in property mortgaged or charged (including a security interest in personal property) to secure the company's debt, then the person preferred shall be subject to the same liabilities and have the same rights as if he had undertaken to be personally liable as surety for the debt to the extent of the charge on the property or the value of his interest, whichever is less.[121] The trustee is entitled to reclaim from the creditor concerned money paid which was a fraudulent preference of a surety or guarantee. The Court has the power to determine any questions regarding payment arising between the person to whom the payment was made and the surety and guarantor and to order repayment by the surety or guarantor to the extent of his liability.[122]

Onerous Property

Onerous property may be disclaimed by the trustee with the leave of the Court within twelve months after the commencement of the winding up or after the trustee becomes aware of the onerous property or such extended period as may be allowed by the Court. Onerous property includes unprofitable contracts and property that is unsaleable, not easily saleable, or gives rise to continuing liability.[123] Although the company is released from liability, the rights of third parties are not affected as they are entitled to prove in the winding up.[124]

The trustee is not entitled to disclaim any property or contract if, in the case of property, he has not given notice to an applicant interested in the property within 28 days of his intention to apply to the Court for leave to disclaim the property or, in the case of a contract, he has not disclaimed the contract.[125] The Court has the power to make a vesting order, however, under-lessees and mortgagees by demise are protected.[126] Any person injured by the operation may prove the amount as a debt in the winding up as a creditor.[127]

Creditors are not entitled to retain the benefit of any execution against goods or lands of the company, or attachment to any debt due to the company,[128] unless:

119. *Sharp v Jackson* [1899], AC 419.
120. Companies Act 2004, s 312(1).
121. Companies Act 2004, s 313(1) amended by the Security Interest in Personal Property Act 2013 to include 'security interest in personal property'.
122. Companies Act 2004, s 313; Magnus and Estrin, *Companies,* 294.
123. Companies Act 2004, s 315(1).
124. Ibid., s 315(2).
125. Ibid., s 315(4).
126. Ibid., s 315(6).
127. Ibid., s 316(8).
128. Ibid., s 316(1).

a. it was completed before the commencement of the winding up or the date on which a creditor had notice of a meeting at which a resolution for voluntary winding up is proposed;[129] or

b. a bona fide purchaser of goods under a sale by a bailiff on which an execution has been levied acquires a good title to them against a trustee.[130]

The rights conferred on the trustee by section 316(1) may be set aside by the Court in favour of the creditor.[131]

III. Receivers and Managers

General and Definition

A receivership is a mechanism for enforcing a debenture where the debenture holder's position is in jeopardy.[132] Receivers may be appointed out of Court or by the Court.

There is no statutory definition of a receiver. At common law, a receiver is defined as a person who receives rent or other income and pays ascertained outgoings but does not manage the property. A manager, however, must be appointed to manage the property.[133] A receiver may also be appointed manager, hence the phrase receiver-manager.[134]

It has also been stated that a receiver, who is appointed by debenture holders, their trustees or the Court, must:

c. get in the assets charged;

c. collect the rents and profits;

d. exercise the debenture holders' powers of realization;

e. pay the net proceeds to the debenture holders.[135]

Receivers are usually appointed when a company is insolvent or in the vicinity of insolvency.

Where a receiver or manager has been appointed, all documents relating to the company must contain a statement that a receiver or manager has been appointed. The company and every officer, trustee, receiver or manager who knowingly authorize or permit the default of the provision relating to notification of appointment will

---

129. Ibid., s 316(1)(a).
130. Ibid., s 316(1)(b).
131. Ibid., s 316 (1)(c).
132. *McMahon v North Kent Ironworks Company* [1891] 2 Ch. 148; *Edwards v Standard Rolling Stock Syndicate* [1893] 1 Ch. 574; *Victoria Steamboats Co, Re* [1897] 1 Ch. 158; *Tilt Cove Copper Co Ltd, Re* [1913] 2 Ch. 588.
133. *Manchester and Milford Ry Co, ex parte Cambrian Ry Co, Re* (1880) LR 14 Ch. D 645.
134. *Newdigate Colliery Ltd, Re* [1912] 1 Ch. 468.
135. LCB Gower, *Gower's Principles of Modern Company Law* (4th edn, Stevens and Sons 1979) 487.

be fined.[136] The Court may fix, vary or amend the remuneration of the receiver or manager on application by the trustee and, in the case of variation or amendment, by the trustee or by the receiver or manager.[137]

Receivers and Managers Appointed Out of Court

A receiver appointed out of Court is an agent of the debenture holders or trustees who have appointed him or of the company as expressly or impliedly stipulated in the debenture.[138] The receiver may, however, apply to the Court for directions if he so wishes. He, similar to the Court appointed receiver or manager, shall be personally liable and entitled to indemnity in respect of any contract entered into by him in the performance of his functions, except in so far as the contract otherwise provides.[139]

Where a receiver or manager over the whole or substantially the whole of the property of the company is appointed on behalf of the holders of any security interest registered under the Security Interests in Personal Property Act (SIPPA) then (subject to the Act) the receiver:

a. must send notice to the company of his appointment;
b. request a statement as to the affairs of the company in the prescribed form;[140]
c. send a copy of the statement as to the affairs of the company and his comments to the Registrar within two months of receipt of the statement;
d. send a copy of any such comments or a notice that he does not see fit to make any comment to the company within two months of receipt of the statement;
e. send a copy of the summary to any trustees for the debenture holders on whose behalf he was appointed within two months of receipt of the statement.[141]

The powers of directors of a company in receivership are only limited to the extent of the powers conferred on receivers by the debenture,[142] which relates only to the company's assets which are covered by the debenture.[143] The board of directors of a company in receivership, however, may be considered as having come to an end

136. Companies Act 2004, s 343.
137. Ibid., s 344.
138. Gower, *Gower's Principles,* 489.
139. Companies Act 2004, s 349.
140. This statement should be made in accordance with section 346 of the Jamaica Companies Act 2004.
141. Companies Act, s 345 (1)(c)(iii).
142. *Newhart Developments Ltd v Co-operative Commercial Bank Ltd* [1978 1 QB 814 (CA); *Arawak Woodworking Establishment Ltd v Jamaica Development Bank* (1987) 24 JLR 15.
143. Andrew D Burgess, *The Law of Corporate Receivers and Receiver-Managers* (Kingston: The Caribbean Law Publishing Company, 2002) 83–84.

if a receiver and manager is appointed over all the undertaking, and winding up will invariably follow.[144] In this case, the trustee will oversee the receiver.

Court Appointed Receivers and Managers

A receiver appointed by the Court is an independent officer of the Court. He is personally liable on any contract entered into by him in the performance of his functions subject to the provisions of the contract and entitled in respect of that liability to indemnity out of the assets.[145]

Where a receiver manager of the property of a company has been appointed, documents issued on behalf of the company or the receiver or manager or the trustee of the company, in which the company's name appears, shall contain a statement that a receiver or manager has been appointed. Once appointed, the receiver or manager over the whole or substantially the whole of the property of the company that is appointed on behalf of the holders of any security interest registered under the SIPPA debentures shall:

a. send notice to the company of his appointment;

b. request a statement as to the affairs of the company in the prescribed form;[146]

c. send a copy of the statement as to the affairs of the company to the Registrar and the Court as well as a statement and his comments to the Registrar within two months of receipt of the statement; send a copy of any such comments or a notice that he does not see fit to make any comment to the company within two months of receipt of the statement; send a copy of the summary to any trustees or debenture holders on whose behalf he was appointed within two months of receipt of the statement.[147]

IV. Winding Up of Unregistered Companies

Unregistered companies include:

1. limited or unlimited partnerships;
2. associations; or
3. companies not registered under the law relating to companies.

Any partnership, association or unregistered company which is not a foreign partnership, association or unregistered company must consist of not less than eight members.[148]

---

144. *Moss Steamship Co Ltd v Whinney* [1912] AC 254 (HL). See also *Newhart Ltd v Co-op Commercial Bank* (n 156) where it was held that the directors could allow the company to sue the debenture-holders where the receiver did not wish to. See also P Davies, *Gower and Davies' Principles of Modern Company Law* (7th edn, Sweet & Maxwell 2003) 846.
145. Companies Act 2004, s 349.
146. This statement should be made in accordance with section 346 of the Jamaica Companies Act 2004.
147. Companies Act 2004, s 345(1).
148. Companies Act 2004, s 355.

All provisions for winding up of registered companies apply with the following exceptions and additions:

1. winding up voluntarily or subject to supervision does not apply to unregistered companies;[149]
2. the circumstances in which an unregistered company may be wound up are:[150]
   a. if the company is dissolved, or has ceased to carry on business, or is carrying on business only for the purpose of winding up its affairs;
   b. if the Court is of the opinion that it is just and equitable that the company should be wound up.
3. A contributory of an unregistered company is every person who is liable to pay or contribute to the payment of:
   a. any debt or liability of the company; or
   b. any sum for the adjustment of the rights of the members among themselves; or
   c. the costs and expenses of winding up the company.

Every contributory shall be liable to contribute to the assets of the company all sums due from him in respect of any such liability as aforesaid.[151] The provisions of the Act with respect to the personal representatives of deceased contributories and to the trustees of bankrupt contributories shall apply in the event of death or bankruptcy.[152]

4. Where the application to wind up an unregistered company is made by a creditor, the provisions of the Act with respect to staying and restraining actions and proceedings against a company at any time after the presentation of an application for winding up and before the making of a winding up order shall extend to actions and proceedings against any contributory of the company.[153]
5. Any action against a contributory shall be stayed on the making of a winding up order of an unregistered company, except where the Court grants leave for the action to be proceeded with.[154]
6. Companies incorporated outside the Island may be wound up as an unregistered company under the Act notwithstanding its dissolution or ceasing to exist as a company[155] under or by virtue of the laws of the country under which it was incorporated.

149. Ibid., s 355 (a).
150. Ibid., s 355 (b).
151. Companies Act 2004, s 356(1).
152. Ibid., s 356(2).
153. Ibid., s 357.
154. Ibid., s 358.
155. Ibid., s 359.

Section 359 has been interpreted as a discretion which the statute confers, and that the discretion should be exercised based on:[156]

a. sufficient connection with the jurisdiction, which may consist of assets within the jurisdiction;

b. a reasonable possibility of benefit to those applying for the winding up order;

c. the Court's exercise of jurisdiction over one or more persons interested in the distribution of the assets of the company.

Section 360 states that the provisions relating to the winding up of unregistered companies shall be in addition to and not in restriction of any of the provisions in the Act with respect to the winding up of companies by the Court. Although an unregistered company is not deemed to be a company under the Act, all provisions relating to the powers of the Court or trustee in the winding up of companies formed and registered under the Act apply to unregistered companies.

The Minister may, from time to time, prescribe modifications in respect of the winding up of limited partnerships and with the substitution of general partners for directors.[157]

156. *Real Estate Development Co, Re* [1991] BCLC 210 (Knox J) followed in *OJSC Ank Yugraneft v Sibir Energy Plc, Re* [2010] BCC 475. See also *Banco Nacional de Cuba v Cosmos Trading Corp* [2000] BCC 910.

157. Companies Act 2004, s 361.

Bibliography

Burgess, A. *Commonwealth Caribbean Company Law*. New York: Routledge, 2013.

Ballantine, H.W. *Ballantine on Corporations*. Chicago: Callaghan and Company, 1946.

Davies, PL. *Gower and Davies' Principles of Modern Company Law*. 7th ed. London: Sweet and Maxwell, 2003.

Dickerson, R.W.V., J.L. Howard and L. Getz. 'Proposals for a New Business Corporations Law for Canada.' *Commentary Ottawa* 1 (1971). Ottawa: Information Canada.

Easson, A.J., and D.A. Soberman. 'Pre-Incorporation Contracts: Common Law Confusion and Statutory Complexity,' *Queens Law Journal* 17 (1992).

Estey, W.M. 'Pre-Incorporation Contracts: The Fog is Finally Lifting'. *Canadian Business Law Journal* 33 (2000): 3–37.

Farrar, J.H., N. Furey and B.M. Hannigan. *Farrar's Company Law*. 3rd ed. Oxford: Butterworths, 1991.

Ffolkes Goldson, S. 'The Corporate Director's Duty of Care, Diligence and Skill: *Soper v The Queen*.' *CaribLB* 2, no. 2 (1997): 53.

———. 'Directors' Duties to Creditors On or Near Insolvency and Duty of Care in the Commonwealth Caribbean: Should the Peoples Decision be Adopted?' *OUCLJ* 6, no.1 (2006): 61.

———. 'The Reform of Jamaica's Insolvency Law: Balancing the Interests of Creditors and Debtors'. *West Indian Law Journal* 32, no. 2 (2007–10): 171.

———. 'The Reform of the Law Relating to the Duties of Directors in the Commonwealth Caribbean.' *Co Lawyer* 24, no. 12 (2003).

———. 'The Use and Misuse of the Oppression Remedy in the Commonwealth Caribbean.' *The Company Lawyer* 35, Issue 7 (2014). London: Thomson Reuters.

Golding, M. 'A Review of the Major Changes to Jamaican Company Law Introduced by the Companies Act.' Paper presented to the Private Sector Organisation of Jamaica on March 25, 2004.

Goldson, P., D. Walker and J. Thompson-James. 'The Security Interests in Person Property Act.' Presented by the Commercial Law Committee of the Bar Association, Jamaica Bar Association Conference, Montego Bay Jamaica, November 16, 2013.

Gower, LCB., *Gower's Principles of Modern Company Law*. 4th ed. London: Stevens and Sons, 1979.

———. *Gower's Principles of Modern Company Law*. 5th ed. London: Sweet & Maxwell, 1992.

Gray, W. *The Annotated Canada Business Corporations Act.* 2nd ed. Toronto: Carswell Corporate Management, 2009.

Greenaway, E. and S. Ffolkes Goldson. 'Booms Need Busts Improving the Legal Framework for Insolvency.' *Caribbean Policy Research Institute* CaPRI Policy Brief B12 (2012).

Kaplan, W., and B. Elwood. 'The Derivative Action: A Shareholder's 'Bleak House.' *UBCL Rev* 36 (2003): 443.

Ladd, M. 'Companies Act 2004 – Corporate Finance Highlights.' Paper presented to Myers Fletcher and Gordon on April 27, 2004.

Magnus, S., and M. Estrin. *Companies Law and Practice.* 4th ed. London Butterworths, 1968.

Maloney, MA. 'Pre-Incorporation Transactions: A Statutory Solution?' *Canadian Business Law Journal* 10 (1985): 409–38.

Morrison, C.D. 'The Companies Act 2004 – Complainants' Remedies.' Faculty of Law Companies Act 2004 Symposium, Kingston, April 2004.

———. 'The Citizen and the Law – Perspectives Old and New.' Grace Kennedy Foundation Lecture 2004, Kingston, March 2004.

Puri, P. 'The Promise of Certainty in the Law of Pre-Incorporation Contracts.' *Canadian Bar Review* 80 (2002).

Welling, B. *Corporate Law in Canada: The Governing Principles.* 2nd ed. Oxford: Butterworths, 1991.

Ziegel, J.S. 'Promoter's Liability and Pre-incorporation Contracts: *Westcom Radio Group Ltd v MacIsaac.*' *Canadian Business Law Journal* 16 (1990).

Index

Accountants 4, 38, 58
Accounts 4, 19, 21, 25–26, 36–37, 42, 47, 76 101–102
Affiliated Company 53, 79, 84
Agency 10, 14, 78,
Arrangements 8, 48, 88–89, 91
Articles of Association 12, 14–15, 18, 30, 44, 71
Articles of Incorporation 1, 7, 14–15, 19, 27, 30, 44
Alteration 26, 30, 96, 105
Auditors 38, 72
Allotted Share Capital 32
Bankruptcy 19, 71, 92–93, 97, 100, 109, 113
Bearer Shares 48–49
Board of Directors 69, 78, 112
Capital Maintenance 30, 34, 47
Civil Liability 39,
Classes of Shares 7, 15–16, 27–28, 30, 37, 45
Closely Held Companies 87
Company Secretary 5, 58–59,
Complainants 8, 78–79, 80–82, 87
Contents 4, 7, 13, 51
Conflict of Interest 7, 67
Conflict of Duty and Interest 6, 61, 66, 68
Constructive Notice Doctrine 13, 60
Corporate Capacity 12
Corporate Name 57
Creditors 1–3, 6, 8–10, 27, 46, 65–66, 71, 75–76, 79, 81, 83, 88–91, 95, 97, 99–107, 109–110
Damages 11, 76
Debentures 7, 21, 38–39, 48–49, 51–52, 69, 85, 90, 112
Defences, 8, 39
Derivative Action 3, 8, 13, 18, 29, 43, 77–82, 87
Directors 1, 3–8, 12–13, 15–16, 25–26, 28–32, 34–35, 38–39, 42–44, 47, 55–72, 74–80, 83–85, 87, 90, 98, 103, 105–106, 112, 114
Disqualification 8, 54, 71
Dividends 1, 3, 25, 27–29, 40, 44, 48, 85, 92, 100
Duties of Directors 3
Employees 2–4, 41, 46, 54, 64
Fiduciary Duty 7, 54, 60–61, 64–68
Fixed Charges 5, 51
Foss v Harbottle 77–80
Fraud 8, 10, 63, 74–75
Fraudulent 11
Fraudulent Certifications 48
Fraudulent Entry 75
Fraudulent Preference 97, 109
Fraudulent Purpose 76, 95–96
Fraudulent Trading 4
General meeting 69, 101, 104, 108
Incorporation 2–3, 5, 7, 10–11, 17, 22–27, 31, 35, 79, 82, 93
Indemnity 8, 69, 71–74, 111–12
Indoor Management Rule 59
Insolvency 4–5, 8, 55, 65–66, 100–11
Insolvency Act 2014 6, 8, 9, 27, 88–89, 91, 93, 95, 97–99, 103–105, 107–108
Insurance 8, 11, 14, 24, 28, 62–63, 74, 79, 84–86, 92, 99
Liability 7–8, 11, 14–16, 22, 38–39, 41, 43, 45–48, 50, 53, 55, 57–58, 68, 71–72, 74, 76, 92–93, 101, 103, 107, 112–13

Liquidation 8, 28, 75, 88, 91, 101, 106
Meetings 104, 108
Meetings of Creditors and Contributories 99, 102
Meetings of Directors 69
Meetings of Shareholders 16
Memorandum of Association 13–15, 30, 41
Offences 57–58, 71, 74–75
Officers 3, 6–8, 48, 55, 60–65, 67, 69–70, 72, 74–76, 78, 83–84, 103
Oppression Remedy 8, 18, 43, 65–66, 78, 80–82, 84, 86–88
Ordinary Resolution 105, 30, 33, 45
Ordinary Shares 28
Pre-emptive Rights 7, 21, 44
Pre-incorporation Agreements 23
Pre-incorporation Contracts 23
Preference Shares 28, 45
Private Companies 21, 32, 34, 41, 54, 59, 67
Promoters 103
Prospectus 7, 25, 37–40, 59
Public Companies 3, 31–32, 58–59, 67, 74
Receivers 110–12
Receivership 8, 88, 110, 112
Receiver-managers 110–12
Registered Office 5, 15, 56–57, 106
Registrar 3–4, 13–17, 26–28, 31, 33–34, 37–38, 42–43, 45–46, 50–52, 57, 59, 71, 74, 81, 86, 89–90, 93, 97, 99, 101–102, 105–108, 111–12
Remedies 3, 8, 18, 22, 77, 79–83, 85, 87–88
Remuneration 59, 99, 106, 108, 111
Resolutions 105
Salomon Principle 10–11
Secret Profit 7, 61
Separate Legal Entity Doctrine 10–11, 14
Separate Legal Personality 11
Shadow Directors 8, 54–58, 75
Share Capital 7, 15–17, 19–20, 24–25, 27–28, 30–32, 35–36, 41, 43–46, 52, 59, 62, 89, 92
Share Premium Account 34, 36
Share Warrants 6, 48–49
Shareholder Agreements 85
Shareholders 1–3, 8, 16, 18–19, 21, 28–29, 36, 41, 43–44, 47, 49, 54, 61, 64, 66, 69–71, 77–79, 87, 91
Shares 2–3, 7, 10, 15–16, 18–22, 25, 27–49, 59, 62, 69, 84–87, 89, 91–92, 95–96, 105–106
Solvency 40, 42, 47, 65, 85
Stamp Duty 15, 30
Stated Capital 2, 25, 30, 35–37, 41–42, 46–47, 53
Statement in Lieu of Prospectus 59
Statutory Declaration 17, 31, 34, 42–43, 47, 59, 101, 105–106
Transfer of Shares 7, 15, 20–21, 47–49, 91, 96, 105
Trusts 88
Turquand's Case 59–60
Ultra Vires Doctrine 3, 13
Unlimited Companies 16–18, 30, 113
Veil of Incorporation 11
Voting Rights 19, 28, 36, 41, 43, 85
Winding Up 1, 4, 8, 27–28, 50, 57, 74–76, 78, 86–89, 91–114

The Companies Act

THE COMPANIES ACT

ARRANGEMENT OF SECTIONS

PART I—*Preliminary*

1. Short title.
2. Interpretation. Amended 2013 and 2017 and by the SIPP Act 2013 and by the Insolvency Act 2014

Incorporation of Companies and Matters Incidental Thereto

3. Mode of forming incorporated company. Amended 2013
4. Capacity and powers.
5. Powers reduced.
6. Validity of Acts.
7. Notice not presumed.

Articles of Incorporation

8. Form of articles. Amended 2017
9. Regulations required in case of unlimited company or company limited by guarantee.
10. Alteration of articles by special resolution.

Registration

11. Registration of articles.
12. Effect of registration.
13. ~~Conclusiveness of certificate of incorporation.~~ ***Repealed and Replaced*** 2013 - Certificate of Incorporation to be Conclusive Evidence
14. Registration of unlimited company as limited.

Provisions with respect to Names of Companies

15. Prohibition of registration of companies by undesirable names.
16. Power to dispense with "limited" in name of charitable and other companies.

17. Change of name.

18. Reservation of name.

General Provisions with respect to Articles

19. Effect of articles.

20. Provision as to articles of companies limited by guarantee.

21. Alterations of articles increasing liability to contribute to share capital not to bind existing members without consent.

22. Copies of articles to be given to members.

Membership of Company

23. Definition of member.

24. Membership of holding company.

Private companies.

26. Statement in lieu of prospectus to be delivered to Registrar by company ceasing to be private company.

27. Consequences of default in complying with conditions constituting company a private company.

Mutual Fund Companies

27A. Mutual Fund companies.

Contracts, etc.

28. Form of contracts.

29. Pre-incorporation contracts.

30. Bills of exchange and promissory.

31. Execution of deeds abroad.

32. Company may have official seal for use abroad.

Authentication of Documents

33. Authentication of documents.

PART II—*Share Capital and Debentures*

34. Minimum share capital.

35. Authorized minimum.

36. Nature of shares.

37. Election to retain par value shares.

38. Consideration.

39. Stated capital accounts.

Prospectus

40. Dating and registration of prospectus.

41. Specific requirements as to particulars in prospectus.

42. Experts consent to issue of prospectus containing statement by him.

43. Restriction on alternation of terms mentioned in prospectus or statement in lieu of prospectus.

44. Civil liability for statements in prospectus.

45. Criminal liability for misstatements in prospectus.

46. Document containing offer of shares or debentures for sale to be deemed prospectus.

47. Interpretation of provisions relating to prospectuses.

Allotment

48. Prohibition of allotment unless minimum subscription received.

49. Prohibition of allotment in certain cases unless statement in lieu of prospectus delivered to Registrar.

50. Effect of irregular allotment.

51. Applications for, and allotment of shares and debentures.

52. Return as to allotments.

53. Power to pay certain commissions and prohibition of payment of all other commissions. etc.

54. Statement in balance sheet. as to commissions.

Construction of References to Offering Shares or Debentures to the Public

55. Construction of references to offering shares or debentures to the public.

Issue of Redeemable Shares

56. Power to issue redeemable shares.

57. Financing, etc., of redemption.

58. Power of company to purchase own shares. ***Amended 2017***

59. Alternative acquisition of company's own shares.

60. Notice to shareholders of purchase by company of own shares. ***Amended 2017***

61 . Pre-emptive rights.

62. Power to issue redeemable preference shares.

Miscellaneous Provisions as to Share Capital

63. Power of company to arrange for different amounts being paid on shares.

64. Reserve liability of limited company.

65. Power of company limited by shares to alter its share capital.

66. Notice to Registrar of consolidation of share capital, conversion of shares into stock, etc.

67. Notice of increase of share capital

68. Power of unlimited company to provide for reserve capital share on registration.

69. Power of company to pay interest out of capital in certain cases.

70. Redemption or cancellation of shares under Employees Share Ownership Plan Act.

Reduction of Share Capital

71. Reduction of stated capital.

72. Effect of redemption, purchase, etc.

Variation of Shareholders' Rights

73. Rights of holders of special classes of shares.

Transfer of Shares and Debentures, Evidence of Title, etc.

74. Nature and numbering of shares.

75. Transfer not to be registered except on production of instrument of transfer.

76. Registration of transfer on request of transferor.

77. Notice of refusal to register transfer.

78. Certification of transfers.

79. Duties of company with respect to issue of certificates.

80. Certificate evidence of title.

81. Evidence of grant of probate.

82. ~~Issue and effect of share warrants to bearer.~~ ***Repealed 2017***

83. Penalty for personation of shareholder.

Special Provisions as to Debentures

84. Register of debenture holders.

85. Consequences of failure to comply with requirements as to register of debenture holders owing to agent's default.

86. Inspection of register of debenture holders.

87. Application to registers of debenture holders of certain provisions relating to registers of members.

88. Liability of trustees for debenture holders.

89. Perpetual debentures.

90. Power to re-issue redeemed debentures in certain cases.

91. Specific performance of contracts to subscribe for debentures.

92. Payments of certain debts out of assets subject to floating charge in priority to claims under the charge.

PART III—*Registration of Charges Registration of Charges with Registrar*

93. Registration of charges. ***Amended by SIPP Act 2013***

94. ~~Effect of registration.~~ ***Repealed by SIPP Act 2013***

95. Duty of company to register charges created by company. ***Amended by SIPP Act 2013***

96. Duty of company to register charges existing on property acquired.

97. Registrar to keep register charges. ***Amended by SIPP Act 2013***

98. ~~Indorsement of certificate of registration on debenturees.~~ ***Repealed by SIPP Act 2013***

99. Entries of satisfaction and release of property from charge.

100. Rectification of register of charges.

101. Registration of enforcement of security.

Provisions as to Company's Register of Charges and as to Copies of Instruments creating Charges

102. Copies of instruments creating charges to be kept by company. Amended by SIPP Act 2013

103. Company's register of charges.

104. Right to inspect copies of instruments creating charges and company's register of charges.

Application of Part III to Companies incorporated outside ~~the Island~~ ***Jamaica***

105. Application of Part III to charges created, and charges on property subject to charges acquired, by company incorporated outside the Island.

PART IV—*Management And Administration*

Registered Office and Name

106. Registered office of company. ***Amended 2013***

107. Publication of name by company.

108. Restriction on commencement of business.

Register of Members

109. Register of members. ***Amended 2017***

110. Index of members of company.

111. ~~Provisions as to entries in register in relation to share warrants.~~ ***Repealed 2017***

112. Inspection of register of members and index.

113. Consequences of failure to comply with requirements as to register owing to agent's default.

114. Power to close register.

115. Power of Court to rectify register.

116. ~~Trusts not to be entered on register.~~ ***Repealed and replaced 2017 – Notice of Trusts***

117. Register to be evidence.

Branch Register

118. Power for company to keep branch register.

119. Regulation as to branch register.

120. Provisions as to branch registers of companies incorporated abroad kept in ~~the Island.~~ ***Jamaica.***

121. Duty to deliver annual returns.

Annual Reports

122. Annual return to be made by company having a share capital. ***Amended 2017***

123. Annual return to be made by company not having share capital. ***Amended by SIPP Act 2013***

124. General provisions as to annual returns.

125. Certificates to be sent by private company with annual return.

Meetings and Proceedings

126. Annual general meeting.

127. Statutory meeting and statutory report.

128. Convening of extraordinary general meeting on requisition.

129. Length of notice for calling meetings.

130. General provisions as to meetings and votes.

131. Proxies.

132. Right to demand a poll.

133. Voting on a poll.

134. Representation of companies at meetings of other companies and of other creditors.

135. Circulation of members' resolutions.

136. Circulation of members' circulars.

137. General provisions affecting sections 135 and 136.

138. Provisions as to extraordinary and special resolutions.

139. Registration and copies of certain resolutions and agreements.

140. Resolutions passed at adjourned meetings.

141. Participation by electronic means.

142. Minutes of proceedings of meetings of company and of directors and managers.

143. Inspection of minute books.

Accounts and Audit

144. Books and documents of account.

145. Profit and loss account and balance sheet.

146. General provisions as to contents and form of accounts.

147. Obligation to lay group accounts before holding company.

148. Form of group accounts.

149. Contents of group accounts.

150. Financial year of holding company and subsidiary.

151. Meaning of "holding company" and "subsidiary".

152. Requirements relating to balance sheets.

153. Right to receive copies of balance Sheets and auditors's report.

154. Appointment and remuneration of auditors.

155. Qualification for appointment as auditor.

156. Disqualification for appointment as auditor.

157. Auditor's report and right of access to books and to attend and be heard at general meetings.

158. Dividends.

159. Exception from the provision of Audited reports.

Inspection

160. Investigation of company's affairs on application of members.

161. Investigation of company's affairs in other cases.

162. Power of inspectors to carry investigation into affairs of related companies.

163. Production of documents, and evidence on investigation.

164. Inspector's report.

165. Proceedings on inspector's report.

166. Expenses of investigation of company's affairs.

167. Inspector's report to be evidence.

168. Appointment and powers of inspectors to investigate ownership of company.

169. Power to require information as to persons interested in shares or debentures.

170. Power to impose restrictions on shares or debentures.

171. Saving for attorneys and bankers.

Directors and other Officers

172. Number of directors and secretary. ***Amended 2013*** and ***2017***

173. Avoidance of acts done by persons in dual capacity as director and secretary

174. Duty of care.

174A. Duty to avoid conflict of interest. Added 2017

175. Restrictions on appointment or advertisement of director.

176. Validity of acts of directors.

177. Share qualifications of directors. ***Amended 2017***

178. Appointments of directors to be voted on individually.

179. Removal of directors.

180. Court disqualified directors.

181. Provisions as to undischarged bankrupts acting as directors.

182. Disqualification for persistent breaches of Act.

183. Register of directors. ***Amended 2013***

184. Illicit loans by company.

185. Permitted loans.

186. Approval of company requisite for payment in connection with transfer of property to director for loss of office, etc.

187. Approval of company required for any payment re transfer of its property to director for loss of office, etc.

188. Duty of director to disclose payment for loss of office, etc. made in connection with transfer of shares in company.

189. Provisions supplementary to sections 186, 187 and 188.

190. Particulars in accounts of directors salaries, pensions, etc.

191. Particulars in accounts of loans to officers, etc.

192. General duty to make disclosure for purposes of sections 190 and 191.

193. Disclosure by directors of interest in contracts.

194. Particulars with respect to directors in trade catalogues, circulars, etc.

195. Director's service contracts to be open to inspection.

196. Duty of directors to disclose shareholdings in own company.

197. Register of interest notified under section 196.

198. Sanctions for non-compliance.

199. Application of section 196 to spouse and child.

200. Provisions as to assignment of office by directors.

201. Indemnifying directors, etc. ***Amended 2017***

202. For derivative action.

203. Right to indemnity.

204. Insurance of directors, etc.

205. Court approval of indemnity.

205A. Application in relation to proposals under Insolvency Act

Arrangements and Reconstructions

206. Power to compromise with creditors and members.

207. Information as to compromises with creditors and members.

208. Provisions for facilitating reconstruction and amalgamation of companies.

209. Power to acquire shares of shareholders dissenting from scheme or contract approved by majority. ***Amended 2017***

210. Scheme of arrangement company and connected person.

211. Power of Court to order pooling of assets.

212. Derivative actions.

213. Court powers. ***Amended 2017***

213A. Remedy in case of Oppression. ***Amended 2017***

213B Non-Application to Companies that are Insolvent under Insolvency Act

PART V—*WINDING UP*

(i) PRELIMINARY

Modes of Winding Up

214. Modes of Winding up.

Contributories

215. Liability as contributories of present and past members.

216. Definition of contributory.

217. Nature of liability of contributory.

218. Contributories in case of death of member.

219. Contributories in case of bankruptcy of member. ***Amended by the Insolvency Act 2014***

(ii) WINDING UP BY THE COURT

Cases in which Company may be wound up by Court

220. Circumstances in which companies may be wound up by Court. ***Amended by the Insolvency Act 2014***

~~221. Definition of inability to pay debts.~~ ***Repealed by Insolvency Act 2014***

Application ~~*Petition*~~ *for Winding Up and Effects thereof*

222. Provisions as to applications for winding up. Amended 2017 and by the Insolvency Act 2014

223. Power of Court on hearing ~~petition~~ application.

224. Power to stay or restrain proceedings against companies.

225. Avoidance of dispositions of property, etc. after commencement of winding up.

226. Avoidance of attachments, etc.

Commencement of Winding Up

227. Commencement of winding up by the Court.

Consequences of Winding Up Order

228. Copy of order to be forwarded to Registrar.

229. Actions stayed on winding up order.

230. Effect of winding up order.

Trustee in Bankruptcy

~~231. Trustee in Bankruptcy to be Trustee for winding up purposes.~~ ***Repealed and replaced by the Insolvency Act 2014 – Meaning of "Government Trustee" and "Supervisor"***

232. Statement of company's affairs to be submitted to Trustees.

233. Report by Trustees.

~~*Liquidators*~~ ***Trustees***

234. Power of Court to appoint trustees.

235. Appointment and powers of provisional trustee.

236. Appointment, style, etc. of trustees. ***Amended by the Insolvency Act 2014***

237. Provisions where person other than Trustee is appointed trustee.

238. General provisions as to trustees.

239. Custody of company's property.

240. Vesting of company's property in trustee.

241. Powers of trustee.

242. Exercise and control of trustee's powers.

243. Books to be kept by trustee.

244. Payments of trustee into bank.

245. Audit of trustee's accounts.

246. Control of Registrar over trustees.

247. Release of trustee.

Committees of Inspection

248. Meetings of creditors and contributories to determine whether committee of inspection shall be appointed.

249. Constitution and proceedings of committee of inspection.

250. Power of Minister where no committee of inspection.

General Powers of Court in case of Winding Up by Court

251. Power to stay winding up.

252. Settlement of list of contributories and application of assets.

253. Delivery of property to trustee.

254. Payment of debts due by contributory to company and extent to which set-off allowed.

255. Power of Court to make calls.

256. Payment into bank of moneys due to company.

257. Order on contributory conclusive evidence.

258. Appointment of special manager.

259. Power to exclude creditors not proving in time.

260. Adjustment of rights of contributories.

261. Inspection of books by creditors and contributories.

~~262. Power to order costs of winding up to be paid out of assets.~~ ***Repealed and replaced by the Insolvency Act 2014 – Power to order application by trustee for assignment under Insolvency Act***

263. Power to summon persons suspected of having company property.

264. Power to order public examination of promoters, directors, etc.

265. Procedure at examination.

266. Power to arrest absconding contributory.

267. Powers of Court cumulative.

268. Delegation to trustee of certain powers of Court.

269. Dissolution of company.

Enforcement of, and appeal from, orders

270. Power to enforce orders.

271. Appeal from orders.

(iii) VOLUNTARY WINDING UP

Resolution for, and Commencement of, Voluntary Winding Up

272. Circumstances in which company may be wound up voluntarily. ***Amended by the Insolvency Act 2014***

273. Notice of resolution to wind up voluntarily.

274. Commencement of voluntary winding up.

Consequences of Voluntary Winding Up

275. Effect of voluntary winding up on business and status of company.

276. Avoidance of transfers, etc., after commencement of voluntary winding up.

Declaration of Solvency

277. Statutory declaration of solvency in case of proposal to wind up voluntarily.

Provisions applicable to a Members' Voluntary Winding Up

278. Provisions applicable to members' winding up.

279. Power of company to appoint and fix remuneration of trustees.

280. Power to fill vacancy in office of trustee.

281. Power of trustee to accept shares, etc. as consideration for sale of company.

282. Duty of trustee to call creditors' meeting in case of insolvency. ***Amended by the Insolvency Act 2014***

283. Duty of trustee to call general meeting at end of each year.

284. Final meeting and dissolution.

~~285. Alternative provisions as to annual and final meetings in case of insolvency.~~

~~*Provisions applicable to a Creditors' Voluntary Winding Up*~~

~~286. Provisions applicable to creditor's winding up.~~

~~287. Meeting of creditors.~~

~~288. Appointment of trustee.~~

289. Appointment of committee of inspection.

290. Fixing of trustees' remuneration and cesser of directors' powers.

291. Power to fill vacancy in office of trustee.

292. Application of section 305 to creditors' winding up.

293. Duty of trustee to call meetings of company and of creditors at end of each year. ***Repealed by the Insolvency Act 2014***

294. Final meeting and dissolution.

Provisions applicable to every Voluntary Winding Up

295. Provision applicable to every voluntary winding up.

296. Distribution of company's property. ***Amended by the Insolvency Act 2014***

297. Powers and duties of trustee in voluntary winding up.

298. Power of Court to appoint and remove trustee in voluntary winding up.

299. Notice by trustee of his appointment. ***Amended by the Insolvency Act 2014***

300. Arrangement when binding on creditors. ***Repealed by the Insolvency Act 2014***

301. Power to apply to Court to have questions determined or powers exercised.

302. Costs of voluntary winding up.

303. Saving for rights of creditors and contributories.

(iv) WINDING UP SUBJECT TO SUPERVISION OF COURT

304. Power to order winding up subject to supervision.

305. Effect of petition ***application*** for winding up subject to supervision.

306. Application of sections 225 and 226 to winding up subject to supervision.

307. Power of Court to appoint or remove trustees.

308. Effect of supervision order.

(v) PROVISIONS APPLICABLE TO EVERY MODE OF WINDING UP

Proof and Ranking of Claims

309. Debts of all descriptions to be proved.

~~310. Application of bankruptcy rules in winding up of insolvent companies.~~ ***Repealed by the Insolvency Act 2014***

~~311. Preferential payments~~ ***Amended by SIPP Act 2013; Repealed and replaced by the Insolvency Act 2014 – Ranking of claims for distribution***

Effect of Winding Up on Antecedent and other Transaction

312. Fraudulent preference.

313. Liabilities and rights of certain fraudulently preferred person. ***Amended by SIPP Act 2013***

~~314. Effect of floating charge.~~ ***Repealed by the Insolvency Act 2014***

315. Disclaimer of onerous property.

316. Restriction of rights of creditor as to execution or attachment.

317. Duties of bailiff as to goods taken in execution.

Offences Antecedent to or in Course of Winding Up

318. Offences by officers of companies in liquidation.

319. Penalty for falsification of books.

320. Fraud by officers of companies which have gone into liquidation. ***Amended by SIPP Act 2013***

321. Liability where proper accounts not kept.

322. Responsibility for fraudulent trading of persons concerned.

323. Power of Court to assess damages against delinquent directors, etc.

324. Prosecution of delinquent officers and members of company.

Supplementary Provisions as to Winding Up

~~325. Disqualification for appointment trustee.~~ ***Repealed by the Insolvency Act 2014***

326. Enforcement of duty of trustee to make returns, etc.

327. Notification that company is in liquidation.

328. Exemption of certain documents from stamp duty on winding up of companies

329. Books of company to be evidence.

330. Disposal of books and papers of company.

331. Information as to pending liquidations.

332. Unclaimed assets.

333. Resolutions passed at adjourned meetings of creditors and contributories.

Supplementary Powers of Court

334. Meetings to ascertain wishes of creditors or contributories.

335. Affidavits, etc.

Provisions as to Dissolution

336. Power of Court to declare dissolution of company void.

337. Registrar may strike defunct company off register.

338. Property of dissolved company to be bona vacantia.

339. Power of Crown to disclaim title to property vesting under section 337.

Rules and Fees

340. Rules and fees for winding up. ***Amended by the Insolvency Act 2014***

PART VI—*Receivers and Managers*

~~341. Disqualification for appointment as receiver and for acting as receiver or manager.~~ ***Repealed by the SIPP Act 2014***

~~342. Power to appoint Trustee as receiver for debenture holders or creditors.~~ ***Amended by SIPP Act 2013 then Repealed by the Insolvency Act 2014***

343. Notification that receiver or manager appointed.

344. Power of Court to fix remuneration on application of trustee.

345. Provisions as to information where receiver or manager appointed. ***Amended by the SIPP Act 2013***

346. Special provisions as to statement submitted to receiver.

347. Delivery to Registrar of accounts of receivers and managers.

348. Enforcement of duty of receivers and managers to make returns, etc.

349. Liability of receiver for contracts, etc.

350. Construction of references to receivers and managers.

PART VII—*Registration Office and Fees*

351. Registrar of Companies and registration office.

351A. Powers of the Registrar re Form BRF1

352. Inspection, production and evidence of documents kept by Registrar.

353. Enforcement of duty of company to make returns to Registrar.

PART VIII—*Application of Act to Existing Companies*

354. Application of Act to existing companies.

PART IX—*Winding Up of Unregistered Companies*

355. Meaning and winding up of unregistered company. ***Amended by the Insolvency Act 2014***

356. Contributories in winding up of unregistered company.

357. Power of Court to stay or restrain proceedings.

358. Action stayed on winding up order.

359. Winding up company incorporated outside ~~the Island~~ Jamaica.

360. Provisions of Part IX cumulative.

361. Winding up of limited partnership.

PART X—*Companies Incorporated Outside the ~~Island~~* ***Jamaica*** *Carrying on Business Within ~~the Island~~* ***Jamaica***

362. Companies to which Part X applies.

363. Documents, etc. to be delivered to Registrar by companies carrying on business in ~~the Island~~ ***Jamaica.***

363A. Register of Members to be Kept by Companies Incorporated Outside Jamaica. Amended 2017

364. Power of companies incorporated outside Island to hold lands.

365. Return to be delivered to Registrar where documents, etc. altered. ***Amended 2017***

366. Accounts of company carrying on business in Island. ***Amended 2017***

367. Obligation to state name of company, whether limited and country where incorporated.

368. Service on company to which Part X applies.

369. Removing company's name from register.

370. Penalties. ***Amended 2017***

371. Interpretation of Part X.

PART XI—Restrictions on Sale of Shares and Offers of Shares for Sale

372. Provisions with respect to prospectuses of foreign companies inviting subscriptions for shares or offering shares for sale.

373. Additional requirements as to prospectus.

374. Provisions as to expert's consent and allotment.

375. Penalty for contravention of sections 373, 374 and 375.

376. Civil liability for misstatements in prospectus.

377. Interpretation of provisions as to prospectus.

PART XII—Miscellaneous

Prohibition of Partnership with more than Twenty Members

378. Prohibition of partnerships with more than twenty members.

Provisions relating to Banks

379. Prohibition of banking partnerships with more than ten members.

Application of certain Provisions of this Act to Unregistered Companies

380. Application of certain provisions of this Act to unregistered companies.

Form of registers, etc.

381. Form of registers, etc.

Miscellaneous Offences

382. Penalty for false statement.

383. Penalty for improper use of word "Limited".

383A. Share Warrants Prohibited

Provisions as to Offences

384. Provision with respect to default fines and meaning of "officer in

385. Prosecution of offences punishable by fine.

386. Production and inspection of books where offence suspected.

Service of Documents and Legal Proceedings

387. Service of documents on company.

388. Costs in actions by certain limited companies.

389. Power of Court to grant relief in certain cases.

390. Saving for privileged communications.

390A. Records

Savings, etc.

391. Savings.

392. Power to alter or add to certain requirements.

393. Power to make rules. ***Amended 2013***

394. Fees.

395. Repeal.

396. Transitional.

396* Transitional arrangements for share warrants

397. Registrar to give notice of prohibition to bearers of share warrants

398. Definition of share warrants

FIRST SCHEDULE	Tables, A, B, C and D
SECOND SCHEDULE	Form of Statement in lieu of Prospectus to bedelivered to Registrar by a Private Company on becoming a Public Company and Reports to be set out therein.
THIRD SCHEDULE	Matters to be specified in Prospectus and Reports to be set out therein.
FOURTH SCHEDULE	Form of Statement in lieu of Prospectus to be delivered to Registrar by a Company which does not issue a Prospectus or which does not go to allotment on a Prospectus issued, and Reports to be set out therein.
FIFTH SCHEDULE	Contents (Required by Section 119 (3)) and form of Annual Return of a Company having a Share Capital.
SIXTH SCHEDULE	Provisions which do not apply in the case of a winding up subject to supervision of the Court.
SEVENTH SCHEDULE	Financial Disclosure - Form and content of Company Accounts.
EIGHTH SCHEDULE	Matters to be expressly stated in Auditors Report.
NINTH SCHEDULE	Provisions referred to in Section 382.
TENTH SCHEDULE	Procedure in cases of applications for licences under Section 16.
ELEVENTH SCHEDULE	Provisions of this Act applied to the Unregistered companies.
TWELFTH SCHEDULE	Exceptions referred to at paragraph (e) of subsection (1) of Section 25.
THIRTEENTH SCHEDULE	Exceptions referred to at subsection (3) of Section 25.
FOURTEENTH SCHEDULE	Provisions supplementing and interpreting Section 196.
FIFTEENTH SCHEDULE	Table of Fees.
SIXTEENTH SCHEDULE	***Form BRF1***

THE COMPANIES ACT

Act 10 of 2004

[*1st February, 2005.*]

PART I—*Preliminary*

1. This Act may be cited as the Companies Act. Short title.

2.—(1) In this Act unless the context otherwise requires— Interpretation.

"accounts" includes a company's group accounts whether prepared in the form of accounts or not;

"affiliated" in relation to two or more companies means that—

(*a*) one of them is the subsidiary of the other;

(*b*) each of them is a subsidiary of the same company;

(*c*) each of them is controlled directly or indirectly by the same person; or

(*d*) each of them by virtue of paragraph (*a*), (*b*) or (*c*) has a relationship with the same company at the same time;

"agent" does not include a person's counsel acting as such;

"annual return" means the return required to be made, in the case of a company having a share capital, under section 122, and, in the case of a company not having a share capital, under section 123;

"appointed day" means the 1st day of February, 2005;

"articles" means the articles of incorporation of a company as originally framed or as altered by special resolution;

"associate" in relation to any person means—

(*a*) a company or body corporate of which that person beneficially owns or controls, directly or indirectly, shares or debentures convertible into shares, that carry more than twenty per cent of the voting rights—

(i) under all circumstances;

(ii) by reason of the occurrence of an event that is continuing; or

(iii) by reason of a currently exercisable option or right to purchase those shares or those convertible debentures;

(*b*) a partner of that person acting on behalf of the partnership of which they are partners;

(*c*) a trust or estate in which that person has a substantial beneficial interest or in respect of which he serves as a trustee or in a similar capacity;

(*d*) a spouse of that person;

(*e*) a child, step-child or adopted child of that person;

(*f*) an immediate relative of that person or of his spouse;

"book and paper" and "book or paper" include accounts, deeds, writings and documents;

"company" means a company formed and registered under this Act or an existing company;

"the Court" used in relation to a company means the Supreme Court;

"debenture" includes debenture stock, bonds and any other securities of a company whether constituting a charge on the assets of the company or not;

"director" includes any person occupying the position of director by whatever name called;

"document" includes, in addition to a document in writing—

(*a*) any map, plan, graph or drawing;

(*b*) any photograph;

(*c*) any disc, tape, sound track or other device in which sounds or other data are embodied so as to be capable (with or without the aid of some other equipment) of being reproduced therefrom;

"existing company" means a company formed and registered before the 1st day of February, 2005, under the Law in force before that date;

"file accounts" has the meaning assigned to that expression by subsection (4) of section 25;

"financial year" means, in relation to any body corporate, the period in respect of which any profit and loss account of the body corporate laid before it in general meeting is made up, whether that period is a year or not;

"issued generally" means, in relation to a prospectus, issued to persons who are not existing members or debenture holders of the company;

"immediate relative", as respects any person, means his spouse, or his children (including step-children) and their spouses, his parents, his brother or sister;

"officer" in relation to a body corporate includes a director, manager or secretary;

"prescribed" means, as respects the provisions of this Act relating to procedure, winding up, and the costs; and fees in connection therewith, prescribed by rules of court, and as respects the other provisions of this Act, prescribed by the Minister;

"prospectus" means any prospectus, notice, circular, advertisement, or other invitation, offering to the public for subscription or purchase any shares or debentures of a company;

"Registrar" or "Registrar of Companies" means the public officer referred to in section 351;

"rules" means rules provided for in this Act, and includes rules of court and forms;

"shadow director" in relation to a company, means a person in accordance with whose directions or instructions the directors of the company are accustomed to act, so, however, that a person is not deemed a shadow director by reason only that the directors act on advice given by him in a professional capacity;

"share" means a share in the share capital of a company, and includes stock except where a distinction between stock and shares is expressed or implied;

"share warrant" has the meaning assigned to that expression by subsection (2) of section 82;

"stated capital" includes—

(*a*) the total issue price (including consideration other than cash) of all classes of shares;

(*b*) the full value of transfers to capital by the company from profit, or revenue reserves, including the total issue price of bonus shares issued upon a capitalization of profits or revenue reserves;

First Schedule. "Table A" means Table A in the First Schedule;

"time of the opening of the subscription lists" has the meaning assigned to that expression by subsection (2) of section 51;

"Trustee" has the meaning assigned to it by section 231.

(2) A person shall not be deemed, within the meaning of any provision in this Act, to be a person in accordance with whose directions or instructions the directors of a company are accustomed to act, by reason only that the directors of the company act on advice given by him in a professional capacity.

(3) Wherever in this Act or in any rules a copy of an order of the Court is required to be served on or delivered to the Registrar the copy so to be served or delivered shall be an office copy.

(4) References in this Act to a body corporate or to a corporation shall be construed as not including a corporation sole but as including a company incorporated outside Jamaica.

(5) Any document filed with the Registrar shall be capable of being read.

Incorporation of Companies and Matters Incidental thereto

3.—(1) One or more persons may form a company by signing and sending articles of incorporation to the Registrar and otherwise complying with the requirements of this Act in respect of registration. Mode of forming incorporated company.

(2) Such a company may be either—

(*a*) a company having the liability of its members limited by the articles to the amount, if any, unpaid on the shares respectively held by them (in this Act termed "a company limited by shares"); or

(*b*) a company having the liability of its members limited by the articles to such amount as the members may respectively thereby undertake to contribute to the assets of the company in the event of its being wound up (in this Act termed "a company limited by guarantee") whether or not such a company has a share capital; or (*c*) a company not having any limit on the liability of its members (in this Act termed "an unlimited company").

Capacity and powers.

4.—(1) A company has the capacity, and, subject to this Act, the rights, powers and privileges of an individual.

(2) A company has the capacity to carry on its business, conduct its affairs and exercise its powers in any jurisdiction outside Jamaica to the extent that the laws of Jamaica and of that jurisdiction permit.

(3) It is not necessary for a bylaw to be passed to confer any particular power on a company or its directors.

(4) This section does not authorize any company to carry on any business or activity in breach of—

(*a*) any enactment prohibiting or restricting the carrying on of the business or activity; or

(*b*) any provision requiring any permission or licence for the carrying on of the business or activity.

Powers reduced.

5. A company shall not carry on any business or exercise any power that it is restricted by its articles from carrying on or exercising, nor shall a company exercise any of its powers in a manner contrary to its articles.

Validity of acts.

6. For the avoidance of doubt, it is hereby declared that, unless otherwise specifically provided in this Act or any other enactment, an act of a company that is contrary to its articles (including any transfer of property to or by a company) shall not be invalid by reason only that the act is contrary to its articles.

Notice not presumed.

7. No person shall be affected by, or presumed to have notice or knowledge of, the contents of a document concerning a company by reason only that the document has been filed with the Registrar or is available for inspection at any office of the company.

Articles of Incorporation

8.—(1) Articles of incorporation of a company shall be in the prescribed form and shall set out in respect of the company— Form of articles.

(*a*) the name of the company with "limited" as the last word of the name in the case of a company limited by shares or by guarantee;

(*b*) that the registered office of the company is to be situated in the Island;

(*c*) in the case of a company having a share capital, the classes of shares, if any, and the maximum number of shares, if any, that the company is authorized to issue;

(*d*) if the right to transfer shares in the company is to be restricted, a statement to that effect and giving the nature of the restriction;

(*e*) the number of directors, or the maximum or minimum number of directors of the company;

(*f*) any restrictions on the business that the company may carry on.

(2) Articles shall—

(*a*) be printed or typewritten or be in some legible form or other form acceptable to the Registrar;

(*b*) be divided into paragraphs numbered consecutively;

(*c*) bear the same stamp as if they were contained in a deed;

(*d*) be signed by each subscriber of the articles in the presence of at least one witness who must attest the signature.

(3) Nothing in this section shall operate to prevent the inclusion in the articles of a company, of provisions with respect to any matter not required by this section to be included in the articles.

(4) The articles of a company referred to in section 11 (*a*) and (*b*) shall state that the liability of its members is limited.

(5) The articles of a private company shall contain the matters specified in section 25 (1).

(6) The form of the articles of—

(*a*) a company limited by shares;

(*b*) a company limited by guarantee and not having a share capital;

(*c*) a company limited by guarantee and having a share capital;

(*d*) an unlimited company having a share capital,

First Schedule.

may be respectively in accordance with the forms set out in Tables A, B, C and D in the First Schedule, except to the extent that they are excluded in whole or in part or modified.

(7) A company having a share capital shall, where applicable, file a document with the Registrar setting out the following—

(*a*) if two or more classes of shares are issued, the rights, privileges, restrictions and conditions attaching to each class of shares; and

(*b*) if a class of shares may be issued in a series, the authority given to the directors to fix the number of shares in, and to determine the designation of, and the rights, privileges, restrictions and conditions attaching to the shares of each series.

Regulations required in case of unlimited company or company limited by guarantee.

9.—(1) In the case of an unlimited company or a company limited by guarantee the articles must state the number of members with which the company proposes to be registered and, if the company has a share capital, the amount of share capital with which the company proposes to be registered.

(2) Where an unlimited company or a company limited by guarantee has increased the number of its members beyond the registered number, it shall, within fifteen days after the increase was resolved on or took place, give to the Registrar notice of the increase, and the Registrar shall record the increase.

(3) If default is made in complying with subsection (2), the company and every officer of the company who is in default shall be liable to a fine not exceeding fifty thousand dollars.

10.—(1) Subject to the provisions of this Act, a company may by special resolution alter or add to its articles. Alteration of articles by special resolution.

(2) Any alteration or addition so made in the articles shall, subject to the provisions of this Act, be as valid as if originally contained therein, and be subject in like manner to alteration by special resolution.

Registration

11. The articles shall be delivered to the Registrar who shall— Registration of articles.

(*a*) retain and register them if the articles comply with the provisions of this Act; or

(*b*) where the articles are not in compliance, require that they be amended to ensure such compliance.

12.—(1) On the registration of the articles of a company the Registrar shall certify under his hand that the company is incorporated and, in the case of a limited company, that the company is limited. Effect of registration.

(2) From the date of incorporation mentioned in the certificate of incorporation, the subscribers of the articles, together with such other persons as may from time to time

become members of the company, shall be a company by the name contained in the articles, capable forthwith of exercising all the functions of an incorporated company, and having perpetual succession and a common seal, but with such liability on the part of the members to contribute to the assets of the company in the event of its being wound up as is mentioned in this Act.

Conclusiveness of certificate of incorporation.

13.—(1) A certificate of incorporation given by the Registrar in respect of any association shall be conclusive evidence that all the requirements of this Act in respect of registration and of matters precedent and incidental thereto have been complied with, and that the association is a company authorized to be registered and duly registered under this Act.

(2) A statutory declaration by an attorney-at-law engaged in the formation of the company, or by a person named in the articles as a director or secretary of the company, or by a person who is a member of the Institute of Chartered Secretaries and Administrators engaged in the formation of the company, of compliance with all or any of the said requirements shall be produced to the Registrar, and the Registrar may accept such a declaration as sufficient evidence of compliance.

Registration of unlimited company as limited.

14.—(1) Subject to the provisions of this section, a company registered as unlimited may register under this Act as limited, or a company already registered as a limited company may re-register under this Act, but the registration of an unlimited company as a limited company shall not affect the rights or liabilities of the company in respect of any debt or obligation incurred, or any contract entered into, by, to, with or on behalf of the company before the registration, and those rights or liabilities may be enforced as provided by this Act in the same manner in all respects as if no such change of registration had taken place.

(2) On registration in pursuance of this section the Registrar shall close the former registration of the company, and may dispense with the delivery to him of copies of any documents with copies of which he was furnished on the occasion of the original registration of the company, but, save as aforesaid, the registration shall take place in the same manner and shall have effect as if it were the first registration of the company under this Act.

(3) Where a company limited by shares re-registers as a company limited by guarantee, the amount of the guarantee shall not be less than the amount remaining unpaid on the shares.

Provisions with respect to Names of Companies

15.—(1) No company shall be registered by a name which in the opinion of the Registrar is undesirable having regard to such provisions as may be prescribed.

Prohibition of registration of companies by undesirable names.

(2) If, through inadvertence or otherwise, a company on its first registration or on its registration by a new name is registered by a name which in the opinion of the Registrar too closely resembles the name by which a company in existence is previously registered, the first mentioned company may, with the sanction of the Registrar, change its name, and shall, if the Registrar so directs within six months of its being registered by that name, change its name within six weeks of the date of such direction or within such longer period as the Registrar may think fit to allow.

(3) If at any time after a company has been registered it appears to the Registrar that the name under which it is registered is undesirable, the Registrar may notify the company accordingly and may in such notification direct the company to change its name, and the company shall change its name within six weeks of such direction unless within that time it has lodged an appeal to the Court against such direction.

(4) The Court shall thereupon either cancel or confirm such direction and its decision shall be final and conclusive.

(5) If the direction is confirmed the company shall change its name within six weeks of such confirmation.

(6) If a company makes default in complying with a direction under subsection (2) or, except where an appeal has not been disposed of, under subsection (3), it shall be liable to a fine not exceeding one thousand dollars for every day during which the default continues.

(7) Subsections (3), (4) and (5) of section 17 shall apply to a change of name under this section as they apply to a change of name under that section.

Power to dispense with "limited" in name of charitable and other companies.

16.—(1) Where it is proved to the satisfaction of the Minister that an association about to be formed as a limited company is to be formed for promoting commerce, art, science, religion, charity or any other useful object, and intends to apply its profits, if any, or other income in promoting its objects, and to prohibit the payment of any dividend to its members, the Minister may by licence direct that the association may be registered as a company with limited liability, without the addition of the word "limited" to its name, and the association maybe registered accordingly and shall, on registration,enjoy all the privileges and (subject to the provisions of this section) be subject to all the obligations of limited companies.

(2) Where it is proved to the satisfaction of the Minister—

(*a*) that the objects of a company registered under this Act as a limited company or of an existing company, being a limited company, is restricted to the matters specified in subsection (1) and to objects incidental or conducive thereto; and (*b*) that by its constitution the company is required to apply its profits, if any, or other income in promoting its objects and is prohibited from paying any dividend to its members,

the Minister may by licence authorize the company to make by special resolution a change in its name including or consisting of the omission of the word "limited", and subsections (4), (5) and (6) of section 17 shall apply to a change of name under this subsection as they apply to a change of name under that section.

(3) A licence by the Minister under this section may be granted on such conditions and subject to such regulations as the Minister thinks fit, and those conditions and regulations shall be binding on the body to which the licence is granted, and, where the grant is under subsection (1), shall, if the Minister so directs, be inserted in the articles.

(4) A body to which a licence is granted under this section shall be exempted from the provisions of this Act relating to the use of the word "limited" as any part of its name, the publishing of its name and the sending of lists of members to the Registrar.

(5) A licence under this section may at any time be revoked by the Minister, and upon revocation the Registrar shall enter upon the register the word "limited" at the end of the name of the body to which it was granted, and the body shall cease to enjoy the exemptions and privileges or, as the case may be, the exemptions granted by this section:

Provided that, before a licence is so revoked, the Minister shall give to the body notice in writing of his intention, and shall afford the body an opportunity of being heard in opposition to the revocation.

(6) Where a body in respect of which a licence under this section is in force alters the provisions of its articles with

respect to its business, the Minister may (unless he sees fit to revoke the licence) vary the licence by making it subject to such conditions and regulations as the Minister thinks fit, in lieu of or in addition to the conditions and regulations, if any, to which the licence was formerly subject.

(7) Where a licence granted under this section to a body the name of which contains the words "Chamber of Commerce" is revoked, the notice to be given under the proviso to subsection (5) shall include a statement of the effect of the provisions of subsection (2) of section 17.

(8) The procedure in cases of applications for licences under this section shall be in accordance with that set out in the Tenth Schedule.

Tenth Schedule.

Change of name.

17.—(1) A company may, by special resolution and with the approval of the Registrar signified in writing, change its name.

(2) Where a licence granted pursuant to section 16 to a body the name of which contains the words "Chamber of Commerce" is revoked, the body shall, within a period of six weeks from the date of the revocation or such longer period as the Registrar may think fit to allow, change its name to a name which does not contain those words.

(3) If such a body makes default in complying with the requirements of subsection (2), it shall be liable to a fine not exceeding two thousand dollars for every day during which the default continues.

(4) Where a company or a body changes its name under this section the Registrar shall enter the new name on the register in place of the former name, and shall issue a certificate of incorporation altered to meet the circumstances of the case.

(5) The change of name shall not affect any rights or obligations of the company or body, or render defective any legal proceedings by or against it, and any legal proceedings that might have been continued or commenced against it by its former name may be continued or commenced against it by its new name.

(6) Where a company or body changes its name under this section it shall cause notice of the change of name to be published in the *Gazette* and in a daily newspaper printed and circulating in the Island within thirty days after the date on which the Registrar approves the change and if default is made in complying with this subsection the company or body and every director, manager, secretary or other officer of the company or body who knowingly and wilfully authorizes or permits the default shall be liable to a fine not exceeding fifty thousand dollars.

18. The Registrar may, upon request and upon payment of the prescribed fee, reserve for ninety days a name for an intended company or for a company about to change its name. Reservation of name.

General Provisions with respect to Articles

19.—(1) Subject to the provisions of this Act, the articles shall, when registered, bind the company and the members thereof to the same extent as if they respectively had been signed and sealed by each member, and contained covenants on the part of each member to observe all the provisions of the articles. Effect of articles.

(2) All money payable by any member to the company under the articles shall be a debt due from him to the company, and in this Island be of the nature of a specialty debt.

Provision as to articles of companies limited by guarantee.

20.—(1) In the case of a company limited by guarantee and not having a share capital, every provision in the articles or in any resolution of the company purporting to give any person a right to participate in the divisible profits of the company otherwise than as a member shall be void unless such provision was in existence at the appointed day.

(2) For the purpose of the provisions of this Act relating to the articles of a company limited by guarantee and of this section, every provision in the articles or in any resolution, of a company limited by guarantee purporting to divide the undertaking of the company into shares or interests shall be treated as a provision for a share capital notwithstanding that the number of the shares or interests is not specified thereby.

Alterations of articles increasing liability to contribute to share capital not to bind existing members without consent.

21. Notwithstanding anything in the articles of a company, no member of the company shall be bound by an alteration made in the articles after the date on which he became a member, if and so far as the alteration requires him to take or subscribe for more shares than the number held by him at the date on which the alteration is made, or in any way increases his liability as at that date to contribute to the share capital of, or otherwise to pay money to, the company:

Provided that this section shall not apply in any case where the member agrees in writing, either before or after the alteration is made, to be bound thereby.

Copies of articles to be given to members.

22.—(1) A company shall, on being so required by any member, send to him a copy of the articles, subject to payment of such sum as may be prescribed.

(2) If a company makes default in complying with this section, the company and every officer of the company who is in default shall be liable to a fine not exceeding two thousand dollars.

Membership of Company

Definition of member.

23.—(1) The following persons are members of a company and shall be entered as members on its register of members—

(*a*) persons who subscribe to the company's articles whose names shall, on the registration of the company, be entered in the company's register;

(*b*) the personal representatives of a deceased member and the trustee in bankruptcy of a bankrupt member;

(*c*) persons named as a principal account holder or subsidiary account holder, as the case may be, during any period in respect of which eligible securities carrying voting rights are entered against their names in the register of the licensed central securities depository for that company's shares.

(2) Every other person who agrees to become a member of a company, and whose name is entered in its register of members, shall be a member of the company.

(3) For the purposes of this section—

"licensed central securities depository" means a company licensed under section 67B of the Securities Act to operate a central securities depository;

"principal account holder" means a person who maintains an account with a licensed central securities depository;

"subsidiary account holder" means the person in whose name a subsidiary account is opened and maintained by the principal account holder.

24.—(1) Except in the cases hereafter in this section mentioned, a body corporate cannot be a member of a company which is its holding company, and any allotment or transfer of shares in a company to its subsidiary shall be void. Membership of holding company.

(2) Nothing in this section shall apply where the subsidiary is concerned as personal representative, or where it is concerned as trustee, unless the holding company or a subsidiary thereof is beneficially interested under the trust and is

not so interested only by way of security for the purposes of a transaction entered into by it in the ordinary course of a business which includes the lending of money.

(3) This section shall not prevent—

(*a*) a subsidiary which is, on the appointed day, a member of its holding company; or

(*b*) a company which, being a member of another company, becomes a subsidiary of that company,

from continuing to be a member but, subject to subsection (2), the subsidiary shall have no right to vote at meetings of the holding company or any class of members thereof.

(4) Subject to subsection (2), subsections (1) and (3) shall apply in relation to a nominee for a body corporate which is a subsidiary, as if references in subsections (1) and (3) to such a body corporate included references to a nominee for it.

(5) In relation to a company limited by guarantee or unlimited which is a holding company, the reference in this section to shares, whether or not it has a share capital, shall be construed as including a reference to the interest of its members as such, whatever the form of that interest.

Private Companies

Private companies.

25.—(1) For the purposes of this Act, the expression "private company" means a company which by its articles—

(*a*) restricts the right to transfer its shares; and

(*b*) limits the number of its members to twenty, not including persons who are in the employment of the company and persons who, having been formerly in the employment of the company were, while in that employment, and have continued after the determination of that employment to be, members of the company; and (*c*) prohibits any invitation to the public to subscribe for any shares or debentures of the company; and

(*d*) prohibits any invitation to the public to deposit money for fixed periods or payable on call whether bearing or not bearing interest; and

(*e*) subject to the exceptions provided for in the Twelfth Schedule, prohibits any person other than the holder from having any interest in any of the company's shares. Twelfth Schedule.

(2) Where two or more persons hold one or more shares of a company jointly, they shall, for the purposes of this section, be treated as a single member.

(3) Subject to subsection (4), a private company shall not be obliged to file accounts unless, but shall be so obliged if, any of its shares is held by a body corporate, so, however, that any obligation to file accounts imposed upon a private company by virtue of this subsection shall be subject to the exceptions provided for in the Thirteenth Schedule. Thirteenth Schedule.

(4) In this Act the expression "file accounts" in relation to a company means to include in its annual return pursuant to subsection (3) of section 124 the documents and information mentioned in that subsection.

(5) The provisions of paragraph (*b*) of subsection (1) shall not apply to a company which is a foreign sales corporation operating under the Foreign Sales Corporations Act.

(6) For the purposes of this Act a public company is a company that is not a private company.

Statement in lieu of prospectus to be delivered to Registrar by company ceasing to be private company.

26.—(1) If a company, being a private company, alters its articles in such manner that they no longer include the provisions which, under section 25, are required to be included in the articles of a company in order to constitute it a private company, the company shall, as on the date of the alteration, cease to be a private company and shall, within a period of fourteen days after that date, deliver to the Registrar for registration a prospectus or a statement in lieu of prospectus in the form and containing the particulars set out in Part I of the Second Schedule and, in the cases mentioned in Part II of that Schedule, setting out the reports specified therein, and the said Parts I and II shall have effect subject to the provisions contained in Part III of that Schedule: Second Schedule.

Provided that a statement in lieu of prospectus need not be delivered under this subsection if within the period of fourteen days aforesaid a prospectus relating to the company which complies with the Third Schedule is issued and is delivered to the Registrar as required by section 40. Third Schedule.

(2) Every statement in lieu of prospectus delivered under subsection (1) shall, where the persons making any such reports as aforesaid have made therein or have, without giving the reasons, indicated therein any such adjustments as are mentioned in paragraph 5 of Part III of the Second Schedule, have endorsed thereon or attached thereto a written statement signed by those persons setting out the adjustments and giving the reasons therefor.

(3) If default is made in complying with subsection (1) or (2) the company and every officer of the company who is in default shall be liable to a fine not exceeding fifty thousand dollars.

(4) Where a statement in lieu of prospectus delivered to the Registrar under subsection (1) includes any untrue statement, any person who authorized the delivery of the statement in lieu of prospectus for registration shall be liable—

(*a*) on conviction on indictment, to imprisonment with or without hard labour for a term not exceeding two years or a fine not exceeding fifty thousand dollars, or both such fine and imprisonment; or (*b*) on summary conviction before a Resident Magistrate, to imprisonment with or without hard labour for a term not exceeding three months or a fine not exceeding fifty thousand dollars or both such fine and imprisonment,

unless he proves either that the untrue statement was immaterial or that he had reasonable ground to believe and did up to the time of the delivery for registration of the statement in lieu of prospectus believe that the untrue statement was true.

(5) For the purposes of this section—

(*a*) a statement included in a statement in lieu of prospectus shall be deemed to be untrue if it is misleading in the form and context in which it is included; and

(*b*) a statement shall be deemed to be included in a statement in lieu of prospectus if it is contained therein or in any report or memorandum appearing on the face thereof or by reference incorporated therein.

Consequences of default in complying with conditions constituting company a private company.

27. Where the articles of a company include the provisions which under section 25 are required to be included in the articles of a company in order to constitute it a private company but default is made in complying with any of those provisions, the company shall cease to be entitled to the privileges and exemptions conferred on private companies under the provisions contained in subsection (3) of that section, and thereupon those provisions shall apply to the company as if it were not a private company:

Provided that the Court, on being satisfied that the failure to comply with the conditions was accidental or due to inadvertence or to some other sufficient cause, or that on other grounds it is just and equitable to grant relief, may on the application of the company or any other person interested and on such terms and conditions as may seem to the Court just and expedient, order that the company be relieved from such consequences as aforesaid.

Mutual Fund Companies

Mutual fund company.

27A.—(1) A "mutual fund company" means a company having a share capital and incorporated for the purpose of investing the moneys of its members for their mutual benefit, stating in its articles that it is a mutual fund, having the power to redeem or purchase for cancellation its shares without reducing its authorized share capital and is registered under the Securities Act as a mutual fund.

(2) A mutual fund company may, on the redemption of its own shares, repay the capital paid up on such shares out of its stated capital account or reserves, on such terms and in such manner and at such price as may be determined having regard to the asset values of shares as ascertained in accordance with the articles of the company.

(3) The redemption or purchase of its own shares by a mutual fund company shall not be taken as reducing its authorized share capital, and a mutual fund shall have the power to issue shares equal in aggregate value to the aggregate value of the shares so redeemed or purchased as if those shares had never been issued and the issuance of such shares under the power herein contained shall not be taken as increasing the amount of its issued share capital.

(4) The powers of a mutual fund company referred to in subsection (3) shall be exercisable by the directors of the mutual fund company or in accordance with the policies and procedures established by the directors.

(5) No shares of a mutual fund company shall be redeemed by the mutual fund company or purchased by another mutual fund company unless such shares are fully paid.

(6) A mutual fund company shall be exempt from the provisions of sections 41, 42, 43, and 46 of this Act in relation to a prospectus and the offering of shares for sale or subscription to the public; and sections 44, 45 and 47 of this Act and the provisions of the Securities Act shall apply to such company in

relation to a prospectus and the offering of shares for sale or subscription to the public.

(7) Sections 112 and 113 (inspection of register of members by public) shall not apply to a mutual fund company.

Contracts, etc.

Form of contracts.

28.—(1) Contracts on behalf of a company may be made as follows—

(*a*) a contract which if made between private persons would be by law required to be in writing and if made according to the law of Jamaica to be under seal, may be made on behalf of the company in writing under the common seal of the company;

(*b*) a contract which if made between private persons would be by law required to be in writing, signed by the parties to be charged therewith may be made on behalf of the company in writing signed by any person acting under its authority express or implied;

(*c*) a contract which if made between private persons would by law be valid although made by parol only, and not reduced into writing, may be made by parol on behalf of the company by any person acting under its authority, express or implied.

(2) A contract made according to this section shall be effectual in law, and shall bind the company and its successors and all other parties thereto.

(3) A contract made according to this section may be varied or discharged in the same manner in which it is authorized by this section to be made.

Pre-incorporation contracts.

29.—(1) Except as provided in this section, a person who enters into an oral or written agreement or contract in the name of or on behalf of a company before it comes into existence or who purports to enter into such an agreement or contract, is personally bound by the agreement or contract and is entitled to the benefits of that agreement or contract.

(2) Within a reasonable time after a company comes into existence, it may, by any action or conduct signifying its intention to be bound thereby, adopt an oral or written agreement or contract made in its name or on its behalf before it came into existence.

(3) When a company adopts an agreement or contract under subsection (2)—

(*a*) the company is bound by the agreement or contract and is entitled to the benefits thereof as if the company had been in existence at the date of the contract and had been a party to it; and

(*b*) a person who purported to act in the name of the company or on its behalf ceases, except as provided in subsection (4), to be bound by or entitled to the benefits of the agreement or contract.

(4) Except as provided in subsection (5), whether or not an oral or written agreement or contract made before the company came into existence is adopted by the company, a party to the agreement or contract may apply to the court for an order—

(*a*) fixing obligations under the contract as joint or joint and several; or

(*b*) apportioning liability between or among the company and a person who purported to act in the name of the company or on its behalf,

and the court may, upon the application, make any order it thinks fit.

(5) If expressly so provided in an agreement or contract, a person who purported to act for or on behalf of a company before it came into existence is not in any event bound by the agreement or contract or entitled to the benefits thereof.

Bills of exchange and promissory notes.

30. A bill of exchange or promissory note shall be deemed to have been made, accepted or endorsed on behalf of a company if made, accepted or endorsed in the name of, or by or on behalf or on account of, the company by any person acting under its authority.

Execution of deeds abroad.

31.—(1) A company may, by writing under its common seal, empower any person, either generally or in respect of any specified matters, as its attorney, to execute deeds on its behalf in any place not situated in the Island.

(2) A deed signed by such an attorney on behalf of the company and under his seal shall bind the company and have the same effect as if it were under its common seal.

Company may have official seal for use abroad.

32.—(1) A company whose business requires or comprises the transaction of business out of the Island may, if authorized by its articles, have for use in any territory, district, or place not situated in the Island, an official seal, which shall be a facsimile of the common seal of the company, with the addition on its face of the name of every territory, district or place where it is to be used.

(2) A deed or other document to which an official seal is duly affixed shall bind the company as if it had been sealed with the common seal of the company.

(3) A company having an official seal for use in any such territory, district or place may, by writing under its common seal, authorize any person appointed for the purpose in that territory, district or place to affix the official seal to any deed or other document to which the company is party in that territory, district or place.

(4) The authority of any such agent shall, as between the company and any person dealing with the agent, continue during the period, if any, mentioned in the instrument conferring the authority, or if no period is so mentioned, then until notice of the revocation or determination of the agent's authority has been given to the person dealing with him.

(5) The person affixing any such official seal shall, by writing under his hand, certify on the deed or other instrument to which the seal is affixed, the date on which and the place at which it is affixed.

Authentication of Documents

Authentication of documents.

33. A document or proceeding requiring authentication by a company may be signed by a director, secretary or other authorized officer of the company, and need not be under its common seal.

PART II—*Share Capital and Debentures*

Minimum share capital

34.—(1) A company registered as a public company having a share capital on its original incorporation shall not do business or exercise any borrowing powers unless the Registrar has issued it with a certificate under this section or the company is re-registered as a private company.

(2) The Registrar shall issue a company with such a certificate if, on an application by the company in the prescribed form, he is satisfied that the value of the company's allotted share capital is not less than the authorized minimum, and there is delivered to the Registrar a statutory declaration in accordance with subsection (3).

(3) The statutory declaration shall be in the prescribed form and be signed by a director or secretary of the company and shall—

(*a*) state that the value of the company's allotted share capital is not less than the authorized minimum;

(*b*) specify the amount paid up, at the time of the application, on the company's allotted share capital;

(*c*) specify the amount, or estimated amount, of the company's preliminary expenses and the persons by whom any of those expenses have been paid or are payable; and

(*d*) specify the amount or benefit paid or given, or intended to be paid or given, to any promoter of the company, and the consideration for the payment or benefit.

35.—(1) In section 34 "authorized minimum" means five hundred thousand dollars or such other sum as the Minister may, by order, prescribe. Authorized minimum.

(2) An order under subsection (1) which increases the authorized minimum may—

(*a*) require any public company having an allotted share capital of which the value is less than the amount specified in the order as the authorized minimum to increase that value to not less than that amount or make application to be re-registered as a private company;

(*b*) make, in connection with any such requirement, provision for any of the matters for which provision is made by this Act relating to—

(i) a company's registration, re-registration or change of name;

(ii) payment for any share comprised in a company's capital and offers of shares in or debentures of a company to the public, including provision as to the consequences (whether in criminal law or otherwise) of a failure to comply with any requirement of the order; and (*c*) contain such supplemental and transitional provisions as the Minister thinks appropriate, make different provisions for different cases and in particular, provide for any provision of the order to come into operation on different days for different purposes.

(3) An order under this section shall be subject to affirmative resolution.

Nature of shares.

36. Subject to section 37—

(*a*) from the appointed day shares in a company shall be issued without nominal or par value;

(*b*) a share with a nominal or par value issued before the appointed day shall be deemed to be a share without nominal or par value.

Election to retain par value shares.

37.—(1) An existing company may by ordinary resolution within six months of the appointed day, elect under this section to retain its existing shares with a nominal or par value and may continue to issue shares with a nominal or par value.

(2) An existing company which fails to make an election pursuant to subsection (1), shall be deemed to have converted at the end of the six months period referred to in that subsection, its existing shares to shares without nominal or par value and any shares issued thereafter shall be issued without a nominal or par value.

(3) An existing company which makes an election pursuant to subsection (1) shall serve the Registrar with notice of that Resolution.

(4) Where an existing company makes an election pursuant to subsection (1)—

(*a*) the provisions of the repealed Act specified in subsection (5) shall, to the extent that they are relevant to the shares having a nominal or par value (and to that extent only), continue to apply to that company; and (*b*) the provisions of this Act which provide for a determination of the value of shares without reference to a nominal or par value shall not apply to that company.

(5) The provisions of the repealed Act mentioned in subsection (4) (*a*) are as follows—

Section 56 (Application of premiums received on issue of shares);

Section 57 (Power to issue redeemable preference shares);

Section 58 (Power to issue shares at a discount);

Section 64 (Power of unlimited company to provide for reserve share capital on registration);

Section 66 (Special resolution for reduction of share capital);

Section 67 (Application to Court for confirming order, objections by creditors, and settlement of list of objecting creditors);

Section 68 (Order confirming reduction and powers of Court on making such order);

Section 69 (Registration of order and minute of reduction);

TABLE A

Paragraph 11 (First and paramount lien);

Paragraphs 15—21 (Calls on shares).

(6) Where an existing company has made an election pursuant to subsection (1), that company shall at the end of eighteen months from the date of the election, be deemed to have converted its existing shares to shares without a nominal or par value and any shares issued thereafter shall be shares issued without a nominal or par value.

38.—(1) A share may be paid for— Considera-tion.

(*a*) in money; or

(*b*) in property or past service rendered for value that is the fair equivalent of the money that the company would have received if the share had been issued for money.

(2) In determining whether property or past service is the fair equivalent of money consideration, the directors may take into account reasonable charges and expenses of organization and reorganization, and payments for property and past services reasonably expected to benefit the company.

(3) For the purposes of this section "property" does not include a debt security other than—

(*a*) a debt security of a company as part of a merger, acquisition, amalgamation or scheme of arrangement, reorganization or reconstruction.

(*b*) promises to pay that are comprised of government securities or debt instruments that are guaranteed by a financial institution.

(4) Subject to this section, no allotment by a company of shares for a consideration other than cash shall be made unless—

(*a*) the directors of the company have passed a resolution that the allotment be made; and

(*b*) the resolution states the nature of the consideration, its value and the extent to which the shares to be issued in respect of it will be credited as paid up by virtue of it;

(5) Befoie passing a resolution pursuant to subsection (4) (*a*), the directors of the company shall—

(*a*) where the consideration consists of services, have a qualified accountant estimate the value of the services to the company in money terms; or

(*b*) in any other case, have the consideration valued by a qualified accountant, valuer or surveyor.

(6) No allotment as aforesaid shall be made unless, not more than one hundred and twenty days before the allotment, the accountant, or as the case may be, valuer or surveyor reports that in his opinion the value of the services to the company in money terms or the value of the other consideration in question is worth at least as much as the amount which will be credited as paid up on the shares to be allocated in respect of those services or that consideration.

(7) Where, pursuant to a pre-incorporation arrangement, consideration other than cash is made for any allotment, the nature and value of that consideration shall be stated in the company's articles and the allotment shall be approved by a general meeting of the company.

(8) In subsection (3) (*b*)—

"financial institution" means—

(*a*) a company licensed under the Banking Act, the Financial Institutions Act or the Securities Act; or

(*b*) a society registered under the Co-operative Societies Act or incorporated under the Building Societies Act;

"Government securities" include securities by a body corporate that is owned or controlled by the Government.

Stated capital accounts.

39.—(1) A company shall maintain a separate stated capital account for each class and series of shares issued by it.

(2) A company shall add to the appropriate stated capital account, the full amount of the consideration received by it for any shares issued by the company.

(3) A company shall not reduce its stated capital or any stated capital account except in the manner provided by this Act.

(4) A company shall not, in respect of a share issued by it, add to a stated capital account, an amount greater than the amount of the consideration received by the company for the share.

(5) When a company proposes to add an amount to a stated capital account maintained by it in respect of a class or series of shares, that addition to the stated capital account shall be approved by special resolution if—

(*a*) bonus shares are not being apportioned rateably among all shareholders; and

(*b*) the effect of the bonus issue on voting rights is such that the holders of one class of shares assume control of the company or are able to pass a resolution which, prior to the bonus issue, they did not have sufficient voting rights to carry if the other shareholders were against it.

(6) Notwithstanding section 38 and subsection (2) of this section—

(*a*) when, in exchange for property, a company issues shares—

(i) to a body corporate that was an affiliate of the company immediately before the exchange; or

(ii) to a person who controlled the company immediately before the exchange,

the company, subject to subsection (4), may add to the stated capital accounts that are maintained for the shares of the classes or series issued, the amount agreed, by the company and the body corporate or person, to be the consideration for the shares so exchanged;

(*b*) when a company issues shares in exchange for shares of a body corporate referred to in paragraph (*a*) (i) the company may, subject to subsection (4), add to the stated capital accounts maintained for the shares of the classes or series issued, the whole or any part of the consideration it received in exchange; or

(*c*) when a company issues shares in exchange for shares of a body corporate that becomes the company's affiliate because of the exchange, the company may, subject to subsection (4), add to the stated capital accounts that are maintained for the classes or series issued, an amount that is not less than the amount set out, in respect of the acquired shares of the body corporate, in the stated capital or equivalent accounts of the body corporate immediately before the exchange.

(7) When a company which was incorporated before the appointed day continues in existence after that date then, notwithstanding subsection (2), it is not required to add to a stated capital account, any consideration received by it before that date, unless the shares in respect of which the consideration is received are issued after that date.

Prospectus

40.—(1) A prospectus issued by or on behalf of a company or in relation to an intended company shall be dated. Dating and registration of prospectus.

(2) No prospectus shall be issued by or on behalf of a company or in relation to an intended company unless before the date of its issue—

(*a*) there has been delivered to the Registrar for the purpose of securing registration of the prospectus a copy thereof signed by every person who is named therein as director or proposed director of the company or by his agent authorized in writing; and (*b*) pursuant thereto registration has been effected.

(3) Every prospectus shall state on the face of it that the prospectus has been registered as required by subsection (2).

(4) The Registrar shall not register any prospectus unless it is dated, and the copy thereof signed, in manner required by this section, and he may refuse to register a prospectus if—

(*a*) in any case where he considers that on the face of it the prospectus is misleading, within fourteen days of the delivery of the copy of the prospectus (or such longer period as may be prescribed) he by notice in writing informs the company or any other person who has delivered the copy of the prospectus pursuant to this section that in his opinion the prospectus is misleading for the reasons stated in the notice; or

(*b*) in any case where he considers it necessary or expedient for him to carry out an investigation as to whether the prospectus is misleading, he by notice in writing—

(i) within fourteen days of the delivery of the copy of the prospectus (or such longer period as may be prescribed) so informs the company or any other person as aforesaid; and

(ii) within six weeks of the delivery of the copy of the prospectus (or such longer period as may be prescribed) informs the company or any other person as aforesaid that in his opinion the prospectus is misleading for the reasons stated in the notice.

(5) In any case where the Registrar acting under the power given by paragraph (*a*) or (*b*) of subsection (4) refuses to register a prospectus, the company or any other person who has delivered the copy of the prospectus pursuant to this section may

apply to the Court, which, after hearing the applicant and the Registrar, and such evidence as they may call, may either order the Registrar to register the prospectus or may dismiss the application.

(6) Whenever the Registrar has registered a prospectus under this section he shall in writing inform the company or any other person who has delivered the copy of the prospectus pursuant to this section of the fact of registration and the date thereof, and every prospectus issued by or on behalf of a company or in relation to an intended company shall show on its face, in addition to the date required by subsection (1), the date of registration.

(7) If a prospectus is issued without having been registered as required by this section, the company, and every person who is knowingly a party to the issue of the prospectus, shall be liable to a fine not exceeding five thousand dollars for every day from the date of the issue of the prospectus until it is withdrawn in a manner which either is reasonable having regard to all the circumstances of the case or accords with the reasonable directions of the Registrar.

41.—(1) Every prospectus issued by or on behalf of a company, or by or on behalf of any person who is or has been engaged or interested in the formation of the company, must state the matters specified in Part I of the Third Schedule and set out the reports specified in Part II of that Schedule. Specific requirements as to particulars in prospectus. Third Schedule.

(2) A condition requiring or binding an applicant for shares in or debentures of a company to waive compliance with any requirement of this section, or purporting to affect him with notice of any contract, document, or matter not specifically referred to in the prospectus shall be void.

(3) It shall not be lawful to issue any form of application for shares in or debentures of a company unless the form is issued with a prospectus which complies with the requirements of this section:

Provided that this subsection shall not apply if it is shown that the form of application was issued either—

(*a*) in connection with a *bona fide* invitation to a person to enter into an underwriting agreement with respect to the shares or debentures; or

(*b*) in relation to shares or debentures which were not offered to the public.

(4) If any person acts in contravention of the provisions of subsection (3), he shall be liable to a fine not exceeding five thousand dollars for every day during which the contravention continues.

(5) In the event of non-compliance with or contravention of any of the requirements of this section a director or other person responsible for the prospectus shall not incur any liability by reason of the non-compliance or contravention, if—

(*a*) as regards any matter not disclosed, he proves that he was not cognizant thereof; or

(*b*) he proves that the non-compliance or contravention arose from an honest mistake of fact on his part; or

(*c*) the non-compliance or contravention was in respect of matters which in the opinion of the Court dealing with the case were immaterial or was otherwise such as ought, in the opinion of that Court, having regard to all the circumstances of the case, reasonably to be excused:

Third Schedule.

Provided that, in the event of failure to include in a prospectus a statement with respect to the matters specified in paragraph 16 of the Third Schedule, no director or other person shall incur any liability in respect of the failure unless it be proved that he had knowledge of the matters not disclosed.

(6) This section shall not apply to the issue, to existing members or debenture holders of a company, of a prospectus or form of application relating to shares in or debentures of the company, whether an applicant for shares or debentures will or will not have the right to renounce in favour of other persons, but subject as aforesaid, this section shall apply to a prospectus or a form of application whether issued on or with reference to the formation of a company or subsequently.

(7) Nothing in this section shall limit or diminish any liability which any person may incur under the general law or this Act apart from this section.

Expert's consent to issue of prospectus containing statement by him.

42.—(1) A prospectus inviting persons to subscribe for shares in or debentures of a company and including a statement purporting to be made by an expert shall not be issued unless—

(*a*) he has given and has not, before delivery of a copy of the prospectus for registration, withdrawn his written consent to the issue thereof with the statement included in the form and context in which it is included; and

(*b*) a statement that he has given and has not withdrawn his consent as aforesaid appears in the prospectus.

(2) If any prospectus is issued in contravention of this section, the company and every person who is knowingly a party to the issue thereof shall be liable to a fine not exceeding one hundred thousand dollars.

(3) In this section the expression "expert" includes engineer, valuer, accountant and any other person whose profession gives authority to a statement made by him.

Restriction on alteration of terms mentioned in prospectus or statement in lieu of pros-

43.—(1) A company limited by shares or a company limited by guarantee and having a share capital shall not, prior to the statutory meeting, vary the terms of a contract referred to in the prospectus, or statement in lieu of prospectus, except subject to the approval of the statutory meeting.

(2) This section shall not apply to a private company.

(3) If default is made in complying with the provisions of subsection (1), the company and every officer of the company who is in default shall be liable to a fine not exceeding fifty thousand dollars.

Civil liability for statements in prospectus.

44.—(1) Subject to the provisions of this section, where a prospectus invites persons to subscribe for shares in or debentures of a company, the following persons shall be liable to pay compensation to all persons who subscribe for any shares or debentures on the faith of the prospectus for the loss or damage they may have sustained by reason of any untrue statement included therein, that is to say—

(*a*) every person who is a director of the company at the time of the issue of the prospectus;

(*b*) every person who has authorized himself to be named and is named in the prospectus as a director or as having agreed to become a director either immediately or after an interval of time;

(*c*) every person who is a promoter of the company; and

(*d*) every person who has authorized the issue of the prospectus:

Provided that where, under section 42, the consent of a person is required to the issue of a prospectus and he has given that consent, he shall not by reason of his having given it be liable under this subsection as a person who has authorized the issue of the prospectus except in respect of an untrue statement purporting to be made by him as an expert.

(2) No person shall be liable under subsection (1) if he proves—

(*a*) that, having consented to become a director of the company, he withdrew his consent before the issue of the prospectus, and that it was issued without his authority or consent; or (*b*) that the prospectus was issued without his knowledge or consent, and that on becoming aware of its issue he forthwith gave reasonable public notice that it was issued without his knowledge or consent; or

(*c*) that, after the issue of the prospectus and before allotment thereunder, he, on becoming aware of any untrue statement therein, withdrew his consent thereto and gave reasonable public notice of the withdrawal and of the reason therefor; or

(*d*) that—

(i) as regards every untrue statement not purporting to be made on the authority of an expert or of a public official document or statement, he had reasonable ground to believe, and did up to the time of the allotment of the shares or debentures, as the case may be, believe, that the statement was true; and

(ii) as regards every untrue statement purporting to be a statement by an expert or contained in what purports to be a copy of or extract from a report or valuation of an expert, it fairly represented the statement, or was a correct and fair copy of or extract from the report or valuation, and he had reasonable ground to believe and did up to the time of the issue of the prospectus believe that the person making the statement was competent to make it and that person had given the consent required by section 42 to the issue of the prospectus and had not withdrawn that consent before delivery of a copy of the prospectus for registration or, to the defendant's knowledge, before allotment thereunder; and

(iii) as regards every untrue statement purporting to be a statement made by an official person or contained in what purports to be a copy of or extract from a public official document, it was a correct and fair representation of the statement or copy of or extract from the document:

Provided that this subsection shall not apply in the case of a person liable, by reason of his having given a consent required of him by section 42, as a person who has authorized the issue of the prospectus in respect of an untrue statement purporting to be made by him as an expert.

(3) A person who, apart from this subsection, would under subsection (1) be liable, by reason of his having given a consent required of him by section 42, as a person who has authorized the issue of a prospectus in respect of an untrue statement purporting to be made by him as an expert shall not be so liable if he proves—

(*a*) that, having given his consent under that section to the issue of the prospectus, he withdrew it in writing before delivery of a copy of the prospectus for registration; or

(*b*) that, after delivery of a copy of the prospectus for registration and before allotment thereunder, he, on becoming aware of the untrue statement, withdrew his consent in writing and gave reasonable public notice of the withdrawal, and of the reason therefor; or

(*c*) that he was competent to make the statement and that he had reasonable ground to believe and did up to the time of the allotment of the shares or debentures, as the case may be, believe that the statement was true.

(4) Where—

(*a*) the prospectus contains the name of a person as a director of the company, or as having agreed to become a director thereof, and he has not consented to become a director, or has withdrawn his consent before the issue of the prospectus, and has not authorized or consented to the issue thereof; or

(*b*) the consent of a person is required under section 42 to the issue of the prospectus and he either has not given that consent or has withdrawn it before the issue of the prospectus,

the directors of the company, except and without whose knowledge or consent the prospectus was issued, and any other person who authorized the issue thereof shall be liable to indemnify the person named as aforesaid or whose consent was required as aforesaid, as the case may be, against all damages, costs and expenses to which he may be made liable by reason of his name having been inserted in the prospectus or of the inclusion therein of a statement purporting to be made by him as an expert, as the case maybe, or in defending himself against any action or legal proceeding brought against him in respect thereof:

Provided that a person shall not be deemed for the purposes of this subsection to have authorized the issue of a prospectus by reason only of his having given the consent required by section 42 to the inclusion therein of a statement purporting to be made by him as an expert.

(5) For the purposes of this section—

(*a*) "expert" has the same meaning as in section 42; and

(*b*) "promoter" means a promoter who was a party to the preparation of the prospectus, or of the portion thereof containing the untrue statement, but does not include any person by reason of his acting in a professional capacity for persons engaged in procuring the formation of the company.

Criminal liability for misstatements in prospectus.

45.—(1) Where a prospectus issued after the appointed day includes any untrue statement, any person who authorized the issue of the prospectus shall be liable—

(*a*) on conviction on indictment, to imprisonment with or without hard labour for a term not exceeding two years, or a fine or both such imprisonment and fine; or

(*b*) on summary conviction before a Resident Magistrate, to imprisonment with or without hard labour for a term not exceeding three months, or a fine not exceeding one hundred thousand dollars, or both such imprisonment and fine,

unless he proves either that the statement was immaterial or that he had reasonable ground to believe and did, up to the time of the issue of the prospectus, believe that the statement was true.

(2) A person shall not be deemed for the purposes of this section to have authorized the issue of a prospectus by reason only of his having given the consent required by section 42 to the inclusion therein of a statement purporting to be made by him as an expert.

Document containing offer of shares or debentures for sale to be deemed prospectus.

46.—(1) Where a company allots or agrees to allot any shares in or debentures of the company with a view to all or any of those shares or debentures being offered for sale to the public—

(*a*) any document by which the offer for sale to the public is made shall for all purposes be deemed to be a prospectus issued by the company; and

(*b*) all enactments and rules of law as to the contents of prospectuses and to liability in respect of statements in and omissions from prospectuses, or otherwise relating to prospectuses,

shall apply and have effect accordingly, as if the shares or debentures had been offered to the public for subscription and as if persons accepting the offer in respect of any shares or debentures were subscribers for those shares or debentures, but without prejudice to the liability, if any, of the persons by whom the offer is made, in respect of misstatements contained in the document or otherwise in respect thereof.

(2) For the purposes of this Act, it shall, unless the contrary is proved, be evidence that an allotment of, or an agreement to allot, shares or debentures was made with a view to the shares or debentures being offered for sale to the public if it is shown—

(*a*) that an offer of the shares or debentures or of any of them for sale to the public was made within six months after the allotment or agreement to allot; or

(*b*) that at the date when the offer was made the whole consideration to be received by the company in respect of the shares or debentures had not been so received.

(3) Section 40 as applied by this section shall have effect as though the persons making the offer were persons named in a prospectus as directors of a company, and section 41 as applied by this section shall have effect as if it required a prospectus to state in addition to the matters required by that section to be stated in a prospectus—

(*a*) the net amount of the consideration received or to be received by the company in respect of the shares or debentures to which the offer relates; and

(*b*) the place and time at which the contract under which those shares or debentures have been or are to be allotted may be inspected.

(4) Where a person making an offer to which this section relates is a company or a firm, it shall be sufficient if the document aforesaid is signed on behalf of the company or firm by two directors of the company or not less than half of the partners, as the case may be, and any such director or partner may sign by his agent authorized in writing.

47. For the purposes of the foregoing provisions of this Part— Interpretation of provisions relating to prospectuses.

(*a*) a statement included in a prospectus shall be deemed to be untrue if it is misleading in the form and context in which it is included; and (*b*) a statement shall be deemed to be included in a prospectus if it is contained therein or in any report or memorandum appearing on the face thereof or by reference incorporated therein or issued therewith.

Allotment

Prohibition of allotment unless minimum subscription received.

48.—(1) No allotment shall be made of any share capital of a company offered to the public for subscription unless the amount stated in the prospectus as the minimum amount which, in the opinion of the directors must be raised by the issue of share capital in order to provide for the matters specified in paragraph 4 of the Third Schedule has been subscribed, and the sum payable on application for the amount so stated has been paid to and received by the company.

Third Schedule.

(2) For the purposes of subsection (1), a sum shall be deemed to have been paid to and received by the company if a cheque for that sum has been received in good faith by the company and the directors of the company have no reason for suspecting that the cheque will not be paid.

(3) The amount so stated in the prospectus shall be reckoned exclusively of any amount payable otherwise than in cash and is in this Act referred to as "the minimum subscription".

(4) If the conditions aforesaid have not been complied with on the expiration of forty days after the first issue of the prospectus, all money received from applicants for shares shall be forthwith repaid to them without interest, and, if any such money is not so repaid within forty-eight days after the issue of the prospectus, the directors of the company shall be jointly and severally liable to repay that money with interest at the rate of six *per centum* per annum from the expiration of the forty-eighth day:

Provided that a director shall not be liable if he proves that the default in the repayment of the money was not due to any misconduct or negligence on his part.

(5) Any condition requiring or binding any applicant for shares to waive compliance with any requirement of this section shall be void.

(6) This section shall not apply to any allotment of shares subsequent to the first allotment of shares offered to the public for subscription.

Prohibition of allotment in certain cases unless statement in lieu of prospectus delivered to Registrar.

49.—(1) A company having a share capital which does not issue a prospectus on or with reference to its formation, or which has issued such a prospectus but has not proceeded to allot any of the shares offered to the public for subscription, shall not allot any of its shares or debentures unless at least three days before the first allotment of either shares or debentures there has been delivered to the Registrar for registration a statement in lieu of prospectus, signed by every person who is named therein as a director or a proposed director of the company or by his agent authorized in writing, in the form and containing the particulars set out in Part I of the Fourth Schedule and, in the cases mentioned in Part II of that Schedule, setting out the reports specified therein, and those Parts shall have effect subject to the provisions contained in Part III of that Schedule.

Fourth Schedule.

(2) Every statement in lieu of prospectus delivered under subsection (1) shall, where the persons making any such report as aforesaid have made therein or have, without giving the reasons, indicated therein any such adjustments as are mentioned in paragraph 5 of the Fourth Schedule, have endorsed thereon or attached thereto a written statement signed by those persons setting out the adjustments and giving the reasons therefor.

(3) This section shall not apply to a private company.

(4) If a company acts in contravention of subsection (1) or (2), the company and every director of the company who knowingly authorizes or permits the contravention shall be liable to a fine not exceeding fifty thousand dollars.

(5) Where a statement in lieu of prospectus delivered to the Registrar under subsection (1) includes any untrue statement, any person who authorized the delivery of the statement in lieu of prospectus for registration shall be liable—

(*a*) on conviction on indictment, to imprisonment with or without hard labour for a term not exceeding two years or a fine or both such imprisonment and fine; or

(*b*) on summary conviction before a Resident Magistrate, to imprisonment with or without hard labour for a term not exceeding three months or a fine not exceeding one hundred thousand dollars, or both such imprisonment and fine,

unless he proves either that the untrue statement was immaterial or that he had reasonable ground to believe and did up to the time of the delivery for registration of the statement in lieu of prospectus believe that the untrue statement was true.

(6) For the purposes of this section—

(*a*) a statement included in a statement in lieu of prospectus shall be deemed to be untrue if it is misleading in the form and context in which it is included; and

(*b*) a statement shall be deemed to be included in a statement in lieu of prospectus if it is contained therein or in any report or memorandum appearing on the face thereof or by reference incorporated therein.

Effect of irregular allotment.

50.—(1) An allotment made by a company to an applicant in contravention of the provisions of sections 48 and 49 shall be voidable at the instance of the applicant within one month after the holding of the statutory meeting of the company and not later, or, in any case where the company is not required to hold a statutory meeting, or where the allotment is made after the holding of the statutory meeting, within one month after the date of the allotment, and not later, and shall be so voidable notwithstanding that the company is in course of being wound up.

(2) If any director of a company knowingly contravenes, or permits or authorizes the contravention of, any of the provisions of sections 48 and 49 with respect to allotment, he shall be liable to compensate the company and the allottee respectively for any loss, damages, or costs which the company or the allottee may have sustained or incurred thereby:

Provided that proceedings to recover any such loss, damages or costs shall not be commenced after the expiration of two years from the date of the allotment.

Applications for, and allotment of shares and debentures.

51.—(1) No allotment shall be made of any shares in or debentures of a company in pursuance of a prospectus issued generally and no proceedings shall be taken on applications made in pursuance of a prospectus so issued, until the beginning of the third day after that on which the prospectus is first so issued or such later time (if any) as may be specified in the prospectus.

(2) The beginning of the third day or such later time as aforesaid is hereafter in this Act referred to as "the time of the opening of the subscription lists".

(3) In subsection (1) the reference to the day on which the prospectus is first issued generally shall be construed as referring to the day on which it is first so issued as a newspaper advertisement:

Provided that, if it is not so issued as a newspaper advertisement before the third day after that on which it is first so issued in any other manner, the reference shall be construed as referring to the day on which it is first so issued in any manner.

(4) The validity of an allotment shall not be affected by any contravention of the foregoing provisions of this section but, in the event of any such contravention, the company and every officer of the company who is in default shall be liable to a fine not exceeding fifty thousand dollars.

(5) In the application of this section to a prospectus offering shares or debentures for sale, subsections (1), (3) and (4) shall have effect with the substitution of references to sale for references to allotment, and with the substitution for the reference to the company and every officer of the company who is in default of a reference to any person by or through whom the offer is made and who knowingly and wilfully authorizes or permits the contravention.

(6) An application for shares in or debentures of a company which is made in pursuance of a prospectus issued generally shall not be revocable until after the expiration of the third day after the time of the opening of the subscription lists, or the giving before the expiration of that third day, by some person responsible under section 44 for the prospectus, of a public notice having the effect under that section of excluding or limiting the responsibility of the person giving it.

Return as to allotments.

52.—(1) Whenever a company limited by shares or a company limited by guarantee and having a share capital makes any allotment of its shares, the company shall within one month thereafter deliver to the Registrar for registration—

(*a*) a return of the allotments stating the number of shares comprised in the allotment, the names, addresses and descriptions of the allottees, and the amount, if any, paid or due and payable on each share; and

(*b*) in the case of shares allotted as fully or partly paid up otherwise than in cash, a contract in writing constituting the title of the allottee to the allotment together with any contract of sale, or for services or other consideration in respect of which that allotment was made, such contracts being duly stamped, and a return stating the number of shares so allotted, the extent to which they are to be treated as paid up, and the consideration for which they have been allotted.

(2) Where such a contract is not reduced to writing, the company shall within one month after the allotment deliver to the Registrar for registration the prescribed particulars of the contract stamped with the same stamp duty as would have been payable if the contract had been reduced to writing, and those particulars shall be deemed to be an instrument within the meaning of the Stamp Duty Act.

(3) If default is made in complying with this section, every officer of the company who is in default shall be liable to a fine not exceeding one thousand dollars for every day during which the default continues:

Provided that, in the case of default in delivering to the Registrar within one month after the allotment any document required to be delivered by this section, the company, or any person liable for the default, may apply to the Court for relief and the Court, if satisfied that the omission to deliver the document was accidental or due to inadvertence or that it is just and equitable to grant relief, may make an order extending the time for the delivery of the document for such period as the Court may think proper.

Commissions, etc.

Power to pay certain commissions and prohibition of payment of all other commissions, etc.

53.—(1) It shall be lawful for a company to pay a commission to any person in consideration of his subscribing or agreeing to subscribe, whether absolutely or conditionally, for any shares in the company, or procuring or agreeing to procure subscriptions, whether absolute or conditional, for any shares in the company if—

(*a*) the payment of the commission is authorized by the articles; and

(*b*) the commission paid or agreed to be paid does not exceed ten *per centum* of the price at which the shares are issued or the amount or rate authorized by the articles, whichever is the less; and (*c*) the amount or rate *per centum* of the commission paid or agreed to be paid is—

(i) in the case of shares offered to the public for subscription, disclosed in the prospectus; or

(ii) in the case of shares not offered to the public for subscription, disclosed in the statement in lieu of prospectus, or in a statement in the prescribed form signed in like manner as a statement in lieu of prospectus and delivered before the payment of the commission to the Registrar for registration, and, where a circular or notice, not being a prospectus, inviting subscription for the shares is issued, also disclosed in that circular or notice; and

(*d*) the number of shares which persons have agreed for a commission to subscribe absolutely is disclosed in manner aforesaid.

(2) Save as aforesaid, no company shall apply any of its shares or capital money either directly or indirectly in payment of any commission, or allowance, to any person in consideration of his subscribing or agreeing to subscribe, whether absolutely or conditionally, for any shares of the company, or procuring or agreeing to procure subscriptions, whether absolute or conditional, for any shares in the company, whether the shares or money be so applied by being added to the purchase money of any property acquired by the company or to the contract price of any work to be executed for the company, or the money be paid out of the purchase money or contract price, or otherwise.

(3) Nothing in this section shall affect the power of any company to pay such brokerage as it has heretofore been lawful for a company to pay.

(4) A vendor to, promoter of, or other person who receives payment in money or shares from, a company shall have and shall be deemed always to have had power to apply

any part of the money or shares so received in payment of any commission, the payment of which, if made directly by the company, would have been legal under this section.

(5) A company which contravenes any of the provisions of this section and every officer of the company who knowingly authorizes or permits the contravention shall be liable to a fine not exceeding fifty thousand dollars.

54.—(1) Where a company has paid any sums by way of commission in respect of any shares or debentures, as the total amount so paid, or so much thereof as has not been written off, shall be stated in every balance sheet of the company until the whole amount thereof has been written off. Statement in balance sheet, as to commissions.

(2) If default is made in complying with this section, the company and every officer of the company who is in default shall be liable to a fine not exceeding fifty thousand dollars.

Construction of References to Offering Shares or Debentures to the Public

55.—(1) Any reference in this Act to offering shares or debentures to the public shall, subject to any provision to the contrary contained therein, be construed as including a reference to offering them to any section of the public, whether selected as members or debenture holders of the company concerned or as clients of the person issuing the prospectus or in any other manner, and references in this Act or in a company's articles to invitations to the public to subscribe for shares or debentures shall, subject as aforesaid, be similarly construed. Construction of references to offering shares or debentures to the public.

(2) Subsection (1) shall not be taken as requiring any offer or invitation to be treated as made to the public if it can properly be regarded, in all the circumstances, as not being calculated to result, directly or indirectly, in the shares or debentures becoming available for subscription or purchase by persons other than those receiving the offer or invitation, or otherwise as being a domestic concern of the persons making and receiving it, and in particular—

(*a*) a provision in a company's articles prohibiting invitations to the public to subscribe for shares or debentures shall not be taken as prohibiting the making to members or debenture holders of an invitation which can properly be regarded as aforesaid; and

(*b*) the provisions of this Act relating to private companies shall be construed accordingly.

Issue of Redeemable Shares

Power to issue redeemable shares.

56.—(1) Subject to this section, a company may, if so authorized by its articles, issue shares which by the terms of the issue will be redeemed or, at the option of the company, may be redeemed.

(2) No redeemable shares may be issued at a time when there are no issued shares of the company which are not redeemable.

(3) Redeemable shares may not be redeemed unless they are fully paid and the terms of redemption must provide for payment on redemption.

(4) Notwithstanding anything in the company's article—

(*a*) no shares issued as provided in subsection (1) shall be redeemed except out of the company's profits or revenue reserves which would otherwise be available for the payment of dividends, or out of proceeds of a fresh issue of shares made for the purpose of the redemption; and

(*b*) the minimum premium (if any) payable on redemption shall be provided out of the company's profits or revenue reserves which would otherwise be available for the payment of dividends or out of a fresh issue of shares before the shares are redeemed.

(5) If a company acts in contravention of this section, the company and every officer thereof who knowingly authorizes the contravention shall be liable to a fine not exceeding fifty thousand dollars.

57.—(1) Subject to this Act, redemption of shares may be effected on such terms and in such manner as may be provided by the company's articles. Financing, etc., of redemption

(2) Where shares are redeemed under this section, the voting rights attaching to those shares shall be suspended and the amount of the company's issued share capital shall be diminished by the value attributed to those shares in the stated capital account accordingly, but the redemption of shares by a company is not to be taken as reducing the amount of the company's authorized number of shares.

(3) Without prejudice to subsection (1), where a company is about to redeem shares, it has power to issue shares up to the value of the shares to be redeemed as if those shares had never been issued.

58.—(1) Subject to subsection (4) and its articles, a company may purchase or otherwise acquire shares issued by it. Power of company to purchase own shares.

(2) Section 57 shall apply to the purchase by a company under this section of its own shares as it applies to the redemption of redeemable shares, save that the terms and manner of purchase need not be determined by the articles as required by section 57(1).

(3) A company may not under this section purchase its shares if as a result of the purchase there would no longer be any member of the company holding shares other than redeemable shares.

(4) A company shall not make any payment to purchase or otherwise acquire shares issued by it unless a statutory declaration is made by the company's directors in accordance with this Act and lodged with the Registrar, to the effect that there are no reasonable grounds for believing that—

(*a*) the company is, or would after the payment be, unable to pay its liabilities as they become due; or

(*b*) the realizable value of the company's assets would, after the payment, be less than the aggregate of its liabilities and stated capital.

(5) The statutory declaration under subsection (4) shall be based on—

(*a*) the company's audited accounts made up no more than twelve months before the date of the statutory declaration;

(*b*) the company's unaudited accounts made up no more than forty-five days before the date of the statutory declaration; and

(*c*) any other relevant facts of which the directors are aware.

(6) This section does not apply to a purchase or acquisition of a kind referred to in section 59.

(7) The directors of a company who willfully or recklessly make a declaration under subsection (4), a statement which is false in any material particular, shall be liable on summary conviction before a Resident Magistrate, to a fine not exceeding one million dollars or to imprisonment for a term not exceeding two years or to both such fine and imprisonment.

Alternative acquisition of company's own shares.

59.—(1) Subject to subsection (3) and if permitted by its articles, a company may purchase or otherwise acquire shares issued by it—

(*a*) to settle or compromise a debt or claim asserted by or against the company;

(*b*) to eliminate fractional shares; or

(*c*) to fulfil the terms of a non-assignable agreement under which the company has an option or is obliged to purchase shares owned by an officer or an employee of the company.

(2) Section 57 shall apply to the purchase or other acquisition by a company under this section of its own shares as it applies to the redemption of redeemable shares, save that the terms and manner of purchase or other acquisition need not be determined by the articles as required by section 57 (1).

(3) A company may purchase or otherwise acquire shares issued by it to comply with an order under section 213.

(4) A company shall not make any payment to purchase or acquire under subsection (1) shares issued by it unless a statutory declaration is made by the company's directors and lodged with the Registrar for registration to the effect that there are no reasonable grounds for believing that—

(*a*) the company is, or would after the payment be, unable to pay its liabilities as they become due; or

(*b*) the realizable value of the company's assets would after the payment be less than the aggregate of its liabilities and the amount required for payment on a redemption or in a winding up of all shares the holders of which have the right to be paid prior to or rateably with the holders of the shares to be purchased or acquired.

(5) The declaration under subsection (4) shall be based on—

(*a*) the company's audited accounts made up no more than twelve months before the date of the statutory declaration;

(*b*) the company's unaudited accounts made up no more than forty-five days before the date of the statutory declaration; and

(*c*) any other relevant facts of which the directors are aware.

(6) A company may accept from any shareholder a share in the company surrendered to it as a gift, but may not extinguish or reduce a liability in respect of an amount unpaid on any such share, except in accordance with section 71.

(7) The directors of a company who wilfully or recklessly make a declaration under subsection (4), a statement which is false in any material particular, shall be liable on summary conviction before a Resident Magistrate, to a fine not exceeding one million dollars or to imprisonment for a term not exceeding two years or to both such fine and imprisonment.

Notice to shareholders of purchase by company of own shares.

60. A company shall, within thirty days of the purchase of any of its issued shares, notify its shareholders of—

(*a*) the number of shares it has purchased;

(*b*) the names of the shareholders from whom it has purchased the shares;

(*c*) the price paid for the shares;

(*d*) if the consideration was other than cash, the nature of the consideration and the value attributed to it; and

(*e*) the balance, if any, remaining due to shareholders or those shareholders from whom it purchased the shares.

Pre-emptive rights.

61.—(1) If the articles so provide, no shares or a class of shares may be issued unless the shares have first been offered to the shareholders of the company holding shares of that class.

(2) The shareholders mentioned in subsection (1) have a pre-emptive right to acquire the offered shares in proportion to their holding at such price and on such terms as those shares are to be offered to others.

(3) Notwithstanding that the articles provide the pre-emptive right referred to in subsection (1), the shareholders of the company have no pre-emptive right in respect of shares to be issued by the company—

(*a*) for consideration other than cash;

(*b*) pursuant to the exercise of conversion privileges, options or rights previously granted by the company.

62.—(1) Subject to the provisions of this section, a company limited by shares may, if so authorized by its articles, issue preference shares which are, or at the option of the company, are to be liable to be redeemed: Power to issue redeemable preference shares.

Provided that—

(*a*) no such shares shall be redeemed except out of profits of the company which would otherwise be available for dividend or out of the proceeds of a fresh issue of shares for the purposes of the redemption;

(*b*) no such shares shall be issued unless they are fully paid;

(*c*) the premium, if any, payable on redemption, must have been provided for out of the company's profits before the shares are redeemed;

(*d*) where any such shares are redeemed otherwise than out of the proceeds of a fresh issue, there shall out of profits that would otherwise have been available for dividend be transferred to a reserve fund to be called "the capital redemption reserve fund", a sum equal to the amount of the shares to be redeemed, and the provisions of this Act relating to the reduction of a company's share capital shall, except as provided in this section, apply as if the capital redemption reserve fund were the company's paid up share capital.

(2) Subject to the provisions of this section, the redemption of preference shares thereunder may be effected on such terms and in such manner as may be provided by the articles.

(3) The redemption of preference shares by a company under this section shall not be taken as reducing the amount of the company's stated capital.

(4) Where in pursuance of this section a company has redeemed or is about to redeem any preference shares, it shall have power to issue shares up to the amount of the shares redeemed or to be redeemed as if those shares had never been issued, and accordingly the company's share capital shall not for the purposes of the Stamp Duty Act be deemed to be increased by the issue of shares in pursuance of this subsection:

Provided that, where new shares are issued before the redemption of the old shares, the new shares, shall not, so far as relates to stamp duty, be deemed to have been issued in pursuance of this section unless the old shares are redeemed within a month after the issue of the new shares.

(5) The capital redemption reserve fund may, notwithstanding anything in this section, be applied by the company in paying up the company's unissued shares to be issued to the company's members as fully paid bonus shares.

(6) If a company acts in contravention of this section, the company and every officer of the company who knowingly authorizes or permits the contravention shall be liable to a fine not exceeding fifty thousand dollars.

Miscellaneous Provisions as to Share Capital

Power of company to arrange for different amounts being paid on shares.

63. A company, if so authorized by its articles, may do any one or more of the following—

(*a*) make arrangements on the issue of shares for a difference between the shareholders in the amounts and times of payment of calls on their shares;

(*b*) accept from any member the whole or a part of the amount remaining unpaid on any shares held by him, although no part of that amount has been called up;

(*c*) pay dividend in proportion to the amount paid up on each share where a larger amount is paid up on some shares than on others.

64. A limited company may by special resolution determine that any portion of its share capital which has not been already called up shall not be capable of being called up, except in the event and for the purposes of the company being wound up, and thereupon the portion of its share capital shall not be capable of being called up except in the event and for the purposes aforesaid. Reserve liability of limited company.

65.—(1) A company limited by shares or a company limited by guarantee and having a share capital, if so authorized by its articles, may alter the conditions of its articles as follows, that is to say, it may— Power of company limited by shares to alter its share capital.

(*a*) increase its share capital by new shares of such amount as it thinks expedient;

(*b*) consolidate and divide all or any of its share capital into shares of larger amount than its existing shares;

(*c*) convert all or any of its paid up shares into stock, and reconvert that stock into paid up shares of any denomination;

(*d*) subdivide its shares, or any of them, into shares of smaller amount than is fixed by the articles, so, however, that in the subdivision the proportion between the amount paid and the amount, if any, unpaid on each reduced share shall be the same as it was in the case of the share from which the reduced share is derived;

(*e*) cancel shares which, at the date of the passing of the resolution in that behalf, have not been taken or agreed to be taken by any person, and diminish the amount of its share capital by the amount of the shares so cancelled.

(2) The powers conferred by this section must be exercised by the company in general meeting.

(3) A cancellation of shares in pursuance of this section shall not be deemed to be a reduction of share capital within the meaning of this Act.

Notice to Registrar of consolidation of share capital, conversion of shares into stock, etc.

66.—(1) If a company having a share capital has—

(*a*) consolidated and divided its share capital into shares of larger amount than its existing shares; or

(*b*) converted any shares into stock; or

(*c*) re-converted stock into shares; or

(*d*) subdivided its shares or any of them; or

(*e*) redeemed any redeemable preference shares; or

(*f*) cancelled any shares, otherwise than in connection with a reduction of share capital under section 71,

it shall within one month after so doing give notice thereof to the Registrar specifying, as the case may be, the shares consolidated, divided, converted, subdivided, redeemed or cancelled, or the stock re-converted.

(2) If default is made in complying with this section, the company and every officer of the company who is in default shall be liable to a fine not exceeding fifty thousand dollars.

Notice of increase of share capital.

67.—(1) Where a company having a share capital, whether its shares have or have not been converted into stock, has increased its share capital beyond the registered capital, it shall within fifteen days after the passing of the resolution authorizing the increase, give to the Registrar notice of the increase, and the Registrar shall record the increase.

(2) The notice to be given as aforesaid shall include such particulars as may be prescribed with respect to the classes of shares affected and the conditions subject to which the new shares have been or are to be issued, and there shall be forwarded to the Registrar together with the notice and a copy of the resolution authorizing the increase.

(3) If default is made in complying with this section, the company and every officer of the company who is in default shall be liable to a fine not exceeding fifty thousand dollars.

Power of unlimited company to provide for reserve capital share on registration.

68. An unlimited company having a share capital may, by its resolution for registration as a limited company in pursuance of this Act, do either or both of the following, namely—

(*a*) increase the amount of its share capital by increasing the amount of its shares, subject to the condition that no part of the increased capital shall be capable of being called up except in the event and for the purposes of the company being wound up;

(*b*) provide that a specified portion of its uncalled share capital shall not be capable of being called up except in the event and for the purposes of the company being wound up.

Power of company to pay interest out of capital in certain cases.

69.—(1) Where any shares of a company are issued for the purpose of raising money to defray the expenses of the construction of any works or buildings or the provision of any plant which cannot be made profitable for a lengthened period, the company may pay interest on so much of that share capital as is for the time being paid up for the period and subject to the conditions and restrictions mentioned in this section, and may charge the sum so paid by way of interest to capital as part of the cost of construction of the work or building, or the provision of plant:

Provided that—

(*a*) no such payment shall be made unless it is authorized by the articles or by special resolution;

(*b*) no such payment, whether authorized by the articles or by special resolution, shall be made without the previous sanction of the Minister;

(*c*) before sanctioning any such payment the Minister may, at the expense of the company, appoint a person to inquire and report to him as to the circumstances of the case, and may, before making the appointment, require the company to give security for the payment of the costs of the inquiry;

(*d*) the payment shall be made only for such period as may be determined by the Minister, and that period shall in no case extend beyond the close of the half year next after the half year during which the works or buildings have been actually completed or the plant provided;

(*e*) the rate of interest shall in no case exceed six *per centum* per annum or such other rate as may for the time being be prescribed by the Minister;

(*f*) the accounts of the company shall show the share capital on which, and the rate at which, interest has been paid out of capital during the period to which the accounts relate.

(2) If default is made in complying with proviso (*f*) to subsection (1), the company and every officer of the company who is in default shall be liable to a fine not exceeding fifty thousand dollars.

Redemption or cancellation of shares under Employees Share Ownership Plan Act.

70.—(1) A company limited by shares may, if so authorized by its articles, purchase its own shares out of profits available for distribution or out of a fresh issue of shares for that purpose and in accordance with the provisions of this section.

(2) Where a company, in the operation of an employee share ownership plan approved under the Employees Share Ownership Plan Act—

(*a*) purchases its shares and such shares are thereupon either cancelled or transferred to the trustees of the plan; or

(*b*) otherwise cancels its shares,

in the exercise of the company's rights or obligations under that Act or any plan thereunder, such purchase or cancellation of its shares by the company shall not be deemed to be a reduction of the company's capital.

(3) The purchase of shares in accordance with this section shall not be taken as reducing the amount of the company's stated capital.

Reduction of Share Capital

Reduction of stated capital.

71.—(1) Subject to subsection (3), a company may by special resolution—

(*a*) extinguish or reduce a liability in respect of an amount unpaid on any shares;

(*b*) reduce its stated capital by an amount that is not represented by realizable assets; or

(*c*) return to its shareholders any of its assets which are in excess of the wants of the company.

(2) The stated capital of a company shall be reduced in accordance with any resolution under subsection (1) which reduces or has the effect of reducing the stated capital.

(3) A company shall not reduce its stated capital under subsection (1) (*a*) or return assets pursuant to subsection (1) (*c*) unless a statutory declaration is made by the directors of the company to the effect that there were no reasonable grounds for believing—

(*a*) that after the reduction or, as the case may be, return, the company would be unable to pay its liabilities as they become due; or

(*b*) that the realizable value of the company's assets would thereby be less than the aggregate of its liabilities and the stated capital remaining after the reduction in accordance with subsection (2).

86 COMPANIES

(4) The declaration under subsection (3) shall be based on—

(*a*) the company's audited accounts made up no more than twelve months before the date of the statutory declaration;

(*b*) the company's unaudited accounts made up no more than forty-five days before the date of the statutory declaration; and

(*c*) any other relevant facts of which the directors are aware.

(5) A company shall at two intervals at least seven days apart, give notice in a daily newspaper circulating in the Island of—

(*a*) any reduction of its stated capital pursuant to subsection (1) (*b*); or

(*b*) any intention to reduce its stated capital under subsection (1) (*a*) or (*c*).

(6) A company shall not return assets to shareholder under subsection (1) (*c*) until the expiration of one hundred and eighty days after the publication of the second notice required under subsection (5).

(7) A director of a company who wilfully or recklessly makes, in any declaration under subsection (3), a statement which is false in a material particular shall be liable on summary conviction in a Resident Magistrate's Court to a fine not exceeding one million dollars or to imprisonment for a term not exceeding two years or to both such fine and imprisonment.

Effect of redemption, purchase, etc.

72.—(1) Subject to subsection (2), no redemption, purchase, acquisition or forfeiture by a company of its shares nor the cancellation of shares so redeemed, purchased, acquired or

(2) The stated capital of a company shall be reduced by the amount by which a redemption of redeemable shares is made out of a fresh issue of shares made for the purpose of the redemption not more than twelve months before the date of the redemption.

(3) Subject to this section, a company may not reduce its stated capital except as provided in section 71.

(4) The provisions of section 71 shall not apply to a redemption, purchase, acquisition or forfeiture.

Variation of Shareholders' Rights

73.—(1) If in the case of a company the share capital of which is divided into different classes of shares— Rights of holders of special classes of shares.

(*a*) provision is made by the articles for authorizing the variation of the rights attached to any class of shares in the company, subject to—

(i) the consent of any specified proportion of the holders of the issued shares of that class; or

(ii) the sanction of a resolution passed at a separate meeting of the holders of those shares; and

(*b*) in pursuance of the said provision the rights attached to any such class of shares are at any time varied,

the holders of not less in the aggregate than fifteen *per centum* of the issued shares of that class, being persons who did not consent to or vote in favour of the resolution for the variation, may apply to the Court to have the variation cancelled, and, where any such application is made, the variation shall not have effect unless and until it is confirmed by the Court.

(2) An application under this section must be made within twenty-eight days after the date on which the consent was given or the resolution was passed, as the case may be, and may be made on behalf of the shareholders entitled to make the application by such one or more of their number as they may appoint in writing for the purpose.

(3) On any such application the Court, after hearing the applicant and any other persons who apply to the Court to be heard and appear to the Court to be interested in the application, may, if it is satisfied, having regard to all the circumstances of the case, that the variation would unfairly prejudice the shareholders of the class represented by the applicant, disallow the variation and shall, if not so satisfied, confirm the variation.

(4) The decision of the Court on any such application shall be final.

(5) The company shall within fifteen days after the making of an order by the Court on any such application forward a copy of the order to the Registrar, and, if default is made in complying with this provision, the company and every officer of the company who is in default shall be liable to a fine not exceeding fifty thousand dollars.

(6) In this section the expression "variation" includes abrogation, and for the purposes of this Act any resolution of a company the implementation of which would have the effect of diminishing the proportion of the total votes exercisable at a general meeting of the company by the holders of the existing shares of a class, or of reducing the proportion of the dividends or distributions payable at any time to the holders of the existing shares of a class, shall be deemed to be a variation of the rights of that class.

Transfer of Shares and Debentures, Evidence of Title, etc.

Nature and numbering of shares.

74.—(1) The shares or other interest of any member in a company shall be personal estate, transferable in manner provided by the articles of the company, and shall not be of the nature of real estate.

(2) Each share in a company having a share capital shall be distinguished by its appropriate number.

Transfer not to be registered except on production of instrument of transfer.

75.—(1) Notwithstanding anything in the articles of a company, it shall not be lawful for the company to register a transfer of shares in or debentures of the company unless a proper instrument of transfer has been delivered to the company:

Provided that nothing in this section shall prejudice any power of the company to register as shareholder or debenture holder any person to whom the right to any shares in or debentures of the company has been transmitted by operation of law.

(2) If a company contravenes the provisions of this section the company and every officer of the company who knowingly authorizes or permits the contravention shall be liable to a fine not exceeding fifty thousand dollars.

Registration of transfer on request of transferor.

76. On the application of the transfer of any share or interest in a company, the company shall enter in its register of members the name of the transferee in the same manner and subject to the same conditions as if the application for the entry were made by the transferee.

Notice of refusal to register transfer.

77.—(1) If a company refuses to register a transfer of any shares or debentures, the company shall, within three months after the date on which the transfer was lodged with the company, send to the transferee notice of the refusal.

(2) If default is made in complying with this section, the company and every officer of the company who is in default shall be liable to a fine not exceeding two thousand dollars for every day during which the default continues.

Certification of transfers.

78.—(1) The certification by a company of any instrument of transfer of shares in or debentures of the company shall be taken as a representation by the company to any person acting on the faith of the certification that there have been produced to the company such documents as on the face of them show a *prima facie* title to the shares or debentures in the transferor named in the instrument of transfer, but not as a representation that the transferor has any title to the shares or debentures.

(2) Where any person acts on the faith of a false certification by a company made negligently, the company shall be under the same liability to him as if the certification had not been made fraudulently.

(3) For the purposes of this section—

(*a*) an instrument of transfer shall be deemed to be certificated if it bears the words "certificate lodged" or words to the like effect;

(*b*) the certification of an instrument of transfer shall be deemed to be made by a company if—

(i) the person issuing the instrument is a person authorized to issue certificated instruments of transfer on the company's behalf; and

(ii) the certification is signed by a person authorized to certify transfers on the company's behalf or by any officer or servant either of the company or of a body corporate so authorized;

(*c*) a certification shall be deemed to be signed by any person if—

(i) it purports to be authenticated by his signature or initials (whether handwritten or not); and

(ii) it is not shown that the signature or initials was or were placed there neither by himself nor by any person authorized to use the signature or initials for the purpose of certifying transfers on the company's behalf.

79.—(1) Every company shall, within two months after the allotment of any of its shares, debentures, or debenture stock and within three months after the date on which a transfer of any such shares, debentures, or debenture stock, is lodged with the company, complete and have ready for delivery the certificates of all shares, the debentures, and the certificates of all debenture stock allotted or transferred, unless the conditions of issue of the shares, debentures, or debenture stock otherwise provide. Duties of company with respect to issue of certificates.

(2) In subsection (1) "transfer" means a transfer duly stamped and otherwise valid, and does not include such a transfer as the company is for any reason entitled to refuse to register and does not register.

(3) If default is made in complying with this section, the company and every officer who is in default shall be liable to a fine not exceeding fifty thousand dollars.

(4) If any company on whom a notice has been served requiring the company to make good any default in complying with the provisions of subsection (1) fails to make good the default within ten days after the service of the notice, the Court may, on the application of the person entitled to have the certificates or the debentures delivered to him, make an order directing the company and any officer of the company to make good the default within such time as may be specified in the order, and any such order may provide that all costs of and incidental to the application shall be borne by the company or by any officer of the company responsible for the default.

80. A certificate, under the common seal of the company, specifying any shares held by any member, shall be *prima facie* evidence of the title of the member to the shares. Certificate evidence of title.

Evidence of grant of probate.

81. The production to a company of any document which is by law sufficient evidence of probate of the will, or letters of administration of the estate, of a deceased person having been granted to some person shall be accepted by the company, notwithstanding anything in its articles, as sufficient evidence of the grant.

Issue and effect of share warrants to bearer.

82.—(1) A company limited by shares, if so authorized by its articles, may, with respect to any fully paid up shares, issue under its common seal a warrant stating that the bearer of the warrant is entitled to the shares therein specified, and may provide, by coupons or otherwise, for the payment of the future dividends on the shares included in the warrant.

(2) Such a warrant as aforesaid is in this Act termed a "share warrant".

(3) A share warrant shall entitle the bearer thereof to the shares therein specified, and the shares may be transferred by delivery of the warrant.

Penalty for personation of shareholders.

83. If any person falsely and deceitfully personates any owner of any share or interest in any company, or of any share warrant or coupon, issued in pursuance of this Act, and thereby obtains or endeavours to obtain any such share or interest or share warrant or coupon, or receives or endeavours to receive any money due to any such owner, as if the offender were the true and lawful owner, he shall be guilty of a felony, and shall on conviction on indictment be liable to be imprisoned with or without hard labour for fourteen years or to a fine.

Special Provisions as to Debentures

Register of debenture holders.

84.—(1) A company which issues or has issued debentures shall keep, in one or more books, a register of holders of debentures and shall enter therein the following particulars—

(*a*) the names and addresses of the debenture holders;

(*b*) the debentures held by each debenture holder, together with the amount paid or agreed to be considered as paid thereon, and any other prescribed particulars;

(*c*) the date at which each person was entered in the register as a debenture holder; and

(*d*) the date at which any person ceased to be a debenture holder:

Provided that—

(i) in the application of paragraph (*b*) to debenture stock and holders thereof it shall not be necessary for the register to show the amount paid or agreed to be considered as paid on such stock; and

(ii) nothing in this subsection shall apply in relation to debentures which are transferable by delivery.

(2) The register of holders of debentures shall be kept at the registered office of the company:

Provided that—

(*a*) if the work of making it up is done at another office of the company, it may be kept at that other office; and

(*b*) if the company arranges with some other person for the making up of the register to be undertaken on behalf of the company by that other person, it may be kept at the office of that other person at which the work is done,

so, however, that it shall not be kept at a place outside the Island.

(3) Every company shall send notice to the Registrar of the place where its register of holders of debentures is kept and of any change in that place:

Provided that a company shall not be bound to send notice under this subsection where the register has, at all times since it came into existence or, in the case of a register in existence on the appointed day, at all times since then been kept at the registered office of the company.

(4) If default is made in complying with this section, the company and every officer of the company who is in default shall be liable to a fine not exceeding fifty thousand dollars.

Consequences of failure to comply with requirements as to register of debenture holders owing to agent's default.

85. Where, by virtue of proviso (*b*) to subsection (2) of section 84, the register of holders of debentures is kept at the office of some person other than the company, and by reason of any default of his the company fails to comply with subsection (3) of that section or section 86 or with any of the requirements of this Act as to the production of the register, that other person shall be liable to the same penalties as if he were an officer of the company who was in default, and the power of the Court under subsection (6) of section 86 shall extend to the making of orders against that other person and his officers and servants.

Inspection of register of debenture holders.

86.—(1) Every register of holders of debentures of a company shall, except when duly closed, be open to the inspection without charge of the registered holder of any such debentures and of any holder of shares in the company and, on payment of fifty dollars or such less sum as the company may specify for each inspection, of any other person, but subject to such reasonable restrictions as the company may in general meeting impose, so that not less than two hours in each day shall be allowed for inspection.

(2) For the purposes of subsection (1), a register shall be deemed to be duly closed if closed in accordance with provisions contained in the articles or in the debentures or, in the case of debenture stock, in the stock certificates, or in the trust deed or other document securing the debentures or debenture stock, during such period or periods, not exceeding in the whole thirty days in any year, as may be therein specified.

(3) Any person may require a copy of the register of holders of debentures of the company or any part thereof on payment of twenty dollars for every page required to be copied.

(4) A copy of any trust deed or other document securing any issue of debentures shall be forwarded to every holder of any such debentures at his request on payment of twenty dollars for every page required to be copied.

(5) If inspection is refused, or a copy is refused or not forwarded, the company and every officer of the company who is in default shall be liable to a fine not exceeding fifty thousand dollars.

(6) Where a company is in default as aforesaid, the Court may by order compel an immediate inspection of the register or direct that the copies required shall be sent to the person requiring them.

Application to registers of debenture holders of certain provisions relating to registers of members.

87.—(1) The provisions of section 115 (except subsection (4)) and sections 116 and 117 shall apply to and in relation to registers of holders of debentures as they apply to and in relation to registers of members.

(2) The provisions of sections 118 and 119 shall apply to and in relation to the keeping by companies (whether having a share capital or not) whose business comprise the transaction of business in countries outside the Island of branch registers of holders of debentures resident outside the Island and the registering of holders of debentures therein as they apply to and in relation to the keeping by companies referred to in section 118 of branch registers of members so resident and the registering of members therein, so, however, that—

(*a*) so much of subsection (2) of section 119 as relates to advertisement before closing a register shall not apply; and (*b*) there shall be substituted for the reference in subsection (7) of section 119 to proviso (*b*) to subsection (2) of section 109 a reference to proviso (*b*) to subsection (2) of section 84.

Liability of trustees for debenture holders.

88.—(1) Subject to the following provisions of this section, any provision contained in a trust deed for securing an issue of debentures, or in any contract with the holders of debentures secured by a trust deed, shall be void in so far as it would have the effect of exempting a trustee thereof from or indemnifying him against liability for breach of trust where he fails to show the degree of care and diligence required of him as trustee, having regard to the provisions of the trust deed conferring on him any powers, authorities or discretions.

(2) Subsection (1) shall not invalidate—

(*a*) any release otherwise validly given in respect of anything done or omitted to be done by a trustee before the giving of the release; or

(*b*) any provision enabling such a release to be given—

(i) on the agreement thereto of a majority of not less than three-fourths in value of the debenture holders present and voting in person or, where proxies are permitted, by proxy at a meeting summoned for the purpose; and

(ii) either with respect to specific acts or omissions or on the trustee dying or ceasing to act.

(3) Subsection (1) shall not operate—

(*a*) to invalidate any provision in force on the appointed day so long as any person then entitled to the benefit of that provision or afterwards given the benefit thereof under subsection (4) remains a trustee of the deed in question; or (*b*) to deprive any person of any exemption or right to be indemnified in respect of anything done or omitted to be done by him while any such provision was in force.

(4) While any trustee of a trust deed remains entitled to the benefit of a provision saved by subsection (3), the benefit of that provision may be given either—

(*a*) to all trustees of the deed, present and future; or

(*b*) to any named trustees or proposed trustees thereof, by resolution passed by a majority of not less than three-fourths in value of the debenture holders present in person or, where proxies are permitted, by proxy at a meeting summoned for the purpose in accordance with the provisions of the deed or, if the deed makes no provision for summoning meetings, a meeting summoned for the purpose in any manner approved by the Court.

89. A condition contained in any debentures or in any deed for securing any debentures, whether issued or executed before or after the appointed day, shall not be invalid by reason only that the debentures are thereby made irredeemable or redeemable only on the happening of a contingency, however remote, or on the expiration of a period, however long, any rule of equity to the contrary notwithstanding. Perpetual debentures.

90.—(1) Where either before or after the appointed day a company has redeemed any debentures previously issued, then— Power to re-issue redeemed debentures in certain cases.

(*a*) unless any provision to the contrary whether express or implied, is contained in the articles or in any contract entered into by the company; or

(*b*) unless the company has, by passing a resolution to that effect or by some other act, manifested its intention that the debentures shall be cancelled, the company shall have, and shall be deemed always to have had, power to re-issue the debentures, either by re-issuing the same debentures or by issuing other debentures in their place.

(2) On a re-issue of redeemed debentures the person entitled to the debentures shall have, and shall be deemed always to have had, the same priorities as if the debentures had never been redeemed.

(3) Where a company has power to re-issue debentures which have been redeemed, particulars with respect to the debentures which can be so re-issued shall be included in every balance sheet of the company.

(4) Where a company has either before or after the appointed day deposited any of its debentures to secure advances from time to time on current account or otherwise, the debentures shall not be deemed to have been redeemed by reason only of the account of the company having ceased to be in debit whilst the debentures remained so deposited.

(5) The re-issue of a debenture or the issue of another debenture in its place under the power by this section given to, or deemed to have been possessed by, a company, whether the re-issue or issue was made before or after the appointed day, shall be treated as the issue of a new debenture for the purposes of stamp duty, but it shall not be so treated for the purposes of any provision limiting the amount or number of debentures to be issued:

Provided that any person lending money on the security of a debenture re-issued under this section which appears to be duly stamped may give the debenture in evidence in any proceedings for enforcing his security without payment of the stamp duty or any penalty in respect thereof, unless he had notice or, but for his negligence might have discovered, that the debenture was not duly stamped, but in any such case the company shall be liable to pay the proper stamp duty and penalty.

(6) Where any debentures which have been redeemed before the appointed day are re-issued subsequently to that date, the re-issue of the debentures shall not prejudice any right or priority which any person would have had under or by virtue of any mortgage or charge created before that date.

91. A contract with a company to take up and pay for any debentures of the company may be enforced by an order for specific performance. Specific performance of contracts to subscribe for debentures.

92.—(1) Where either a receiver is appointed on behalf of the holders of any debentures of the company secured by a floating charge, or possession is taken by or on behalf of those debentures of any property comprised in or subject to the charge, then, if the company is not at the time in course of being wound up, the debts which in every winding up are under the provisions of Part V relating to preferential payments to be paid in priority to all other debts, shall be paid out of any assets coming to the hands of the receiver or other person taking possession as aforesaid in priority to any claim for principal or interest in respect of the debentures. Payment of certain debts out of assets subject to floating charge in priority to claims under the charge.

(2) The periods of time mentioned in the said provisions of Part V shall be reckoned from the date of the appointment of the receiver or of possession being taken as aforesaid, as the case may be.

(3) Any payments made under this section shall be recouped as far as may be out of the assets of the company available for payment of general creditors.

PART III—*Registration of Charges*

Registration of Charges with Registrar

93.—(1) Every charge created after the appointed day by a company registered in the Island, being a charge to which this section applies shall, so far as any security on the company's Registration of charges.

property or undertaking is conferred thereby, be void against the liquidator and any creditor of the company, unless the prescribed particulars of the charge, together with the original or a copy certified in the prescribed manner of the instrument, if any, by which the charge is created or evidenced, are delivered to or received by the Registrar for registration in the manner required by this Act prior to the commencement of the winding up of the company, but without prejudice to any contract or obligation for repayment of the money secured; and when a charge becomes void under this section, the money secured thereby shall immediately become payable.

(2) Where—

(*a*) a charge to which subsection (3) applies is registered within twenty-one days of its creation, that charge shall for the purposes of priority (and subject to any agreement altering priorities) rank in priority to any charge created after it;

(*b*) a charge to which subsection (3) applies is created and is not registered until after twenty-one days after its creation, that charge shall for purposes of priority (and subject to any agreement altering priorities) be deemed to have been created on the date of registration.

(3) This section applies to the following charges—

(*a*) a charge for the purpose of securing any issue of debentures;

(*b*) a charge on uncalled share capital of the company;

(*c*) a charge created or evidenced by an instrument which, if executed by an individual, would require registration as a bill of sale;

(*d*) a charge on land, wherever situated, or any interest therein but not including a charge for any rent or other periodical sum issuing out of land;

(*e*) a charge on book debts of the company;

(*f*) a floating charge on the undertaking or property of the company;

(*g*) a charge on calls made but not paid;

(*h*) a charge on a ship or any share in a ship;

(*i*) a charge on goodwill, on a patent or a licence under a patent, on a trade mark or on a copyright or a licence under a copyright.

(4) Where a charge is created outside of the Island comprising property situated outside the Island, for the purpose of calculating the period for registration, the twenty-one days shall commence after the date on which the instrument or copy would, in due course of post, and if dispatched with due diligence, have been received in the Island.

(5) Where a charge is created in the Island but comprises property outside the Island, the instrument creating or purporting to create the charge or the copy thereof, as the case may be, may be sent for registration under this section notwithstanding that further proceedings maybe necessary to make the charge valid or effectual according to the law of the country in which the property is situated.

(6) Where a negotiable instrument has been given to secure the payment of any book debts of a company the deposit of the instrument for the purpose of securing an advance to the company shall not for the purposes of this section be treated as a charge on those book debts.

(7) Where a series of debentures containing, or giving by reference to any other instrument, any charge to the benefit of which the debenture holders of that series are entitled *pari passu* is created by a company, it shall for the purposes of this section be sufficient if there are delivered to or received by the Registrar within twenty-one days after the execution of the deed containing the charge or if there is no such deed, after the execution of any debentures of the series, the following particulars—

(*a*) the total amount secured by the whole series; and

(*b*) the dates of the resolutions authorizing the issue of the series and the date of the covering deed, if any, by which the security is created or defined; and

(*c*) a general description of the property charged; and

(*d*) the names of the trustees, if any, for the debenture holders,

together with a copy of the deed containing the charge, certified to be a true copy by an attorney-at-law or an officer of the company, or, if there is no such deed, one of the debentures of the series:

Provided that, where more than one issue is made of debentures in the series, there shall be sent to the Registrar for entry in the register particulars of the date and amount of each issue, but an omission to do this shall not affect the validity of the debentures issued.

(8) Where any commission, allowance or discount has been paid or made either directly or indirectly by a company to any person in consideration of his subscribing or agreeing to subscribe, whether absolutely or conditionally, for any debentures of the company, or procuring or agreeing to procure subscriptions, whether absolute or conditional, for any such debentures, the particulars required to be sent for registration under this section shall include particulars as to the amount or rate *per centum* of the commission, discount, or allowance so paid or made, but omission to do this shall not affect the validity of the debentures issued:

Provided that the deposit of any debentures as security for any debt of the company shall not for the purposes of this subsection be treated as the issue of the debentures at a discount.

(9) If default is made in complying with subsection (1), the company and every officer thereof who is in default shall be liable to a fine not exceeding fifty thousand dollars.

(10) In this Part the expression "charge" includes mortgage.

94.—(1) Where a charge requiring registration under this Act is created then— Effect of registration.

(*a*) the registration of that charge in accordance with this Act shall constitute notice to the world of the existence of that charge;

(*b*) where a subsequent charge is registered in accordance with this Act in respect of the same property or undertaking and written notice thereof is given to the prior chargee, the amount secured by the prior charge shall not be increased to the prejudice of the later charge notwithstanding any provision to the contrary contained in the document creating the earlier charge.

(2) Where the amount secured by a charge is increased after the charge is registered, the particulars of the increase shall be sent to the Registrar for registration in the prescribed manner.

95.—(1) It shall be the duty of a company to send to the Registrar for registration the particulars of every charge created by the company and of the issues of debentures of a series requiring registration under section 93, but registration of any such charge may be effected on the application of any person interested therein. Duty of company to register charges created by company.

(2) Where registration is effected on the application of some person other than the company, that person shall be entitled to recover from the company the amount of any fees properly paid by him to the Registrar on the registration.

(3) If any company makes default in sending to the Registrar for registration the particulars of any charge created by the company, or of the issues of debentures of a series requiring registration as aforesaid, then, unless the registration has been effected on the application of some other person, the company and every officer of the company

who is in default shall be liable to a default fine not exceeding fifty thousand dollars.

Duty of company to register charges existing on property acquired.

96.—(1) Where after the appointed day a company registered in the Island acquires any property which is subject to a charge of any such kind as would, if it had been created by the company after the acquisition of the property, have been required to be registered under this Part, the company shall cause the prescribed particulars of the charge, together with a copy (certified in the prescribed manner to be a correct copy) of the instrument, if any, by which the charge was created or is evidenced, to be delivered to the Registrar for registration in manner required by this Act within twenty-one days after the date on which the acquisition is completed:

Provided that, if the property is situated and the charge was created outside the Island, twenty-one days after the date on which the copy of the instrument could in due course of post, and if dispatched with due diligence, have been received in the Island shall be substituted for twenty-one days after the completion of the acquisition as the time within which the particulars and the copy of the instrument are to be delivered to the Registrar.

(2) If default is made in complying with this section, the company and every officer of the company who is in default shall be liable to a default fine not exceeding fifty thousand dollars.

Registrar to keep register of charges.

97.—(1) The Registrar shall keep, with respect to each company, a register in the prescribed form of all the charges requiring registration under this Part and shall, on payment of the prescribed fee, enter in the register with respect to such charges the following particulars—

(*a*) in the case of a charge to the benefit of which the holders of a series of debentures are entitled, such particulars as are specified in subsection (7) of section 93;

(*b*) in the case of any other charge—

(i) if the charge is a charge created by the company, the date of its creation, and if the charge was a charge existing on property acquired by the company, the date of the acquisition of the property; and

(ii) the amount secured by the charge; and

(iii) short particulars of the property charged; and

(iv) the persons entitled to the charge

(2) The Registrar shall give a certificate under his hand of the registration of any charge registered in pursuance of this Part, stating the amount thereby secured, and the certificate shall be conclusive evidence that the requirements of this Part as to registration have been complied with.

(3) The register kept in pursuance of this section shall be open to inspection by any person on payment of the prescribed fee for each inspection.

(4) The Registrar shall keep a chronological index, in the prescribed form and with the prescribed particulars, of the charges entered in the register.

Indorsement of certificate of registration on debentures.

98.—(1) The company shall cause a copy of every certificate of registration given under section 97 to be indorsed on every debenture or certificate of debenture stock which is issued by the company, and the payment of which is secured by the charge so registered:

Provided that nothing in this subsection shall be construed as requiring a company to cause a certificate of registration of any charge so given to be indorsed on any debenture or certificate of debenture stock issued by the company before the charge was created.

(*b*) in the case of any other charge—

(i) if the charge is a charge created by the company, the date of its creation, and if the charge was a charge existing on property acquired by the company, the date of the acquisition of the property; and

(ii) the amount secured by the charge; and

(iii) short particulars of the property charged; and

(iv) the persons entitled to the charge

(2) The Registrar shall give a certificate under his hand of the registration of any charge registered in pursuance of this Part, stating the amount thereby secured, and the certificate shall be conclusive evidence that the requirements of this Part as to registration have been complied with.

(3) The register kept in pursuance of this section shall be open to inspection by any person on payment of the prescribed fee for each inspection.

(4) The Registrar shall keep a chronological index, in the prescribed form and with the prescribed particulars, of the charges entered in the register.

Indorsement of certificate of registration on debentures.

98.—(1) The company shall cause a copy of every certificate of registration given under section 97 to be indorsed on every debenture or certificate of debenture stock which is issued by the company, and the payment of which is secured by the charge so registered:

Provided that nothing in this subsection shall be construed as requiring a company to cause a certificate of registration of any charge so given to be indorsed on any debenture or certificate of debenture stock issued by the company before the charge was created.

(2) If any person knowingly and wilfully authorizes or permits the delivery of any debenture or certificate of debenture stock which under the provisions of this section is required to have indorsed on it a copy of a certificate of registration without the copy being so indorsed upon it, he shall, without prejudice to any other liability, be liable to a fine not exceeding fifty thousand dollars.

Entries of satisfaction and release of property from charge.

99. The Registrar, on evidence being given to his satisfaction with respect to any registered charge—

(*a*) that the debt for which the charge was given has been paid or satisfied in whole or in part; or

(*b*) that part of the property or undertaking charged has been released from the charge or has ceased to form part of the company's property or undertaking,

may enter on the register a memorandum of satisfaction in whole or in part, or of the fact that part of the property or undertaking has been released from the charge or has ceased to form part of the company's property or undertaking, as the case may be, and where he enters a memorandum of satisfaction in whole he shall, if required, furnish the company with a copy thereof.

Rectification of register of charges.

100. The Court, on being satisfied that the omission or mis-statement of any particular with respect to any such charge or in a memorandum of satisfaction was accidental, or due to inadvertence or to some other sufficient cause, or is not of a nature to prejudice the position of creditors or shareholders of the company, or that on other grounds it is just and equitable to grant relief, may, on the application of the company or any person interested, and on such terms and conditions as seem to the Court just and expedient, order that the omission or mis-statement shall be rectified.

101.—(1) If any person obtains an order for the appointment of a receiver or manager of the property of a company, or appoints such a receiver or manager under any powers contained in any instrument, he shall, within seven days from the date of the order or of the appointment under the said powers, give notice of the fact to the Registrar and the Registrar shall, on payment of the prescribed fee enter the fact in the register of charges. Registration of enforcement of security.

(2) Where any person appointed receiver or manager of the property of a company under the powers contained in any instrument, ceases to act as such receiver or manager, he shall, on so ceasing, give the Registrar notice to that effect, and the Registrar shall enter the notice in the register of charges.

(3) If any person makes default in complying with the requirements of this section he shall be liable to a fine not exceeding two thousand dollars for every day during which the default continues.

Provisions as to Company's Register of Charges and as to Copies of Instruments creating Charges

102.—(1) Every company shall cause a copy of every instrument creating any charge requiring registration under this Part to be certified in the prescribed manner and kept at the registered office of the company: Copies of instruments creating charges to be kept by company.

Provided that, in the case of a series of uniform debentures, a copy certified as aforesaid of one debenture of the series shall be sufficient.

(2) If default is made by a company in complying with subsection (1), the company and every officer of the company who is in default shall be liable to a fine not exceeding two thousand dollars.

103.—(1) Every limited company shall keep at the registered office of the company a register of charges and enter therein all charges specifically affecting property of the company and all Company's register of charges.

floating charges on the undertaking or any property of the company, giving in each case a short description of the property charged, the amount of the charge, and, except in the case of securities to bearer, the names of the persons entitled thereto.

(2) If any officer of the company knowingly and wilfully authorizes or permits the omission of any entry required to be made in pursuance of this section, he shall be liable to a fine not exceeding one hundred thousand dollars.

Right to inspect copies of instruments creating charges and company's register of charges.

104.—(1) The copies of instruments creating any charge requiring registration under this Part with the Registrar, and the register of charges kept in pursuance of section 103 shall be open during business hours (but subject to such reasonable restrictions as the company in general meeting may impose, so that not less than two hours in each day shall be allowed for inspection) to the inspection of any creditor or member of the company without fee, and the register of charges shall also be open to the inspection of any other person on payment of such fee, not exceeding fifty dollars for each inspection, as the company may specify.

(2) If inspection of the said copies or register is refused, any officer of the company who is in default shall be liable to a fine not exceeding fifty thousand dollars and where the default continues to a further fine not exceeding two thousand dollars for every day during which the refusal continues.

(3) If any such refusal occurs in relation to a company, the Court may by order compel an immediate inspection of the copies or register.

Application of Part III to Companies incorporated outside the Island

105. The provisions of this Part shall extend to charges on property in the Island which are created, and to charges on property in the Island which is acquired, after the appointed day, by a company (whether a company within the meaning of this Act or not) incorporated outside the Island which has an established place of business in the Island.

Application of Part III to charges created, and charges on property subject to charges acquired, by company incorporated outside the Island.

PART IV—*Management and Administration*

Registered Office and Name

106.—(1) A company shall have a registered office to which all communications and notices may be addressed.

Registered office of company.

(2) Notice of the situation of the registered office shall be given at the date of the company's incorporation or within seven days of any change in such situation, as the case may be, to the Registrar, who shall record the same. The inclusion in the annual return of a company of a statement as to the address of its registered office shall not be taken to satisfy the obligation imposed by this subsection.

(3) If default is made in complying with this section, the company and every officer of the company who is in default shall be liable to a fine not exceeding fifty thousand dollars.

107.—(1) Every company—

Publication of name by company.

(*a*) shall paint or affix, and keep painted or affixed, its name on the outside of every office or place in which its business is carried on, in a conspicuous position, in letters easily legible;

(*b*) shall have its name engraven in legible characters on its seal;

(*c*) shall have its name mentioned in legible characters in all business letters of the company and in all notices and other official publications of the company, and in all bills of exchange, promissory notes, indorsements, cheques and orders for money or goods purporting to be signed by or on behalf of the company, and in all bills of parcels, invoices, receipts and letters of credit of the company.

(2) If a company does not paint or affix its name in manner directed by this Act, the company and every officer of the company who is in default shall be liable to a fine not exceeding fifty thousand dollars, and if a company does not keep its name painted or affixed in manner so directed, the company and every officer of the company who is in default shall be liable to a fine not exceeding two thousand dollars for every day during which the default continues.

(3) If a company fails to comply with paragraph (*b*) or paragraph (*c*) of subsection (1), the company shall be liable to a fine not exceeding fifty thousand dollars.

(4) If an officer of a company or any person on its behalf—

(*a*) uses or authorizes the use of any seal purporting to be a seal of the company whereon its name is not so engraven as aforesaid; or

(*b*) issues or authorizes the issue of any business letter of the company or any notice or other official publication of the company, or signs or authorizes to be signed on behalf of the company any bill of exchange, promissory note, indorsement, cheque or order for money or goods wherein its name is not mentioned in the manner aforesaid; or (*c*) issues or authorizes the issue of any bill of parcels, invoice, receipt or letter of credit of the company wherein its name is not mentioned in the manner aforesaid,

he shall be liable to a fine not exceeding fifty thousand dollars, and shall further be personally liable to the holder of the bill of exchange, promissory note, cheque or order for money or goods for the amount thereof unless it is duly paid by the company.

Restriction on commencement of business.

108.—(1) Where a company having a share capital has issued a prospectus inviting the public to subscribe for its shares, the company shall not commence any business or exercise any borrowing powers unless—

(*a*) shares held subject to the payment of the whole amount thereof in cash have been allotted to an amount not less in the whole than the minimum subscription; and

(*b*) every director of the company has paid to the company, on each of the shares taken or contracted to be taken by him and for which he is liable to pay in cash, a proportion equal to the proportion payable on application and allotment on the shares offered for public subscription; and

(*c*) there has been delivered to the Registrar for registration a statutory declaration by the secretary or one of the directors, in the prescribed form, that the conditions specified in paragraphs (*a*) and (*b*) have been complied with.

(2) Where a company having a share capital has not issued a prospectus inviting the public to subscribe for its shares, the company shall not commence any business or exercise any borrowing powers unless—

(*a*) there has been delivered to the Registrar for registration a statement in lieu of prospectus; and (*b*) every director has paid to the company, on each of the shares taken or contracted to be taken by him and for which he is liable to pay in cash, a proportion equal to the proportion payable on application and allotment on the shares payable in cash;

(*c*) there has been delivered to the Registrar for registration a statutory declaration by the secretary or one of the directors, in the prescribed form, that paragraph (*b*) has been complied with.

(3) The Registrar shall, on the delivery to him of the statutory declaration, and, in the case of a company which is required by this section to deliver a statement in lieu of prospectus, of such a statement, certify that the company is entitled to commence business; and that certificate shall be conclusive evidence that the company is so entitled.

(4) Any contract made by a company before the date at which it is entitled to commence business shall be provisional only, and shall not be binding on the company until that date, and on that date it shall become binding.

(5) Nothing in this section shall prevent the simultaneous offer for subscription or allotment of any shares and debentures or the receipt of any money payable on application for debentures.

(6) If any company commences business or exercises borrowing powers in contravention of this section, every person who is responsible for the contravention shall, without prejudice to any other liability, be liable to a fine not exceeding fifty thousand dollars for every day during which the contravention continues.

(7) Nothing in this section shall apply to a private company.

Register of Members

109.—(1) Every company shall keep in one or more documents a register of its members, and enter therein the following particulars— Register of members.

(*a*) the names and addresses and the occupation, if any, of the members, and in the case of a company having a share capital a statement of the shares held by each member, distinguishing each share by its number, and of the amount paid or agreed to be considered as paid on the shares of each member;

(*b*) the date at which each person was entered in the register as a member;

(*c*) the date at which any person ceased to be a member:

Provided that where the company has converted any of its shares into stock and given notice of the conversion to the Registrar, the register shall show the amount of stock held by each member instead of the amount of shares and the particulars relating to shares specified in paragraph (*a*).

(2) The register of members shall be kept at the registered office of the company:

Provided that—

(*a*) if the work of making it up is done at another office of the company, it may be kept at that other office; and

(*b*) if the company arranges with some other person for the making up of the register to be undertaken on behalf of the company by that other person, it may be kept at the office of that other person at which the work is done,

so, however, that it shall not be kept at a place outside the Island.

(3) Every company shall send notice to the Registrar of the place where its register of members is kept and of any change in that place:

Provided that a company shall not be bound to send notice under this subsection where the register has, at all times since it came into existence or, in the case of a register in existence at the appointed day, at all times since then been kept at the registered office of the company.

(4) Where a company makes default in complying with subsection (1) or makes default for fourteen days in complying with subsection (3), the company and every officer of the company who is in default shall be liable to a fine not exceeding fifty thousand dollars.

Index of members of company.

110.—(1) Every company having more than fifty members shall, unless the register of members is in such a form as to constitute in itself an index, keep an index of the names of the members of the company and shall, within fourteen days after the date on which any alteration is made in the register of members, make any necessary alteration in the index.

(2) The index, which may be in the form of a card index, shall in respect of each member contain a sufficient indication to enable the account of that member in the register to be readily found.

(3) The index shall at all times be kept at the same place as the register of members.

(4) If default is made in complying with this section, the company and every officer of the company who is in default shall be liable to a fine not exceeding fifty thousand dollars.

Provisions as to entries in register in relation to share warrants.

111.—(1) On the issue of a share warrant the company shall strike out of its register of members the name of the member then entered therein as holding the shares specified in the warrant as if he had ceased to be a member, and shall enter in the register the following particulars, namely—

(*a*) the fact of the issue of the warrant;

(*b*) a statement of the shares included in the warrant, distinguishing each share by its number; and

(*c*) the date of the issue of the warrant.

(2) The bearer of a share warrant shall, subject to the articles of the company, be entitled, on surrendering it for cancellation, to have his name entered as a member in the register of members.

(3) The company shall be responsible for any loss incurred by any person by reason of the company entering in the register the name of a bearer of a share warrant in respect of the shares therein specified without the warrant being surrendered and cancelled.

(4) Until the warrant is surrendered, the particulars specified in subsection (1) shall be deemed to be the particulars required by this Act to be entered in the register of members, and, on the surrender, the date of the surrender must be entered.

(5) Subject to the provisions of this Act, the bearer of a share warrant may, if the articles of the company so provide, be deemed to be a member of the company within the meaning of this Act, either to the full extent or for any purposes defined in the articles.

Inspection of register of members and index of names.

112.—(1) The register of members, commencing from the date of the registration of the company, and the index of the names of members, except when the register is closed under the provisions of this Act, shall during business hours (subject to such reasonable restrictions as the company in general meeting may impose, so that not less than two hours in each day be allowed for inspection) be open to the inspection of any member without charge and of any other person on payment of fifty dollars, or such less sum as the company may specify, for each inspection.

(2) Any member or other person may request a copy of the register, or of any part thereof, on payment of fifty dollars, or such less sum as the company may specify, for every hundred words or fractional part thereof required to be copied. The company shall cause any copy so required by any person to be

sent to that person within a period of ten days commencing on the day next after the day on which the request is received by the company.

(3) If any inspection required under this section is refused or if any copy required under this section is not sent within the proper period, the company and every officer of the company who is in default shall be liable in respect of each offence to a fine not exceeding fifty thousand dollars.

(4) In the case of any such refusal or default, the Court may by order compel an immediate inspection of the register and index or direct that the copies required shall be sent to the persons requiring them.

Consequences of failure to comply with requirements as to register owing to agent's default.

113. Where, by virtue of proviso (*b*) to subsection (2) of section 109 the register of members is kept at the office of some person other than the company, and by reason of default of that other person the company fails to comply with subsection (3) of that section, subsection (3) of section 110 or subsection (1) of section 112 or with any requirements of this Act as to the production of the register, that other person shall be liable to the same penalties as if he were an officer of the company who was in default, and the power of the Court under subsection (3) of section 112 shall extend to the making of orders against that other person and his officers and servants.

Power to close register.

114. A company may, on giving notice by advertisement in a daily newspaper printed and circulating in the Island close the register of members for any time or times not exceeding in the whole thirty days in each year.

Power of Court to rectify register.

115.—(1) If—

(*a*) the name of any person is, without sufficient cause, entered in or omitted from the register of members of a company; or (*b*) default is made or unnecessary delay takes place in entering on the register the fact of any person having ceased to be a member,

the person aggrieved, or any member of the company, or the company, may apply to the Court for rectification of the register.

(2) Where an application is made under this section, the Court may either refuse the application or may order rectification of the register and payment by the company of any damages sustained by any party aggrieved.

(3) On an application under this section the Court may decide any question relating to the title of any person who is a party to the application to have his name entered in or omitted from the register, whether the question arises between members or alleged members, or between members or alleged members on the one hand and the company on the other hand, and generally may decide any question necessary or expedient to be decided for rectification of the register.

(4) In the case of a company required by this Act to send a list of its members to the Registrar, the Court when making an order for rectification of the register, shall by its order direct notice of the rectification to be given to the Registrar.

116. No notice of any trust, express, implied, or constructive, shall be entered on the register, or be receivable by the Registrar, in the case of companies registered in the Island. Trusts not to be entered on register.

117. The register of members shall be *prima facie* evidence of any matters by this Act directed or authorized to be inserted therein. Register to be evidence.

Branch Register

118.—(1) A company having a share capital which carries on business in any country outside the Island may cause to be kept in that part of any such country in which it transacts business, a register of members resident in such part (in this Act called a "branch register"). Power for company to keep branch register.

(2) The company shall give to the Registrar notice of the situation of the office where any branch register is kept and of any change in its situation, and if it is discontinued of its discontinuance, and any such notice shall be given within fourteen days of the opening of the office or of the change or discontinuance, as the case may be.

(3) If default is made in complying with subsection (2), the company and every officer of the company who is in default shall be liable to a fine not exceeding fifty thousand dollars.

Regulations as to branch register.

119.—(1) A branch register shall be deemed to be part of the company's register of members (in this section called "the principal register").

(2) The branch register shall be kept in the same manner in which the principal register is by this Act required to be kept, except that the advertisement before closing the register shall be inserted in a newspaper circulating in the district where the branch register is kept, and that any competent court in the country where the register is kept may exercise the same jurisdiction of rectifying the register as is under this Act exercisable by the Court.

(3) The company shall transmit to its registered office a copy of every entry in its branch register as soon as may be after the entry is made, and shall cause to be kept at the place where the company's principal register is kept, duly entered up from time to time, a duplicate of its branch register and every such duplicate shall, for all the purposes of this Act, be deemed to be part of the principal register.

(4) Subject to the provisions of this section with respect to the duplicate register, the shares registered in a branch register shall be distinguished from the shares registered in the principal register, and no transaction with respect to any shares registered in a branch register shall, during the continuance of that registration, be registered in any other register.

(5) A company may discontinue to keep a branch register, and thereupon all entries in that register shall be transferred to some other branch register kept by the company in the country concerned or to the principal register.

(6) Subject to the provisions of this Act, any company may, by its articles, make such provisions as it may think fit respecting the keeping of branch registers.

(7) If default is made in complying with subsection (3)—

(*a*) the company and every officer of the company who is in default shall be liable to a fine not exceeding fifty thousand dollars; and

(*b*) where, by virtue of proviso (*b*) to subsection (2) of section 109, the principal register is kept at the office of some person other than the company and by reason of any default of that other person the company fails to comply with the requirements of subsection (3) of this section relating to the keeping of a duplicate of its branch register, he shall be liable to the same penalty as if he were an officer of the company who was in default.

(8) An instrument of transfer of a share registered in a branch register shall be deemed to be a transfer of property situated out of the Island, and unless executed in this Island, shall be exempt from stamp duty chargeable in the Island.

Provisions as to branch registers of companies incorporated abroad kept in the Island.

120. If by virtue of the law in force in any country, outside the Island companies incorporated under that law have power to keep in the Island branch registers of their members resident in the Island, the Minister may by order direct that sections 112 and 115 shall, subject to any modifications and adaptations specified in the order, apply to and in relation to any such branch registers kept in the Island as they apply to and in relation to the registers of companies within the meaning of this Act.

Annual Returns

Duty to deliver annual returns.

121.—(1) Every company shall deliver to the Registrar successive annual returns each of which is made up to a date not later than the date which is from time to time the company's return date, that is—

(*a*) the anniversary of the company's incorporation; or

(*b*) if the company's last return delivered in accordance with this section was made up to a different date, the anniversary of that date.

(2) Each return shall—

Fifth Schedule.

(*a*) be in the prescribed form as set out in the Fifth Schedule;

(*b*) contain the information required by or under the provisions of sections 122, 123 and 124 and shall be delivered to the Registrar within twenty-eight days after the date to which it is made up.

(3) If a company fails to deliver an annual return in accordance with this section—

(*a*) that company shall be liable on default to a penalty of one hundred dollars for each day the default continues, subject to a maximum penalty of ten thousand dollars; and

(*b*) such penalty shall be payable to the Registrar.

Annual return to be made by a company having a share capital.

122.—(1) Every company having a share capital shall make a return stating the date to which it is made up and containing a list of all persons who, on the date of the return, are members of the company, and of all persons who have ceased to be members since the date of the last return or, in the case of the first return, of the incorporation of the company.

(2) The list shall—

(*a*) state the names, addresses and occupations of all past and present members therein mentioned;

(*b*) state the number of shares held by each of the existing members at the date of the return, specifying shares transferred since the date of the last return or, in the case of the first return, of the incorporation of the company by persons who have ceased to be members respectively and the dates of registration of the transfers; and

(*c*) if the names therein are not arranged in alphabetical order, have annexed to it an index sufficient to enable the name of any person in the list to be readily found:

Provided that, where the company has converted any of its shares into stock and given notice of the conversion to the Registrar, the list shall state the amount of stock held by each of the existing members instead of the amount of shares and the particulars relating to shares hereinbefore required.

(3) The return shall contain with respect to the registered office of the company, registers of members and debenture holders, shares and debentures indebtedness, and persons who are directors of the company, the matters specified in Part I of the Fifth Schedule and shall be in accordance with the form set out in Part II of that Schedule or as near thereto as circumstances permit. Fifth Schedule.

(4) In the case of a company keeping a branch register, the particulars of the entries in that register shall, so far as they relate to matters which are required to be stated in the return, be included in the return made next after copies of those entries are received at the registered office of the company.

Annual return to be made by a company not having a share capital.

123.—(1) Every company not having a share capital shall make a return stating—

(*a*) the date to which it is made up;

(*b*) the address of the registered office of the company;

(c) all particulars with respect to the persons who at the date of the return are the directors of the company as are by this Act required to be contained with respect to directors on the register of directors of a company.

(2) There shall be annexed to the return a statement containing particulars of the total indebtedness of the company in respect of all mortgages and charges which are required to be registered under this Act.

General provisions as to annual return

124.—(1) The annual return shall be contained in a separate part of the register of members.

(2) Section 111 shall apply to the annual return as it applies to the register of members.

(3) The annual return shall, in the case of every company which is not a private company and every private company which is obliged to file accounts, include a written copy, certified by a director, the manager or secretary of the company to be a true copy, of the last balance sheet and profit and loss account laid before the company in general meeting, including every document required by law to be annexed thereto, together with a copy of the report of the auditors thereon certified as aforesaid, and if any such balance sheet is in a foreign language, there shall also be annexed to it a translation thereof in English, certified in the prescribed manner to be a correct translation:

Provided that, if the balance sheet did not comply with the requirements of the law as in force at the date of the audit with respect to the form of balance sheets, there shall be made such additions to and corrections in the copy as would have been required to be made in the balance sheet in order to make it comply with those requirements, and the fact that the copy has been so amended shall be stated thereon.

Certificates to be sent by private company with annual return.

125. A private company shall send with the annual return required by section 121—

(*a*) a certificate signed both by a director and by the secretary of the company that the company has not since the date of the last return, or since, in the case of a first return, the date of the incorporation of the company or, in the case of an existing company which became a private company, the date on which it became a private company, issued any invitation to the public to subscribe for any shares or debentures of the company or to deposit money for fixed periods whether bearing or not bearing interest;

(*b*) where the annual return discloses the fact that the number of members of the company exceeds twenty, also a certificate so signed that the excess consists wholly of persons who under paragraph (*b*) of subsection (1) of section 25 are not to be included in reckoning the number of twenty;

(*c*) a certificate signed by the persons aforesaid that, to the best of their knowledge and belief, no person other than the holder thereof except in cases provided for in the Twelfth Schedule has had any interest in any of the company's shares since the date of the last return or since, in the case of a first return, the date of the incorporation of the company or, in the case of an existing company which became a private company, the date on which it became a private company; Twelfth Schedule.

(*d*) where the company claims to be a private company which is not obliged to file accounts, a certificate signed by the persons aforesaid in the prescribed form.

Meetings and Proceedings

Annual general meeting.

126.—(1) Every company shall in each year hold a general meeting as its annual general meeting in addition to any other meetings in that year, and shall specify the meeting as such in the notices calling it; and not more than fifteen months shall elapse between the date of one annual general meeting of a company and that of the next.

Provided that, so long as a company holds its first annual general meeting within eighteen months of its incorporation, it need not hold it in the year of its incorporation or in the following year.

(2) If default is made in holding a meeting of the company in accordance with subsection (1), the Minister may, on the application of any member of the company, call, or direct the calling of, a general meeting of the company and give such ancillary or consequential directions as he may think expedient, including directions modifying or supplementing, in relation to the calling, holding and conducting of the meeting, the operation of the company's articles; and it is hereby declared that the directions that may be given under this subsection include a direction that one member of the company present in person or by proxy shall be deemed to constitute a meeting.

(3) A general meeting held in pursuance of subsection (2) shall, subject to any directions of the Minister, be deemed to be an annual general meeting of the company; but, where a meeting so held is not held in the year in which the default in holding the company's annual general meeting occurred, the meeting so held shall not be treated as the annual general meeting for the year in which it is held unless at that meeting the company resolves that it shall be so treated.

(4) Where a company resolves that a meeting shall be so treated, a copy of the resolution shall, within fifteen days after the passing thereof, be forwarded to the Registrar and recorded by him.

(5) If default is made in—

(*a*) holding a meeting of the company in accordance with subsection (1); or

(*b*) complying with any directions of the Minister under subsection (2);

(*c*) complying with subsection (4),

the company and every officer of the company who is in default shall be liable to a fine not exceeding fifty thousand dollars.

127.—(1) Every company limited by shares and every company limited by guarantee and having a share capital shall, within a period of not less than one month nor more than three months from the date at which the company is entitled to commence business, hold a general meeting of the members of the company, which shall be called "the statutory meeting". Statutory meeting and statutory report.

(2) The directors shall, at least seven days before the day on which the meeting is held, forward a report (in this Act referred to as "the statutory report") to every member of the company.

(3) The statutory report shall be certified by not less than two directors of the company or where there are less than two directors, by the sole director and shall state—

(*a*) the total number of shares allotted, distinguishing shares allotted as fully or partly paid up otherwise than in cash, and stating in the case of shares partly paid up the extent to which they are so paid up, and in either case, the consideration for which they have been allotted;

(*b*) the total amount of cash received by the company in respect of all the shares allotted, distinguished as aforesaid;

(*c*) an abstract of the receipts of the company and of the payments made thereout, up to a date within seven days of the date of the report, exhibiting under distinctive headings the receipts of the company from shares and debentures and other sources, the payments made thereout, and particulars concerning the balance remaining in hand, and an account or estimate of the preliminary expenses of the company;

(*d*) the names, addresses and descriptions of the directors, auditors, if any, managers, if any, and secretary of the company; and

(*e*) the particulars of any contract the modification of which is to be submitted to the meeting for its approval, together with the particulars of the modification or proposed modification.

(4) The statutory report shall, so far as it relates to the shares allotted by the company, and to the cash received in respect of such shares, and to the receipts and payments of the company on capital account, be certified as correct by the auditors, if any, of the company.

(5) The directors shall cause a copy of the statutory report, certified as required by this section, to be delivered to the Registrar for registration forthwith after the sending thereof to the members of the company.

(6) The directors shall cause a list showing the names, descriptions and addresses of the members of the company, and the number of shares held by them respectively, to be produced at the commencement of the meeting and to remain open and accessible to any member of the company during the continuance of the meeting.

(7) The members of the company present at the meeting shall be at liberty to discuss any matter relating to the formation of the company, or arising out of the statutory report, whether previous notice has been given or not, but no resolution of which notice has not been given in accordance with the articles may be passed.

(8) The meeting may adjourn from time to time, and at any adjourned meeting any resolution of which notice has been given in accordance with the articles, either before or subsequent to the former meeting, may be passed, and the adjourned meeting shall have the same powers as an original meeting.

(9) In the event of any default in complying with the provisions of this section, every director of the company who is knowingly and wilfully guilty of the default or, in the case of default by the company, every officer of the company who is in default shall be liable to a fine not exceeding fifty thousand dollars.

(10) This section shall not apply to a private company.

Convening of extra-ordinary general meeting on requisition.

128.—(1) The directors of a company, notwithstanding anything in its articles, shall, on the requisition of members of the company holding, at the date of the deposit of the requisition, not less than one-tenth of such of the paid up capital of the company, as at the date of the deposit, which carries the right of voting at general meetings of the company, or, in the case of a company not having a share capital, members of the company representing not less than one-tenth of the total voting rights of all the members having at that date aright to vote at general meetings of the company, forthwith proceed duly to convene an extraordinary general meeting of the company.

(2) The requisition shall state the objects of the meeting, and shall be signed by the requisitionists and deposited at the registered office of the company, and may consist of several documents in like form, each signed by one or more requisitionists.

(3) If the directors do not within twenty-one days from the date of the deposit of the requisition proceed duly to convene a meeting, the requisitionists, or any of them representing more than one-half of the total voting rights of all of them, may themselves convene a meeting, but any meeting so convened shall not be held after the expiration of three months from that date.

(4) A meeting convened under this section by the requisitionists shall be convened in the same manner, as nearly as possible, as that in which meetings are to be convened by directors.

(5) Any reasonable expenses incurred by the requisitionists by reason of the failure of the directors duly to convene a meeting shall be repaid to the requisitionists by the company, and any sum so repaid shall be retained by the company out of any sums due or to become due from the company by way of fees or other remuneration in respect of their services to such of the directors as were in default.

(6) For the purposes of this section the directors shall, in the case of a meeting at which a resolution is to be proposed as a special resolution, be deemed not to have duly convened the meeting if they do not give such notice thereof as required by section 138.

Length of notice for calling meetings.

129.—(1) Any provision of a company's articles shall be void in so far as it provides for the calling of a meeting of the company (other than an adjourned meeting) by a shorter notice than—

(*a*) in the case of the annual general meeting, twenty-one days' notice in writing; and

(*b*) in the case of a meeting other than an annual general meeting or a meeting for the passing of a special resolution, fourteen days' notice in writing in the case of a company other than an unlimited company and seven days' notice in writing in the case of an unlimited company.

(2) Save in so far as the articles of a company make other provision in that behalf (not being a provision avoided by subsection (1)) a meeting of the company (other than an adjourned meeting) may be called—

(*a*) in the case of the annual general meeting by twenty-one days' notice in writing; and

(*b*) in the case of a meeting other than an annual general meeting or a meeting for the passing of a special resolution, by fourteen days' notice in writing in the case of a company other than an unlimited company and by seven days' notice in writing in the case of an unlimited company

(3) A meeting of a company shall, notwithstanding that it is called by shorter notice than that specified in subsection (2) or in the company's articles, as the case may be, be deemed to have been duly called if it is so agreed—

(*a*) in the case of a meeting called as the annual general meeting, by all the members entitled to attend and vote thereat; and

(*b*) in the case of any other meeting, by a majority in number of the members having a right to attend and vote at the meeting, being a majority, together holding not less than ninety-five *per centum* in value of the shares giving a right to attend and vote at the meeting, or, in the case of a company not having a share capital, together representing not less than ninety-five *per centum* of the total voting rights at that meeting of all the members.

130.—(1) The following provisions shall have effect in so far as the articles of the company do not make other provision in that behalf— General provisions as to meetings and votes.

(*a*) notice of the meeting of a company shall be served on every member of the company in the manner in which notices are required to be served by Table A and for the purpose of this paragraph the expression "Table A" means that Table as for the time being in force;

(*b*) two or more members holding not less than one-tenth of the issued share capital or, if the company has not a share capital, not less than five *per centum* in number of the members of the company may call a meeting;

(*c*) in the case of a private company two members, and in the case of any other company three members, personally present shall be a quorum;

(*d*) any member elected by the members present at a meeting may be chairman thereof;

(*e*) in the case of a company originally having a share capital, every member shall have one vote in respect of each share or each thousand dollars of stock held by him, and in any other case every member shall have one vote.

(2) If for any reason it is impracticable to call a meeting of a company in any manner in which meetings of that company may be called, or to conduct the meeting of the company in a manner prescribed in the company's articles, the Court may, either of its own motion or on the application of any director of the company or of any member of the company who would be entitled to vote at the meeting, order a meeting of the company to be called, held and conducted in such manner as the Court thinks fit, and where any such order is made may give such ancillary or consequential directions as it thinks expedient, and any meeting called, held and conducted in accordance with any such order shall for all purposes be deemed to be a meeting of the company duly called, held and conducted.

(3) It is hereby declared that the directions that may be given under subsection (2) include a direction that one member of the company present in person or by proxy shall be deemed to constitute a meeting.

(4) Where by any provision contained in this Act special notice is required of a resolution, the resolution shall not be effective unless notice of the intention to move it has been given to the company not less than twenty-eight days before the meeting at which it is moved, and the company shall give its members notice of any such resolution at the same time in the same manner as it gives notice of the meeting or, if that is not practicable, shall give them notice thereof, either by advertisement in a newspaper having an appropriate circulation or in any other mode allowed by the articles, not less than twenty-one days before the meeting.

Provided that if, after notice of the intention to move such a resolution has been given to the company, a meeting is called for a date twenty-eight days or less after the notice has been given, the notice, though not given within the time required by this subsection, shall be deemed to have been properly given for the purposes thereof.

131.—(1) Any member of a company entitled to attend and vote at a meeting of the company shall be entitled to appoint another person (whether a member or not) as his proxy to attend and vote instead of him, and a proxy appointed to attend and vote instead of a member (or, where more than one proxy has been so appointed, one of their number named by the member for the purpose) shall also have the same right as the member to speak at the meeting: Proxies.

Provided that, unless the articles otherwise provide—

(*a*) this subsection shall not apply in the case of a company not having a share capital; and

(*b*) a member shall not be entitled to appoint more than one proxy to attend on the same occasion; and

(*c*) a proxy shall not be entitled to vote except on a poll.

(2) In every notice calling a meeting of a company having a share capital there shall appear with reasonable prominence a statement that a member entitled to attend and vote is entitled to appoint a proxy to attend and vote instead of him, and that a proxy need not also be a member and if default is made in complying with this subsection as respects any meeting, every officer of the company who is in default shall be liable to a fine not exceeding fifty thousand dollars.

(3) Any provision contained in a company's articles shall be void in so far as it would have the effect of requiring the instrument appointing a proxy, or any other document necessary to show the validity or otherwise relating to the appointment of a

proxy, to be received by the company or any other person more than forty-eight hours before a meeting or adjourned meeting in order that the appointment may be effective thereat.

(4) Where any such instruments or documents appointing or relating to proxies as are mentioned in subsection (3) are received by or on behalf of a company, any person entitled, in his own right or as proxy for another member or members or partly in one way and partly in another to more than ten *per centum* of the total voting rights of all the members having a right to vote at the meeting or adjourned meeting affected, and also any person authorized in writing in that behalf by any person, or by any number of persons together, so entitled, shall have the right, at any time during business hours prior to the conclusion of the meeting but subject to such reasonable restrictions as the company may impose, to inspect such instruments or documents.

(5) If for the purpose of any meeting of a company invitations to appoint as proxy a person or one of a number of persons specified in the invitations are issued at the company's expense—

(*a*) to some only of the members entitled to be sent a notice of the meeting and to vote thereat by proxy; or

(*b*) without being accompanied by forms for the appointment of a proxy which entitle the members to direct the proxy to vote either for or against each resolution,

every officer of the company who knowingly and wilfully authorizes or permits their issue as aforesaid shall be liable to a fine not exceeding fifty thousand dollars:

Provided that an officer shall not be liable under this subsection by reason only of the issue to a member at his request in writing of a form of appointment naming the proxy or of a list of persons willing to act as proxy if the form or list is available on request in writing to every member entitled to vote at the meeting by proxy.

(6) This section shall apply to meetings of any class of members of a company as it applies to general meetings of the company.

132.—(1) Any provision contained in a company's articles shall be void in so far as it would have the effect either— Right to demand a poll.

(*a*) of excluding the right to demand a poll at a general meeting on any question other than the election of the chairman of the meeting or the adjournment of the meeting; or

(*b*) of making ineffective a demand for a poll on any such question which is made either—

(i) by not less than five members having the right to vote at the meeting; or

(ii) by a member or members representing not less than one-tenth of the total voting rights of all the members having the right to vote at the meeting; or

(iii) by a member or members holding shares in the company, being shares on which an aggregate sum has been paid up equal to not less than one-tenth of the total sum paid up on all the shares conferring that right; or

(iv) by a member holding shares in the company as a trustee of an approved employee share ownership plan as defined in section 2 of the Employees Share Ownership Plan Act, being shares conferring a right to vote at the meeting.

(2) The instrument appointing a proxy to vote at a meeting of a company shall be deemed also to confer authority to demand or join in demanding a poll, and for the purposes of subsection (1) a demand by a person as proxy for a member shall be the same as a demand by the member.

Voting on a poll.

133. On a poll taken at a meeting of a company or a meeting of any class of members of a company, a member entitled to more than one vote need not, if he votes, use all his votes or cast all the votes he uses in the same way.

Representation of companies at meetings of other companies and of creditors.

134.—(1) A corporation, whether a company within the meaning of this Act or not may—

(*a*) if it is a member of another corporation, being a company within the meaning of this Act, by resolution of its directors or other governing body authorize such person as it thinks fit to act as its representative at any meeting of the company or at any meeting of any class of members of the company.

(*b*) if it is a creditor (including a holder of debentures) of another corporation, being a company within the meaning of this Act, by resolution of its directors or other governing body, authorize such person as it thinks fit to act as its representative at any meeting of any creditors of the company held in pursuance of this Act or of any rules made thereunder, or in pursuance of the provisions contained in any debenture or trust deed, as the case may be.

(2) A person authorized as aforesaid shall be entitled to exercise the same powers on behalf of the corporation which he represents as that corporation could exercise if it were an individual shareholder, creditor, or holder of debentures, of that other company.

Circulation of members' resolutions.

135.—(1) A company shall at its own expense on the request in writing of any member entitled to attend and vote at an annual general meeting, include in the notice of that annual general meeting notice of any resolution consisting of not more than five hundred words which may properly be moved and is intended to be moved at that meeting:

Provided that if the proposed resolution is not passed at that meeting the same resolution or one substantially to the same effect shall not be moved at any annual general meeting within three years thereafter unless the directors shall otherwise agree or unless the request within three years is supported in writing by members of the company representing between them not less than one-twentieth of the total voting rights of all the members having at the date of the request a right to vote on the resolution to which the request relates.

(2) A company shall not be bound to give notice of any such resolution unless the written request or requests, signed by the member or members concerned, together with the resolution are deposited at the registered office of the company not less than six weeks before the meeting:

Provided that if, after any such resolution has been deposited, an annual general meeting is called for a date six weeks or less thereafter, the resolution shall be deemed to have been properly deposited.

Circulation of members' circulars.

136.—(1) A company shall, at the request in writing of any member entitled to attend and vote at an annual general meeting but (unless the company otherwise resolves or section 135 applies) at the expense of that member, circulate to members of the company a statement (whether in the form of a resolution or not) of not more than one thousand words with respect to any business to be dealt with at that meeting.

(2) Such a statement shall be circulated to members of the company in any manner permitted for service of notice of the annual general meeting, and, so far as practicable, at the same time as notice of the meeting, or, if that is impracticable, as soon as possible after the circulation of such notice.

(3) A company shall not be bound to circulate such a statement unless—

(*a*) the written request, signed by the member concerned, together with the statement, is deposited at the registered office of the company not less than ten days before the meeting; and

(*b*) there is also deposited with the request a sum reasonably sufficient to meet the company's expenses in giving effect thereto.

General provisions affecting sections 135 and 136.

137.—(1) A company shall not be bound under either section 135 or section 136 to circulate any resolution or statement if, on the application either of the company or of any other person who claims to be aggrieved, the Court is satisfied that the rights conferred by those sections are being abused to secure needless publicity for defamatory matter; and the Court may order the company's costs on an application under this section to be paid in whole or in part by the member making the request, notwithstanding that he is not a party to the application.

(2) In the event of any default in complying with section 135 or section 136, every officer of the company who is in default shall be liable to a fine not exceeding fifty thousand dollars.

Provisions as to extraordinary and special resolutions.

138.—(l) A resolution shall be an extraordinary resolution when it has been passed by a majority of not less than three-fourths of such members as, being entitled so to do, vote in person or, where proxies are allowed, by proxy, at a general meeting of which notice specifying the intention to propose the resolution as an extraordinary resolution has been duly given.

(2) A resolution shall be a special resolution when it has been passed by such a majority as is required for the passing of an extraordinary resolution and at a general meeting of which not less than twenty-one days' notice, specifying the intention to propose the resolution as a special resolution, has been duly given:

Provided that, if ninety-five *per centum* of the members entitled to attend and vote at any such meeting so agree, a resolution may be proposed and passed as a special resolution at a meeting of which less than twenty-one days' notice has been given.

(3) At any meeting at which an extraordinary resolution or a special resolution is submitted to be passed, a declaration of the chairman that the resolution is carried shall, unless a poll is demanded, be conclusive evidence of the fact without proof of the number or proportion of the votes recorded in favour of or against the resolution.

(4) At any meeting at which an extraordinary resolution or a special resolution is submitted to be passed a poll shall be taken to be effectively demanded, if demanded—

(*a*) by such number of members for the time being entitled under the articles to vote at the meeting as may be specified in the articles, so, however, that it shall not in any case be necessary for more than five members to make the demand; or

(*b*) if no provision is made by the articles with respect to the right to demand the poll, by three members so entitled or by one member or two members so entitled, if that member holds or those two members together hold not less than fifteen *per centum* of the paid up share capital of the company.

(5) When a poll is demanded in accordance with this section, in computing the majority on the poll reference shall be had to the number of votes to which each member is entitled by virtue of this Act or of the articles of the company.

(6) For the purposes of this section, notice of a meeting shall be deemed to be duly given and the meeting to be duly held when the notice is given and the meeting held in manner provided by this Act or articles.

Registration and copies of certain resolutions and agreements.

139.—(1) A copy of every resolution or agreement to which this section applies shall, within fifteen days after the passing or making thereof, be forwarded to the Registrar and recorded by him.

(2) Where articles have been registered, a copy of every such resolution or agreement for the time being in force shall be embodied in or annexed to every copy of the articles issued after the passing of the resolution or the making of the agreement.

(3) Where articles have not been registered, a copy of every such resolution or agreement shall be forwarded to any member at his request, on payment of fifty dollars or such less sum as the company may direct.

(4) This section shall apply to—

(*a*) special resolutions;

(*b*) extraordinary resolutions;

(*c*) resolutions which have been agreed to by all the members of a company, but which, if not so agreed to, would not have been effective for their purpose unless, as the case may be, they had been passed as special resolutions or as extraordinary resolutions;

(*d*) resolutions or agreements which have been agreed to by all the members of some class of shareholders, but which, if not so agreed to, would not have been effective for their purpose unless they had been passed by some particular majority or otherwise in some particular manner, and all resolutions or agreements which effectively bind all the members of any class of shareholders though not agreed to by all those members;

(*e*) resolutions requiring a company to be wound up voluntarily, passed under paragraph (a) of subsection (1) of section 272.

(5) If a company fails to comply with subsection (1) the company and every officer of the company who is in default shall be liable to a default fine of fifty thousand dollars.

(6) If a company fails to comply with subsection (2) or subsection (3) the company and every officer of the company who is in default shall be liable to a fine not exceeding one thousand dollars for each copy in respect of which default is made.

(7) For the purposes of subsections (5) and (6) a liquidator of the company shall be deemed to be an officer of the company.

Resolutions passed at adjourned meetings.

140. Where after the appointed day a resolution is passed at an adjourned meeting of—

(*a*) a company;

(*b*) the holders of any class of shares in a company;

(*c*) the directors of a company,

the resolution shall for all purposes be treated as having been passed on the date on which it was in fact passed, and shall not be deemed to have been passed on any earlier date.

Participation by electronic means.

141.—(1) Unless the articles of a company otherwise provides, a director may if all the directors of the company consent, participate in a meeting of directors of the company or of a committee of the directors by means of such telephone or other communicating facilities as permit all persons participating in the meeting to hear each other.

(2) A director who participates in a meeting of directors by such means as are described in subsection (1), is, for the purposes of this Act, present at the meeting, and unless the articles so provide, shall count to constitute a quorum.

(3) For the purposes of this section, the laws of Jamaica shall apply to any meeting of directors of a company incorporated in Jamaica and the meeting is deemed to take place in Jamaica.

Minutes of proceedings of meetings of company and of directors and managers.

142.—(1) Every company shall cause minutes of all proceedings of general meetings, all proceedings at meetings of its directors and, where there are managers, all proceedings at meetings of its managers, to be entered in books kept for the purpose.

(2) Any such minute if purporting to be signed by the chairman of the meeting at which the proceedings were had, or by the chairman of the next succeeding meeting, shall be evidence of the proceedings.

(3) Where minutes have been made in accordance with the provisions of this section of the proceedings at any general meeting of the company or meeting of directors or managers, then, until the contrary is proved, the meeting shall be deemed to have been duly held and convened, and all proceedings had thereat to have been duly had, and all appointments of directors, managers, or liquidators, shall be deemed to be valid.

(4) If a company fails to compiy with subsection (1), the company and every officer of the company who is in default shall be liable to a fine not exceeding fifty thousand dollars.

Inspection of minute books.

143.—(1) The books containing the minutes of proceedings of any general meeting of a company held after the appointed day shall be kept at the registered office of the company, and shall during business hours (subject to such reasonable restrictions as the company may by its articles or in general meeting impose, so that not less than two hours in each day be allowed for inspection) be open to the inspection of any member without charge.

(2) Any member shall be entitled to be furnished within seven days after he has made a request in that behalf to the company with a copy of any such minutes as aforesaid at a charge not exceeding fifty dollars for every hundred words.

(3) If any inspection required under this section is refused or if any copy required under this section is not sent within the proper time, the company and every officer of the

company who is in default shall be liable in respect of each offence to a fine not exceeding two thousand dollars and further to a default fine of fifty thousand dollars.

(4) In the case of any such refusal or default, the Court may by order compel an immediate inspection of the books in respect of all proceedings of general meetings or direct that the copies required shall be sent to the persons requiring them.

Accounts and Audit

144.—(1) Every company shall cause to be kept proper books and documents of account with respect to— Books and documents of account.

(*a*) all sums of money received and expended by the company and the matters in respect of which the receipt and expenditure takes place;

(*b*) all sales and purchases of goods by the company;

(*c*) the assets and liabilities of the company.

(2) For the purposes of subsection (1), proper books and documents of account shall not be deemed to be kept with respect to the matters aforesaid if there are not kept such books and documents as are necessary to give a true and fair view of the state of the company's affairs and to explain its transactions.

(3) Subject to the provisions of subsection (4) relating to books and documents of account kept outside the Island, books and documents of account shall be kept at the registered office of the company or at such other place as the directors think fit, and shall at all times be open to inspection by the directors.

(4) If books and documents of account are kept at a place outside the Island there shall be sent to, and kept at a place in the Island and be at all times open to inspection by the directors such accounts and returns with respect to the business dealt with in the books and documents of account so kept as will disclose with reasonable accuracy the financial position of that business at intervals not exceeding six months and will enable to be prepared in accordance with this Act the company's balance

sheet, its profit and loss account or income and expenditure account, and any document annexed to any of those documents giving information which is required by this Act and is thereby allowed to be so given:

Provided that the Minister, if, having regard to the nature and volume of the business done in the Island by any company, he is satisfied that it is just to do so, may by order grant, subject to such conditions as may be specified in the order, exemption from any of the obligations imposed by this subsection.

(5) If any person being a director of a company fails to take all reasonable steps to secure compliance by the company with the requirements of this section, or has by his own wilful act been the cause of any default by the company thereunder, he shall, in respect of each offence, be liable on summary conviction before a Resident Magistrate to imprisonment with or without hard labour for a term not exceeding six months or to a fine not exceeding fifty thousand dollars:

Provided that—

(*a*) in any proceedings against a person in respect of an offence under this section consisting of a failure to take reasonable steps to secure compliance by the company with the requirements of this section, it shall be a defence to prove that he had reasonable ground to believe and did believe that a competent and reliable person was charged with the duty of seeing that those requirements were complied with and was in a position to discharge that duty; and

(*b*) a person shall not be sentenced to imprisonment for such an offence unless, in the opinion of the Court dealing with the case, the offence was committed wilfully.

145.—(1) The directors of every company shall, at some date not later than eighteen months after the incorporation of the company and subsequently at least once in every calendar year, lay before the company in general meeting a profit and loss account or, in the case of a company not trading for profit, an income and expenditure account for the period, in the case of the first account, since the incorporation of the company, and, in any other case, since the preceding account, made up to a date not earlier than the date of the meeting by more than nine months, or, in the case of a company carrying on business or having interests abroad by more than twelve months: Profit and loss account and balance sheet.

Provided that the Minister, if for any special reason he thinks fit so to do, may, in the case of any company, extend the period of eighteen months aforesaid, and in the case of any company and with respect to any year extend the periods of nine and twelve months aforesaid.

(2) The directors shall cause to be made out in every calendar year, and to be laid before the company in general meeting, a balance sheet as at the date to which the profit and loss account, or the income and expenditure account, as the case may be, is made up and there shall be attached to every such balance sheet a report by the directors with respect to the state of the company's affairs, the amount, if any, which they recommend should be paid by way of dividend, and the amount, if any, which they propose to carry to the reserve fund, general reserve or reserve account shown specifically on the balance sheet, or to a reserve fund, general reserve or reserve account to be shown specifically on a subsequent balance sheet.

(3) If any person being a director of a company fails to take all reasonable steps to comply with the provisions of this section, he shall, in respect of each offence, be liable on summary conviction before a Resident Magistrate to imprisonment with or without hard labour for a term not exceeding six months or to a fine not exceeding fifty thousand dollars:

Provided that—

(*a*) in any proceedings against a person in respect of an offence under this section, it shall be a defence to prove that he had reasonable ground to believe and did believe that a competent and reliable person was charged with the duty of seeing that the provisions of this section were complied with and was in a position to discharge that duty; and

(*b*) a person shall not be sentenced to imprisonment for such an offence unless, in the opinion of the Court dealing with the case, the offence was committed wilfully.

General provisions as to content and form of accounts. Seventh Schedule.

146.—(1) Subject to the provisions of the Seventh Schedule, the accounts of a company shall give a true and fair view of the state of affairs of the company as at the end of its financial year.

(2) The accounts of a company shall comply with the requirements of the Seventh Schedule, so far as applicable thereto.

(3) Save as expressly provided in the following provisions of this section or in the Seventh Schedule the requirements of section 145 and the Seventh Schedule shall be without prejudice either to the general requirements of subsection (1) or to any other requirements of this Act.

(4) The Minister may, on the application or with the consent of a company's directors, modify in relation to that company any of the requirements of this Act as to the matters to be stated in a company's balance sheet or profit and loss account (except the requirements of subsection (1)) for the purpose of adapting them to the circumstances of the company.

(5) Subsections (1) and (2) shall not apply to a company's profit and loss account if—

(*a*) the company has subsidiaries; and

(*b*) the profit and loss account is framed as a consolidated profit and loss account dealing with all or any of the company's subsidiaries as well as the company and—

(i) complies with the requirements of this Act relating to consolidated profit and loss accounts; and

(ii) shows how much of the consolidated profit or loss for the financial year is dealt with in the accounts of the company.

(6) If any person being a director of a company fails to take all reasonable steps to secure compliance as respects any accounts laid before the company in general meeting with the provisions of this section and with the other requirements of this Act as to the matters to be stated in accounts, he shall, in respect of each offence, be liable on summary conviction before a Resident Magistrate to imprisonment with or without hard labour for a term not exceeding six months or to a fine not exceeding fifty thousand dollars:

Provided that—

(*a*) in any proceedings against a person in respect of an offence under this section, it shall be a defence to prove that he had reasonable ground to believe and did believe that a competent and reliable person was charged with the duty of seeing that those provisions or those other requirements, as the case may be, were complied with and was in a position to discharge that duty; and

(*b*) a person shall not be sentenced to imprisonment for any such offence unless, in the opinion of the Court dealing with the case, the offence was committed wilfully.

(7) For the purposes of this section and the following provisions of this Act, except where the context otherwise requires—

(*a*) any reference to a balance sheet or profit and loss account shall include any notes thereon or document annexed thereto giving information which is required by this Act and is thereby allowed to be so given; and

(*b*) any reference to a profit and loss account shall be taken, in the case of a company not trading for profit, as referring to its income and expenditure account, and references to profit or to loss and, if the company has subsidiaries, references to a consolidated profit and loss account shall be construed accordingly.

Obligation to lay group accounts before holding company.

147.—(1) Where at the end of its financial year a company has subsidiaries, accounts or statements (in this Act referred to as "group accounts") dealing as hereinafter mentioned with the state of affairs and profit or loss of the company and the subsidiaries shall, subject to subsection (2), be laid before the company in general meeting when the company's own balance sheet and profit and loss account are so laid.

(2) Notwithstanding anything in subsection (1)—

(*a*) group accounts shall not be required where the company is at the end of its financial year the wholly owned subsidiary of another body corporate incorporated in the Island; and

(*b*) group accounts need not deal with a subsidiary of the company if the company's directors are of opinion that—

(i) it is impracticable, or would be of no real value to members of the company, in view of the insignificant amounts involved, or would involve expense or delay out of proportion to the value to members of the company; or

(ii) the result would be misleading, or harmful to the business of the company or any of its subsidiaries; or

(iii) the business of the holding company and that of the subsidiary are so different that they cannot reasonably be treated as a single undertaking,

and, if the directors are of such an opinion about each of the company's subsidiaries, group accounts shall not be required:

Provided that the approval of the Minister shall be required for not dealing in group accounts with a subsidiary on the ground that the result would be harmful or on the ground of the difference between the business of the holding company and that of the subsidiary.

(3) If any person being a director of a company fails to take all reasonable steps to secure compliance as respects the company with the provisions of this section, he shall, in respect of each offence, be liable on summary conviction before a Resident Magistrate to imprisonment with or without hard labour for a term not exceeding six months or to a fine not exceeding fifty thousand dollars:

Provided that—

(*a*) in any proceedings against a person in respect of an offence under this section, it shall be a defence to prove that he had reasonable ground to believe and did believe that a competent and reliable person was charged with the duty of seeing that the requirements of this section were complied with and was in a position to discharge that duty; and

(*b*) a person shall not be sentenced to imprisonment for an offence under this section unless, in the opinion of the Court dealing with the case, the offence was committed wilfully.

(4) For the purposes of this section a body corporate shall be deemed to be the wholly owned subsidiary of another if it has no members except that other and that other's wholly owned subsidiaries and its or their nominees.

Form of group accounts.

148.—(1) Subject to subsection (2), the group accounts laid before a holding company shall be consolidated accounts comprising—

(*a*) a consolidated balance sheet dealing with the state of affairs of the company and all the subsidiaries to be dealt with in group accounts;

(*b*) a consolidated profit and loss account dealing with the profit or loss of the company and those subsidiaries.

(2) If the company's directors are of opinion that it is better for the purpose—

(*a*) of presenting the same or equivalent information about the state of affairs and profit or loss of the company and those subsidiaries; and

(*b*) of so presenting it that it may be readily appreciated by the company's members,

the group accounts may be prepared in a form other than that required by subsection (1), and in particular may consist of more than one set of consolidated accounts dealing respectively with the company and one group of subsidiaries and with other groups of subsidiaries or of separate accounts dealing with each of the subsidiaries, or of statements expanding the information about the subsidiaries in the company's own accounts, or any combination of those forms.

(3) The group accounts may be wholly or partly incorporated in the company's own balance sheet and profit and loss account.

Contents of group accounts.

149.—(1) The group accounts laid before a company shall give a true and fair view of the state of affairs and profit or loss of the company and the subsidiaries dealt with thereby as a whole, so far as concerns members of the company.

(2) Where the financial year of a subsidiary does not coincide with that of the holding company, the group accounts shall, unless the Minister on the application or with the consent of the holding company's directors otherwise directs, deal with the subsidiary's state of affairs as at the end of its financial year ending with or last before that of the holding company, and with the subsidiary's profit or loss for that financial year.

Seventh Schedule.

(3) Without prejudice to subsection (1), the group accounts, if prepared as consolidated accounts, shall comply with the requirements of the Seventh Schedule so far as applicable thereto, and if not so prepared shall give the same or equivalent information:

Provided that the Minister may, on the application or with the consent of a company's directors, modify those requirements in relation to that company for the purpose of adapting them to the circumstances of the company.

Financial year of holding company and subsidiary.

150.—(1) A holding company's directors shall secure that except where in their opinion there are good reasons against it, the financial year of each of its subsidiaries shall coincide with the company's own financial year.

(2) Where it appears to the Minister desirable for a holding company or a holding company's subsidiary to extend its financial year so that the subsidiary's financial year may end with that of the holding company, and for that purpose to postpone the submission of the relevant accounts to a general meeting from one calendar year to the next, the Minister may on the application or with the consent of the directors of the company whose financial year is to be extended direct that, in the case of that company, the submission of accounts to a

general meeting, the holding of an annual general meeting or the making of an annual return shall not be required in the earlier of those calendar years.

Meaning of "holding company" and "subsidiary"

151.—(1) For the purposes of this Act, a company shall, subject to the provisions of subsection (3), be deemed to be a subsidiary of another if, but only if—

(*a*) that other either—

(i) is a member of it and controls the composition of its board of directors; or

(ii) holds more than half in value of its equity share capital; or

(*b*) the first-mentioned company is a subsidiary of any company which is that other's subsidiary.

(2) For the purposes of subsection (1), the composition of a company's board of directors shall be deemed to be controlled by another company, if, but only if, that other company by the exercise of some power exercisable by it without the consent or concurrence of any other person can appoint or remove the holders of all or a majority of the directorships; but for the purposes of this provision that other company shall be deemed to have power to appoint to a directorship with respect to which any of the following conditions is satisfied, that is to say—

(*a*) that a person cannot be appointed thereto without the exercise in his favour by that other company of such a power as aforesaid; or

(*b*) that a person's appointment thereto follows necessarily from his appointment as director of that other company; or

(*c*) that the directorship is held by that other company itself or by a subsidiary of it.

(3) In determining whether one company is a subsidiary of another—

(*a*) any shares held or power exercisable by that other in a fiduciary capacity shall be treated as not held or exercisable by it;

(*b*) subject to paragraphs (*c*) and (*d*) any shares held or power exercisable—

(i) by any person as a nominee for that other (except where that other is concerned only in a fiduciary capacity); or

(ii) by, or by a nominee for, a subsidiary of that other, not being a subsidiary which is concerned only in a fiduciary capacity, shall be treated as held or exercisable by that other;

(*c*) any shares held or power exercisable by any person by virtue of the provisions of any debentures of the first-mentioned company or of a trust deed for securing any issue of such debentures shall be disregarded;

(*d*) any shares or power exercisable by, or by a nominee for, that other or its subsidiary (not being held or exercisable as mentioned in paragraph (*c*)) shall be treated as not held or exercisable by that other if the ordinary business of that other or its subsidiary, as the case may be, includes the lending of money and the shares are held or power is exercisable as aforesaid by way of security only for the purposes of a transaction entered into in the ordinary course of that business.

(4) For the purpose of this Act, a company shall be deemed to be another's holding company if, but only if, that other is its subsidiary.

(5) In this section the expression "company" includes any body corporate, and the expression "equity share capital" means, in relation to a company, its issued share capital excluding any part thereof which, neither as respects dividends nor as respects capital, carries any rights to participate beyond a specified amount in a distribution.

Requirements relating to balance sheets.

152.—(1) Every balance sheet of a company shall be signed on behalf of the board by two of the directors of the company or, if there is only one director, by that director.

(2) In the case of a banking company the balance sheet shall be signed by the secretary and where there are more than three directors of the company by at least three of those directors, and where there are not more than three directors by all directors.

(3) The profit and loss account and, so far as not incorporated in the balance sheet or profit and loss account, any group accounts laid before the company in general meeting, shall be annexed to the balance sheet, and the auditors' report shall be attached thereto.

(4) Any accounts annexed pursuant to subsection (3) shall be approved by the board of directors before the balance sheet is signed on their behalf.

(5) If any copy of a balance sheet which has not been signed as required by this section is issued, circulated or published, or if any copy of a balance sheet is issued, circulated or published without having annexed thereto a copy of the profit and loss account or any group accounts required by this section to be so annexed, or without having attached thereto a copy of the auditors' report, the company, and every officer of the company who is in default shall be liable to a fine not exceeding one hundred thousand dollars.

153.—(1) In the case of every company, a copy of every balance sheet, including every document required by law to be annexed thereto which is to be laid before the company in general meeting, together with a copy of the auditors' report, shall, not less than twenty-one days before the date of the meeting, be sent to every member of the company (whether or not he is entitled to receive notice of general meetings of the company), every holder of debentures of the company (whether or not he is so entitled) and all persons other than members or holders of debentures of the company, being persons so entitled.

Right to receive copies of balance sheets and auditor's report.

(2) In the case of a company not being a private company any member of the company, and any holder of debentures of the company, shall be entitled to be furnished on demand without charge with a copy of the last balance sheet of the company, including every document required by law to be annexed thereto, together with a copy of the auditors' report on the balance sheet.

(3) If default is made in complying with subsection (1), the company and every officer of the company who is in default, shall be liable to a fine not exceeding one hundred thousand dollars, and if, where any person makes a demand for a document with which he is by virtue of subsection (2) entitled to be furnished, default is made in complying with the demand within ten days after the making thereof, the company and every officer of the company who is knowingly a party to the default shall be liable to a fine not exceeding two thousand dollars for every day during which the default continues, unless it is proved that that person has already made a demand for and been furnished with a copy of the document.

(4) In the case of a private company, any member of the company and any holder of debentures thereof shall be entitled to be furnished, within ten days after he has made a request in that behalf to the company, with a copy of the balance sheet and auditors' report at a charge not exceeding two hundred dollars or such amount as may be prescribed by regulations made by the Minister.

(5) If default is made in furnishing such a copy to any member of the company or, as the case may be, any holder of debentures thereof who demands it and tenders to the company the amount of the proper charge therefor, the company and every officer of the company who is in default shall be liable to a fine not exceeding fifty thousand dollars.

Appointment and remuneration of auditors.

154.—(1) Every company shall at each annual general meeting appoint an auditor or auditors to hold office from the conclusion of that, until the conclusion of the next, annual general meeting.

(2) At any annual general meeting a retiring auditor, however appointed, shall be reappointed without any resolution being passed unless—

(*a*) he is not qualified for reappointment; or

(*b*) a resolution has been passed at that meeting appointing somebody instead of him or providing expressly that he shall not be reappointed; or

(*c*) he has given the company notice in writing of his unwillingness to be reappointed:

Provided that where notice is given of an intended resolution to appoint some person or persons in place of a retiring auditor, and by reason of the death, incapacity or disqualification of that person or of all those persons, as the case may be, the resolution cannot be proceeded with, the retiring auditor shall not be automatically reappointed by virtue of this subsection.

(3) Where at an annual general meeting no auditors are appointed or reappointed, the Minister may appoint a person to fill the vacancy.

(4) The company shall, within seven days of the Minister's power under subsection (3) becoming exercisable, give him notice of that fact, and if a company fails to give notice as required by this subsection the company and every officer of the company who is in default shall be liable to a fine not exceeding fifty thousand dollars.

(5) Special notice shall be required for a resolution at a company's annual general meeting appointing as auditor a person other than a retiring auditor or providing expressly that a retiring auditor shall not be reappointed.

(6) On receipt of notice of such an intended resolution as aforesaid, the company shall forthwith send a copy thereof to the retiring auditor (if any).

(7) Where notice is given of such an intended resolution as aforesaid and the retiring auditor makes with respect to the intended resolution representations in writing to the company (not exceeding a reasonable length) and requests their notification to members of the company, the company shall, unless the representations are received by it too late for it to do so—

(*a*) in any notice of the resolution given to the members of the company, state the fact of the representations having been made; and

(*b*) send a copy of the representations to every member of the company to whom notice of the meeting is sent (whether before or after receipt of the representations by the company),

and if a copy of the representations is not sent as aforesaid because received too late or because of the company's default, the auditor may (without prejudice to his right to be heard orally) require that the representations shall be read out at the meeting;

Provided that copies of the representations need not be sent out and the representations need not be read out at the meeting if, on the application either of the company or of any other person who claims to be aggrieved, the Court is satisfied that the rights conferred by this section are being abused to secure needless publicity for defamatory matter; and the Court may order the company's costs on an application under this section to be paid in whole or in part by the auditor, notwithstanding that he is not a party to the application.

(8) Subsection (7) shall apply to a resolution to remove the first auditors by virtue of subsection (9) as it applies in relation to a resolution that a retiring auditor shall not be reappointed.

(9) Subject as hereinafter provided, the first auditors of a company may be appointed by the directors at any time before the first annual general meeting, and the auditors so appointed shall hold office until the conclusion of that meeting:

Provided that—

(*a*) the company may at a general meeting of which notice has been served on the auditors in the same manner as on members of the company remove any such auditors and appoint in their place any other persons being persons who have been nominated for appointment by any member of the company and of whose nomination notice has been given to the members of the company not less than seven days before the date of the meeting; and

(*b*) if the directors fail to exercise their powers under this subsection, the company in general meeting may appoint the first auditors, and thereupon those powers of the directors shall cease.

(10) The directors may fill any casual vacancy in the office of auditor, but while any such vacancy continues the surviving or continuing auditor or auditors, if any, may act.

(11) The remuneration of the auditors of a company shall be fixed by the company in general meeting or in such manner as the company in general meeting may determine, except that the remuneration of an auditor appointed before the first annual general meeting, or of an auditor appointed to fill a casual vacancy, may be fixed by the directors, and that the remuneration of an auditor appointed by the Minister may be fixed by the Minister.

(12) For the purposes of this subsection, any sums paid or to be paid by the company in respect of the auditors' expenses shall be deemed to be included in the expression "remuneration".

155. A person shall not be qualified for appointment as auditor of a company which is not a private company or of a private company which is obliged to file accounts unless he is a registered public accountant as defined in section 2 of the Public Accountancy Act.

Qualification for appointment as auditor.

156. None of the following persons shall be qualified for appointment as auditor of a company—

Disqualification for appointment as auditor.

(*a*) an officer or servant of the company;

(*b*) a person who is a partner of or in the employment of an officer or servant of the company;

(*c*) a body corporate.

157.—(1) The auditors shall make a report to the members on the accounts examined by them, and on every balance sheet, every profit and loss account and all group accounts laid before the company in general meeting during their tenure of office, and the report shall contain statements as to the matters mentioned in the Seventh and Eighth Schedules.

Auditor's report and right of access to books and to attend and be heard at general meetings. Seventh and Eighth Schedules.

(2) The auditors' report shall be read before the company in general meeting and shall be open to inspection by any member.

(3) Every auditor of a company shall have aright of access at all times to the books and accounts and vouchers of the company, and shall be entitled to require from the officers of the company such information and explanation as he thinks necessary for the performance of the duties of the auditors.

(4) The auditors of a company shall be entitled to attend any general meeting of the company and to receive all notices of and other communications relating to any general meeting which any member of the company is entitled to receive and to be heard at any general meeting which they attend on any part of the business of the meeting which concerns them as auditors.

(5) If any person makes default in complying with any of the requirements of this section, he shall be liable to a fine not exceeding one hundred thousand dollars.

Dividends.

158.—(1) Subject to this section, a company may, in general meeting, declare dividends in respect of any year or other period.

(2) Where, pursuant to the articles of a company, the recommendation of the directors of a company with respect to the declaration of a dividend is rejected or varied by the company in general meeting, a statement to that effect shall be included in the relevant directors' annual report.

(3) No dividend shall be payable to the shareholders of a company except out of profits.

(4) A company shall not declare or pay a dividend if there are reasonable grounds for believing that—

(*a*) the company is, or would be after the payment, unable to pay its liabilities as they become due; or

(*b*) the realizable value of the company's assets would thereby be less than the aggregate of its liabilities and stated capital.

159.—(1) A company, which meets the criteria specified in paragraph 7 of Part II of the Seventh Schedule in a given financial year and in respect of which a resolution is passed in accordance with subsection (2) and is not— Exemption from the provisions of audited reports Seventh Schedule.

(*a*) a public company;

(*b*) a private company whose articles provide otherwise;

(*c*) a company licensed under the Banking Act;

(*d*) an insurance company registered under the Insurance Act;

(*e*) a company licensed under the Securities Act;

(*f*) a company licensed under the Financial Institutions Act;

(*g*) a society registered under the Building Societies Act or the Cooperative Societies Act;

(*h*) a subsidiary of a company, falling within any of the categories in paragraphs (*a*) to (*g*),

shall be exempt from providing audited financial statements and an auditor's report as required under this Act with respect to that financial year.

(2) A resolution referred to in subsection (1) shall be a resolution passed unanimously at a general meeting of the company in relation to the financial year referred to in that subsection.

Inspection

160.—(1) The Minister may appoint one or more competent inspectors to investigate the affairs of a company and to report thereon in such manner as he may direct— Investigation of company's affairs on application of members.

(*a*) in the case of a company having a share capital, on the application either of not less than two hundred members or of members holding not less than one-tenth of the shares issued;

(*b*) in the case of a company not having a share capital, on the application of not less than one-fifth in number of the persons on the company's register of members.

(2) The application shall be supported by such evidence as the Minister may require for the purpose of showing that the applicants have good reason for requiring the investigation, and the Minister may, before appointing an inspector, require the applicants to give security, to an amount not exceeding two hundred thousand dollars, for payment of the costs of the investigation.

Investigation of company's affairs in other cases

161. Without prejudice to his powers under section 164 the Minister—

(*a*) shall appoint one or more competent inspectors to investigate the affairs of a company and to report thereon in such manner as he may direct, if—

(i) the company by special resolution; or

(ii) the Court by order,

declares that its affairs ought to be investigated by an inspector appointed by the Minister; and

(*b*) may do so if it appears to the Minister that there are circumstances suggesting—

(i) that its business is being conducted with intent to defraud its creditors or the creditors of any other person or otherwise for a fraudulent or unlawful purpose or in a manner oppressive of any part of its members or that it was formed for any fraudulent or unlawful purpose; or

(ii) that persons concerned with its formation or the management of its affairs have in connection therewith been guilty of fraud, misfeasance or other misconduct towards it or towards its members; or

(iii) that its members have not been given all the information with respect to its affairs which they might reasonably expect.

162. If an inspector appointed under either section 160 or section 161 to investigate the affairs of a company thinks it necessary for the purposes of his investigation to investigate also the affairs of any other body corporate which is or has at any relevant time been the company's subsidiary or holding company or a subsidiary of its holding company or a holding company of its subsidiary, he shall have power so to do, and shall report on the affairs of the other body corporate so far as he thinks the results of his investigation thereof are relevant to the investigation of the affairs of the first-mentioned company. Power of inspectors to carry investigation into affairs of related companies.

163.—(1) It shall be the duty of all officers and agents of the company and of all officers and agents of any other body corporate whose affairs are investigated by virtue of section 162 to produce to the inspectors all books and documents of or relating to the company or, as the case may be, the other body corporate which are in their custody or power and otherwise to give to the inspectors all assistance in connection with the investigation which they are reasonably able to give. Production of documents, and evidence on investigation.

(2) An inspector may examine on oath the officers and agents of the company or other body corporate in relation to its business, and may administer an oath accordingly.

(3) If any officer or agent of the company or other body corporate refuses to produce to the inspectors any book or document which it is his duty under this section so to produce, or refuses to answer any question which is put to him by the inspectors with respect to the affairs of the company or other body corporate, as the case may be, the inspectors may certify the refusal under their hand to the Court, and the Court may thereupon inquire into the case, and after hearing any witnesses who may be produced against or on behalf of the alleged

offender and after hearing any statement which may be offered in defence, punish the offender in like manner as if he had been guilty of contempt of the Court.

(4) If an inspector thinks it necessary for the purpose of his investigation that a person whom he has no power to examine on oath should be so examined, he may apply to the Court and the Court may if it sees fit order that person to attend and be examined on oath before it on any matter relevant to the investigation, and on any such examination—

(*a*) the inspector may take part therein either personally or by an attorney-at-law;

(*b*) the Court may put such questions to the person examined as the Court thinks fit;

(*c*) the person examined shall answer all such questions as the Court may put or allow to be put to him, but may at his own cost employ an attorney-at-law who shall be at liberty to put to him such questions as the attorney-at-law may deem just for the purpose of enabling him to explain or qualify any answers given by him,

and notes of the examination shall be taken down in writing, and shall be read over to or by, and signed by, the person examined, and may thereafter be used in evidence against him:

Provided that, notwithstanding anything in paragraph (c) of this subsection, the Court may allow the person examined such costs as in its discretion it may think fit, and any costs so allowed shall be paid as part of the expenses of the investigation.

(5) In this section, any reference to officers or to agents shall include past, as well as present, officers or agents, as the case maybe, and for the purposes of this section the expression "agents", in relation to a company or other body corporate shall include the bankers and attorneys of the company or other body corporate and any persons employed by the company or other body corporate as auditors, whether or not those persons are officers of the company or other body corporate.

Inspectors' report.

164.—(1) The inspectors may, and, if so directed by the Minister, shall, make interim reports to the Minister, and on the conclusion of the investigation shall make a final report to the Minister.

(2) Any such report shall be written or printed, as the Minister may direct.

(3) The Minister shall—

(*a*) forward a copy of any report made by the inspectors to the registered office of the company;

(*b*) if the Minister thinks fit, furnish a copy thereof on request and on payment of the prescribed fee to any other person who is a member of the company or of any other body corporate dealt with in the report by virtue of section 162 or whose interests as a creditor of the company or of any such other body corporate as aforesaid appear to the Minister to be affected;

(*c*) where the inspectors are appointed under section 160, furnish, at the request of the applicants for the investigation, a copy to them; and

(*d*) where the inspectors are appointed under section 161 in pursuance of an order of the Court, furnish a copy to the Court,

and may also cause the report to be printed and published.

Proceedings on inspector's report

165.—(1) If from any report made under section 164 it appears to the Minister that any person has, in relation to the company or to any other body corporate whose affairs have been investigated by virtue of section 162 been guilty of any offence for which he is criminally liable, the Minister shall, if it appears to him that the case is one in which the prosecution ought to be undertaken by the Director of Public Prosecutions refer the matter to him.

(2) If, where any matter is referred to the Director of Public Prosecutions under this section, he considers that the case is one in which a prosecution ought to be instituted, he shall institute proceedings accordingly, and it shall be the duty of all officers and agents of the company or other body corporate as aforesaid, as the case may be (other than the defendant in the proceedings), to give him all assistance in connection with the prosecution which they are reasonably able to give.

(3) Subsection (5) of section 163 shall apply for the purposes of this subsection as it applies for the purposes of that section.

(4) If, in the case of any body corporate liable to be wound up under this Act, it appears to the Minister from any such report as aforesaid that it is expedient so to do by reason of any such circumstances as are referred to in sub-paragraph (i) or (ii) of paragraph (*b*) of section 161, the Minister may, unless the body corporate is already being wound up by the Court, present a petition for it to be so wound up if the Court thinks it just and equitable that it should be wound up or a petition for an order under section 213 or both.

(5) If from any such report as aforesaid it appears to the Minister that proceedings ought in the public interest to be brought by any body corporate dealt with by the report for the recovery of damages in respect of any fraud, misfeasance or other misconduct in connection with the promotion or formation of that body corporate or the management of its affairs, or for the recovery of any property of the body corporate which has been misapplied or wrongfully retained, the Minister may himself bring proceedings for that purpose in the name of the body corporate.

(6) The Minister shall indemnify the body corporate against any costs or expenses incurred by it or in connection with any proceedings brought by virtue of subsection (5).

166.—(1) The expenses of and incidental to an investigation by an inspector appointed by the Minister under the foregoing provisions of this Act shall be defrayed in the first instance by the Minister, but the following persons shall, to the extent mentioned, be liable to repay the Minister— Expenses of investigation of company's affairs.

(*a*) any person who is convicted on a prosecution instituted as a result of the investigation by the Director of Public Prosecutions, or who is ordered to pay damages or restore any property in proceedings brought by virtue of subsection (5) of section 165, may in the same proceedings be ordered to pay the expenses to such extent as may be specified in the order;

(*b*) any body corporate in whose name proceedings are brought as aforesaid shall be liable to the amount or value of any sums or property recovered by it as a result of those proceedings; and

(*c*) unless as a result of the investigation a prosecution is instituted by the Director of Public Prosecutions—

(i) any body corporate dealt with by the report, where the inspector was appointed otherwise than of the Minister's own motion, shall be liable, except so far as the Minister otherwise directs; and

(ii) the applicants for the investigation, where the inspector was appointed under section 161, shall be liable to such extent (if any) as the Minister may direct, and any amount for which a body corporate is liable by virtue of paragraph (*b*) of this subsection shall be a first charge on the sums or property mentioned in that paragraph.

(2) The report of an inspector appointed otherwise than of the Minister's own motion may, if the inspector thinks fit, and

shall, if the Minister so directs, include a recommendation as to the directions (if any) which the inspector thinks appropriate, in the light of his investigation, to be given under paragraph (*c*) of subsection (1).

(3) For the purposes of this section, any costs or expenses incurred by the Minister in or in connection with proceedings brought by virtue of subsection (5) of section 165 (including expenses incurred by virtue of subsection (6) thereof) shall be treated as expenses of the investigation giving rise to the proceedings.

(4) Any liability to repay the Minister imposed by paragraphs (*a*) and (*b*) of subsection (1) shall, subject to satisfaction of the Minister's right to repayment, be a liability also to indemnify all persons against liability under paragraph (*c*) thereof, and any such liability imposed by paragraph (*a*) shall, subject as aforesaid, be a liability also to indemnify all persons against liability under paragraph (*b*); and any person liable under paragraph (*a*) or (*b*) or either sub-paragraph of paragraph (*c*) shall be entitled to contribution from any other person liable under the same paragraph or subparagraph, as the case may be, according to the amount of their respective liabilities thereunder.

(5) The expenses incurred by the Minister under this section shall, so far as not recovered thereunder, be paid out of moneys provided by Parliament.

Inspectors' report to be evidence.

167. A copy of any report of any inspectors appointed under the foregoing provisions of this Act, authenticated by the seal of the company whose affairs they have investigated, shall be admissible in any legal proceeding as evidence of the opinion of the inspectors in relation to any matter contained in the report.

Appointment and powers of inspectors to investigate ownership of company.

168.—(1) Where it appears to the Minister that there is good reason so to do, he may appoint one or more competent inspectors to investigate and report on the membership of any company and otherwise with respect to the company for the purpose of determining the true persons who are or have been financially interested in the success or failure (real or apparent) of the company or able to control or materially to influence the policy of the company.

(2) The appointment of an inspector under this section may define the scope of his investigation, whether as respects the matters or the period to which it is to extend or otherwise, and in particular may limit the investigation to matters connected with particular shares or debentures.

(3) Where an application for an investigation under this section with respect to particular shares or debentures of a company is made to the Minister by members of the company, and the number of applicants or the amount of the shares held by them is not less than that required for an application for the appointment of an inspector under section 160, the Minister shall appoint an inspector to conduct the investigation unless he is satisfied that the application is vexatious, and the inspector's appointment shall not exclude from the scope of his investigation any matter which the application seeks to have included therein, except in so far as the Minister is satisfied that it is unreasonable for that matter to be investigated.

(4) Subject to the terms of an inspector's appointment his powers shall extend to the investigation of any circumstances suggesting the existence of an arrangement or understanding which, though not legally binding, is or was observed or likely to be observed in practice and which is relevant to the purposes of his investigation.

(5) For the purposes of any investigation under this section, sections 162 to 164 shall apply with the necessary modifications of references to the affairs of the company or to those of any other body corporate, so, however, that—

(*a*) those sections shall apply in relation to all persons who are or have been, or whom the inspector has reasonable cause to believe to be or have been, financially interested in the success or failure or the apparent success or failure of the company or any other body corporate whose membership is investigated with that of the company, or able to control or materially to influence the policy thereof, including persons concerned only on behalf of others, as they apply in relation to officers and agents of the company or of the other body corporate, as the case may be; and

(*b*) the Minister shall not be bound to furnish the company or any other person with a copy of any report by an inspector appointed under this section or with a complete copy thereof if he is of opinion that there is good reason for not divulging the contents of the report or of parts thereof, but shall cause to be kept by the Registrar a copy of any such report or, as the case may be, the parts of any such report, as respects which he is not of that opinion.

(6) The expenses of any investigation under this section shall be paid out of moneys provided by Parliament.

Power to require information as to persons interested in shares or debentures.

169.—(1) Where it appears to the Minister that there is good reason to investigate the ownership of any shares in or debentures of a company and that it is unnecessary to appoint an inspector for the purpose, he may require any person whom he has reasonable cause to believe—

(*a*) to be or to have been interested in those shares or debentures; or

(*b*) to act or have acted in relation to those shares or debentures as the attorney or agent of someone interested therein,

to give to the Minister any information which such person has or can reasonably be expected to obtain as to the present and past interests in those shares or debentures and the names and addresses of the persons interested and of any persons who act or have acted on their behalf in relation to the shares or debentures.

(2) For the purposes of this section, a person shall be deemed to have an interest in a share or debenture if he has any right to acquire or dispose of the share or debenture or any interest therein or to vote in respect thereof, or if his consent is necessary for the exercise of any of the rights of other persons interested therein, or if other persons interested therein can be required or are accustomed to exercise their rights in accordance with his instructions.

(3) Any person who fails to give any information required of him under this section, or who in giving any such information makes any statement which he knows to be false in a material particular, or recklessly makes any statement which is false in a material particular, shall be liable on summary conviction before a Resident Magistrate to imprisonment with or without hard labour for a term not exceeding six months or to a fine not exceeding fifty thousand dollars or to both such imprisonment and fine.

Power to impose restrictions on shares or debentures.

170.—(1) Where in connection with an investigation under either section 168 or 169 it appears to the Minister that there is difficulty in finding out the relevant facts about any shares (whether issued or to be issued), and that the difficulty is due wholly or mainly to the unwillingness of the persons concerned or any of them to assist the investigation as required by this Act, the Minister may by order direct that the shares shall until further order be subject to the restrictions imposed by this section.

(2) So long as any shares are directed to be subject to the restrictions imposed by this section—

(*a*) any transfer of those shares, or in the case of unissued shares any transfer of the right to be issued therewith and any issue thereof, shall be void;

(*b*) no voting rights shall be exercisable in respect of those shares;

(*c*) no further shares shall be issued in right of those shares or in pursuance of any offer made to the holder thereof;

(*d*) except in a liquidation no payment shall be made of any sums due from the company on those shares, whether in respect of capital or otherwise.

(3) Where the Minister makes an order directing that shares shall be subject to the said restrictions, or refuses to make an order directing that shares shall cease to be subject thereto, any person aggrieved thereby may apply to the Court, and the Court may, if it sees fit, direct that the shares shall cease to be subject to those restrictions.

(4) Any order (whether of the Minister or of the Court) directing that shares shall cease to be subject to restrictions which is expressed to be made with a view to permitting a transfer of those shares may continue the restrictions mentioned in paragraphs (*c*) and (*d*) of subsection (2), either in whole or in part, so far as they relate to any right acquired or offer made before the transfer.

(5) Any person who—

(*a*) exercises or purports to exercise any right to dispose of any shares which, to his knowledge, are for the time being subject to those restrictions or of any right to be issued with any such shares; or

(*b*) votes in respect of any such shares, whether as holder or proxy, or appoints a proxy to vote in respect thereof; or

(*c*) being the holder of any such shares, fails to notify of their being subject to those restrictions any person whom he does not know to be aware of that fact but knows to be entitled, apart from the restrictions, to vote in respect of those shares whether as holder or proxy, shall be liable on summary conviction before a Resident Magistrate to imprisonment with or without hard labour for a term not exceeding six months or to a fine not exceeding fifty thousand dollars or to both such imprisonment and fine.

(6) Where shares in any company are issued in contravention of the restrictions, the company and every officer of the company who is in default shall be liable to a fine not exceeding fifty thousand dollars.

(7) A prosecution shall not be instituted under this section by any person other than the Director of Public Prosecutions except by or with the consent of the Minister.

(8) This section shall apply in relation to debentures as it applies in relation to shares.

171. Nothing in the foregoing provisions of this Part shall require disclosure to the Minister or to any inspector appointed by him— Saving for attorneys and bankers.

(*a*) by an attorney of any privileged communication made to him in that capacity, except as respects the name and address of his client; or

(*b*) by a company's bankers as such of any information as to the affairs of any of their customers other than the company.

Directors and other Officers

172.—(1) A private company shall have at least one director, but a public company shall have at least three directors, at least two of whom are not employees of the company or any of its affiliates. Number of directors and secretary.

(2) Every company shall have a secretary.

(3) A sole director of a company shall not also be secretary thereof and no company shall—

(*a*) have as secretary to the company, a corporation the sole director of which is a sole director of the company; or

(*b*) have as sole director of the company, a corporation the sole director of which is secretary to the company.

(4) It is the duty of the directors of a public company to take all reasonable steps to ensure that the secretary or each joint secretary of the company is a person who appears to them to have the requisite knowledge and experience to discharge the functions of secretary of the company.

(5) Anything required or authorized to be done by or to the secretary of a company may, if the office is vacant or there is for any other reason no secretary capable of acting, be done by or to any assistant or deputy secretary, or, if there is no assistant or deputy secretary capable of acting, by or to any officer of the company authorized generally or specially in that behalf by the directors.

(6) Notice of the appointment of a secretary to a company shall be given to the Registrar in the prescribed form within fifteen days after the date of that appointment.

Avoidance of acts done by persons in dual capacity as director and secretary.

173. A provision requiring or authorizing a thing to be done by or to a director and the secretary shall not be satisfied by its being done by or to the same person acting both as director and as, or in place of, the secretary.

Duty of care.

174.—(1) Every director and officer of a company in exercising his powers and discharging his duties shall—

(*a*) act honestly and in good faith with a view to the best interest of the company; and

(*b*) exercise the care, diligence and skill that a reasonably prudent person would exercise in comparable circumstances, including, but not limited to the general knowledge, skill and experience of the director or officer.

(2) A director or officer of a company shall not be in breach of his duty under this section if the director or officer exercised due care, diligence and skill in the performance of that duty or believed in the existence of facts that, if true, would render the director's or officer's conduct reasonably prudent.

(3) For the purposes of this section, a director or officer shall be deemed to have acted with due care, diligence and skill where, in the absence of fraud or bad faith, the director or officer reasonably relied in good faith on documents relating to the company's affairs, including financial statements, reports of experts or on information presented by other directors or, where appropriate, other officers and professionals.

(4) In determining what are the best interests of the company, a director or officer may have regard to the interests of the company's shareholders and employees and the community in which the company operates.

(5) The duties imposed by subsection (1) on the directors or officers of a company is owed to the company alone.

(6) Where pursuant to a contract of service with a company, a director or officer is required to perform management functions, the terms of that contract may require the director or officer in the exercise of those functions, to observe a higher standard than that specified in subsection (1).

Restrictions on appointment or advertisement of director.

175.—(1) A person shall not be capable of being appointed director of a company by the articles, and shall not be named as a director or proposed director of a company in a prospectus issued by or on behalf of the company, or as proposed director of an intended company in a prospectus issued in relation to that intended company, or in a statement in lieu of prospectus delivered to the Registrar by or on behalf of a company, unless, before the registration of the articles or the publication of the prospectus, or the delivery of the statement in lieu of prospectus, as the case may be, he has by himself or by his agent authorized in writing—

(*a*) signed and delivered to the Registrar for registration a consent in writing to act as such director; and

(*b*) either—

(i) signed the articles for a number of shares not less than his qualification, if any; or

(ii) taken from the company and paid or agreed to pay for his qualification shares, if any; or

(iii) signed and delivered to the Registrar for registration an undertaking in writing to take from the company and pay for his qualification shares, if any; or

(iv) made and delivered to the Registrar for registration a statutory declaration to the effect that a number of shares, not less than his qualification, if any, are registered in his name.

(2) Where a person has signed and delivered as aforesaid an undertaking to take and pay for his qualification shares, he shall, as regards those shares, be in the same position as if he had signed the articles for that number of shares.

(3) On the application for registration of the articles of a company the applicant shall deliver to the Registrar a list of the persons who have consented to be directors of the company, and if this list contains the name of any person who has not so consented, the applicant shall be liable to a fine not exceeding one hundred thousand dollars.

(4) This section shall not apply to—

(*a*) a company not having a share capital; or

(*b*) a private company; or

(*c*) a company which was a private company before becoming a public company; or (*d*) a prospectus issued by or on behalf of a company after the expiration of one year from the date on which the company was entitled to commence business.

176. The acts of a director or manager shall be valid notwithstanding any defect that may afterwards be discovered in his appointment or qualification. Validity of acts of directors.

177.—(1) Without prejudice to the restrictions imposed by section 175, it shall be the duty of every director who is by the articles of the company required to hold a specified share qualification, and who is not already qualified, to obtain his qualification within two months after his appointment, or such shorter time as may be fixed by the articles. Share qualifications of directors.

(2) For the purpose of any provision in the articles requiring a director or other officer to hold a specified share qualification, the bearer of a share warrant shall not be deemed to be the holder of the share specified in the warrant.

(3) The office of director of a company shall be vacated if the director does not within two months from the date of his appointment, or within such shorter time as may be fixed by the articles, obtain his qualification, or if after the expiration of that period or shorter time he ceases at any time to hold his qualification.

(4) A person vacating office under this section shall be incapable of being reappointed director of the company until he has obtained his qualification.

(5) If after the expiration of the period or shorter time any unqualified person acts as a director of the company, he shall be liable to a fine not exceeding two thousand dollars for every day between the expiration of the period or shorter time or the day on which he ceased to be qualified, as the case may be, and the last day on which it is proved that he acted as a director.

Appointment of directors to be voted on individually.

178.—(1) At a general meeting of a company other than a private company, a motion for the appointment of two or more persons as directors of the company by a single resolution shall not be made, unless a resolution that it shall be so made has first been agreed to by the meeting without any vote being given against it.

(2) A resolution moved in contravention of this section shall be void, whether or not its being so moved was objected to at the time:

Provided that—

(*a*) this subsection shall not be taken as excluding the operation of section 176; and

(*b*) where a resolution so moved is passed, no provision for the automatic reappointment of retiring directors in default of another appointment shall apply.

(3) For the purposes of this section, a motion for approving a person's appointment or for nominating a person for appointment shall be treated as a motion for his appointment.

(4) Nothing in this section shall apply to a resolution altering the company's articles.

Removal of directors.

179.—(1) A company may by ordinary resolution remove a director before the expiration of his period of office notwithstanding anything in its articles or in any agreement between it and him:

Provided that this subsection shall not, in the case of a private company, authorize the removal of a director holding office for life on the 5th of February, 1963, whether or not subject to retirement under an age limit by virtue of the articles or otherwise.

(2) Special notice shall be required of any resolution to remove a director under this section or to appoint somebody instead of a director so removed at the meeting at which he is removed, and on receipt of notice of an intended resolution to remove a director under this section the company shall forthwith send a copy thereof to the director concerned, and the director (whether or not he is a member of the company) shall be entitled to be heard on the resolution at the meeting.

(3) Where notice is given of an intended resolution to remove a director under this section and the director concerned makes with respect thereto representations in writing to the company (not exceeding a reasonable length) and requests their notification to members of the company, the company shall, unless the representations are received by it too late for it to do so—

(*a*) in any notice of the resolution given to members of the company state the fact of the representations having been made; and

(*b*) send a copy of the representations to every member of the company to whom notice of the meeting is sent (whether before or after receipt of the representations by the company),

and if a copy of the representations is not sent as aforesaid because received too late or because of the company's default, the director may (without prejudice to his right to be heard orally) require that the representations shall be read out at the meeting:

Provided that copies of the representations need not be sent out and the representations need not be read out at the meeting if, on the application either of the company or of any other person who claims to be aggrieved, the Court is satisfied that the rights conferred by this section are being abused to secure needless publicity for defamatory matter; and the Court may order the company's costs on an application under this section to be paid in whole or in part by the director, notwithstanding that he is not a party to the application.

(4) A vacancy created by the removal of a director under this section, if not filled at the meeting at which he is removed, may be filled as a casual vacancy.

(5) A person appointed director in place of a person removed under this section shall be treated, for the purpose of determining the time at which he or any other director is to retire, as if he had become director on the day on which the person in whose place he is appointed was last appointed a director.

(6) Nothing in this section shall be taken as depriving a person removed thereunder of compensation or damages payable to him in respect of the termination of his appointment as director or of any appointment terminating with that as director or as derogating from any power to remove a director which may exist apart from this section.

Court disqualified directors.

180.—(1) Where, pursuant to subsection (2), a complaint is made to the Registrar by—

(*a*) shareholders of a company;

(*b*) members of the board of directors of a company or creditors of a company, as the case may be; or

(*c*) the liquidator of the company, or the Trustee,

that person is unfit to be concerned in the management of a company, the Registrar shall act in accordance with subsection (3).

(2) A complaint referred to in subsection (1) shall be in writing and shall state the grounds on which it is made.

(3) Upon receipt of such a complaint the Registrar shall—

(*a*) investigate the matter and afford to the complainants an opportunity to be heard; and (*b*) if satisfied that there are sufficient grounds for a hearing of the matter by the Court, issue a certificate to that effect to the shareholders, liquidator, Trustee, members or creditors, as the case may be, who shall, subject to subsection (7), have the right to make an application to the Court on the matter.

(4) Any shareholder, member or creditor, as the case maybe, who is aggrieved by a refusal of the Registrar to issue a certificate referred to in subsection (3) (*b*), may appeal against that decision to the Master in Chambers.

(5) Where the Registrar is satisfied that a person is unfit to be concerned in the management of a company, the Registrar may make an application to the Court on the matter.

(6) Where, on an application made pursuant to subsection (3) (*b*) or (5), it is made to appear to the Court that a person is unfit to be concerned in the management of a company, the Court may order that, without the prior leave of the Court, that person may not be a director of the company, or in any way, directly or indirectly, be concerned with the management of the company for such period as may be specified in the order—

(*a*) beginning with the date of the order or, if the person is serving, or is to serve, a term of imprisonment and the Court so directs, beginning with the date on which he completes that term of imprisonment or is otherwise released from prison; and

(*b*) not exceeding five years.

(7) In determining whether or not to make an order under subsection (6) the Court shall have regard to the following—

(*a*) any misfeasance or breach of any fiduciary or other duty by the director in relation to the company;

(*b*) any misapplications or retention by the director of, or any conduct by the director giving rise to an obligation to account for, any money or other property of the company;

(*c*) the extent of the director's responsibility for any failure by the company to comply with the provisions of this Act in relation to the keeping and maintenance of accounting records;

(*d*) whether the director has knowingly been party to carrying on the business of the company in a manner for which he may be liable (whether he has been convicted or not) under section 322;

(*e*) such other circumstances as may be prescribed.

(8) Before making an application under this section in relation to any person, the Registrar or any other person intending to apply shall give to the person concerned not less than ten days' notice of the intention to make the application.

(9) On the hearing of an application made under this section or, as the case may be, an application for leave as mentioned in subsection (6), any person concerned with the application may appear and call attention to any matters that are relevant, and may give evidence, call witnesses and be represented by an attorney-at-law.

Provisions as to undischarged bankrupts acting as directors.

181.—(1) If any person being an undischarged bankrupt acts as director of, or directly or indirectly takes part in, or is concerned in the management of, any company except with the leave of the Court, he shall be liable on conviction on indictment to imprisonment with or without hard labour for a term not exceeding two years, or on summary conviction before a Resident Magistrate to imprisonment with or without hard labour for a term not exceeding two years or to a fine not exceeding two hundred thousand dollars, or to both such imprisonment and fine:

Provided that a person shall not be guilty of an offence under this section by reason that he, being an undischarged bankrupt, has acted as director of, or taken part or been concerned in the management of a company, if he was on the appointed day acting as director of, or taking part or being concerned in the management of, that company and has continuously so acted, taken part, or been concerned since that date and the bankruptcy was prior to that date.

(2) Leave of the Court for the purposes of this section shall not be given unless notice of intention to apply therefor has been served on the Trustee, and it shall be the duty of the Trustee, if he is of opinion that it is contrary to the public interest that any such application should be granted, to attend on the hearing of and oppose the granting of the application.

(3) In this section the expression "company" includes an unregistered company and a company incorporated outside the Island which has an established place of business within the Island.

182.—(1) The Court may make a disqualification order against a person where it appears to the Court that he has been persistently in default in relation to provisions of this Act requiring any return, account or other document to be filed with, delivered or sent, or notice of any matter to be given, to the Registrar.

Disqualification for persistent breaches of Act.

(2) On an application to the Court for an order to be made under this section, the fact that a person has been persistently in default in relation to such provisions as are mentioned in subsection (1) may be conclusively proved by showing that in the five years ending with the date of the application he has been adjudged guilty (whether or not on the same occasion) of three or more defaults in relation to those provisions.

(3) A person is to be treated under subsection (2) as being adjudged guilty of a default in relation to any provision as aforesaid if—

(*a*) he is convicted (whether on indictment or summarily) of an offence consisting in a contravention of or failure on his part to comply with that provision; or

(*b*) a default order is made against him under any provision of this Act requiring the submission of returns, notices or other documents to the Registrar, in respect of any such contravention of or failure on his part to comply with that provision.

(4) In this section "Court" means any court having jurisdiction to wind up any of the companies in relation to which the offence or other default has been or is alleged to have been committed.

(5) A disqualification order may be made under this section for a period not exceeding five years.

Register of directors.

183.—(1) Every company shall keep at its registered office a register of its directors or managers and secretary containing with respect to each of them the following particulars, that is to say—

(*a*) in the case of an individual, his present Christian name and surname, any former Christian name or surname, his usual residential address, his nationality, and, if that nationality is not the nationality of origin, his nationality of origin, and his business occupation, if any, or, if he has no business occupation but holds any other directorship or directorships, particulars of that directorship or of some one of those directorships; and

(*b*) in the case of a corporation, its corporate name and registered or principal office.

(2) The company shall, within the periods respectively mentioned in this subsection, send to the Registrar a return in the prescribed form containing the particulars specified in the register and a notification in the prescribed form of any change among its directors or in any of the particulars contained in the register specifying the date of the change.

(3) The return shall be sent within fourteen days from the appointment of the first directors of the company, and the notification of a change shall be sent within fourteen days from the happening thereof.

(4) The register to be kept under this section shall during business hours (subject to such reasonable restrictions as the company may by its articles or in general meeting impose, so that not less than two hours in each day be allowed for inspection) be open to the inspection of any member of the company without charge and of any other person on payment of fifty dollars, or such less sum as the company may specify, for each inspection.

(5) If any inspection required under this section is refused or if default is made in complying with subsection (1) or subsection (2), the company and every officer of the company who is in default shall be liable to a fine not exceeding fifty thousand dollars.

(6) In the case of any such refusal, the Court may by order compel an immediate inspection of the register.

(7) For the purposes of this section, a shadow director shall be deemed to be a director and officer of the company.

Illicit loans by company.

184.—(1) Where circumstances prejudicial to the company exist, the company or any company with which it is affiliated shall not, directly or indirectly, give financial assistance by means of a loan, guarantee or otherwise—

(*a*) to a shareholder, director, officer or employee of the company or affiliated company, or to an associate of any such person for any purpose; or

(*b*) to any person for the purpose of, or in connection with, a purchase of a share issued or to be issued by the company or a company with which it is affiliated.

(2) Circumstances prejudicial to the company exist in respect of financial assistance mentioned in subsection (1) where there are reasonable grounds for believing that—

(*a*) the company is unable or would, after giving the financial assistance, be unable to pay its liabilities as they become due; or

(*b*) the realizable value of the company's assets, excluding the amount of any financial assistance in the form of a loan and in the form of assets pledged or encumbered to secure a guarantee, would, after giving the financial assistance, be less than the aggregate of the company's liabilities and stated capital of all classes.

(3) For the avoidance of doubt, a contract made by a company or by a person giving financial assistance in contravention of this section shall not, by reason only of that contravention, be rendered void, or unenforceable by the company or person giving financial assistance.

(4) An officer of a company who acts in contravention of this section shall, on summary conviction before a Resident Magistrate, be liable to a fine not exceeding one million dollars or to imprisonment for a term not exceeding two years, or to both such fine and imprisonment and the Resident Magistrate may order that officer to restore to the company, an amount equal to the value of the financial assistance given in contravention of this section.

Permitted loans.

185. Subject to the provisions of this Act and the company's articles, a company may give financial assistance to any person by means of a loan, guarantee or otherwise—

(*a*) in the ordinary course of business, if the lending of money is part of the ordinary business of the company;

(*b*) on account of expenditure incurred or to be incurred on behalf of the company;

(*c*) to a holding body corporate if the company is a wholly owned subsidiary of the holding body corporate;

(*d*) to any of the company's subsidiaries;

(*e*) to employees of the company to enable them to purchase shares in an employee share ownership plan approved under the Employee Share Ownership Plan Act.

Approval of company requisite for payment in connection with transfer of property to director for loss of office, etc.

186.—(1) It shall not be lawful for a company to make to any director of the company any payment by way of compensation for loss of office, or as consideration for or to in connection with his retirement from office, without particulars with respect to the proposed payment (including the amount thereof) being disclosed to members of the company and the proposal being approved by the company.

(2) If any payment is made to a director of a company in contravention of this section the company and every officer of the company who is in default shall be liable to a fine not exceeding fifty thousand dollars.

Approval of company required for any payment re transfer of its property to director for loss of office, etc.

187.—(1) It is hereby declared that it is not lawful in connection with the transfer of the whole or any part of the undertaking or property of a company for any payment to be made to any director of the company by way of compensation for loss of office, or as consideration for or in connection with his retirement from office, unless particulars with respect to the proposed payment (including the amount thereof) have been disclosed to the members of the company and the proposal approved by the company.

(2) Where a payment which is hereby declared to be illegal is made to a director of the company, the amount received shall be deemed to have been received by him in trust for the company, so, however, that in any proceeding instituted by virtue of this subsection for the recovery of any payment, the

Court shall have power when justice so requires to order that any sum found to be payable by a director shall be restored in whole or in part to members or former members of the company instead of to the company itself and in that event may order that the necessary inquiries shall be made to ascertain the identity of the members and former members and may give such consequential directions as may be necessary or expedient.

Duty of director to disclose payment for loss of office, etc., made in connection with transfer of shares in company.

188.—(1) Where, in connection with the transfer to any persons of all or any of the shares in a company, being a transfer resulting from—

(*a*) an offer made to the general body of shareholders;

(*b*) an offer made by or on behalf of some other body corporate with a view to the company becoming its subsidiary or a subsidiary of its holding company;

(*c*) an offer made by or on behalf of an individual with a view to his obtaining the right to exercise or control the exercise of not less than one-third of the voting power at any general meeting of the company; or

(*d*) any other offer which is conditional on acceptance to a given extent,

a payment is to be made to a director of the company by way of compensation for loss of office, or as consideration for or in connection with his retirement from office, it shall be the duty of that director to take all reasonable steps to secure that particulars with respect to the proposed payment (including the amount thereof) shall be included in or sent with any notice of the offer made for their shares which is given to any shareholders.

(2) If—

(*a*) any such director fails to take reasonable steps as aforesaid; or (*b*) any person who has been properly required by any such director to include the said particulars in or send them with any such notice as aforesaid fails so to do,

he shall be liable to a fine not exceeding fifty thousand dollars.

(3) If—

(*a*) the requirements of subsection (1) are not complied with in relation to any such payment as is therein mentioned; or

(*b*) the making of the proposed payment is not, before the transfer of any shares in pursuance of the offer, approved by a meeting summoned for the purpose of the holders of the shares to which the offer relates and of other holders of shares of the same class as any of those shares,

any sum received by the director on account of the payment shall be deemed to have been received by him in trust for any persons who have sold their shares as a result of the offer made, and the expenses incurred by him in distributing that sum amongst those persons shall be borne by him and not retained out of that sum.

(4) Where the shareholders referred to in paragraph (*b*) of subsection (3) are not all the members of the company and no provision is made by the articles for summoning or regulating such a meeting as is mentioned in that paragraph, the provisions of this Act and of the company's articles relating to general meetings of the company shall, for that purpose, apply to the meeting either without modification or with such modifications as the Minister on the application of any person concerned may direct for the purpose of adapting them to the circumstances of the meeting.

(5) If at a meeting summoned for the purpose of approving any payment as required by paragraph (*b*) of subsection (3) a quorum is not present and, after the meeting has

been adjourned to a later date, a quorum is again not present, the payment shall be deemed for the purposes of that subsection to have been approved.

Provisions supplementary to sections 186, 187 and 188.

189.—(1) Where in proceedings for the recovery of any payment as having, by virtue of subsections (1) and (2) of section 186 or subsections (1) and (3) of section 187, been received by any person in trust, it is shown that—

(*a*) the payment was made in pursuance of any arrangement entered into as part of the agreement for the transfer in question, or within one year before or two years after that agreement or the offer leading thereto; and

(*b*) the company or any person to whom the transfer was made was privy to that arrangement,

the payment shall be deemed, except in so far as the contrary is shown, to be one to which the subsections apply.

(2) If in connection with any such transfer as is mentioned in either section 187 or 188—

(*a*) the price to be paid to a director of the company whose office is to be abolished or who is to retire from office for any shares in the company held by him is in excess of the price which could at the time have been obtained by other holders of the like shares; or

(*b*) any valuable consideration is given to any such director,

the excess or the money value of the consideration, as the case may be, shall, for the purposes of that section, be deemed to have been a payment made to him by way of compensation for loss of office or as consideration for or in connection with his retirement from office.

(3) It is hereby declared that references in sections 186, 187 and 188 to payments made to any director of a company by way of compensation for loss of office, or as consideration for or in connection with his retirement from office, do not include any *bona fide* payment by way of damages for breach of contract or by way of pension in respect of past services, and for the purposes of this subsection the expression "pension" includes any superannuation allowance, superannuation gratuity or similar payment.

(4) Nothing in section 186 or 187 shall be taken to prejudice the operation of any rule of law requiring disclosure to be made with respect to any such payments as are therein mentioned or with respect to any other like payments made or to be made to the directors of a company.

Particulars in accounts of directors' salaries, pensions, etc.

190.—(1) In any accounts of a company laid before it in general meeting, or in a statement annexed thereto, there shall, subject to and in accordance with the provisions of this section, be shown so far as the information is in the company's books and papers or the company has the right to obtain it from the persons concerned—

(*a*) the aggregate amount of the directors' emoluments;

(*b*) the aggregate amount of directors' or past directors' pensions; and

(*c*) the aggregate amount of any compensation to directors or past directors in respect of loss of office.

(2) The amount to be shown under paragraph (*a*) of subsection (1)—

(*a*) shall include any emoluments paid to or receivable by any person in respect of his services as director of the company or in respect of his services, while director of the company, as director of any subsidiary thereof or otherwise in connection with the management of the affairs of the company or any subsidiary thereof; and (*b*) shall distinguish between emoluments in respect of services as director whether of the company or its subsidiary, and other emoluments.

(3) The amount to be shown under paragraph (*b*) of subsection (1)—

(a) shall not include any pension paid or receivable under a pension scheme if the scheme is such that the contributions thereunder are substantially adequate for the maintenance of the scheme, but save as aforesaid shall include any pension paid or receivable in respect of any such services of a director or past director of the company as are mentioned in subsection (2), whether to or by him or, on his nomination or by virtue of dependence on or other connection with him, to or by any other person; and

(*b*) shall distinguish between pensions in respect of services as director, whether of the company or its subsidiary, and other pensions.

(4) The amount to be shown under paragraph (*c*) of subsection (1)—

(*a*) shall include any sums paid to or receivable by a director or past director by way of compensation for the loss of office as director of the company or for the loss, while director of the company or on or in connection with his ceasing to be a director of the company, of any other office in connection with the management of the company's affairs or of any office as director or otherwise in connection with the management of the affairs of any subsidiary thereof; and

(*b*) shall distinguish between compensation in respect of the office of director, whether of the company or its subsidiary, and compensation in respect of other offices, and for the purposes of this section references to compensation for loss of office shall include sums paid as consideration for or in connection with a person's retirement from office.

(5) The amounts to be shown under each paragraph of subsection (1)—

(*a*) shall include all relevant sums paid by or receivable from—

(i) the company; and

(ii) the company's subsidiaries; and

(iii) any other person,

except sums to be accounted for to the company or any of its subsidiaries or, by virtue of section 188, to past or present members of the company or any of its subsidiaries or any class of those members; and

(*b*) shall distinguish, in the case of the amount to be shown under paragraph (*c*) of subsection (1), between the sums respectively paid by or receivable from the company, the company's subsidiaries and persons other than the company and its subsidiaries.

(6) The amounts to be shown under this section for any financial year shall be the sums receivable in respect of that year, whenever paid, or, in the case of sums not receivable in respect of a period, the sums paid during that year, so, however, that where—

(*a*) any sums are not shown in the accounts for the relevant financial year on the ground that the person receiving them is liable to account therefor as mentioned in paragraph (*a*) of subsection (5), but the liability is thereafter wholly or partly released or is not enforced within a period of two years; or

(*b*) any sums paid by way of expenses allowance are charged to income tax after the end of the relevant financial year, those sums shall, to the extent to which the liability is released or not enforced or they are charged as aforesaid, as the case may be, be shown in the first accounts in which it is practicable to show them or in a statement annexed thereto and shall be distinguished from the amounts to be shown therein apart from this provision.

(7) Where it is necessary so to do for the purpose of making any distinction required by this section in any amount to be shown thereunder, the directors may apportion any payments between the matters in respect of which they have been paid or are receivable in such manner as they think appropriate.

(8) If in the case of any accounts the requirements of this section are not complied with, it shall be the duty of the auditors of the company by whom the accounts are examined to include in their report thereon, so far as they are reasonably able to do so, a statement giving the required particulars.

(9) In this section—

(*a*) "contribution", in relation to a pension scheme, means any payment (including an insurance premium) paid for the purposes of the scheme by or in respect of persons rendering services in respect of which pensions will or may become payable under the scheme, except that it does not include any payment in respect of two or more persons if the amount paid in respect of each of them is not ascertainable;

(*b*) "emoluments", in relation to a director, means the gross sum subject to income tax payable to him as emoluments and includes fees and percentages, any sums paid by way of expenses allowance insofar as those sums are charged to income tax, any contribution paid in respect of him under any pension scheme and the estimated money value of any other benefits received by him otherwise than in cash;

(*c*) "income tax" means the tax payable by individuals and companies under the law for the time being relating to income tax;

(*d*) "pension" includes any superannuation allowance, superannuation gratuity or similar payment;

(*e*) "pension scheme" means a scheme for the provision of pensions in respect of services as director or otherwise, which is maintained in whole or in part by means of contributions;

(*f*) any reference to a company's subsidiary—

(i) in relation to a person who is or was, while a director of the company, a director also, by virtue of the company's nomination, direct or indirect, of any other body corporate, shall, subject to sub-paragraph (ii), include that body corporate, whether or not it is or was in fact the company's subsidiary; and

(ii) shall for the purposes of subsections (2) and (3) be taken as referring to a subsidiary at the time the services were rendered, and for the purposes of subsection (4) be taken as referring to a subsidiary immediately before the loss of office as director of the company;

Particulars in accounts of loans to officers, etc.

191.—(1) The accounts which, in pursuance of this Act, are to be laid before every company in general meeting shall, subject to the provisions of this section, contain particulars showing—

(*a*) the amount of any loans made during the company's financial year to—

(i) any officer of the company;

(ii) any person who, after the making of the loan, became during that year an officer of the company, by the company or a subsidiary thereof or by any other person under a guarantee from or on a security provided by the company or a subsidiary thereof (including any such loans which were repaid during that year); and

(*b*) the amount of any loans made in manner aforesaid to any such officer or person as aforesaid at any time before the company's financial year and outstanding at the expiration thereof.

(2) Subsection (1) shall not require the inclusion in accounts of particulars of—

(*a*) a loan made in the ordinary course of its business by the company or a subsidiary thereof, where the ordinary business of the company or, as the case may be, the subsidiary, includes the lending of money; or

(*b*) a loan made by the company or a subsidiary thereof to an employee of the company or subsidiary, as the case maybe, if the loan does not exceed five hundred thousand dollars and is certified by the directors of the company or subsidiary, as the case may be, to have been made in accordance with any practice adopted or about to be adopted by the company or subsidiary with respect to loans to its employees,

not being, in either case, a loan made by the company under a guarantee from or on a security provided by a subsidiary thereof or a loan made by a subsidiary of the company under a guarantee from or on a security provided by the company or any other subsidiary thereof.

(3) If in the case of any such accounts as aforesaid the requirements of this section are not complied with, it shall be the duty of the auditors of the company by whom the accounts are examined to include in their report on the balance sheet of the company, so far as they are reasonably able to do so, a statement giving the required particulars.

(4) References in this section to a subsidiary shall be taken as referring to a subsidiary at the end of the company's financial year (whether or not a subsidiary at the date of the loan).

192.—(1) It shall be the duty of any director of a company to give notice to the company of such matters relating to himself as may be necessary for the purposes of sections 189 and 190 except so far as it relates to loans made by the company or by any other person under a guarantee from or on a security provided by the company, to an officer thereof. General duty to make disclosure for purposes of sections 189 and 190.

(2) Any such notice given for the purposes of section 189 shall be in writing and, if it is not given at a meeting of the directors, the director giving it shall take reasonable steps to secure that it is brought up and read at the next meeting of directors after it is given.

(3) Subsection (1) shall apply

(*a*) for the purposes of section 192, in relation to officers other than directors; and

(*b*) for the purposes of sections 191 and 192, in relation to persons who are or have at any time during the preceding five years been officers,

as it applies in relation to directors.

(4) Any person who makes default in complying with the foregoing provisions of this section shall be liable to a fine not exceeding fifty thousand dollars.

193.—(1) A director or officer of a company who is— Disclosure by directors of interest in contracts.

(*a*) a party to a contract or proposed contract with the company; or

(*b*) a director or an officer of any body or has an interest in any body that is a party to a contract or proposed contract with the company; or (*c*) an associate of a person who is a party to a contract, proposed contract or has an interest in any body that is a party to a contract or proposed contract with the company,

shall disclose in writing to the company or request to have entered in the minutes of meetings of directors the nature and extent of his interest.

First Schedule.

(2) The contract referred to in subsection (1) shall be subject to the approval of the board of directors of the company and, subject to the provisions of the First Schedule, the director concerned shall not be present during any proceedings of the board in connection with that approval.

(3) A record of such contract shall be kept at the registered office of the company.

(4) The disclosure required by subsection (1) shall be made—

(*a*) in the case of a director of a company—

(i) at the meeting at which a proposed contract is first considered;

(ii) if the director was not then interested in a proposed contract, at the first meeting after he becomes so interested; or

(iii) if a person who is interested in a contract later becomes a director of the company, at the first meeting after he becomes a director;

(*b*) in the case of an officer of the company who is not a director—

(i) forthwith after he becomes aware that the contract or proposed contract is to be considered, or has been considered, at a meeting of directors of the company;

(ii) if the officer becomes interested after a contract is made, forthwith after he becomes so interested; or

(iii) if a person who is interested in a contract later becomes an officer of the company, forthwith after he becomes an officer;

(iv) if the director becomes interested after a contract is made, at the first meeting after he becomes so interested.

(5) If a contract or proposed contract is one that, in the ordinary course of the company's business, would not require approval by the directors or shareholders of the company, a director or officer of the company shall disclose in writing to the company, or request to have entered in the minutes of meetings of directors, the nature and extent of his interest forthwith after the director or officer becomes aware of the contract or proposed contract.

(6) For the purposes of this section, a general notice to the directors of a company by a director or an officer of the company declaring that he is a director or officer of, or has an interest in, another body, and is to be regarded as interested in any type of contract with that body, is a sufficient declaration of interest in relation to any such contract.

(7) A contract between a company and one or more of its directors or officers, or between a company and another body of which a director or officer of the company is a director or officer, or in which he has an interest, is neither void nor voidable—

(*a*) by reason only of that relationship;

(*b*) by reason only that a director with an interest in the contract is present at, or is counted to determine the presence of a quorum at a meeting of directors or a committee of directors that authorized the contract, if the director or officer disclosed his interest in accordance with this section and the contract was approved by the directors and was reasonable and fair to the company at the time it was approved.

(8) Where a director or officer of a company fails to disclose in accordance with this section, his interest in a material contract made by the company, the Court may, upon the application of the company, set aside the contract on such terms as the Court thinks fit.

Particulars with respect to directors in trade catalogues, circulars, etc.

194.—(1) Every company to which this section applies shall, in all trade catalogues, trade circulars, showcards and business letters on or in which the company's name appears and which are issued or sent by the company to any person whether within or without the Island, state in legible characters with respect to every director being a corporation, the corporate name, and with respect to every director being an individual, the following particulars—

(*a*) his present Christian name, or the initials thereof, and present Surname; and

(*b*) any former Christian names, and Surnames:

Provided that, if special circumstances exist which render it in the opinion of the Minister expedient that such an exemption should be granted, the Minister may by order grant, subject to such conditions as may be specified in the order, exemption from the obligations imposed by this subsection.

(2) This section shall apply to—

(*a*) every company registered under this Act and every existing company; and

(*b*) every company incorporated outside the Island which has an established place of business within the Island.

(3) If a company makes default in complying with this section every officer of the company who is in default shall be liable on summary conviction before a Resident Magistrate for each offence to a fine not exceeding fifty thousand dollars, and for the purposes of this subsection, where a corporation is an officer of the company, any officer of the corporation shall be deemed to be an officer of the company:

Provided that no proceedings shall be instituted under this section by any person other than the Director of Public Prosecutions except by, or with the consent of, the Minister.

(4) For the purposes of this section—

(*a*) "director" includes any person in accordance with whose directions or instructions the directors of the company are accustomed to act and the expression "officer" shall be construed accordingly;

(*b*) "initials" includes a recognized abbreviation of a Christian name; and

(*c*) "showcards" means cards containing or exhibiting articles dealt with, or samples or representations thereof.

195.—(1) Subject to this section, every company shall keep at an appropriate place— Director's service contracts to be open to inspection.

(*a*) in the case of each director whose contract of service with the company is in writing, a copy of that contract;

(*b*) in the case of each director whose contract of service with the company is not in writing, a written memorandum setting out its terms; and

(*c*) in the case of each director who is employed under a contract of service with a subsidiary of the company, a copy of that contract or, if it is not in writing, a written memorandum setting out its terms.

(2) All copies and memoranda kept by a company in pursuance of subsection (1) shall be kept at the same place and for the purposes of subsection (1) the following places are appropriate—

(*a*) the company's registered office;

(*b*) the place where its register of members is kept (if other than its registered office);

(*c*) its principal place of business in Jamaica.

(3) Every company shall send notice in the prescribed form to the Registrar of the place where copies and memoranda are kept in compliance with subsection (1) and of any change in that place, save in a case in which they have at all times been kept at the company's registered office.

(4) Subsection (1) shall not apply to a director's contract of service with the company or with any of its subsidiaries if that contract required him to work wholly or mainly outside Jamaica; but the company shall keep, at the same place where copies and memoranda are kept in accordance with subsection (1), a memorandum—

(*a*) in the case of a contract of service with the company, giving the director's name and setting out the provisions of the contract relating to its duration;

(*b*) in the case of a contract of service with a subsidiary, giving the director's name and the name and place of incorporation of the subsidiary, and setting out the provisions of the contract relating to its duration.

(5) For the purposes of this section, a shadow director shall be treated as a director.

(6) Every copy and memorandum required to be kept by subsection (1) or (4) shall during business hours, be open to inspection by members of the company without charge.

(7) If—

(*a*) default is made in complying with subsection (1) or (5);

(*b*) an inspection required under subsection (6) is refused; or

(*c*) default is made for fourteen days in complying with subsection (3),

the company and every officer thereof who is in default is liable on summary conviction before a Resident Magistrate to a fine not exceeding two hundred thousand dollars.

(8) In the case of a refusal of an inspection of a copy or memorandum required under subsection (6), the Court may by order compel an immediate inspection thereof.

(9) Subsections (1) and (4) shall apply to a variation of a director's contract of service as they apply to the contract.

(10) This section does not require that there be kept a copy of, or memorandum setting out the terms of, a contract (or its variation) at a time when the unexpired portion of the term for which the contract is to be in force is less than twelve months, or at a time at which the contract can, within the next ensuing twelve months, be terminated by the company without payment of compensation.

196.—(1) A person who becomes a director of a company and at the time when he does so he is interested in shares in, or debentures of, the company or any other body corporate, being the company's subsidiary or holding company or a subsidiary of the company's holding company, (hereinafter in this section referred to as a specified body corporate) is under obligation to notify the company in writing of— Duty of directors to disclose shareholdings in own company.

(*a*) the subsistence of his interests at that time; and

(*b*) the number of shares of each class in, and the amount of debentures of each class of, the company or other such body corporate in which each interest of his subsists at that time.

(2) A director of a company is under obligation to notify the company in writing of the occurrence, while he is a director, of any of the following events—

(*a*) any event in consequence of whose occurrence he becomes, or ceases to be, interested in shares in, or debentures of the company or any specified body corporate;

(*b*) the entering into by him of a contract to sell any such shares or debentures;

(*c*) the assignment by him of a right granted to him by the company to subscribe for shares in, or debentures of, the company; or

(*d*) the grant to him by a specified body corporate, of a right to subscribe for shares in, or debentures of, that specified body corporate, the exercise of such a right granted to him and the assignment by him of such a right,

and notification to the company shall state the number or amount and class of, shares or debentures involved.

Fourteenth Schedule.

(3) Subsections (1) and (2) shall have effect subject to such exceptions as may be prescribed in regulations made under this Act and the provisions of the Fourteenth Schedule shall have effect in relation to those subsections.

(4) Subsection (2) does not require a person to notify a company of the occurrence of any event which comes to his knowledge after he has ceased to be a director.

(5) This section shall apply to a shadow director as to a director but nothing in this section shall be construed as imposing an obligation with respect to shares in a body corporate which is the wholly owned subsidiary of another body corporate.

(6) A person who—

(*a*) fails, within the proper period, to discharge an obligation to which he is subject under subsection (1) or (2); or

(*b*) in purported discharge of such an obligation, makes to the company a statement which he knows to be false, or recklessly makes to it a false statement,

is guilty of an offence and liable on conviction thereof to a fine not exceeding five hundred thousand dollars or to imprisonment for a term not exceeding two years or to both such fine and imprisonment.

(7) The provisions of this section shall not apply to a director of a company licensed under the Securities Act and to whom sections 54 and 55 of that Act apply.

Register of interests notified under section 196.

197.—(1) Every company shall keep a register for the purposes of section 196.

(2) A company is under obligation to enter in the register, against a director's name, the following information—

(*a*) any information received by the company from that director, being information given in fulfilment of an obligation imposed on him by section 196 and the date of the entry;

(*b*) information concerning the grant by a company to that director of a right to subscribe for shares in, or debentures of, the company, that is to say—

(i) the date on which the right was granted;

(ii) the period during which, and a time at which, it is exercisable;

(iii) the consideration for the grant (or, if there is no consideration, that fact); and

(iv) the description of shares or debentures involved and the number or amount of them, and the price to be paid for them (or the consideration, if otherwise than in money).

(3) Whenever such a right as mentioned in subsection (2) (*b*) is exercised by a director, the company is under obligation to enter in the register against his name that fact (identifying the right), the number or amount of shares or debentures in respect of which it is exercised and, if they were registered in his name, that fact and, if not, the name or names of the person or persons in whose name or names they were registered and, if they were registered in the names of two or more persons, the number or amount of the shares or debentures registered in the name of each of them.

Fourteenth Schedule.

(4) Part IV of the Fourteenth Schedule shall have effect with respect to the register to be kept under this section, the way in which entries in it are to be made, the right of inspection and generally.

(5) For the purposes of this section, a shadow director shall be treated as a director.

(6) The company may, on giving notice by advertisement in a daily newspaper circulating in the Island, close the register for any time not exceeding a total of thirty days in each year.

Sanctions for non-compliance.

198.—(1) The following provisions of this section shall apply with respect to defaults in complying with, and contraventions of, section 197 and Part IV of the Fourteenth Schedule.

(2) If default is made in complying with—

(*a*) subsection (1), (2) or (3) of section 197;

(*b*) paragraph 18,19 or 25 of the Fourteenth Schedule,

the company and every officer thereof who is in default is liable to a fine not exceeding two thousand dollars in respect of every day during which the default continues.

(3) If an inspection of the register required under paragraph 22 of the Fourteenth Schedule is refused, or a copy required under paragraph 23 is not sent within the proper period, the company and every officer thereof who is in default is liable to a daily default fine not exceeding two thousand dollars in respect of every day during which the default continues. Fourteenth Schedule.

(4) If default is made for fourteen days in complying with paragraph 24 of the Fourteenth Schedule (notice to the Registrar of where register is kept), the company and every officer thereof who is in default is liable to a fine not exceeding four thousand dollars in respect of every day during which the default continues.

(5) If default is made in complying with paragraph 23 of the Fourteenth Schedule (register to be produced at annual general meeting), the company and every officer thereof is liable to a default fine not exceeding two thousand dollars.

(6) In the case of a refusal of an inspection of the register required under paragraph 22 of the Fourteenth Schedule, the Court may, by order compel an immediate inspection of it; and in the case of failure to send, within the proper period, a copy required under paragraph 26, the Court may, by order, direct that the copy be sent to the person requiring it.

Application of section 194 to spouse and child.

199.—(1) For the purpose of section 196—

(*a*) an interest of the wife, husband or minor child of a director of a company (not being herself or himself a director thereof) in shares or debentures shall be treated as the director's interest;

(*b*) a contract, assignment or right of subscription entered into, exercised or made by, or a grant made to, the wife, husband or minor child of a director of a company (not being herself or himself a director thereof) shall be treated as having been entered into, exercised or made by, or, as the case may be, as having been made to, the director.

(2) A director of a company is under obligation to notify the company in writing of the occurrence while he or she is a director of either of the following events, namely—

(*a*) the grant by the company to his or her spouse or minor child, of a right to subscribe for shares in, or debentures of, the company; and

(*b*) the exercise by his or her spouse or minor child of such a right granted by the company to the wife, husband or minor child.

(3) A notice given to the company under subsection (2) shall state—

(*a*) in the case of the grant of a right, the like information as is required by section 196 to be stated by the director on the grant to him by another body corporate of a right to subscribe for shares in, or debentures of, that other body corporate; and

(*b*) in the case of the exercise of a right, the like information as is required by that section to be stated by the director on the exercise of a right granted to him by another body corporate to subscribe for shares in, or debentures of, that other body corporate.

(4) An obligation imposed by subsection (2) on a director shall be fulfilled by him before the end of five days beginning with the day following that on which the occurrence of the event giving rise to it comes to his knowledge.

(5) A person who—

(*a*) fails to fulfil, within the proper period, an obligation to which he is subject under subsection (4) is guilty of an offence and liable on conviction to a fine not exceeding two hundred thousand dollars; or (*b*) in purported fulfilment of such an obligation, makes to a company a statement which he knows to be false, or recklessly makes to a company a false statement, is guilty of an offence and liable on conviction thereof to a fine not exceeding five hundred thousand dollars or to imprisonment for a term not exceeding two years or to both such fine and imprisonment.

(6) For the purposes of section 197, an obligation imposed on a director by this section shall be treated as if it were imposed by section 196.

Provisions as to assignment of office by directors.

200. If in the case of any company provision is made by the articles or by any agreement entered into between any person and the company for empowering a director or manager of the company to assign his office as such to another person, any assignment of office made in pursuance of that provision shall, notwithstanding anything to the contrary contained in that provision, be of no effect unless and until it is approved by a special resolution of the company.

Indemnifying directors, etc.

201.—(1) Except in respect of an action by or on behalf of a company or body corporate to obtain a judgment in its favour, a company may indemnify—

(*a*) a director or officer of the company or any person employed by the company as an auditor;

(*b*) a former director, officer or auditor of the company; or

(*c*) a person who acts or acted at the company's request as a director or officer of a body corporate of which the company is or was a shareholder or creditor,

and his legal representatives, against all costs, charges and expenses (including an amount paid to settle an action or satisfy a judgment) reasonably incurred by him in respect of any civil, criminal or administrative action or proceeding to which he is made a party by reason of being, or having been, a director or officer of that company or body corporate, or any person employed by a company or body corporate as an auditor.

(2) Subsection (1) does not apply unless the director or officer to be so indemnified—

(*a*) acted honestly and in good faith with a view to the best interests of the company; and

(*b*) in the case of a criminal or administrative action or proceeding that is enforced by a monetary penalty, had reasonable grounds for believing that his conduct was lawful.

(3) The provisions of subsection (2) shall apply to any person employed to the company as an auditor if the act or omission for which he is to be indemnified did not arise due to a breach of duty on his part.

For derivative action.

202. A company may with the approval of the Court indemnify a person referred to in section 201 in respect of an action—

(*a*) by or on behalf of the company or body corporate to obtain a judgment in its favour; and

(*b*) to which he is made a party by reason of being or having been a director or an officer of the company or body corporate,

against all costs, charges and expenses reasonably incurred by him in connection with the action, if he fulfils the conditions set out in subsection (2) of section 201.

Right to indemnity.

203. Notwithstanding anything in section 201 or 202, a person described in section 201 is entitled to indemnity from the company in respect of all costs, charges and expenses reasonably incurred by him in connection with the defence of any civil, criminal or administrative action or proceeding to which he is made a party by reason of being, or having been, a director or officer of the company or body corporate, if the person seeking indemnity—

(*a*) was substantially successful on the merits in his defence of the action or proceeding;

(*b*) qualified in accordance with the standards set out in section 201 or 202; and

(*c*) is fairly and reasonably entitled to indemnity.

204. A company may purchase and maintain insurance for the benefit of any person referred to in section 201 against any liability incurred by him in his capacity as a director or officer of the company other than liability for fraud. Insurance of directors, etc.

205.—(1) A company or person referred to in section 201 may apply to the Court for an order approving an indemnity under section 202; and the Court may so order and make any further order it thinks fit. Court approval of indemnity.

(2) An applicant under subsection (1) shall give the Registrar notice of the application; and the Registrar may appear and be heard in person or by an attorney-at-law.

(3) An application under subsection (1) in the case of a public company, shall give to the Financial Services Commission notice of the application, and the Financial Services Commission may appear and be heard.

(4) Upon an application under subsection (1), the Court may order notice to be given to any interested person; and that person may appear and be heard in person or by an attorney-at-law.

Arrangements and Reconstructions

206.—(1) Where a compromise or arrangement is proposed between a company and its creditors or any class of them, or with creditors between the company and its members or any class of them, the Court may, on the application in a summary way of the company or of any creditor or member of the company, or, in the case of a company being wound up, of the Power to compromise with creditors and members.

liquidator, order a meeting of the creditors or class of creditors, or of the members of the company or class of members, as the case may be, to be summoned in such manner as the Court directs.

(2) If a majority in number representing three-fourths in value of the creditors or class of creditors, or members or class of members, as the case may be, present and voting either in person or by proxy at the meeting agree to any compromise or arrangement, the compromise or arrangement shall, if sanctioned by the Court, be binding on all the creditors or the class of creditors, or on the members or class of members, as the case may be, and also on the company or, in the case of a company in the course of being wound up, on the liquidator and contributories of the company.

(3) An order made under subsection (2) shall have no effect until a copy of the order has been delivered to the Registrar for registration, and a copy of every such order shall be annexed to every copy of the articles of the company issued after the order has been made.

(4) If a company makes default in complying with subsection (3) the company and every officer of the company who is in default shall be liable to a fine not exceeding one thousand dollars for each copy in respect of which default is made.

(5) In this section and in section 207—

"arrangement" includes a reorganization of the share capital of the company by the consolidation of shares of different classes or by the division of shares of different classes or by both those methods;

"company" means any company liable to be wound up under this Act.

Information as to compromises with creditors and members.

207.—(1) Where a meeting of creditors or any class of creditors or of members or any class of members is summoned under section 206 there shall (*a*) with every notice summoning the meeting which is sent to a creditor or member, be sent also a statement explaining the effect of the compromise or arrangement and in particular stating any material interests of the directors of the company, whether as directors or as members or as creditors of the company or otherwise, and the effect thereon, of the compromise or arrangement, in so far as it is different from the effect on the like interests of other persons; and

(*b*) in every notice summoning the meeting which is given by advertisement, be included either such a statement as aforesaid or a notification of the place at which and the manner in which creditors or members entitled to attend the meeting may obtain copies of such a statement as aforesaid.

(2) Where the compromise or arrangement affects the rights of debenture holders of the company, the statement shall give the like explanation as respects the trustees of any deed for securing the issue of the debentures as it is required to give as respects the company's directors.

(3) Where a notice given by advertisement includes a notification that copies of a statement explaining the effect of the compromise or arrangement proposed can be obtained by creditors or members entitled to attend the meeting, every such creditor or member shall, on making application in the manner indicated by the notice, be furnished by the company free of charge with a copy of the statement.

(4) Where a company makes default in complying with any requirements of this section, the company and every officer of the company who is in default shall be liable to a fine not exceeding fifty thousand dollars, and for the purpose of this subsection any liquidator of the company and any trustee of a deed for securing the issue of debentures of the company shall be deemed to be an officer of the company:

Provided that a person shall not be liable under this subsection if that person shows that the default was due to the refusal of any other person, being a director or trustee for debenture holders, to supply the necessary particulars as to his interests.

(5) It shall be the duty of any director of the company and of any trustee for debenture holders of the company to give notice to the company of such matters relating to himself as may be necessary for the purposes of this section, and any person who makes default in complying with this subsection shall be liable to a fine not exceeding fifty thousand dollars.

Provisions for facilitating reconstruction and amalgamation of companies.

208.—(1) Where an application is made to the Court under section 206 for the sanctioning of a compromise or arrangement proposed between a company and any such persons as are and mentioned in that section, and it is shown to the Court that the compromise or arrangement has been proposed for the purposes of or in connection with a scheme for the reconstruction of any company or companies or the amalgamation of any two or more companies, and that under the scheme the whole or any part of the undertaking or the property of any company concerned in the scheme (in this section referred to as "a transferor company") is to be transferred to another company (in this section referred to as "the transferee company") the Court may, either by the order sanctioning the compromise or arrangement or by any subsequent order, make provision for all or any of the following matters—

(*a*) the transfer to the transferee company of the whole or any part of the undertaking and of the property or liabilities of any transferor company;

(*b*) the allotting or appropriation by the transferee company of any shares, debentures, policies, or other like interests in that company which under the compromise or arrangement are to be allotted or appropriated by that company to or for any person;

(*c*) the continuation by or against the transferee company of any legal proceedings pending by or against any transferor company;

(*d*) the dissolution, without winding up, of any transferor company,

(*e*) the provision to be made for any person, who within such time and in such manner as the Court may direct, dissent from the compromise or arrangement;

(*f*) such incidental, consequential and supplemental matters as are necessary to secure that the reconstruction or amalgamation shall be fully and effectively carried out.

(2) Where an order under this section provides for the transfer of property or liabilities, that property shall, by virtue of the order, be transferred to and vest in, and those liabilities shall, by virtue of the order, be transferred to and become the liabilities of, the transferee company, and in the case of any property, if the order so directs, freed from any charge which is by virtue of the compromise or arrangement to cease to have effect.

(3) Where an order is made under this section, every company in relation to which the order is made shall cause a copy thereof to be delivered to the Registrar for registration within seven days after the making of the order, and if default is made in complying with this subsection, the company and every officer of the company who is in default shall be liable to a fine not exceeding fifty thousand dollars.

(4) In this section the expression "property" includes property, rights and powers of every description, and the expression "liabilities" includes duties.

(5) Notwithstanding the provisions of subsection (5) of section 206, the expression "company" in this section does not include any company other than a company within the meaning of this Act.

Power to acquire shares of shareholders dissenting from scheme or contract approved by majority.

209.—(1) Where a scheme or contract involving the transfer of shares or any class of shares in a company (in this section referred to as "the transferor company") to another company, whether a company within the meaning of this Act or not (in this section referred to as "the transferee company"), has, within four months after the making of the offer in that behalf by the transferee company been approved by the holders of not less than nine-tenths in value of the shares whose transfer is involved (other than shares already held at the date of the offer by, or by a nominee for, the transferee company or its subsidiary)—

(*a*) the transferee company may, at any time within two months after the expiration of the four months, give notice in the prescribed manner to any dissenting shareholder that it desires to acquire his shares; and

(*b*) when such a notice is given the transferee company shall, unless on an application made by the dissenting shareholder within one month from the date on which the notice was given the Court thinks fit to order otherwise, be entitled and bound to acquire those shares on the terms on which, under the scheme or contract, the shares of the approving shareholders are to be transferred to the transferee company:

Provided that where shares in the transferor company of the same class or classes as the shares whose transfer is involved are already held as aforesaid to a value greater than one-tenth of the aggregate of their value and that of the shares (other than those already held as aforesaid) whose transfer is involved, the foregoing provisions of this subsection shall not apply unless—

(*a*) the transferee company offers the same terms to all holders of the shares (other than those already held as aforesaid) whose transfer is involved, or, where those shares include shares of different classes, of each class of them; and (*b*) the holders who approve the scheme or contract, besides holding not less than nine-tenths in value of the shares (other than those already held as aforesaid) whose transfer is involved, are not less than three-fourths in number of the holders of those shares.

(2) Where, in pursuance of any such scheme or contract as aforesaid, shares in a company are transferred to another company or its nominee, and those shares together with any other shares in the first-mentioned company held by, or by a nominee for, the transferee company or its subsidiary at the date of the transfer comprise or include nine-tenths in value of the shares in the first-mentioned company or of any class of those shares, then—

(*a*) the transferee company shall within one month from the date of the transfer (unless on a previous transfer in pursuance of the scheme or contract it has already complied with this requirement) give notice of that fact in the prescribed manner to the holders of the remaining shares or of the remaining shares of that class, as the case may be, who have not assented to the scheme or contract; and

(*b*) any such holder may within three months from the giving of the notice to him require the transferee company to acquire the shares in question,

and where a shareholder gives notice under paragraph (*b*) of this subsection with respect to any shares, the transferee company shall be entitled and bound to acquire those shares on the terms on which under the scheme or contract the shares of the approving shareholders were transferred to it, or on such other terms as may be agreed or as the Court on the application of either the transferee company or the shareholder thinks fit to order.

(3) Where a notice has been given by the transferee company under subsection (1) and the Court has not, on an application made by the dissenting shareholder, ordered to the contrary, the transferee company shall, on the expiration of one month from the date on which the notice has been given, or, if an application to the Court by the dissenting shareholder is then pending, after that application has been disposed of—

(*a*) transmit a copy of the notice to the transferor company together with an instrument of transfer executed on behalf of the shareholder by any person appointed by the transferee company and on its own behalf by the transferee company; and

(*b*) pay or transfer to the transferor company the amount or other consideration representing the price payable by the transferee company for the shares which by virtue of this section that company is entitled to acquire,

and the transferor company shall thereupon register the transferee company as the holder of those shares:

Provided that an instrument of transfer shall not be required for any share for which a share warrant is for the time being outstanding.

(4) Any sums received by the transferor company under this section shall be paid into a separate bank account, and any such sums and any other consideration so received shall be held by that company on trust for the several persons entitled to the shares in respect of which those sums or other consideration were respectively received.

(5) In this section the expression "dissenting shareholder" includes a shareholder who has not assented to the scheme or contract and any shareholder who has failed or refused to transfer his shares to the transferee company in accordance with the scheme or contract.

(6) In relation to an offer made by the transferee company to shareholders of the transferor company before the appointed day, this section shall have effect—

(*a*) with the substitution, in subsection (1), for the words "the shares whose transfer is involved (other than shares already held at the date of the offer by, or by a nominee for, the transferee company or its subsidiary)," of the words "the shares affected" and with the omission of the proviso to that subsection;

(*b*) with the omission of subsection (2); and

(*c*) with the omission, in subsection (3), of the words "together with an instrument of transfer executed on behalf of the shareholder by any person appointed by the transferee company and on its own behalf by the transferee company" and of the proviso to that subsection.

Scheme of arrangement re company and connected person.

210.—(1) Without prejudice to the operation of sections 206 to 209—

(*a*) the provisions of subsection (2) of this section shall apply in any case where a compromise or arrangement is proposed in relation to a company which is a member of a group of connected bodies corporate in respect of any or all of which a compromise or arrangement is proposed; and

(*b*) for the purposes of this section, a group of connected bodies corporate shall be deemed to exist where the same persons or individuals have the effective control, direction or management of the members of the group or have had such effective control, direction or management at any time within the period of twenty-four months immediately preceding—

(i) the date on which the compromise or arrangement is proposed; or

(ii) the date of appointment, pursuant to any enactment, of a temporary manager or liquidator, as the case may be, in relation to any member of the group.

(2) A compromise or arrangement in relation to a company may provide that—

(*a*) the assets and liabilities of the company and any or all of the connected bodies corporate be combined as if the company and the connected person were a single undertaking; and

(*b*) the members and creditors of the company and any or all of the connected bodies corporate were members and creditors of that single undertaking.

Power of Court to order pooling of assets.

211. The Court may, in respect of an application for the sanctioning of a compromise or arrangement in respect of a company, order that the assets of that company be combined with the assets of any other body corporate, if the Court is satisfied that—

(*a*) the assets of the company are so intermingled with the assets of the other body corporate that it is just and equitable that they should be treated as a single undertaking; or

(*b*) the same persons or individuals have the effective control, direction or management of the company and the other body corporate or have had such effective control, direction or management at any time during the period of twenty-four months immediately preceding—

(i) the date on which the compromise or arrangement is proposed; or

(ii) the date of appointment pursuant to any enactment of a temporary manager or liquidator, as the case may be, in relation to the company or other body corporate.

Complainant Remedies

212.—(1) Subject to subsection (2), a complainant may, for the purpose of prosecuting, defending or discontinuing an action on behalf of a company, apply to the Court for leave to bring a derivative action in the name and on behalf of the company or any of its subsidiaries, or intervene in an action to which any such company or any of its subsidiaries is a party. Derivative actions.

(2) No action may be brought, and no intervention in an action may be made under subsection (1) unless the Court is satisfied that—

(*a*) the complainant has given reasonable notice to the directors of the company or its subsidiary of his intention to apply to the Court under subsection (1) if the directors of the company or its subsidiary do not bring, diligently prosecute or defend, or discontinue, the action;

(*b*) the complainant is acting in good faith; and

(*c*) it appears to be in the interests of the company or its subsidiary that the action be brought, prosecuted, defended or discontinued.

(3) In this section and sections 213 and 213A, "complainant" means—

(*a*) a shareholder or former shareholder of a company or an affiliated company;

(*b*) a debenture holder or former debenture holder of a company or an affiliated company;

(*c*) a director or officer or former director or officer of a company or an affiliated company.

Court powers

213.—(1) The Court may, in connection with an action brought or intervened in under section 212, make such order as it thinks fit, including an order—

(*a*) authorizing the complainant, the Registrar or any other person to control the conduct of the action;

(*b*) giving directions for the conduct of the action;

(*c*) directing that any amount adjudged payable by a defendant in the action be paid, in whole or in part, directly to former and present shareholders or debenture holders of the company or its subsidiary, instead of to the company or its subsidiary; or

(*d*) requiring the company or its subsidiary to pay reasonable legal fees incurred by the complainant in connection with the action.

(2) An action brought or intervened in under section 212 shall not be stayed or dismissed by reason only that it is shown that an alleged breach of a right or duty owed to the company or its subsidiary has been or may be approved by the shareholders, but evidence of approval by the shareholders may be taken into account by the Court in making an order under that section.

Remedy in case of oppression.

213A.—(1) A complainant may apply to the Court for an order under this section.

(2) If upon an application under subsection (1), the Court is satisfied that in respect of a company or of any of its affiliates—

(*a*) any act or omission of the company or any of its affiliates effects a result;

(*b*) the business or affairs of the company or any of its affiliates are or have been carried on or conducted in a manner;

(*c*) the powers of the directors of the company or any of its affiliates are or have been exercised in a manner,

that is oppressive or unfairly prejudicial to, any shareholder or debenture holder, creditor, director or officer of the company, the Court may make an order to rectify the matters complained of.

(3) The Court may, in connection with an application under this section make any interim or final order it thinks fit, including an order—

(*a*) restraining the conduct complained of;

(*b*) appointing a receiver or receiver-manager;

(*c*) to regulate a company's affairs by amending its articles or by-laws, or creating or amending a unanimous shareholder agreement;

(*d*) directing an issue or exchange of shares or debentures;

(*e*) appointing directors in place of, or in addition to, all or any of the directors then in office;

(*f*) directing a company, subject to subsection (4), or any other person to purchase the shares or debentures of a holder thereof;

(*g*) directing a company, subject to subsection (4), or any other person to pay to a shareholder or debenture holder any part of the moneys paid by him for his shares or debentures;

(*h*) varying or setting aside a transaction or contract to which a company is a party, and compensating the company or any other party to the transaction or contract;

(*i*) requiring a company, within the time specified by the Court, to produce to the Court or an interested person, financial statements or an accounting in such forms as the Court may determine;

(*j*) compensating an aggrieved person;

(*k*) directing rectification of the registers or other records of the company;

(*l*) liquidating and dissolving the company;

(*m*) directing an investigation to be made; or

(*n*) requiring the trial of any issue.

(4) A company shall not make a payment to a shareholder under paragraph (*f*) or (*g*) of subsection (3) if there are reasonable grounds for believing that—

(*a*) the company is unable or would, after that payment, be unable to pay its liabilities as they become due; or

(*b*) the realizable value of the company's assets would thereby be less than the aggregate of its liabilities.

PART V—WINDING UP

(i) PRELIMINARY

Modes of Winding Up

Modes of winding up.

214.—(1) The winding up of a company may be either—

(*a*) by the Court; or

(*b*) voluntary; or

(*c*) subject to the supervision of the Court.

(2) The provisions of this Act with respect to winding up apply, unless the contrary appears, to the winding up of a company in any of those modes.

Contributories

215.—(1) In the event of a company being wound up, every present and past member shall be liable to contribute to the assets of the company to an amount sufficient for payment of its debts and liabilities, and the costs, charges, and expenses of the winding up, and for the adjustment of the rights of the contributories among themselves, subject to the following qualifications— Liability as contributories of present and past members.

(*a*) a past member shall not be liable to contribute if he has ceased to be a member for one year or upwards before the commencement of the winding up;

(*b*) a past member shall not be liable to contribute in respect of any debt or liability of the company contracted after he ceased to be a member;

(*c*) a past member shall not be liable to contribute unless it appears to the Court that the existing members are unable to satisfy the contributions required to be made by them in pursuance of this Act;

(*d*) in the case of a company limited by shares, no contribution shall be required from any member exceeding the amount, if any, unpaid on the shares in respect of which he is liable as a present or past member;

(*e*) in the case of a company limited by guarantee, no contribution shall, subject to the provisions of subsection (2), be required from any member exceeding the amount undertaken to be contributed by him to the assets of the company in the event of its being wound up;

(*f*) nothing in this Act shall invalidate any provision contained in any policy of insurance or other contract whereby the liability of individual members on the policy or contract is restricted, or whereby the funds of the company are alone made liable in respect of the policy or contract;

(g) a sum due to any member of a company, in his character of a member, by way of dividends, profits or otherwise, shall not be deemed to be a debt of the company, payable to that member in a case of competition between himself and any other creditor not a member of the company, but any such sum may be taken into account for the purpose of the final adjustment of the rights of the contributories among themselves.

(2) In the winding up of a company limited by guarantee which has a share capital, every member of the company shall be liable, in addition to the amount undertaken to be contributed by him to the assets of the company in the event of its being wound up, to contribute to the extent of any sums unpaid on any shares held by him.

Definition of contributory.

216. The term "contributory" means every person liable to contribute to the assets of a company in the event of it being wound up, and for the purposes of all proceedings for determining, and all proceedings prior to the final determination of, the persons who are to be deemed contributories, include any person alleged to be a contributory.

Nature of liability of contributory.

217. The liability of a contributory shall create a debt in the nature of a specialty accruing due from him at the time when his liability commenced, but payable at the times when calls are made for enforcing the liability.

Contributories in case of death of member.

218.—(1) If a contributory dies either before or after he has been placed on the list of contributories, his personal representatives shall be liable in a due course of administration to contribute to the assets of the company in discharge of his liability and shall be contributories accordingly.

(2) If the personal representatives make default in paying any money ordered to be paid by them, proceedings may be taken for administering the estate of the deceased contributory, and for compelling payment out of the money due.

219. If a contributory becomes bankrupt, either before or after he has been placed on the list of contributories— Contributories in case of bankruptcy of member

(*a*) the Trustee shall represent him for all the purposes of the winding up, and shall be a contributory accordingly, and may be called on to admit to proof against the estate of the bankrupt, or otherwise to allow to be paid out of his assets in due course of law, any money due from the bankrupt in respect of his liability to contribute to the assets of the company; and

(*b*) there may be proved against the estate of the bankrupt the estimated value of his liability to future calls as well as calls already made.

(ii) WINDING UP BY THE COURT

Cases in which Company may be wound up by Court

220. A company may be wound up by the Court if— Circumstances in which companies may be wound up by Court.

(*a*) the company has by special resolution resolved that the company be wound up by the Court;

(*b*) default is made in delivering the statutory report to the Registrar or in holding the statutory meeting;

(*c*) the company does not commence its business within a year from its incorporation, or suspends its business for a whole year;

(*d*) the company is unable to pay its debts;

(*e*) the Court is of opinion that it is just and equitable that the company should be wound up.

Definition of inability to pay debts.

221. A company shall be deemed to be unable to pay its debts—

(*a*) if a creditor, by assignment or otherwise, to whom the company is indebted in a sum exceeding five hundred thousand dollars then due, has served on the company, by leaving it at the registered office of the company, a demand under his hand requiring the company to pay the sum so due, and the company has for three weeks thereafter neglected to pay the sum, or to secure or compound for it to the reasonable satisfaction of the creditor; or

(*b*) if execution or other process issued on a judgment, decree or order of any Court in favour of a creditor of the company is returned unsatisfied in whole or in part; or

(*c*) if it is proved to the satisfaction of the Court that the company is unable to pay its debts, and, in determining whether a company is unable to pay its debts, the Court shall take into account the contingent and prospective liabilities of the company.

Petition for Winding Up and Effects thereof

Provisions as to applications for winding up.

222.—(1) An application to the Court for the winding up of a company shall be by petition, presented subject to the provisions of this section either by the company, or by any creditor or creditors (including any contingent or prospective creditor or creditors) contributory or contributories, or by all or any of those parties, together or separately:

Provided that—

(*a*) a contributory shall not be entitled to present a winding up petition unless the shares in respect of which he is a contributory, or some of them, either were originally allotted to him or have been held by him, and registered in his name, for at least six months during the eighteen months before the commencement of the winding up, or have devolved on him through the death of a former holder; and (*b*) a winding up petition shall not, if the ground of the petition is default in delivering the statutory report to the Registrar or in holding the statutory meeting, be presented by any person except a shareholder, nor before the expiration of fourteen days after the last day on which the meeting ought to have been held; and

(*c*) the Court shall not give a hearing to a winding up petition presented by a contingent or prospective creditor until such security for costs has been given as the Court thinks reasonable and until a *prima facie* case for winding up has been established to the satisfaction of the Court; and

(*d*) in a case falling within subsection (4) of section 165, a winding up petition may be presented by the Minister.

(2) Where a company is being wound up voluntarily or subject to supervision, a winding up petition may be presented by the Trustee as well as by any other person authorized in that behalf under the other provisions of this section, but the Court shall not make a winding up order on the petition unless it is satisfied that the voluntary winding up or winding up subject to supervision cannot be continued with due regard to the interests of the creditors or contributories.

Power of Court on hearing petition.

223.—(1) On hearing a winding up petition the Court may dismiss it, or adjourn the hearing conditionally or unconditionally, or make any interim order, or any other order that it thinks fit, but the Court shall not refuse to make a winding up order on the ground only that the assets of the company have been mortgaged to an amount equal to or in excess of those assets, or that the company has no assets.

(2) Where the petition is presented by members of the company as contributories on the ground that it is just and equitable that the company should be wound up, the Court, if it is of opinion—

(*a*) that the petitioners are entitled to relief either by winding up the company or by some other means; and

(*b*) that in the absence of any other remedy it would be just and equitable that the company should be wound up,

shall make a winding up order, unless it is also of the opinion both that some other remedy is available to the petitioners and that they are acting unreasonably in seeking to have the company wound up instead of pursuing that other remedy.

(3) Where the petition is presented on the ground of default in delivering the statutory report to the Registrar in holding the statutory meeting, the Court may—

(*a*) instead of making a winding up order, direct that the statutory report shall be delivered or that a meeting shall be held; and

(*b*) order the costs to be paid by any persons who, in the opinion of the Court, are responsible for the default.

Power to stay or restrain proceedings against company.

224. At any time after the presentation of a winding up petition, and before a winding up order has been made, the company, or any creditor or contributory, may, where any action or proceeding is pending against the company, apply to the Court to restrain further proceedings in the action or proceeding, and the Court may stay or restrain the proceedings accordingly on such terms as it thinks fit.

Avoidance of dispositions of property, etc., after commencement of winding up.

225. In a winding up by the Court, any disposition of the property of the company, including things in action, and any transfer of shares, or alteration in the status of the members of the company, made after the commencement of the winding up, shall, unless the Court otherwise orders, be void.

Avoidance of attachments, etc.

226. Where any company is being wound up by the Court, any attachment, sequestration, distress, or execution put in force against the estate or effects of the company after the commencement of the winding up shall be void to all intents.

Commencement of Winding Up

227.—(1) Where before the presentation of a petition for the winding up of a company by the Court a resolution has been passed by the company for voluntary winding up, the winding up of the company shall be deemed to have commenced at the time of passing of the resolution, and unless the Court, on proof of fraud or mistake, thinks fit otherwise to direct, all proceedings taken in the voluntary winding up shall be deemed to have been validly taken.

(2) In any other case, the winding up of a company by the Court shall be deemed to commence at the time of the presentation of the petition for the winding up.

Consequences of Winding Up Order

Copy of order to be forwarded to Registrar.

228.—(1) On the making of a winding up order, a copy of the order shall forthwith be forwarded by the company, or otherwise as may be prescribed, to the Registrar, who shall make a minute thereof in his books relating to the company.

(2) If default is made in forwarding a copy of a winding up order to the Registrar as required by subsection (1), every officer of the company or other person who knowingly and wilfully authorizes or permits the default shall be liable to a fine not exceeding fifty thousand dollars.

Actions stayed on winding up order.

229. When a winding up order has been made, or a provisional liquidator has been appointed, no action or proceeding shall be proceeded with or commenced against the company except by leave of the Court, and subject to such terms as the Court may impose.

Effect of winding up order.

230. An order for winding up a company shall operate in favour of all the creditors and of all the contributories of the company as if made on the joint petition of a creditor and of a contributory.

Trustee in Bankruptcy

Trustee in Bankruptcy to be Trustee for winding up purposes.

231. For the purposes of this Act, the term "Trustee" means the Trustee in Bankruptcy attached to the Court for bankruptcy purposes as provided for in section 14 of the Bankruptcy Act.

Statement of company's affairs to be submitted to trustee.

232.—(1) Where the Court has made a winding up order or appointed a provisional liquidator, there shall, unless the Court thinks fit to order otherwise and so orders, be made out and submitted to the Trustee a statement as to the affairs of the company in the prescribed form, verified by affidavit, and showing the particulars of its assets, debts and liabilities, the names, residences, and occupations of its creditors, the securities held by them respectively, the dates when the securities were respectively given, and such further or other information as may be prescribed or as the Trustee may require.

(2) The statement shall be submitted and verified by one or more of the persons who are at the relevant date the directors and by the person who is, at that date, the secretary or other chief officer of the company, or by such of the persons hereinafter mentioned in this subsection as the Trustee, subject to the direction of the Court, may require to submit and verify the statement, that is to say, persons—

(*a*) who are or have been directors or officers of the company;

(*b*) who have taken part in the formation of the company at any time within one year before the relevant date;

(*c*) who are in the employment of the company, or have been in the employment of the company within that year, and are in the opinion of the Trustee capable of giving the information required;

(*d*) who are or have been within that year officers of or in the employment of a company, which is, or within the said year was, an officer of the company to which the statement relates.

(3) The statement shall be submitted within fourteen days from the relevant date, or within such extended time as the Trustee or the Court may for special reasons appoint.

(4) Any person making or concurring in making the statement and affidavit required by this section shall be allowed, and shall be paid by the Trustee or provisional liquidator, as the case may be, out of the assets of the company, such costs and expenses incurred in and about the preparation and making of the statement and affidavit as the Trustee may consider reasonable, subject to an appeal to the Court.

(5) If any person, without reasonable excuse, makes default in complying with the requirements of this section, he shall be liable to a fine not exceeding two thousand dollars for every day during which the default continues.

(6) Any person stating himself in writing to be a creditor or contributory of the company shall be entitled by himself or by his agent at all reasonable times, on payment of the prescribed fee, to inspect the statement submitted in pursuance of this section, and to a copy thereof or extract therefrom.

(7) Any person untruthfully so stating himself to be a creditor or contributory shall be guilty of a contempt of court and shall, on the application of the liquidator or of the Trustee, be punishable accordingly.

(8) In this section the expression "the relevant date" means in a case where a provisional liquidator is appointed, the date of his appointment, and, in a case where no such appointment is made, the date of the winding up order.

233.—(1) In a case where a winding up order is made, the Trustee shall, as soon as practicable after receipt of the statement to be submitted under section 232, or, in a case where the Court orders that no statement shall be submitted, as soon as practicable after the date of the order, submit a preliminary report to the Court— Report by Trustee.

(*a*) as to the amount of capital issued, subscribed, and paid up, and the estimated amount of assets and liabilities; and

(*b*) if the company has failed, as to the causes of the failure; and

(*c*) whether in his opinion further inquiry is desirable as to any matter relating to the promotion, formation or failure of the company, or the conduct of the business thereof.

(2) The Trustee may also, if he thinks fit, make a further report, or further reports, stating the manner in which the company was formed and whether in his opinion any fraud has been committed by any person in its promotion or formation, or by any director or other officer of the company in relation to the company since the formation thereof, and any other matters which in his opinion it is desirable to bring to the notice of the Court.

(3) If the Trustee states in any such further report as aforesaid that in his opinion a fraud has been committed as aforesaid, the Court shall have the further powers provided in sections 265 and 266.

Liquidators

Power of Court to appoint liquidators.

234. For the purpose of conducting the proceedings in winding up a company and performing such duties in reference thereto as the Court may impose, the Court may appoint a liquidator or liquidators.

Appointment and powers of provisional liquidator.

235.—(1) Subject to the provisions of this section, the Court may appoint a liquidator provisionally at any time after the presentation of a winding up petition, and either the Trustee or any other fit person may be appointed.

(2) Where a liquidator is provisionally appointed by the Court, the Court may limit and restrict his powers by the order appointing him.

236.—(1) The following provisions with respect to liquidators shall have effect on a winding up order being made— Appoint-ment, style, etc., of liquidators.

(*a*) the Trustee shall by virtue of his office become the provisional liquidator and shall continue to act as such until he or another person becomes liquidator and is capable of acting as such;

(*b*) the Trustee shall summon separate meetings of the creditors and contributories of the company for the purpose of determining whether or not an application is to be made to the Court for appointing a liquidator in the place of the Trustee;

(*c*) the Court may make any appointment and order required to give effect to any such determination, and, if there is a difference between the determinations of the meetings of the creditors and contributories in respect of the matter aforesaid, the Court shall decide the difference and make such order thereon as the Court may think fit;

(*d*) in a case where a liquidator is not appointed by the Court, the Trustee shall be the liquidator of the company;

(*e*) the Trustee shall by virtue of his office be the liquidator during any vacancy;

(*f*) a liquidator shall be described, where a person other than the Trustee is liquidator, by the style of "the liquidator", and, where the Trustee is liquidator, by the style of "the Trustee and liquidator", of the particular company in respect of which he is appointed, and not by his individual name.

(2) The Trustee may charge such fees as may be prescribed by the Minister for duties carried out by him as provisional liquidator.

Provisions where person other than Trustee is appointed liquidator.

237.—(1) Where in the winding up of a company by the Court a person other than the Trustee is appointed liquidator, that person—

(*a*) shall not be capable of acting as liquidator until he has notified his appointment to the Registrar and given security in such manner as the Court may direct;

(*b*) shall give the Trustee such information and such access to and facilities for inspecting the books and documents of the company and generally such aid as may be requisite for enabling that officer to perform his duties under this Act.

(2) If a liquidator contravenes the provisions of paragraph (*b*) of subsection (1), he shall be liable to a fine not exceeding fifty thousand dollars.

General provisions as to liquidators.

238.—(1) A liquidator appointed by the Court may resign or, on cause shown, be removed by the Court.

(2) Where a person other than the Trustee is appointed liquidator, he shall receive such salary or remuneration by way of percentage or otherwise as the Court may direct, and, if more than one such person are appointed liquidators, their remuneration shall be distributed among them in such proportions as the Court directs.

(3) A vacancy in the office of a liquidator appointed by the Court shall be filled by the Court.

(4) If more than one liquidator is appointed by the Court, the Court shall declare whether any act by this Act required or authorized to be done by the liquidator is to be done by all or any one or more of the persons appointed.

(5) Subject to the provisions of section 325, the acts of a liquidator shall be valid notwithstanding any defects that may afterwards be discovered in his appointment or qualification.

Custody of company's property.

239. Where a winding up order has been made or where a provisional liquidator has been appointed, the liquidator, or the provisional liquidator, as the case may be, shall take into his custody, or under his control, all the property and things in action to which the company is or appears to be entitled.

Vesting of company's property in liquidator.

240. Where a company is being wound up by the Court, the Court may on the application of the liquidator by order direct that all or any part of the property of whatever description belonging to the company or held by trustees on its behalf shall vest in the liquidator by his official name, and thereupon the property to which the order relates shall vest accordingly, and the liquidator may, after giving such indemnity, if any, as the Court may direct, bring or defend in his official name any action or other legal proceeding which relates to that property or which it is necessary to bring or defend for the purpose of effectually winding up the company and recovering its property.

Powers of liquidator.

241.—(1) The liquidator in a winding up by the Court shall have power with the sanction either of the Court or of the committee of inspection—

(*a*) to bring or defend any action or other legal proceeding in the name and on behalf of the company;

(*b*) to carry on the business of the company, so far as may be necessary for the beneficial winding up thereof;

(*c*) to appoint an attorney-at-law or other agent to assist him in the performance of his duties;

(*d*) to pay any classes of creditors in full;

(*e*) to make any compromise or arrangement with creditors or persons claiming to be creditors, or having or alleging themselves to have any claim, present or future, certain or contingent, ascertained or sounding only in damages against the company, or whereby the company may be rendered liable;

(*f*) to compromise all calls and liabilities to calls, debts, and liabilities capable of resulting in debts, and all claims, present or future, certain or contingent, ascertained or sounding only in damages, subsisting or supposed to subsist between the company and a contributory, or alleged contributory, or other debtor or person apprehending liability to the company, and all questions in any way relating to or affecting the assets or the winding up of the company, on such terms as may be agreed, and take any security for the discharge of any such debt, liability or claim, and give a complete discharge in respect thereof.

(2) The liquidator in a winding up by the Court shall have power—

(*a*) to sell the real and personal property and things in action of the company by public auction or private contract, with power to transfer the whole thereof to any person or company, or to sell the same in parcels;

(*b*) to do all acts and to execute, in the name and on behalf of the company, all deeds, receipts, and other documents, and for that purpose to use, when necessary, the company's seal;

(*c*) to prove, rank, and claim in the bankruptcy, insolvency, or sequestration of any contributory, for any balance against his estate, and to receive dividends in the bankruptcy, insolvency, or sequestration in respect of that balance, as a separate debt due from the bankrupt or insolvent, and rateably with the other separate creditors;

(*d*) to draw, accept, make, and indorse any bill of exchange or promissory note in the name and on behalf of the company, with the same effect with respect to the liability of the company as if the bill or note had been drawn, accepted, made, or indorsed by or on behalf of the company in the course of its business;

(*e*) to raise on the security of the assets of the company any money requisite;

(*f*) to take out in his official name letters of administration to any deceased contributory, and to do in his official name any other act necessary for obtaining payment of any money due from a contributory or his estate which cannot be conveniently done in the name of the company, and in all such cases the money due shall, for the purpose of enabling the liquidator to take out the letters of administration or recover the money, be deemed to be due to the liquidator himself;

(*g*) to appoint an agent to do any business which the liquidator is unable to do himself;

(*h*) to do all such other things as may be necessary for winding up the affairs of the company and distributing its assets.

(3) The exercise by the liquidator in a winding up by the Court of the powers conferred by this section shall be subject to the control of the Court, and any creditor or contributory may apply to the Court with respect to any exercise or proposed exercise of any of those powers.

242.—(1) Subject to the provisions of this Act, the liquidator of a company which is being wound up by the Court shall, in the administration of the assets of the company and in the distribution thereof among its creditors, have regard to any directions that may be given by resolution of the creditors or contributories, at any general meeting, or by the committee of inspection, and any directions given by the creditors or contributories at any general meeting shall in case of conflict be deemed to override any directions given by the committee of inspection. Exercise and control of liquidator's powers.

(2) The liquidator may summon general meetings of the creditors or contributories for the purpose of ascertaining their wishes, and it shall be his duty to summon meetings at such times as the creditors or contributories, by resolution, either at the meeting appointing the liquidator or otherwise, may direct, or whenever requested in writing to do so by one-tenth in value of the creditors or contributories as the case may be.

(3) The liquidator may apply to the Court in manner prescribed for directions in relation to any particular matter arising under the winding up.

(4) Subject to the provisions of this Act, the liquidator shall use his own discretion in the management of the estate and its distribution among the creditors.

(5) Any person aggrieved by any act or decision of the liquidator, may apply to the Court, and the Court may confirm, reverse, or modify the act or decision complained of, and make such order in the premises as it thinks just.

Books to be kept by liquidator.

243.—(1) Every liquidator of a company which is being wound up by the Court shall keep, in the prescribed manner, proper books in which he shall cause to be made entries or minutes of proceedings at meetings, and of such other matters as may be prescribed, and any creditor or contributory may, subject to the control of the Court, personally or by his agent inspect any such books.

(2) If a liquidator fails to keep proper books as required by subsection (1) or refuses to allow any inspection permitted thereby, he shall be liable to a fine not exceeding fifty thousand dollars.

Payments of liquidator into bank.

244.—(1) Every liquidator of a company which is being wound up by the Court shall pay the money received by him into such bank as the Court may direct.

(2) If any such liquidator at any time retains for more than ten days a sum exceeding one hundred thousand dollars, or such other amount as the Court in any particular case authorizes him to retain, then, unless he explains the retention to the satisfaction of the Court, he shall pay interest on the amount so retained in excess at the rate of twenty *per centum* per annum, and shall be liable to disallowance of all or such part of his remuneration as the Court may think just, and to be removed from his office by the Court, and shall be liable to pay any expenses occasioned by reason of his default

(3) A liquidator of a company which is being wound up by the Court shall not pay any sums received by him as liquidator into his private banking account.

(4) If a liquidator contravenes the provisions of subsection (3), he shall be liable to a fine not exceeding fifty thousand dollars.

245.—(1) Every liquidator of a company which is being wound up by the Court shall, at such times as may be prescribed but not less than twice in each year during his tenure of office, send to the Registrar an account of his receipts and payments as liquidator. Audit of liquidator's accounts.

(2) The account shall be in a prescribed form, shall be made in duplicate, and shall be verified by an affidavit or a statutory declaration in the prescribed form.

(3) The Registrar shall cause the account to be audited and for the purpose of the audit the liquidator shall furnish the Registrar with such vouchers and information as the Registrar may require, and the Registrar may at any time require the production of and inspect any books or accounts kept by the liquidator.

(4) When the account has been audited, one copy thereof shall be filed and kept by the Registrar, and the other copy shall be delivered to the Court for filing, and each copy shall be open to the inspection of any creditor or of any person interested.

(5) The Registrar shall cause the account when audited or a summary thereof to be printed, and shall send a printed copy of the account or summary by post to every creditor and contributory.

(6) If a liquidator fails to comply with any of the duties imposed upon him by this section, he shall be liable to a fine not exceeding fifty thousand dollars.

Control of Registrar over liquidators.

246.—(1) The Registrar shall take cognizance of the conduct of liquidators of companies which are being wound up by the Court, and, if a liquidator does not faithfully perform his duties and duly observe all the requirements imposed on him by statute, rules, or otherwise with respect to the performance of his duties, or if any complaint is made to the Registrar by any creditor or contributory in regard thereto, the Registrar shall inquire into the matter, and take such action thereon as he may think expedient.

(2) The Registrar may at any time require any liquidator of a company which is being wound up by the Court to answer any inquiry in relation to any winding up in which he is engaged, and may if the Registrar thinks fit, apply to the Court to examine him or any other person on oath concerning the winding up.

(3) The Registrar may also direct an investigation to be made of the books and vouchers of the liquidator.

Release of liquidator.

247.—(1) When the liquidator of a company which is being wound up by the Court has realized all the property of the company, or so much thereof as can, in his opinion, be realized without needlessly protracting the liquidation, and has distributed a final dividend, if any, to the creditors, and adjusted the rights of the contributories among themselves, and made a final return, if any, to the contributories, or has resigned, or has been removed from his office, the Registrar shall, on his application, cause a report on his accounts to be prepared, and, on his complying with all the requirements of the Registrar, shall take into consideration the report, and any objection which may be urged by any creditor or contributory or person interested against the release of the liquidator, and shall either grant or withhold the release accordingly, subject nevertheless to an appeal to the Court.

(2) Where the release of a liquidator is withheld, the Court may, on the application of any creditor or contributory, or person interested, make such order as it thinks just, charging the liquidator with the consequences of any act or default which he may have done or made contrary to his duty.

(3) An order of the Registrar releasing the liquidator shall discharge him from all liability in respect of any act done or default made by him in the administration of the affairs of the company, or otherwise in relation to his conduct as liquidator, but any such order may be revoked on proof that it was obtained by fraud or by suppression or concealment of any material fact.

(4) Where the liquidator has not previously resigned or been removed, his release shall operate as a removal of him from his office.

Meetings of creditors and contributories to determine whether committee of inspection shall be appointed.

248.—(1) When a winding up order has been made by the Court, it shall be the business of the separate meetings of creditors and contributories summoned for the purpose of determining whether or not an application should be made to the Court for appointing a liquidator in place of the Trustee, to determine further whether or not an application is to be made to the Court for the appointment of a committee of inspection to act with the liquidator and who are to be members of the committee if appointed.

(2) The Court may make any appointment and order required to give effect to any such determination, and if there is a difference between the determinations of the meetings of the creditors and contributories in respect of the matters aforesaid the Court shall decide the difference and make such order thereon as the Court may think fit.

Constitution and proceedings of committee of inspection.

249.—(1) A committee of inspection appointed in pursuance of this Act shall consist of creditors and contributories of the company or persons holding general powers of attorney from creditors or contributories in such proportions as may be agreed on by the meetings of creditors and contributories, or as, in case of difference, may be determined by the Court.

(2) The committee shall meet at such times as they from time to time appoint, and, failing such appointment, at least once a month and the liquidator or any member of the committee may also call a meeting of the committee as and when he thinks necessary.

(3) The committee may act by a majority of their members present at a meeting, but shall not act unless a majority of the committee are present.

(4) A member of the committee may resign by notice in writing signed by him and delivered to the liquidator.

(5) If a member of the committee becomes bankrupt, or compounds or arranges with his creditors, or is absent from five consecutive meetings of the committee without the leave of those members who together with himself represent the creditors or contributories, as the case may be, his office shall thereupon become vacant.

(6) A member of the committee may be removed by an ordinary resolution at a meeting of creditors, if he represents creditors, or of contributories, if he represents contributories of which seven days' notice has been given, stating the object of the meeting.

(7) On a vacancy occurring in the committee the liquidator shall forthwith summon a meeting of creditors or of contributories, as the case may require, to fill the vacancy, and the meeting may, by resolution, reappoint the same or appoint another creditor or contributory to fill the vacancy:

Provided that if the liquidator, having regard to the position in the winding up, is of the opinion that it is unnecessary for the vacancy to be filled he may apply to the Court which may make an order that the vacancy shall not be filled, or shall not be filled except in such circumstances as may be specified in the order.

(8) The continuing members of the committee, if not less than two, may act notwithstanding any vacancy in the committee.

250. Where in the case of a winding up there is no committee of inspection, the Minister may, on the application of the liquidator, do any act or thing or give any direction or permission which is by this Act authorized or required to be done or given by the committee. Powers of Minister where no committee of inspection.

General Powers of Court in case of Winding up by Court

251.—(1) The Court may at any time after an order for winding up, on the application either of the liquidator, or the Trustee, or any creditor or contributory, and on proof to the satisfaction of the Court that all proceedings in relation to the winding up ought to be stayed, make an order staying the proceedings, either altogether or for a limited time on such terms and conditions as the Court thinks fit. Power to stay winding up.

(2) On any application under this section the Court may, before making an order, require the Trustee to furnish to the Court a report with respect to any facts or matters which are in his opinion relevant to the application.

(3) A copy of every order made under this section shall forthwith be forwarded by the company, or otherwise as may be prescribed, to the Registrar, who shall make a minute of the order in his books relating to the company.

Settlement of list of contributories and application of assets.

252.—(1) As soon as may be after making a winding up order, the Court shall settle a list of contributories, with power to rectify the register of members in all cases where rectification is required in pursuance of this Act, and shall cause the assets of the company to be collected, and applied in discharge of its liabilities:

Provided that, where it appears to the Court that it will not be necessary to make calls on or adjust the rights of contributories, the Court may dispense with the settlement of a list of contributories.

(2) In settling the list of contributories, the Court shall distinguish between persons who are contributories in their own right and persons who are contributories as being representatives of or liable for the debts of others.

Delivery of property to liquidator.

253. The Court may, at any time after making a winding up order, require any contributory for the time being on the list of contributors, and any trustee, receiver, banker, agent or officer of the company to pay, deliver, convey, surrender, or transfer forthwith, or within such time as the Court directs, to the liquidator any money, property, or books and papers in his hands to which the company is *prima facie* entitled.

Payment of debts due by contributory to company and extent to which set-off allowed.

254.—(1) The Court may, at any time after making a winding up order, make an order on any contributory for the time being on the list of contributories to pay, in manner directed by the order, any money due from him or from the estate of the person whom he represents to the company, exclusive of any money payable by him or the estate by virtue of any call in pursuance of this Act.

(2) The Court in making such an order may, in the case of an unlimited company, allow to the contributory by way of set-off any money due to him or the estate which he represents from the company on any independent dealing or contract with the company, but not any money due to him as a member of the company in respect of any dividend or profit.

(3) In the case of any company, whether limited or unlimited, when all the creditors are paid in full, any money due on any account whatever to a contributory from the company may be allowed to him by way of set-off against any subsequent call.

Power of Court to make calls.

255.—(1) The Court may, at any time after making a winding up order, and either before or after it has ascertained the sufficiency of the assets of the company, make calls on all or any of the contributories for the time being settled on the list of the contributories to the extent of their liability, for payment of any money which the Court considers necessary to satisfy the debts and liabilities of the company, and the costs, charges, and expenses of winding up, and for the adjustment of the rights of the contributories, among themselves, and make an order for payment of any calls so made.

(2) On making a call the Court may take into consideration the probability that some of the contributories may partly or wholly fail to pay the call.

Payment into bank of moneys due to company.

256.—(1) The Court may order any contributory, purchaser or other person from whom money is due to the company to pay the amount due into a bank to the account of the liquidator instead of to the liquidator, and any such order may be enforced in the same manner as if it had directed payment to the liquidator.

(2) All moneys and securities paid or delivered into such bank in the event of a winding up by the Court shall be subject in all respects to the orders of the Court.

Order on contributory conclusive evidence.

257.—(1) An order made by the Court on a contributory shall, subject to any right of appeal, be conclusive evidence that the money, if any, thereby appearing to be due or ordered to be paid is due.

(2) All other pertinent matters stated in the order shall be taken to be truly stated as against all persons and in all proceedings.

Appointment of special manager.

258.—(1) Where in any proceedings the Trustee becomes the liquidator of a company, whether provisionally or otherwise, he may, if satisfied that the nature of the estate or business of the company, or the interests of the creditors or contributories generally, require the appointment of a special manager of the estate or business of the company other than himself, apply to the Court, and the Court may on such application appoint a special manager of that estate or business to act during such time as the Court may direct, with such powers, including any of the powers of a receiver or manager, as may be entrusted to him by the Court.

(2) The special manager shall give such security and account in such manner as the Court directs.

(3) The special manager shall receive such remuneration as may be fixed by the Court.

Power to exclude creditors not proving in time.

259. The Court may fix a time or times within which creditors are to prove their debts or claims or to be excluded from the benefit of any distribution made before those debts are proved.

Adjustment of rights of contributories.

260. The Court shall adjust the rights of the contributories among themselves, and distribute any surplus among the persons entitled thereto.

Inspection of books by creditors and contributories.

261.—(1) The Court may, at any time after making a winding up order, make such order for inspection of the books and papers of the company by creditors and contributories as the Court thinks just, and any books and papers in the possession of the company may be inspected by creditors or contributories accordingly, but not further or otherwise.

(2) Nothing in this section shall be taken as excluding or restricting any statutory rights of a Government Department or person acting under the authority of a Government Department.

262. The Court may, in the event of the assets being insufficient to satisfy the liabilities, make an order as to the payment out of the assets of the costs, charges and expenses incurred in the winding up in such order of priority as the Court thinks just.

Power to order costs of winding up to be paid out of assets.

263.—(1) The Court may, at any time after the appointment of a provisional liquidator or the making of a winding up order, summon before it any officer of the company or person known or suspected to have in his possession any property of the company, or supposed to be indebted to the company, or any person whom the Court deems capable of giving information concerning the promotion, formation, trade, dealings, affairs, or property of the company.

Power to summon persons suspected of having company property.

(2) The Court may examine him on oath concerning the matters aforesaid, either by word of mouth or on written interrogatories, and may reduce his answers to writing and require him to sign them.

(3) The Court may require him to produce any books and papers in his custody or power relating to the company, but, where he claims any lien on books or papers produced by him, the production shall be without prejudice to that lien, and the Court shall have jurisdiction in the winding up to determine all questions relating to that lien.

(4) If any person so summoned, after being tendered a reasonable sum for his expenses, refuses to come before the Court at the time appointed, not having a lawful impediment (made known to the Court at the time of its sitting, and allowed by it), the Court may cause him to be apprehended and brought before the Court for examination.

Power to order public examination of promoters, directors, etc.

264. Where an order has been made for winding up a company by the Court, and the Trustee has made a further report under this Act stating that in his opinion a fraud has been committed by any person in the promotion or formation of the company, or by any director or other officer of the company in relation to the company since its formation, the Court may, after consideration of the report, direct that the person, director or officer shall attend before the Court on a day appointed by the Court for that purpose, and be publicly examined as to the promotion or formation or the conduct of the business of the company, or as to his conduct and dealings as director or officer thereof.

Procedure at examination.

265.—(1) The Trustee shall take part in the examination, and for that purpose may, if specially authorized by the Court in that behalf, employ an attorney-at-law.

(2) The liquidator, where the Trustee is not the liquidator, and any creditor or contributory, may also take part in the examination either personally or by an attorney-at-law.

(3) The Court may put such questions to the person examined as the Court thinks fit.

(4) The person examined shall be examined on oath, and shall answer all such questions as the Court may put or allow to be put to him.

(5) A person ordered to be examined shall at his own cost, before his examination, be furnished with a copy of the Trustee's report, and may at his own cost employ an attorney-at-law, who shall be at liberty to put to him such questions as the Court may deem just for the purpose of enabling him to explain or qualify any answers given by him:

Provided that, if any such person applies to the Court to be exculpated from any charges made or suggested against him, it shall be the duty of the Trustee to appear on the hearing of the application and call the attention of the Court to any matters which appear to the Trustee to be relevant, and if the Court, after hearing any evidence given or witnesses called by the Trustee, grants the application, the Court may allow the applicant such costs as in its discretion it may think fit.

(6) Notes of the examination shall be taken down in writing, and shall be read over to or by, and signed by, the person examined, and may thereafter be used in evidence against him, and shall be open to the inspection of any creditor or contributory at all reasonable times.

(7) The Court may, if it thinks fit, adjourn the examination from time to time.

Power to arrest absconding contributory.

266. The Court, at any time either before or after making a winding up order, on proof of probable cause for believing that a contributory is about to quit the Island or otherwise to abscond or to remove or conceal any of his property for the purpose of evading payment of calls, or of avoiding examination respecting the affairs of the company, may cause the contributory to be arrested, and his books and papers and movable personal property to be seized, and him and them to be safely kept until such time as the Court may order.

Powers of Court cumulative.

267. Any powers by this Act conferred on the Court shall be in addition to and not in restriction of any existing powers of instituting proceedings against any contributory or debtor of the company, or the estate of any contributory or debtor, for the recovery of any call or other sums.

Delegation to liquidator of certain powers of Court.

268. Provision may be made by rules for enabling or requiring all or any of the powers and duties conferred and imposed on the Court by this Act in respect of the following matters—

(*a*) the holding and conducting of meetings to ascertain the wishes of creditors and contributories;

(*b*) the settling of lists of contributories and the rectifying of the register of members where required, and the collecting and applying of the assets;

(*c*) the paying, delivering, conveyance, surrender or transfer of money, property, books or papers to the liquidator;

(*d*) the making of calls;

(*e*) the fixing of a time within which debts and claims must be proved, to be exercised or performed by the liquidator as an officer of the Court, and subject to the control of the Court:

Provided that the liquidator shall not, without the special leave of the Court, rectify the register of members, and shall not make any call without either the special leave of the Court or the sanction of the committee of inspection.

Dissolution of company.

269.—(1) When the affairs of a company have been completely wound up, the Court, if the liquidator makes an application in that behalf, shall make an order that the company be dissolved from the date of the order, and the company shall be dissolved accordingly.

(2) The order shall within fourteen days from the date thereof be forwarded by the liquidator to the Registrar who shall make in his books a minute of the dissolution of the company.

(3) If the liquidator makes default in complying with the requirements of this section, he shall be liable to a fine not exceeding two thousand dollars for every day during which he is in default.

Enforcement of, and appeal from, orders

Power to enforce orders.

270. Orders made by the Court under this Act may be enforced in the same manner as orders made in any action pending therein.

271. Subject to rules of court, an appeal from any order or decision made or given in the winding up of a company by the Court under this Act shall lie in the same manner and subject to the same conditions as an appeal from any order or decision of the Court. Appeal from orders.

(iii) VOLUNTARY WINDING UP

Resolutions for, and Commencement of, Voluntary Winding Up

272.—(1) A company may be wound up voluntarily— Circumstances in which company may be wound up voluntarily.

(*a*) when the period, if any, fixed for the duration of the company by the articles expires, or the event, if any, occurs, on the occurrence of which the articles provide that the company is to be dissolved, and the company in general meeting has passed a resolution requiring the company to be wound up voluntarily,

(*b*) if the company resolves by special resolution that the company be wound up voluntarily;

(*c*) if the company resolves by extraordinary resolution to the effect that it cannot by reason of its liabilities continue its business, and that it is advisable to wind up.

(2) In this Act the expression "a resolution for voluntary winding up" means a resolution passed under any of the provisions of subsection (1).

273.—(1) When a company has passed a resolution for voluntary winding up, it shall, within fourteen days after the passing of the resolution, give notice of the resolution by advertisement in the *Gazette* and in writing to the Registrar. Notice of resolution to wind up voluntarily.

(2) If default is made in complying with this section, the company and every officer of the company who is in default shall be liable to a default fine not exceeding one hundred thousand dollars, and for the purposes of this subsection the

liquidator of the company shall be deemed to be an officer of the company.

Commencement of voluntary winding up.

274. A voluntary winding up shall be deemed to commence at the time of the passing of the resolution for voluntary winding up.

Consequences of Voluntary Winding Up

Effect of voluntary winding up on business and status of company.

275. In case of a voluntary winding up, the company shall, from the commencement of the winding up, cease to carry on its business, except so far as may be required for the beneficial winding up thereof:

Provided that the corporate state and corporate powers of the company shall, notwithstanding anything to the contrary in its articles, continue until it is dissolved.

Avoidance of transfer, etc., after commencement of voluntary winding up.

276. Any transfer of shares not being a transfer made to or with the sanction of the liquidator, and any alteration in the status of the members of the company, made after the commencement of a voluntary winding up, shall be void.

Declaration of Solvency

Statutory declaration of solvency in case of proposal to wind up voluntarily.

277.—(1) Where it is proposed to wind up a company voluntarily, the directors of the company or, in the case of a company having more than two directors, the majority of the directors, may, at a meeting of the directors make a statutory declaration to the effect that they have made a full inquiry into the affairs of the company, and that, having so done, they have formed the opinion that the company will be able to pay its debts in full within such period not exceeding twelve months from the commencement of the winding up as may be specified in the declaration.

(2) A declaration made as aforesaid shall have no effect for the purposes of this Act unless—

(*a*) it is made within the five weeks immediately preceding the date of the passing of the resolution for winding up the company and is delivered to the Registrar for registration before that date; and

(*b*) it embodies a statement of the company's assets and liabilities as at the latest practicable date before the making of the declaration.

(3) Any director of a company making a declaration under this section without having reasonable grounds for the opinion that the company will be able to pay its debts in full within the period specified in the declaration, shall be liable to imprisonment with or without hard labour for a period not exceeding six months or to a fine not exceeding fifty thousand dollars or to both such imprisonment and fine; and if the company is wound up in pursuance of a resolution passed within the period of five weeks after the making of the declaration, but its debts are not paid or provided for in full within the period stated in the declaration, it shall be presumed until the contrary is shown that the director did not have reasonable grounds for his opinion.

(4) A winding up in the case of which a declaration has been made and delivered in accordance with this section is in this Act referred to as "a members' voluntary winding up", and a winding up in the case of which a declaration has not been made and delivered as aforesaid is in this Act referred to as "a creditors' voluntary winding up".

Provisions applicable to a Members' Voluntary Winding Up

278. The provisions contained in sections 280 to 286 (inclusive) shall apply in relation to a members' voluntary winding up.

Provisions applicable to members' winding up.

Power of company to appoint and fix remuneration of liquidators.

279.—(1) The company in general meeting shall appoint one or more liquidators for the purpose of winding up the affairs and distributing the assets of the company, and may fix the remuneration to be paid to him or them.

(2) On the appointment of a liquidator all the powers of the directors shall cease, except so far as the company in general meeting, or the liquidator, sanctions the continuance thereof.

Power to fill vacancy in office of liquidator.

280.—(1) If a vacancy occurs by death, resignation, or otherwise in the office of liquidator appointed by the company, the company in general meeting may, subject to any arrangement with its creditors, fill the vacancy.

(2) For that purpose a general meeting may be convened by any contributory or, if there were more than one liquidator, by the continuing liquidators.

(3) The meeting shall be held in manner provided by this Act or by the articles, or in such manner as may, on application by any contributory or by the continuing liquidators, be determined by the Court.

Power of liquidator to accept shares, etc., as consideration for sale of property of company.

281.—(1) Where a company is proposed to be, or is in the course of being wound up altogether voluntarily, and the whole or part of its business or property is proposed to be transferred or sold to another company, whether a company within the meaning of this Act or not (in this section called "the transferee company") the liquidator of the first-mentioned company (in this section called "the transferor company") may—

(*a*) with the sanction of a special resolution of that company, conferring either a general authority on the liquidator or an authority in respect of any particular arrangement, receive, in compensation or part compensation for the transfer or sale, shares, policies, or other like interests in the transferee company, for distribution among the members of the transferor company; or (*b*) enter into any other arrangement whereby the members of the transferor company may, in lieu of receiving cash, shares, policies, or other like interests, or in addition thereto, participate in the profits of or receive any other benefit from the transferee company.

(2) Any sale or arrangement in pursuance of this section shall be binding on the members of the transferor company, and where the whole or part of the compensation or benefit accruing to the members of the transferor company in respect of any such sale or arrangement consists of fully paid shares in the transferee company each such member shall be deemed to have agreed with the transferee company for the acceptance of the fully paid shares to which he is entitled under the distribution referred to in subsection (1).

(3) If any member of the transferor company who did not vote in favour of the special resolution express his dissent therefrom in writing addressed to the liquidator, and left at the registered office of the company within seven days after the passing of the resolution, he may require the liquidator either to abstain from carrying the resolution into effect, or to purchase his interest at a price to be determined by agreement or by arbitration in manner provided by the Arbitration Act.

(4) If the liquidator elects to purchase the member's interest, the purchase money shall be paid before the company is dissolved, and be raised by the liquidator in such manner as may be determined by special resolution.

(5) A special resolution shall not be invalid for the purposes of this section by reason that it is passed before or concurrently with a resolution for voluntary winding up or for appointing liquidators, but, if an order is made within a year for winding up the company by or subject to the supervision of the Court, the special resolution shall not be valid unless sanctioned by the Court.

Duty of liquidator to call creditors' meeting in case of insolvency.

282.—(1) If, in the case of a winding up commenced after the appointed day, the liquidator is at any time of opinion that the company will not be able to pay its debts in full within the period stated in the declaration under section 277, he shall forthwith summon a meeting of the creditors, and shall lay before the meeting a statement of the assets and liabilities of the company.

(2) If the liquidator fails to comply with this section, he shall be liable to a fine not exceeding fifty thousand dollars or to imprisonment for a term not exceeding six months or to both such fine and imprisonment.

Duty of liquidator to call general meeting at end of each year.

283.—(1) Subject to the provisions of section 286, in the event of the winding up continuing for more than one year, the liquidator shall summon a general meeting of the company at the end of the first year from the commencement of the winding up and of each succeeding year, or at the first convenient date within three months (or such longer period as the Minister may allow) from the end of the year, and shall lay before the meeting an account of his acts and dealings and of the conduct of the winding up during the preceding year.

(2) If the liquidator fails to comply with this section, he shall be liable to a fine not exceeding fifty thousand dollars.

Final meeting and dissolution.

284.—(1) Subject to the provisions of section 285, as soon as the affairs of the company are fully wound up, the liquidator shall make up an account of the winding up, showing how the winding up has been conducted and the property of the company has been disposed of, and thereupon shall call a general meeting of the company for the purpose of laying before it the account, and giving any explanation thereof.

(2) The meeting shall be called by advertisement in the *Gazette* and in one daily newspaper printed and circulating in the Island, specifying the time, place, and object thereof, and published one month at least before the meeting.

(3) Within one week after the meeting, the liquidator shall send to the Registrar a copy of the account, and shall make a return to him of the holding of the meeting and of its date, and if the copy is not sent or the return is not made in accordance with this subsection the liquidator shall be liable to a fine not exceeding two thousand dollars for every day during which the default continues:

Provided that, if a quorum is not present at the meeting, the liquidator shall, in lieu of the return as aforesaid, make a return that the meeting was duly summoned and that no quorum was present thereat, and upon such a return being made the provisions of this subsection as to the making of the return shall be deemed to have been complied with.

(4) The Registrar on receiving the account and either of the returns hereinbefore mentioned shall forthwith register them, and on the expiration of three months from the registration of the return, the company shall be deemed to be dissolved:

Provided that the Court may, on the application of the liquidator or of any other person who appears to the Court to be interested, make an order deferring the date at which the dissolution of the company is to take effect for such time as the Court thinks fit.

(5) It shall be the duty of the person on whose application an order of the Court under this section is made, within seven days after the making of the order, to deliver to the Registrar a copy of the order for registration, and if that person fails so to do he shall be liable to a fine not exceeding two thousand dollars for every day during which the default continues.

(6) If the liquidator fails to call a general meeting of the company as required by this section, he shall be liable to a fine not exceeding fifty thousand dollars.

Alternative provisions as to annual and and final meetings in case of insolvency.

285. Where section 282 has effect, sections 293 and 294 shall apply to the winding up to the exclusion of sections 283 and 284, as if the winding up were a creditors' voluntary winding up and not a members' voluntary winding up:

Provided that the liquidator shall not be required to summon a meeting of creditors under section 293 at the end of the first year from the commencement of the winding up, unless the meeting held under section 282 is held more than three months before the end of that year.

Provisions applicable to a Creditors' Voluntary Winding Up

Provisions applicable to creditors' winding up.

286. The provisions contained in sections 287 to 294 (inclusive) shall apply in relation to a creditors' voluntary winding up.

Meeting of creditors.

287.—(1) The company shall cause a meeting of the creditors of the company to be summoned for the day, or the day next following the day, on which there is to be held the meeting at which the resolution for voluntary winding up is to be proposed, and shall cause the notices of the meeting of creditors to be sent by post to the creditors simultaneously with the sending of the notices of the meeting of the company.

(2) The company shall cause notice of the meeting of the creditors to be advertised once in the *Gazette* and once at least in one daily newspaper printed and circulating in the Island.

(3) The directors of the company shall—

(*a*) cause a full statement of the position of the company's affairs together with a list of the creditors of the company and the estimated amount of their claims to be laid before the meeting of creditors to be held as aforesaid; and

(*b*) appoint one of their number to preside at that meeting.

(4) It shall be the duty of the director appointed to preside at the meeting of creditors to attend the meeting and preside thereat.

(5) If the meeting of the company at which the resolution for voluntary winding up is to be proposed is adjourned and the resolution is passed at an adjourned meeting, any resolution passed at the meeting of the creditors held in pursuance of subsection (1) shall have effect as if it had been passed immediately after the passing of the resolution for winding up the company.

(6) If default is made—

(*a*) by the company in complying with subsections (1) and (2);

(*b*) by the directors of the company in complying with subsection (3);

(*c*) by any director of the company in complying with subsection (4),

the company, directors or director, as the case may be, shall be liable to a fine not exceeding fifty thousand dollars, and, in the case of default by the company, every officer of the company who is in default shall be liable to the like penalty.

288. The creditors and the company at their respective meetings mentioned in section 287 may nominate a person to be liquidator for the purpose of winding up the affairs and distributing the assets of the company, and if the creditors and the company nominate different persons, the person nominated by the creditors shall be liquidator, and if no person is nominated by the creditors the person, if any, nominated by the company shall be liquidator: Appointment of liquidator.

Provided that in the case of different persons being nominated any director, member, or creditor of the company may, within seven days after the date on which the nomination was made by the creditors, apply to the Court for an order either directing that the person nominated as liquidator by the company shall be liquidator instead of or jointly with the person nominated by the creditors, or appointing some other person to be liquidator instead of the person appointed by the creditors.

Appointment of committee of inspection.

289.—(1) The creditors at the meeting to be held in pursuance of section 287 or at any subsequent meeting, may, if they think fit, appoint a committee of inspection consisting of not more than five persons, and if such a committee is appointed the company may, either at the meeting at which the resolution for voluntary winding up is passed or at any time subsequently in general meeting, appoint such number of persons as they think fit to act as members of the committee not exceeding five in number:

Provided that—

(*a*) the creditors may, if they think fit, resolve that all or any of the persons so appointed by the company ought not to be members of the committee of inspection; and

(*b*) if the creditors so resolve, the persons mentioned in the resolution shall not, unless the Court otherwise directs, be qualified to act as members of the committee; and

(*c*) on any application to the Court under this provision the Court may, if it thinks fit, appoint other persons to act as such members in place of the persons mentioned in the resolution.

(2) Subject to the provisions of this section and to rules, the provisions of section 249 (except subsection (1)) shall apply with respect to a committee of inspection appointed under this section as they apply with respect to a committee of inspection appointed in a winding up by the Court.

Fixing of liquidators' remuneration and cesser of directors' powers.

290.—(1) The committee of inspection, or if there is no such committee, the creditors, may fix the remuneration to be paid to the liquidator or liquidators.

(2) On the appointment of a liquidator, all the powers of the directors shall cease, except so far as the committee of inspection, or if there is no such committee, the creditors, sanction the continuance thereof.

Power to fill vacancy in office of liquidator.

291. If a vacancy occurs, by death, resignation or otherwise, in the office of a liquidator, other than a liquidator appointed by, or by the direction of, the Court, the creditors may fill the vacancy.

Application of section 281 to creditors' winding up.

292. The provisions of section 281 shall apply in the case of a creditors' voluntary winding up as in the case of a members' voluntary winding up, with the modification that the powers of the liquidator under that section shall not be exercised except with the sanction either of the Court or of the committee of inspection.

Duty of liquidator to call meetings of company and of creditors at end of each year.

293.—(1) In the event of the winding up continuing for more than one year, the liquidator shall summon a general meeting of the company and a meeting of creditors at the end of the first year from the commencement of the winding up, and of each succeeding year, or at the first convenient date within three months (or such longer period as the Minister may allow) from the end of the year, and shall lay before the meetings, an account of his acts and dealings and of the conduct of the winding up during the preceding year.

(2) If the liquidator fails to comply with this section, he shall be liable to a fine not exceeding fifty thousand dollars.

Final meeting and dissolution.

294.—(1) As soon as the affairs of the company are fully wound up, the liquidator shall make up an account of the winding up, showing how the winding up has been conducted and the property of the company has been disposed of, and thereupon shall call a general meeting of the company and a meeting of the creditors, for the purpose of laying the account before the meetings, and giving any explanation thereof.

(2) Each such meeting shall be called by advertisement in the *Gazette* and in one daily newspaper printed and circulating in the Island specifying the time, place, and object thereof, and published one month at least before the meeting.

(3) Within one week after the date of the meetings, or, if the meetings are not held on the same date, after the date of the later meeting, the liquidator shall send to the Registrar a copy of the account, and shall make a return to him of the holding of the meetings and of their dates, and if the copy is not sent or the return is not made in accordance with this subsection the liquidator shall be liable to a fine not exceeding two hundred dollars for every day during which the default continues:

Provided that, if a quorum is not present at either such meeting, the liquidator shall, in lieu of the return hereinbefore mentioned, make a return that the meeting was duly summoned and that no quorum was present thereat, and upon such a return being made the provisions of this subsection as to the making of the return shall, in respect of that meeting, be deemed to have been complied with.

(4) The Registrar on receiving the account and in respect of each such meeting either of the returns hereinbefore mentioned shall forthwith register them, and on the expiration of three months from the registration thereof the company shall be deemed to be dissolved:

Provided that the Court may, on the application of the liquidator or of any other person who appears to the Court to be interested, make an order deferring the date at which the dissolution of the company is to take effect for such time as the Court thinks fit.

(5) It shall be the duty of the person on whose application an order of the Court under this section is made, within seven days after the making of the order, to deliver to the Registrar a copy of the order for registration, and if that person fails so to do he shall be liable to a fine not exceeding two thousand dollars for every day during which the default continues.

(6) If the liquidator fails to call a general meeting of the company or a meeting of the creditors as required by this section, he shall be liable to a fine not exceeding fifty thousand dollars.

Provisions Applicable to every Voluntary Winding up

295. The provisions contained in sections 294 to 298 (inclusive) shall apply to every voluntary winding up whether a members' or a creditors' winding up. Provision applicable to every voluntary winding up.

296. Subject to the provisions of this Act as to preferential payments, the property of a company shall, on its winding up, be applied in satisfaction of its liabilities *pari passu*, and, subject to such application, shall, unless the articles otherwise provide, be distributed among the members according to their rights and interests in the company. Distribution of company's property.

297.—(1) The liquidator may— Powers and duties of liquidator in voluntary winding up.

(*a*) in the case of a members' voluntary winding up, with the sanction of an extraordinary resolution of the company, and, in the case of a creditors' voluntary winding up, with the sanction of either the Court or the committee of inspection, exercise any of the powers given by paragraphs (*d*), (*e*) and (*f*) of subsection (1) of section 239 to a liquidator in a winding up by the Court;

(*b*) without sanction, exercise any of the other powers by this Act given to the liquidator in a winding up by the Court;

(*c*) exercise the power of the Court under this Act of settling a list of contributories, and the list of contributories shall be *prima facie* evidence of the liability of the persons named therein to be contributories;

(*d*) exercise the power of the Court of making calls;

(*e*) summon general meetings of the company for the purpose of obtaining the sanction of the company by special or extraordinary resolution or for any other purpose he may think fit.

(2) The liquidator shall pay the debts of the company and shall adjust the rights of the contributories among themselves.

(3) When several liquidators are appointed, any power given by this Act may be exercised by such one or more of them as may be determined at the time of their appointment, or, in default of such determination, by any number not less than two.

Power of Court to appoint and remove liquidator in voluntary winding up.

298.—(1) If from any cause whatever there is no liquidator acting, the Court may appoint a liquidator.

(2) The Court may, on cause shown, remove a liquidator and appoint another liquidator.

Notice by liquidator of his appointment.

299.—(1) The liquidator shall, within twenty-one days after his appointment, publish in the *Gazette* and in one daily newspaper printed and circulating in the Island, and deliver to the Registrar for registration a notice of his appointment in the prescribed form.

(2) If the liquidator fails to comply with the requirements of this section he shall be liable to a fine not exceeding two thousand dollars for every day during which the default continues.

Arrangement when binding on creditors.

300.—(1) Any arrangement entered into between a company about to be, or in the course of being, wound up and its creditors shall, subject to the right of appeal under this section, be binding on the company if sanctioned by an extraordinary resolution, and on the creditors if acceded to by three-fourths in number and value of the creditors.

(2) Any creditor or contributory may, within three weeks from the completion of the arrangement, appeal to the Court against it, and the Court may thereupon, as it thinks just, amend, vary, or confirm the arrangement.

301.—(1) The liquidator or any contributory or creditor may apply to the Court to determine any question arising in the winding up of a company, or to exercise as respects the enforcing of calls, or any other matter, all or any of the powers which the Court might exercise if the company were being wound up by the Court. Power to apply to Court to have questions determined or powers exercised.

(2) The Court, if satisfied that the determination of the question or the required exercise of power will be just and beneficial, may accede wholly or partially to the application on such terms and conditions as it thinks fit, or may make such other order on the application as it thinks just.

(3) A copy of an order made by virtue of this section staying the proceedings in the winding up shall forthwith be forwarded by the company, or otherwise as may be prescribed, to the Registrar, who shall make a minute of the order in his books relating to the company.

302. All costs, charges and expenses properly incurred in the winding up, including the remuneration of the liquidator, shall be payable out of the assets of the company in priority to all other claims. Costs of voluntary winding up.

303. The winding up of a company shall not bar the right of any creditor or contributory to have it wound up by the Court, but in the case of an application by a contributory the Court must be satisfied that the rights of the contributories will be prejudiced by a voluntary winding up. Saving for rights of creditors and contributories.

(iv) WINDING UP SUBJECT TO SUPERVISION OF COURT

Power to order winding up subject to supervision.

304. When a company has passed a resolution for voluntary winding up, the Court may make an order that the voluntary winding up shall continue but subject to such supervision of the Court, and with such liberty for creditors, contributories, or others to apply to the Court, and generally on such terms and conditions, as the Court thinks just.

Effect of petition for winding up subject to supervision.

305. A petition for the continuance of a voluntary winding up subject to the supervision of the Court shall, for the purpose of giving jurisdiction to the Court over actions, be deemed to be a petition for winding up by the Court.

Application of sections 225 and 226 to winding up subject to supervision.

306. A winding up subject to the supervision of the Court shall, for the purposes of sections 225 and 226, be deemed to be a winding up by the Court.

Power of Court to appoint or remove liquidators.

307.—(1) Where an order is made for a winding up subject to supervision, the Court may by that or any subsequent order appoint an additional liquidator.

(2) A liquidator appointed by the Court under this section shall have the same powers, be subject to the same obligations, and in all respects stand in the same position, as if he had been duly appointed in accordance with the provisions of this Act with respect to the appointment of liquidators in a voluntary winding up.

(3) The Court may remove any liquidator so appointed by the Court or any liquidator continued under the supervision order and fill any vacancy occasioned by the removal, or by death or resignation.

308.—(1) Where an order is made for a winding up subject to supervision, the liquidator may, subject to any restrictions imposed by the Court, exercise all his powers, without the sanction or intervention of the Court, in the same manner as if the company were being wound up altogether voluntarily: Effect of supervision order.

Provided that the powers specified in paragraphs (*d*), (*e*) and (*f*) of subsection (1) of section 241 shall not be exercised by the liquidator except with the sanction of the Court or, in a case where before the order the winding up was a creditors' voluntary winding up, with the sanction of either the Court or the committee of inspection or (if there is no such committee) a meeting of the creditors.

(2) A winding up subject to the supervision of the Court is not a winding up by the Court for the purpose of the provisions of this Act which are set out in the Sixth Schedule, but, subject as aforesaid, an order for a winding up subject to supervision shall for all purposes be deemed to be an order for winding up by the Court: Sixth Schedule.

Provided that where the order for winding up subject to supervision was made in relation to a creditors' voluntary winding up in which a committee of inspection had been appointed, the order shall be deemed to be an order for winding up by the Court for the purpose of section 249 (except subsection (1) thereof) except in so far as the operation of that section is excluded in a voluntary winding up by rules.

(v) PROVISIONS APPLICABLE TO EVERY MODE OF WINDING UP

Proof and Ranking of Claims

309. In every winding up (subject in the case of insolvent companies to the application in accordance with the provisions of this Act of the law of bankruptcy) all debts payable on a contingency, and all claims against the company, present or Debts of all description to be proved.

future, certain or contingent, ascertained or sounding only in damages, shall be admissible to proof against the company, a just estimate being made, so far as possible, of the value of such debts or claims as may be subject to any contingency or sound only in damages or for some other reason do not bear a certain value.

Application of bankruptcy rules in winding up of insolvent companies.

310. In the winding up of an insolvent company the same rules shall prevail and be observed with regard to the respective rights of secured and unsecured creditors and to debts provable and to the valuation of annuities and future and contingent liabilities as are in force for the time being under the law of bankruptcy with respect to the estates of persons adjudged bankrupt, and all persons who in any such case would be entitled to prove for and receive dividends out of the assets of the company may come in under the winding up, and make such claims against the company as they respectively are entitled to by virtue of this section.

Preferential payments.

311.—(1) In a winding up there shall be paid in priority to all other debts—

(*a*) all rates, charges, taxes, assessments, or impositions, whether imposed or made by the Government or by any public authority under the provisions of any law, and having become due and payable within twelve months next before the relevant date and not exceeding in the whole one year's assessment;

(*b*) all wages or salary (whether or not earned wholly or in part by way of commission) of any clerk or servant in respect of services rendered to the company during four months next before the relevant date, and all wages (whether payable for time or for piece work), of any workman or labourer in respect of services so rendered:

Provided that the sum to which priority is to be given under this paragraph shall not, in the case of any one claimant, exceed two hundred thousand dollars;

(*c*) unless the company is being wound up voluntarily merely for the purposes of reconstruction or of amalgamation with another company, or unless the company has at the commencement of the winding up under such a contract with insurers as is mentioned in section 21 of the Workmen's Compensation Act, rights capable of being transferred to and vested in the workman, all amounts due in respect of any compensation or liability for compensation under that Act accrued before the relevant date;

(*d*) all amounts by way of contributions for which the company is liable pursuant to sections 4, 5 and 6 of the National Insurance Act and which have become due and payable before the relevant date;

(*e*) redundancy payments payable under the Employment (Termination and Redundancy Payments) Act whether such payments fall due before or after the appointment of a liquidator;

(*f*) all amounts by way of contributions for which the company is liable pursuant to sections 11 and 12 of the National Housing Trust Act and which have become due and payable before the relevant date.

(2) Where any compensation under the Workmen's Compensation Act is a weekly payment, the amount due in respect thereof shall, for the purposes of paragraph (*c*) of subsection (1), be taken to be the amount of the lump sum for which the weekly payment could, if redeemable, be redeemed if the employer made an application for that purpose under that Act.

(3) Where any payment on account of wages or salary has been made to any clerk, servant, workman or labourer in the employment of a company out of money advanced by some person for that purpose, that person shall in a winding up have a right of priority in respect of the money so advanced and paid up to the amount by which the sum in respect of which that clerk, servant, workman or labourer would have been entitled to priority in the winding up has been diminished by reason of the payment having been made.

(4) The foregoing debts shall—

(*a*) rank equally among themselves and be paid in full, unless the assets are insufficient to meet them, in which case they shall abate in equal proportions; and

(*b*) in the case of a company registered in the Island, so far as the assets of the company available for payment of general creditors are insufficient to meet them, have priority over the claims of holders of debentures under any floating charge created by the company, and be paid accordingly out of any property comprised in or subject to that charge.

(5) Subject to the retention of such sums as may be necessary for the costs and expenses of the winding up, the foregoing debts shall be discharged forthwith so far as the assets are sufficient to meet them.

(6) In this section the expression "the relevant date" means—

(*a*) in the case of a company ordered to be wound up compulsorily which had not previously commenced to be wound up voluntarily, the date of the winding up order; and

(*b*) in any other case, the date of the commencement of the winding up.

Effect of Winding Up on Antecedent and other Transactions

312.—(1) Any conveyance, mortgage, delivery of goods, payment, execution, or other act relating to property which would, if made or done by or against an individual, be deemed in his bankruptcy a fraudulent preference, or a fraudulent conveyance, assignment, transfer, sale or disposition, shall, if made or done by or against a company, be deemed, in the event of its being wound up, a fraudulent preference of its creditors, or a fraudulent conveyance, assignment, transfer, sale or disposition, as the case may be, and be invalid accordingly. Fraudulent preference.

(2) For the purposes of this section, the commencement of the winding up shall be deemed to correspond with the presentation of the bankruptcy petition in the case of an individual.

(3) Any conveyance or assignment by a company of all its property to trustees for the benefit of all its creditors shall be void to all intents.

313.—(1) Where, in the case of a company wound up in the Island, anything made or done after the appointed day is void under section 312 as a fraudulent preference of a person interested in property mortgaged or charged to secure the company's debt, then (without prejudice to any rights or liabilities arising apart from this provision) the person preferred shall be subject to the same liabilities, and shall have the same rights, as if he had undertaken to be personally liable as surety for the debt to the extent of the charge on the property or the value of his interest, whichever is the less. Liabilities and rights of certain fraudulently preferred person.

(2) The value of that person's interest shall be determined as at the date of the transaction constituting the fraudulent preference, and shall be determined as if the interest were free of all incumbrances other than those to which the charge for the company's debt was then subject.

(3) On any application made to the Court with respect to any payment on the ground that the payment was a fraudulent preference of a surety or guarantor, the Court shall have jurisdiction to determine any questions with respect to the payment arising between the person to whom the payment was made and the surety or guarantor and to grant relief in respect thereof, notwithstanding that it is not necessary so to do for the purposes of the winding up, and for that purpose may give leave to bring in the surety or guarantor as a third party as in the case of an action for the recovery of the sum paid.

(4) Subsection (3) shall apply, with the necessary modifications, in relation to transactions other than the payment of money as it applies in relation to payments.

Effect of floating charge.

314. Where a company is being wound up, a floating charge on the undertaking or property of the company created within twelve months of the commencement of the winding up shall, unless it is proved that the company immediately after the creation of the charge was solvent, be invalid, except to the amount of any cash paid to the company at the time of or subsequently to the creation of, and in consideration for, the charge, together with interest on that amount at the rate of six *per centum* per annum or such other rate as may for the time being be prescribed by order of the Minister.

Disclaimer of onerous property.

315.—(1) Where any part of the property of a company which is being wound up consists of land of any tenure burdened with onerous covenants, of shares or stock in companies, unprofitable contracts, or any other property that is unsaleable, or not readily saleable, by reason of its binding the possessor thereof to the performance of any onerous act, or to the payment of any sum of money, the liquidator of the company, notwithstanding that he has endeavoured to sell or has taken possession of the property, or exercised any act of ownership in relation thereto, may, with the leave of the Court and subject to the provisions of this section, by writing signed by him, at any time within twelve months after the commencement of the winding up or such extended period as may be allowed by the Court, disclaim the property:

Provided that, where any such property has not come to the knowledge of the liquidator within one month after the commencement of the winding up, the power under this section of disclaiming the property may be exercised at any time within twelve months after he has become aware thereof or such extended period as may be allowed by the Court.

(2) The disclaimer shall operate to determine, as from the date of disclaimer, the rights, interest, and liabilities of the company, and the property of the company, in or in respect of the property disclaimed, but shall not, except so far as is necessary for the purpose of releasing the company and the property of the company from liability, affect the rights or liabilities of any other person.

(3) The Court, before or on granting leave to disclaim, may require such notices to be given to persons interested, and impose such terms as a condition of granting leave, and make such other order in the matter as the Court thinks just.

(4) The liquidator shall not be entitled to disclaim any property under this section in any case where an application in writing has been made to him by any persons interested in the property requiring him to decide whether he will or will not disclaim, and the liquidator has not, within a period of twenty-eight days after the receipt of the application or such further period as may be allowed by the Court, given notice to the applicant that he intends to apply to the Court for leave to disclaim, and, in the case of a contract, if the liquidator, after such an application as aforesaid, does not within that period or further period disclaim the contract, the company shall be deemed to have adopted it.

(5) The Court may, on the application of any person who is, as against the liquidator, entitled to the benefit or subject to the burden of a contract made with the company, make an order rescinding the contract on such terms as to payment by or to either party of damages for the non-performance of the contract, or otherwise as the Court thinks just, and any damages payable under the order to any such person may be proved by him as a debt in the winding up.

(6) The Court may, on an application by any person who either claims any interest in any disclaimed property or is under any liability not discharged by this Act in respect of any disclaimed property and on hearing any such persons as it thinks fit, make an order for the vesting of the property in or the delivery of the property to any persons entitled thereto, or to whom it may seem just that the property should be delivered by way of compensation for such liability as aforesaid, or a trustee for him, and on such terms as the Court thinks just, and on any such vesting order being made, the property comprised therein shall vest accordingly in the person therein named in that behalf without any conveyance or assignment for the purpose:

Provided that, where the property disclaimed is of a leasehold nature, the Court shall not make a vesting order in favour of any person claiming under the company, whether as under-lessee or as mortgagee by demise, except upon the terms of making that person—

(*a*) subject to the same liabilities and obligations as those to which the company was subject under the lease in respect of the property at the commencement of the winding up; or

(*b*) if the Court thinks fit, subject only to the same liabilities and obligations as if the lease had been assigned to that person at that date,

and in either event (if the case so require) as if the lease had comprised only the property comprised in the vesting order.

(7) Any mortgagee or under-lessee declining to accept a vesting order upon the terms referred to in paragraphs (*a*) and (*b*) of the proviso to subsection (6) shall be excluded from all interest in and security upon the property, and, if there is no person claiming under the company who is willing to accept an order upon such terms, the Court shall have power to vest the estate and interest of the company in the property in any person liable either personally or in a representative character, and either alone or jointly with the company to perform the lessee's covenants in the lease, freed and discharged from all estates, incumbrances and interests created therein by the company.

(8) Any person injured by the operation of a disclaimer under this section shall be deemed to be a creditor of the company to the amount of the injury, and may accordingly prove the amount as a debt in the winding up.

316.—(1) Where a creditor has issued execution against the goods or lands of a company or has attached any debt due to the company, and the company is subsequently wound up, he shall not be entitled to retain the benefit of the execution or attachment against the liquidator in the winding up of the company unless he has completed the execution or attachment before the commencement of the winding up: Restriction of rights of creditor as to execution or attachment.

Provided that—

(*a*) where any creditor has had notice of a meeting having been called at which a resolution for voluntary winding up is to be proposed, the date on which the creditor so had notice shall for the purposes of the foregoing provision be substituted for the date of the commencement of the winding up;

(*b*) a person who purchases in good faith under a sale by a bailiff any goods of a company on which an execution has been levied shall in all cases acquire a good title to them against the liquidator; and (*c*) the rights conferred by this subsection on the liquidator may be set aside by the Court in favour of the creditor to such extent and subject to such terms as the Court may think fit.

(2) For the purposes of this section, an execution against goods shall be taken to be completed by seizure and sale, and an attachment of a debt shall be deemed to be completed by receipt of the debt and an execution against land shall be deemed to be completed from the date of the order for sale or by seizure as the case may be, and, in the case of an equitable interest, by the appointment of a receiver.

(3) In this section and in section 317 the expression "goods" includes all chattels personal, and the expression "bailiff" includes any officer charged with the execution of a writ or other process.

Duties of bailiff as to goods taken in execution

317.—(1) Subject to the provisions of subsection (3), where any goods of a company are taken in execution, and, before the sale thereof or the completion of the execution by the receipt or recovery of the full amount of the levy, notice is served on the bailiff that a provisional liquidator has been appointed or that a winding up order has been made or that a resolution for voluntary winding up has been passed, the bailiff shall, on being so required, deliver the goods and any money seized or received in part satisfaction of the execution to the liquidator, but the costs of the execution shall be a first charge on the goods or money so delivered, and the liquidator may sell the goods, or a sufficient part thereof, for the purpose of satisfying that charge.

(2) Subject to the provisions of subsection (3), where under an execution in respect of a judgment for a sum exceeding two hundred thousand dollars the goods of a company are sold or money is paid in order to avoid sale, the bailiff shall deduct the costs of the execution from the proceeds of the sale or the money paid and retain the balance for fourteen days, and if

within that time notice is served on him of a petition for the winding up of the company having been presented or of a meeting having been called at which there is to be proposed a resolution for the voluntary winding up of the company and an order is made or a resolution is passed, as the case may be, for the winding up of the company, the bailiff shall pay the balance to the liquidator, who shall be entitled to retain it as against the execution creditor.

(3) The rights conferred by this section on the liquidator may be set aside by the Court in favour of the creditor to such extent and subject to such terms as the Court thinks fit.

Offences Antecedent to or in Course of Winding up

Offences by officers of companies in liquidation

318.—(1) If any person, being a past or present officer of a company which at the time of the commission of the alleged offence is being wound up, whether by or under the supervision of the Court or voluntarily, or is subsequently ordered to be wound up by the Court or subsequently passes a resolution for voluntary winding up—

(*a*) does not to the best of his knowledge and belief fully and truly discover to the liquidator all the property, real and personal, of the company, and how and to whom and for what consideration and when the company disposed of any part thereof, except such part as has been disposed of in the ordinary way of the business of the company; or

(*b*) does not deliver up to the liquidator, or as he directs, all such part of the real and personal property of the company as is in his custody or under his control, and which he is required by law to deliver up; or

(*c*) does not deliver up to the liquidator, or as he directs, all books and papers in his custody or under his control belonging to the company and which he is required by law to deliver up; or (*d*) within twelve months next before the commencement of the winding up or at any time thereafter conceals any part of the property of the company to the value of five thousand dollars or upwards, or conceals any debt due to or from the company; or

(*e*) within twelve months next before the commencement of the winding up or at any time thereafter fraudulently removes any part of the property of the company to the value of five thousand dollars or upwards; or

(*f*) makes any material omission in any statement relating to the affairs of the company; or

(*g*) knowing or believing that a false debt has been proved by any person under the winding up, fails for the period of a month to inform the liquidator thereof; or

(*h*) after the commencement of the winding up prevents the production of any book or paper affecting or relating to the property or affairs of the company; or

(*i*) within twelve months next before the commencement of the winding up or at any time thereafter, conceals, destroys, mutilates, or falsifies, or is privy to the concealment, destruction, mutilation, or falsification of, any book or paper affecting or relating to the property or affairs of the company; or

(*j*) within twelve months next before the commencement of the winding up or at any time thereafter makes or is privy to the making of any false entry in any book or paper affecting or relating to the property or affairs of the company; or

(*k*) within twelve months next before the commencement of the winding up or at any time thereafter fraudulently parts with, alters, or makes any omission in, or is privy to the fraudulent parting with, altering, or making any omission in, any document affecting or relating to the property or affairs of the company; or (*l*) after the commencement of the winding up or at any meeting of the creditors of the company within twelve months next before the commencement of the winding up attempts to account for any part of the property of the company by fictitious losses or expenses; or

(*m*) has within twelve months next before the commencement of the winding up or at any time thereafter, by any false representation or other fraud, obtained any property for or on behalf of the company on credit which the company does not subsequently pay for; or

(*n*) within twelve months next before the commencement of the winding up or at any time thereafter, under the false pretence that the company is carrying on its business, obtains on credit, for or on behalf of the company, any property which the company does not subsequently pay for; or

(*o*) within twelve months next before the commencement of the winding up or at any time thereafter pawns, pledges, or disposes of any property of the company which has been obtained on credit and has not been paid for, unless such pawning, pledging, or disposing is in the ordinary way of the business of the company; or

(*p*) is guilty of any false representation or other fraud for the purpose of obtaining the consent of the creditors of the company or any of them to an agreement with reference to the affairs of the company or to the winding up,

he shall be guilty of an offence.

(2) A person convicted of an offence—

(*a*) under paragraph (*a*), (*b*), (*c*), (*d*), (*e*), (*f*), (*g*), (*h*), (*i*), (*j*), (*k*), (*l*) or (*p*) of subsection (1) shall be liable—

(i) on conviction in a Circuit Court, to a fine or to imprisonment for a term not exceeding two years or to both such fine and imprisonment;

(ii) on summary conviction before a Resident Magistrate, to a fine not exceeding three million dollars or to imprisonment for a term not exceeding twelve months or to both such fine and imprisonment;

(*b*) under paragraph (*m*), (*n*) or (*o*) of that subsection shall be liable—

(i) on conviction in a Circuit Court to a fine or to imprisonment for a term not exceeding five years or to both such fine and imprisonment;

(ii) on summary conviction before a Resident Magistrate, to a fine not exceeding five million dollars or to imprisonment for a term not exceeding twelve months or to both such fine and imprisonment.

(3) It shall be a good defence to a charge under any of paragraphs (*a*), (*b*), (*c*), (*d*), (*f*), (*n*) and (*o*), if the accused proves that he had no intent to defraud, and to a charge under any of paragraphs (*h*), (*i*) and (*j*), if he proves that he had no intent to conceal the state of affairs of the company or to defeat the law.

(4) Where any person pawns, pledges or disposes of any property in circumstances which amount to an offence under paragraph (*o*) of subsection (1), every person who takes in pawn or pledge or otherwise receives the property knowing it to be pawned, pledged, or disposed of in such circumstances as aforesaid shall be guilty of an offence, and shall be liable—

(*a*) on conviction in a Circuit Court to a fine or to imprisonment for a term not exceeding five years or to both such fine and imprisonment;

(*b*) on summary conviction before a Resident Magistrate to a fine not exceeding three million dollars or to imprisonment for a term not exceeding twelve months or to both such fine and imprisonment.

(5) For the purposes of this section, the expression "officer" shall include any person in accordance with whose directions or instructions the directors of a company have been accustomed to act.

Penalty for falsification of books.

319. If any officer or contributory of any company being wound up destroys, mutilates, alters, or falsifies any books, papers, or securities, or makes or is privy to the making of any false or fraudulent entry in any register, book of account, or document belonging to the company with intent to defraud or deceive any person, he shall be guilty of an offence and on conviction thereof he shall be liable to a fine not exceeding two million dollars or to imprisonment with or without hard labour for a term not exceeding two years or to both such fine and imprisonment.

Fraud by officers of companies which have gone into liquidation.

320. If any person, being at the time of the commission of the alleged offence an officer of a company which is subsequently ordered to be wound up by the Court or subsequently passes a resolution for voluntary winding up—

(*a*) has by false pretences or by means of any other fraud induced any person to give credit to the company;

(*b*) with intent to defraud creditors of the company, has made or caused to be made any gift or transfer of or charge on, or has caused or connived at the levying of any execution against, the property of the company;

(*c*) with intent to defraud creditors of the company, has concealed or removed any part of the property of the company since, or within two months before, the date of any unsatisfied judgment or order for payment of money obtained against the company, he shall be guilty of an offence and shall be liable—

(i) on conviction in a Circuit Court to a fine or to imprisonment with or without hard labour for a term not exceeding two years or to both such fine and imprisonment; or

(ii) on summary conviction before a Resident Magistrate to a fine not exceeding three million dollars or to imprisonment with or without hard labour for a term not exceeding twelve months or to both such fine and imprisonment.

Liability where proper accounts not kept.

321.—(1) If where a company is wound up it is shown that proper books of account were not kept by the company throughout the period of two years immediately preceding the commencement of the winding up, or the period between the incorporation of the company and the commencement of the winding up, whichever is the shorter, every officer of the company who was knowingly a party to or connived at the default of the company shall, unless he shows that he acted honestly and that in the circumstances in which the business of the company was carried on the default was excusable, be guilty of an offence and shall be liable—

(*a*) on conviction in a Circuit Court to a fine or to imprisonment with or without hard labour for a term not exceeding one year; or

(*b*) on summary conviction before a Resident Magistrate to a fine not exceeding two million dollars or to imprisonment for a term not exceeding six months.

(2) For the purposes of this section, proper books of account shall be deemed not to have been kept in the case of any company if there have not been kept such books or accounts as are necessary to exhibit and explain the transactions and financial position of the trade or business of the company,

including books containing entries from day to day in sufficient detail of all cash received and cash paid, and, where the trade or business has involved dealings in goods, statements of the annual stock takings and (except in the case of goods sold by way of ordinary retail trade) of all goods sold and purchased, showing the goods and the buyers and sellers thereof in sufficient detail to enable those goods and those buyers and sellers to be identified.

322.—(1) If in the course of the winding up of a company it appears that any business of the company has been carried on with intent to defraud creditors of the company, creditors of any other person or for any fraudulent purpose, the Court, on the application of the Trustee, or the liquidator or any creditor or contributory of the company, may, if it thinks proper so to do, declare that any persons who were knowingly parties to the carrying on of the business in manner aforesaid shall be personally responsible, without any limitation of liability, for all or any of the debts or other liabilities of the company as the Court may direct.

Responsibility for fraudulent trading of persons concerned.

(2) On the hearing of an application under subsection (1) the Trustee or the liquidator, as the case may be, may himself give evidence or call witnesses.

(3) Where the Court makes any such declaration, it may give such further directions as it thinks proper for the purpose of giving effect to that declaration, and in particular may make provision for making the liability of any such person under the declaration a charge on any debt or obligation due from the company to him, or on any mortgage or charge or any interest in any mortgage or charge on any assets of the company held by or vested in him, or any company or person on his behalf, or any person claiming as assignee from or through the person liable or any company or person acting on his behalf, and may from time to time make such further order as may be necessary for the purpose of enforcing any charge imposed under this subsection.

(4) For the purpose of subsection (3), the expression "assignee" includes any person to whom or in whose favour, by the directions of the person liable, the debt, obligation, mortgage or charge was created, issued or transferred or the interest created, but does not include an assignee for valuable consideration (not including consideration by way of marriage) given in good faith and without notice of any of the matters on the ground of which the declaration is made.

(5) Where any business of a company is carried on with such intent or for such purpose as is mentioned in subsection (1), every person who was knowingly a party to the carrying on of the business in manner aforesaid, shall be liable on conviction on indictment to imprisonment with or without hard labour for a term not exceeding two years or to a fine not exceeding fifty thousand dollars or to both such imprisonment and fine.

(6) The provisions of this section shall have effect notwithstanding that the person concerned may be criminally liable in respect of the matters on the ground of which the declaration is to be made, and where the declaration under subsection (1) is made in the case of a winding up, the declaration shall be deemed to be a final judgment within the meaning of paragraph (*h*) of section 19 of the Bankruptcy Act.

Power of Court to assess damages against delinquent directors, etc.

323.—(1) If in the course of winding up a company it appears that any person who has taken part in the formation or promotion of the company, or any past or present officer or liquidator of the company, has misapplied or retained or become liable or accountable for any money or property of the company, or been guilty of any misfeasance or breach of trust in relation to the company, the Court may, on the application of the Trustee, or of the liquidator, or of any creditor or contributory, examine into the conduct of the promoter, liquidator, or officer, and compel him to repay or restore the money or property or any part thereof respectively with interest at such rate as the Court thinks just, or to contribute such sum to the assets of the company by way of compensation in respect of the mis-application, retainer, misfeasance, or breach of trust as the Court thinks just.

(2) The provisions of this section shall have effect notwithstanding that the offence is one for which the offender may be criminally liable.

(3) Where in the case of a winding up an order for payment of money is made under this section, the order shall be deemed to be a final judgment within the meaning of paragraph (*h*) of section 19 of the Bankruptcy Act.

Prosecution of delinquent officers and members of company.

324.—(1) If it appears to the Court in the course of a winding up by, or subject to the supervision of, the Court that any past or present officer, or any member, of the company has been guilty of any offence in relation to the company for which he is criminally liable, the Court may, either on the application of any person interested in the winding up or of its own motion, direct the liquidator to refer the matter to the Director of Public Prosecutions.

(2) If it appears to the liquidator in the course of a voluntary winding up that any past or present officer, or any member, of a company has been guilty of any offence in relation to the company for which he is criminally liable, he shall forthwith report the matter to the Director of Public Prosecutions, and shall furnish to the Director such information and give to him such access to and facilities for inspecting and taking copies of any documents, being information or documents in the possession or under the control of the liquidator and relating to the matter in question, as the Director may require.

(3) Where any report is made under subsection (2) to the Director of Public Prosecutions, he may, if he thinks fit, refer the matter to the Minister for further enquiry, and the Minister shall thereupon investigate the matter and may, if he thinks it expedient, apply to the Court for an order conferring on the Minister or any person designated by the Minister for the purpose with respect to the company concerned all such powers of investigating the affairs of the company as are provided by this Act in the case of a winding up by the Court.

(4) If it appears to the Court in the course of a voluntary winding up that any past or present officer, or any member, of the company has been guilty as aforesaid, and that no report with respect to the matter has been made by the liquidator to the Director of Public Prosecutions under subsection (2), the Court may, on the application of any person interested in the winding up or of its own motion, direct the liquidator to make such a report, and on a report being made accordingly the provisions of this section shall have effect as though the report had been made in pursuance of the provisions of subsection (2).

(5) Where any matter is reported or referred to the Director of Public Prosecutions under this section, if he considers that the case is one in which a prosecution ought to be instituted, he shall institute proceedings accordingly, and it shall be the duty of the liquidator and of every officer and agent of the company past and present (other than the defendant in the proceedings) to give him all assistance in connection with the prosecution which he is reasonably able to give.

(6) For the purposes of subsection (5) the expression "agent" in relation to a company shall be deemed to include any banker or attorney-at-law of the company and any person employed by the company as auditor, whether that person is or is not an officer of the company.

(7) If any person fails or neglects to give assistance in manner required by subsection (5), the Court may, on the application of the Director of Public Prosecutions, direct that person to comply with the requirements of that subsection, and where any such application is made with respect to a liquidator the Court may, unless it appears that the failure or neglect to comply was due to the liquidator not having in his hands sufficient assets of the company to enable him so to do, direct that the costs of the application shall be borne by the liquidator personally.

Supplementary Provisions as to Winding up

325. A body corporate shall not be qualified for appointment as liquidator of a company, whether in a winding up by or under the supervision of the Court or in a voluntary winding up, and— Disqualification for appointment as liquidator.

(*a*) any appointment made in contravention of this provision shall be void; and

(*b*) any body corporate which acts as liquidator of a company shall be liable to a fine not exceeding fifty thousand dollars.

326.—(1) If any liquidator, who has made any default in filing, delivering or making any return, account or other document, or in giving any notice which he is by law required to file, deliver, make or give, fails to make good the default within fourteen days after the service on him of a notice requiring him to do so, the Court may, on an application made to the Court by any contributory or creditor of the company or by the Registrar, make an order directing the liquidator to make good the default within such time as may be specified in the order. Enforcement of duty of liquidator to make returns, etc.

(2) Any such order may provide that all costs of and incidental to the application shall be borne by the liquidator.

(3) Nothing in this section shall be taken to prejudice the operation of any enactment imposing penalties on a liquidator in respect of any such default as aforesaid.

Notification that company is in liquidation.

327.—(1) Where a company is being wound up, whether by or under the supervision of the Court or voluntarily, every invoice, order for goods or business letter issued by or on behalf of the company or a liquidator of the company, or a receiver or manager of the property of the company, being a document on or in which the name of the company appears, shall contain a statement that the company is being wound up.

(2) If default is made in complying with this section the company and every officer of the company, and every liquidator of the company and every receiver or manager, who knowingly and wilfully authorizes or permits the default shall be liable to a fine not exceeding fifty thousand dollars.

Exemption of certain documents from stamp duty on winding up of companies.

328.—(1) In the case of a winding up by the Court, or of a creditors' voluntary winding up, of a company—

(*a*) every assurance relating solely to freehold or leasehold property, or to any mortgage, charge or other incumbrance on, or any estate, right or interest in, any real or personal property, which forms part of the assets of the company and which, after the execution of the assurance, either at law or in equity, is or remains part of the assets of the company; and

(*b*) every power of attorney, proxy paper, writ, order, certificate, affidavit, bond or other instrument or writing relating solely to the property of any company which is being so wound up, or to any proceeding under any such winding up,

shall be exempt from duties chargeable under the enactments relating to stamp duties.

(2) In subsection (1) the expression "assurance" includes deed, conveyance, assignment, transfer and surrender.

329. Where a company is being wound up, all books and papers of the company and of the liquidators shall, as between the contributories of the company, be *prima facie* evidence of the truth of all matters purporting to be therein recorded. Books of company to be evidence.

330.—(1) When a company has been wound up and is about to be dissolved, the books and papers of the company and of the liquidators may be disposed of as follows, that is to say— Disposal of books and papers of company.

(*a*) in the case of a winding up by or subject to the supervision of the Court, in such way as the Court directs;

(*b*) in the case of a members' voluntary winding up, in such way as the company by extraordinary resolution directs, and, in the case of a creditors' voluntary winding up, in such way as the committee of inspection or, if there is no such committee, as the creditors of the company, may direct.

(2) After five years from the dissolution of the company no responsibility shall rest on the company, the liquidators, or any person to whom the custody of the books and papers has been committed, by reason of any book or paper not being forthcoming to any person claiming to be interested therein.

(3) Provision may be made by rules for enabling the Court to prevent, for such period (not exceeding five years from the dissolution of the company) as the Court thinks proper, the destruction of the books and papers of a company which has been wound up, and for enabling any creditor or contributory of the company to make representations to the Court.

(4) If any person acts in contravention of any rules made for the purposes of this section or of any direction of the Court thereunder, he shall be liable to a fine not exceeding three thousand dollars.

Information as to pending liquidations.

331.—(1) If the winding up of a company is not concluded within one year after its commencement, the liquidator shall, at such intervals as may be prescribed, until the winding up is concluded, send to the Registrar a statement in the prescribed form and containing the prescribed particulars with respect to the proceedings in and position of the liquidation.

(2) Any person stating himself in writing to be a creditor or contributory of the company shall be entitled, by himself or by his agent, at all reasonable times, on payment of the prescribed fee, to inspect the statement, and to receive a copy thereof or extract therefrom.

(3) If a liquidator fails to comply with this section, he shall be liable to a fine not exceeding five hundred dollars for each day during which the default continues, and any person untruthfully stating himself as aforesaid to be a creditor or contributory shall be guilty of a contempt of court, and shall, on the application of the liquidator or of the Trustee, be punishable accordingly.

Unclaimed assets.

332.—(1) If it appears either from any statement sent to the Registrar under section 331 or otherwise that a liquidator has in his hands or under his control any money representing unclaimed or undistributed assets of the company which have remained unclaimed or undistributed for six months after the date of their receipt or any money held by the company in trust in respect of dividends or other sums due to any person as a member of the company, the liquidator shall forthwith pay that money into Court, and shall be entitled to the prescribed certificate of receipt for the money so paid, and that certificate shall be an effectual discharge to him in respect thereof.

(2) Any person claiming to be entitled to any money paid into Court in pursuance of this section may apply to the Court for payment thereof, and the Court may, on a certificate by the liquidator that the person claiming is entitled, make an order for the payment to that person of the sum due.

333. Where after the appointed day a resolution is passed at an adjourned meeting of any creditors or contributories of a company, the resolution shall, for all purposes, be treated as having been passed on the date on which it was in fact passed, and shall not be deemed to have been passed on any earlier date. Resolutions passed at adjourned meetings of creditors and contributors.

Supplementary Powers of Court

334.—(1) The Court may, as to all matters relating to the winding up of a company, have regard to the wishes of the creditors or contributories of the company, as proved to it by any sufficient evidence, and may, if it thinks fit, for the purpose of ascertaining those wishes, direct meetings of the creditors or contributories to be called, held, and conducted in such manner as the Court directs, and may appoint a person to act as chairman of any such meeting and to report the result thereof to the Court. Meetings to ascertain wishes of creditors or contributories.

(2) In the case of creditors, regard shall be had to the value of each creditor's debt.

(3) In the case of contributories, regard shall be had to the number of votes conferred on each contributory by this Act or the articles.

335.—(1) Any affidavit required to be sworn under the provisions or for the purposes of this Part may be sworn in the Island, or elsewhere within the Commonwealth, before any court, judge, or person lawfully authorized to take and receive affidavits, or, in any place outside the Commonwealth, before any of Her Majesty's consuls or vice-consuls or a notary public, subject to the like restrictions as apply in relation to the power of a notary public in a foreign state or country under section 152 of the Registration of Titles Act to attest instruments and powers of attorney under that Act. Affidavits, etc.

(2) All courts, judges, justices, commissioners and persons acting judicially shall take judicial notice of the seal or stamp or signature, as the case may be, of any such court, judge,

person, consul, vice-consul or notary public attached, appended, or subscribed to any such affidavit, or to any other document to be used for the purposes of this Part.

Provisions as to Dissolution

Power of Court to declare dissolution of company void

336.—(1) Where a company has been dissolved, the Court may at any time within two years of the date of the dissolution, on an application being made for the purpose by the liquidator of the company or by any other person who appears to the Court to be interested, make an order, upon such terms as the Court thinks fit, declaring the dissolution to have been void, and thereupon such proceedings maybe taken as might have been taken if the company had not been dissolved.

(2) It shall be the duty of the person on whose application the order was made, within seven days after the making of the order, or such further time as the Court may allow, to deliver to the Registrar for registration a copy of the order, and if that person fails so to do he shall be liable to a fine not exceeding two thousand dollars for every day during which the default continues.

Registrar may strike defunct company off register.

337.—(1) Where the Registrar has reasonable cause to believe that a company is not carrying on business or in operation, he may send to the company by post a letter inquiring whether the company is carrying on business or in operation.

(2) If the Registrar does not within one month of sending the letter receive any answer thereto, he shall within fourteen days after the expiration of the month send to the company by post a registered letter referring to the first letter, and stating that no answer thereto has been received, and that if an answer is not received to the second letter within one month from the date thereof, a notice will be published in the *Gazette* and in a daily newspaper circulating in the Island with a view to striking the name of the company off the register.

(3) If the Registrar either receives an answer to the effect that the company is not carrying on business or in operation, or does not within one month after sending the second letter receive any answer, he may publish in the *Gazette* and in a daily newspaper circulating in the Island, and send to the company by post, a notice that at the expiration of three months from the date of that notice the name of the company mentioned therein will, unless cause is shown to the contrary, be struck off the register and the company will be dissolved.

(4) If, in any case where a company is being wound up, the Registrar has reasonable cause to believe either that no liquidator is acting, or that the affairs of the company are fully wound up, and the returns required to be made by the liquidator have not been made for a period of six consecutive months, the Registrar shall publish in the *Gazette* and send to the company or the liquidator, if any, a like notice as is provided in subsection (3).

(5) At the expiration of the time mentioned in the notice the Registrar may, unless cause to the contrary is previously shown by the company, strike its name off the register, and shall publish notice thereof in the *Gazette*, and on the publication in the *Gazette* of that notice the company shall be dissolved:

Provided that—

(*a*) the liability, if any, of every director, managing officer, and member of the company shall continue and may be enforced as if the company had not been dissolved; and

(*b*) nothing in this subsection shall affect the power of the Court to wind up a company the name of which has been struck off the register.

(6) If a company or any member or creditor thereof feels aggrieved by the company having been struck off the register, the Registrar on an application made by the company or

member or creditor before the expiration of twenty years from the publication in the *Gazette* of the notice aforesaid may, if satisfied that—

(*a*) the company was at the time of the striking off, carrying on business or in operation; or

(*b*) otherwise that it is just that the company be restored to the register,

order the name of the company to be restored to the register and upon such registration, the company shall be deemed to have continued in existence as if its name had not been struck off.

(7) A notice to be sent under this section to a liquidator may be addressed to the liquidator at his last known place of business, and a letter or notice to be sent under this section to a company shall be addressed—

(*a*) to the company at its registered office and to some director or other officer of the company; or

(*b*) if there is no director or other officer whose name and address are known to the Registrar, to each of the persons who subscribed the articles, addressed to him at the address mentioned in the articles.

Property of dissolved company to be *bona vacantia*.

338.—(1) Where a company is dissolved, all property and rights whatsoever vested in or held on trust for the company immediately before its dissolution (including leasehold property but not including property held by the company on trust for any other person) shall, subject and without prejudice to any order which may at any time be made by the Court under section 336 or by the Registrar under section 337—

(*a*) prior to the expiration of two years referred to in section 336 (1) be held on trust by the Crown for the members of that company for the duration of two years; or (*b*) prior to the expiration of the period of twenty years referred to in section 337 (6) be held on trust by the Crown for the members of that company for the duration of the twenty years; and

(*c*) after the expiration of the relevant period be deemed to be *bona vacantia* and shall accordingly belong to the Crown, and shall vest and may be dealt with in the same manner as other *bona vacantia* accruing to the Crown.

(2) Where a company is restored, the trust referred to in subsection (1) shall be extinquished and the property shall revert to the company.

(3) Where the Crown holds property for a dissolved Company on trust, the Crown shall not be liable—

(*a*) to manage the property;

(*b*) for any loss or damage to the property;

(*c*) for waste; or

(*d*) in respect of any claim by a third party.

(4) Where the Crown holds property for a dissolved company on trust in the case of—

(*a*) real property, it shall be held by the Commissioner of Lands;

(*b*) personalty, it shall be held by the Accountant General.

Power of Crown to disclaim title to property vesting under section 338

339.—(1) Where any property vests in the Crown under section 338 (1) (*c*) the Crown's title thereto under that section may be disclaimed by a notice signed by the Administrator-General.

(2) Where a notice of disclaimer under this section is executed as respects any property, that property shall be deemed not to have vested in the Crown under section 338 (1) (*c*), and

subsections (2) and (6) of section 315 shall apply in relation to the property as if it had been disclaimed under subsection (1) of that section immediately before the dissolution of the company.

(3) The right to execute a notice of disclaimer under this section may be waived by or on behalf of the Crown either expressly or by taking possession or other act evincing that intention.

(4) A notice of disclaimer under this section shall be of no effect unless it is executed within twelve months of the date on which the vesting of the property as aforesaid came to the notice of the Administrator-General or, if an application in writing is made to the Administrator-General by any person interested in the property requiring him to decide whether he will or will not disclaim, within a period of three months after the receipt of the application or such further period as may be allowed by the Court.

(5) A statement in a notice of disclaimer of any property under this section that the vesting of the property came to the notice of the Administrator-General on a specified date or that no such application as aforesaid was received by him with respect to the property before a specified date shall, until the contrary is proved, be sufficient evidence of the fact stated.

(6) A notice of disclaimer under this section shall be delivered to the Registrar and retained and registered by him, and copies thereof shall be published in the *Gazette* and sent to any persons who have given the Administrator-General notice that they claim to be interested in the property.

Rules and Fees

Rules and fees for winding up.

340.—(1) The Rules Committee of the Supreme Court established by section 3 of the Judicature (Rules of Court) Act, may, with the concurrence of the Minister, make rules for carrying into effect the objects of this Act so far as they relate to the winding up of companies, and all such rules shall be judicially noticed and shall have effect as if enacted in this Act.

(2) There shall be paid in respect of proceedings under this Act in relation to the winding up of companies such fees as the Rules Committee may, with the sanction of the Minister responsible for finance, by order direct, and that Minister may direct by whom and in what manner the same are to be collected and accounted for.

(3) All rules made under subsection (1) and all orders made under subsection (2) shall be subject to negative resolution.

(4) Until varied or revoked pursuant to the powers given by subsection (1) or, as the case may be, subsection (2), the Companies (Winding up) Rules, 1949, made under the 11 and 12 Companies Act, 1948, of the United Kingdom and the scale of winding up fees in force under the said Act are declared to be in force in the Island and shall be read with and construed as part of this Act: 11 and 12 Geo. 6 Cap. 38.

Provided that it shall be lawful for any court to make such alterations to those Rules as may be deemed expedient to render the same applicable to any matters before such court, so, however, that any such alteration shall not be inconsistent with the provisions of this Act.

(5) Notwithstanding anything to the contrary, the Judicature (Rules of Court) Act shall not apply in relation to any matter for which provision is made in this section.

PART VI—RECEIVERS AND MANAGERS

Disqualification for appointment as receiver and for acting as receiver or manager.

341.—(1) A body corporate shall not be qualified for appointment as receiver of the property of a company and any body corporate which acts as such a receiver shall be liable to a fine not exceeding fifty thousand dollars.

(2) If any person being an undischarged bankrupt acts as receiver or manager of the property of a company on behalf of debenture holders, he shall, subject to subsection (3), be

liable on conviction on indictment to imprisonment with or without hard labour for a term not exceeding two years, or on summary conviction before a Resident Magistrate to imprisonment with or without hard labour for a term not exceeding six months or to a fine not exceeding fifty thousand dollars or to both such imprisonment and fine.

(3) Subsection (2) shall not apply to a receiver or manager where—

(*a*) the appointment under which he acts and the bankruptcy were both before the appointed day; or

(*b*) he acts under an appointment made by order of a court.

Power to appoint Trustee as receiver for debenture holders or creditors.

342. Where an application is made to the Court to appoint a receiver on behalf of the debenture holders or other creditors of a company which is being wound up by the Court, the Trustee may be so appointed.

Notification that receiver or manager appointed.

343.—(1) Where a receiver or manager of the property of a company has been appointed, every invoice, order for goods or business letter issued by or on behalf of the company or the receiver or manager or the liquidator of the company, being a document on or in which the name of the company appears, shall contain a statement that a receiver or manager has been appointed.

(2) If default is made in complying with the requirements of this section, the company and every officer of the company, and every liquidator of the company, and every receiver or manager, who knowingly and wilfully authorizes or permits the default, shall be liable to a fine not exceeding fifty thousand dollars.

Power of Court to fix remuneration on application of liquidator.

344.—(1) The Court may, on an application made to the Court by the liquidator of a company, by order fix the amount to be paid by way of remuneration to any person who, under the powers contained in any instrument, has been appointed as receiver or manager of the property of the company.

(2) The power of the Court under subsection (1) shall, where no previous order has been made with respect thereto under that subsection—

(*a*) extend to fixing the remuneration for any period before the making of the order or the application therefor; and

(*b*) be exercisable notwithstanding that the receiver or manager has died or ceased to act before the making of the order or the application therefor; and

(*c*) where the receiver or manager has been paid or has retained for his remuneration for any period before the making of the order any amount in excess of that so fixed for that period, extend to requiring him or his personal representatives to account for the excess or such part thereof as may be specified in the order:

Provided that the power conferred by paragraph (*c*) shall not be exercised as respects any period before the making of the application for the order unless in the opinion of the Court there are special circumstances making it proper for the power to be so exercised.

(3) The Court may from time to time on an application made either by the liquidator or by the receiver or manager, vary or amend an order made under subsection (1).

(4) This section shall apply whether the receiver or manager was appointed before or after the appointed day, and to periods before, as well as to periods after, such day.

Provisions as to information where receiver or manager appointed.

345.—(1) Where a receiver or manager of the whole or substantially the whole of the property of the company (hereafter in this section and in section 346 referred to as "the receiver") is appointed on behalf of the holders of any debentures of the company secured by a floating charge, then subject to the provisions of this section and section 346—

(*a*) the receiver shall forthwith send notice to the company of his appointment; and

(8) If the receiver makes default in complying with the requirements of this section, he shall be liable to a fine not exceeding two thousand dollars for every day during which the default continues.

Special provisions as to statement submitted to receiver.

346.—(1) The statement as to the affairs of a company required by section 345 to be submitted to the receiver (or his successor) shall show as at the date of the receiver's appointment the particulars of the company's assets, debts and liabilities, the names, residences and occupations of its creditors, the securities held by them respectively, the dates when the securities were respectively given and such further or other information as may be prescribed.

(2) The statement shall be submitted by, and be verified by affidavit of, one or more of the persons who are at the date of the receiver's appointment the directors and by the person who is at that date the secretary of the company, or by such of the persons hereafter in this subsection mentioned as the receiver (or his successor), subject to the direction of the Court, may require to submit and verify the statement, that is to say, persons—

(*a*) who are or have been officers of the company;

(*b*) who have taken part in the formation of the company at any time within one year before the date of the receiver's appointment;

(*c*) who are in the employment of the company, or have been in the employment of the company within that year, and are in the opinion of the receiver capable of giving the information required;

(*d*) who are or have been within that year officers of or in the employment of a company which is, or within that year was, an officer of the company to which the statement relates.

from the end of the period to which the last preceding abstract related up to the date of his so ceasing, and the aggregate amounts of his receipts and of his payments during all preceding periods since his appointment.

(3) Where the receiver is appointed under the powers contained in any instrument, this section shall have effect—

(*a*) with the omission of the references to the Court in subsection (l);and

(*b*) with the substitution for the references to the Court in subsection (2) of references to the Registrar.

(4) Subsection (1) shall not apply in relation to the appointment of a receiver or manager to act with an existing receiver or manager or in place of a receiver or manager dying or ceasing to act, except that, where that subsection applies to a receiver or manager who dies or ceases to act before it has been fully complied with, the references in paragraphs (*b*) and (*c*) thereof to the receiver shall (subject to subsection (5)) include references to his successor and to any continuing receiver or manager.

(5) Nothing in subsection (4) shall be taken as limiting the meaning of the expression "the receiver" where used in, or in relation to, subsection (2).

(6) This section and section 346, where the company is being wound up, shall apply notwithstanding that the receiver or manager and the liquidator are the same person, but with any necessary modifications arising from that fact.

(7) Nothing in subsection (2) shall be taken to prejudice the duty of the receiver to render proper accounts of his receipts and payments to the persons to whom, and at the times at which, he may be required to do so apart from that subsection.

(*b*) there shall, within fourteen days after receipt of the notice, or such longer period as may be allowed by the Court or by the receiver, be made out and submitted to the receiver in accordance with section 346 a statement in the prescribed form as to the affairs of the company; and

(*c*) the receiver shall within two months after receipt of that statement send—

(i) to the Registrar and to the Court, a copy of the statement and of any comments he sees fit to make thereon and in the case of the Registrar also a summary of the statement and of his comments (if any) thereon; and

(ii) to the company, a copy of any such comments as aforesaid or, if he does not see fit to make any comment, a notice to that effect; and

(iii) to any trustees for the debenture holders on whose behalf he was appointed and, so far as he is aware of their addresses, to all such debenture holders, a copy of the said summary.

(2) The receiver shall within two months, or such longer period as the Court may allow, after the expiration of the period of twelve months from the date of his appointment and of every subsequent period of twelve months, and within two months or such longer period as the Court may allow after he ceases to act as receiver or manager of the property of the company, send to the Registrar, to any trustees for debenture holders of the company on whose behalf he was appointed, to the company and (so far as he is aware of their addresses) to all such debenture holders an abstract in the prescribed form showing his receipts and payments during that period of twelve months, or where he ceases to act as aforesaid, during the period

(3) Any person making the statement and affidavit shall be allowed, and shall be paid by the receiver (or his successor) out of his receipts, such costs and expenses incurred in and about the preparation and making of the statement and affidavit as the receiver (or his successor) may consider reasonable, subject to an appeal to the Court.

(4) Where the receiver is appointed under the powers contained in any instrument, this section shall have effect with the substitution for references to the Court of references to the Registrar and for references to an affidavit of references to a statutory declaration.

(5) If any person without reasonable excuse makes default in complying with the requirements of this section, he shall be liable to a fine not exceeding three thousand dollars for every day during which the default continues.

(6) References in this section to the receiver's successor shall include a continuing receiver or manager.

Delivery to Registrar of accounts of receivers and managers.

347.—(1) Except where subsection (2) of section 345 applies, every receiver or manager of the property of a company who has been appointed under the powers contained in any instrument shall, within one month, or such longer period as the Registrar may allow, after the expiration of the period of six months from the date of his appointment and of every subsequent period of six months, and within one month after he ceases to act as receiver or manager, deliver to the Registrar for registration an abstract in the prescribed form showing his receipts and his payments during that period of six months, or, where he ceases to act as aforesaid, during the period from the end of the period to which the last preceding abstract related up to the date of his so ceasing, and the aggregate amount of his receipts and of his payments during all preceding periods since his appointment.

(2) Every receiver or manager who makes default in complying with the provisions of this section shall be liable to a fine not exceeding two thousand dollars for every day during which the default continues.

Enforcement of duty of receivers and managers to make returns, etc.

348.—(1) If any receiver or manager of the property of a company—

(*a*) having made default in filing, delivering or making any return, account or other document, or in giving any notice, which a receiver or manager is by law required to file, deliver, make or give, fails to make good the default within fourteen days after the service on him of a notice requiring him to do so; or

(*b*) having been appointed under the powers contained in any instrument, has, after being required at any time by the liquidator of the company so to do, failed to render proper accounts of his receipts and payments and to vouch the same and to pay over to the liquidator the amount payable to him,

the Court may, on an application made for the purpose, make an order directing the receiver or manager, as the case may be, to make good the default within such time as may be specified in the order.

(2) In the case of any such default as is mentioned in paragraph (*a*) of subsection (1) an application for the purposes of this section may be made by any member or creditor of the company or by the Registrar, and in the case of any such default as is mentioned in paragraph (*b*) of that subsection the application shall be made by the liquidator, and in either case the order may provide that all costs of and incidental to the application shall be borne by the receiver or manager, as the case may be.

(3) Nothing in this section shall be taken to prejudice the operation of any enactments imposing penalties on receivers or managers in respect of any such default as is mentioned in subsection (1).

349.—(1) A receiver or manager of the property of a company appointed under the powers contained in any instrument shall, to the same extent as if he had been appointed by order of a court, be personally liable on any contract entered into by him in the performance of his functions, except in so far as the contract otherwise provides, and entitled in respect of that liability to indemnity out of the assets; but nothing in this subsection shall be taken as limiting any right to indemnity which he would have apart from this subsection, or as limiting his liability on contracts entered into without authority or as conferring any right to indemnity in respect of that liability. Liability of receiver for contracts, etc.

(2) This section shall apply whether the receiver or manager was appointed before or after the appointed day but subsection (1) shall not apply to contracts entered into before that day.

350. It is hereby declared that, except where the context otherwise requires— Construction of references to receivers and managers.

(*a*) any reference in this Act to a receiver or manager of the property of a company, or to a receiver thereof, includes a reference to a receiver or manager, or (as the case may be) to a receiver, of part only of the property and to a receiver only of the income arising from that property or from part thereof; and

(*b*) any reference in this Act to the appointment of a receiver or manager under powers contained in any instrument includes a reference to an appointment made under powers which, by virtue of any enactment, are implied in and have effect as if contained in an instrument.

PART VII—REGISTRATION OFFICE AND FEES

351.—(1) For the purposes of this Act there shall be a Registrar of Companies whose office shall be a public office, and the Minister shall establish in the Island a registration office of companies Registrar of Companies and registration office.

(2) The Registrar may in writing authorize any officer of his department to execute, subject to the Registrar's directions and to prescribe conditions (if any), functions assigned to the Registrar by any enactment.

(3) Anything executed by any officer to whom authority is given under this section and in accordance with such authority shall be as valid and effectual as if it were executed by the Registrar.

(4) Notice of any authority given under this section and of any extension or revocation of such authority shall be published in the *Gazette* but failure to publish such notice shall not affect the validity of the authority conferred, or any extension or revocation thereof, as the case may be.

Inspection, production, evidence and retention of documents kept by Registrar.

352.—(1) Any person may inspect the documents kept by the Registrar on payment of the prescribed fees, and any person may require a certificate of the incorporation of any company, or a copy or extract of any other document or any part of any other document, to be certified by the Registrar, on payment of the prescribed fees.

(2) No process for compelling the production of any document kept by the Registrar shall issue from any Court except with the leave of that Court, and any such process if issued shall bear thereon a statement that it is issued with the leave of the Court.

(3) A copy of or extract from any document kept and registered at the office for the registration of companies, certified to be a true copy under the hand of the Registrar (whose official position it shall not be necessary to prove), shall in all legal proceedings be admissible in evidence as of equal validity with the original document.

(4) The Minister may make rules subject to affirmative resolution, prescribing the maximum period for which the Registrar is required to retain any documents or category thereof kept and registered at the office.

353.—(1) If a company, having made default in complying with any provision of this Act which requires it to file with, or deliver or send to, the Registrar any return, account or other document, or to give notice to him of any matter, fails to make good the default within fourteen days after the service of a notice on the company requiring it to do so, a Judge in Chambers may, on an application made to him by any member or creditor of the company or by the Registrar, make an order directing the company and any officer thereof to make good the default within such time as may be specified in the order: Enforcement of duty of company to make returns to Registrar.

Provided that the Judge may refer the application for hearing in open Court.

(2) Any such order may provide that all costs of and incidental to the application shall be borne by the company or by any officers of the company responsible for the default.

(3) Nothing in this section shall be taken to prejudice the operation of any enactment imposing penalties on a company or its officers in respect of any such default as aforesaid.

PART VIII—APPLICATION OF ACT TO EXISTING COMPANIES

354. In the application of this Act to existing companies it shall apply in the same manner— Application of Act to existing companies.

(*a*) in the case of a limited company, other than a company limited by guarantee, as if the company had been formed and registered under this Act as a company limited by shares;

(*b*) in the case of a company limited by guarantee, as if the company had been formed and registered under this Act as a company limited by guarantee; and

(*c*) in the case of a company other than a limited company, as if the company had been formed and registered under this Act as an unlimited company.

Provided that reference, express or implied, to the date of registration or recording shall be construed as a reference to the date at which the company was registered or recorded before the 1st day of February, 2005.

PART IX—WINDING UP OF UNREGISTERED COMPANIES

Meaning and winding up of unregistered company.

355. For the purposes of this Part, the expression "unregistered company" shall not include a friendly society registered and established under the Friendly Societies Act, or a society established under the Building Societies Act, but shall include any partnership whether limited or not, association or company not registered under the law relating to companies before the 1st day of February, 2005 or under this Act, so, however, that any such partnership, association or company which is not a foreign partnership, association or company shall consist of not less than eight members, and all the provisions of this Act with respect to winding up shall apply to such a company, with the following exceptions and additions, that is to say—

(*a*) no unregistered company shall be wound up under this Act voluntarily or subject to supervision;

(*b*) the circumstances in which an unregistered company may be wound up are as follows, that is to say—

(i) if the company is dissolved, or has ceased to carry on business, or is carrying on business only for the purpose of winding up its affairs;

(ii) if the company is unable to pay its debts;

(iii) if the Court is of opinion that it is just and equitable that the company should be wound up;

(*c*) an unregistered company shall, for the purposes of this Act, be deemed to be unable to pay its debts—

(i) if a creditor, by assignment or otherwise, to whom the company is indebted in a sum exceeding two hundred thousand dollars then due, has served on the company, by leaving at its principal place of business, or by delivering to the secretary or some director, manager or principal officer of the company, or by otherwise serving in such manner as the Court may approve or direct, a demand under his hand requiring the company to pay the sum so due, and the company has, for three weeks after the service of the demand, neglected to pay the sum or to secure or compound for it to the satisfaction of the creditor;

(ii) if any action or other proceeding has been instituted against any member for any debt or demand due or claimed to be due from the company, or from him in his character of member, and notice in writing of the institution of the action or proceeding having been served on the company by leaving the same at its principal place of business, or by delivering it to the secretary or some director, manager or principal officer of the company, or by otherwise serving the same in such manner as the Court may approve or direct, the company has not, within ten days after service of the notice, paid, secured, or compounded for the debt or demand, or procured the action or proceeding to be stayed, or indemnified the defendant to his reasonable satisfaction against the action or proceeding and against all costs, damages, and expenses to be incurred by him by reason of the same;

(iii) if execution or other process issued on a judgment, decree, or order obtained in the Court in favour of a creditor against the company, or any member thereof as such, or any person authorized to be sued as nominal defendant on behalf of the company, is returned unsatisfied;

(iv) if it is otherwise proved to the satisfaction of the Court that the company is unable to pay its debts.

Contributories in winding up of unregistered company.

356.—(1) In the event of an unregistered company being wound up, every person shall be deemed to be a contributory who is liable to pay or contribute to the payment of any debt or liability of the company, or to pay or contribute to the payment of any sum for the adjustment of the rights of the members among themselves, or to pay or contribute to the payment of the costs and expenses of winding up the company, and every contributory shall be liable to contribute to the assets of the company all sums due from him in respect of any such liability as aforesaid.

(2) In the event of the death or bankruptcy of any contributory, the provisions of this Act with respect to the personal representatives of deceased contributories, and to the trustees of bankrupt contributories, shall apply.

Power of Court to stay or restrain proceedings.

357. The provisions of this Act with respect to staying and restraining actions and proceedings against a company at any time after the presentation of a petition for winding up and before the making of a winding up order, shall, in the case of an unregistered company, where the application to stay or restrain is by a creditor, extend to actions and proceedings against any contributory of the company.

358. Where an order has been made for winding up an unregistered company, no action or proceeding shall be proceeded with or commenced against any contributory of the company in respect of any debt of the company, except by leave of the Court, and subject to such terms as the Court may impose. Action stayed on winding up order.

359. Where a company incorporated outside the Island which has been carrying on business in the Island ceases to carry on business in the Island, it may be wound up as an unregistered company under this Part, notwithstanding that it has been dissolved or otherwise ceased to exist as a company under or by virtue of the laws of the country under which it was incorporated. Winding up company incorporated outside Island.

360. The provisions of this Part with respect to unregistered companies shall be in addition to and not in restriction of any provisions hereinbefore in this Act contained with respect to winding up companies by the Court, and the Court or liquidator may exercise any powers or do any act in the case of unregistered companies which might be exercised or done by it or him in winding up companies formed and registered under this Act; but an unregistered company shall not, except in the event of its being wound up, be deemed to be a company under this Act, and then only to the extent provided by this Part. Provisions of Part IX cumulative.

361. In the case of a limited partnership the provisions of this Act with respect to winding up shall apply with such modifications, if any, as may from time to time be prescribed by the Minister and with the substitution of general partners for directors. Winding up of limited partnership.

PART X—COMPANIES INCORPORATED OUTSIDE THE ISLAND CARRYING ON BUSINESS WITHIN THE ISLAND

362. This Part shall apply to all companies incorporated outside the Island which, after the appointed day, establish a place of business within the Island, and to all companies Companies to which Part X applies.

incorporated outside the Island which have, before the appointed day, established a place of business within the Island and continue to have an established place of business within the Island after the appointed day.

Documents, etc., to be delivered to Registrar by companies carrying on business in the Island.

363.—(1) Companies incorporated outside the Island which after the appointed day establish a place of business within the Island, shall within one month (or, in the case of any of the documents mentioned in paragraph (*a*) of this subsection or such longer period not exceeding four months as the Minister may allow) from the establishment of the place of business, deliver to the Registrar for registration—

(*a*) a certified copy of the charter, statutes or articles of the company, or other instrument constituting or defining the constitution and containing the name of the company, and, if the instrument is not written in the English language, a certified translation thereof;

(*b*) a list of the directors of the company, containing such particulars with respect to the directors as are by this Act required to be contained with respect to directors in the register of the directors of a company;

(*c*) the names and addresses of some one or more persons resident in the Island authorized to accept on behalf of the company service of process and any notices required to be served on the company.

(2) The provisions of subsection (1) shall apply in relation to companies to which this Part applies, other than companies mentioned in that subsection, as they apply in relation to companies so mentioned with the substitution for the words "one month" of the words "three months", for the words "four months" of the words "six months", and for the words "the establishment of the place of business" of the words "the appointed day".

(3) If within six months of the delivery to the Registrar pursuant to subsection (1) by any such company as is mentioned in that subsection of the instrument containing the name of the company it appears to the Registrar that such name too closely resembles the name registered in respect of any other company (whether incorporated within or outside Jamaica) in the documents registered at the office for the registration of companies, the Registrar may direct such first-mentioned company within six weeks of the date of the direction (or within such longer period as the Registrar may think fit to allow) in addition to or in place of its principal name to take an alternative name approved by the Registrar as the name in which it proposes to carry on business in Jamaica.

(4) Where a direction has been given to a company pursuant to subsection (3) the company shall—

(*a*) on or before the expiration of the time given by the Registrar notify in writing to the Registrar for the purpose of registration by him the approved alternative name taken by the company pursuant to the direction; and

(*b*) after the date of such notification carry on business in Jamaica solely in that alternative name.

Power of companies incorporated outside Island to hold lands.

364. A company incorporated outside the Island shall have the same power to hold lands in the Island as if it were a company incorporated under this Act.

Return to be delivered to Registrar where documents, etc., altered.

365.—(1) If in the case of any company to which this Part applies any alteration is made in—

(*a*) the charter, statutes, or articles of the company or any such instrument as aforesaid; or

(*b*) the directors of the company or the particulars contained in the list of the directors; or

(*c*) the names or addresses of the persons authorized to accept service on behalf of the company, the company shall, within twenty-one days after the date on which particulars of the alterations could, in due course of post and if despatched with due diligence, have been received in the Island from the place where the company is incorporated, deliver to the Registrar for registration a return containing the prescribed particulars of the alteration.

(2) Where an alteration made to the name of any company to which this Part applies is shown in a return delivered to the Registrar for registration pursuant to subsection (1), the provisions of subsections (3) and (4) of section 363 shall apply with the necessary modifications in relation to the name of the company as altered as they apply in relation to the name of a company contained in the relevant instrument delivered to the Registrar pursuant to paragraph (*a*) of subsection (1) of that section.

Accounts of company carrying on business in Island.

366.—(1) Subject to the provisions of this section, every company to which this Part applies shall in every calendar year make out a balance sheet and profit and loss account and, if the company is a holding company, group accounts in such form, and containing such particulars and including such documents, as under the provisions of this Act it would, if it had been a company incorporated under this Act, have been required to make out and lay before the company in general meeting, and deliver a copy of those documents to the Registrar for registration.

(2) Subject to the provisions of this section, a company to which this Part applies may in any calendar year, at the option of the company, in lieu of complying with the requirements of subsection (1) in relation to that year, deliver to the Registrar for registration a copy of its balance sheet and profit and loss account or, if the company is a subsidiary company, a copy of the balance sheet of its holding company, prepared in the form required under the law of the place of the company's incorporation, but in the event of exercising the option given by this subsection the company shall also deliver to the Registrar for registration—

(*a*) a profit and loss account, prepared in the English language and to the satisfaction of the Registrar made out as nearly as maybe in the form and containing the particulars required by this Act in relation to the profit and loss account of a company incorporated under this Act, on the company's operations in Jamaica as if such operations had been conducted by a separate company incorporated under this Act, so, however, that the company shall be entitled to make such apportionments and to add such notes and explanations as shall in its opinion be necessary or desirable to give a true and fair view of the profit or loss on its operations in Jamaica and for this purpose may debit a reasonable rate of interest on capital employed in Jamaica;

(*b*) a statement as at the date to which the company's profit and loss account is made up prepared in the English language and showing the company's assets locally situated in Jamaica classified, distinguished and valued in accordance with the provisions of this Act affecting the classifying, distinguishing and valuing of the assets of a company incorporated under this Act and the nature and amount of any specific charges on such assets;

(*c*) a report prepared in the English language on the account and statement referred to in paragraphs (*a*) and (*b*) by an accountant qualified under this Act for appointment as auditor of a company which is not a private company or of a private company which is obliged to file accounts stating that in his opinion and to the best of his information such account and statement are in accordance with the books and records of the company and give the information required by this Act in the manner therein required and give a true and fair view of the matters therein stated.

(3) Subject to subsection (5), if any document mentioned in subsection (1), or if any document mentioned in subsection (2) which is not required by subsection (2) to be in the English language, is not in the English language, there shall be annexed thereto a certified translation thereof.

(4) In relation to the balance sheets, accounts and statements referred to in this section the Minister shall have the same powers to modify any of the requirements imposed by virtue of this section as he has to modify the requirements imposed by this Act in relation to the balance sheets and profit and loss accounts of a company incorporated under this Act.

(5) The Minister, if, having regard to the nature and volume of the business done in the Island by the company or class of companies affected, he is satisfied that it is expedient so to do, may by order grant, to such extent and subject to such conditions as may be specified in the order, exemption—

(*a*) to any holding company, or class of holding companies, to which this Part applies, from the provisions of subsection (1) requiring the making out of group accounts, and the delivery to the Registrar of a copy of any documents relating to such accounts; and

(*b*) to any company, or class of companies, to which this Part applies, from the provisions of subsection (3) requiring the annexing of a certified translation to any document.

Obligation to state name of company, whether limited and country where incorporated.

367.—(1) Every company to which this Part applies shall—

(*a*) in every prospectus inviting subscriptions for its shares or debentures in the Island state the country in which the company is incorporated; and

(*b*) conspicuously exhibit on every place where it carries on business in the Island the name of the company and the country in which the company is incorporated; and (*c*) cause the name of the company and of the country in which the company is incorporated to be stated in legible characters in all bill-heads and letter paper, and in all notices and other official publications of the company; and

(*d*) if the liability of the members of the company is limited, cause notice of that fact to be stated in legible characters in every such prospectus as aforesaid and in all bill-heads, letter paper, notices and other official publications of the company in the Island, and to be affixed on every place where it carries on its business.

(2) In their application to any company in respect of which there has been registered an alternative name pursuant to the provisions of subsections (3) and (4) of section 363 or by virtue of the provisions of subsection (2) of section 365, the provisions of paragraphs (*b*) and (*c*) of subsection (1) of this section requiring the exhibiting and stating of the name of the company shall be taken to require the exhibiting and stating of the alternative name as well as the principal name of the company on the places and in the documents specified in those paragraphs in the manner respectively so specified.

Service on company to which Part X applies.

368. Any process or notice required to be served on a company to which this Part applies shall be sufficiently served if addressed to any person whose name has been delivered to the Registrar under this Part and left at or sent by post to the address which has been so delivered:

Provided that—

(*a*) where any such company makes default in delivering to the Registrar the name and address of a person resident in the Island who is authorized to accept on behalf of the company service of process or notices; or (*b*) if at any time all the persons whose names and addresses have been so delivered are dead or have ceased so to reside, or refuse to accept service on behalf of the company, or for any reason cannot be served,

a document may be served on the company by leaving it at or sending it by post to any place of business established by the company in the Island.

Removing company's name from register.

369. If any company to which this Part applies ceases to have a place of business in the Island it shall forthwith give notice of the fact to the Registrar, and as from the date on which notice is so given the obligation of the company to deliver any document to the Registrar under this Act shall cease:

Provided that in case the Registrar is satisfied by any other means that the company has ceased to have a place of business in the Island it shall be lawful for him to close the file of the company unless it is necessary to maintain the file for the purposes of the Transfer Tax Act, and upon such closure the obligation of the company to deliver any document to the Registrar under this Act shall cease.

Penalties.

370. If any company to which this Part applies fails to comply with any of the foregoing provisions of this Part the company, and every officer or agent of the company who knowingly or wilfully authorizes or permits the default shall be liable to a fine not exceeding fifty thousand dollars, or, in the case of a continuing offence, two thousand dollars for every day during which the default continues.

Interpretation of Part X.

371. For the purposes of this Part—

"certified" means certified in the manner prescribed to be a true copy or a correct translation;

"director" in relation to a company includes any person in accordance with whose directions or instructions the directors of the company are accustomed to act;

"place of business" includes a share transfer or share registration office;

"principal name" means—

(*a*) in relation to a company to which a direction has been given pursuant to subsection (3) of section 363, the name of the company contained in the relevant instrument delivered to the Registrar pursuant to paragraph (*a*) of subsection (1) of that section; and

(*b*) in relation to a company to which a direction has been given by virtue of the provisions of subsection (2) of section 365, the altered name of the company as shown in the return delivered to the Registrar pursuant to subsection (1) of that section;

"prospectus" has the same meaning as when used in relation to a company incorporated under this Act.

PART XI—RESTRICTIONS ON SALE OF SHARES AND OFFERS OF SHARES FOR SALE

Provisions with respect to prospectuses of foreign companies inviting subscriptions for shares or offering shares for sale.

372.—(1) The provisions of subsections (2) to (6) of this section shall have effect in relation to the issuing, circulating or distributing in the Island by any person of any prospectus offering for subscription shares in or debentures of a company incorporated or to be incorporated outside the Island, whether the company has or has not established, or when formed will or will not establish, a place of business in the Island.

(2) Every such prospectus shall be dated.

(3) No such prospectus shall be issued, circulated or distributed in the Island unless before the date of such issue, circulation or distribution—

(*a*) there has been delivered to the Registrar for the purpose of securing registration of the prospectus a copy thereof certified by the chairman and two other directors of the company as having been approved by resolution of the managing body; and

(*b*) pursuant thereto registration has been effected.

(4) Every such prospectus shall state on the face of it that the prospectus has been registered as required by this subsection.

(5) The Registrar shall not register any such prospectus unless it is dated, and the copy thereof certified, in manner required by this section and there is endorsed on or attached to the copy—

(*a*) any consent to the issue of the prospectus required by section 374;

Third Schedule.

(*b*) a copy of any contract required by paragraph 11 of the Third Schedule to be stated in the prospectus or, in the case of a contract not reduced into writing, a memorandum giving full particulars thereof; and

(*c*) where the persons making any report required by Part II of that Schedule have made therein or have, without giving the reasons, indicated therein any such adjustments as are mentioned in paragraph 21 of that Schedule, a written statement signed by those persons setting out the adjustments and giving the reasons therefor.

(6) The reference in paragraph (*b*) of subsection (5) to the copy of a contract required thereby to be endorsed on or attached to a copy of the prospectus shall, in the case of a contract wholly or partly in a foreign language, be taken as a reference to a copy of a translation of the contract in English or a copy embodying a translation in English of the parts in a foreign language, as the case may be, being a translation certified in the prescribed manner to be a correct translation.

(7) The provisions of subsection (4) of section 40 which relate to the power of the Registrar to refuse to register prospectuses and the provisions of subsection (5) of that section shall, with the necessary modifications, apply in relation to prospectuses referred to in subsection (1) of this section as they apply in relation to prospectuses referred to in that section.

(8) Whenever the Registrar has registered a prospectus under this section he shall in writing inform the company or any other person who has delivered the copy of the prospectus pursuant to this section, of the fact of registration and the date thereof, and every prospectus referred to in subsection (1) issued, circulated or distributed in the Island by any person shall show on its face, in addition to the date required by subsection (2), the date of registration.

(9) It shall not be lawful for any person to issue to any person in the Island a form of application for shares in or debentures of such a company or intended company as is mentioned in subsection (1) unless the form is issued with a prospectus which complies with this Part and the issue whereof does not contravene the provisions of section 374:

Provided that this subsection shall not apply if it is shown that the form of application was issued in connection with a *bona fide* invitation to a person to enter into an underwriting agreement with respect to the shares or debentures.

(10) This section shall not apply to the issue to existing members or debenture holders of a company of a prospectus or form of application relating to shares in or debentures of the company, whether an applicant for shares or debentures will or will not have the right to renounce in favour of other persons, but, subject as aforesaid, this section shall apply to a prospectus or form of application whether issued on or with reference to the formation of a company or subsequently.

Additional require-ments as to prospectus

373.—(1) Any such prospectus as is mentioned in subsection (1) of section 372 shall also—

(*a*) contain particulars with respect to the following matters—

(i) any restrictions on the business that the company can conduct;

(ii) the instrument constituting or defining the constitution of the company;

(iii) the enactments, or provisions having the force of an enactment, by or under which the incorporation of the company was effected;

(iv) an address in the Island where those instruments, enactments or provisions, or copies thereof, and if, the same are in a foreign language a translation thereof certified in the prescribed manner, can be inspected;

(v) the date on which and the country in which the company was incorporated;

(vi) whether the company has established a place of business in the Island, and, if so, the address of its office in the Island:

Provided that the provisions of sub-paragraphs (i), (ii), (iii) and (iv) shall not apply in the case of a prospectus issued more than two years after the date at which the company is entitled to commence business;

Third Schedule.

(*b*) subject to the provisions of this section, state the matters specified in Part I of the Third Schedule and set out the reports specified in Part II of that Schedule:

Provided that in paragraph 1 of the Third Schedule a reference to the constitution of the company shall be substituted for the reference to the articles.

(2) Any condition requiring or binding any applicant for shares or debentures to waive compliance with any requirement of this section, or purporting to affect him with notice of any contract, document, or matter not specifically referred to in the prospectus, shall be void.

(3) In the event of non-compliance with or contravention of any of the requirements of this section, a director or other person responsible for the prospectus shall not incur any liability by reason of the non-compliance or contravention, if—

(*a*) as regards any matter not disclosed, he proves that he was not cognizant thereof; or

(*b*) he proves that the non-compliance or contravention arose from an honest mistake of fact on his part; or

(*c*) the non-compliance or contravention was in respect of matters which, in the opinion of the Court dealing with the case, were immaterial or were otherwise such as ought, in the opinion of that Court, having regard to all the circumstances of the case, reasonably to be excused:

Provided that—

(*a*) where any prospectus is published as a newspaper advertisement, it shall be a sufficient compliance with the requirement that the prospectus must specify the objects of the company if the advertisement specifies the primary object with which the company was formed; and

(*b*) in paragraph 2 of the Third Schedule a reference to the constitution of the company shall be substituted for the reference to the articles. Third Schedule.

(4) This section shall not apply to the issue to existing members or debenture holders of a company of a prospectus or form of application relating to shares in or debentures of the company, whether an applicant for shares or debentures will or will not have the right to renounce in favour of other persons, but, subject as aforesaid, this section shall apply to a prospectus or form of application whether issued on or with reference to the formation of a company or subsequently.

(5) Nothing in this section or section 372 shall limit or diminish any liability which any person may incur under the general law or this Act, apart from those sections.

Provisions as to expert's consent and allotment.

374.—(1) It shall not be lawful for any person to issue, circulate or distribute in the Island any prospectus offering for subscription shares in or debentures of a company incorporated or to be incorporated outside the Island, whether the company has or has not established, or when formed will or will not establish, a place of business in the Island—

(*a*) if, where the prospectus includes a statement purporting to be made by an expert, he has not given, or has before delivery of the prospectus for registration withdrawn, his written consent to the issue of the prospectus with the statement included in the form and context in which it is included or there does not appear in the prospectus a statement that he has given and has not withdrawn his consent as aforesaid; or

(*b*) if the prospectus does not have the effect, where an application is made in pursuance thereof, of rendering all persons concerned bound by all the provisions (other than penal provisions) of section 51 as far as applicable.

(2) In this section the expression "expert" includes engineer, valuer, accountant and any other person whose profession gives authority to a statement made by him, and for the purposes of this section a statement shall be deemed to be included in a prospectus if it is contained therein or in any report or memorandum appearing on the face thereof or by reference incorporated therein or issued therewith.

Penalty for contravention of sections 372, 373 and 374.

375. Any person who is knowingly responsible for the issue, circulation or distribution of a prospectus, or for the issue of a form of application for shares or debentures, in contravention of any of the provisions of sections 372, 373 and 374 shall be liable to a fine not exceeding fifty thousand dollars.

Civil liability for misstatements in prospectus.

376. Section 44 shall extend to every prospectus offering for subscription shares in or debentures of a company incorporated or to be incorporated outside the Island, whether the company has or has not established, or when formed will or will not establish, a place of business in the Island, with the substitution, for references to section 42 of references to section 374.

Interpretation of provisions as to prospectuses.

377.—(1) Where any document by which any shares in or debentures of a company incorporated outside the Island are offered for sale to the public would, if the company concerned had been a company within the meaning of this Act, have been deemed by virtue of section 46 to be a prospectus issued by the company, that shall be deemed to be, for the purposes of this Part, a prospectus issued by the company.

(2) An offer of shares or debentures for subscription or sale to any person whose ordinary business is to buy or sell shares or debentures, whether as principal or agent, shall not be deemed an offer to the public for the purposes of this Part.

(3) In this Part the expressions "prospectus", "shares" and "debentures" have the same meanings as when used in relation to a company incorporated under this Act.

PART XII—MISCELLANEOUS

Prohibition of Partnerships with more than Twenty Members

Prohibition of partnerships with more than twenty members.

378.—(1) No company, association, or partnership consisting of more than twenty persons shall be formed for the purpose of carrying on any business (other than the business of banking) for the acquisition of gain by the company, association, or partnership, or by the individual members thereof, unless it is registered as a company under this Act, or is formed in pursuance of some other local statute, or of letters patent.

(2) Nothing in subsection (1) prohibits the formation—

(*a*) for the purpose of carrying on practice as attorneys-at-law, of a partnership consisting of persons each of whom is an attorney-at-law;

(*b*) for the purpose of carrying on practice as accountants, of a partnership consisting of persons each of whom is registered as a public accountant under the Public Accountancy Act;

(*c*) of a partnership consisting of persons each of whom is a member of such profession as may be prescribed in regulations made under this Act for the purpose.

Provisions relating to Banks

Prohibition of banking partnerships with more than ten members.

379. No company, association, or partnership consisting of more than ten persons shall be formed for the purpose of carrying on the business of banking, unless it is registered as a company under this Act, or is formed in pursuance of some other local statute, or of letters patent.

Application of certain Provisions of this Act to Unregistered Companies

Application of certain provisions of this Act to unregistered com-

380.—(1) The provisions of this Act specified in the second column of the Eleventh Schedule (which respectively relate to the matters referred to in the first column of that Schedule) shall apply to all bodies corporate incorporated in and having a principal place of business in the Island, other than those mentioned in subsection (2), as if they were companies registered under this Act, but subject to any limitations mentioned in relation to those provisions respectively in the third column of that Schedule and to such adaptations and modifications (if any) as may be specified by regulations made by the Minister. Eleventh Schedule.

(2) The provisions of that Schedule shall not apply by virtue of this section to any of the following, that is to say—

(*a*) any body incorporated by or registered under any local statute; and

(*b*) any body not formed for the purpose of carrying on a business which has for its object the acquisition of gain by the body or by the individual members thereof; and

(*c*) any body for the time being exempted by direction of the Minister.

(3) This section shall not repeal or revoke in whole or in part any enactment, royal charter or other instrument constituting or regulating any body in relation to which those provisions are applied by virtue of this section, or restrict the power of Her Majesty to grant a charter in lieu of or supplementary to any such charter as aforesaid, but, in relation to any such body, the operation of any such enactment, charter or instrument shall be suspended in so far as it is inconsistent with any of those provisions as they apply for the time being to that body.

(4) Any regulations made under this section or the Eleventh Schedule shall be subject to negative resolution.

Form of Registers, etc.

Forms of registers, etc.

381.—(1) Any register, index, minute book or book of account required by this Act to be kept by a company may be kept either by making entries in bound books or by recording the matters in question in any other manner.

(2) Where any such register, index, minute book or book of account is not kept by making entries in a bound book, but by some other means, adequate precautions shall be taken for guarding against falsification and facilitating its discovery, and where default is made in complying with this subsection the company and every officer of the company who is in default shall be liable to a fine not exceeding fifty thousand dollars.

Miscellaneous Offences

Penalty for false statement. Ninth Schedule.

382. If any person in any return, report, certificate, balance sheet, or other document, required by or for the purposes of any of the provisions of this Act specified in the Ninth Schedule, wilfully makes a statement which is false in any material particular, knowing it to be false, he shall be guilty of a misdemeanour, and shall be liable on conviction on indictment to imprisonment with or without hard labour for a term not exceeding two years and be liable on summary conviction before a Resident Magistrate to imprisonment with or without hard labour for a term not exceeding four months, and in either case to a fine in lieu of or in addition to such imprisonment as aforesaid:

Provided that—

(*a*) the fine imposed on summary conviction shall not exceed fifty thousand dollars;

(*b*) nothing in this section shall affect the provisions of the Perjury Act.

383. If any person or persons trade or carry on business under any name or title of which "Limited", or any contraction or imitation of that word, is the last word, that person or those persons shall, unless duly incorporated with limited liability, be liable to a fine not exceeding five hundred dollars for every day upon which that name or title has been used.

Penalty for improper use of word "Limited".

Provisions as to Offences

384.—(1) Where by any enactment in this Act it is provided that a company and every officer of the company who is in default shall be liable to a fine, the company and every such officer shall, for every day during which the default, refusal or contravention continues, be liable to a fine not exceeding such amount as is specified in that enactment, or if the amount of the fine is not so specified, to a fine not exceeding fifty thousand dollars.

Provision with respect to default fines and meaning of "officer in default".

(2) For the purpose of any enactment in this Act which provides that an officer of a company who is in default shall be liable to a fine or penalty, the expression "officer who is in default" means any director, manager, secretary or other officer of the company, who knowingly and wilfully authorizes or permits the default, refusal or contravention mentioned in the enactment.

385. All offences under this Act made punishable by fine may be prosecuted in the Resident Magistrate's Court in a summary manner; and any person upon whom a fine is imposed in respect of any such offence shall in default of payment thereof be liable to imprisonment with or without hard labour for a term not exceeding twelve months.

Prosecution of offences punishable by fine.

386.—(1) If on an application made to a Judge in Chambers by the Director of Public Prosecution or the Minister there is shown to be reasonable cause to believe that any person has, while an officer of a company, committed an offence in connection with the management of the company's affairs

Production and inspection of books where offence suspected.

and that evidence of the commission of the offence is to be found in any books or papers of or under the control of the company, an order may be made

(*a*) authorizing any person named therein to inspect the said books or papers or any of them for the purpose of investigating and obtaining evidence of the offence; or

(*b*) requiring the secretary of the company or such other officer thereof as may be named in the order to produce those books or papers or any of them to a person named in the order at a place so named.

(2) Subsection (1) shall apply also in relation to any books or papers of a person carrying on the business of banking so far as they relate to the company's affairs, as it applies to any books or papers of or under the control of the company, except that no such order as is referred to in paragraph (*b*) thereof shall be made by virtue of this subsection.

(3) The decision of a Judge on an application under this section shall not be appealable.

Service of Documents and Legal Proceedings

Service of documents on company.

387. A document may be served on a company by leaving it at or sending it by post to the registered office of the company.

Costs in actions by certain limited companies.

388. Where a limited company is plaintiff in any action or other legal proceeding, any judge having jurisdiction in the matter may, if it appears by credible testimony that there is reason to believe that the company will be unable to pay the costs of the defendant if successful in his defence, require sufficient security to be given for those costs, and may stay all proceedings until the security is given.

389.—(1) If in any proceeding for negligence, default, breach of duty, or breach of trust against a person to whom this section applies it appears to the Court hearing the case that the person is or may be liable in respect of the negligence, default, breach of duty or breach of trust, but that he has acted honestly and reasonably, and that, having regard to all the circumstances of the case, including those connected with his appointment, he ought fairly to be excused for the negligence, default, breach of duty or breach of trust, that Court may relieve him, either wholly or partly, from his liability on such terms as the Court may think fit.

Power of Court to grant relief in certain cases.

(2) Where any person to whom this section applies has reason to apprehend that any claim will or might be made against him in respect of any negligence, default, breach of duty or breach of trust, he may apply to the Court for relief, and the Court on any such application shall have the same power to relieve him as under this section it would have had if it had been a court before which proceedings against that person for negligence, default, breach of duty or breach of trust had been brought.

(3) Where any case to which subsection (1) applies is being tried by a judge with a jury, the judge, after hearing the evidence, may, if he is satisfied that the defendant ought in pursuance of that subsection to be relieved either in whole or in part from the liability sought to be enforced against him, withdraw the case in whole or in part from the jury and forthwith direct judgment to be entered for the defendant on such terms as to costs or otherwise as the judge may think proper.

(4) The persons to whom this section applies are the following—

(*a*) directors of a company;

(*b*) officers of a company;

(*c*) persons employed by a company as auditors whether they are or are not officers of the company.

Saving for privileged communications

390. Where proceedings are instituted under this Act against any person, nothing in this Act shall be taken to require any person who has acted as attorney for the defendant to disclose any privileged communication made to him in that capacity.

Saving, etc.

Saving.

391. Nothing in this Act shall affect the incorporation of any company registered under the Companies Act (repealed by this Act), and the provisions of this Act with respect to winding up shall not apply to any company of which the winding up has commenced before the appointed day, but every such company shall be wound up in the same manner and with the same incidents as if this Act had not been passed, and, for the purposes of the winding up, the law under which the winding up commenced shall be deemed to remain in full force.

Power to alter or add to certain requirements. Seventh Schedule.

392.—(1) The Minister shall have power by regulations to alter or add to the requirements of this Act as to the matters to be stated in a company's balance sheet, profit and loss account and group accounts and the requirements specified in the Seventh Schedule and any reference in this Act to the Schedule shall be construed as a reference to that Schedule with any alterations or additions made by regulations for the time being in force under this subsection.

First Schedule. Fifth Schedule.

(2) The Minister may by regulations alter or add to Tables A, B, C and D in the First Schedule and the form in Part II of the Fifth Schedule.

(3) Any regulations made under subsection (1) which render more onerous the requirements therein referred to shall be subject to affirmative resolution.

(4) Regulations made under this section not being regulations to which subsection (3) applies, shall be subject to negative resolution.

393.—(1) In addition to the powers conferred upon the Minister by section 392 the Minister may make rules providing for all or any of the other matters which by this Act are to be prescribed by his authority. Power to make rules.

(2) Notwithstanding the provisions of subsection (1), the Minister may make particular rules—

(*a*) prescribing the format and contents of returns, notices or other documents required to be sent to the Registrar or to be issued by the Registrar;

(*b*) prescribing the retention period for company records held by the Registrar; and

(*c*) respecting any other matter required for the efficient administration of this Act.

(3) Any rules made under this section shall be subject to affirmative resolution.

394.—(1) There shall be paid to the Registrar of Companies in respect of the several matters mentioned in the Fifteenth Schedule the several fees therein specified. Fees. Fifteenth Schedule.

(2) All fees paid under this section shall be paid into the Consolidated Fund.

(3) The Minister may by order amend the Fifteenth Schedule.

(4) An order made pursuant to subsection (3) shall be subject to negative resolution.

395.—(1) Section 177 applies to an existing company upon the appointed day. Transitional.

(2) Where, on application by an existing company or its members, the Registrar determines that it is not practicable to change a reference to the nominal or par value of shares of a class or series that the existing company was authorized to issue

before the appointed day, the Registrar may permit the company to continue to refer in its articles to those shares, whether issued or not, as shares having a nominal or par value.

(3) A share of an existing company issued before the appointed day shall be deemed to have been issued in compliance with this Act, irrespective of—

(*a*) whether the share is fully paid;

(*b*) any designation, rights, privileges, restrictions or conditions attached to the share or set out on, or referred to in, the certificate representing the share,

and the provisions of this Act shall not be construed as depriving a shareholder of any right or privilege that he claims under an issued share of the company nor as relieving him of any liability in respect of such a share.

(4) Where any person is aggrieved by a decision of the Registrar, that person may appeal to the Supreme Court.

SCHEDULES

FIRST SCHEDULE (Sections 2, 8 and 392)

Tables A, B, C and D

TABLE A

PART I

Articles for Management of a Company Limited by Shares

THE COMPANIES ACT

ARTICLES OF INCORPORATION

Company Limited by Shares

Articles for Management of a Company Limited by Shares

1. Name of Company ....

Situation of Registered Office ....

2. Main Business of Company ....

....

3. Liability of Members—

☐ Limited by Shares

4. Form of Company: ☐ Public

☐ Private

The company is a private company and accordingly—

(*a*) the right to transfer shares is restricted in manner hereinafter prescribed;

(*b*) subject to section 25 (1) (*b*) of the Act, the number of members of the company (exclusive of persons who are in the employment of the company and of persons who having been formerly in the employment of the company were while in such employment and have continued after the determination of such employment to be members of the company) is limited to twenty:

Provided that where two or more persons hold one of more shares in the company jointly they shall for the purpose of this regulation be treated as a single member;

(*c*) any invitation to the public to subscribe for any shares or debentures of the company is prohibited;

(*d*) any invitation to the public to deposit money for fixed periods or payable on call whether bearing or not bearing interest is prohibited;

(*e*) subject to the exceptions provided for in the Twelfth Schedule any person other than the holder is prohibited from having any interest in any of the company's shares; and

(*f*) the company shall not have power to issue share warrants to bearer.

5. Authorized Capital (if any) ....

(Public Companies should have an authorized minimum share capital of at least $500,000.00)

6. Article(s) .... shall apply ☐

shall not apply ☐

7. In these articles—

"the Act" means the Companies Act;

"the seal" means the common seal of the company;

"secretary" means any person appointed to perform the duties of the secretary of the company.

Expressions referring to writing shall, unless the contrary intention appears, be construed as including references to printing, lithography, photography, and other modes of representing or reproducing words in a visible form.

Unless the context otherwise requires, words or expressions contained in these articles shall bear the same meaning as in the Act or any statutory modification thereof in force at the date at which these articles become binding on the company.

Share Capital and Variation of Rights

8. Without prejudice to any special rights previously conferred on the holders of any existing shares or class of shares, any share in the company may be issued with such preferred, deferred or other special rights or such restrictions, whether in regard to dividend, voting, return of capital or otherwise as the company may from time to time by ordinary resolution determine.

9. Subject to the provisions of section 56 of the Act, any preference shares may, with the sanction of an ordinary resolution, be issued on the terms that they are, or at the option of the company are liable, to be redeemed on such terms and in such manner as the company before the issue of the shares may by special resolution determine.

10. If at any time the share capital is divided into different classes of shares, the rights attached to any class (unless otherwise provided by the terms of issue of the shares of that class) may, whether or not the company is being wound up, be varied with the consent in writing of the holders of three-fourths of the issued shares of that class, or with the sanction of an extra-ordinary resolution passed at a separate general meeting of the holders of the shares of the class. To every such separate general meeting the provisions of these articles relating to general meetings shall apply, but so that the necessary quorum shall be two persons at least holding or representing by proxy one-third of the issued shares of the class and that any holder of shares of the class present in person or by proxy may demand a poll.

11. The rights conferred upon the holders of the shares of any class issued with preferred or other rights shall be deemed to be varied by the creation or issue of further shares ranking *pari passu* therewith.

12. The company may exercise the powers of paying commissions conferred by section 53 of the Act, provided that the rate *per centum* or the amount of the commission paid or agreed to be paid shall be disclosed in the manner required by that section and the rate of commission shall not exceed the rate of ten *per centum* of the price at which the shares in respect whereof the same is paid are issued or an amount equal to ten *per centum* of such price (as the case may be). Such commission may be satisfied by the payment of cash or the allotment of fully paid shares or partly in one way and partly in the other. The company may also on any issue of shares pay such brokerage as may be lawful.

13. Except as required by law, no person shall be recognized by the company as holding any share upon any trust, and the company shall not be bound by or be compelled in any way to recognize (even when having notice thereof) any equitable, contingent, future or partial interest in any share or any interest in any fractional part of a share or (except only as by these articles or by law otherwise provided) any other rights in respect of any share except an absolute right to the entirety thereof in the registered holder.

14. Every person whose name is entered as a member in the register of members shall be entitled without payment to receive within two months after allotment or lodgment of transfer (or within such other period as the conditions of issue shall provide) one certificate for all his shares or several certificates each for one or more of his shares upon payment of Two Dollars for every certificate after the first or such less sum as the directors shall from time to time determine. Every certificate shall be under the seal and shall specify the shares to which it relates and the amount paid up thereon. Provided that in respect of a share or shares held jointly by several persons the company shall not be bound to issue more than one certificate, and delivery of a certificate for a share to one of several joint holders shall be sufficient delivery to all such holders.

15. If a share certificate be defaced lost or destroyed, it may be renewed on payment of a fee of Two Dollars or such less sum and on such terms (if any) as to evidence and indemnity and the payment of out-of-pocket expenses of the company of investigating evidence as the directors think fit.

16. The company shall not give, whether directly or indirectly, and whether by means of a loan, guarantee, the provision of security or otherwise, any financial assistance for the purpose of or in connection with a purchase or subscription made or to be made by any person of or for any shares in the company or in its holding company nor shall the company make a loan for any purpose whatsoever on the security of its shares or those of its holding company.

Lien

17. The company shall have a first and paramount lien on every share (not being a fully paid share) for all moneys (whether presently payable or not) called or payable at a fixed time in respect of that share, and the company shall also have a first and paramount lien on all shares (other than fully paid shares) standing registered in the name of a single person for all moneys presently payable by him or his estate to the company; but the directors may at any time declare any share to be wholly or in part exempt from the provisions of this article. The company's lien, if any, on a share shall extend to all dividends payable thereon.

18. The company may sell, in such manner as the directors think fit, any shares on which the company has a lien, but no sale shall be made unless a sum in respect of which the lien exists is presently payable, nor until the expiration of fourteen days after a notice in writing, stating and demanding payment of such part of the amount in respect of which the lien exists as is presently payable, has been given to the registered holder for the time being of the share, or the person entitled thereto by reason of his death or bankruptcy.

19. To give effect to any such sale the directors may authorize some person to transfer the shares sold to the purchaser thereof. The purchaser shall be registered as the holder of the shares comprised in any such transfer, and he shall not be bound to see to the application of the purchase money, nor shall his title to the share be affected by any irregularity or invalidity in the proceedings in reference to the sale.

20. The proceeds of the sale shall be received by the company and applied in payment of such part of the amount in respect of which the lien exists as is presently payable, and the residue, if any, shall (subject to a like lien for sums not presently payable as existed upon the shares before the sale) be paid to the person entitled to the shares at the date of the sale.

Calls on Shares

21. The directors may from time to time make calls upon the members in respect of any moneys unpaid on their shares and not by the conditions of allotment thereof made payable at fixed times, provided that no call shall exceed one-fourth of the nominal value of the share or be payable at less than one month from the date fixed for the payment of the last preceding call, and each member shall (subject to receiving at least fourteen days' notice specifying the time or times and place of payment) pay to the company at the time or times and place so specified the amount called on his shares. A call may be revoked or postponed as the directors may determine.

22. A call shall be deemed to have been made at the time when the resolution of the directors authorizing the call was passed and may be required to be paid by instalments.

23. The joint holders of a share shall be jointly and severally liable to pay all calls in respect thereof.

24. If a sum called in respect of a share is not paid before or on the day appointed for payment thereof, the person from whom the sum is due shall pay interest on the sum from the day appointed for payment thereof to the time of actual payment at such rate not exceeding five *per centum* per annum as the directors may determine, but the directors shall be at liberty to waive payment of such interest wholly or in part.

25. Any sum which by the terms of issue of a share becomes payable on allotment or at any fixed date, whether on account of the nominal value of the share or by way of premium, shall for the purposes of these articles be deemed to be a call duly made and payable on the date on which by the terms of issue the same becomes payable, and in case of non-payment all the relevant provisions of these articles as to payment of interest and expenses, forfeiture or otherwise shall apply as if such sum had become payable by virtue of a call duly made and notified.

26. The directors may, on the issue of shares, differentiate between the holders as to the amount of calls to be paid and the times of payment.

27. The directors may, if they think fit, receive from any member willing to advance the same, all or any part of the moneys uncalled and unpaid upon any shares held by him, and upon all or any of the moneys so advanced may (until the same would, but for such advance, become payable) pay interest at such rate not exceeding (unless the company in general meeting shall otherwise direct) five *per centum* per annum, as may be agreed upon between the directors and the member paying such sum in advance.

Transfer of Shares

28. The instrument of transfer of any share shall be executed by or on behalf of the transferor and transferee, and the transferor shall be deemed to remain a holder of the share until the name of the transferee is entered in the register of members in respect thereof.

29. Subject to such of the restrictions of these articles as may be applicable, any member may transfer all or any of his shares by instrument in writing in any usual or common form or any other form which the directors may approve.

30. The directors may decline to register the transfer of a share (not being a fully paid share) to a person of whom they shall not approve, and they may also decline to register the transfer of a share on which the company has a lien.

31. The directors may also decline to recognize any instrument of transfer unless—

(*a*) a fee of Two Dollars or such lesser sum as the directors may from time to time require is paid to the company in respect thereof;

(*b*) the instrument of transfer is accompanied by the certificate of the shares to which it relates, and such other evidence as the directors may reasonably require to show the right of the transferor to make the transfer, and

(*c*) the instrument of transfer is in respect of only one class of share.

32. If the directors refuse to register a transfer they shall within two months after the date on which the transfer was lodged with the company send to the transferee notice of the refusal.

33. The registration of transfers may be suspended at such times and for such periods as the directors may from time to time determine, provided always that such registration shall not be suspended for more than thirty days in any year.

34. The company shall be entitled to charge a fee not exceeding Two Dollars on the registration of every probate, letters of administration, certificate of death or marriage, power of attorney, notice in lieu of *distringas*, or other instrument.

Transmission of Shares

35. In case of the death of a member the survivor or survivors where the deceased was a joint holder, and the legal personal representatives of the deceased, where he was a sole holder, shall be the only persons recognized by the company as having any title to his interest in the shares: but nothing herein contained shall release the estate of a deceased joint holder from any liability in respect of any share which had been jointly held by him with other persons.

36. Any person becoming entitled to a share in consequence of the death or bankruptcy of a member may, upon such evidence being produced as may from time to time properly be required by the directors and subject as hereinafter provided, elect either to be registered himself as holder of the share or to have some person nominated by him registered as the transferee thereof.

37. If the person so becoming entitled shall elect to be registered himself, he shall deliver or send to the company a notice in writing signed by him stating that he so elects. If he shall elect to have another person registered he shall testify his election by executing to that person a transfer of the share. All the limitations, restrictions and provisions of these articles relating to the right to transfer and the registration of transfers of shares shall be applicable to any such notice or transfer as aforesaid as if the death or bankruptcy of the member had not occurred and the notice or transfer were a transfer signed by that member.

38. A person becoming entitled to a share by reason of the death or bankruptcy of the holder shall be entitled to the same dividends and other advantages to which he would be entitled if he were the registered holder of the share, except that he shall not, before being registered as a member in respect of the share, be entitled in respect of it to exercise any right conferred by membership in relation to meetings of the company:

Provided always that the directors may at any time give notice requiring any such person to elect either to be registered himself or to transfer the share, and if the notice is not complied with within ninety days the directors may thereafter withhold payment of all dividends, bonuses or other moneys payable in respect of the share until the requirements of the notice have been complied with.

Forfeiture of Shares

39. If a member fails to pay any call or instalment of a call on the day appointed for payment thereof, the directors may, at any time thereafter during such time as any part of the call or instalment remains unpaid, serve a notice on him requiring payment of so much of the call or instalment as is unpaid, together with any interest which may have accrued.

40. The notice shall name a further day (not earlier than the expiration of fourteen days from the date of service of the notice) on or before which the payment required by the notice is to be made, and shall state that in the event of non-payment at or before the time appointed the shares in respect of which the call was made will be liable to be forfeited.

41. If the requirements of any such notice as aforesaid are not complied with, any share in respect of which the notice has been given may at any time thereafter, before the payment required by the notice has been made, be forfeited by a resolution of the directors to that effect.

42. A forfeited share may be sold or otherwise disposed of on such terms and in such manner as the directors think fit, and at any time before a sale or disposition the forfeiture may be cancelled on such terms as the directors think fit.

43. A person whose shares have been forfeited shall cease to be a member in respect of the forfeited shares, but shall, notwithstanding, remain liable to pay to the company all moneys which, at the date of forfeiture were payable by him to the company in respect of the shares, but his liability shall cease if and when the company shall have received payment in full of all such moneys in respect of the shares.

44. A statutory declaration in writing that the declarant is a director or the secretary of the company, and that a share in the company has been duly forfeited on a date stated in the declaration, shall be conclusive evidence of the facts therein stated as against all persons claiming to be entitled to the share. The company may receive the consideration, if any, given for the share on any sale or disposition thereof and may execute a transfer of the share in favour of the person to whom the share is sold or disposed of and he shall thereupon be registered as the holder of the share, and shall not be bound to see to the application of the purchase money, if any, nor shall his title to the share be affected by any irregularity or invalidity in the proceedings in reference to the forfeiture, sale or disposal of the share.

45. The provisions of these articles as to forfeiture shall apply in the case of non-payment of any sum which, by the terms of issue of a share, becomes payable at a fixed time, as if the same had been payable by virtue of a call duly made and notified.

Conversion of Shares into Stock

46. The company may by ordinary resolution convert any paid-up shares into stock, and reconvert any stock into paid-up shares of any denomination.

47. The holders of stock may transfer the same, or any part thereof, in the same manner, and subject to the same articles, as and subject to which the shares from which the stock arose might previously to conversion have been transferred, or as near thereto as circumstances admit; and the directors may from time to time fix the minimum amount of stock transferable but so that such minimum shall not exceed the value of the shares from which the stock arose.

48. The holders of stock shall, according to the amount of stock held by them, have the same rights, privileges and advantages as regards dividends, voting at meetings of the company and other matters as if they held the shares from which the stock arose, but no such privilege or advantage (except participation in the dividends and profits of the company and in the assets on winding up) shall be conferred by an amount of stock which would not, if existing in shares, have conferred that privilege or advantage.

49. Such of the articles of the company as are applicable to paid-up shares shall apply to stock, and the words "share" and "shareholder" therein shall include "stock" and "stockholder".

Alteration of Capital

50. The company may from time to time by ordinary resolution increase the share capital by such sum, to be divided into shares of such amount, as the resolution shall prescribe.

51. The company may by ordinary resolution—

(*a*) consolidate and divide all or any of its share capital into shares of larger amount than its existing shares;

(*b*) subdivide its existing shares, or any of them, into shares of smaller amount than is fixed by the articles subject nevertheless to the provisions of section 65 (1)(*d*) of the Act;

(*c*) cancel any shares which, at the date of the passing of the resolution, have not been taken or agreed to be taken by any person.

52. The company may by special resolution reduce its share capital, any capital redemption reserve fund in any manner and with, and subject to, any incident authorized, and consent required, by law.

General Meetings

53. The company shall in each year hold a general meeting as its annual general meeting in addition to any other meetings in that year, and shall specify the meeting as such in the notices calling it; and not more than fifteen months shall elapse between the date of one annual general meeting of the company and that of the next. Provided that so long as the company holds it first annual general meeting within eighteen months of its incorporation, it need not hold it in the year of its incorporation or in the following year. The annual general meeting shall be held at such time and place as the directors shall appoint.

54. All general meetings other than annual general meetings shall be called extraordinary general meetings.

55. The directors may, whenever they think fit, convene an extraordinary general meeting, an extraordinary general meeting shall also be convened on such requisition, or, in default, may be convened by such requisitionists, as provided by section 128 of the Act. If at any time there are not within the Island sufficient directors capable of acting to form a quorum, any director or any two members of the company may convene an extraordinary general meeting in the same manner as nearly as possible as that in which meetings may be convened by the directors.

Notice of General Meetings

56. An annual general meeting and a meeting called for the passing of a special resolution shall be called by twenty-one days' notice in writing at the least, and a meeting of the company other than an annual general meeting or a meeting for the passing of a special resolution shall be called by fourteen days' notice in writing at the least. The notice shall be exclusive of the day on which it is served or deemed to be served and of the day for which it is given, and shall specify the place, the day and the hour of meeting and, in case of special business, the general nature of that business, and shall be given in manner hereinafter mentioned or in such other manner, if any, as may be prescribed by the company in general meeting, to such persons as are, under the regulations of the company, entitled to receive such notices from the company:

Provided that a meeting of the company shall, notwithstanding that it is called by shorter notice than that specified in this article, be deemed to have been duly called if it is so agreed—

(*a*) in the case of a meeting called as the annual general meeting, by all the members entitled to attend and vote thereat; and (*b*) in the case of any other meeting, by a majority in number of the members having a right to attend and vote at the meeting, being a majority together holding not less than ninety-five *per centum* of the shares giving that right.

57. The accidental omission to give notice of a meeting to, or the non-receipt of notice of a meeting by, any person entitled to receive notice shall not invalidate the proceedings at that meeting.

Proceedings at General Meetings

58. All business shall be deemed special that is transacted at an extraordinary general meeting, and also all that is transacted at an annual general meeting, with the exception of declaring a dividend, the consideration of the accounts, balance sheets, and the reports of the directors and auditors, the election of directors in the place of those retiring and the appointment of, and the fixing of the remuneration of, the auditors.

59. No business shall be transacted at any general meeting unless a quorum of members is present at the time when the meeting proceeds to business; save as herein otherwise provided, three members present in person shall be a quorum.

60. If within half an hour from the time appointed for the meeting a quorum is not present, the meeting, if convened upon the requisition of members, shall be dissolved; in any other case it shall stand adjourned to the same day in the next week, at the same time and place or to such other day and at such other time and place as the directors may determine, and if at the adjourned meeting a quorum is not present within half an hour from the time appointed for the meeting, the members present shall be a quorum.

61. The chairman, if any, of the board of directors shall preside as chairman at every general meeting of the company, or if there is no such chairman, or if he shall not be present within fifteen minutes after the time appointed for the holding of the meeting or is unwilling to act the directors present shall elect one of their number to be chairman of the meeting.

62. If at any meeting no director is willing to act as chairman or if no director is present within fifteen minutes after the time appointed for holding the meeting, the members present shall choose one of their number to be chairman of the meeting.

63. The chairman may, with the consent of any meeting at which a quorum is present (and shall if so directed by the meeting), adjourn the meeting from time to time and from place to place, but no business shall be transacted at any adjourned meeting other than the business left unfinished at the meeting from which the adjournment took place. When a meeting is adjourned for thirty days or more, notice of the adjourned meeting shall be given as in the case of an original meeting. Save as aforesaid it shall not be necessary to give any notice of an adjournment or of the business to be transacted at an adjourned meeting.

64. At any general meeting a resolution put to the vote of the meeting shall be decided on a show of hands unless a poll is (before or on the declaration of the result of the show of hands) demanded—

(*a*) by the chairman; or

(*b*) by at least three members present in person or by proxy; or

(*c*) by any member or members present in person or by proxy and representing not less than one-tenth of the total voting rights of all the members having the right to vote at the meeting; or

(*d*) by a member or members holding shares in the company conferring a right to vote at the meeting being shares on which an aggregate sum has been paid up equal to not less than one-tenth of the total sum paid up on all the shares conferring that right.

Unless a poll be so demanded a declaration by the chairman that a resolution has on a show of hands been carried or carried unanimously, or by a particular majority, or lost and an entry to that effect in the book containing the minutes of the proceedings of the company shall be conclusive evidence of the fact without proof of the number or proportion of the votes recorded in favour of or against such resolution.

The demand for a poll may be withdrawn.

65. Except as provided in article 67, if a poll is duly demanded it shall be taken in such manner as the chairman directs, and the result of the poll shall be deemed to be the resolution of the meeting at which the poll was demanded.

66. In the case of an equality of votes, whether on a show of hands or on a poll, the chairman of the meeting at which the show of hands takes place or at which the poll is demanded, shall be entitled to a second or casting vote.

67. A poll demanded on the election of a chairman or on a question of adjournment shall be taken forthwith. A poll demanded on any other question shall be taken at such time as the chairman of the meeting directs, and any business other than that upon which a poll has been demanded may be proceeded with pending the taking of the poll.

Votes of Members

68. Subject to any rights or restrictions for the time being attached to any class or classes of shares, on a show of hands every member present in person shall have one vote, and on a poll every member shall have one vote for each share of which he is the holder.

69. In the case of joint holders the vote of the senior who tenders a vote, whether in person or by proxy, shall be accepted to the exclusion of the votes of the other joint holders; and for this purpose seniority shall be determined by the order in which the names stand in the register of members.

70. A member of unsound mind, or in respect of whom an order has been made by any court having jurisdiction in lunacy, may vote, whether on a show of hands or on a poll, by his committee, receiver, or other person in the nature of a committee or receiver appointed by that court, and any such committee, receiver, or other person may on a poll vote by proxy.

71. No member shall be entitled to vote at any general meeting unless all calls or other sums presently payable by him in respect of shares in the company have been paid.

72. No objection shall be raised to the qualification of any voter except at the meeting or adjourned meeting at which the vote objected to is given or tendered, and every vote not disallowed at such meeting shall be valid for all purposes. Any such objection made in due time shall be referred to the chairman of the meeting, whose decision shall be final and conclusive.

73. On a poll votes may be given either personally or by proxy.

74. The instrument appointing a proxy shall be in writing under the hand of the appointer or of his attorney duly authorized in writing, or, if the appointer is a corporation, either under seal, or under the hand of an officer or attorney duly authorized. A proxy need not be a member of the company.

75. The instrument appointing a proxy and the power of attorney or other authority, if any, under which it is signed, or a notarially certified copy, of that power or authority shall be deposited at the registered office of the company or at such other place within the Island as is specified for that purpose in the notice convening the meeting, not less than forty-eight hours before the time for holding the meeting or adjourned meeting, at which the person named in the instrument proposes to vote, or in the case of a poll

not less than twenty-four hours before the time appointed for the taking of the poll, and in default the instrument of proxy shall not be treated as valid.

76. An instrument appointing a proxy shall be in the following form or a form as near thereto as circumstances admit—

" Company Limited.

I/ We . of . being a member/members of the abovenamed company, hereby appoint of .or failing him. of . as my/our proxy to vote for me/us on my/our behalf at the [annual or extraordinary, as the case may be] general meeting of the company to be held on the day of . and at any adjournment thereof.

Signed this day of "

77. Where it is desired to afford members an opportunity of voting for or against a resolution the instrument appointing a proxy shall be in the following form or a form as near thereto as circumstances admit—

" Company Limited.

I/We .of . being a member/members of the abovenamed company, hereby appoint

of , or failing him, of , as my/our proxy to vote for me/us on my/our behalf at the [annual or extraordinary, as the case may be] general meeting of the company to be held on the day of , and at any adjournment thereof.

Signed this day of

This form is to be used * in favour of / against the resolution. Unless otherwise instructed, the proxy will vote as he thinks fit.

* **Strike out whichever is not desired.**"

78. The instrument appointing a proxy shall be deemed to confer authority to demand or join in demanding a poll.

79. A vote given in accordance with the terms of an instrument of proxy shall be valid notwithstanding the previous death or insanity of the principal

or revocation of the proxy or of the authority under which the proxy was executed, on the transfer of the share in respect of which the proxy is given, provided that no intimation in writing of such death, insanity, revocation or transfer as aforesaid shall have been received by the company at the office before the commencement of the meeting or adjourned meeting at which the proxy is used.

Corporations acting by Representatives at Meetings

80. Any corporation which is a member of the company may by resolution of its directors or other governing body authorize such person as it thinks fit to act as its representative at any meeting of the company or of any class of members of the company, and the person so authorized shall be entitled to exercise the same powers on behalf of the corporation which he represents as that corporation could exercise if it were an individual member of the company.

Directors

81. The number of directors and the names of the first directors shall be determined in writing by the subscribers of the articles or a majority of them.

82. The remuneration of the directors shall from time to time be determined by the company in general meeting. Such remuneration shall be deemed to accrue from day to day. The directors may also be paid all travelling, hotel and other expenses properly incurred by them in attending and returning from meetings of the directors or any committee of the directors or general meetings of the company or in connection with the business of the company.

83. The shareholding qualification for directors may be fixed by the company in general meeting, and unless and until so fixed no qualification shall be required.

84. A director of the company may be or become a director or other officer of, or otherwise interested in, any company promoted by the company or in which the company may be interested as shareholder or otherwise, and no such director shall be accountable to the company for any remuneration or other benefits received by him as a director or officer of, or from his interest in, such other company unless the company otherwise direct.

Borrowing Powers

85. The directors may exercise all the powers of the company to borrow money, and to mortgage or charge its undertaking, property and uncalled capital, or any part thereof, and to issue debentures, debenture stock, and other securities whether outright or as security for any debt, liability or obligation of the company or of any third party:

Provided that the amount for the time being remaining undischarged of moneys borrowed or secured by the directors as aforesaid (apart from temporary loans obtained from the company's bankers in the ordinary course of business) shall not at any time, without the previous sanction of the company in general meeting, exceed the amount of the share capital of the company for the time being issued, but nevertheless no lender or other person dealing with the company shall be concerned to see or inquire whether this limit is observed. No debt incurred or security given in excess of such limit shall be invalid or ineffectual except in the case of express notice to the lender or the recipient of the security at the time when the debt was incurred or security given that the limit hereby imposed had been or was thereby exceeded.

Powers and Duties of Directors

86. The business of the company shall be managed by the directors, who may pay all expenses incurred in promoting and registering the company, and may exercise all such powers of the company as are not, by the Act or by these articles, required to be exercised by the company in general meeting, subject, nevertheless, to any of these articles, to the provisions of the Act and to such articles, being not inconsistent with the aforesaid articles or provisions, as may be prescribed by the company in general meeting; but no articles made by the company in general meeting shall invalidate any prior act of the directors which would have been valid if that article had not been made.

87. The directors may from time to time and at any time by power of attorney appoint any company, firm or person or body of persons, whether nominated directly or indirectly by the directors, to be the attorney or attorneys of the company for such purposes and with such powers, authorities and discretions (not exceeding those vested in or exercisable by the directors under these articles) and for such period and subject to such conditions as they may think fit and any such powers of attorney may contain such provisions for the protection and convenience of persons dealing with any such attorney as the directors may think fit and may also authorize any such attorney to delegate all or any of the powers, authorities and discretions vested in him.

88. The company may exercise the powers conferred by section 32 of the Act with regard to having an official seal for use abroad, and such powers shall be vested in the directors.

89. The company may exercise the powers conferred upon the company by virtue of sections of the Act with regard to the keeping of branch registers of holders of debentures and members and the directors may (subject to the provisions of those sections) make and vary such articles as they may think fit respecting the keeping of any such registers.

90.—(1) A director who is, in any way, whether directly or indirectly, interested in a contract or proposed contract with the company shall declare the nature and extent of his interest at a meeting of the directors in accordance with section 193 of the Act.

(2) A director shall not vote in respect of any contract or arrangement in which he is interested, and if he shall do so his vote shall not be counted, nor shall he be counted in the quorum present at the meeting, but neither of these prohibitions shall apply to—

(*a*) any arrangement for giving any director any security or indemnity in respect of money lent by him to or obligations undertaken by him for the benefit of the company; or

(*b*) any arrangement for the giving by the company of any security to a third party in respect of a debt or obligation of the company for which the director himself has assumed responsibility in whole or in part under a guarantee or indemnity or by the deposit of a security; or

(*c*) any contract by a director to subscribe for or underwrite shares or debentures of the company; or

(*d*) any contract or arrangement with any other company in which he is interested only as an officer of the company or as holder of shares or other securities,

and these prohibitions may at any time be suspended or relaxed to any extent, and either generally or in respect of any particular contract, arrangement or transaction, by the company in general meeting.

(3) A director may hold any other office or place of profit under the company (other than the office of auditor) in conjunction with his office of director for such period and on such terms (as to remuneration and otherwise) as the directors may determine and no director or intending director shall be disqualified by his office from contracting with the company either with regard to his tenure of any such other office or place of profit or as vendor, purchaser or otherwise, nor shall any such contract, or any contract or arrangement entered into by or on behalf of the company in which any director is in any way interested, be liable to be avoided, nor shall any

director so contracting or being so interested be liable to account to the company for any profit realized by any such contract or arrangement by reason of such director holding that office or of the fiduciary relation thereby established.

(4) A director, notwithstanding his interest, may be counted in the quorum present at any meeting whereat he or any other director is appointed to hold any such office or place of profit under the company or whereat the terms of any such appointment are arranged, and he may vote on any such appointment or arrangement other than his own appointment or the arrangement of the terms thereof.

(5) Any director may act by himself or his firm in a professional capacity for the company, and he or his firm shall be entitled to remuneration for professional services as if he were not a director; provided that nothing herein contained shall authorize a director or his firm to act as auditor to the company.

91. All cheques, promissory notes, drafts, bills of exchange and other negotiable instruments, and all receipts for moneys paid to the company, shall be signed, drawn, accepted, indorsed, or otherwise executed, as the case may be, in such manner as the directors shall from time to time by resolution determine.

92. The directors shall cause minutes to be made in books provided for the purpose—

(*a*) of all appointments of officers made by the directors;

(*b*) of the names of the directors present at each meeting of the directors and of any committee of the directors;

(*c*) of all resolutions and proceedings at all meetings of the company, and of the directors, and of committees of directors, and every director present at any meeting of directors or committee of directors shall sign his name in a book to be kept for that purpose.

93. The directors on behalf of the company may pay a gratuity or pension or allowance on retirement to any director who has held any other salaried office or place of profit with the company or to his widow or dependants and may make contributions to any fund and pay premiums for the purchase or provision of any such gratuity, pension or allowance.

Disqualification of Directors

94. The office of director shall be vacated, if the director—

(*a*) ceases to be a director by virtue of section 177 of the Act; or

(*b*) becomes bankrupt or makes any arrangement or composition with his creditors generally; or

(*c*) becomes prohibited from being a director by reason of any order made under sections 180 and 182 of the Act; or

(*d*) becomes of unsound mind; or

(*e*) resigns his office by notice in writing to the company; or

(*f*) shall for more than six months have been absent without permission of the directors from meetings of the directors held during that period.

Rotation of Directors

95. At the first annual general meeting of the company, all the directors shall retire from office, and at the annual general meeting in every subsequent year one-third of the directors for the time being or, if their number is not three or a multiple of three, then the number nearest one-third, shall retire from office.

96. The directors to retire in every year shall be those who have been longest in office since their last election, but as between persons who became directors on the same day those to retire shall (unless they otherwise agree among themselves) be determined by lot.

97. A retiring director shall be eligible for re-election.

98. The company at the meeting at which a director retires in manner aforesaid may fill the vacated office by electing a person thereto, and in default the retiring director shall if offering himself for re-election be deemed to have been re-elected, unless at such meeting it is expressly resolved not to fill such vacated office or unless a resolution for the re-election of such director shall have been put to the meeting and lost.

99. No person other than a director retiring at the meeting shall unless recommended by the directors be eligible for election to the office of director at any general meeting unless not less than three nor more than twenty-one days before the date appointed for the meeting there shall have been left at the registered office of the company notice in writing, signed by a member duly qualified to attend and vote at the meeting for which such notice is given, of his intention to propose such person for election, and also notice in writing signed by that person of his willingness to be elected.

100. The company may from time to time by ordinary resolution increase or reduce the number of directors, and may also determine in what rotation the increased or reduced number is to go out of office.

101. The directors shall have power at any time, and from time to time, to appoint any person to be a director, either to fill a casual vacancy or as an addition to the existing directors, but so that the total number of directors shall not at any time exceed the number fixed in accordance with these articles. Any director so appointed shall hold office only until the next following annual general meeting, and shall then be eligible for re-election but shall not be taken into account in determining the directors who are to retire by rotation at such meeting.

102. The company may by ordinary resolution remove any director before the expiration of his period of office notwithstanding anything in these articles or in any agreement between the company and such director. Such removal shall be without prejudice to any claim such director may have for damages for breach of any contract of service between him and the company.

103. The company may by ordinary resolution appoint another person in place of a director removed from office under article 102, and without prejudice to the powers of the directors under article 101 the company in general meeting may appoint any person to be a director either to fill a casual vacancy or as an additional director. A person appointed in place of a director so removed or to fill such a vacancy shall be subject to retirement at the same time as if he had become a director on the day on which the director in whose place he is appointed was last elected a director.

Proceedings of Directors

104. The directors may meet together for the despatch of business, adjourn, and otherwise regulate their meetings, as they think fit. Questions arising at any meeting shall be decided by a majority of votes. In case of an equality of votes, the chairman shall have a second or casting vote. A director may, and the secretary on the requisition of a director shall, at any time summon a meeting of the directors. It shall not be necessary to give notice of a meeting of directors to any director for the time being absent from the Island.

105. The quorum necessary for the transaction of the business of the directors may be fixed by the directors, and unless so fixed shall be two.

106. The continuing directors may act notwithstanding any vacancy in their body, but, if and so long as their number is reduced below the number fixed by or pursuant to the articles of the company as the necessary quorum of directors, the continuing directors or director may act for the purpose of increasing the number of directors to that number, or of summoning a general meeting of the company, but for no other purpose.

107. The directors may elect a chairman of their meetings and determine the period for which he is to hold office; but if no such chairman is elected, or if at any meeting the chairman is not present within five minutes after the time appointed for holding the same, the directors present may choose one of their number to be chairman of the meeting.

108. The directors may delegate any of their powers to committees consisting of such member or members of their body as they think fit; any committee so formed shall in the exercise of the powers so delegated conform to any articles that may be imposed on it by the directors.

109. A committee may elect a chairman of its meetings; if no such chairman is elected, or if at any meeting the chairman is not present within five minutes after the time appointed for holding the same, the members present may choose one of their number to be chairman of the meeting.

110. A committee may meet and adjourn as it thinks proper. Questions arising at any meeting shall be determined by a majority of votes of the members present, and in the case of an equality of votes the chairman shall have a second or casting vote.

111. All acts done by any meeting of the directors or of a committee of directors or by any person acting as a director shall, notwithstanding that it be afterwards discovered that there was some defect in the appointment of any such director or person acting as aforesaid, or that they or any of them were disqualified, be as valid as if every such person had been duly appointed and was qualified to be a director.

112. A resolution in writing, signed by all the directors for the time being entitled to receive notice of a meeting of the directors, shall be as valid and effectual as if it had been passed at a meeting of the directors duly convened and held.

Managing Director

113. The directors may from time to time appoint one or more of their body to the office of managing director for such period and on such terms as they think fit, and, subject to the terms of any agreement entered into in any particular case, may revoke such appointment. A director so appointed shall not, whilst holding that office, be subject to retirement by rotation or be taken into account in determining the rotation of retirement of directors, but his appointment shall be automatically determined if he ceases from any cause to be a director.

114. A managing director shall receive such remuneration (whether by way of salary, commission or participation in profits, or partly in one way and partly in another) as the directors may determine.

115. The directors may entrust to and confer upon a managing director any of the powers exercisable by them upon such terms and conditions and with such restrictions as they may think fit, and either collaterally with or to the exclusion of their own powers and may from time to time revoke, withdraw, alter or vary all or any of such powers.

Secretary

116. The secretary shall be appointed by the directors for such term, at such remuneration and upon such conditions as they may think fit; and any secretary so appointed may be removed by them.

117. No person shall be appointed or hold office as secretary who is—

(*a*) the sole director of the company; or

(*b*) a corporation the sole director of which is the sole director of the company; or

(*c*) the sole director of a corporation which is the sole director of the company.

118. A provision of the Act or these articles requiring or authorizing a thing to be done by or to a director and the secretary shall not be satisfied by its being done by or to the same person acting both as director and as, or in place of, the secretary.

The Seal

119. The directors shall provide for the safe custody of the seal, which shall only be used by the authority of the directors or of a committee of the directors authorized by the directors in that behalf, and every instrument to which the seal shall be affixed shall be signed by a director and shall be countersigned by the secretary or by a second director or by some other person appointed by the directors for the purpose.

Dividends and Reserve

120. The company in general meeting may declare dividends but no dividend shall exceed the amount recommended by the directors.

121. The directors may from time to time pay to the members such interim dividends as appear to the directors to be justified by the profits of the company.

122. No dividend shall be paid otherwise than out of profits.

123. The directors may, before recommending any dividend, set aside out of the profits of the company such sums as they think proper as a reserve or reserves which shall, at the discretion of the directors, be applicable for any purpose to which the profits of the company may be properly applied, and pending such application may, at the like discretion, either be employed in the business of the company or be invested in such investments (other than shares of the company) as the directors may from time to time think fit. The directors may also without placing the same to reserve carry forward any profits which they may think prudent not to divide.

124. Subject to the rights of persons, if any, entitled to shares with special rights as to dividend, all dividends shall be declared and paid according to the amounts paid or credited as paid on the shares in respect whereof the dividend is paid, but no amount paid or credited as paid on a share in advance of calls shall be treated for the purposes of this article as paid on the share. All dividends shall be apportioned and paid proportionately to the amounts paid or credited as paid on the shares during any portion or portions of the period in respect of which the dividend is paid; but if any share is issued on terms providing that it shall rank for dividend as from a particular date such share shall rank for dividend accordingly.

125. The directors may deduct from any dividend payable to any member all sums of money (if any) presently payable by him to the company on account of calls or otherwise in relation to the shares of the company.

126. Any general meeting declaring a dividend or bonus may direct payment of such dividend or bonus wholly or partly by the distribution of specific assets and in particular of paid up shares, debentures or debenture stock of any other company or in any one or more of such ways and the directors shall give effect to such resolution, and where any difficulty arises in regard to such distribution, the directors may settle the same as they think expedient, and in particular may issue fractional certificates and fix the value for distribution of such specific assets or any part thereof and may determine that cash payments shall be made to any members upon the footing of the value so fixed in order to adjust the rights of all parties, and may vest any such specific assets in trustees as may seem expedient to the directors

127. Any dividend, interest or other moneys payable in cash in respect of shares may be paid by cheque or warrant sent through the post directed to the registered address of the holder or, in the case of joint holders, to the registered address of that one of the joint holders who is first named on the register of members or to such person and to such address as the holder or joint holders may in writing direct. Every such cheque or warrant shall be made payable to the order of the person to whom it is sent. Any one of two or more joint holders may give effectual receipts for any dividends, bonuses or other moneys payable in respect of the shares held by them as joint holders.

128. No dividend shall bear interest against the company.

Accounts

129. The directors shall cause proper books of account to be kept with respect to—

(*a*) all sums of money received and expended by the company and the matters in respect of which the receipt and expenditure takes place;

(*b*) all sales and purchases of goods by the company; and

(*c*) the assets and liabilities of the company.

Proper books shall not be deemed to be kept if there are not kept such books of account as are necessary to give a true and fair view of the state of the company's affairs and to explain its transactions.

130. The books of account shall be kept at the registered office of the company, or, subject to subsections (3) and (4) of section 144 of the Act, at such other place or places as the directors think fit, and shall always be open to the inspection of the directors.

131. The directors shall from time to time determine whether and to what extent and at what time and places and under what conditions or articles the accounts and books of the company or any of them shall be open to the inspection of members not being directors, and no member (not being a director) shall have any right of inspecting any account or book or document of the company except as conferred by law or authorized by the directors or by the company in general meeting.

132. The directors shall from time to time, in accordance with sections 145 and 147 of the Act, cause to be prepared and to be laid before the company in general meeting such profit and loss accounts, balance sheets, group accounts (if any) and reports as are referred in those sections.

133. A copy of every balance sheet (including every document required by law to be annexed thereto) which is to be laid before the company in general meeting, together with a copy of the auditor's report, shall not less than twenty-one days before the date of the meeting be sent to every member of, and every holder of debentures of, the company and to every person registered under article 37. Provided that this article shall not require a copy of those documents to be sent to any person of whose address the company is not aware or to more than one of the joint holders of any shares or debentures.

Capitalization of Profits

134. The company in general meeting may upon the recommendation of the directors resolve that it is desirable to capitalize any part of the amount for the time being standing to the credit of any of the company's reserve accounts or to the credit of the profit and loss account or otherwise available for distribution, and accordingly that such sum be set free for distribution amongst the members who would have been entitled thereto if distributed by way of dividend and in the same proportions on condition that the same be not paid in cash but be applied either in or towards paying up any amounts for the time being unpaid on any shares held by such members respectively or towards paying up in full unissued shares or debentures of the company to be allotted and distributed and credited as fully paid up to and amongst such members in the proportion aforesaid or partly in the one way and partly in the other, and the directors shall give effect to such resolution:

Provided that a share premium account and a capital redemption reserve fund may, for the purposes of this article, only be applied in the paying up of unissued shares to be issued to members of the company as fully paid bonus shares.

135. Whenever such a resolution as aforesaid shall have been passed the directors shall make all appropriations and applications of the undivided profits resolved to be capitalized thereby, and all allotments and issues of fully paid shares or debentures, if any, and generally shall do all acts and things required to give effect thereto, with full power to the directors to make such provision by the issue of fractional certificates or by payment in cash or otherwise as they think fit for the case of shares or debentures becoming distributable in fractions, and also to authorize any person to enter on behalf of all the members entitled thereto into an agreement with the company providing for the allotment to them respectively, credited as fully paid up, of any further shares or debentures to which they may be entitled upon such capitalization or (as the case may require) for the payment by the company on their behalf, by the application thereto of their respective profits resolved to be capitalized, of the amounts as any part of the amounts remaining unpaid on their existing shares, and any agreement made under such authority shall be effective and binding on all such members.

Audit

136. Auditors shall be appointed and their duties regulated in accordance with sections 154 to 157 of the Act.

Notices

137. A notice may be given by the company to any member either personally or by sending it by post to him or to his registered address or (if he has no registered address within the Island) to the address if any, within the Island supplied by him to the company for the giving of notice to him. Where a notice is sent by post, service of the notice shall be deemed to be effected by properly addressing, prepaying, and posting a letter containing the notice, and to have been effected in the case of a notice of a meeting at the expiration of twenty-four hours after the letter containing the same is posted, and in any other case at the time at which the letter would be delivered in the ordinary course of post.

138. A notice may be given by the company to the joint holders of a share by giving the notice to the joint holder first named in the register of members in respect of the share.

139. A notice may be given by the company to the persons entitled to a share in consequence of the death or bankruptcy of a member by sending it through the post in a prepaid letter addressed to them by name, or by the title of representatives of the deceased, or trustee of the bankrupt, or by any like description, at the address, if any, within the Island supplied for the purpose by the persons claiming to be so entitled, or (until such an address has been so supplied) by giving the notice in any manner in which the same might have been given if the death or bankruptcy had not occurred.

140. Notice of every general meeting shall be given in any manner hereinbefore authorized to—

(*a*) every member except those members who (having no registered address within the Island) have not supplied to the company an address within the Island for the giving of notices to them;

(*b*) every person upon whom the ownership of a share devolves by reason of his being a legal personal representative or a trustee in bankruptcy of a member where the member but for his death or bankruptcy would be entitled to receive notice of the meeting; and

(*c*) the auditor for the time being of the company.

No other person shall be entitled to receive notices of general meetings.

Winding up

141. If the company shall be wound up the liquidator may, with the sanction of an extraordinary resolution of the company and any other sanction required by the Act, divide amongst the members in specie or kind the whole or any part of the assets of the company (whether they shall consist of property of the same kind or not) and may, for such purpose set such value as he deems fair upon any property to be divided as aforesaid and may determine how such division shall be carried out as between the members or different classes of members. The liquidator may, with the like sanction, vest the whole or any part of such assets in trustees upon such trusts for the benefit of the contributories as the liquidator, with the like sanction, shall think fit, but so that no member shall be compelled to accept any shares or other securities whereon there is any liability.

Indemnity

142. Every director, managing director, agent, auditor, secretary and other officer for the time being of the company shall be indemnified out of the assets of the company against any liability incurred by him in defending any proceedings, whether civil or criminal, in which judgment is given in his favour or in which he is acquitted or in connection with any application under section 389 of the Act in which relief is granted to him by the Court.

PART II

Regulations for the Management of a Private Company Limited by Shares

1. The regulations contained in Part I of Table A (with the exception of articles 30 and 59) shall apply.

2. The company is a private company and accordingly—

(*a*) the right to transfer shares is restricted in manner hereinafter prescribed;

(*b*) the number of members of the company (exclusive of persons who are in the employment of the company and of persons who having been formerly in the employment of the company were while in such employment and have continued after the determination of such employment to be members of the company) is limited to twenty:

Provided that where two or more persons hold one or more shares in the company jointly they shall for the purpose of this regulation be treated as a single member;

(*c*) any invitation to the public to subscribe for any shares or debentures of the company is prohibited:

(*d*) any invitation to the public to deposit money for fixed periods or payable on call whether bearing or not bearing interest is prohibited:

(*e*) subject to the exceptions provided for in the Twelfth Schedule to the Act any person other than the holder is prohibited from having any interest in any of the company's shares:

(*f*) the company shall not have power to issue share warrants to bearer.

3. The directors may, in their absolute discretion and without assigning any reason therefor, decline to register any transfer of any share whether or not it is a fully paid up share.

4. No business shall be transacted at any general meeting unless a quorum of members are present at the time when the meeting proceeds to business: save as herein otherwise provided two members present in person or by proxy shall be a quorum.

5. Subject to the provisions of the Act, a resolution in writing signed by all the members for the time being entitled to receive notice of and to attend and vote at general meetings (or being corporations by their duly authorized representatives) shall be as valid and effective as if the same had been passed at a general meeting of the company duly convened and held.

TABLE B

Form of Articles of a Company Limited by Guarantee, and not having a Share Capital

Form........................

THE COMPANIES ACT

ARTICLES OF INCORPORATION

(Company Limited by Guarantee without Share Capital pursuant S. 20.)

1. Name of Company ....

(hereinafter referred to as the association)

2. Situation of Registered Office...

3. Main Business of Company...

Commerce ☐ Art ☐ Science ☐ Religion ☐

Charity ☐ Other ☐

4. (*a*) State proposed number of members at time of

Registration..

(*b*) State terms of undertaking and extent of Guarantee:

Every member of the association undertakes to contribute to the assets of the association in the event of the same being wound up during the time that he is a member, or within one year afterwards, for payment of the debts and liabilities of the association contracted before the time at which he ceases to be a member, and of the costs, charges, and expenses of winding-up of the same, and for the adjustment of the rights of the contributors amongst themselves, such amount as may be required not exceeding dollars.

5. Form of Company: ☐ Private ☐ Public

6. No part of the net earnings of the Association shall inure to the benefit of, or be distributable to its members, directors, officers, or other private persons, except that the Association shall be authorized and empowered to pay reasonable compensation for services rendered and make payments and distributions in furtherance of the purposes set forth in Article 3 hereof. The Association shall not support with its fund any purpose or object, or impose on or procure to be observed by its members or others any regulations, restrictions or conditions which if an object of the Association would make it a Trade Union.

TABLE B. *contd.*

7. The form of articles set forth in the Tenth Schedule is followed.

Yes ☐ No ☐

8. Restriction. if any on powers to amend articles:

No addition. alteration. or amendment shall be made to or in the regulations contained in Articles for the time being in force. unless the same shall have been previously submitted to and approved by the Minister.

9. Number (or minimum/maximum number) of directors.................

....

10. Indicate name(s) of first directors for the time being. if any:

....

11A. Restrictions. if any. on business the company may carry on:

....

11B. The Corporation is formed exclusively for promotion of:

12. If upon the winding up or dissolution of the association there remains after the satisfaction of all its debts and liabilities, any property whatsoever, the same shall not be paid to or distributed among the members of the association. but shall be given or transferred to some other institution or institutions, having objects similar to the objects of the association and which shall prohibit the distribution of its or their income and property among its or their members to an extent at least as great as is imposed on the association under or by virtue of article 5 hereof, such institution or institutions to be determined by the members of the association at or before the time of dissolution or in default thereof by such Judge of the Supreme Court as may have or acquire jurisdiction in the matter and if and so far as effect cannot be given to the aforesaid provision then to some charitable object.

13. True accounts shall be kept of the sums of money received and expended by the association and the matters in respect of which such receipts and expenditure take place and of the property, credits and liabilities of the association, and subject to any reasonable restrictions as to the time and manner of inspecting the same that may be imposed in accordance with the articles of the association for the time being shall be opened to the inspection of the members. Once at least in every year the accounts of the association shall be examined and the correctness of the balance sheet ascertained by one or more properly qualified auditor or auditors.

Interpretation

14. In these articles—

"the Act" means the Companies Act;

"the seal" means the common seal of the company;

"secretary" means any person appointed to perform the duties of the secretary of the company.

Expressions referring to writing shall, unless the contrary intention appears, be construed as including references to printing, lithography, photography, and other modes of representing or reproducing words in a visible form.

Unless the context otherwise requires, words or expressions contained in these articles shall bear the same meaning as in the Act or any statutory modification thereof in force at the date at which these articles become binding on the company.

Members

15. The subscribers to the Articles of Association and such other persons as the directors shall admit to membership shall be members of the company.

General Meetings

16. The company shall in each year hold a general meeting as its annual general meeting in addition to any other meetings in that year, and shall specify the meeting as such in the notices calling it; and not more than fifteen months shall elapse between the date of one annual general meeting of the company and that of the next. Provided that so long as the company holds its first annual general meeting within eighteen months of its incorporation, it need not hold it in the year of its incorporation or in the following year. The annual general meeting shall be held at such time and place as the directors shall appoint.

17. All general meetings other than annual general meetings shall be called extraordinary general meetings.

18. The directors may, whenever they think fit, convene an extraordinary general meeting and extraordinary general meetings shall also be convened on such requisition, or, in default may be convened by such requisitionists, as provided by section 128 of the Act. If at any time there are not within the Island sufficient directors capable of acting to form a quorum, any director or any two members of the company may convene an extraordinary general meeting in the same manner as nearly as possible as that in which meetings may be convened by the directors.

Notice of General Meetings

19. An annual general meeting and a meeting called for the passing of a special resolution shall be called by twenty-one days' notice in writing at the least, and a meeting of the company other than an annual general meeting or a meeting for the passing of a special resolution shall be called by fourteen days' notice in writing at the least. The notice shall be exclusive of the day on which it is served or deemed to be served and of the day for which it is given, and shall specify the place, the day and the hour of meeting and, in case of special business, the general nature of that business and shall be given, in manner hereinafter mentioned or in such other manner, if any, as may be prescribed by the company in general meeting, to such persons as are, under the articles of the company, entitled to receive such notices from the company:

Provided that a meeting of the company shall, notwithstanding that it is called by shorter notice than that specified in this article be deemed to have been duly called if it is so agreed—

(*a*) in the case of a meeting called as the annual general meeting, by all the members entitled to attend and vote thereat; and

(*b*) in the case of any other meeting, by a majority in number of the members having a right to attend and vote at the meeting, being a majority together representing not less than ninety-five per cent of the total voting rights at that meeting of all the members.

20. The accidental omission to give notice of a meeting to, or the non-receipt of notice of a meeting by, any person entitled to receive notice shall not invalidate the proceedings at that meeting.

Proceedings at General Meetings

21. All business shall be deemed special that is transacted at an extraordinary general meeting, and also all that is transacted at an annual general meeting, with the exception of declaring a dividend, the consideration of the accounts, balance sheets, and the reports of the directors and auditors, the election of directors in the place of those retiring and the appointment of, and the fixing of the remuneration, of the auditors.

22. No business shall be transacted at any general meeting unless a quorum of members is present at the time when the meeting proceeds to business; save as herein otherwise provided, three members present in person shall be a quorum.

23. If within half an hour from the time appointed for the meeting a quorum is not present, the meeting, if convened upon the requisition of members, shall be dissolved; in any other case it shall stand adjourned to the same day in the next week, at the same time and place, or to such other day and at such other time and place as the directors may determine, and if at the adjourned meeting a quorum is not present within half an hour from the time appointed for the meeting the members present shall be a quorum.

24. The chairman, if any, of the board of directors shall preside as chairman at every general meeting of the company, or if there is no such chairman, or if he shall not be present within fifteen minutes after the time appointed for the holding of the meeting or is unwilling to act the directors present shall elect one of their number to be chairman of the meeting.

25. If at any meeting no director is willing to act as chairman or if no director is present within fifteen minutes after the time appointed for holding the meeting, the members present shall choose one of their number to be chairman of the meeting.

26. The chairman may, with the consent of any meeting at which a quorum is present (and shall if so directed by the meeting), adjourn the meeting from time to time and from place to place, but no business shall be transacted at any adjourned meeting other than the business left unfinished at the meeting from which the adjournment took place. When a meeting is adjourned for thirty days or more, notice of the adjourned meeting shall be given as in the case of an original meeting. Save as aforesaid it shall not be necessary to give any notice of an adjournment or of the business to be transacted at an adjourned meeting.

27. At any general meeting a resolution put to the vote of the meeting shall be decided on a show of hands unless a poll is (before or on the declaration of the result of the show of hands) demanded—

(*a*) by the chairman; or

(*b*) by at least three members present in person or by proxy; or

(*c*) by any member or members present in person or by proxy and representing not less than one-tenth of the total voting rights of all the members having the right to vote at the meeting.

Unless a poll be so demanded a declaration by the chairman that a resolution has on a show of hands been carried or carried unanimously, or by a particular majority, or lost and an entry to that effect in the book containing the minutes of proceedings of the company shall be conclusive evidence of the fact without proof of the number or proportion of the votes recorded in favour of or against such resolution.

The demand for a poll may be withdrawn.

28. Except as provided in article 30, if a poll is duly demanded it shall be taken in such manner as the chairman directs, and the result of the poll shall be deemed to be the resolution of the meeting at which the poll was demanded.

29. In the case of an equality of votes, whether on a show of hands or on a poll, the chairman of the meeting at which the show of hands takes place or at which the poll is demanded, shall be entitled to a second or casting vote.

30. A poll demanded on the election of a chairman, or on a question of adjournment, shall be taken forthwith. A poll demanded on any other question shall be taken at such time as the chairman of the meeting directs, and any business other than that upon which a poll has been demanded may be proceeded with pending the taking of the poll.

31. Subject to the provisions of the Act a resolution in writing signed by all the members for the time being entitled to receive notice of and to attend and vote at general meetings (or being corporations by their duly authorized representatives) shall be as valid and effective as if the same had been passed at a general meeting of the company duly convened and held.

Votes of Members

32. Every member shall have one vote.

33. A member of unsound mind, or in respect of whom an order has been made by any court having jurisdiction in lunacy, may vote, whether on a show of hands or on a poll, by his committee, receiver or other person in the nature of a committee, or receiver, appointed by that court, and any such committee, receiver or other person may, on a poll, vote by proxy.

34. No member shall be entitled to vote at any general meeting unless all moneys presently payable by him to the company have been paid.

35. On a poll votes may be given either personally or by proxy.

36. The instrument appointing a proxy shall be in writing under the hand of the appointer or of his attorney duly authorized in writing, or, if the appointer is a corporation, either under seal or under the hand of an officer or attorney duly authorized. A proxy need not be a member of the company.

37. The instrument appointing a proxy and the power of attorney or other authority, if any, under which it is signed or a notarially certified copy of that power or authority shall be deposited at the registered office of the company or at such other place within the Island as is specified for that purpose in the notice convening the meeting, not less than forty-eight hours before the time for holding the meeting or adjourned meeting at which the person named in the instrument proposes to vote, or, in the case of a poll, not less than twenty-four hours before the time appointed for the taking of the poll, and in default the instrument of proxy shall not be treated as valid.

38. An instrument appointing a proxy shall be in the following form or a form as near thereto as circumstances admit—

" Company Limited.

I/We , of , being a member/ members of the abovenamed company, hereby appoint of , or failing him of , as my/our proxy to vote for me/us on my/our behalf at the [annual or extraordinary, as the case may be] general meeting of the company to be held on the day of , and at any adjournment thereof.

Signed this day of ."

39. Where it is desired to afford members an opportunity of voting for or against a resolution the instrument appointing a proxy shall be in the following form or a form as near thereto as circumstances admit—

" Company Limited.

I/We , of , being a member/ members of the abovenamed company, hereby appoint of , or failing him of , as my/our proxy to vote for me/us on my/our behalf at the [annual or extraordinary, as the case may be] general meeting of the company to be held on the day of , and at any adjournment thereof.

Signed this day of ."

*used in favour of

This form is to be ______________________________ the resolution. Unless

*against

otherwise instructed, the proxy will vote as he thinks fit.

***Strike out whichever is not desired.**"

40. The instrument appointing a proxy shall be deemed to confer authority to demand or join in demanding a poll.

41. A vote given in accordance with the terms of an instrument of proxy shall be valid notwithstanding the previous death or insanity of the principal or revocation of the proxy or of the authority under which the proxy was executed, provided that no intimation in writing of such death, insanity or revocation as aforesaid shall have been received by the company at the office before the aforesaid shall have been received by the company at the office before the commencement of the meeting or adjourned meeting at which proxy is used.

Corporations acting by Representatives at Meetings

42. Any corporation which is a member of the company may by resolution of its directors or other governing body authorize such person as it thinks fit to act as its representative at any meeting of the company, and the person so authorized shall be entitled to exercise the same powers on behalf of the corporation which he represents as that corporation could exercise if it were an individual member of the company.

Directors

43. The number of the directors and the names of the first directors shall be determined in writing by the subscribers of the articles or a majority of them.

44. The remuneration of the directors shall from time to time be determined by the company in general meeting. Such remuneration shall be deemed to accrue from day to day. The directors shall also be paid all travelling, hotel and other expenses properly incurred by them in attending and returning from meetings of the directors or any committee of the directors or general meetings of the company or in connection with the business of the company.

Borrowing Powers

45. The directors may exercise all the powers of the company to borrow money, and to mortgage or charge its undertaking and property, or any part thereof, and to issue debentures, debenture stock and other securities, whether outright or as security for any debt, liability or obligation of the company or of any third party.

Powers and Duties of Directors

46. The business of the company shall be managed by the directors who may pay all expenses incurred in promoting and registering the company, and may exercise all such powers of the company as are not, by the Act or by these articles, required to be exercised by the company in general meeting, subject nevertheless to the provisions of the Act or these articles and to such regulations, being not inconsistent with the aforesaid provisions, as may be prescribed by the company in general meeting; but no regulation made by the company in general meeting shall invalidate any prior act of the directors which would have been valid if that regulation had not been made.

47. The directors may from time to time and at any time by power of attorney appoint any company, firm or person or body of persons, whether nominated directly or indirectly by the directors, to be the attorney or attorneys of the company for such purposes and with such powers, authorities and discretions (not exceeding those vested in or exercisable by the directors under these articles) and for such period and subject to such conditions as they may think fit, and any such powers of attorney may contain such provisions for the protection and convenience of persons dealing with any such attorney as the directors may think fit and may also authorize any such attorney to delegate all or any of the powers, authorities and discretions vested in him.

48. All cheques, promissory notes, drafts, bills of exchange and other negotiable instruments, and all receipts for moneys paid to the company, shall be signed, drawn, accepted, endorsed, or otherwise executed, as the case may be, in such manner as the directors shall from time to time by resolution determine.

49. The directors shall cause minutes to be made in books provided for the purpose—

(*a*) of all appointments of officers made by the directors;

(*b*) of the names of the directors present at each meeting of the directors and of any committee of the directors;

(*c*) of all resolutions and proceedings at all meetings of the company, and of the directors, and of committees of directors and every director present at any meeting of directors or committee of directors shall sign his name in a book to be kept for that purpose.

Disqualification of Directors

50. The office of director shall be vacated if the director—

(*a*) without the consent of the company in general meeting holds any other office of profit under the company; or

(*b*) becomes bankrupt or makes any arrangement or composition with his creditors generally; or

(*c*) becomes prohibited from being a director by reason of any order made under sections 180 and 182 of the Act; or

(*d*) becomes of unsound mind; or

(*e*) resigns his office by notice in writing to the company; or

(*f*) is directly or indirectly interested in any contract with the company and fails to declare the nature of his interest in manner required by section 193 of the Act.

A director shall not vote in respect of any contract in which he is interested or any matter arising thereout, and if he does so vote his vote shall not be counted.

Rotation of Directors

51. At the first annual general meeting of the company all the directors shall retire from office, and at the annual general meeting in every subsequent year one-third of the directors for the time being, or, if their number is not three or a multiple of three, then the number nearest one-third, shall retire from office.

52. The directors to retire in every year shall be those who have been longest in office since their last election, but as between persons who became directors on the same day those to retire shall (unless they otherwise agree among themselves) be determined by lot.

53. A retiring director shall be eligible for re-election.

54. The company at the meeting at which a director retires in manner aforesaid may fill the vacated office by electing a person thereto, and in default the retiring director shall, if offering himself for re-election, be deemed to have been re- elected, unless at such meeting it is expressly resolved not to fill such vacated office or unless a resolution for the re-election of such director shall have been put to the meeting and lost.

55. No person other than a director retiring at the meeting shall unless recommended by the directors be eligible for election to the office of director at any general meeting unless, not less than three nor more than twenty-one days before the date appointed for the meeting, there shall have been left at the registered office of the company notice in writing, signed by a member duly qualified to attend and vote at the meeting for which such notice is given, of his intention to propose such person for election, and also notice in writing signed by that person of his willingness to be elected.

56. The company may from time to time by ordinary resolution increase or reduce the number of directors, and may also determine in what rotation the increased or reduced number is to go out of office.

57. The directors shall have power at any time, and from time to time, to appoint any person to be a director, either to fill a casual vacancy or as an addition to the existing directors, but so that the total number of directors shall not at any time exceed the number fixed in accordance with these articles. Any director so appointed shall hold office only until the next following annual general meeting, and shall then be eligible for re-election, but shall not be taken into account in determining the directors who are to retire by rotation at such meeting.

58. The company may by ordinary resolution remove any director before the expiration of his period of office notwithstanding anything in these articles or any agreement between the company and such director. Such removal shall be without prejudice to any claim such director may have for damages for breach of any contract of service between him and the company.

59. The company may by ordinary resolution appoint another person in place of a director removed from office under article 58. Without prejudice to the powers of the directors under article 57 the company in general meeting may appoint any person to be director either to fill a casual vacancy or as an additional director. The person appointed to fill such a vacancy shall be subject to retirement at the same time as if he had become a director on the day on which the director in whose place he is appointed was last elected a director.

Proceedings of Directors

60. The directors may meet together for the despatch of business, adjourn, and otherwise regulate their meetings, as they think fit. Questions arising at any meeting shall be decided by a majority of votes. In the case of an equality of votes the chairman shall have a second or casting vote. A director may, and the secretary on the requisition of a director shall, at any time summon a meeting of the directors. It shall not be necessary to give notice of a meeting of directors to any director for the time being absent from the Island.

61. The quorum necessary for the transaction of the business of the directors may be fixed by the directors, and unless so fixed shall be two.

62. The continuing directors may act notwithstanding any vacancy in their body, but, if and so long as their number is reduced below the number fixed by or pursuant to the articles of the company as the necessary quorum of directors, the continuing directors or director may act for the purpose of increasing the number of directors to that number, or of summoning a general meeting of the company, but for no other purpose.

63. The directors may elect a chairman of their meetings and determine the period for which he is to hold office; if no such chairman is elected, or if at any meeting the chairman is not present within five minutes after the time appointed for holding the same, the directors present may choose one of their number to be chairman of the meeting.

64. The directors may delegate any of their powers to committees consisting of such member or members of their body as they think fit; any committee so formed shall in the exercise of the powers so delegated conform to any regulations that may be imposed on it by the directors.

65. A committee may elect a chairman of its meetings; if no such chairman is elected, or if at any meeting the chairman is not present within five minutes after the time appointed for holding the same, the members present may choose one of their number to be chairman of the meeting.

66. A committee may meet and adjourn as it thinks proper. Questions arising at any meeting shall be determined by a majority of votes of the members present, and in the case of an equality of votes the chairman shall have a second or casting vote.

67. All acts done by any meeting of the directors or of a committee of directors, or by any person acting as a director, shall, notwithstanding that it be afterwards discovered that there was some defect in the appointment of any such director or person acting as aforesaid, or that they or any of them were disqualified, be as valid as if every such person had been duly appointed and was qualified to be a director.

68. A resolution in writing, signed by all the directors for the time being entitled to receive notice of a meeting of the directors, shall be as valid and effectual as if it had been passed at a meeting of the directors duly convened and held.

Secretary

69. The secretary shall be appointed by the directors for such term, at such remuneration and upon such conditions as they may think fit; and any secretary so appointed may be removed by them.

70. A provision of the Act or these articles requiring or authorizing a thing to be done by or to a director and the secretary shall not be satisfied by its being done by or to the same person acting both as director and as, or in place of, the secretary.

The Seal

71. The directors shall provide for the safe custody of the seal which shall only be used by the authority of the directors or of a committee of the directors authorized by the directors in that behalf, and every instrument to which the seal shall be affixed shall be signed by a director and shall be countersigned by the secretary or by a second director or by some other person appointed by the directors for the purpose.

Accounts

72. The directors shall cause proper books of account to be kept with respect to—

(*a*) all sums of money received and expended by the company and the matters in respect of which the receipt and expenditure takes place;

(*b*) all sales and purchases of goods by the company; and

(*c*) the assets and liabilities of the company.

Proper books shall not be deemed to be kept if they are not kept such books of account as are necessary to give a true and fair view of the state of the company's affairs and to explain its transactions.

73. The books of account shall be kept at the registered office of the company, or, subject to subsections (3) and (4) of section 144 of the Act, at such other place or places as the directors think fit, and shall always be open to the inspection of the directors.

74. The directors shall from time to time determine whether and to what extent and at what times and places and under what conditions or regulations the accounts and books of the company or any of them shall be open to the inspection of members not being directors, and no member (not being a director) shall have any right of inspecting any account or book or document of the company except as conferred by statute or authorized by the directors or by the company in general meeting.

75. The directors shall from time to time, in accordance with sections 145 and 147 of the Act, cause to be prepared and to be laid before the company in general meeting such profit and loss accounts, balance sheets, group accounts (if any) and reports as are referred to in those sections.

76. A copy of every balance sheet (including every document required by law to be annexed thereto) which is to be laid before the company in general meeting, together with a copy of the auditor's report, shall not less than twenty-one days before the date of the meeting be sent to every member of, and every holder of debentures of, the company:

Provided that this article shall not require a copy of those documents to be sent to any person of whose address the company is not aware or to more than one of the joint holders of any debentures.

Audit

77. Auditors shall be appointed and their duties regulated in accordance with sections 154 to 157 of the Act.

Notices

78. A notice may be given by the company to any member either personally or by sending it by post to him or to his registered address, or (if he has no registered address within the Island) to the address, if any, within the Island supplied by him to the company for the giving of notice to him. Where a notice is sent by post, service of the notice shall be deemed to be effected by properly addressing, pre-paying and posting a letter containing the notice, and to have been effected in the case of a notice of a meeting at the expiration of twenty-four hours after the letter containing the same is posted, and in any other case at the time at which the letter would be delivered in the ordinary course of post.

79. Notice of every general meeting shall be given in any manner hereinbefore authorized to—

(*a*) every member except those members who (having no registered address within the Island) have not supplied to the company an address within the Island for the giving of notices to them;

(*b*) every person being a legal-personal representative or a trustee in bankruptcy of a member where the member but for his death or bankruptcy would be entitled to receive notice of the meeting; and

(*c*) the auditor for the time being of the company.

No other person shall be entitled to receive notices of general meetings.

TABLE C

Articles of Incorporation of a Company Limited by Guarantee, and having a Share Capital

Form........................

THE COMPANIES ACT

ARTICLES OF INCORPORATION

(Company Limited by Guarantee with Share Capital pursuant to section 20 (2))

1. Name of Company..

2. Situation of Registered Office...

3. Main Business of Company...

....

4. *a.* State proposed number of members at time of registration

....

b. State terms of undertaking and extent of Guarantee

....

5. Form of Company

Private ☐ Public ☐

6. Share Capital..

7. Classes of shares and any maximum number of shares the company is authorized to issue..

8. Restrictions, if any, on share transfer or share ownership

....

9. Pre-emptive rights granted Yes ☐ No ☐

If yes, indicate nature of rights granted with any variation, if any

....

....

10. Rights, privileges, restrictions and conditions (if any) attaching to each class of shares and directors' authority with respect to any class of shares which may be issued

11. Articles set forth in Tables C and D of the First Schedule are adopted

Yes ☐ No ☐

12. Restrictions, if any, on powers to amend articles

....

13. Number (or minimum/maximum number) of directors:

....

....

14. Indicate name(s) of first directors for the time being, if any:

....

....

15. Restrictions, on business the company may carry on (if any):

....

16. Other provisions (if any):

....

The number of members with which the company proposes to be registered is [ ] but the directors may from time to time register an increase of members.

Subscribers Name and occupation	Address	Signatures

Dated the.......................day of..................................20..........

Witness to the signatures of the above subscribers

Signature...

(Name)

Address...

	Names, Addresses and Descriptions of Subscribers		Number of shares taken by each Subscriber
1.	John Jones of	merchant	200
2.	John Smith of	"	25
3.	Thomas Green of	"	30
4.	John Thompson of	"	40
5.	Caleb White of	"	15
6.	Andrew Brown of	"	5
7.	Caesar White of	"	10
		Total shares taken	325

Dated the day of 20

Witness to the above signatures,
A. B., No. 13, XYZ Street, Kingston, Jamaica.

TABLE D

Articles of Incorporation of an Unlimited Company having a Share Capital

Form........................

THE COMPANIES ACT

ARTICLES OF INCORPORATION OF UNLIMITED COMPANY HAVING A SHARE CAPITAL

1. Name of Company...

2. Situation of Registered Office...

3. Main Business of Company...

....

4. Form of Company ☐ Public

☐ Private

The company is a private company and accordingly—

(*a*) the right to transfer shares is restricted in manner hereinafter prescribed;

(*b*) subject to section 25 (1) (*b*) of the Act, the number of members of the company (exclusive of persons who are in the employment of the company and of persons who having been formerly in the employment of the company were while in such employment and have continued after the determination of such employment to be members of the company) is limited to twenty:

Provided that where two or more persons hold one or more shares in the company jointly they shall for the purpose of this article be treated as a single member;

(*c*) any invitation to the public to subscribe for any shares or debentures of the company is prohibited;

(*d*) any invitation to the public to deposit money for fixed periods or payable on call whether bearing or not bearing interest is prohibited;

(*e*) subject to the exceptions provided for in the Twelfth Schedule any person other than the holder is prohibited from having any interest in any of the company's shares; and

(*f*) the company shall not have power to issue share warrants to bearer.

5. The number of members with which the company proposes to be registered is [ ]. but the directors may from time to time register an increase of members.

6. The company may by special resolution—

(*a*) increase the share capital by such amount as the resolution may prescribe:

(*b*) increase the number of its shares:

(*c*) reduce the number of its shares:

(*d*) cancel any shares which at the date of the passing of the resolution have not been taken or agreed to be taken by any person:

(*e*) reduce its share capital in any way.

7. The articles in Table A. set out in the First Schedule (other than articles [ ] to [ ] inclusive). shall be deemed to be incorporated with these articles and shall apply to the company.

Name and Occupation	Address	Signatures

DATED the............................day of ....

WITNESS TO THE SIGNATURES OF THE ABOVE SUBSCRIBERS

Signature...
(Name)

Address..

SECOND SCHEDULE (Section 26)

Form of Statement in lieu of Prospectus to be delivered to Registrar by a Private Company on becoming a Public Company and Reports to be set out therein

PART I

Form of Statement and Particulars to be contained therein

THE COMPANIES ACT

Statement in lieu of Prospectus delivered for registration by

[Insert the name of the company]

Pursuant to section 26 of the Companies Act

Delivered for registration by The share capital of the company $	
Amount (if any) of above capital which consists of redeemable preference shares.	
The date on or before which these shares are, or are liable, to be redeemed.	
Names, descriptions and addresses of directors or proposed directors.	
Amount of shares issued ...	Shares
Amount of commissions paid in connection therewith.	
Unless more than one year has elapsed since the date on which the Company was entitled to commence business—	
Amount of preliminary expenses ...	$ Name of promoter—
Amount paid to any promoter ...	Amount $
Consideration for the payment ...	Consideration—
Any other benefit given to any promoter	Name of promoter Nature of value of benefit—

SECOND SCHEDULE, *contd.*

If the share capital of the company is divided into different classes of shares, the right of voting at meetings of the company conferred by, and the rights in respect of capital and dividends attached to, the several classes of shares respectively.	
Number and amount of shares and debentures issued within the two years preceding the date of this statement as fully or partly paid up otherwise than for cash or agreed to be so issued at the date of this statement.	
Consideration for the issue of those shares or debentures ...	Debenture $ Consideration—
Number, description and amount of any shares or debentures which any person has or is entitled to be given an option to subscribe for, or to acquire from a person to whom they have been allotted or agreed to be allotted with a view to his offering them for sale.	———Shares of $.................... and ....Debentures of $......................
Period during which option is exercisable	Until
Price to be paid for shares or debentures subscribed for or acquired under option.	
Consideration for option or right to option ...	Consideration—
Persons to whom option or right to option was given or, if given to existing shareholders or debenture holders as such, the relevant shares or debentures.	Names and Addresses—
Names and addresses of vendors of property (1) purchased or acquired by the company within the two years preceding the date of this statement or (2) agreed or proposed to be purchased or acquired by the company except where the contract for its purchase or acquisition was entered into in the ordinary course of business and there is no connection between the contract and	

SECOND SCHEDULE. *contd.*

the company ceasing to be a private company or where the amount of the purchase money is not material.	
Amount (in cash, shares or debentures) paid or payable to each separate vendor.	
Amount paid or payable in cash, shares or debentures for any such property specifying the amount paid or payable for goodwill.	Total purchase price $ Cash ... $ Shares ... $ Debenture ... $ Goodwill ... $
Short particulars of any transaction relating to any such property which was completed within the two preceding years and in which any vendor to the company or any person who is, or was at the time thereof, a promoter, director or proposed director of the company had any interest direct or indirect.	
Dates of, parties to, and general nature of every material contract (other than contracts entered into in the ordinary course of business or entered into more than two years before the delivery of this statement).	
Time and place at which the contracts or copies thereof may be inspected.	
Names and addresses of the auditors of the company.	
Full particulars of the nature and extent of the interest of every director in any property purchased or acquired by the company within the two years preceding the date of this statement or proposed to be purchased or acquired by the company or, where the interest of such a director consists in being a partner in a firm, the nature and extent of the interest of the firm, with a statement of all sums paid or agreed to be paid to him or to the firm in cash or shares, or otherwise, by any person either to induce him to become or to qualify him as a	

SECOND SCHEDULE, *contd.*

director, or otherwise for services rendered or to be rendered to the company by him or by the firm.

Rates of the dividends (if any) paid by the company in respect of each class of shares in the company in each of the three financial years immediately preceding the date of this statement or since the incorporation of the company whichever period is the shorter.

Particulars of the cases in which no dividends have been paid in respect of any class of shares in any of these years.

Signatures of the persons above named as directors or proposed directors or of their agents authorized in writing.

____
____
____

Date: ____________________

PART II

Reports to be Set Out

1. If unissued shares or debentures of the company are to be applied in the purchase of a business, a report made by accountants (who shall be named in the statement) upon—

(*a*) the profits or losses of the business in respect of each of the three financial years immediately preceding the delivery of the statement to the Registrar; and

(*b*) the assets and liabilities of the business at the last date to which the accounts of the business were made up.

2.—(1) If unissued shares or debentures of the company are to be applied directly or indirectly in any manner resulting in the acquisition of shares in a body corporate which by reason of the acquisition or anything to be done in consequence thereof or in connection therewith will become a subsidiary of the

SECOND SCHEDLUE, *contd.*

company, a report made by accountants (who shall be named in the statement) with respect to the profits and losses and assets and liabilities of the other body corporate in accordance with sub-paragraph (2) or (3) as the case requires, indicating how the profits or losses of the other body corporate dealt with by the report would, in respect of the shares to be acquired, have concerned members of the company, and what allowance would have fallen to be made, in relation to assets and liabilities so dealt with, for holders of other shares, if the company had at all material times held the shares to be acquired.

(2) If the other body corporate has no subsidiaries, the report referred to in sub-paragraph (1) shall—

(*a*) so far as regards profits and losses, deal with the profits or losses of the body corporate in respect of each of the three financial years immediately preceding the delivery of the statement to the Registrar; and

(*b*) so far as regards assets and liabilities, deal with the assets and liabilities of the body corporate at the last date to which the accounts of the body corporate were made up.

(3) If the other body corporate has subsidiaries, the report referred to in the said sub-paragraph (1) shall—

(*a*) so far as regards profits and losses, deal separately with the other body corporate's profits or losses as provided by sub-paragraph (2) and in addition deal either—

(i) as a whole with the combined profits or losses of its subsidiaries, so far as they concern members of the other body corporate; or

(ii) individually with the profits or losses of each subsidiary, so far as they concern members of the other body corporate.

or, instead of dealing separately with the other body corporate's profits or losses, deal as a whole with the profits or losses of the other body corporate and, so far as they concern members of the other body corporate, with the contained profits or losses of its subsidiaries; and

(*b*) so far as regards assets and liabilities, deal separately with the other body corporate's assets and liabilities as provided by sub-paragraph (2) and in addition, deal either—

SECOND SCHEDULE, *contd.*

(i) as a whole with the combined assets and liabilities of its subsidiaries, with or without the other body corporate's assets and liabilities; or

(ii) individually with the assets and liabilities of each subsidiary,

and shall indicate as respects the assets and liabilities of .the subsidiaries the allowance to be made for persons other than members of the company.

PART III

Provisions applying to Parts 1 and II of this Schedule

3. In this Schedule the expression "vendor" includes a vendor as defined in Part I of the Third Schedule and the expression "financial year" has the meaning assigned to it in Part II of that Schedule.

4. If in the case of a business which has been carried on, or of a body corporate which has been carrying on business, for less than three years, the accounts of the business or body corporate have only been made up in respect of two years or one year, Part II shall have effect as if references to two years or one year, as the case may be, were substituted for references to three years.

5. Any report required by Part II shall either indicate by way of note any adjustments as respects the figures of any profits or losses or assets and liabilities dealt with by the report which appear to the persons making the report necessary or shall make those adjustments and indicate that adjustments have been made.

6. Any report by accountants required by Part II shall be made by accountants qualified under this Act for appointment as auditors of a company and shall not be made by any accountant who is an officer or servant or, except where the company is a private company, a person who is a partner of or in the employment of an officer or servant of the company; and for the purposes of this paragraph the expression "officer" shall include a proposed director but not an auditor.

THIRD SCHEDULE (Sections 26, 41, 47, 48, 49, 372 and 373)

Matters to be specified in Prospectus and Reports to be set out therein

PART I

Matters to be specified

The company's proprietorship, management and its capital requirements

1.—(1) The prospectus must state—

(*a*) the number of founders or management or deferred shares, if any, and the nature and extent of the interest of the holders in the property and profits of the company;

(*b*) the number of shares, if any, fixed by the articles as the qualification of a director, and any provision in the articles as to the remuneration of the directors;

(*c*) the names, descriptions and addresses of the directors or proposed directors.

(2) Sub-paragraphs (1)(*b*) and (1)(*c*) do not apply in the case of a prospectus issued more than two years after the date at which the company is entitled to commence business.

2. Where shares are offered to the public for subscription, particulars as to—

(*a*) the minimum amount which, in the opinion of the directors must be raised by the issue of those shares in order to provide the sums, or, if any part thereof is to be defrayed in any other manner, the balance of the sums, required to be provided in respect of each of the following matters—

(i) the purchase price of any property purchased or to be purchased which is to be defrayed in whole or in part out of the proceeds of the issue;

(ii) any preliminary expenses payable by the company, and any commission so payable to any person in consideration of his agreeing to subscribe for, or of his procuring or agreeing to procure subscriptions for, any shares in the company;

(iii) the repayment of any moneys borrowed by the company in respect of any of the foregoing matters;

(iv) working capital; and

THIRD SCHEDULE. *contd.*

(*b*) the amounts to be provided in respect of the matters aforesaid otherwise than out of the proceeds of the issue and the sources out of which those amounts are to be provided.

Details relating to the offer

3.—(1) The prospectus must state—

(*a*) the time of the opening of the subscription lists;

(*b*) the amount payable on application and allotment on each share (including the amount, if any, payable by way of premium).

(2) In the case of a second or subsequent offer of shares, the amount offered for subscription on each previous allotment made within the two preceding years, the amount actually allotted and the amount if any, paid on the shares so allotted.

4.—(1) There must be stated the number, description and amount of any shares in or debentures of the company which any person has, or is entitled to be given, an option to subscribe for.

(2) The following particulars of the option must be given—

(*a*) the period during which it is exercisable;

(*b*) the price to be paid for shares or debentures subscribed for under it;

(*c*) the consideration (if any) given or to be given for it or for the right to it;

(*d*) the names and addresses of the persons to whom it or the right to it was given or, if given to existing shareholders or debenture holders as such, the relevant shares or debentures.

(3) References in this paragraph to subscribing for shares or debentures include acquiring them from a person to whom they have been allotted with a view to his offering them for sale.

5.—(1) There shall be shown under separate headings—

(*a*) the aggregate amounts respectively of the company's trade investments, quoted investments other than trade investments and unquoted investments other than trade investments;

THIRD SCHEDULE. *contd.*

(*b*) if the amount of the goodwill and of any patents and trade marks or part of that amount is shown as a separate item in or is otherwise ascertainable from the books of the company, or from any contract for the sale or purchase of any property to be acquired by the company, or from any documents in the possession of the company relating to the stamp duty payable in respect of any such contract or the conveyance of any such property, the said amount so shown or ascertained so far as not written off or, as the case may be, the said amount so far as it is shown or ascertainable and as so shown or ascertained, as the case may be;

(*c*) the aggregate amount of bank loans and overdrafts;

(*d*) the net aggregate amount (after deduction of income tax) which is recommended for distribution by way of dividend.

(2) Nothing under heading (*b*) of sub-paragraph (1) shall be taken as requiring the amount of the goodwill, patents and trade marks to be stated otherwise than as a single item.

(3) The heading showing the amount of the quoted investments other than trade investments shall be subdivided, where necessary, to distinguish the investments as respects which there has, and those as respects which there has not, been granted a quotation or permission to deal on a recognized stock exchange.

6.—(1) For the purposes of paragraphs 7 and 8 relevant property is property purchased or acquired by the company, or proposed so to be purchased or acquired—

(*a*) which is to be paid for wholly or partly out of the proceeds of the issue offered for subscription by the prospectus; or

(*b*) the purchase or acquisition of which has not been completed at the date of the issue of the prospectus.

(2) Paragraphs 7 and 8 do not apply to property—

(*a*) the contract for the purchase or acquisition of which was entered into in the ordinary course of the company's business, not being a contract made in contemplation of the issue nor the issue in contemplation of the contract; or

(*b*) as respects which the amount of the purchase money is not material.

THIRD SCHEDULE, *contd.*

7.—(1) As respects any property to which this paragraph applies the prospectus must state—

(*a*) the names and addresses of the vendors;

(*b*) the amount payable in cash, shares or debentures to the vendor and, where there is more than one separate vendor, or the company is a sub-purchaser, the amount so payable to each vendor;

(*c*) short particulars of any transaction relating to the property completed within the two preceding years in which any vendor of the property to the company or any person who is, or was at the time of the transaction, a promoter or a director or proposed director of the company had any interest direct or indirect.

8. There must be stated the amount, if any, paid or payable as purchase money in cash, shares or debentures for any relevant property, specifying the amount, if any, payable for goodwill.

9.—(1) The following applies for the interpretation of paragraphs 6, 7 and 8.

(2) Every person is deemed a vendor who has entered into any contract (absolute or conditional) for the sale or purchase, or for any option of purchase, of any property to be acquired by the company, in any case where—

(*a*) the purchase money is not fully paid at the date of the issue of the prospectus;

(*b*) the purchase money is to be paid or satisfied wholly or in part out of the proceeds of the issue offered for subscription by the prospectus;

(*c*) the contract depends for its validity or fulfilment on the result of that issue.

(3) Where any property to be acquired by the company is to be taken on lease, paragraphs 6, 7 and 8 apply as if "vendor" included the lessor, "purchase money" included the consideration for the lease and "sub-purchaser" included a sub-lessee.

(4) For the purposes of paragraph 7, where the vendors or any of them are a firm, the members of the firm are not to be treated as separate vendors.

Commissions, Preliminary Expenses, etc.

10.—(1) The prospectus must state—

THIRD SCHEDULE, *contd.*

(*a*) the amount, if any, paid within the two preceding years, or payable, as commission (but not including commission to sub-underwriters) for subscribing or agreeing to subscribe, or procuring or agreeing to procure subscriptions, for any shares in or debentures of the company, or the rate of any such commission;

(*b*) the amount or estimated amount of any preliminary expenses and the persons by whom any of those expenses have been paid or are payable, and the amount of estimated amount or the expenses of the issue and the persons by whom any of those expenses have been paid or are payable;

(*c*) any amount or benefit paid or given within the two preceding years or intended to be paid or given to any promoter, and the consideration for the payment or the giving of the benefit.

(2) Sub-paragraph (1) (*b*), so far as it relates to preliminary expenses, does not apply in the case of a prospectus issued more than two years after the date at which the company is entitled to commence business.

Contracts

11.—(1) The prospectus must give the dates of, parties to, and general nature of every material contract.

(2) Sub-paragraph (1) does not apply to a contract entered into in the ordinary course of the business carried on or intended to be carried on by the company or a contract entered into more than two years before the date of issue of the prospectus.

Auditors

12. The prospectus must state the names and addresses of the company's auditors, if any.

Interests of Directors

13.—(1) The prospectus must give full particulars of—

(*a*) the nature and extent of the interest, if any, of every director in the promotion of, or in the property proposed to be acquired by, the company; or

(*b*) where the interest of such a director consists in being a partner in a firm, the nature and extent, of the interest of the firm.

THIRD SCHEDULE, *contd.*

(2) The particulars required under sub-paragraph (1) (*b*) must be accompanied by a statement of all sums paid or agreed to be paid to the director or to the firm in cash or shares or otherwise by any person either to induce him to become, or to qualify him as, a director, or otherwise for services rendered by him or by the firm in connection with the promotion or formation of the company.

(3) This paragraph does not apply in the case of a prospectus issued more than two years after the date at which the company is entitled to commence business.

Other Matters

14. If the prospectus invites the public to subscribe for shares in the company and the share capital of the company is divided into different classes of shares, the right of voting at meetings of the company conferred by, and the rights in respect of capital and dividends attached to, the several classes of shares respectively.

15. In the case of a company which has been carrying on business, or of a business which has been carried on for less than three years, the prospectus must state the length of time during which the business of the company or the business to be acquired, as the case may be, has been carried on.

PART II

Auditors' and Accountants' Reports to be set out in Prospectus

Auditors' Report

16.—(1) The prospectus shall set out a report by the company's auditors with respect to—

(*a*) profits and losses and assets and liabilities, in accordance with sub-paragraph (2) or (3) as the case requires; and

(*b*) the rates of the dividends, if any, paid by the company in respect of each class of shares in the company in respect of each of the five financial years immediately preceding the issue of the prospectus, giving particulars of each such class of shares on which such dividends have been paid and particulars of the cases in which no dividends have been paid in respect of any class of shares in respect of any of those years, and, if no accounts have been made up in respect of any part of the period of five years ending on the date three months before the issue of the prospectus, containing a statement of the fact.

THIRD SCHEDULE, *contd.*

(2) If the company has no subsidiaries, the report shall—

(*a*) deal with profits and losses of the company in respect of each of the five financial years immediately preceding the issue of the prospectus; and

(*b*) deal with the assets and liabilities of the company at the last date to which the accounts of the company were made up.

(3) If the company has subsidiaries, the report shall—

(*a*) deal separately with the company's profits or losses as provided by sub-paragraph (2), and in addition, deal either—

(i) as a whole with the combined profits or losses of its subsidiaries, so far as they concern members of the company; or

(ii) individually with the profits or losses of each subsidiary so far as they concern members of the company,

or, instead of dealing separately with the company's profits or losses, deal as a whole with the profits or losses of the company and, so far as they concern members of the company, with the combined profits or losses of its subsidiaries; and

(*b*) deal separately with the company's assets and liabilities as provided by sub-paragraph (2) and, in addition, deal either—

(i) as a whole with the combined assets and liabilities of its subsidiaries, with or without the company's assets and liabilities; or

(ii) individually with the assets and liabilities of each subsidiary,

indicating, as respects the assets and liabilities of the subsidiaries the allowance to be made for persons other than members of the company.

Accountants' Reports

17. If the proceeds of the issue of the shares or debentures are to be applied directly or indirectly in the purchase of any business, or any part of the proceeds of the issue is to be so applied, there shall be set out in the prospectus a report made by accountants upon—

(*a*) the profits or losses of the business in respect of each of the five financial years immediately preceding the issue of the prospectus, and

THIRD SCHEDULE. *contd.*

(*b*) the assets and liabilities of the business at the last date to which the accounts of the business were made up.

18.—(1) The following provisions apply if—

(*a*) the proceeds of the issue are to be applied directly or indirectly in any manner resulting in the acquisition by the company of shares in any other undertaking, or any part of the proceeds is to be so applied; and

(*b*) by reason of that acquisition or anything to be done in consequence thereof or in connection therewith that undertaking will become a subsidiary of the company.

(2) There shall be set out in the prospectus a report made by accountants upon—

(*a*) the profits or losses of the other undertaking in respect of each of the five financial years immediately preceding the issue of the prospectus; and

(*b*) the assets and liabilities of the other undertaking at the last date to which its accounts were made up.

(3) The report shall—

(*a*) indicate how the profits or losses of the other body corporate dealt with by the report, would, in respect of the shares to be acquired, have concerned members of the company and what allowance would have fallen to be made, in relation to assets and liabilities so dealt with, for holders of other shares if the company had at all material times held the shares to be acquired; and

(*b*) where the other undertaking is a parent undertaking, deal with the profits or losses and the assets and liabilities of the undertaking and its subsidiaries in the manner provided by sub-paragraph (3) of paragraph 16 in relation to the company and its subsidiaries.

Provisions interpreting preceding paragraphs and modifying them in certain cases

19. If in the case of a company which has been carrying on business, or of a business which has been carried on, for less than five years, the accounts of the company or business have only been made up in respect of four years, three years or one year, the preceding paragraphs of this Part shall have effect as if references to four years, three years or one year, as the case may be, were substituted for references to five years.

THIRD SCHEDULE, *contd.*

20. The expression "financial year" means the year in respect of which the accounts of the company or of the business, as the case may be, are made up, and where by reason of any alteration of the date on which the financial year of the company or business terminates the accounts of the company or business have been made up for a period greater or less than a year, that greater or less period shall for the purpose of this Part be deemed to be a financial year.

21. Any report required by this Part shall either indicate by way of note any adjustments as respects the figures of any profits or losses or assets and liabilities dealt with by the report which appear to the persons making the report necessary or shall make those adjustments and indicate that adjustments have been made.

22.—(1) A report required by paragraph 17 or 18 shall be made by accountants qualified under this Act for appointment as auditors of a company.

(2) Such a report shall not be made by any accountant who is an officer or servant or partner of or in the employment of an officer or servant of—

(*a*) the company or any of its subsidiaries;

(*b*) a parent undertaking of the company or any subsidiary of such an undertaking.

(3) The accountants making any report required for purposes of paragraph 17 or 18 shall be named in the prospectus.

FOURTH SCHEDULE (Section 49)

Form of Statement in lieu of Prospectus to be delivered to Registrar by a Company which does not issue a Prospectus or which does not go to Allotment on a Prospectus issued, and Reports to be set out therein

PART I

Form of Statement and Particulars to be contained therein

The Companies Act

Statement in lieu of Prospectus delivered for registration by

[Insert the name of the company]

Pursuant to section 49 of the Companies Act.

FOURTH SCHEDULE, *contd.*

Delivered for registration by	
The share capital of the company	
Amount (if any) of above capital which consists of redeemable preference shares	
The earliest date on which the company has power to redeem these shares	
Names, descriptions and addresses of directors or proposed directors	
If the share capital of the company is divided into different classes of shares, the right of voting at meetings of the company conferred by, and the rights in respect of capital and dividends attached to, the several classes of shares respectively	
Number and amount of shares and debentures agreed to be issued as fully or partly paid up otherwise than in cash	
The consideration for the intended issue of those shares and debentures	Debenture $
Number, description and amount of any shares or debentures which any person has or is entitled to be given an option to subscribe for, or to acquire from a person to whom they have been allotted or agreed to be allotted with a view to his offering them for sale	Consideration Share of $ and Debentures of $
Period during which option is exercisable	Until
Price to be paid for shares or debentures subscribed for or acquired under option	
Consideration for option or right to option	Consideration:
Persons to whom option or right to option was given or, if given to existing shareholders or debenture holders as such, the relevant shares or debentures	Names and Addresses: —

FOURTH SCHEDULE, *contd.*

Names and addresses of vendors of property purchased or acquired, or proposed to be purchased or acquired by the company except where the contract for its purchase or acquisition was entered into in the ordinary course of the business intended to be carried on by the company or the amount of the purchase money is not material	
Amount (in cash, shares or debentures) payable to each separate vendor	
Amount (if any) paid or payable (in cash or shares or debentures) for any such property, specifying amount (if any) or payable for goodwill	Total purchase price $ Cash ... $ Shares ... $ Debentures $ Goodwill $
Short particulars of any transaction relating to such property which was complete within the two preceding years and in which any vendor to the company or any person who is, or was at the time thereof, a promoter, director or proposed director of the company had any interest direct or indirect	
Amount (if any) paid or payable as commission for subscribing or agreeing to subscribe or procuring or agreeing to procure subscriptions for any shares or debentures in the company; or	Amount paid Amount payable
Rate of the commission	Rate *per centum*
The number of shares, if any, which persons have agreed for a commission to subscribe absolutely	
Estimated amount of preliminary expenses	$
By whom those expenses have been paid or are payable	
Amount paid or intended to be paid to any promoter	Name of promoter Amount $
Consideration for the payment	Consideration:

FOURTH SCHEDULE. *contd.*

Any other benefit given or intended to be given to any promoter	Name of promoter:— Nature and value of benefit:—
Consideration for giving of benefit	Consideration:—
Dates of, parties to, and general nature of, every material contract (other than contracts entered into in the ordinary course of the business intended to be carried on by the company or entered into more than two years before the delivery of this statement)	
Time and place at which the contracts or copies thereof may be inspected	
Names and addresses of the auditors of the company (if any)	
Full particulars of the nature and extent of the interest of every director in the promotion of or in the property proposed to be acquired by the company, or where the interest of such a director consists in being a partner in a firm, the nature and extent of the interest of the firm, with a statement of all sums paid or agreed to be paid to him or to the firm in cash or shares, or otherwise, by any person either to induce him to become, or to qualify him as, a director, or otherwise for services rendered by him or by the firm in connection with the promotion or formation of the company	

(Signatures of the persons above named as directors or proposed directors, or of their agents authorized in writing).	....

Date.................................

PART II

Reports to be Set Out

1. Where it is proposed to acquire a business, a report made by accountants (who shall be named in the statement) upon—

FOURTH SCHEDULE, *contd.*

(*a*) the profits or losses of the business in respect of each of the three financial years immediately preceding the delivery of the statement to the Registrar; and

(*b*) the assets and liabilities of the business at the last date to which the accounts of the business were made up.

2.—(1) Where it is proposed to acquire shares in an undertaking which by reason of the acquisition or anything to be done in consequence thereof or in connection therewith will become a subsidiary of the company, a report made by accountants (who shall be named in the statement) with respect to the profits and losses and assets and liabilities of the other undertaking in accordance with sub-paragraph (2) or (3) as the case requires, indicating how the profits or losses of the other body corporate dealt with by the report would, in respect of the shares to be acquired, have concerned members of the company and what allowance would have fallen to be made, in relation to assets and liabilities so dealt with, for holders of other shares, if the company had at all material times held the shares to be acquired.

(2) If the other undertaking has no subsidiaries, the report referred to in sub-paragraph (1) shall—

(*a*) so far as regards profits and losses, deal with the profits or losses of the undertaking in respect of each of the three financial years immediately preceding the delivery of the statement to the Registrar; and

(*b*) so far as regards assets and liabilities, deal with the assets and liabilities of the undertaking at the last date to which the accounts of the undertaking were made up.

(3) If the other body corporate has subsidiaries, the report referred to in sub-paragraph (1) shall—

(*a*) so far as regards profits and losses, deal separately with the other undertaking's profits or losses as provided by sub-paragraph (2), and in addition deal either—

(i) as a whole with the combined profits or losses of its subsidiaries, so far as they concern members of the other undertaking; or

(ii) individually with the profits or losses of each subsidiary, so far as they concern members of the other undertaking,

FOURTH SCHEDULE. *contd.*

or, instead of dealing separately with the other undertaking's profits or losses, deal as a whole with the profits or losses of the other undertaking and, so far as they concern members of the other undertaking, with the combined profits or losses of its subsidiaries; and

(*b*) so far as regards assets and liabilities, deal separately with the other undertaking's assets and liabilities as provided by sub-paragraph (2) and, in addition, deal either—

(i) as a whole with the combined assets and liabilities of its subsidiaries, with or without the other undertaking's assets and liabilities; or

(ii) individually with the assets and liabilities of each subsidiary,

and shall indicate as respects the assets and liabilities of the subsidiaries the allowance to be made for persons other than members of the company.

PART III

Provisions Applying to Parts I and II of this Schedule

3. In this Schedule the expression "vendor" includes a vendor as defined in Part I of the Third Schedule, and the expression "financial year" has the meaning assigned to it in Part II of that Schedule.

4. If in the case of a business which has been carried on, or of a body corporate which has been carrying on business, for less than three years, the accounts of the business or body corporate have only been made up in respect of two years or one year, Part II shall have effect as if references to two years or one year, as the case may be, were substituted for references to three years.

5. Any report required by Part II shall either indicate by way of note any adjustments as respects the figures of any profits or losses or assets and liabilities dealt with by the report which appear to the persons making the report necessary or shall make those adjustments and indicate that adjustments have been made.

6. Any report by accountants required by Part II shall be made by accountants qualified under this Act for appointment as auditors of a company and shall not be made by any accountant who is an officer or servant or, except where the company is a private company, a person who is a partner of or in the employment of an officer or servant of the company; and for the purposes of this paragraph the expression "officer" shall include a proposed director but not an auditor.

FIFTH SCHEDULE (Sections 121 and 392)

Contents (Required by section 121 (2)) and form of Annual Return of a Company having a Share Capital

PART I

1. The address of the registered office of the company.

2. If the register of members or the register of debenture holders is under the provisions of this Act kept elsewhere than at the registered office of the company, the address of the place where such register is kept.

3. A summary, distinguishing between shares issued for cash and shares issued as fully or partly paid up otherwise than in cash, specifying the following particulars—

(*a*) the amount of the share capital of the company;

(*b*) the number of shares taken from the commencement of the company up to the date of the return;

(*c*) the amount called upon each shares;

(*d*) the total amount of calls received;

(*e*) the total amount of calls unpaid;

(*f*) the total amount of shares for which share warrants are outstanding at the date of the return;

(*g*) the total amount of share warrants issued and surrendered respectively since the date of the last return;

(*h*) the number of shares comprised in each share warrant.

4. All such particulars with respect to the persons who at the date of the return are the directors of the company as are by this Act required to be contained with respect to directors in the register of the directors of a company.

5. Particulars of the total amount of the indebtedness of the company in respect of all mortgages and charges which are required to be registered with the Registrar under this Act.

FIFTH SCHEDULE, *contd.*

L.N. 6/2005.

PART II—*Form of Annual Return*

FORM 19A
INSTRUCTIONS ON REVERSE

JAMAICA
THE COMPANIES ACT
ANNUAL RETURN
COMPANY HAVING A SHARE CAPITAL
[Pursuant to sections 121, 122 & 124]

1. NAME OF COMPANY

1A. COMPANY NUMBER

1B. COMPANY TAXPAYER REGISTRATION NUMBER

1C. COMPANY FAX NUMBER

1D. TYPE OF COMPANY:
PRIVATE ☐ PUBLIC ☐

2. LOCATION OF REGISTERED OFFICE

STREET	
TOWN	
POST OFFICE	
PARISH	

3. MAILING ADDRESS

STREET	
TOWN	
POST OFFICE	
PARISH	

3A. LOCATION OF REGISTER OF MEMBERS IF NOT KEPT AT THE REGISTERED OFFICE

STREET	
TOWN	
POST OFFICE	
PARISH	

FIFTH SCHEDULE, *contd.*

FORM 19A, *contd.*

3B. LOCATION OF REGISTER OF DEBENTURE HOLDERS IF NOT KEPT AT REGISTERED OFFICE

STREET	
TOWN	
POST OFFICE	
PARISH	

3C. LOCATION OF REGISTER OF DIRECTOR SHAREHOLDINGS IF NOT KEPT AT THE REGISTERED OFFICE

STREET	
TOWN	
POST OFFICE	
PARISH	

3D. LOCATION OF THE DIRECTOR'S SERVICE CONTRACTS IF NOT KEPT AT REGISTERED OFFICE

STREET	
TOWN	
POST OFFICE	
PARISH	

4. HAS THERE BEEN A CHANGE OF REGISTERED OFFICE? YES ☐ NO ☐

4A. IF YES, HAS FORM 17 BEEN FILED ☐ ATTACHED ☐

5. HAS THERE BEEN A CHANGE OF DIRECTOR (S) ? YES ☐ NO ☐

5A. IF YES, HAS FORM 23 BEEN FILED ☐ ATTACHED ☐

6. DATE OF LAST ANNUAL RETURN

YEAR	MONTH	DAY

6A DATE UP TO WHICH PRESENT ANNUAL RETURN IS MADE

YEAR	MONTH	DAY

7. HAS THERE BEEN A CHANGE IN STATED CAPITAL? YES ☐ NO ☐

INCREASE ☐ REDUCTION ☐

[The inclusion of this page is authorized by L.N. 180A/2006]

[The inclusion of this page is authorized by L.N. 180A/2006]

FIFTH SCHEDULE, *contd.*

FORM 19A, *contd.*

7A. THE COMPANY HAS RECEIVED THE FOLLOWING SHARES AS A GIFT FROM SHAREHOLDERS PURSUANT TO SECTION 59(6) OF THE COMPANIES ACT

NAME OF SHAREHOLDER	AMOUNT / SERIES OF SHARES SURRENDERED	VALUE OF SHARES ($)

FIFTH SCHEDULE, *contd.*

FORM 19A, *contd.*

7B PARTICULARS OF SHARE CAPITAL

	CLASS OF SHARES	STATED CAPITAL AS OF i)____ DATE $____ (AMOUNT)		SHARES ISSUED DURING THE PERIOD STARTING ii)____ DATE AND ENDING ____ DATE		SHARES PURCHASED /REDEEMED DURING THE PERIOD STARTING iii)____ DATE AND ENDING ____ DATE			STATED CAPITAL AS OF iv)____ DATE $____ (AMOUNT)	
		NUMBER OF SHARES NOT FULLY PAID UP	VALUE OF ISSUED SHARES $	NUMBER OF SHARES	VALUE OF ISSUED SHARES $	NUMBER OF SHARES	VALUE OF ISSUED SHARES $ PURCHASED	VALUE OF ISSUED SHARES $ REDEEMED	NUMBER OF SHARES NOT FULLY PAID UP	VALUE OF ISSUED SHARES $
A										
B										
C										
D										
E										

FIFTH SCHEDULE, *contd.*

FORM 19A, *contd.*

7C. i) THE AMOUNT OF SHARE CAPITAL

ii)

	CLASS OF SHARES	NUMBER OF SHARES TAKEN UP FROM INCORPORATION TO ______ DATE	NUMBER OF SHARES FULLY OR PARTLY PAID UP IN CASH	AMOUNT CALLED UPON EACH SHARE	TOTAL AMOUNT OF CALLS RECEIVED	TOTAL AMOUNT OF CALLS UNPAID	TOTAL AMOUNT OF SHARES FOR WHICH SHARE WARRANTS ARE OUTSTANDING	TOTAL AMOUNT OF SHARE WARRANTS ISSUED AND SURRENDERED SINCE THE LAST RETURN		NUMBER OF SHARES COMPRISED IN EACH SHARE WARRANT
								ISSUED	SURRENDERED	
A										
B										
C										
D										
E										

FIFTH SCHEDULE, *contd.*

FORM 19A, *contd.*

iii)

	CLASS OF SHARES	NUMBER OF SHARES TAKEN UP FROM INCORPORATION TO DATE	NUMBER OF SHARES FULLY OR PARTLY PAID UP OTHERWISE THAN IN CASH	AMOUNT CALLED UPON EACH SHARE	TOTAL AMOUNT OF CALLS RECEIVED	TOTAL AMOUNT OF CALLS UNPAID	TOTAL AMOUNT OF SHARES FOR WHICH SHARE WARRANTS ARE OUTSTANDING	TOTAL AMOUNT OF SHARE WARRANTS ISSUED AND SURRENDERED SINCE THE LAST RETURN		NUMBER OF SHARES COMPRISED IN EACH SHARE WARRANT
								ISSUED	SURRENDERED	
A										
B										
C										
D										
E										

8. CLASSES AND MAXIMUM NUMBER OF SHARES THAT THE COMPANY IS AUTHORIZED TO ISSUE:

CLASS OF SHARES	NUMBER OF SHARES IN EACH CLASS

FIFTH SCHEDULE, *contd.*

FORM 19A, *contd.*

9. LIST OF PERSON HOLDING SHARES IN THE COMPANY ON THE DAY OF AND OF PERSON WHO HAVE HELD SHARES THEREIN AT ANY TIME SINCE THE DATE OF THE LAST RETURN, OR IN THE CASE OF THE FIRST RETURN OF THE INCORPORATION OF THE COMPANY, SHOWING THEIR NAMES AND ADDRESSES AND AN ACCOUNT OF THE SHARES HELD.

NAME	ADDRESS	NATIONALITY	CLASS OF SHARES	SHARES HELD AT A)_____	SHARES ACQUIRED SINCE (B)_____	SHARES DISPOSED SINCE (C)_____	DATE OF TRANSFER/ FORFEITURE	BALANCE AT (D)_____

10. TOTAL AMOUNT OF INDEBTEDNESS OF THE COMPANY IN RESPECT OF ALL MORTGAGES AND CHARGES OF THE KIND WHICH ARE REQUIRED TO BE REGISTERED WITH THE REGISTRAR UNDER SECTION 93 OF THE COMPANIES ACT: $

FIFTH SCHEDULE, *contd.*

FORM 19A, *contd.*

11. THE DIRECTORS AND SHADOW DIRECTORS OF THE COMPANY AS OF THE DATE OF THE ANNUAL RETURN WERE:

NAME	ADDRESS	OCCUPATION	NATIONALITY	DATE OF APPOINTMENT

(SHADOW DIRECTORS SHOULD BE IDENTIFIED WITH AN (*) BESIDE THEIR NAMES)

12. THE SECRETARY OF THE COMPANY AS OF THE DATE OF THE ANNUAL RETURN WAS:

NAME	ADDRESS	OCCUPATION	NATIONALITY	DATE OF APPOINTMENT

FIFTH SCHEDULE, *contd.*

FORM 19A, *contd.*

13. Certificates

A. "We certify that the Company has not since the date of the last Annual Return issued any invitation to the Public to subscribe for any shares or debentures of the Company or to deposit money for fixed period or payable on call whether bearing or not bearing interest and we also certify that to the best of our knowledge and belief since the above-mentioned date no person other than the holder has except in cases provided for in the Fourteenth Schedule, had any interest in any of the Company's shares".

Signed.. Director

Signed.. Secretary

B. Should the number of the members exceed twenty the following certificates are also required:-

"We certify that the excess of the members of the Company above twenty consists wholly of persons who are in the employment of the company, and/or of persons who, having formerly in the employment of the company, were while in such employment and have continued after the determination of such employment to be, members of the Company".

Signed..Director

Signed.. Secretary

C. Should the Company be a private company not obliged to file accounts the following certificate is also required:-

"We certify that to the best of our knowledge and belief, subject to the exceptions provided for in the Fifteenth Schedule, no body corporate holds any shares in the Company, and that this has been the positions all times since the date of the last Annual Return."*

Signed.. Director

Signed..Secretary

*In the case of the first Annual Return strike out the words "last Annual Return" and substitute therefor the words "Incorporation of the Company" or, in the case of an existing company which became a private company, the date on which it became a private company.

D. "We certify that there is annexed hereto a true copy of every Balance Sheet laid before the Company in general meeting during the period to which this Return relates (including every document required by Law to be annexed to the Balance Sheet) and a true copy of the report of the Auditors on and of the report of the Directors accompanying each Balance Sheet.

Signed.. Director

Signed..Secretary

E. Any company which falls within the exceptions outlined in section 159 (1) and the criteria outlined in the 7th Schedule Part I Paragraph 7of the Companies Act 2004 must also complete the following certificate:

"We certify that the company is neither a public company, a private company whose articles provide otherwise, a bank licensed under the Banking Act, an insurance company registered under the Insurance Act, a company licensed under the Securities Act, a company licensed under the Financial Institutions Act, a society registered under the Building Societies Act, a society registered under the Cooperative Societies Act or a subsidiary of a company falling within any of the categories outlined in section 159 (1) of the Companies Act 2004 and that the company has passed the requisite unanimous resolution for the period to which this return relates to exempt the company from producing audited reports for the period to which this return relates and that the company has:

A. ☐ a turnover of less than $40 million;

a balance sheet total of less than $30 million; and

the total number of employees is less than 25.

FIFTH SCHEDULE, *contd.*

FORM 19A, *contd.*

OR

B. ☐ a group turnover of less than $80 million;

the group's balance sheet total is less than $60 million; and

the total number of employees is less than 50.

Signed.. Director

Signed..Secretary

NOTE: Banking Companies must add a list of all their places of business.

14.

I HEREBY CERTIFY THAT THE CONTENTS OF THIS RETURN ARE CORRECT			
DATE	PRINTED NAME	SIGNATURE	CONTACT #
CAPACITY: ☐ DIRECTOR ☐ SECRETARY ☐ AUTHORIZED OFFICIAL			

15. FILED BY

NAME:		
ADDRESS:	STREET	
	TOWN	
	POST OFFICE	
	PARISH	
E-MAIL ADDRESS:		
CONTACT NUMBER:		
FAX NUMBER:		

FIFTH SCHEDULE, *contd.*

FORM 19A, *contd.*

16. **PARTICULARS OF DIRECTORS**

NAME OF DIRECTOR)	EMAIL ADDRESS	TAX REGISTRATION NUMBER

17. **PARTICULARS OF SECRETARY**

NAME OF SECRETARY	EMAIL ADDRESS	TAX REGISTRATION NUMBER

"FOR OFFICIAL USE ONLY"

COMPANY NUMBER: ______________________

FILED: _____/__________/_____

JAMAICA

THE COMPANIES ACT

ANNUAL RETURNS

COMPANY HAVING A SHARE CAPITAL

FORM 19A

INSTRUCTIONS

GENERAL

This document should indicate in its title its specific purpose and is required to be filed with the Office of the Registrar of Companies and must conform to the requirement under the Act. Where any provision required to be set out is too long for the space provided in the form, the form may incorporate the provisions by annexing a schedule in such manner as may be prescribed under the Act.

ITEMS 1, 1A, 1B, 1C & 1D

- Set out the full legal name of the company.
- Set out Company number assigned by the Registrar of Companies.
- Set out Company Taxpayer Registration Number. (The Company Taxpayer Registration Number will be photocopied by the Registrar of Companies and returned. Individuals may, instead of bringing the Taxpayer Registration Card into the Offices of the Registrar of Companies, provide a certified copy of the

FIFTH SCHEDULE, *contd.*

FORM 19A, *contd.*

same). An Attorney -at - Law, a Justice of the Peace, or a Notary Public may certify the copy of the Taxpayer Registration Number. Where the copy is certified by a Justice of the Peace or a Notary Public they must affix the relevant seal of their office.

- Set out, where applicable the company fax number.
- Indicate whether the company is a private or a public company.

NOTE: Once certified copies of the Taxpayer Registration Number have been supplied to the Registrar of Companies or the Registrar of Companies has seen the original Taxpayer Registration Card and made a copy of the same the company need only affix the number to any documents being subsequently filed.

ITEM 2

Set out in full the location at which the registered office is situated, including the street, and if located in a multi- office building, the relevant room number. The registered office must be an actual physical location and might include the relevant district and parish. However it cannot be a post office box.

ITEMS 3, 3A 3B, 3C & 3D

- Set out the mailing address of the company. The mailing address may include a post office box number, if the mailing address is same as the registered office, state 'SAME AS ABOVE AT ITEM 2'
- Set out, where applicable, the location of the register of members if this register is not kept at the registered office.
- Set out, where applicable, the location of the register of debenture holders if this register is not kept at the registered office.
- Set out, where applicable, the location of the register of director shareholdings if this register is not kept at the registered office.
- Set out, where applicable, the location of the director's service contracts if they are not kept at the registered office.

ITEMS 4 & 4A

Indicate whether the registered office has changed since the last annual return. If there has been a change indicate whether **Form 17** has been filed or will it be submitted along with the present form. If **Form 17** will be submitted along with the present form put a tick in the box marked attached.

NOTE: **A Form 17 must be filed within 7 days of any change in the situation of registered office.** (Section 106 (2))

ITEMS 5 & 5A

Indicate whether there has been a change of directors since the last annual return. If there has been a change indicate whether **Form 23** has been filed or will it be submitted along with the present form. If **Form 23** will be submitted along with the present form put a tick in the box marked attached.

NOTE: **A Form 23 must be filed where there has been a change of directors.** (Section 183 (3))

ITEMS 6 & 6A

Indicate the date of the last return filed on behalf of the company and also the date up to, which the present annual return relates.

ITEMS 7 & 7A

Indicate whether there has been a reduction or an increase in the stated capital of the company during the period to which the annual return relates. Also indicate, where applicable, the particulars of any shares received from a shareholder as a gift pursuant to section 59 (6) of the Companies Act.

ITEM 7B

Section (i) relates to the beginning of the period to which the return relates. [According to section 121 (1) of the Companies Act annual returns should be made up to a date not later than the anniversary of the company's incorporation or the date of the last return.] Section (ii) and (iii) relate to the entire period. While section (iv) relates to the end of the period.

For Example: If the date of incorporation is Dec. 31, 2003 Section (i) would be January 1, 2004, sections (ii) and (iii) would be January 1, 2004 to December 31, 2004. While section (iv) would be December 31, 2004.

Set out in relation to all classes of shares, the number of shares not fully paid up at the beginning of the period to which the return relates, the value of all shares issued by the company as at the beginning of the period, the number and value of shares issued, purchased or redeemed during the period to which the return relates, the number of any shares not fully paid up at the end of the period and the value of all shares issued by the company, as at the end of the period to which the return relates.

In the first column "Class of Shares", the following key should be used:

Ordinary Shares	O	Ordinary A Shares	OA	Ordinary B Shares	OB
Cumulative Shares	C	Preference Shares	P	Redeemable Shares	(R)

For Example: If ordinary shares are redeemable, this will be indicated by O (R)

FIFTH SCHEDULE, *contd.*

FORM 19A, *contd.*

ITEM 7C (i), (ii) and (iii)

State the amount of share capital of the company.

State in respect of each class of shares issued as fully or partly paid up for cash or for consideration other than cash the following:

a) the number of shares taken from the commencement of the company up to the date of this annual return.
b) the amount called upon each share.
c) The total amount of calls received.
d) The total amount of calls unpaid.
e) The total amount of shares for which share warrants are outstanding at the date of this annual return.
f) The total amount of share warrants issued and surrendered respectively since the date of the last annual return.
g) The number of shares comprised in each share warrant.

In the first column the "Class of Shares", the following key should be used:

Ordinary Shares	O	Ordinary A Shares	OA	Ordinary B Shares	OB
Cumulative Shares	C	Preference Shares	P	Redeemable Shares	(R)

For Example: If ordinary shares are redeemable, this will be indicated by O (R)

The date that should be inserted in the second column is the date of the present annual return.

ITEM 8

Set out in full the classes and maximum number of shares that the company is authorized to issue.

ITEM 9

Set out in relation to every shareholder having shares at the end of the period to which the annual return relates the following.

- Name
- Residential Address
- Nationality
- Class of shares held
- Amount of shares held at the beginning of the period to which the return relates
- Amount of shares acquired since the beginning of the period to which the return relates
- Amount of shares disposed of since the beginning of the period to which the return relates
- Date of any transfer or forfeiture of shares
- Amount of shares held at the end of the period to which the return relates.

Shareholders holding a particular class of shares should be grouped together in alphabetical order.

NOTE: The date to be inserted in the caption is the last day of the period for which the return is being made.

(A) is the date of the beginning of the period for which the return is being made.
(B) is the date of the beginning of the period for which the return is being made.
(C) is the date of the beginning of the period for which the return is being made.
(D) is the date at the end of the period for which the return is being made.

For Example: If the date of incorporation is Dec. 31, 2003. (A), (B) and (C) would be 1/1/04 While (D) would be 31/12/04.

ITEM 10

Set out the total amount of indebtedness of the company.

ITEM 11

Set out the names, residential addresses, occupation, nationality and date of appointment of all directors. Also set out the names, residential addresses, occupation and nationality of all shadow directors. (Shadow directors must be identified by an asterisk (*) after their names).

ITEM 12

Set out the name, residential address, occupation, nationality and date of appointment of the company secretary.

ITEM 13

Certificate A should be completed by private companies which have not since the date of the last annual return offered any of its shares to the public.

Certificate B should be completed by private companies who have over 20 members, but this number consists of persons who are in the employment of the company.

Certificate C should be completed by private companies which do not have any body corporate as shareholders.

FIFTH SCHEDULE, *contd.*

FORM 19A, *contd.*

Certificate D should be completed if the form will be accompanied by a true copy of every Balance Sheet laid before the Company in general meeting during the period to which this Annual Return relates (including every document required by Law to be annexed to the Balance Sheet) and a true copy of the report of the Auditors on and of the report of the Directors accompanying each Balance Sheet.

Certificate E should be completed by any company which does not fall within the categories listed in section 159 (1) of the Companies Act 2004 but falls within the criteria outlined in 7th Schedule Part I Paragraph 7of the Companies Act 2004.

- These categories are namely that the company is neither a public company, a private company whose articles provide otherwise, a bank licensed under the Banking Act, an insurance company registered under the Insurance Act, a company licensed under the Securities Act, a company licensed under the Financial Institutions Act, a society registered under the Building Societies Act, a society registered under the Cooperative Societies Act or a subsidiary of a company falling within any of these categories.

- The company must also have

  A. a turnover of less than$40 million, its balance sheet total is less than $30 million and the number of employees is less than 25 and that the company have passed the requisite unanimous resolution for the period to which this return relates to exempt the company from producing audited reports for the period to which this return relates. OR

  B. a group turnover of less than$80 million, its balance sheet total is less than $60 million and the number of employees is less than 50 and that the company have passed the requisite unanimous resolution for the period to which this return relates to exempt the company from producing audited reports for the period to which this return relates.

director and the secretary of the company must sign these certificates.

ITEM 14

director, secretary or an authorized officer of the company must certify the accuracy of the contents of the form.

ITEM 15

t out the name, residential address, telephone number, fax number and email address of the person filing the form with the Registrar of Companies.

ITEM 16

t out in relation to each director their name, email address and Taxpayer Registration Number. (See instructions at Item 1 above in relation to Taxpayer gistration cards)

ITEM 17

t out in relation to the secretary his/ her/ its name, email address and Taxpayer Registration Number. (See instructions at Item 1 above in relation to Taxpayer gistration cards)

OTE:

Where the company making the return is not a private company, or is a private company which is obliged to file accounts this form must be accompanied by a written copy, certified by a director, manager or secretary of the company to be a true copy, of the last balance sheet and profit and loss account laid before the company in a general meeting including every document required by law to be annexed.

IIS FORM AND THE PRESCRIBED FEE AT THE DATE OF FILING SHOULD BE DEPOSITED WITH THE REGISTRAR OF OMPANIES.

** ANY PERSON WHO WILFULLY MAKES A FALSE STATEMENT KNOWING IT TO BE FALSE IS LIABLE ON CONVICTION TO IMPRISONMENT FOR UP TO TWO YEARS AND/OR A FINE NOT EXCEEDING $50,000 PURSUANT TO THE PROVISIONS OF SECTION 382 AND THE 9TH SCHEDULE OF THE COMPANIES ACT 2004.

*** EVERY OFFICER OF THE COMPANY IN DEFAULT OF THE PROVISIONS OF THE COMPANIES ACT IS LIABLE TO THE PRESCRIBED PENALTY AND WHERE NO PENALTY IS PRESCRIBED BY THE RELEVANT SECTION IN THE ACT TO A FINE NOT EXCEEDING $50,000. (SECTION 384 COMPANIES ACT)

FIFTH SCHEDULE, *contd.*

FORM 19B
INSTRUCTIONS ON REVERSE

JAMAICA
THE COMPANIES ACT
ANNUAL RETURN
COMPANY NOT HAVING A SHARE CAPITAL
(Pursuant to sections 123 & 124)

1. NAME OF COMPANY

1A. COMPANY NUMBER

1B. COMPANY TAXPAYER REGISTRATION NUMBER

1C. COMPANY FAX NUMBER

1D. TYPE OF COMPANY:

PRIVATE ☐ PUBLIC ☐

2. LOCATION OF REGISTERED OFFICE

STREET	
TOWN	
POST OFFICE	
PARISH	

2A. MAILING ADDRESS

STREET	
TOWN	
POST OFFICE	
PARISH	

2B. LOCATION OF REGISTER OF MEMBERS IF NOT KEPT AT THE REGISTERED OFFICE

STREET	
TOWN	
POST OFFICE	
PARISH	

3. HAS THERE BEEN A CHANGE OF REGISTERED OFFICE? YES ☐ NO ☐

3A. IF YES, HAS **FORM 17** BEEN FILED ☐ ATTACHED ☐

4. HAS THERE BEEN A CHANGE OF DIRECTOR (S) ? YES ☐ NO ☐

4A. IF YES, HAS **FORM 23** BEEN FILED ☐ ATTACHED ☐

FIFTH SCHEDULE, *contd.*

FORM 19B, *contd.*

5. HAS THERE BEEN AN INCREASE IN THE NUMBER OF REGISTERED MEMBERS? YES ☐ NO ☐

5A. HAS NOTICE BEEN GIVEN TO THE REGISTRAR OF COMPANIES? YES ☐ NO ☐

6. DATE OF LAST ANNUAL RETURN

YEAR	MONTH	DAY

6A. DATE UP TO WHICH PRESENT ANNUAL RETURN IS MADE

YEAR	MONTH	DAY

7. TOTAL AMOUNT OF INDEBTEDNESS OF THE COMPANY IN RESPECT OF ALL MORTGAGES AND CHARGES OF THE KIND WHICH ARE REQUIRED TO BE REGISTERED WITH THE REGISTRAR UNDER SECTION 93 OF THE COMPANIES ACT: $

8. THE DIRECTORS AND SHADOW DIRECTORS OF THE COMPANY AS OF THE DATE OF THE ANNUAL RETURN WERE:

NAME	ADDRESS	OCCUPATION	NATIONALITY	DATE OF APPOINTMENT

[SHADOW DIRECTORS SHOULD BE IDENTIFIED WITH AN ASTERICK (*) BESIDE THEIR NAMES]

FIFTH SCHEDULE, *contd.*

FORM 19B, *contd.*

9. THE SECRETARY OF THE COMPANY AS OF THE DATE OF THE ANNUAL RETURN WAS:

NAME	ADDRESS	OCCUPATION	NATIONALITY	DATE OF APPOINTMENT

10.

I HEREBY CERTIFY THAT THE CONTENTS OF THIS RETURN ARE CORRECT			
DATE	PRINTED NAME	SIGNATURE	CONTACT #
CAPACITY: ☐ DIRECTOR ☐ SECRETARY ☐ AUTHORIZED OFFICIAL			

FIFTH SCHEDULE, *contd.*

FORM 19B, *contd.*

11. FILED BY

NAME:		
ADDRESS:	STREET	
	TOWN	
	POST OFFICE	
	PARISH	
E-MAIL ADDRESS:		
CONTACT NUMBER:		
FAX NUMBER:		

12. PARTICULARS OF DIRECTORS

NAME OF DIRECTOR)	EMAIL ADDRESS	TAX REGISTRATION NUMBER

13. PARTICULARS OF SECRETARY

NAME OF SECRETARY	EMAIL ADDRESS	TAX REGISTRATION NUMBER

"FOR OFFICIAL USE ONLY"

COMPANY NUMBER: ____________

FILED: ______/__________/______

FIFTH SCHEDULE, *contd.*

FORM 19B, *contd.*

JAMAICA
THE COMPANIES ACT

ANNUAL RETURNS

COMPANY NOT HAVING A SHARE CAPITAL

FORM 19B

INSTRUCTIONS

GENERAL

This document should indicate in its title its specific purpose and is required to be filed with the Office of the Registrar of Companies and must conform to the requirement under the Act. Where any provision required to be set out is too long for the space provided in the form, the form may incorporate the provisions by annexing a schedule in such manner as may be prescribed under the Act.

ITEMS 1, 1A, 1B, 1C & 1D

- Set out the full legal name of the company.
- Set out Company number assigned by the Registrar of Companies
- Set out Company Taxpayer Registration Number. (The Company Taxpayer Registration Number will be photocopied by the Registrar of Companies and returned. Individuals may, instead of bringing the Taxpayer Registration Card into the Offices of the Registrar of Companies, provide a certified copy of the same). An Attorney –at – Law, a Justice of the Peace, or a Notary Public may certify the copy of the Taxpayer Registration Number. Where the copy is certified by a Justice of the Peace or a Notary Public they must affix the relevant seal of their office
- Set out, where applicable the company tax number
- Indicate whether the company is a private or a public company.

NOTE: Once certified copies of the Taxpayer Registration Number have been supplied to the Registrar of Companies or the Registrar of Companies has seen the original Taxpayer Registration Card and made a copy of the same the company need only affix the number to any documents being subsequently filed

ITEM 2

Set out in full the location at which the registered office is situated, including the street, and if located in a multi- office building, the relevant room number. The registered office must be an actual physical location and might include the relevant district and parish. However it cannot be a post office box.

ITEMS 2A & 2B

- Set out the mailing address of the company. The mailing address may include a post office box number, if the mailing address is same as the registered office, state 'SAME AS ABOVE AT ITEM 2'
- Set out, where applicable, the location of the register of members if this register is not kept at the registered office.

ITEMS 3 & 3A

Indicate whether the registered office has changed since the last return. If there has been a change indicate whether **Form 17** has been filed or will it be submitted along with the present form. If **Form 17** will be submitted along with the present form put a tick in the box marked attached.

NOTE: **A Form 17 must be filed within 7 days of any change in the situation of registered office. (Section 106 (2))**

ITEMS 4 & 4A

Indicate whether there has been a change of directors since the last return. If there has been a change indicate whether **Form 23** has been filed or will it be submitted along with the present form. If **Form 23** will be submitted along with the present form put a tick in the box marked attached.

NOTE: **A Form 23 must be filed where there has been a change of directors. (Section 183 (3))**

ITEMS 5 & 5A

Indicate whether there has been an increase in the number of registered members. If there has been an increase indicate whether notice has been given to the Registrar of Companies.

ITEMS 6 & 6A

Indicate the date of the last return filed on behalf of the company and also the date up to, which the present return relates.

FIFTH SCHEDULE, *contd.*

FORM 19B, *contd.*

ITEM 7

Set out the total amount of indebtedness of the company

ITEM 8

Set out the names, residential addresses, occupation, nationality and date of appointment of all directors. Also set out the names, residential addresses, occupation and nationality of all shadow directors. (Shadow directors must be identified by an asterisk (*) after their names)

ITEM 9

Set out the name, residential address, occupation, nationality and date of appointment of the company secretary.

ITEM 10

A director, secretary or an authorized officer of the company must certify the accuracy of the contents of the form.

ITEM 11

Set out the name, residential address, telephone number, fax number and email address of the person filing the form with the Registrar of Companies

ITEM 12

Set out in relation to each director their name, email address and Taxpayer Registration Number. (See instructions at Item 1 above in relation to Taxpayer Registration cards)

ITEM 13

Set out in relation to the secretary their name, email address and Taxpayer Registration Number. (See instructions at Item 1 above in relation to Taxpayer Registration cards)

NOTE:

Where the company making the return is not a private company, or is a private company which is obliged to file accounts this form must be accompanied by a written copy, certified by a director, manager or secretary of the company to be a true copy, of the last balance sheet and profit and loss account laid before the company in a general meeting including every document required by law to be annexed.

THIS FORM AND THE PRESCRIBED FEE AT THE DATE OF FILING SHOULD BE DEPOSITED WITH THE REGISTRAR OF COMPANIES.

** ANY PERSON WHO WILFULLY MAKES A FALSE STATEMENT KNOWING IT TO BE FALSE IS LIABLE ON CONVICTION TO IMPRISIONMENT FOR UP TO TWO YEARS AND/OR A FINE NOT EXCEEDING $50,000 PURSUANT TO THE PROVISIONS OF SECTION 382 AND THE 9TH SCHEDULE OF THE COMPANIES ACT 2004.

*** EVERY OFFICER OF THE COMPANY IN DEFAULT OF THE PROVISIONS OF THE COMPANIES ACT IS LIABLE TO THE PRESCRIBED PENALTY AND WHERE NO PENALTY IS PRESCRIBED BY THE RELEVANT SECTION IN THE ACT TO A FINE NOT EXCEEDING $50,000. (SECTION 384 COMPANIES ACT)

SIXTH SCHEDULE (Section 308(2))

Provisions which do not apply in the case of a winding up subject to supervision of the Court

Section

232. Statement of Company's affairs to be submitted to Trustee.

233. Report by Trustee.

234. Power of Court to appoint liquidators.

235. Appointment and powers of provisional liquidator.

236. Appointment style, etc., of liquidators.

237. Provisions where person other than Trustee is appointed liquidator.

238. General provisions as to liquidators (except subsection (5)).

242. Exercise and control of liquidator's powers.

243. Books to be kept by liquidator in winding up.

244. Payments of liquidator into bank.

245. Audit of liquidator's accounts.

246. Control of Registrar over liquidators.

247. Release of liquidator.

248. Meetings of creditors and contributories to determine whether committee of inspection shall be appointed.

249. Constitution and proceedings of committee of inspection.

250. Powers of Minister where no committee of inspection.

258. Appointment of special manager.

264. Power to order public examination of promoters, directors, etc.

265. Procedure at examination.

268. Delegation to liquidator of certain powers of Court.

342. Power to appoint Trustee as receiver for debenture holders or creditors.

SEVENTH SCHEDULE (Sections 53, 149, 152, 157, 159 and 392)

Financial Disclosure—Form and Content of Company Accounts

PART I

Interpretation

1. In this Schedule—

"small company" means a company that qualifies under Part II of this Schedule, to be treated as a small company;

"small group" means a group that qualifies under Part II of this Schedule, to be treated as a small group.

General Rules

2. The accounts referred to in sections 146 (2) and 157 of the Act shall, except as otherwise provided in Part II of this Schedule in relation to small companies or small groups—

(*a*) be prepared in accordance with generally accepted accounting principles promulgated by the Institute of Chartered Accountants of Jamaica, from time to time, or such other body as the Minister may prescribe;

(*b*) contain—

(i) a balance sheet;

(ii) a statement of changes in equity;

(iii) a profit and loss account;

(iv) a statement of changes in financial position;

(v) notes to the accounts;

(vi) such other variation or addition to the above list as may be promulgated by the Institute of Chartered Accountants of Jamaica,

but the contents need not be designated by the respective names specified in items (i)—(v).

3. If accounts prepared in accordance with the requirements of paragraph 2 do not (in the opinion of the directors) give a true and fair view of the matters to which they relate, then the directors of the company concerned may depart from those requirements to such extent as may in their opinion be necessary to give a true and fair view of those matters, and particulars of the departure and the reasons for it shall be given in a note to the accounts.

SEVENTH SCHEDULE, *contd.*

PART II

Small Companies

4.—(1) A small company is not required to comply with the generally accepted accounting principles referred to in paragraph 2, unless—

(*a*) otherwise decided by the directors; or

(*b*) disqualified under paragraph 8.

(2) The fact of such non-compliance shall be disclosed in notes to the accounts.

5. A small company shall present accounts in accordance with accounting principles that are appropriate to its circumstances having regard to the requirement for those accounts to present a true and fair view of the state of affairs and the results of operation of the company.

6. A company shall be treated as qualifying as small in relation to a financial year if it is not disqualified under paragraph 8 or 12, and meets two or more of the criteria specified in paragraph 7—

(*a*) in the current year, if that is the first financial year of the company;

(*b*) in the current year and the immediately preceding financial year.

7. The criteria referred to in paragraph 6 in relation to a small company are that—

(*a*) its turnover is less than $40 million;

(*b*) its balance sheet total is less than $30 million;

(*c*) the total number of employees is less than 25.

8. A small company is disqualified for the purposes of this Part if it is or was at anytime within the financial year to which the accounts relate—

(*a*) a public company;

(*b*) a company licensed under the Banking Act;

(*c*) an insurance company registered under the Insurance Act;

(*d*) a licensee under the Securities Act;

(*e*) a company licensed under the Financial Institutions Act;

(*f*) a society registered under the Building Societies Act or the Cooperative Societies Act.

SEVENTH SCHEDULE, *contd.*

Small Groups

9. Group accounts need not be prepared with respect to a holding company in relation to a financial year in which the holding company and its subsidiaries qualify as a small group and the holding company is not disqualified under paragraph 11.

10. A holding company and its subsidiaries qualify as a small group in relation to a financial year if they meet on a consolidated basis, two or more of the following criteria for that financial year and the immediately preceding financial years—

(*a*) the groups turnover is less than $80 million;

(*b*) the balance sheet total is less than $60 million;

(*c*) the total number of employees is less than 50.

11. A group of companies is disqualified for the purposes under this Part if any of the companies within that group is—

(*a*) public company;

(*b*) a company licensed under the Banking Act;

(*c*) an insurance company registered [or exempted from registration] under the Insurance Act;

(*d*) a licensee under the Securities Act;

(*e*) a company licensed under the Financial Institutions Act;

(*f*) a society registered under the Building Societies Act or the Cooperative Societies Act.

12. A holding company shall not be treated as qualifying as a small company in relation to a financial year unless it and its subsidiaries qualifies as a small group in relation to a financial year.

EIGHTH SCHEDULE (Section 157)

Matters to be expressly stated in Auditors' Report

1. Whether they have obtained all the information and explanations which to the best of their knowledge and belief were necessary for the purposes of their audit.

2. Whether, in their opinion, proper books of account have been kept by the company, so far as appears from their examination of those books, and proper returns adequate for the purposes of their audit have been received from branches not visited by them.

EIGHTH SCHEDULE, *contd.*

3.—(1) Whether the company's balance sheet and (unless it is framed as a consolidated profit and loss account) profit and loss account dealt with by the report are in agreement with the books of account and returns.

(2) Whether, in their opinion and to the best of their information and according to the explanations given them, the said accounts give the information required by the Act in the manner so required and give a true and fair view—

(*a*) in the case of the balance sheet, of the state of the company's affairs as at the end of its financial year;

(*b*) in the case of the profit and loss account, of the profit or loss for its financial year;

(*c*) a statement of change in equity for its financial year; and

(*d*) a statement of change in finances for its financial year,

or, as the case may be, give a true and fair view thereof subject to the non-disclosure of any matters (to be indicated in the report) which by virtue of Part III of the Seventh Schedule are not required to be disclosed.

4. In the case of a holding company submitting group accounts whether, in their opinion, the group accounts have been properly prepared in accordance with the provisions of the Act so as to give a true and fair view of the state of affairs and profit or loss of the company and its subsidiaries dealt with thereby, so far as concerns members of the company, or, as the case may be, so as to give a true and fair view thereof.

NINTH SCHEDULE (Section 382)

Provisions referred to in section 382

Section or Provision of Schedule	Subject Matter
13	Conclusiveness of certificate of incorporation.
26	Statement in lieu of prospectus to be delivered to Registrar by company on ceasing to be private company.

NINTH SCHEDULE. *contd.*

Section or Provision of Schedule	Subject Matter
41	Specific requirements as to particulars in prospectus.
49	Prohibition of allotment in certain cases unless statement in lieu of prospectus delivered to Registrar.
52	Return as to allotments.
93	Registrations of charges.
95	Duty of company to register charges created by company.
96	Duty of company to register charges existing on property acquired.
102	Copies of instruments creating charges to be kept by company.
105	Application of Part III to charges created, and charges on property subject to charges acquired, by company incorporated outside the Island.
123	Annual return to be made by company not having share capital.
125	Certificates to be sent by private company with annual return.
127	Statutory meeting and statutory report.
157(1), (3)	Auditors' report and right to information and explanations.
175	Restrictions on appointment or advertisement of director.
299	Notice by liquidator of his appointment.
345(2)	Abstract to receiver's receipts and payments.
347	Delivery to Registrar of accounts of receivers and managers.

NINTH SCHEDULE, contd.

Section or Provision of Schedule	Subject Matter
363	Documents, etc., to be delivered to Registrar by companies carrying on business in the Island.
365	Return to be delivered to Registrar where documents, etc., altered.
366	Accounts of company carrying on business in the Island.
367	Obligation to state name of company, whether limited, and country where incorporated.
5th Schedule Part I paras. 2, 4 and 5.	Particulars in annual return of company having a share capital.

TENTH SCHEDULE (Section 16)

Procedure in cases of applications for licences under section 16

1. The accompanying draft in the form marked "A" hereinafter set out have been prepared to show generally the manner in which the articles of incorporation should be framed where an association about to be formed as a limited company proposes to apply to the Minister for a licence under section 16 of the Act.

2. Under section 16 of the Act any chamber, institute, society, or other association formed for the purpose of promoting commerce, art, science, religion, charity, or any other useful object which does not involve the division of profit, may, if it obtains the licence of the Minister be incorporated by registration with limited liability, but without the addition of the word "limited" to its name.

3. It is to be understood that the drafts of the articles of incorporation are subject to such additions, alterations and omissions as the circumstances of the association desiring incorporation may render necessary or the Minister may require.

TENTH SCHEDULE, *contd.*

4. An association seeking to obtain the benefits of the said section should make a written application to the Minister for his licence and, together with such application, should transmit for consideration a draft in duplicate of the proposed articles of incorporation, together with a list of the promoters and proposed governing body of the association, and a report or statement of its previous proceedings as an unincorporated body. If the Minister is satisfied that the application may be entertained he will give instructions for a notice of such application in the form marked "B" hereinafter set out to be inserted in a daily newspaper printed and circulating in the Island for the information of the public once a week for two successive weeks and if after the expiration of fourteen days from the date of the last insertion there appears to be no sufficient reason why the licence should not be granted the Minister will accept the articles of incorporation with such amendment, if any, as may be necessary, and grant a licence. The fees for registration of the association are set out in the Fifteenth Schedule.

5. The Minister will not be responsible for the articles of incorporation being properly framed as regards the interests of the association. No fees or charges in respect of the licence are payable.

6. In the event of any proposed addition, alteration or amendment of the articles being required, the same shall be submitted to the Minister for his approval.

7. The procedure set forth in paragraph 4 with respect to the publication of a notice in a local daily newspaper is to apply in relation to an application by a company under section 16 (2) of the Act as it applies in relation to an application by an association under section 16 (1) thereof with the omission of all the words appearing after the words "for his licence" in the first sentence of the paragraph and with the substitution for the words "will accept the articles of incorporation with such amendment" of the words "will accept the application subject to such conditions".

(A)

Articles of Incorporation

(1) These articles are to be construed with reference to the provisions of the Companies Act, and terms used in these articles shall be taken as having the same respective meanings as they have when used in that Act.

(2) Qualification of members.

(3) Admission of members.

TENTH SCHEDULE, *contd.*

Names, addresses and descriptions of subscribers (as in articles).

*All names should be in full, and the addresses should be definite giving, where practicable, the name of the street and the number of the house.

It is proposed to adopt the style "Chamber" "society", etc., throughout, and to avoid the use of the word "company".

(4) Retirement of members.

(5) Rights of members.

(6) Honorary officers and their elections.

(7) Management of chamber.

(8) Powers of chamber (or of the council or governing body thereof).

Dated the day of

Witness

(B)

Notice of application for a licence from the Minister under section 16 of the Companies Act

Notice is hereby given that in pursuance of section 16 of the Companies Act, application has been made to the Minister for a licence whereby the Limited (or an association about to be formed under the name of) may operate with limited liability without the addition of the word "limited" to its name.

* The objects for which the association is proposed to be established are

Notice is hereby further given that any person, company or corporation objecting to this application may bring such objection before the Minister on or before the next by letter addressed to the Minister at the Ministry of Commerce and Technology, Kingston, Jamaica.

Dated this day of

Permanent Secretary,
Ministry of Industry, Commerce and Technology.

* Strike out in case of application by limited company.

ELEVENTH SCHEDULE (Section 391)

Provisions of this Act applied to unregistered companies

Subject matter	Provisions applied	Limitations on application
Prospectuses and allotments	Sections 40 to 47, 51, 55 and the Third Schedule	To apply so far only as may be specified by regulations made by the Minister and to such bodies corporate as may be so specified.
Annual return	Sections 121 to 125 and the Fifth Schedule	Not to apply so as to require particulars in respect of any period before the appointed day, and as respects any period thereafter to apply so far only as may be specified as aforesaid and to, such bodies corporate as may be so specified.
Accounts and audit	Sections 144 to 157, 190 and 191, the Eighth Schedule (except sub-paragraphs (*a*) to (*d*) of paragraph 2, sub-paragraphs (*c*), (*d*) and (*e*) of paragraph 3 and sub-paragraph (1) (*c*) of paragraph 8 and the Seventh Schedule	To apply so far only as may be specified as aforesaid and to such bodies corporate as may be so specified.
Investigations	Sections 160 to 171	—
Register of directors	Section 183.	—

ELEVENTH SCHEDULE. *contd.*

Subject matter	Provisions applied	Limitations on application
Registration of documents, enforcement and other supplemental matters	Sections 2, 192, 353 to 354, 381, 382, 389, 384, 385, 386, 387, 396 (1) and the Ninth Schedule and Fifteenth Schedule	To apply so far only as they have effect in relation to provisions applying by virtue of the foregoing entries in this Schedule.

TWELFTH SCHEDULE (Sections 25 (1)(e), 125)

Exceptions referred to in sections 25(1)(e) and 125(1)

1. The exceptions referred to at paragraph (e) of subsection (1) of section 25 of the Act to the requirement that a private company's articles shall prohibit any person other than the holder from having any interest in any of the company's shares (hereinafter referred to as the relevant requirement) are those provided for in the following paragraphs of this Schedule.

Interpretation

2. In this Schedule—

(*a*) the expression "banking or finance company" means any body corporate or partnership whose ordinary business includes the business of banking and any other body corporate whose ordinary business includes the business of lending money or of subscribing for shares, except, that it does not include any such other body corporate unless either—

(i) its shares are quoted or dealt in on a recognized stock exchange; or

(ii) it is designated for the purposes of this paragraph by order of the Minister; or

(iii) it is a subsidiary of a body corporate whose shares are so quoted or dealt in or which is so designated; and

TWELFTH SCHEDULE, *contd.*

(*b*) the expression "recognized stock exchange" means any body of persons carrying on business whether in Jamaica or elsewhere declared by an order of the Minister to be a recognized stock exchange for the purposes of this paragraph.

Exceptions for normal Dealings of a Business Nature

3.—(1) The rules contained in the following sub-paragraphs of this paragraph shall apply for the purposes both of the relevant requirement and of the exceptions from that requirement.

(2) Where any share or any interest in any share is subject to a charge in favour of a banking or finance company by way of security for the purposes of a transaction entered into in the ordinary course of its business as such—

(*a*) any interest under the charge, whether of the banking or finance company or a nominee for it, shall be disregarded; and

(*b*) if the banking or finance company or its nominee is the holder of the share, the person entitled to the equity of redemption shall be treated as the holder, whether he has a present right to redeem or not.

(3) Any interest under a contract for the transfer of any share or of any interest in any share shall, until execution of an instrument of transfer by the parties, be disregarded unless execution thereof is unreasonably delayed.

(4) Subject to sub-paragraph (2) of this paragraph, on execution of an instrument of transfer of a share, the transferee and not the transferor shall be treated as the holder, notwithstanding that the transfer requires registration with the company, unless registration is refused.

(5) Any interest of the company itself in any of its shares, and any lien or charge arising by operation of law and affecting any of the shares shall be disregarded.

Exceptions for Cases of Death and for Family Settlements

4.—(1) The relevant requirement shall be subject to exceptions for—

(*a*) any shares forming part of the estate of a deceased holder thereof, so long as administration of his estate has not been completed; and

(*b*) any shares held by trustees on the trusts of a will or family settlement disposing of the shares, so long as no body corporate has for the time being any immediate interest under the said trusts other than—

TWELFTH SCHEDULE. *contd.*

(i) a body corporate established for charitable purposes only and having no right to exercise or control the exercise of any part of the voting power at any general meeting of the company;

(ii) a body corporate which is a trustee of the said trusts and has such an interest only by way of remuneration for acting as trustee thereof.

(2) For the purposes of this paragraph—

(*a*) shares held by trustees on trusts arising on an intestacy shall, if the shares or an interest therein formed part of the intestate's estate at the time of his death, be treated as if the trusts arose under a will disposing of the shares;

(*b*) the expression "family settlement" means a settlement made either—

(i) in consideration or contemplation of an intended marriage of the settler or any of the settler's issue or in pursuance of a contract entered into in consideration or contemplation of any such marriage; or

(ii) otherwise in favour of any of the following persons, that is to say, the settler, his parents and grandparents, and any other individual who at the date of the settlement is a member of the company, and the wife or husband and issue, and the wife or husband of any issue, of the settler, his parents, or any such other individual, and persons taking in the event of a failure of the issue or any class of the issue of any person taking under the settlement;

(*c*) the expressions "parent", "grandparent" and "issue" shall be construed as if the stepchild, adopted child or illegitimate child of any person were that person's child;

(*d*) any reference to a wife or husband shall include a former wife or husband and a reputed wife or husband;

(*e*) the expression "will" includes any testamentary disposition;

(*f*) any reference to a will or family settlement disposing of any shares shall include a will or family settlement disposing of an interest under another will or family settlement disposing of the shares.

TWELFTH SCHEDULE, *contd.*

Exception for Cases of Disability

5. Where the person entitled to any share or any interest in any share is of unsound mind or otherwise under any disability, and by reason thereof the share or interest is vested in an administrator or other person on behalf of the person entitled thereto, then in relation to the share or interest the person in whom it is so vested and the person entitled thereto shall be treated for the purposes of this Schedule as if they were the same person.

Exception for Trusts for Employees

6. The relevant requirement shall be subject to an exception for any shares held by trustees for the purposes of a scheme maintained for the benefit of employees of the company, including any director holding a salaried employment or office in the company.

Exceptions for Bankruptcies, Liquidations, etc.

7. The relevant requirement shall be subject to exceptions for—

(*a*) any shares forming part of the assets in a bankruptcy or liquidation of a holder thereof; and

(*b*) any shares held either—

(i) on trusts created for the benefit of his creditors generally by a person having an interest therein; or

(ii) otherwise for the purposes of any composition or scheme made or approved under any statute by a court or an officer of a court for arranging the affairs of such a person.

Exception for Holdings of Nominees for Banking or Finance Companies providing Capital

8. The relevant requirement shall be subject to an exception for any shares held by a nominee for a banking or finance company where the interest of the banking or finance company in the shares was required in the ordinary course of the business of the banking or finance company as such, and by arrangement with the company or its promoters:

Provided that this exception shall not apply if the banking or finance company has the right (or, where there is more than one such company having an interest in shares to which this exception applies, they have between them the right) to control the exercise of one-fifth or more of the total voting power at any general meeting of the company.

TWELFTH SCHEDULE, *contd.*

Limited Exception for Certain Other Nominee Holdings

9. The relevant requirement shall be subject to an exception for any share held by not more than one member (hereinafter referred to as the relevant shareholder) of the company holding such share in trust for a member of the company or subject to any arrangement whereby a member of the company has any right to become holder thereof (whether on payment or not):

Provided that this exception shall not apply if the relevant shareholder holds more than a single share.

THIRTEENTH SCHEDULE (Section 25 (3))

Exceptions referred to at subsection (3) of section 25

1. The exceptions referred to at subsection (3) of section 25 to the obligation imposed upon a private company to file accounts if any of its shares is held by a body corporate (hereinafter referred to as the relevant obligation) are those provided for in the following paragraphs of this Schedule.

2. The provisions of paragraph 2 of the Twelfth Schedule and the exceptions specified in paragraphs 3 to 7 inclusive of that Schedule shall, with the necessary modifications, apply in relation to the relevant obligation as they apply in relation to the relevant requirement mentioned in paragraph 1 of that Schedule.

Exception for Shares held by Private Companies

3.—(1) The relevant obligation shall also be subject to an exception for shares held by another private company which is not obliged to file accounts:

Provided that this exception shall not apply if taking all the following companies together, that is to say—

(*a*) the company whose obligation to file accounts is in question (hereafter in this Schedule referred to as the relevant company);

(*b*) any company holding shares to which this exception has to be applied in determining the relevant company's right to be treated as a private company which is not obliged to file accounts; and

(*c*) any further company taken into account for the purposes of this proviso in determining the right to be so treated of any company holding any such shares as aforesaid.

THIRTEENTH SCHEDULE, *contd.*

the total number of persons holding shares in those companies is more than twenty, joint shareholders being treated as a single person and the companies themselves and (subject to sub-paragraph (3)) their employees and former employees being disregarded.

(2) Where the relevant company and another company hold shares in each other, the other company shall be treated for the purposes of sub-paragraph (1) as a private company which is not obliged to file accounts if—

(*a*) in determining its right to be so treated the exception in that sub-paragraph would apply to the shares in it held by the relevant company, on the assumption that the relevant company was a private company which is not obliged to file accounts; and

(*b*) in all other respects the other company is entitled to be so treated,

and where another company's right to be so treated depends on the application to any shares in it of that sub-paragraph, and the application thereof to those shares depends indirectly on the relevant company's right to be so treated, this sub-paragraph shall apply as if those shares were held by the relevant company.

(3) In the proviso to sub-paragraph (1) the direction that employees and former employees of the companies shall be disregarded in computing the number of shareholders shall not apply to a person holding shares in a company of which he is not for the time being an employee unless, having been formerly in the employment of that company, he held, while in that employment, and has continued after the termination of that employment to hold shares in that company.

Exception for Banking or Finance Companies Providing Capital

4. The relevant obligation shall also be subject to an exception for any shares held by a banking or finance company, where the banking or finance company acquired the shares in the ordinary course of its business as such and by arrangement with the relevant company or its promoters:

Provided that this exception shall not apply if the banking or finance company has the right (or, where there is more than one such company holding shares to which this exception has to be applied in determining the relevant company's right to be treated as a private company which is not obliged to file accounts, they have between them the right) to exercise or control the exercise of one-fifth or more of the total voting power at any general meeting of the relevant company.

FOURTEENTH SCHEDULE (Section 196)

Provisions supplementing and interpreting section 196

PART I

Rules for interpretation of the sections

1.—(1) A reference to an interest in shares or debentures is to be read as including any interest of any kind whatsoever in shares or debentures.

(2) Accordingly, there are to be disregarded any restraints or restrictions to which the exercise of any right attached to the interest is or may be subject.

2. Where property is held on trust and any interest in shares or debentures is comprised in the property, any beneficiary of the trust who (apart from this paragraph) does not have an interest in the shares or debentures is to be taken as having such an interest; but this paragraph is without prejudice to the following provisions of this Part of this Schedule.

3.—(1) A person is taken to have an interest in shares or debentures if—

(*a*) he enters into a contract for their purchase by him (whether for cash or other consideration); or

(*b*) not being the registered holder, he is entitled to exercise any right conferred by the holding of the shares or debentures or is entitled to control the exercise of any such right.

(2) For the purposes of sub-paragraph (1) (*b*), a person is taken to be entitled to exercise or control the exercise of a right conferred by the holding of shares or debentures if he—

(*a*) has a right (whether subject to conditions or not) the exercise of which would make him so entitled; or

(*b*) is under an obligation (whether or not so subject) the fulfilment of which would make him so entitled.

(3) A person is not by virtue of sub-paragraph (1) (b) taken to be interested in shares or debentures by reason only that he—

(*a*) has been appointed a proxy to vote at a specified meeting of a company or of any class of its members and at any adjournment of that meeting; or

(*b*) has been appointed by a corporation to act as its representative at any meeting of a company or of any class of its members.

(4) A person is taken to be interested in shares or debentures if a body corporate is interested in them and—

FOURTEENTH SCHEDULE. *contd.*

(*a*) that body corporate or its directors are accustomed to act in accordance with his directions or instructions; or

(*b*) he is entitled to exercise or control the exercise of one-third or more of the voting power at general meetings of that body corporate.

4. Where a person is entitled to exercise or control the exercise of one-third or more of the voting power at general meetings of a body corporate and that body corporate is entitled to exercise or control the exercise of any of the voting power at general meetings of another body corporate ("the effective voting power") then, for the purposes of paragraph 4 (*b*), the effective voting power is taken to be exercisable by that person.

5.—(1) A person is taken to have an interest in shares or debentures if, otherwise than by virtue of having an interest under a trust—

(*a*) he has a right to call for delivery of the shares or debentures to himself or to his order; or

(*b*) he has a right to acquire an interest in shares or debentures or is under an obligation to take an interest in shares or debentures, whether in any case the right or obligation is conditional or absolute.

(2) Rights or obligations to subscribe for shares or debentures are not to be taken, for purposes of sub-paragraph (1), to be rights to acquire, or obligations to take, an interest in shares or debentures.

6. Persons having a joint interest are each deemed to have that interest.

7. It is immaterial that shares or debentures in which a person has an interest are unidentifiable.

8. So long as a person is entitled to receive, during the lifetime of himself or another, income from trust property comprising shares or debentures, an interest in the shares or debentures in reversion or remainder are to be disregarded.

9. A person is to be treated as uninterested in shares or debentures if, and so long as, he holds them as a trustee.

10. Delivery to a person's order of shares or debentures in fulfilment of a contract for the purchase of them by him or in satisfaction of a right of his to call for their delivery, or failure to deliver shares or debentures in accordance with the terms of such a contract or on which such a right falls to be satisfied, is deemed to constitute an event in consequence of the occurrence of which he ceases to be interested in them, and so is the lapse of a person's right to call for delivery of shares or debentures.

FOURTEENTH SCHEDULE, *contd.*

PART II

Periods within which obligations imposed by section 196 must be fulfilled

11.—(1) An obligation imposed on a person by section 196 (1) to notify an interest must, if he knows of the existence of the interest on the day on which he becomes a director, be fulfilled before the expiration of the period of five days beginning with the day following that day.

(2) Otherwise, the obligation must be fulfilled before the expiration of the period of five days beginning with the day following that on which the existence of the interest comes to his knowledge.

12.—(1) An obligation imposed on a person by section 196 (2) to notify the occurrence of an event must, if at the time at which the event occurs he knows of its occurrence and of the fact that its occurrence gives rise to the obligation, be fulfilled before the expiration of the period of five days beginning with the day following that on which the event occurs.

(2) Otherwise, the obligation must be fulfilled before the expiration of a period of five days beginning with the day following that on which the fact that the occurrence of the event gives rise to the obligation comes to his knowledge.

PART III

Circumstances in which obligation imposed by section 196 not discharged

13.—(1) Where an event of whose occurrence a director is, by virtue of section 196 (2) (a), under an obligation to notify a company consists of his entering into a contract for the purchase by him of shares or debentures, the obligation is not discharged in the absence of inclusion in the notice of a statement of the price to be paid by him under the contract.

(2) An obligation imposed on a director by section 196 (2) (*b*) is not discharged in the absence of inclusion in the notice of the price to be received by him under the contract.

14.—(1) An obligation imposed on a director by virtue of section 196 (2) (*c*) to notify a company is not discharged in the absence of inclusion in the notice of a statement of the consideration for the assignment (or, if it be the case that there is no consideration, that fact).

(2) Where an event of whose occurrence a director is, by virtue of section 196 (2) (d), under obligation to notify a company consists in his assigning a right, the obligation is not discharged in the absence of inclusion in the notice of a similar statement.

FOURTEENTH SCHEDULE, *contd.*

15.—(1) Where an event of whose occurrence a director is, by virtue of section 196 (2) (d), under an obligation to notify a company consists in the grant to him of a right to subscribe for shares or debentures, the obligation is not discharged in the absence of inclusion in the notice of a statement of—

(*a*) the date on which the right was granted;

(*b*) the period during which or the time at which the right is exercisable;

(*c*) the consideration for the grant (or, if it be the case that there is no consideration, that fact); and

(*d*) the price to be paid for the shares or debentures.

(2) Where an event of whose occurrence a director is, by section 196 (2) (d), under obligation to notify a company consists in the exercise of a right granted to him to subscribe for shares or debentures, the obligation is not discharged in the absence of inclusion in the notice of a statement of—

(*a*) the number of shares or amount of debentures in respect of which the right was exercised; and

(*b*) if it be the case that they were registered in his name, that fact, and, if not, the name or names of the person or persons in whose name or names they were registered, together (if they were registered in the names of two persons or more) with the number or amount registered in the name of each person.

16. In this Part, a reference to price paid or received includes any consideration other than money.

PART IV

Provisions with respect to Register of Directors' interests to be kept under section 196

17. The register must be so made up that the entries in it against the several names appear in chronological order.

18. An obligation imposed by section 196 (2) to (4) must be fulfilled before the expiration of the period of three days beginning with the day after that on which the obligation arises.

19. The nature and extent of an interest recorded in the register of a director in any shares or debentures shall, if he so requires, be recorded in the register.

FOURTEENTH SCHEDULE, *contd.*

20. The company is not, by virtue of anything done for the purposes of section 196 or this Part of this Schedule, affected with notice of, or put upon enquiry as to, the rights of any person in relation to any shares or debentures.

21. The register shall—

(*a*) if the company's register of members is kept at its registered office, be kept there;

(*b*) if the company's register of members is not so kept, be kept at the company's registered office or at the place where its register of members is kept,

and shall, during business hours, be open to inspection of any member of the company without charge and of any other person on payment of Fifty Dollars.

22.—(1) Any member of the company or other person may require a copy of the register, or of any part of it, on payment of Fifty Dollars.

(2) The company shall cause any copy so required by a person to be sent to him within the period of ten days beginning with the day after that on which the requirement is received by the company.

23. The company shall send notice in the prescribed form to the Registrar of the place where the register is kept and of any change in that place except in a case in which it has at all times been kept at its registered office.

24. Unless the register is in such a form as to constitute in itself an index, the company shall keep an index of the names inscribed in it, which shall—

(*a*) in respect of each name, contain a sufficient indication to enable the information entered against to be readily found; and

(*b*) be kept at the same place as the register,

and the company shall, within fourteen days after the date on which a name is entered in the register, make any necessary alteration in the index.

25. The register shall be produced at the commencement of the company's annual general meeting and remain open and accessible during the continuance of the meeting to any person attending the meeting.

FIFTEENTH SCHEDULE (Section 394)(3)) L.N. 7/2005.

Matter in respect of which fee is payable	Fee
For registration of a company limited by shares ...	$10,000.00
For registration of a company not having share capital	$10,000.00
For the registration of a company limited by guarantee and having a share capital or an unlimited company having a share capital	$10,000.00
For the registration of an increase in the share capital of any company—	
Notice of increase of share capital ...	$ 3,000.00
Statement of increase of share capital ...	$ 3,000.00
Ordinary Resolution for increase in share capital	$ 3,000.00
Overseas Company	$18,000.00
For registering Annual Return	$ 4,000.00
For registering any charge	$ 3,000.00
For registering Amended Memorandum or Articles of Incorporation	$ 3,000.00
For registering any other document by the Act required or authorized to be registered or required to be delivered, sent or forwarded to the Registrar other than the Memorandum or the abstract required to be delivered to the Registrar by a receiver or manager or the statement required to be sent to the Registrar by the Liquidator in a winding up	$ 2,000.00
For making a record of any fact by the Act required or authorized to be recorded by the Registrar	$ 2,000.00
For inspection of documents kept by the Registrar ...	$ 200.00 for 1 hour
For a certified copy of a Certificate of Incorporation	$ 1,000.00

FIFTEENTH SCHEDULE, *contd.*

Matter in respect of which fee is payable	Fee
For a certified copy of any document or part of any document kept by the Registrar or extract therefrom	$ 150.00 per page
For change of name of company	$3,000.00
For an uncertified copy of any document or part of any document kept by the Registrar ...	$ 100.00 per page
For registering a prospectus	$20,000.00
For registering a rights issue	$10,000.00
For a certificate of Good Standing from the Registrar of Companies	$ 2,000.00
For a Registrar's report on the status of a company	$ 2,000.00
Fee for removal of a company at the request of the company (not including the cost of advertisement)	$ 3,000.00
For the late registration of any document required to be filed	$ 1,000.00
For the expedition of registration	$ 3,000.00
For supplying information via facsimile (per page)	
U.S., Canada, Caribbean	$ 500.00
Jamaica	$ 100.00
Other countries	$ 600.00
Filing of document pertaining to shares along with Articles of Incorporation	$ 2,000.00
Company name reservation	$ 2,000.00
Registration of mutual fund companies ...	$10,000.00
Examination of Statutory Declaration and issuance of Registrar's Certificate regarding public companies allotted share capital to be not less than the authorized minimum ...	$ 5,000.00

FIFTEENTH SCHEDULE, *contd.*

Matter in respect of which fee is payable	Fee
For filing of ordinary resolution and notification to the Registrar that company intends to retain its existing shares with nominal or par value ...	$2,000.00
Notice to the Registrar of allotment by company of shares for other than monetary considera-tion along with directors' resolution and accountant's estimate of the value of the consideration	$4,000.00 (filing fee for the resolution and notice)
For filing of special resolution regarding the addition to the company's stated capital account (where the effect of the issuance of bonus shares is to allow one class of shareholders to obtain control of the company or pass a resolution which they could not have done before the issue)	$ 2,000.00
For filing of directors' declaration of solvency and audited or unaudited accounts prior to purchasing or otherwise acquiring a company's own shares	$ 4,000.00
For filing directors' declaration of solvency, special resolution and audited or unaudited accounts prior to a company reducing its stated capital	$ 4,000.00
For filing of notice of increase in the amount secured by a registered charge	$ 2,000.00
For filing of notice of resolution that company agrees not to produce audited reports within a particular financial year	$ 2,000.00
For filing of notice of Secretary's appointment ...	$ 2,000.00
For filing of complaint regarding unfitness of director or officer of a company	$ 5,000.00
Fee to conduct investigation	$10,000.00

FIFTEENTH SCHEDULE, *contd.*

Matter in respect of which fee is payable	Fee
Fee to conduct hearing	$2,000.00 per hour or part thereof
Fee to issue Certificate of Unfitness ...	No fee
Fee payable to Registrar to make application to the Court	According to court fees set out in the Civil Procedure Rules
For filing of notice of the location of directors' contracts and memoranda or any change in the location	$2,000.00
For filing of notice of the place where the register of directors' interests is kept or any change in location	$2,000.00
For filing of notice of application to be made to the Court regarding indemnification ...	$2,000.00 in addition to court fees set out in the Civil Procedure Rules
Fee to restore a company to the Companies Registry	$15,000.00 in addition to filing fees
Fee for the filing of documents to support the company's request for permission to continue to refer in its articles to shares as having a nominal or par value and issuance of Registrar's certificate granting permission ...	$5,000.00 in addition to fees for professional opinion

Amendments No. 40 – 2013

JAMAICA

No. 40– 2013

I assent.

[L.S.]

PATRICK LINTON ALLEN,
Governor-General.

30th day of December, 2013

AN ACT to Amend the Companies Act to prescribe a single form for business registration; to make consequential amendments to other enactments; and for related matters.

[*30th December, 2013.*]

BE IT ENACTED by The Queen's Most Excellent Majesty, by and with the advice and consent of the Senate and House of Representatives of Jamaica, and by the authority of the same, as follows:—

1. This Act may be cited as the Companies (Amendment) Act, 2013, and shall be read and construed as one with the Companies Act (hereinafter referred to as the "principal Act") and all amendments thereto. Short title and construction.

Amendment of section 2 of principal Act.

2. Section 2 of the principal Act is amended by inserting next after subsection (5) the following—

" (6) Where rules made under section 393(2)(b) require or permit articles of incorporation, forms, returns, notices or other documents to be sent to the Registrar, to be created, stored or communicated electronically, references in this Act to signing shall, in relation thereto, include the use of electronic signatures.".

Amendment of section 3 of principal Act.

3. Section 3 of the principal Act is amended by deleting subsection (1) and substituting therefor the following—

" (1) One or more persons may form a company by—

(a) signing and sending to the Registrar—

(i) articles of incorporation;

(ii) an application in the form set out as Form BRF 1 in the Sixteenth Schedule; and

Sixteenth Schedule.

(b) otherwise complying with the requirements of this Act in respect of registration.".

Repeal and replacement of section 13 of principal Act.

4. Section 13 of the principal Act is repealed and the following substituted therefor—

" Certificate of incorporation to be conclusive evidence.

13. A certificate of incorporation given by the Registrar in respect of any company shall be conclusive evidence that all the requirements of this Act in respect of registration and of matters precedent and incidental thereto have been complied with, and that the company is authorised to be registered and has been duly registered under this Act.".

Amendment of section 106 of principal Act.

5. Section 106 of the principal Act is amended—

(a) in subsection (1), by inserting next after the word "addressed" the words "and notice thereof shall be included in the form set out as Form BRF1 in the Sixteenth Schedule"; and

(b) by deleting subsection (2) and substituting therefor the following—

" (2) Notice of any change in the situation of a registered office, shall be given to the Registrar in the prescribed form within fourteen days of any change in such situation; and the Registrar shall record the change or cause the change to be recorded.

(2A) The inclusion in the annual return of a company of a statement as to the address of its registered office shall not be taken to satisfy the obligation imposed by subsection (2).".

6. Section 172 (6) of the principal Act is amended by deleting the word "fifteen" and substituting therefor the word "fourteen". Amendment of section 172 of principal Act.

7. Section 183 of the principal Act is amended by deleting— Amendment of section 183 of principal Act.

(a) paragraph (a) and substituting therefor the following—

"(a) in the case of an individual—

(i) his Christian name;

(ii) his surname;

(iii) his usual address;

(iv) his nationality, and if that nationality is not the nationality of origin, his nationality of origin;

(v) his business occupation, if any, or, if he has no business occupation but holds any other directorship or directorships, particulars of that directorship or of some one of those directorships;"; and

(b) subsection (3) and substituting therefor the following—

"(3) A company shall, within fourteen days of any change in the appointment of a director, give notice to the Registrar of the change in the prescribed form.

(3A) The inclusion in the annual return of a company of a statement of the names of a company's directors shall not be taken to satisfy the duty imposed by subsection (3).".

nsertion of new section 351A in principal Act.

8. The principal Act is amended by inserting next after section 351 the following—

" Powers of Registrar *re* Form BRF 1.

Sixteenth Schedule.

351A.—(1) Where the Registrar receives an application in the form set out as Form BRF 1 in the Sixteenth Schedule, the Registrar shall—

(a) use such of the information on the form BRF 1 as is relevant to the functions of the Registrar under the Companies Act or Registration of Business Names Act; and

(b) transmit the relevant portions of the information to each public body that is by law required to perform the function for which the applicant is applying, as is indicated on the duly completed Form BRF 1.

(2) The delivery to the Registrar of the duly completed Form BRF 1 shall be an application for such of the following as is required by the applicant in the Form—

(a) a taxpayer registration number under the Revenue Administration Act or any subsidiary legislation made thereunder;

(b) registration under the General Consumption Tax Act or any subsidiary legislation made thereunder to facilitate the payment of general consumption tax;

(c) registration under the National Insurance Act;

(d) registration under the National Housing Trust Act as an employer;

(e) a tax compliance certificate for a new company under the Revenue Administration Act; and

(f) such other application as may be made under the Form.

(3) Except as may be required under any other law or as provided for in paragraph (b) of subsection (1), the Registrar shall not disclose the information referred to in that paragraph in any other circumstance.".

Amendment of section 393 of principal Act.

9. Section 393 of the principal Act is amended in subsection (2) by—

(a) re-lettering paragraphs (b) and (c) as paragraphs (c) and (d), respectively; and

(b) inserting next after paragraph (a) the following—

"(b) requiring or permitting articles of incorporation, forms, returns, notices or other documents required to be sent to the Registrar, to be created, stored or communicated electronically;".

Insertion of new Sixteenth Schedule in principal Act.

First Schedule.

10. The principal Act is amended by inserting next after the Fifteenth Schedule the heading and form set out in the First Schedule to this Act, as the Sixteenth Schedule.

Validation and indemnity.

Second Schedule.

11.—(1) Notwithstanding anything to the contrary in any other enactment, the making and use, in good faith, of the forms set out as Forms 2 and 17 in the Second Schedule to this Act by the Registrar of Companies, and the collection of the prescribed fees in connection therewith, during the period commencing from the 1st day of February, 2005 and ending on the date of commencement of this Act, without the same having been made or done in the manner required by law, are declared to have been validly, properly and lawfully made and done with the effect as if made and used in accordance with the procedure prescribed by law.

(2) Every person liable to be legally proceeded against on the ground of any illegality in relation to the making and use of the forms set out as Forms 2 and 17 in the Second Schedule to this Act, and the collection of the prescribed fees in connection therewith, which was done in good faith is hereby freed, acquitted, discharged and indemnified against The Queen's Most Excellent Majesty, Her Heirs and Successors as well as against all other persons whatsoever from liability.

Amendment of enactments.

Third Schedule.

12. The provisions of the enactments referred to in the first column of the Third Schedule are amended in the manner specified in the second column of the Third Schedule.

FIRST SCHEDULE (Section 10)

FORM BRF1

SIXTEENTH SCHEDULE (Sections 3, 106, 183 and 351A)

Business Registration Form No: BRF1

Application for : New Companies, New Business Names, TRN, NIS, TCC, GCT, HEART/NTA & NHT

Under THE REGISTRATION OF BUSINESS NAMES ACT, THE REVENUE ADMINISTRATION ACT, NATIONAL INSURANCE ACT, COMPANIES ACT & THE GENERAL CONSUMPTION TAX ACT

Instructions/Information

Usage: *This form should be used by all customers when creating either a new Company or new Business Name. It is a substitute for the following forms when creating a New Company ONLY:*

+ *Form 20 - Notice of Appointment of/Change of Company Secretary*
+ *Form 2 - Declaration of Compliance*
+ *Form 23 - Notice of Appointment of/Change of Directors*
+ *Form 17 - Notice of Address of Registered Office or Notice of Change of Registered Office*

It also substitutes for the following forms when creating a New Business Name ONLY:

+ *BN1 - Application for Registration by Sole Proprietor (Individual)*
+ *BN2 - Application for Registration by Partnership*
+ *BN3 - Application for Registration by Corporate Proprietor*

Application for TRN, NIS, GCT, TCC, HEART-NTA and NHT will be done automatically for New Companies Only.

Application for TRN, NIS, HEART-NTA and NHT will be done automatically for New Business Name.

The form is broken down as follows:

+ *Section A - Business/Company Information (Basic information required to create new company or business names)*
+ *Section B - Directors/Proprietors Information - Individuals (Data on the individual directors/proprietors for the new entity)*
+ *Section C - Directors/Proprietors Information - Companies (When a company is a director/proprietor for the new entity)*
+ *Section D - Particulars of Company Secretary (Applicable only to New Companies and when a director is not the secretary)*
+ *Section E - GCT Registration (Request for specific data for a successful registration for GCT. Applicable ONLY to New Companies)*
+ *Section F - Tax Compliance Certificate (Applicable to New Company registration Only)*
+ *Section G - Declaration (To be signed by the Principal Officer (or Authorised Official) of the new company or business name)*
+ *Section H - Filed By (To be completed by the person submitting the form at the COJ)*
+ *Section I - Directors/Proprietors TRN (The TRN for each director/proprietor is required in this section)*

General:

* *Please PRINT or TYPE the required information. Use blue or black ink pen only*
* *Tick the appropriate box where required and write in bold capitals in all fields*
* *Underlined prompts indicate mandatory data entry is required*
* *When entering telephone numbers the area code is required*
* *Complete Form 2 if the new Business name or company will have a branch*

When creating a New Company:

* *One of the following forms must also be submitted with this form:*
  + *Form 1A - Articles of Incorporation -Company Limited by Shares*
  + *Form 1B - Articles of Incorporation -Company Limited by Guarantee Without a Share Capital*
  + *Form 1C - Articles of Incorporation -Company Limited by Guarantee with Share Capital*
  + *Form 1D - Articles of Incorporation -Unlimited Company*
* *Also complete the following sections:*
  + *Section A, Section B, Section C, Section D, Section E, Section F, Section G, Section H & Section I - where applicable*
* *Complete Form 2 if Branches will be registered*

When creating a New Business Name:

* *Please complete the following sections: Section A, Section B, Section C, Section G, Section H & Section I - where applicable*
* *Complete Form 2 if Branches will be registered*

Registration for General Consumption Tax(GCT) - Only Applicable to New Company:

* *GCT Registration is determined by a person's business activity. i.e., depending on a person's "Nature of Business". Businesses will be registered as Registered Person and issued with a Notice of Registration. When the business starts to operate if gross sales is above the threshold TAJ is to be informed so that the registration status can be changed to that of Registered Taxpayer. Registered Taxpayers are issued Registration Certificates which authorizes them to collect and account for the tax.*

Registration for Tax Compliance Certificate (TCC) - Only Applicable to New Company:

* *Tax Compliance Certificate is a document issued to a company as proof that payments of tax liabilities and wage-related statutory deductions are up-to-date. Applying for TCC using this form will only be facilitated for new companies, that is companies registered under the Companies Act. TCC will have a tenure of a maximum of 90 days.*

PLEASE SEE OVERLEAF FOR CONTINUATION OF FORM

SECTION A - Business/Company Information *(General information for the Companies or Businesses. This section is mandatory)*

1a Type of Registration/ Incorporation ☐ Company ☐ Business Name

1b. Type of Organisation ☐ Government ☐ Non-Profit ☐ Other

2a.Commencement Date (Business Name) OR Projected Start Date (Companies) ______ *dd/mm/yyyy*

2b. If Company, indicate classification ☐ Private ☐ Public

3a. Name of Business/Company (Primary)

4a. If Business Name, provide any other Name

3b. Justification of Primary Name (where applicable) *See list on page 11*

4b. Justification of Other Name (where applicable) *See list on page 11*

5a. If Business Name, indicate Type ☐ Sole Proprietor -Individual ☐ Sole Proprietor -Company ☐ Partnership

5b. State the number of branches and complete a Form BRF2 for each Branch *(Both Company & Business Name)*

6a. Business Names/ Company Registered Address ☐ Same as Actual Business Location ☐ Same as Mailing Address

Location ______ *Building/Complex/Apt/Suite*

Street ______ *Number* ______ *Name*

Town/District ______ *City/Town/District*

Post Office ______ P. O. Box ______

Parish ______ Postal Code ______

Country ______

6b. Actual Business Location (if different from number 6a)

Location ______ *Building/Complex/Apt/Suite*

Street ______ *Number* ______ *Name*

Town/District ______ *City/Town/District*

Post Office ______ P. O. Box ______

Parish ______ Postal Code ______

Country ______

6c. Location of Office Records ☐ Registered Address ☐ Actual Business Location ☐ Mailing Address *(Use Schedule 5 for Mailing Address)*

7a. Tel ______ 7b. Cell ______ 7c. Fax ______

7d. Email-Address ______

Nature of Business Name/Core Business of Company

8a. Primary Nature ______ 8b. Secondary Nature ______

8c If Business Name, provide nature phrase ______

9a Number of Employees ______

9b. Expecting Payroll Greater Than $14,444 per month? ☐ Yes ☐ No

9c. Will there be a single annual return (SO2) for all branches? ☐ Yes ☐ No

10. If Business Name, complete the following where applicable

10a Date First Employee Commenced Employment ______ *dd/mm/yyyy*

10b Date Accounting Year Begins ______ *mm/yyyy*

10c Name of Auditing Firm/Accountant ______

11. Number of Directors/Proprietors ______

PLEASE SEE OVERLEAF FOR CONTINUATION OF FORM Page 2/13

SECTION B - Directors/Proprietors Information - Individuals *(Data on the individual director/proprietor. This section is mandatory)*

(Note: When creating a new company only ONE Director can be named Company Secretary and if so indicated, than Section D should NOT be completed. Otherwise Section D must be filled in. Also if only one director is named, than a different person must be named secretary)

Principal - Director/Proprietor Only ☐ Yes ☐ No *(Only one Individual or Corporate Director/Proprietor must be indicated. See Page 6)*

12a. Name ______ Last ______ First ______ Middle

Job Title/ Occupation ______

Present Nationality ______ *See page 10 for more details regarding other supporting documentation*

Tel. ______ Cell ______

Original Nationality ______ *(if different from present nationality)*

18 Years & Over ? ☐ Yes ☐ No Sex ☐ Female ☐ Male

Location ______ *Building/Complex/Apt/Suite*

Street ______ *Number* ______ *Name*

Town/District ______ *City/Town/District*

Post Office ______ P. O. Box ______

Parish ______ Postal Code ______

Country ______

To the best of my knowledge and belief, all the requirements of the Companies Act, Registration of Business Name Act, The Revenue Administration Act, National Insurance Act & General Consumption Tax Act, in respect of matters precedent to the formation of a business name and incorporation of a company have been complied with.

Signature ______

(If creating a new company, complete the following fields if applicable)

Is this person also the Company Secretary? ☐ Yes ☐ No

Particulars of Any Other Directorship held *(Complete only if the director has no other business occupation)*

Company Name ______

Company Number ______ Company TRN ______

Location ______ *Building/Complex/Apt/Suite*

Street ______ *Number* ______ *Name*

Town/District ______ *City/Town/District*

Post Office ______ P. O. Box ______

Parish ______ Postal Code ______

Country ______

Only to be completed by applicants required to present certification from a Professional or Regulatory body when certain words referring to a trade, profession or, occupation form part of the business (Example: "Medical", "Engineer/Engineering", "Daycare", "Accounting", "Dental", etc). See complete list on pages 12 &13

Field or Profession ______ Expiry Date ______ *dd/mm/yyyy*

Certifying Body ______ Certification # ______

Have you provided the relevant certification as part of your application ? ☐ Yes ☐ No

12b. Name ______ Last ______ First ______ Middle

Job Title/ Occupation ______

Present Nationality ______ *See page 10 for more details regarding other supporting documentation*

Tel. ______ Cell ______

Original Nationality ______ *(If different from present nationality)*

18 Years & Over ? ☐ Yes ☐ No Sex ☐ Female ☐ Male

PLEASE SEE OVERLEAF FOR CONTINUATION OF FORM Page 5/13

Location __________
Building/Complex/Apt/Suite

Street ____ __________
Number *Name*

Town/District __________
City/Town/District

Post Office __________ P. O. Box ____

Parish __________ Postal Code ____

Country __________

To the best of my knowledge and belief, all the requirements of the Companies Act, Registration of Business Name Act, The Revenue Administration Act, National Insurance Act & General Consumption Tax Act, in respect of matters precedent to the formation of a business name and incorporation of a company have been complied with.

Signature __________

(If creating a new company, complete the following fields if applicable)

Is this person also the Company Secretary? ☐ Yes ☐ No

Particulars of Any Other Directorship held *(Complete only if the director has no other business occupation)*

Company Name __________

Company Number __________ Company TRN __________

Location __________
Building/Complex/Apt/Suite

Street ____ __________
Number *Name*

Town/District __________
City/Town/District

Post Office __________ P. O. Box ____

Parish __________ Postal Code ____

Country __________

Only to be completed by applicants required to present certification from a Professional or Regulatory body when certain words referring to a trade, profession or, occupation form part of the business (Example: "Medical", "Engineer/Engineering", "Daycare", "Accounting", "Dental", etc). See complete list on pages 12 &13

Field or Profession __________ Expiry Date __________ *dd/mm/yyyy*

Certifying Body __________ Certification # __________

Have you provided the relevant certification as part of your application ? ☐ Yes ☐ No

12c. Name __________ __________ __________
Last *First* *Middle*

Job Title/ Occupation __________

Present Nationality __________ *See page 10 for more details regarding other supporting documentation*

Tel. __________ Cell __________

Original Nationality __________ *(if different from present nationality)*

18 Years & Over ? ☐ Yes ☐ No Sex ☐ Female ☐ Male

Location __________
Building/Complex/Apt/Suite

Street ____ __________
Number *Name*

Town/District __________
City/Town/District

Post Office __________ P. O. Box ____

Parish __________ Postal Code ____

Country __________

(If creating a new company, complete the following fields if applicable)

Is this person also the Company Secretary? ☐ Yes ☐ No

Particulars of Any Other Directorship held *(Complete only if the director has no other business occupation)*

Company Name __________

Company Number __________ Company TRN __________

Location __________
Building/Complex/Apt/Suite

PLEASE SEE OVERLEAF FOR CONTINUATION OF FORM

To the best of my knowledge and belief, all the requirements of the Companies Act, Registration of Business Name Act, The Revenue Administration Act, National Insurance Act & General Consumption Tax Act, in respect of matters precedent to the formation of a business name and incorporation of a company have been complied with.

Signature

Street ____ (Number) ____ (Name)

Town/District ____ (City/Town/District)

Post Office ____ P. O. Box ____

Parish ____ Postal Code ____

Country ____

Only to be completed by applicants required to present certification from a Professional or Regulatory body when certain words referring to a trade, profession or, occupation form part of the business (Example: "Medical", "Engineer/Engineering", "Daycare", "Accounting", "Dentist", etc). See complete list on pages 12 & 13

Field or Profession ____ Expiry Date ____ (dd/mm/yyyy)

Certifying Body ____ Certification # ____

Have you provided the relevant certification as part of your application ? ☐ Yes ☐ No

12d. Name ____ (Last) ____ (First) ____ (Middle)

Title/Occupation ____

Present Nationality ____

Tel. ____ Cell ____

Original Nationality ____ *(if different from present nationality)*

See page 10 for more details regarding other supporting documentation

18 Years & Over ? ☐ Yes ☐ No Sex ☐ Female ☐ Male

Location ____ (Building/Complex/Apt/Suite)

Street ____ (Number) ____ (Name)

Town/District ____ (City/Town/District)

Post Office ____ P. O. Box ____

Parish ____ Postal Code ____

Country ____

To the best of my knowledge and belief, all the requirements of the Companies Act, Registration of Business Name Act, The Revenue Administration Act, National Insurance Act & General Consumption Tax Act, in respect of matters precedent to the formation of a business name and incorporation of a company have been complied with.

Signature

(If creating a new company, complete the following fields if applicable)

Is this person also the Company Secretary? ☐ Yes ☐ No

Particulars of Any Other Directorship held *(Complete only if the director has no other business occupation)*

Company Name ____

Company Number ____ Company TRN ____

Location ____ (Building/Complex/Apt/Suite)

Street ____ (Number) ____ (Name)

Town/District ____ (City/Town/District)

Post Office ____ P. O. Box ____

Parish ____ Postal Code ____

Country ____

PLEASE SEE OVERLEAF FOR CONTINUATION OF FORM Page 5/13

Only to be completed by applicants required to present certification from a Professional or Regulatory body when certain words referring to a trade, profession or, occupation form part of the business (Example:"Medical", "Engineer/Engineering", "Daycare", "Accounting", "Dental", etc). *See complete list on pages 12 &13*

Field or Profession ____ Expiry Date ____ dd/mm/yyyy

Certifying Body ____ Certification # ____

Have you provided the relevant certification as part of your application ? ☐ Yes ☐ No

To add more directors/proprietors, fill-in Schedule 1 and attach it to the back of this form Is Schedule Attached? ☐ Yes ☐ No

SECTION C - Directors/Proprietors Information - Companies *(Complete ONLY if there is a Corporate Director/Proprietor)*

Principal - Director/Proprietor Only ☐ Yes ☐ No *(Only one individual or Corporate Director/Proprietor must be indicated. See Page 2)*

13a Company Name ____

Company Number ____ Company TRN. ____ Date Incorporated ____ dd/mm/yyyy Classification of Company ☐ Private ☐ Public

Location ____ *Building/Complex/Apt/Suite*

Tel1 ____ Tel2 ____

Street ____ ____ *Number* *Name*

Fax. ____

Town/District ____ *City/Town/District*

Post Office ____ P. O. Box ____

Parish ____ Postal Code ____

Country ____

(Company Seal Should be Affixed if Required By The Company's Articles/Constitution)

Two Officers are required to sign on behalf of the company (If Required By The Company's Articles/Constitution)	Two Officers are required to sign on behalf of the company (If Required By The Company's Articles/Constitution)
Name(1)	Name(2)
Last ____	Last ____
First ____	First ____
Middle ____	Middle ____
Capacity ☐ Director ☐ Secretary ☐ Authorized Official	Capacity ☐ Director ☐ Secretary ☐ Authorized Official
Signature ____	Signature ____
Date Signed ____	Date Signed ____

13b Company Name ____

Company Number ____ Company TRN. ____ Date Incorporated ____ Classification of Company ☐ Private ☐ Public

Location ____ *Building/Complex/Apt/Suite*

Tel1 ____ Tel2 ____

Street ____ ____ *Number* *Name*

Fax. ____

PLEASE SEE OVERLEAF FOR CONTINUATION OF FORM Page 6/13

Town/District ______ (City/Town/District)

Post Office ______ P. O. Box ______

Parish ______ Postal Code ______

Country ______

(Company Seal Should be Affixed If Required By The Company's Articles/Constitution)

Two Officers are required to sign on behalf of the company
(If Required By The Company's Articles/Constitution)

Name(1)
Last ______
First ______
Middle ______

Capacity ☐ Director ☐ Secretary ☐ Authorized Official

Signature ______

Date Signed ______

Two Officers are required to sign on behalf of the company
(If Required By The Company's Articles/Constitution)

Name(2)
Last ______
First ______
Middle ______

Capacity ☐ Director ☐ Secretary ☐ Authorized Official

Signature ______

Date Signed ______

To add more company directors/proprietors, fill-in Schedule 2 and attach it to the back of this form

Is Schedule Attached? ☐ Yes ☐ No

SECTION D - Particulars of Company Secretary *(When creating a company only, complete this section if no director was identified as the company secretary)*

Type of Secretary ☐ Individual ☐ Company

14. Name ______ (Last) ______ (First) ______ (Middle)

Job Title/ Occupation ______

Tel. ______ Cell ______ Nationality ______

Company Name ______

Individual Address

Location ______ (Building/Complex/Apt/Suite)

Street ______ (Number) ______ (Name)

Town/District ______ (City/Town/District)

Post Office ______ P. O. Box ______

Parish ______ Postal Code ______

Country ______

Company's Registered Address

Location ______ (Building/Complex/Apt/Suite)

Street ______ (Number) ______ (Name)

Town/District ______ (City/Town/District)

Post Office ______ P. O. Box ______

Parish ______ Postal Code ______

Country ______

PLEASE SEE OVERLEAF FOR CONTINUATION OF FORM

Page 7/15

SECTION E - GCT REGISTRATION *(Applying for GCT is ONLY applicable for New Companies)*

15. Applying For GCT ☐ Yes ☐ No *(If No, skip to SECTION F)*

16 Gross Income/Sales *(Ie Projected Sales before Expenses)*

	Monthly	Annual
GCT:		

17. Projected Start Date of Taxable Activities

GCT: ______ dd/mm/yyyy

18. GCT Taxable Activities

Primary Activity ______ Secondary Activity ______

19. Would you like an officer from the Tax Department to contact you in order to explain your tax obligations? ☐ Yes ☐ No

20. If you have more than one place of business, state the number of GCT Certificates required ______

21. Are your accounts computerised? ☐ Yes ☐ No ☐ Partly

SECTION F - TAX COMPLIANCE CERTIFICATE *(Applying for TCC is ONLY applicable for New Companies)*

22. Applying For TCC? ☐ Yes ☑ No *(If No, skip to SECTION G)*

25. Certificate is required for (Select one):

☐ Custom Clearance Only *(Please complete fields 24-28)*

☐ Contracts Only

☐ Multi-Purpose

☐ Other (Specify)

______

24. Vessel ______

25. Date Reported ______ dd/mm/yyyy

26. Document Type

☐ Airway Bill

☐ Bill of Sight

☐ Bill of Lading

☐ Detention Notice

☐ Wharf Order

27.Document Number ______

28. Description of Goods ______

SECTION G - DECLARATION

29. To the best of my knowledge and belief, all the requirements of the Companies Act, Registration of Business Name Act, The Revenue Administration Act, National Insurance Act & General Consumption Tax Act, in respect of matters precedent to the formation of a business name and incorporation of a company have been complied with.

Name ______ First

______ Last

Signature ______

Position ______ *(State whether Proprietor, Partner, Director, Manager, Secretary, Office-holder in Club, Association, etc)*

Date ______ dd/mm/yyyy

ID Type *(Please use Declarant ID in Section I on Page 9)*

Email Address ______

PLEASE SEE OVERLEAF FOR CONTINUATION OF FORM

Page 8/15

SECTION H – FILED BY *(Please indicate who will be submitting this document on behalf of the Company or Business Names)*

30. Name ______ ______ ______
Last First Middle

Company Name

Email Address

Location (Building/Complex/Apt/Suite) Tel. Cell

Street (Number, Name) Fax

Town/District (City/Town/District) TRN

Post Office P. O. Box

Parish P/Code

Country

SECTION I – DIRECTORS/PROPRIETORS/SECRETARY TRN *(Kindly sure the names entered in this section match that in Sections B, C & D)*

31. Name (Directors/Proprietors)	Taxpayer Registration Number

Name (Company Secretary if Applicable)	Taxpayer Registration Number

Declarant ID

☐ Driver's License ☐ National Voter's ID ☐ Passport ID Number

FOR OFFICIAL USE ONLY

Customer Service Officer's Name

Date (dd/mm/yyyy)

Remarks

Customer Service Officer's Signature

Nearest Collectorate to Business Name/Company (See List at the back)

Page 9/13

Data Sheet

List of Tax Offices

Clarendon	- Chapelton - Lionel Town - May Pen
Hanover	- Lucea
Kingston	- Kingston
Manchester	- Christiana - Mandeville
Portland	- Buff Bay - Port Antonio
St. Andrew	- Constant Spring - Cross Roads
St Ann	- Brown's Town - Moneague - St. Anns Bay
St. Catherine	- Linstead - Old Harbour - Spanish Town - Portmore
St. Elizabeth	- Santa Cruz - Black River
St. James	- Montego Bay
St. Mary	- Annotto Bay - Port Maria
St. Thomas	- Morant Bay - Port Morant
Trelawny	- Falmouth - Jackson Town
Westmoreland	- Darliston - Savanna-La-Mar

Requirement: Nationality

- Where owners are not of Jamaican/Caricom nationality. The original /certified copy of the valid work permit is required.
- Where owners have become nationals by naturalization or marriage. The original/certified copy of the naturalization documents or marriage certificate is required.
- Where an individual's name has been changed by either marriage or a deed poll a certified copy of this document must be attached.

PLEASE SEE OVERLEAF FOR CONTINUATION OF FORM

JUSTIFICATION WORDS AND RESPONSIBLE TABLE

- *The use of certain words, in the proposed name of a company/business shall be justified to the Registrar's satisfaction prior to registration where-*
  - *The use of the word suggests a connection with the Crown or members of a royal family or suggests royal patronage, for example "Royal", "King", "Princess", "Prince", or "Crown";*
  - *The name suggests a connection with a Government department, statutory undertaking, local authority, or with any Commonwealth or foreign Government;*

Words used in Name	Justification Reasons
1 Global	a) Conducting business globally
2 "Group"	a) Part of the group of companies
3 Holding/(s)	a) The company will be holding shares in other companies b) The company will own other companies
4 "National"	b) Affiliated with other Jamaican entities
5. International,	c) Will be Trading internationally d) Serving clients locally and overseas
6. Caribbean	e) Operating within the Caribbean f) Trading with the Caribbean
7 CARICOM	g) Trading with CARICOM countries
8 Worldwide	h) Trading worldwide i) Conducting business worldwide j) Buying goods worldwide/globally
9. "King", "Princess", "Prince", Queen or "Crown", "Royal",	k) It is my name; It is my address l) Divine Guidance
10. Crown	m) Only Crowne is allowed. No justification required if "e" is at the end
11. "Royal",	n) Only Royale is allowed. No justification required if "e" is at the end
12. Nationality Names contains Nationality for example "British" or "American" etc;	o) Will be trading goods from this country or will be trading with this country p) Will be affiliated with this country
13. A Parish in the name	q) I live in this parish r) I was born in this parish s) Business Operating in the parish
14. A Personal name	t) This is a family name. u) my mother's name, father's name, my name v) If not "a family name" then permission is needed. Submit permission.
15. "Standard" may not be included in a proposed company name unless the Minister has given his consent pursuant to section 13 of the Standards Act	w) Submit permission
16. "Blue Mountain" may only be used where the Coffee Industry Board has so permitted pursuant to the Coffee Industry Regulation Act	x) Submit permission

PLEASE SEE OVERLEAF FOR CONTINUATION OF FORM Page 11/13

CERTIFICATION TABLE - PART 1 OF 2

- *When selecting a nature/the businesses activity, where the use of these words in the nature makes reference to these professions/ occupations certification is required.*
- *The nature must be for profit making, cannot be a charity.*
- *This requires the production of certification from the relevant professional or regulatory body upon submission for registration.*

THE USE OF THESE WORDS IN THE NATURE OR NAME OF BUSINESS MAKING REFERENCE TO THESE PROFESSIONS/ OCCUPATIONS REQUIRE CERTIFICATION	PROFESSIONAL/ REGULATORY BODY	CERTIFICATION	Justification of Name Required	Certification Required Per Company
ACCOUNTANT (PUBLIC)	PUBLIC ACCOUNTANCY BOARD	License	NO	ALL
ACCOUNTANT (Chartered)	ICAJ	PRACTISING CERTIFICATE	NO	ALL
ARCHITECT	ARCHITECTS REGISTRATION BOARD	CERTIFICATE OF REGISTRATION	NO	ALL
Legal Law	GENERAL LEGAL COUNCIL	PRACTISING CERTIFICATE	NO	ALL
ATTORNEY-AT-LAW	GENERAL LEGAL COUNCIL	PRACTISING CERTIFICATE	NO	ALL
BARBER	LOCAL BOARD OF HEALTH for respective Parish Council	LICENCE	NO	ALL
Bank	Bank of Jamaica	LICENCE	NO	ONLY 1
BEAUTY THERAPIST COSMETOLOGIST HAIR DRESSER	LOCAL BOARD OF HEALTH for respective Parish Council	LICENCE	NO	ALL
TRADER IN SECOND HAND GOLD CASH FOR GOLD	RESIDENT MAGISTRATE COURT	LICENCE	NO	ALL
CREDIT BUREAU	Bank of Jamaica	LICENCE	NO	ONLY 1
CUSTOM BROKER	CUSTOM BROKER ASSOCIATION	LICENCE	NO	ALL
DENTIST	DENTAL COUNCIL OF JAMAICA	PRACTISING CERTIFICATE	NO	ALL
DIETICIAN	COUNCIL FOR PROFESSIONS SUPPLEMENTARY TO MEDICINE	PRACTISING CERTIFICATE	NO	ALL
ELECTRICAL INSTALLATION	BOARD OF ELECTRICIANS	LICENCE	NO	ALL
Engineering	PROFESSIONAL ENGINEERS REGISTRATION BOARD	PRACTISING CERTIFICATE	YES	ALL
ENGINEER	PROFESSIONAL ENGINEERS REGISTRATION BOARD	PRACTISING CERTIFICATE	YES	ALL
LAND SURVEYOR	LAND SURVEYORS BOARD	PRACTISING CERTIFICATE	NO	ALL
LOTTERY AGENTS	BETTING, GAMING AND LOTTERIES COMMISSION	LICENCE	NO	ONLY 1
Medical	MEDICAL COUNCIL OF JAMAICA	PRACTISING CERTIFICATE	NO	ALL
MEDICAL PRACTITIONER	MEDICAL COUNCIL OF JAMAICA	PRACTISING CERTIFICATE	NO	ALL
MEDICAL LABORATORY TECHNICIAN	COUNCIL FOR PROFESSIONS SUPPLEMENTARY TO MEDICINE	PRACTISING CERTIFICATE	NO	ALL

PLEASE SEE OVERLEAF FOR CONTINUATION OF FORM

CERTIFICATION TABLE, PART 2 OF 2

- *When selecting a nature/the businesses activity, where the use of these words in the nature makes reference to these professions/ occupations certification is required.*
- *The nature must be for profit making, cannot be a charity.*
- *This requires the production of certification from the relevant professional or regulatory body upon submission for registration.*

THE USE OF THESE WORDS IN THE NATURE OR NAME OF BUSINESS MAKING REFERENCE TO THESE PROFESSIONS/ OCCUPATIONS REQUIRE CERTIFICATION	PROFESSIONAL/ REGULATORY BODY	CERTIFICATION	Justification of Name Required	Certification Required For
NURSE/MID-WIFE	NURSING COUNCIL	CERTIFICATE OF REGISTRATION	NO	ALL
OCCUPATIONAL THERAPIST	COUNCIL FOR PROFESSIONS SUPPLEMENTARY TO MEDICINE	CERTIFICATE OF REGISTRATION	NO	ALL
OPHTHALMOLOGIST	MEDICAL COUNCIL OF JAMAICA	PRACTISING CERTIFICATE	NO	ALL
OPTICIAN/OPTOMETRY PROFESSIONAL	REGISTRAR GENERAL'S DEPARTMENT	LETTER FROM COUNCIL EVIDENCING REGISTRATION / OR COPY OF MOST RECENT GAZETTE SHOWING REGISTRATION	NO	ALL
PEST CONTROL	PESTICIDE CONTROL AUTHORITY	CERTIFICATE OF REGISTRATION	NO	ALL
PHARMACY	PHARMACY COUNCIL OF JAMAICA	No Objection Letter	NO	ONLY 1
PHARMACIST	PHARMACY COUNCIL OF JAMAICA	CERTIFICATE OF REGISTRATION/ PRACTICING CERTIFICATE	NO	ONLY 1
PHYSIOTHERAPIST	COUNCIL FOR PROFESSIONS SUPPLEMENTARY TO MEDICINE	CERTIFICATE OF REGISTRATION	NO	ALL
PROPERTY DEVELOPER (for specific projects)	REAL ESTATE BOARD	LICENCE	NO	ALL
PROPERTY MANAGEMENT	REAL ESTATE BOARD	LICENCE	NO	ALL
RADIOGRAPHERS	COUNCIL FOR PROFESSIONS SUPPLEMENTARY TO MEDICINE	CERTIFICATE OF REGISTRATION	NO	ALL
REAL ESTATE DEALERS/REAL ESTATE SALESMAN	REAL ESTATE BOARD	LICENCE	NO	ALL
RETIREMENT HOMES	MINISTRY OF HEALTH	LETTER FROM MOH	NO	ONLY 1
SCHOOLS; DAY CARE CENTRES; NURSERIES	MINISTRY OF EDUCATION	LETTER FROM MOE	NO	ONLY 1
SPEECH THERAPIST	COUNCIL FOR PROFESSIONS SUPPLEMENTARY TO MEDICINE	CERTIFICATE OF REGISTRATION	NO	ALL
VETERINARY SURGEON	VETERINARY COUNCIL OF JAMAICA	CERTIFICATE OF REGISTRATION	NO	ALL

END OF FORM

Page 13/13

Business Registration Form

Schedule 1

Application for : New Companies, New Business Names, TRN, NIS, TCC, GCT & SCT, HEART/NTA & NHT

Under THE REGISTRATION BUSINESS NAMES ACT, THE REVENUE ADMINISTRATION ACT, NATIONAL INSURANCE ACT, COMPANIES ACT & THE GENERAL CONSUMPTION TAX ACT

Instructions/Information

Usage:
- *This schedule should only be used once Section B on the Form BR1 is fully utilised*
- *One schedule for each added director/proprietor*

Directors/Proprietors Information - Individuals *(Data on the individual director/proprietor)*

12. Name ______ *Last* ______ *First* ______ *Middle*

Title/Occupation ______

Present Nationality ______

18 Years & Over ? ☐ Yes ☐ No

Sex ☐ Female ☐ Male

Original Nationality ______ *(if different from present nationality)*

Tel. ______ Cell ______

Location ______ *Building/Complex/Apt/Suite*

Street ______ *Number* ______ *Name*

Town/District ______ *City/Town/District*

Post Office ______ P. O. Box ______

Parish ______ Postal Code ______

Country ______

To the best of my knowledge and belief, all the requirements of the Companies Act, Registration of Business Name Act, The Revenue Administration Act, National Insurance Act & General Consumption Tax Act, in respect of matters precedent to the formation of a business names and incorporation of a company have been complied with.

Signature ______

(If creating a new company, complete the following fields if applicable)

Is this personal also the Company Secretary? ☐ Yes ☐ No

Particulars of Any Other Directorship held *(Complete only if the director has no other business occupation)*

Company Name ______

Company Number ______ Company TRN ______

Location ______ *Building/Complex/Apt/Suite*

Street ______ *Number* ______ *Name*

Town/District ______ *City/Town/District*

Post Office ______ P. O. Box ______

Parish ______ Postal Code ______

Country ______

Only to be completed by applicants required to present certification from a Professional or Regulatory body when certain words referring to a trade, profession or, occupation form part of the business (Example: "Medical", "Engineer/Engineering", "Daycare", "Accounting", "Dental", etc). See complete list on pages 12 &13

Field or Profession ______

Expiry Date ______ *dd/mm/yyyy*

Certifying Body ______

Certification # ______

Have you provided the relevant certification as part of your application ? ☐ Yes ☐ No

END OF SCHEDULE 1

Page 1/1

Business Registration Form

Schedule 2

Application for : New Companies, New Business Names, TRN, NIS, TCC, GCT & SCT, HEART/NTA & NHT
Under THE REGISTRATION BUSINESS NAMES ACT, THE REVENUE ADMINISTRATION ACT, NATIONAL INSURANCE ACT, COMPANIES ACT & THE GENERAL CONSUMPTION TAX ACT

Instructions/Information

Usage:

- *This schedule should only be used once Section C on the Form BR1 is fully utilised*
- *One schedule for each added company director/proprietor*

Directors/Proprietors Information - Companies *(When a company is a director/proprietor)*

13 Company Name

Company Number | Company TRN. | Date Incorporated (dd/mm/yyyy) | Classification of Company ☐ Private ☐ Public

Location (*Building/Complex/Apt/Suite*)

Tel1. | Tel2

Street (*Number* / *Name*)

Fax.

Town/District (*City/Town/District*)

Post Office | P. O. Box

Parish | Postal Code

Country

(Company Seal Should be Affixed If Required By The Company's Articles/Constitution)

Two Officers are required to sign on behalf of the company (If Required By The Company's Articles/Constitution)	Two Officers are required to sign on behalf of the company (If Required By The Company's Articles/Constitution)
Name(1)	Name(2)
Last	Last
First	First
Middle	Middle
Capacity ☐ Director ☐ Secretary ☐ Authorized Official	Capacity ☐ Director ☐ Secretary ☐ Authorized Official
Signature	Signature
Date Signed	Date Signed

END OF SCHEDULE 2 Page 1/1

Business Registration Form **Schedule 5**

Application for : New Companies, New Business Names, TRN, NIS, TCC, GCT & SCT, HEART/NTA & NHT
Under THE REGISTRATION BUSINESS NAMES ACT, THE REVENUE ADMINISTRATION ACT, NATIONAL INSURANCE ACT, COMPANIES ACT & THE GENERAL CONSUMPTION TAX ACT

Instructions/Information

Usage:

- *This schedule should only be used once a mailing address is required under Section A on Form BRF1*

Mailing Address

Location

Building/Complex/Apt/Suite

Street

Number *Name*

Town/District

City/Town/District

Post Office P. O. Box

Parish Postal Code

Country

END OF SCHEDULE 5 Page 1/1

Business Registration Form - Branch Information

Schedule 4

New Business Names & Companies

Application for : New Companies, New Business Names, TRN, NIS, TCC, GCT & SCT, HEART/NTA & NHT

Under THE REGISTRATION BUSINESS NAMES ACT, THE REVENUE ADMINISTRATION ACT, NATIONAL INSURANCE ACT, COMPANIES ACT & THE GENERAL CONSUMPTION TAX ACT

INSTRUCTIONS: This form is to be submitted with a Form 1 once Box 5c on the Form BR1 was completed. Please PRINT or TYPE the required information. Use blue or black ink pen only. Tick appropriate box where required. Underline prompts indicate mandatory data entry is required

SECTION A - Branch Information

1. Business Name/Company Name *(Should be the same name entered on the Form BRF1)*

2a. Branch Name

2b. Justification of Branch Name (where applicable) *(This field is only applicable to Business Names registration only)*

(Nature of the Branch for New Business Names Only)

2c. Primary Nature

2d. Secondary Nature

2e. Will this branch be filing a different annual return (SO2) from the parent Company/Business Name? ☐ Yes ☐ No

3a. Tel

3b. Cell

3c. Fax

3d. Email-Address

4a. Branch Address	4b. Branch Mailing Address (if different from 4a)
Location *Building/Complex/Apt/Suite*	Location *Building/Complex/Apt/Suite*
Street *Number* *Name*	Street *Number* *Name*
Town/District *City/Town/District*	Town/District *City/Town/District*
Post Office P. O. Box	Post Office P. O. Box
Parish Postal Code	Parish Postal Code
Country	Country

SECTION B - DECLARATION

5. I declare that the information given in this form is to the best of my knowledge and belief a true and correct statement.

Name

Signature

Position *(State whether Proprietor, Partner, Director, Manager Secretary, Office-holder in Club, Association, etc)*

Date *dd/mm/yyyy*

END OF FORM Page 1/1

SECOND SCHEDULE (Section 11)

FORM 2
INSTRUCTIONS ON REVERSE

JAMAICA
THE COMPANIES ACT
DECLARATION OF COMPLIANCE
(Pursuant to section 13 (2))

1. NAME OF COMPANY ______________________

1A. COMPANY FAX NUMBER ____________ 1B. TYPE OF COMPANY:

PRIVATE ☐ PUBLIC ☐

2. I, ____
(PRINT NAME)

____
(STATE FULL RESIDENTIAL / BUSINESS ADDRESS)

____

____

do solemnly and sincerely declare as follows:

3. ☐ I am an Attorney -at - Law of the Supreme Court of Jamaica engaged in the formation of the company named herein;

☐ I am a person named in the Articles of Incorporation as a director or secretary of the company named herein or

☐ I am a member of the Institute of Chartered Secretaries & Administrators engaged in the formation of the company named herein.

(INDICATE CAPACITY)

To the best of my knowledge and belief, all the requirements of the Companies Act, in respect of matters precedent to the formation and incorporation of a company have been complied with and I make this solemn declaration conscientiously believing the same to be true and by virtue of the Voluntary Declarations Act.

TAKEN AND ACKNOWLEDGED by	)	
the said	)	
at	)	
in the parish of	)	______________________
this day of	)	
Before me:	)	

____

JUSTICE OF THE PEACE ☐
for the parish of:

NOTARY PUBLIC ☐

COMMISSIONER OF OATHS ☐

(INDICATE CAPACITY)

NAME:		
ADDRESS:	STREET	
	TOWN	
	POST OFFICE	
	PARISH	
E-MAIL ADDRESS:		
CONTACT NUMBER:		
FAX NUMBER:		

7. TAXPAYER REGISTRATION NUMBER OF PERSON MAKING THE DECLARATION

TAXPAYER REGISTRATION NUMBER (TRN)	

"FOR OFFICIAL USE ONLY"

COMPANY NUMBER: ______________________

FILED: __________ / ______________ / __________
DAY MONTH YEAR

FORM 17
INSTRUCTIONS ON THE REVERSE

JAMAICA

THE COMPANIES ACT

NOTICE OF ADDRESS OF REGISTERED OFFICE
OR
NOTICE OF CHANGE OF ADDRESS OF REGISTERED OFFICE
(Pursuant to section 106)

1. NAME OF COMPANY

1A. COMPANY NUMBER

1B. COMPANY TAXPAYER REGISTRATION NUMBER

1C. COMPANY FAX NUMBER

1D. TYPE OF COMPANY:

PRIVATE ☐ PUBLIC ☐

2. LOCATION OF REGISTERED OFFICE

STREET	
TOWN	
POST OFFICE	
PARISH	

2A. MAILING ADDRESS

STREET	
TOWN	
POST OFFICE	
PARISH	

3. EFFECTIVE DATE OF CHANGE (if applicable)

4. PREVIOUS ADDRESS OF REGISTERED OFFICE (If applicable)

STREET	
TOWN	
POST OFFICE	
PARISH	

5.

DATE	PRINTED NAME	SIGNATURE	CONTACT #

CAPACITY:

☐ DIRECTOR
☐ SECRETARY
☐ AUTHORIZED OFFICIAL

6. FILED BY:

NAME:		
ADDRESS:	STREET	
	TOWN	
	POST OFFICE	
	PARISH	
E-MAIL ADDRESS:		
CONTACT NUMBER:		
FAX NUMBER:		

"FOR OFFICIAL USE ONLY"

COMPANY NUMBER: ____________________

FILED: ______ / ______ / ______
DAY MONTH YEAR

JAMAICA

THE COMPANIES ACT
NOTICE OF ADDRESS OF REGISTERED OFFICE OR
NOTICE OF CHANGE OF ADDRESS OF REISTERED OFFICE

FORM 17

INSTRUCTIONS

GENERAL

This document is required to be filed with the Office of the Registrar of Companies and must conform to the requirement under the Act. Where any provision required to be set out is too long for the space provided in the form, the form may incorporate the provisions by annexing a schedule in such manner as may be prescribed under the Act.

Complete Items 1, 1C, 1D, 2, 5 and 6 for new companies.
Complete Items 1 – 6 for changes in the address of the registered office of existing companies.

ITEM 1, 1A, 1B, 1C & 1D

- Set out the full legal name of the company.
- Set out Company number assigned by the Registrar of Companies if it is a change of registered office.
- Set out Company Taxpayer Registration Number if it is a change of the registered office. (The Company Taxpayer Registration Number will be photocopied by the Registrar of Companies and returned. Individuals may, instead of bringing the Taxpayer Registration Card into the Offices of the Registrar of Companies, provide a certified copy of the same). An Attorney –at – Law, a Justice of the Peace, or a Notary Public may certify the copy of the Taxpayer Registration Number. Where the copy is certified by a Justice of the Peace or a Notary Public they must affix the relevant seal of their office.
- Set out, where applicable the company fax number.
- Indicate whether the company is a private or a public company.

NOTE: Once certified copies of the Taxpayer Registration Number have been supplied to the Registrar of Companies or the Registrar of Companies has seen the original Taxpayer Registration Card and made a copy of the same the company need only affix the number to any documents being subsequently filed.

ITEM 2 & 2A

(i) Set out in full the location at which the registered office is situated or to which it has been changed, including the name of the street, and if located in a multi- office building, the relevant room number. The registered office must be an actual physical location and might include the relevant district and parish. However it cannot be a post office box. Upon any change in the location of the registered office a new notice will have to be filed.

(ii) The mailing address may include a post office box number, if the mailing address is same as the registered office, state 'SAME AS ABOVE AT ITEM 2'

ITEM 3

State the date when the change of registered office is to take effect.

ITEM 4

Set out the previous address of the registered office, where applicable.

- NOTE THE INSTRUCTIONS SET OUT AT ITEM 2 (i) above.

ITEM 5

- FOR NEW COMPANIES

If this form is filed with Articles of Incorporation in the prescribed form, the director or secretary named in the Articles of Incorporation, the attorney – at – law or chartered secretary and administrator engaged in the formation of the company shall sign the notice.

THIRD SCHEDULE (Section 12)

Amendment of Enactments

Provision	*Amendment*
Companies Act.	
Companies (Forms) Rules, 2005.	Insert in the Schedule in the appropriate numerical sequence as Form 17 the form set out as Form 17 in the Second Schedule to the Companies (Amendment) Act, 2013.
General Consumption Tax Act.	
New section 28A.	Insert next after section 28 the following—
	" Requirement to submit information. 28A. With effect from the date of commencement of the Companies (Amendment) Act, 2013, any person applying to register a company under the Companies Act or a business name under the Registration of Business Names Act shall, if the company will be or the person is required to register as a taxpayer under this Act (and, in the case of a person applying for registration of a business name, if the person is not already registered as a taxpayer under this Act), complete and submit to the Registrar of Companies the appropriate section of the form set out as Form BRF 1 in the Sixteenth Schedule to the Companies Act.".
National Housing Trust Act.	
New section 12A.	Insert next after section 12 the following—
	" Requirement to submit information regarding employees. 12A. With effect from the date of commencement of the Companies (Amendment) Act,

Provision	*Amendment*
	2013, any person applying to register a company under the Companies Act or a business name under the Registration of Business Names Act shall, if the company will be or the person is required to be registered with the Trust as an employer (and, in the case of a person applying for registration of a business name, if the person is not already registered with the Trust as an employer), complete and submit to the Registrar of Companies the appropriate section of the form set out as Form BRF 1 in the Sixteenth Schedule to the Companies Act.".
National Insurance Act.	
New section 6A.	Insert next after section 6 the following—
	" Requirement to register employees. 6A. With effect from the date of commencement of the Companies (Amendment) Act, 2013, any person applying to register a company under the Companies Act or a business name under the Registration of Business Names Act shall if it is intended for the company or person to employ one or more persons (and, in the case of a person applying for registration of a business name, if the person is not already registered as an employer under this Act), complete and submit to the Registrar of Companies the appropriate section of the form set out as Form BRF 1 in the Sixteenth Schedule to the Companies Act.".

Registration of Business Names Act.

Registration of Business Names Rules, 1934.

Rule 11. Insert immediately after the word "Act" the words "so, however, that on or after the date of commencement of the Companies (Amendment) Act, 2013, the form set out as Form BRF 1 in the Sixteenth Schedule to the Companies Act shall be used for the purpose of registration of business names and the forms set out, respectively, as Form B.N.1, Form B.N. 2, and Form B.N. 3 shall be used, as appropriate, for the renewal of registration of business names".

Tax Administration of Jamaica Act.

New section 17O. Insert next after section 17N the following—

" Requirement to submit information regarding TRN and TCC.

17O. With effect from the date of commencement of the Companies (Amendment) Act, 2013, any person applying to register a company under the Companies Act or a business name under the Registration of Business Names Act shall apply for a Taxpayer Registration Number, and may apply for a Tax Compliance Certificate, by completing and submitting to the Registrar of Companies the appropriate sections of the form set out as Form BRF 1 in the Sixteenth Schedule to the Companies Act.".

Amendments No. 11 – 2017

JAMAICA

No. 11–2017

I assent,

[L.S.]

PATRICK LINTON ALLEN,
Governor-General.

21st day of June, 2017.

AN ACT to Amend the Companies Act.

[*21st June, 2017*]

BE IT ENACTED by The Queen's Most Excellent Majesty, by and with the advice and consent of the Senate and House of Representatives of Jamaica, and by the authority of the same, as follows:—

Short title and construction.

1. This Act may be cited as the Companies (Amendment) Act, 2017, and shall be read and construed as one with the Companies Act (hereinafter referred to as the "principal Act") and all amendments thereto.

Amendment of principal Act.

2. The principal Act is amended by deleting the words "the Island", and all its cognate expressions, wherever they appear and substituting therefor, in each case, the word "Jamaica".

Amendment of section 2 of principal Act.

3. Section 2 of the principal Act is amended—

(a) in subsection (1) by—

(i) deleting the definition of "share warrant";

(ii) inserting in the correct alphabetical sequence the following definitions—

" "beneficial owner"—

(a) in relation to shares, means the individual on whose behalf the shares are held or on whose behalf a share transaction is conducted;

(b) in relation to a company, means the individual who exercises ultimate ownership or ultimate effective control;

"specified date" means the date of commencement of the Companies (Amendment) Act, 2017;

"ultimate effective control" means the control exercised by an individual who—

(a) is in a position to determine the policy of the company or to make the final determination as to the decisions to be made by the company; or

(b) by himself or together with a connected person within the meaning of subsection (7) is in a position to control more than fifty percent of the voting power in the company or would hold interest in more than fifty percent of the issued shares of the company;

"ultimate ownership" means any situation in which ownership of a company is exercised by means of control other than direct control, and includes any arrangement utilizing one or more persons through which beneficial ownership of a company is established;";

(b) inserting next after subsection (6) the following—

" (7) For the purposes of subsection (2), the following persons shall be treated as being connected with a given person "A", and the person with A, and shall be so treated notwithstanding that at the relevant time any of the persons in question (not being individuals) had not yet come into existence or ceased to exist—

(a) a holding company or subsidiary of A;

(b) a subsidiary of a holding company of A;

(c) a holding company of a subsidiary of A;

(d) any company of which A has control;

(e) any company of which A and persons connected with A together have control;

(f) any company which together with A constitute a group;

(g) an individual who is a director, manager or a person who has control of A or any partner or any immediate relative of such director, manager or person aforesaid;

(h) any company of which any of the persons referred to in sub-paragraph (g) is a director, manager or has control.

(8) For the purposes of subsection (7)(f), "group" in relation to a company means that company and—

(a) any other company which is its holding company or subsidiary;

(b) any other company which is a subsidiary of the holding company;

(c) any company which is controlled by a person who directly or indirectly controls or is controlled by any company referred to in paragraph (a) or (b);

(d) any company which is controlled by a person referred to in paragraph (a), (b) or (c).

(9) Notwithstanding section 151, for the purposes of subsections (7) and (8), a company is a holding company of any company that is its immediate, intermediate or ultimate subsidiary, whether the holding company holds that other company's shares on trust or is the beneficial owner of such shares.".

Amendment of section 8 of principal Act.

4. Section 8 of the principal Act is amended by deleting subsection (6) and substituting therefor the following—

" (6) As applicable to the case, the articles of—

First Schedule. Tables A, B and D.

(a) a company limited by shares may include the articles specified in Table A of the First Schedule;

(b) a company limited by guarantee and not having a share capital may include the articles specified in Table B of the First Schedule;

(c) a company limited by guarantee and having a share capital may include, as appropriate, the articles specified in Table A or Table B of the First Schedule; and

(d) an unlimited company having a share capital may include the articles specified in Table D of the First Schedule.

except to the extent that they are excluded in whole or in part or modified.".

5. Section 58(4) of the principal Act is amended by deleting the words "by the company's directors" and substituting therefor the words "by not less than seventy-five percent of the company's directors". Amendment of section 58 of principal Act.

6. Section 60 of the principal Act is amended— Amendment of section 60 of principal Act.

(a) by deleting the marginal note and substituting therefor the following—

"Notice to shareholders and Registrar of acquisition by company of its shares.";

(b) by inserting immediately after the words—

(i) "of the purchase" the words "or other acquisition"; and

(ii) "notify its shareholders" the words "and the Registrar";

(c) in paragraphs (a), (b) and (e), by inserting, in each case, immediately after the word "purchased" the words "or acquired".

7. Section 82 of the principal Act is repealed. Repeal of section 82 of principal Act.

8. Section 109 of the principal Act is amended in subsection (1)— Amendment of section 109 of principal Act.

(a) by deleting paragraph (a) and inserting the following as paragraphs (a), (aa) and (ab)—

"(a) the names, nationalities, addresses and occupations of—

(i) the members; and

(ii) the beneficial owners;

(aa) in the case of a company having a share capital, a statement of the shares held by each member and the beneficial owner of the shares, if any, distinguishing each share by its number, and the amount paid or agreed to be considered as paid on the shares of each member;

(ab) in respect of beneficial ownership, the entry relating to the relevant member shall include—

(i) an entry in respect of that member specifying that the ownership of the member is on behalf of a beneficial owner;

(ii) the name of the beneficial owner; and

(iii) such cross-reference, index or information as is necessary for convenient inspection of the particulars of the beneficial owner identified in the entry;";

(b) in paragraph (b), by inserting immediately after the words "a member," the words "or as a beneficial owner, if applicable,";

(c) in paragraph (c), by inserting immediately after the words "a member," the words "or a beneficial owner, if applicable,"; and

(d) in the proviso thereto, by inserting immediately after the words "each member" the words "and each beneficial owner, if any,".

Repeal of section 111 of principal Act.

9. Section 111 of the principal Act is repealed.

Repeal and replacement of section 116 of principal Act.

10. The principal Act is amended by deleting section 116 and substituting therefor the following—

"Notice of Trusts.

116.—(1) Where a company has notice of any trust, whether express, implied, resulting or constructive, affecting the membership of the company, the company shall enter the particulars of the beneficial owner in the register as specified in section 109.

(2) A member who holds property in, or of, a company, including the exercise of any rights or

effecting any transaction in relation to the property, on behalf of or at the direction of another individual, shall notify the company of

(a) the name and particulars of the beneficial owner of the property, as specified in section 109, for inclusion in the register; and

(b) any subsequent change in relation to the legal or beneficial ownership of the property,

within fourteen days of having knowledge thereof.

(3) The beneficial owner, on whose behalf a member holds property in or of a company, shall submit, in writing—

(a) to the member for notification to the company; or

(b) directly to the company,

the particulars required for inclusion in the register under section 109 and of any subsequent change in relation to the company within fourteen days of the change.

(4) Where a company has notice of beneficial ownership of property in or of the company, or of any change in the particulars of any such beneficial owner, and it has not been notified under subsections (2) or (3), the company shall request its members, in writing, to—

(a) advise if the members hold property in or of the company on behalf of a beneficial owner; and

(b) supply the particulars of any beneficial owner required for inclusion in the register under section 109.

(5) Notwithstanding subsection (4), a company shall once per year, or at such times as the

Registrar may direct, in writing, or prescribe, request its members, in writing, to—

(a) advise whether they hold property in the company on behalf of a beneficial owner; and

(b) supply the particulars of any beneficial owner required for inclusion in the register under section 109.

(6) Subject to subsection (7), where, without reasonable excuse—

(a) a company fails to comply with subsection (1), (4) or (5), the company and every officer of the company who caused the failure is liable to a default fine not exceeding five hundred thousand dollars;

(b) a member fails to comply with subsection (2), the member who caused the failure is liable to a default fine not exceeding five hundred thousand dollars;

(c) a beneficial owner fails to comply with subsection (3), the beneficial owner who caused the failure is liable to a default fine not exceeding five hundred thousand dollars.

(7) Subsection (6) shall not apply if the company, the member or the beneficial owner, as the case may be, made the requests referred to in subsections (4) and (5) to obtain, or for the supply of, the relevant particulars for inclusion in the register.".

11. Section 122 of the principal Act is amended— Amendment of section 122 of principal Act.

(a) by deleting subsection (1) and substituting therefor the following—

" (1) Every company having a share capital shall make a return specifying the date to which the return is made up and containing a list of all persons who, on the date of the return—

(a) are members of the company, and all persons who have ceased to be members; and

(b) pursuant to section 116 are beneficial owners of the company, and all persons who have ceased to be beneficial owners, if any,

since the date of the last return or, in the case of a company's first return, of the incorporation of the company."; and

(b) in subsection (2)—

(i) by deleting paragraph (a), and substituting therefor the following—

"(a) state the names, nationalities, addresses and occupations of the past and present members and beneficial owners;";

(ii) in paragraph (b), by inserting immediately after the word "members", wherever it appears, the words "and beneficial owners, if any," in each case;

(iii) in the proviso thereto, by inserting immediately after the word "members" the words "or beneficial owners, if any,".

Amendment of section 172 of principal Act.

12. Section 172 of the principal Act is amended by inserting next after subsection (6), the following subsections —

"(7) Where a company fails, subject to subsection (8), to comply with subsection (1) or subsection (2), the company shall be liable to a default fine not exceeding five hundred thousand dollars.

(8) Subsection (7) shall not apply in respect of a vacancy of the office of director or secretary for a period of less than three months.".

Insertion of new section 174A in principal Act.

13. The principal Act is amended by inserting next after section 174, the following section—

"Duty to avoid conflict of interest.

174A.—(1) Subject to subsection (9), it shall be the duty of the director of a company to avoid circumstances which, whether directly or indirectly, constitute a conflict of interest or may result in a conflict of interest with the interests of the company.

(2) A director who is directly or indirectly interested in a matter which may constitute a conflict of interest or may result in a conflict of interest with the interests of the company—

(a) shall disclose the nature of his interest at a meeting of the directors;

(b) shall not take part in any deliberations at the meeting of the directors in respect to that matter.

(3) The duty under subsection (1) applies in particular to the exploitation of any property, information or opportunity (and it is immaterial whether the company could take advantage of the property, information or opportunity).

(4) The duty referred to in subsection (1) is not infringed—

(a) if the circumstances cannot reasonably be regarded as likely to give rise to a conflict of interest; or

(b) if the matter giving rise to the circumstances has been approved by the directors.

(5) The approval referred to in subsection (4)(b) may be given by the directors, where—

(a) the company is a private company and nothing in the company's articles invalidates such approval, by the matter being proposed to and approved by the directors in accordance with the company's articles; or

(b) the company is a public company and its articles include a provision enabling the directors to approve the matter, by the matter being proposed to and approved by them in accordance with the company's articles.

(6) The approval of the directors is effective only if—

(a) any requirement as to the quorum at the meeting at which the matter is considered is met without counting the director in question or any other interested director; and

(b) the matter was agreed to without their voting or would have been agreed to if their votes had not been counted.

(7) A director of a company shall not accept a benefit from a third party conferred by reason of—

(a) his being a director; or

(b) his doing or not doing an act as a director, unless the acceptance of the benefit cannot reasonably be regarded as likely to give rise to a conflict of interest.

(8) Any reference in this section to a "conflict of interest" includes, a conflict of interest and duty and a conflict of duties.

(9) In this section, "third party" means a person other than the company, its holding company or subsidiary company or any person acting on the behalf of the company, its holding company or subsidiary company.

(10) This section does not apply where the company has only one director and only one shareholder, who is the same individual.".

Amendment of section 177 of principal Act.

14. Section 177 of the principal Act is amended by deleting—

(a) the marginal note and substituting therefor the following—

"Share qualifications of directors.";

(b) subsection (2).

Amendment of section 201 of principal Act.

15. Section 201 of the principal Act is amended—

(a) in subsection (1)(a), by deleting the word "any" and substituting therefor the word "a"; and

(b) in subsection (3), by deleting the words "subsection (2)" and substituting therefor the words "subsection (1)".

16. Section 209(3) of the principal Act is amended by deleting— Amendment of section 209 of principal Act.

(a) the colon and substituting therefor a full stop; and

(b) the proviso thereto.

17. Section 212(3) of the principal Act is amended in paragraph (a) by deleting the words "a shareholder or former shareholder" and substituting therefor the words "a member or former member". Amendment of section 212 of principal Act.

18. Section 213(1) of the principal Act is amended by deleting the words "make such order" and substituting therefor the words "make such interim or final order". Amendment of section 213 of principal Act.

19. Section 213A of the principal Act is amended— Amendment of section 213A of principal Act.

(a) in subsection (2)—

(i) in paragraph (b), by inserting immediately after the words "in a manner;" the word "or";

(ii) by inserting immediately after the words "that is oppressive or unfairly prejudicial to," the words "or unfairly disregards the interest of,"; and

(b) in subsection (3)(c), by deleting the words "or by-laws".

20. Section 222(1) of the principal Act is amended, in paragraph (b), by deleting the word "shareholder," and substituting therefor the word "member,". Amendment of section 222 of principal Act.

21. Section 363(1) of the principal Act is amended by— Amendment of section 363 of principal Act.

(a) deleting the word "or" appearing immediately after the words "of this subsection" and substituting therefor a comma;

(b) renumbering paragraph (c) as paragraph (d) and inserting next after paragraph (b) the following paragraph—

"(c) a list of members and any beneficial owners, containing such particulars as are by this Act required to be entered in the register of members of a company;".

Insertion of section 363A of principal Act.

22. The principal Act is amended by inserting next after section 363 the following section—

"Register of members to be kept by companies incorporated outside Jamaica.

363A.—(1) Subject to subsection (2), a company incorporated outside Jamaica which establishes a place of business within Jamaica, shall keep in Jamaica a register of its members, to be referred to as the "overseas branch register", to which sections 109 to 117 shall apply.

(2) A company referred to in subsection (1) which has established a place of business on or before the specified date, shall comply with subsection (1) within three months of the specified date.".

Amendment of section 365 of principal Act.

23. Section 365 of the principal Act is amended—

(a) in subsection (1)—

(i) by deleting the word "or" wherever it appears after the semi-colon in paragraphs (a) and (b);

(ii) by renumbering paragraph (c) as paragraph (d) and inserting next after paragraph (b), the following paragraph—

"(c) a list of the members and any beneficial owners of the company or the particulars entered in the register of members; or";

(iii) by deleting all the words appearing after the word "within" and substituting therefor the words "twenty-eight days after the date on which the alteration was made, deliver to the Registrar for registration a return containing the prescribed particulars of the alteration and a certified copy of the alteration made.";

(b) by inserting next after subsection (2), the following subsection—

" (3) In this section, "certified" means certified by not less than two directors, or a director and the secretary, or a notary public, to be a true copy.".

Amendment of section 366 of principal Act.

24. Section 366 of the principal Act is amended in subsections (1) and (2), by deleting the words "in every calendar year", wherever they appear, and substituting therefor the words "within eighteen months of the registration of the company, and thereafter, in every calendar year", in each case.

Amendment of section 370 of principal Act.

25. Section 370 of the principal Act is amended by deleting all the words appearing after the word "exceeding" and substituting therefor the words "two million dollars".

Insertion of new section 383A in principal Act.

26. The principal Act is amended by inserting next after section 383 the following sections—

"Share warrants prohibited.

383A.—(1) Subject to section 396, no company shall issue, or have entered on its register of members, a share warrant.

(2) If a company fails to comply with subsection (1) the company and every officer who knowingly caused the failure is liable to a default fine not exceeding three million dollars.

(3) In this section, "share warrant" means, with respect to any fully paid up shares, a warrant issued under the company's common seal, stating that the bearer of the warrant is entitled to the shares therein specified, and may provide by coupons or otherwise, for the payment of dividends on the shares included in the warrant.".

Insertion of new section 390A in principal Act.

27. The principal Act is amended by inserting next after section 390 the following section—

"*Records*

Records.

390A.—(1) Every company shall keep such documents as may be prescribed—

(a) for not less than seven years or for such other period as may be prescribed; and

(b) in such manner as may be prescribed.

(2) A company that contravenes subsection (1) commits an offence and is liable on summary conviction in a Parish Court to a fine not exceeding five hundred thousand dollars.".

Insertion of new sections 396, 397 and 398 in principal Act.

28. The principal Act is amended by inserting next after section 395 the following sections—

"Transitional arrangements for share warrants.

396.—(1) Upon the specified date, a person who is the bearer of a share warrant shall be deemed to be—

(a) the owner of the shares specified in the share warrant; and

(b) a member of the company.

(2) Eighteen months after the specified date a share warrant shall—

(a) be incapable of effecting the transfer of ownership of the shares specified in the share warrant from the bearer thereof to any other person; and

(b) except for the purposes of subsection (1) and (4)(b), be deemed null and void.

(3) Within eighteen months after the specified date, every company which has issued a share warrant to a bearer before the specified date shall—

(a) withdraw the share warrant;

(b) if the bearer of the share warrant presents the share warrant to the company, cause the name of the bearer of the share warrant to be entered as a member in the register of members and shall issue under seal, to that person one or more certificates in respect of that person's ownership of the shares specified in the share warrant, and a certificate issued under this paragraph shall specify the shares to which it relates;

(c) in accordance with this Act, amend its articles of incorporation, to remove any authorization to issue share warrants or to prohibit the issue of share warrants, as the case may require.

(4) If a company fails to comply with subsection (3) the company and every officer who knowingly caused the failure is liable to a default fine not exceeding two million dollars.

Registrar to give notice of prohibition to bearer's of share warrants.

397.—(1) Within three months of the specified date and thereafter, at such times as the Registrar may determine during the period referred to in section 396(2), the Registrar shall cause a notice to be given to the public—

(a) advising the public of the matters referred to in sections 383A and 396; and

(b) requesting the bearers of share warrants to present themselves to the company to which the share warrant relates to be entered in the register of members as a member of the company in respect of the shares specified in the share warrant .

(2) The Registrar shall cause the notice referred to in subsection (1) to be published in a daily newspaper circulated throughout Jamaica and in the *Gazette*.".

Definition of share warrant.

398. For the purposes of sections 397 and 398, "share warrant" shall have the meaning assigned to it by section 383A(3).".

Repeal and replacement of the First Schedule to the principal Act.

29. The First Schedule to the principal Act is amended—

(a) in Part I of Table A—

(i) by deleting paragraphs 1 to 6 and renumbering paragraphs 7 to 142 as paragraphs 1 to 135;

(ii) in paragraph 1, as renumbered, by inserting immediately after the words "photography," the words "electronic documents within the meaning of the *Electronic Transactions Act*";

(b) in Table B, by—

(i) deleting the word "Form ....";

(ii) deleting paragraphs 1 to 14 and inserting the following as paragraphs 1 to 6—

"1. In these articles—

"the Act" means the *Companies Act*;

"company" means, where the context requires, the association on its incorporation under section 13 of the Act;

"the seal" means the common seal of the company;

"secretary" means any person appointed to perform the duties of the secretary of the company.

Expressions referring to writing shall, unless the contrary intention appears, be construed as including references to printing, lithography, photography, electronic documents within the meaning of the *Electronic Transactions Act*, and other modes of representing or reproducing words in a visible form.

Unless the context otherwise requires, words or expressions contained in these articles shall bear the same meaning as in the Act or any statutory modification thereof in force at the date at which these articles become binding on the company.

2. Every member of the association undertakes to contribute to the assets of the association in the event of the same being wound up during the time that he is a member, or within one year afterwards, for payment of the debts and liabilities of the association contracted before the time at which he ceases to be a member, and of the costs, charges, and expenses of winding-up of the same, and for the adjustment of the rights of the contributors amongst themselves, such amount as may be required not exceeding dollars.

3. No part of the net earnings of the association shall inure to the benefit of, or be distributable to its members, directors or officers, or other private persons, except that the association shall be authorized and empowered to pay reasonable compensation for services rendered and to make payments and distributions in furtherance of the purposes set forth in Article 4 hereof. The association shall not support with its fund any purpose or object, or impose on or procure to be

observed by its members or others any regulations, restrictions or conditions which if an object of the association would make it a Trade Union.

4. In the event of any proposed addition, alteration or amendment of the articles being required, the same shall be submitted to the Minister for his approval.

5. If upon the winding up or dissolution of the association there remains after the satisfaction of all its debts and liabilities, any property whatsoever, the same shall not be paid to or distributed among the members of the association, but shall be given or transferred to some other institution or institutions, having objects similar to the objects of the association and which shall prohibit the distribution of its or their income and property among its or their members to an extent at least as great as is imposed on the association under or by virtue of Article 5 hereof, such institution or institutions to be determined by the members of the association at or before the time of dissolution or in default thereof by such Judge of the Supreme Court as may have or acquire jurisdiction in the matter and if and so far as effect cannot be given to the aforesaid provision then to some charitable object.

6. True accounts shall be kept of the sums of money received and expended by the association and the matters in respect of which such receipts and expenditure take place and of the property, credits and liabilities of the association, and subject to any reasonable restrictions as to the time and manner of

inspecting the same that may be imposed in accordance with the articles of the association for the time being shall be opened to the inspection of the members. Once at least in every year the accounts of the association shall be examined and the correctness of the balance sheet ascertained by one or more properly qualified auditor or auditors.";

(iii) re-numbering paragraphs 15 to 79 as paragraphs 7 to 71; and

(iv) in paragraph 7, as renumbered, by deleting the words "Articles of Association" and substituting therefor the words "Articles of Incorporation";

(c) by deleting Table C; and

(d) in Table D—

(i) by deleting the word "Form ....";

(ii) by deleting paragraphs 1 to 3 and renumbering paragraphs 4 to 7 as paragraphs 1 to 4;

(iii) in paragraph 1, as re-numbered, by deleting the following words—

"Form of Company	☐	Public
	☐	Private

The company is a private company and accordingly—" and substituting therefor the words "Where the company is a private company—".

30. The Fifth Schedule to the principal Act is amended— Amendment of Fifth Schedule to principal Act.

(a) in paragraph 3 of Part I by—

(i) deleting paragraphs (f) and (g); and

(ii) renumbering paragraph (h) as (f);

(b) in Part II by deleting Form 19A and Form 19B and substituting therefor the following—

"

☐ **Amended Return** Year: ____________

If the return for the year above was registered in error please indicate the reasons for amendment in this box

FORM 19A

READ INSTRUCTIONS BEFORE COMPLETING

THE COMPANIES ACT

ANNUAL RETURN FOR COMPANIES WITH A SHARE CAPITAL

(Pursuant to sections 121, 122 & 124 of the Companies Act 2004)

COMPLETE THIS FORM IN BLOCK CAPITALS ONLY WITHIN THE PRESCRIBED FIELDS. PUT "N/A" IN FIELDS THAT DO NOT APPLY

1A NAME OF COMPANY

1B COMPANY REGISTRATION NUMBER

1C COMPANY TAXPAYER REGISTRATION NUMBER

1D COMPANY TELEPHONE NUMBER

1E EMAIL ADDRESS

1F TYPE OF COMPANY ☐ Private ☐ Public

2 PERIOD FOR WHICH ANNUAL RETURN IS MADE UP

	Day	Month	Year		Day	Month	Year
(i) START				(ii) END			

3 LOCATION OF REGISTERED OFFICE

Street or District	
Town	
Post Office	
Parish	

3A MAILING ADDRESS (if different from the registered office address)

Street or District	
Town	
Post Office	
Parish	

4 HAS THERE BEEN A CHANGE IN THE REGISTERED OFFICE ADDRESS DURING THE PERIOD FOR WHICH THE ANNUAL RETURN IS MADE UP? *If yes, notice must be given to the Registrar using a Form 17)* ☐ YES ☐ NO

5 IS/ARE THE REGISTER OF MEMBERS/DIRECTORS' SHAREHOLDINGS/DEBENTURE HOLDINGS/DIRECTORS' SERVICE CONTRACTS LOCATED AT AN ADDRESS DIFFERENT FROM THE REGISTERED OFFICE (*If yes, this information must be presented on a schedule and attached to this form.*) ☐ YES ☐ NO

5A (FOR COMPANIES LIMITED BY GUARANTEE HAVING A SHARE CAPITAL ONLY) HAS THERE BEEN AN INCREASE IN THE REGISTERED NUMBER OF MEMBERS? (*If yes, notice must be given to the Registrar using a Form 5)* ☐ YES ☐ NO

6 PLEASE INDICATE THE TOTAL AMOUNT OF INDEBTEDNESS OF THE COMPANY IF ANY

$

FOR OFFICIAL USE ONLY COMPANY #

7 SUMMARY OF SHARE PARTICULARS

7A AUTHORIZED NUMBER OF SHARES	7B CLASSES OF SHARES	7C TOTAL NUMBER OF SHARES IN EACH CLASS
	(i) ORDINARY	
	(ii) PREFERENCE	
	(iii) OTHER State ______	

8 ARE THERE ANY ISSUED SHARES THAT HAVE BEEN PARTIALLY PAID UP? ☐ YES ☐ NO

If yes, please complete items 8A–8C. If no, you must complete items 9–9C.

8A. PARTICULARS OF SHARES THAT HAVE BEEN PARTIALLY PAID UP

CLASS OF SHARES	(i) TOTAL NUMBER OF SHARES ISSUED AT THE BEGINNING OF THE PERIOD	(ii) SHARES ISSUED DURING THE PERIOD	(iii) SHARES PURCHASED FORFEITED SURRENDERED DURING THE PERIOD	(iv) TOTAL NUMBER OF SHARES AT THE END OF THE PERIOD
1				
2				
3				

8B. CASH SHARES THAT HAVE BEEN PARTIALLY PAID UP (Shares which were or are to be paid for in cash)

CLASS OF SHARES	(i) NUMBER OF CASH SHARES PARTLY PAID UP IN CASH	(ii) AMOUNT CALLED UPON EACH SHARE	(iii) TOTAL AMOUNT CALLS RECEIVED FROM CALLS	(iv) TOTAL AMOUNT OF CALLS UNPAID
1				
2				
3				

8C. NON-CASH SHARES THAT HAVE BEEN PARTIALLY PAID UP (Shares which were or are to be paid for in consideration other than in cash, eg services, goods)

CLASS OF SHARES	(i) NUMBER OF NON-CASH SHARES PARTLY PAID UP	(ii) AMOUNT CALLED UPON EACH SHARE	(iii) TOTAL AMOUNT CALLS RECEIVED FROM CALLS	(iv) TOTAL AMOUNT OF CALLS UNPAID
1				
2				
3				

9 ARE THERE ANY ISSUED SHARES WHICH HAVE BEEN FULLY PAID UP? ☐ YES ☐ NO

If yes, please complete items 9A–9C.

9A. PARTICULARS OF SHARES THAT HAVE BEEN FULLY PAID UP

CLASS OF SHARES	(i) TOTAL NUMBER OF SHARES ISSUED AT THE BEGINNING OF THE PERIOD	(ii) SHARES ISSUED DURING THE PERIOD	(iii) SHARES PURCHASED/REDEEMED/SURRENDERED DURING THE PERIOD	(iv) TOTAL NUMBER OF SHARES AT THE END OF THE PERIOD
1				
2				
3				

9B. CASH FULLY PAID UP SHARE PARTICULARS

CLASS	NUMBER

9C. NON-CASH FULLY PAID UP SHARE PARTICULARS

CLASS	NUMBER

FOR OFFICIAL USE ONLY COMPANY #:

10 LIST OF SHAREHOLDERS AND BENEFICIAL HOLDERS AS AT THE DATE OF THIS ANNUAL RETURN

This list should include all shareholders holding shares during the period for which the Annual Return is made up and must reflect **all changes in shareholders**

NOTE: Where shares are transferred/forfeited etc the date of the transaction must be indicated under the relevant column next to the name of the person acquiring/disposing of the shares and the type of transaction (see key at right)

Where shares are issued during the period the details should also be provided on a Return of Allotment (Form 5). This includes newly issued shares and shares re-allotted upon forfeiture

KEY

TYPE OF TRANSACTION
- T = TRANSFER
- F = FORFEITURE
- S = SURRENDERED (to the company)
- P = PURCHASE
- R = REDEMPTION
- RP = REPURCHASE
- TM = TRANSMISSION

NAME (For individuals: FIRST LAST)	ADDRESS	OCCUPATION	CLASS OF SHARES	NUMBER OF SHARES HELD AT BEGINNING OF PERIOD	CHANGES IN SHAREHOLDING DURING THE PERIOD		DATE OF TRANSACTION (dd/mm/yyyy)	TYPE OF TRANSACTION (see key above)	NUMBER OF SHARES HELD AT THE END OF THE PERIOD
					# of shares acquired[1]	# of shares disposed of[2]			

FOR OFFICIAL USE ONLY COMPANY #

11 **LIST OF BENEFICIAL OWNERS**

This list should include all **beneficial owners on whose behalf shares are being held**, during the period for which the Annual Return is made up and must include any changes made to any **beneficial holding**.

NOTE: Where shares are transferred, forfeited etc the date of the transaction must be indicated under the relevant column next to the name of the person acquiring/disposing of the shares and the type of transaction (see key at right).

Where shares are issued during the period, the details should also be provided on a Return of Allotment (Form 5). This includes newly issued shares and shares re-allotted upon forfeiture.

KEY

TYPE OF TRANSACTION
T = TRANSFER
F = FORFEITURE
S = SURRENDERED (as a gift to the company)
P = PURCHASE
R = REDEMPTION
RP = REPURCHASE
TM = TRANSMISSION

NAME (For individuals: FIRST, LAST)	ADDRESS	NATIONALITY	CLASS OF SHARES	NUMBER OF SHARES HELD ON BENEFICIARY'S BEHALF AT BEGINNING OF PERIOD	CHANGES IN SHAREHOLDING DURING THE PERIOD		DATE OF TRANSACTION (dd/mm/yyyy)	TYPE OF TRANSACTION (see key above)	NUMBER OF SHARES HELD AT THE END OF THE PERIOD
					# of shares acquired[1]	# of shares disposed of[2]			
Shareholder holding shares on behalf of beneficiary[3]									
Shareholder holding shares on behalf of beneficiary[3]									
Shareholder holding shares on behalf of beneficiary[3]									

Transmission occurs on the death of the shareholder and the shares that were held by the deceased pass on to his personal representative.
[1] Acquired shares are shares received by shareholders during the period for which the Annual Return is made up, usually by means of transfer or allotment.
[2] Disposed shares are those which no longer belong to the shareholder, usually by means of transfer, forfeiture, purchase or redemption by the company or given as gift to the company.
[3] Beneficial owners are persons who enjoy and have a right to the benefits of ownership of the shares, as the right to dividends, without being registered on the company's books/records as the owner.

12. **HAS THERE BEEN ANY CHANGE IN DIRECTORSHIP (REMOVALS/APPOINTMENTS) DURING THE PERIOD FOR WHICH THE ANNUAL RETURN IS MADE UP?** ☐ YES ☐ NO
(If yes, notice must be given to the Registrar using a Form 23)

FOR OFFICIAL USE ONLY COMPANY #:

12A PARTICULARS OF DIRECTORS AS AT THE DATE OF THIS ANNUAL RETURN

This should be a complete listing of all Directors as at the date of this Annual Return taking into consideration any changes (whether removals or appointments) made during the period. Directors who have been removed during this period should be excluded from this list while those directors who have been appointed since the last annual return and any still directors must be included. Ensure that the Notices of the Appointments of all listed directors have been filed with the Companies Office of Jamaica.

DIRECTOR 1

FULL NAME		CURRENT NATIONALITY	
FORMER NAME(S) (If any)		NATIONALITY OF ORIGIN (if different)	
FULL RESIDENTIAL ADDRESS or REGISTERED OFFICE	STREET & STREET	TOWN	
	POST OFFICE	PARISH	COUNTRY

DIRECTOR 2

FULL NAME		CURRENT NATIONALITY	
FORMER NAME(S) (If any)		NATIONALITY OF ORIGIN (if different)	
FULL RESIDENTIAL ADDRESS or REGISTERED OFFICE	STREET & STREET	TOWN	
	POST OFFICE	PARISH	COUNTRY

DIRECTOR 3

FULL NAME		CURRENT NATIONALITY	
FORMER NAME(S) (If any)		NATIONALITY OF ORIGIN (if different)	
FULL RESIDENTIAL ADDRESS or REGISTERED OFFICE	STREET & STREET	TOWN	
	POST OFFICE	PARISH	COUNTRY

DIRECTOR 4

FULL NAME		CURRENT NATIONALITY	
FORMER NAME(S) (If any)		NATIONALITY OF ORIGIN (if different)	
FULL RESIDENTIAL ADDRESS or REGISTERED OFFICE	STREET & STREET	TOWN	
	POST OFFICE	PARISH	COUNTRY

FOR OFFICIAL USE ONLY	COMPANY #:

13. HAS THERE BEEN ANY CHANGE OF COMPANY SECRETARY DURING THE PERIOD FOR WHICH THE ANNUAL RETURN IS MADE UP? (*If yes, notice must be given to the Registrar using a Form 20*) ☐ YES ☐ NO

13B. PARTICULARS OF COMPANY SECRETARY AS AT THE DATE OF THIS ANNUAL RETURN
Please ensure that the notice of appointment of the secretary has been filed with the Companies Office of Jamaica

NAME (For individuals: FIRST LAST)	RESIDENTIAL ADDRESS (or where a secretary is a company, the registered office)	OCCUPATION

FOR OFFICIAL USE ONLY COMPANY #:

14 **CERTIFICATES**

The relevant certificate is to be signed by both a duly appointed Director and the secretary of the Company. Where a director is also the Secretary he/she may not sign in both capacities

A. **Certificate to be signed by all Private Companies**

"We certify that the Company has not since the date of the last annual return or incorporation as the case may be, issued any invitation to the Public to subscribe for any shares or debentures of the Company or to deposit money for fixed periods or payable on call whether bearing or not bearing interest. We also certify that to the best of our knowledge and belief since the above-mentioned date no person other than the holder has, except in cases provided for in the Fourteenth Schedule, had any interest in any of the Company's shares."

1. Director Print Name ____________________ Signature/Seal of Corporate Director

Officer of Corporate Director ____________________ Signature ____________________

Officer of Corporate Director ____________________ Signature ____________________

2. Secretary Print Name ____________________ Signature/Seal of Corporate Secretary

Officer of Corporate Secretary ____________________ Signature ____________________

Officer of Corporate Secretary ____________________ Signature ____________________

B. **Certificate to be signed by all Private Companies**

"We certify that to the best of our knowledge and belief, no person other than the holder thereof except in cases provided for in the Twelfth Schedule has had any interest in any of the company's shares since the date of the last annual return or incorporation or in the case of an existing company which became a private company, the date on which it became a private company."

1. Director Print Name ____________________ Signature/Seal of Corporate Director

Officer of Corporate Director ____________________ Signature ____________________

Officer of Corporate Director ____________________ Signature ____________________

2. Secretary Print Name ____________________ Signature/Seal of Corporate Secretary

Officer of Corporate Secretary ____________________ Signature ____________________

Officer of Corporate Secretary ____________________ Signature ____________________

C. **Certificate to be signed by a Private Company with more than twenty members**

We certify that the excess of members of the Company above twenty consists wholly of persons who are in the employment of the company, and/or of persons who, having formerly in the employment of the company, were while in such employment and have continued after the determination of such employment to be, members of the Company"

1. Director Print Name ____________________ Signature/Seal of Corporate Director

Officer of Corporate Director ____________________ Signature ____________________

Officer of Corporate Director ____________________ Signature ____________________

2. Secretary Print Name ____________________ Signature/Seal of Corporate Secretary

Officer of Corporate Secretary ____________________ Signature ____________________

Officer of Corporate Secretary ____________________ Signature ____________________

FOR OFFICIAL USE ONLY	COMPANY #:

D. **Certificate to be signed by a Private Company without a corporate shareholder OR with a corporate shareholder not required to file Accounts.**

Should the Company be a private company not obliged to file accounts the following certificate is also required:

I/We certify that to the best of our knowledge and belief, pursuant to the exception provided in the Thirteenth Schedule, no body corporate obliged to file accounts holds any shares in the Company, and that has been the position at all times since the date of the last Annual Return (or the date of incorporation for companies filing first Annual Return, or in the case of an existing company which became a private company, the date on which it became a private company).

Affix the Seal of Corporate Director

Director Print Name ____________________

Officer of Corporate Director ____________________ Signature ____________________

Officer of Corporate Director ____________________ Signature ____________________

Affix the Seal of Corporate Secretary

2. Secretary Print Name ____________________

Officer of Corporate Secretary ____________________ Signature ____________________

Officer of Corporate Secretary ____________________ Signature ____________________

15. DECLARATION OF ACCURACY OF PRESENTED INFORMATION

NAME OF DECLARANT		**SIGNATURE OF DECLARANT**	
CAPACITY	☐ Director ☐ Secretary ☐ Authorized Official	**DATE**	

FOR OFFICIAL USE ONLY	COMPANY #:

F19A

16. FILED BY
PARTICULARS OF INDIVIDUAL/COMPANY FILING THE FORM WITH THE COMPANIES OFFICE OF JAMAICA

NAME:

COMPLETE ADDRESS:

EMAIL ADDRESS:

CONTACT NUMBER

FAX NUMBER

17. ADDITIONAL PARTICULARS OF DIRECTORS LISTED AT ITEM 12A.

NAME OF DIRECTOR	TAXPAYER REGISTRATION NUMBER	EMAIL

18. PARTICULARS OF COMPANY SECRETARY LISTED AT ITEM 14D.

NAME OF SECRETARY	TAXPAYER REGISTRATION NUMBER	EMAIL

FOR OFFICIAL USE ONLY COMPANY #:

☐ **Amended Return** **Year:** ____________

If, the return for the year above was registered in error, please indicate the reason(s) for amendment in this box:

FORM 19B

READ INSTRUCTIONS BEFORE COMPLETING

THE COMPANIES ACT

ANNUAL RETURN FOR COMPANIES LIMITED BY GUARANTEE WITHOUT A SHARE CAPITAL

(Pursuant to sections 121, 123 & 124 of the Companies Act 2004)

COMPLETE THIS FORM IN BLOCK CAPITALS ONLY WITHIN THE PRESCRIBED FIELDS. PUT "N/A" IN FIELDS THAT DO NOT APPLY.

1A. NAME OF COMPANY

____

____

[illegible] **Certificate of Incorporation** [illegible] **Change of Name Certificate** [illegible]

1B. COMPANY REGISTRATION NUMBER ____________

1C. COMPANY TAXPAYER REGISTRATION NUMBER ____________

1D. COMPANY TELEPHONE NUMBER ____________

1E. EMAIL ADDRESS ____________

1F. TYPE OF COMPANY ☐ Private ☐ Public

2. PERIOD FOR WHICH ANNUAL RETURN IS MADE UP

(i) START	Day	Month	Year	(ii) END	Day	Month	Year

3. LOCATION OF REGISTERED OFFICE

Street or District	
Town	
Post Office	
Parish	

3A. MAILING ADDRESS (if different from the registered office address)

Street or District	
Town	
Post Office	
Parish	

4. HAS THERE BEEN A CHANGE IN THE REGISTERED OFFICE ADDRESS DURING THE PERIOD FOR WHICH THE ANNUAL RETURN IS MADE UP? (*If yes, notice must be given to the Registrar using a Form 17*) ☐ YES ☐ NO

5. IS/ARE THE REGISTER OF MEMBERS/DIRECTORS' SHAREHOLDINGS/DEBENTURE HOLDINGS/DIRECTORS' SERVICE CONTRACTS LOCATED AT AN ADDRESS DIFFERENT FROM THE REGISTERED OFFICE (*If yes, this information must be presented on a schedule and attached to this form*) ☐ YES ☐ NO

6. HAS THERE BEEN AN INCREASE IN THE REGISTERED NUMBER OF MEMBERS DURING THE PERIOD FOR WHICH THE ANNUAL RETURN IS MADE UP? (*If yes, notice must be given to the Registrar using a Form 5*) ☐ YES ☐ NO

7. PLEASE INDICATE THE TOTAL AMOUNT OF INDEBTEDNESS OF THE COMPANY, IF ANY

$ ____________

[illegible] Companies Office of Jamaica

FOR OFFICIAL USE ONLY COMPANY #:

3. HAS THERE BEEN ANY CHANGE IN DIRECTORSHIP (REMOVALS/APPOINTMENTS) DURING THE PERIOD FOR WHICH THE ANNUAL RETURN IS MADE UP? (*If yes, notice must be given to the Registrar using a Form 13*) ☐ YES ☐ NO

3A. PARTICULARS OF DIRECTORS AS AT THE DATE OF THIS ANNUAL RETURN

This should be a complete listing of all Directors as at the date of this Annual Return taking into consideration any changes (whether removals or appointments) made during the period. Directors who have been removed during the period should be excluded from this list while those directors who have been appointed since the last annual return and are still directors must be included. Ensure that the Notices of the Appointments of all listed directors have been filed with the Companies Office of Jamaica.

DIRECTOR 1

FULL NAME			CURRENT NATIONALITY	
FORMER NAME(S) (if any)			NATIONALITY OF ORIGIN [illegible]	
FULL RESIDENTIAL ADDRESS or REGISTERED OFFICE	STREET/DISTRICT		TOWN	
	POST OFFICE	PARISH	COUNTRY	

DIRECTOR 2

FULL NAME			CURRENT NATIONALITY	
FORMER NAME(S) (if any)			NATIONALITY OF ORIGIN [illegible]	
FULL RESIDENTIAL ADDRESS or REGISTERED OFFICE	STREET/DISTRICT		TOWN	
	POST OFFICE	PARISH	COUNTRY	

DIRECTOR 3

FULL NAME			CURRENT NATIONALITY	
FORMER NAME(S) (if any)			NATIONALITY OF ORIGIN [illegible]	
FULL RESIDENTIAL ADDRESS or REGISTERED OFFICE	STREET/DISTRICT		TOWN	
	POST OFFICE	PARISH	COUNTRY	

DIRECTOR 4

FULL NAME			CURRENT NATIONALITY	
FORMER NAME(S) (if any)			NATIONALITY OF ORIGIN [illegible]	
FULL RESIDENTIAL ADDRESS or REGISTERED OFFICE	STREET/DISTRICT		TOWN	
	POST OFFICE	PARISH	COUNTRY	

FOR OFFICIAL USE ONLY COMPANY #

9 HAS THERE BEEN ANY CHANGE OF COMPANY SECRETARY DURING THE PERIOD FOR WHICH THE ANNUAL RETURN IS MADE UP? (*If yes, notice must be given to the Registrar using a Form 29*) ☐ YES ☐ NO

9A PARTICULARS OF COMPANY SECRETARY AS AT THE DATE OF THIS ANNUAL RETURN

Please ensure that the notice of appointment of the secretary has been filed with the Companies Office of Jamaica

NAME (For individuals: FIRST LAST)	RESIDENTIAL ADDRESS (or where a secretary is a company, the registered office)	OCCUPATION

10 DECLARATION OF ACCURACY OF PRESENTED INFORMATION

NAME OF DECLARANT		SIGNATURE OF DECLARANT	
CAPACITY	☐ Director ☐ Secretary ☐ Authorized Official	DATE	

FOR OFFICIAL USE ONLY	COMPANY #:

F19B

11 FILED BY
PARTICULARS OF INDIVIDUAL/COMPANY FILING THE FORM WITH THE COMPANIES OFFICE OF JAMAICA

NAME
COMPLETE ADDRESS
EMAIL ADDRESS
CONTACT NUMBER
FAX NUMBER

12 ADDITIONAL PARTICULARS OF DIRECTORS LISTED AT ITEM 8A

NAME OF DIRECTOR	TAXPAYER REGISTRATION NUMBER	EMAIL

13 PARTICULARS OF COMPANY SECRETARY LISTED AT ITEM 9A

NAME OF SECRETARY	TAXPAYER REGISTRATION NUMBER	EMAIL

FOR OFFICIAL USE ONLY COMPANY #:

31. The *Companies (Forms) Rules*, 2005, is amended—

Amendment of the *Companies (Forms) Rules*, 2005

(a) by deleting the words "section 393(3)" and substituting therefor the words "section 393"; and

(b) in the Schedule, by deleting Form 1A, Form 1B, Form 1C and Form 1D and substituting therefor the following forms—

☐ New Incorporation
☐ Amended Articles
☐ Re-registration

FORM 1A
READ INSTRUCTIONS BEFORE COMPLETING

THE COMPANIES ACT
ARTICLES OF INCORPORATION: COMPANY LIMITED BY SHARE CAPITAL
(Pursuant to sections 5 & 25 of the Companies Act)

COMPLETE THIS FORM IN BLOCK CAPITALS ONLY WITHIN THE PRESCRIBED FIELDS. PUT "NA" IN FIELDS THAT DO NOT APPLY

1A. NAME OF COMPANY

1B. JUSTIFICATION FOR PROPOSED NAME (if applicable)

1C. CORE BUSINESS OF THE COMPANY
(The activities of the business are not restricted to the area(s) stated below unless indicated at item 1D)

1D. RESTRICTION ON THE BUSINESS OF THE COMPANY (if applicable)

1E. COMPANY TELEPHONE NUMBER   1F. COMPANY EMAIL ADDRESS   1G. TYPE OF COMPANY
☐ Private ☐ Public

2. THE REGISTERED OFFICE IS LOCATED IN JAMAICA AND THE LIABILITY OF THE MEMBERS IS LIMITED

3. COMPANY'S ARTICLES (RULES) Please check the appropriate box below (ONLY ONE BOX MUST BE CHECKED)

3a. ☐ Standard Articles Articles 1–78, 80–136 with Varied Article 79 and Additional Articles 137–143 SEE SCHEDULE(S) _____
3b. ☐ Standard Articles Articles 1–78, 80–136 with Varied Article 79 only SEE SCHEDULE _____
3c. ☐ Standard Articles Articles 1–136 with Additional Articles 137–143 only SEE SCHEDULE(S) _____
3d. ☐ Standard Articles in their entirety Articles 1–136
3e. ☐ Other

NOTES FOR PRIVATE COMPANIES

- The right to transfer shares is restricted
- Subject to section 26(1)(b) of the Companies Act 2004, the number of members of the company, is limited to twenty.
- Provided that where two or more persons hold one or more shares in the company jointly, they shall for the purpose of this regulation be treated as a single member. Any invitation to the public to subscribe for any shares or debentures of the company is prohibited.
- Any invitation to the public to deposit money for fixed periods or payable on call whether bearing or not interest is prohibited.
- Subject to the exceptions provided for in the Twelfth Schedule to the Act, any person other than a shareholder is prohibited from having any interest in any of the company's shares.
- The company shall not have the power to issue share warrants to bearer.

FOR OFFICIAL USE ONLY   COMPANY #

4 AUTHORIZED NUMBER OF SHARES This is the maximum number of shares that your company is authorized to issue

	The total number of shares in all classes should not exceed the total number of shares, if any, indicated at Item 4.

4A CLASSES OF SHARES (indicate by ticking the class or classes of shares that the company issues on incorporation)	4B TOTAL NUMBER OF SHARES IN EACH CLASS
☐ ORDINARY	
☐ PREFERENCE	
☐ OTHER Specify ________________	

Shares may be issued with different rights, privileges and conditions. Shares with the same rights, privileges and conditions are grouped into classes.

All companies limited by shares must issue at least one class of shares which are non-redeemable (e.g. ordinary shares) and may issue two or more classes of shares. If different classes of shares are issued at incorporation a Form 3 should be completed and attached to this form.

5 RESTRICTIONS ON SHARE TRANSFER (eg Directors must give consent to the transfer of shares)

____

____

____

All private companies must restrict the right to transfer shares (e.g. shares must be first offered to existing shareholders).

A public company may only restrict the right to transfer shares which have not been fully paid up.

6 NON-CASH CONSIDERATION

Were any shares issued for non-cash consideration (that is, as a payment for goods, services, property, good will, shares in other companies etc.) based on a contract that existed before incorporation? (ONLY ONE BOX MUST BE CHECKED)

☐ Yes — Complete Item 6A

☐ No — Continue to Item 7

6A PLEASE INDICATE THE NATURE AND VALUE OF THE NON-CASH CONSIDERATION BELOW

____

____

7 MINIMUM NUMBER OF DIRECTORS ☐

AND/OR

7A MAXIMUM NUMBER OF DIRECTORS ☐

A private company must have at least one director. He/she cannot also be the company secretary. A public company must have a minimum of three (3) directors, two of them however should not be employed by the company or any of its affiliates.

8 PARTICULARS OF DIRECTORS

DIRECTOR 1 (Where the director is an individual the name must be represented as FIRST, MIDDLE, LAST)

FULL NAME			
FULL RESIDENTIAL ADDRESS or REGISTERED OFFICE ADDRESS	STREET/DISTRICT		
	TOWN	POST OFFICE	
	PARISH	COUNTRY	
OCCUPATION		CONTACT	

DIRECTOR 2 (Where the director is an individual the name must be represented as FIRST, MIDDLE, LAST)

FULL NAME			
FULL RESIDENTIAL ADDRESS or REGISTERED OFFICE ADDRESS	STREET/DISTRICT		
	TOWN	POST OFFICE	
	PARISH	COUNTRY	
OCCUPATION		CONTACT	

FOR OFFICIAL USE ONLY COMPANY #

DIRECTOR 3 (Where the director is an individual the name must be represented as FIRST MIDDLE LAST)

FULL NAME			
FULL RESIDENTIAL ADDRESS or REGISTERED OFFICE ADDRESS	STREET DISTRICT		
	TOWN	POST OFFICE	
	PARISH	COUNTRY	
OCCUPATION		CONTACT	

DIRECTOR 4 (Where the director is an individual the name must be represented as FIRST MIDDLE LAST)

FULL NAME			
FULL RESIDENTIAL ADDRESS or REGISTERED OFFICE ADDRESS	STREET DISTRICT		
	TOWN	POST OFFICE	
	PARISH	COUNTRY	
OCCUPATION		CONTACT	

DIRECTOR 5 (Where the director is an individual the name must be represented as FIRST MIDDLE LAST)

FULL NAME			
FULL RESIDENTIAL ADDRESS or REGISTERED OFFICE ADDRESS	STREET DISTRICT		
	TOWN	POST OFFICE	
	PARISH	COUNTRY	
OCCUPATION		CONTACT	

9 PARTICULARS OF COMPANY SECRETARY (Where the secretary is an individual the name must be represented as FIRST MIDDLE LAST)

FULL NAME			
FULL RESIDENTIAL ADDRESS or REGISTERED OFFICE ADDRESS	STREET DISTRICT		
	TOWN	POST OFFICE	
	PARISH	COUNTRY	
OCCUPATION		CONTACT	

FOR OFFICIAL USE ONLY	COMPANY #

10. PARTICULARS OF INDIVIDUAL SUBSCRIBERS (shareholders who are individuals)

SUBSCRIBER PARTICULARS	SUBSCRIBER 1	SUBSCRIBER 2	SUBSCRIBER 3	SUBSCRIBER 4
NAME				
ADDRESS				
OCCUPATION				
SHARES TAKEN UP	The total of the number of shares subscribed by all subscribers may not exceed the authorised number of shares stated at item 4			
CLASS OF SHARES 1. ORDINARY ______ 2. PREFERENCE ______ OTHER 3. ______	AMOUNT OF SHARES 1. ______ 2. ______ 3. ______	AMOUNT OF SHARES 1 ______ 2 ______ 3 ______	AMOUNT OF SHARES 1. ______ 2. ______ 3. ______	AMOUNT OF SHARES 1 ______ 2 ______ 3 ______
SIGNATURE				
DATE				
WITNESS PARTICULARS	WITNESS FOR SUBSCRIBER 1	WITNESS FOR SUBSCRIBER 2	WITNESS FOR SUBSCRIBER 3	WITNESS FOR SUBSCRIBER 4
WITNESSED BY (NAME OF WITNESS)				
AT (LOCATION/ADDRESS)				
SIGNATURE				
DATE				
If a subscriber and a witness are located in different countries "while on visit" must be selected	☐ While on Visit	☐ While on visit	☐ While on Visit	☐ While on Visit

FOR OFFICIAL USE ONLY COMPANY #

11. PARTICULARS OF COMPANY SUBSCRIBERS (shareholders who are companies)

COMPANY PARTICULARS	
COMPANY NAME	
COMPANY REGISTERED OFFICE ADDRESS /OTHER ADDRESS	

SHARES TAKEN UP The total of the number of shares subscribed to by all subscribers must not exceed the authorised number of shares stated at Item 4

CLASS OF SHARES		AMOUNT OF SHARES	
	1 ORDINARY SHARES		1
	2 PREFERENCE SHARES		2
	OTHER 3 Specify		3

SEAL

OFFICER PARTICULARS	OFFICER 1	OFFICER 2
OFFICER NAME		
OFFICE HELD IN COMPANY		
SIGNATURE		
DATE		

WITNESS PARTICULARS	WITNESS FOR OFFICER 1	WITNESS FOR OFFICER 2
BY (NAME OF WITNESS)		
AT (LOCATION/ADDRESS)		
SIGNATURE		
DATE		
If an officer and a witness are located in different countries While on visit must be selected.	☐ While on Visit	☐ While on Visit

12. SUBSCRIBER(S) HOLD(S) SHARES ON BEHALF OF BENEFICIAL OWNER(S): ☐ No ☐ Yes, and schedule(s) detailing beneficial owners is/are attached

Beneficial owners are persons who enjoy, and have a right to the benefits of ownership of the shares eg the right to dividends without being registered on the company's books/records as the owner.

13. DECLARATION OF ACCURACY OF PRESENTED INFORMATION

NAME OF DECLARANT		SIGNATURE OF DECLARANT	
CAPACITY	☐ Director ☐ Secretary ☐ Authorized Official	DATE	

FOR OFFICIAL USE ONLY	COMPANY #:

F1A

14. FILED BY
PARTICULARS OF INDIVIDUAL/COMPANY FILING THE FORM WITH THE COMPANIES OFFICE OF JAMAICA

NAME: ....

COMPLETE ADDRESS: ....

....

EMAIL ADDRESS: ....

CONTACT NUMBER: ....

FAX NUMBER ....

15. ADDITIONAL PARTICULARS OF DIRECTORS

NAME OF DIRECTOR	TAXPAYER REGISTRATION NUMBER	EMAIL
1.		
2.		
3.		
4.		
5.		

16. ADDITIONAL PARTICULARS OF COMPANY SECRETARY

NAME OF SECRETARY	TAXPAYER REGISTRATION NUMBER	EMAIL

FOR OFFICIAL USE ONLY	COMPANY #:

FORM 1A – continuation page
PARTICULARS OF DIRECTORS

THE COMPANIES ACT

ARTICLES OF INCORPORATION: COMPANY LIMITED BY SHARE CAPITAL

(Pursuant to sections 5 & 25 of the Companies Act)

COMPLETE THIS FORM IN BLOCK CAPITALS ONLY WITHIN THE PRESCRIBED FIELDS. PUT "N/A" IN FIELDS THAT DO NOT APPLY.

8. PARTICULARS OF DIRECTORS

DIRECTOR # (Where the director is an individual the name must be represented as FIRST MIDDLE LAST)

FULL NAME			
FULL RESIDENTIAL ADDRESS or REGISTERED OFFICE ADDRESS	STREET/DISTRICT		
	TOWN	POST OFFICE	
	PARISH	COUNTRY	
OCCUPATION		CONTACT	

DIRECTOR # (Where the director is an individual the name must be represented as FIRST MIDDLE LAST)

FULL NAME			
FULL RESIDENTIAL ADDRESS or REGISTERED OFFICE ADDRESS	STREET/DISTRICT		
	TOWN	POST OFFICE	
	PARISH	COUNTRY	
OCCUPATION		CONTACT	

DIRECTOR # ___ (Where the director is an individual the name must be represented as FIRST MIDDLE LAST)

FULL NAME			
FULL RESIDENTIAL ADDRESS or REGISTERED OFFICE ADDRESS	STREET/DISTRICT		
	TOWN	POST OFFICE	
	PARISH	COUNTRY	
OCCUPATION		CONTACT	

DIRECTOR # (Where the director is an individual the name must be represented as FIRST MIDDLE LAST)

FULL NAME			
FULL RESIDENTIAL ADDRESS or REGISTERED OFFICE ADDRESS	STREET/DISTRICT		
	TOWN	POST OFFICE	
	PARISH	COUNTRY	
OCCUPATION		CONTACT	

FOR OFFICIAL USE ONLY COMPANY #:

THE COMPANIES ACT

ARTICLES OF INCORPORATION: COMPANY LIMITED BY SHARE CAPITAL

(Pursuant to sections 8 & 25 of the Companies Act)

FORM 1A – continuation page
PARTICULARS OF INDIVIDUAL SUBSCRIBERS

10. PARTICULARS OF INDIVIDUAL SUBSCRIBERS (**shareholders who are individuals**)

SUBSCRIBER PARTICULARS	SUBSCRIBER 1	SUBSCRIBER 2	SUBSCRIBER 3	SUBSCRIBER 4
NAME				
ADDRESS				
OCCUPATION				
SHARES TAKEN UP	The total of the number of shares subscribed to by all subscribers may not exceed the **authorized number of shares** stated at **item 4.**			
CLASS OF SHARES 1. ORDINARY ______ 2. PREFERENCE ______ OTHER 3. ______	AMOUNT OF SHARES 1. ______ 2. ______ 3. ______	AMOUNT OF SHARES 1. ______ 2. ______ 3. ______	AMOUNT OF SHARES 1. ______ 2. ______ 3. ______	AMOUNT OF SHARES 1. ______ 2. ______ 3. ______
SIGNATURE				
DATE				
WITNESS PARTICULARS	**WITNESS FOR SUBSCRIBER 1**	**WITNESS FOR SUBSCRIBER 2**	**WITNESS FOR SUBSCRIBER 3**	**WITNESS FOR SUBSCRIBER 4**
WITNESSED BY (NAME OF WITNESS)				
AT (LOCATION/ADDRESS)				
SIGNATURE				
DATE				
If a subscriber and a witness are located in different countries "while on visit" must be selected	☐ While on Visit	☐ While on Visit	☐ While on Visit	☐ While on Visit

FOR OFFICIAL USE ONLY COMPANY #:

THE COMPANIES ACT

ARTICLES OF INCORPORATION: COMPANY LIMITED BY SHARE CAPITAL

(Pursuant to sections 3 & 26 of the Companies Act)

FORM 1A – continuation page

PARTICULARS OF COMPANY SUBSCRIBERS

11. PARTICULARS OF COMPANY SUBSCRIBERS (shareholders who are companies)

COMPANY PARTICULARS	
COMPANY NAME	
COMPANY REGISTERED OFFICE ADDRESS /OTHER ADDRESS	

SHARES TAKEN UP The total of the number of shares subscribed to by all subscribers may not exceed the authorized number of shares stated at Item Error! Reference source not found.

CLASS OF SHARES		AMOUNT OF SHARES
	1. ORDINARY SHARES	1.
	2. PREFERENCE SHARES	2.
	OTHER 3. Specify	3.

SEAL

OFFICER PARTICULARS	OFFICER 1	OFFICER 2
OFFICER NAME		
OFFICE HELD IN COMPANY		
SIGNATURE		
DATE		
WITNESSS PARTICULARS	**WITNESS FOR OFFICER 1**	**WITNESS FOR OFFICER 2**
BY (NAME OF WITNESS)		
AT (LOCATION/ADDRESS)		
SIGNATURE		
DATE		
If an officer and a witness are located in different countries while on visit must be selected.	☐ While on Visit	☐ While on Visit

FOR OFFICIAL USE ONLY COMPANY #:

THE COMPANIES ACT

ARTICLES OF INCORPORATION: COMPANY LIMITED BY SHARE CAPITAL

(Pursuant to sections 6 & 25 of the Companies Act)

FORM 1A – SCHEDULE
PARTICULARS OF BENEFICIAL OWNERS

12. PARTICULARS OF BENEFICIAL OWNERS

BENEFICIAL OWNER PARTICULARS	BENEFICIAL OWNER ___	BENEFICIAL OWNER ___	BENEFICIAL OWNER ___	BENEFICIAL OWNER ___
NAME				
ADDRESS				
NATIONALITY				
SHARES HELD ON BEHALF OF BENEFICIARY	[illegible]			
CLASS OF SHARES 1. ORDINARY ___ 2. PREFERENCE ___ OTHER 3. ___	AMOUNT OF SHARES 1. ___ 2. ___ 3. ___	AMOUNT OF SHARES 1. ___ 2. ___ 3. ___	AMOUNT OF SHARES 1. ___ 2. ___ 3. ___	AMOUNT OF SHARES 1. ___ 2. ___ 3. ___

SUBSCRIBER PARTICULARS	SUBSCRIBER HOLDING SHARES ON BEHALF OF BENEFICIARY ABOVE	SUBSCRIBER HOLDING SHARES ON BEHALF OF BENEFICIARY ABOVE	SUBSCRIBER HOLDING SHARES ON BEHALF OF BENEFICIARY ABOVE	SUBSCRIBER HOLDING SHARES ON BEHALF OF BENEFICIARY ABOVE
NAME				

FOR OFFICIAL USE ONLY COMPANY #:

☐ **New Incorporation**

☐ **Amended Articles**

☐ **Re-registration**
Changing from one type of a company to another

FORM 1B
READ INSTRUCTIONS BEFORE COMPLETING

THE COMPANIES ACT

ARTICLES OF INCORPORATION: COMPANY LIMITED BY GUARANTEE AND NOT HAVING A SHARE CAPITAL

(Pursuant to sections 6 & 20 of the Companies Act)

COMPLETE THIS FORM IN BLOCK CAPITALS ONLY WITHIN THE PRESCRIBED FIELDS. PUT "N/A" IN FIELDS THAT DO NOT APPLY.

1A. NAME OF COMPANY

____

____

> The name here must be completely consistent with the name reserved in pursuance of this registration.

1B. JUSTIFICATION FOR PROPOSED NAME (if applicable)

____

____

> The use of words such as "Caribbean", "Global" and "International" must be explained.

1C. COMPANY TELEPHONE NUMBER ______________

1D. COMPANY EMAIL ADDRESS ______________

1E. TYPE OF COMPANY ☐ Private ☐ Public

2. THE REGISTERED OFFICE IS LOCATED IN JAMAICA AND THE LIABILITY OF THE MEMBERS IS LIMITED

3. THIS ASSOCIATION IS FORMED EXCLUSIVELY FOR THE PROMOTION OF

☐ Commerce ☐ Art ☐ Science ☐ Religion ☐ Charity ☐ Other

If OTHER, specify ______________________________

The powers of the company are limited to those necessary to the carrying out of the main business of the company outlined in **item 3** above

3A. RESTRICTIONS, IF ANY, ON THE BUSINESS THE ASSOCIATION MAY CARRY ON

____

____

> You may state the activities that the association can engage in or is prohibited from engaging in.

4. COMPANY'S ARTICLES (RULES) **Please check the appropriate box below (ONLY ONE BOX MUST BE CHECKED)**

4a. ☐ Standard Articles from **Table B** in their entirety: **Articles 1-71** only

4b. ☐ Standard Articles from **Table B Articles 1-35, 37-71** with **Varied Article 36** and **Additional Articles 72-77**
SEE SCHEDULE(S) ______________

4c. ☐ Standard Articles selected from **Table B** (e.g. ***1-30 & 32-71***)
ARTICLES ______________

4d. ☐ Standard Articles selected from **Table B** with varied and/or additional articles
ARTICLES ______________
SEE SCHEDULE(S) ______________

4e. ☐ Other
("Other" is to be used when you do not wish to accept the Standard Articles from Table B and wish to attach your own)
SEE SCHEDULE(S) ______________

> Table B of the First Schedule of the Companies Act 2004 provides standard articles (rules) for the internal management of a company limited by guarantee.
> In Table B
> - Articles 1-71 detail general meetings, votes of members, directors, borrowing powers of the company, the seal, accounts and notices etc.
>
> TO COMPLETE THIS SECTION
> You may choose from Table B
> - All the Rules in their entirety exactly as they are stated, or
> - All the Rules in their entirety with an additional article
> - Some of the Rules
>
> If you do not choose to select any of the options 4a to 4d then you must attach your own articles (rules) for the internal management of the company to this form and select the "Other" option at 4e. You are also required to attach schedules containing the varied or additional articles which you wish to include.
>
> Charities most often choose the option 4b.

NOTES FOR ASSOCIATIONS WISHING TO REMOVE "LIMITED" FROM THEIR NAMES

The Minister may issue a licence which permits the removal of the word "**Limited**" from the name of the company. It is advised that an additional schedule be attached to the articles outlining how the association is to be governed and the manner in which the funds will be used for charitable purposes.

5. **GUARANTEE/MEMBERS' LIABILITY (Mandatory)**
(Every member of the association undertakes to contribute to the assets of the association in the event of the same being wound up or closed.)

STATE THE AMOUNT IN DOLLARS: $ ______________

FOR OFFICIAL USE ONLY COMPANY #:

6. PROPOSED NUMBER OF MEMBERS AT THE TIME OF INCORPORATION ☐

7. PARTICULARS OF INDIVIDUAL SUBSCRIBERS

SUBSCRIBER PARTICULARS	SUBSCRIBER 1	SUBSCRIBER 2	SUBSCRIBER 3	SUBSCRIBER 4
NAME				
ADDRESS				
OCCUPATION				
SIGNATURE				
DATE				
WITNESS PARTICULARS	**WITNESS FOR SUBSCRIBER 1**	**WITNESS FOR SUBSCRIBER 2**	**WITNESS FOR SUBSCRIBER 3**	**WITNESS FOR SUBSCRIBER 4**
BY (NAME OF WITNESS)				
AT (LOCATION/ADDRESS)				
SIGNATURE				
DATE				
If a subscriber and a witness are located in different countries, while on visit must be selected.	☐ While on Visit	☐ While on Visit	☐ While on Visit	☐ While on Visit

FOR OFFICIAL USE ONLY COMPANY #:

8. PARTICULARS OF COMPANY SUBSCRIBERS

COMPANY PARTICULARS		
COMPANY NAME		
COMPANY REGISTERED OFFICE ADDRESS /OTHER ADDRESS		
OFFICER PARTICULARS	**OFFICER 1**	**OFFICER 2**
OFFICER NAME		
OFFICE HELD IN COMPANY		
SIGNATURE		
DATE		
WITNESS PARTICULARS	**WITNESS FOR OFFICER 1**	**WITNESS FOR OFFICER 2**
WITNESSED BY (NAME OF WITNESS)		
AT (LOCATION/ ADDRESS)		
SIGNATURE		
DATE		
	☐ While on Visit	☐ While on Visit

SEAL

If an officer and a witness are located in different countries, 'while on visit' must be selected

9. **MINIMUM NUMBER OF DIRECTORS** ☐

AND/OR

9A. **MAXIMUM NUMBER OF DIRECTORS** ☐

A private company must have at least one director, he/she cannot also be the company secretary. A public company must have a minimum of three (3) directors, two of them however should not be employed by the company or any of its affiliates.

10. **PARTICULARS OF DIRECTORS**

DIRECTOR 1 (**Where the director is an individual the name must be represented as FIRST MIDDLE LAST**)

FULL NAME			
FULL RESIDENTIAL ADDRESS or REGISTERED OFFICE ADDRESS	STREET/DISTRICT		
	TOWN	POST OFFICE	
	PARISH	COUNTRY	
OCCUPATION		**CONTACT**	

FOR OFFICIAL USE ONLY COMPANY #:

DIRECTOR 2 (Where the director is an individual the name must be represented as FIRST MIDDLE LAST)

FULL NAME			
FULL RESIDENTIAL ADDRESS or REGISTERED OFFICE ADDRESS	STREET/DISTRICT		
	TOWN	POST OFFICE	
	PARISH	COUNTRY	
OCCUPATION		CONTACT	

DIRECTOR 3 (Where the director is an individual the name must be represented as FIRST MIDDLE LAST)

FULL NAME			
FULL RESIDENTIAL ADDRESS or REGISTERED OFFICE ADDRESS	STREET/DISTRICT		
	TOWN	POST OFFICE	
	PARISH	COUNTRY	
OCCUPATION		CONTACT	

DIRECTOR 4 (Where the director is an individual the name must be represented as FIRST MIDDLE LAST)

FULL NAME			
FULL RESIDENTIAL ADDRESS or REGISTERED OFFICE ADDRESS	STREET/DISTRICT		
	TOWN	POST OFFICE	
	PARISH	COUNTRY	
OCCUPATION		CONTACT	

11. PARTICULARS OF COMPANY SECRETARY (Where the secretary is an individual the name must be represented as FIRST MIDDLE LAST)

FULL NAME			
FULL RESIDENTIAL ADDRESS or REGISTERED OFFICE ADDRESS	STREET/DISTRICT		
	TOWN	POST OFFICE	
	PARISH	COUNTRY	
OCCUPATION		CONTACT	

12. DECLARATION OF ACCURACY OF PRESENTED INFORMATION

NAME OF DECLARANT			
CAPACITY	☐ Director ☐ Secretary ☐ Authorized Official		
SIGNATURE		DATE	

FOR OFFICIAL USE ONLY	COMPANY #.

F1B

13. FILED BY
PARTICULARS OF INDIVIDUAL/COMPANY FILING THE FORM WITH THE COMPANIES OFFICE OF JAMAICA

NAME:

COMPLETE ADDRESS:

EMAIL ADDRESS:

CONTACT NUMBER:

14. ADDITIONAL PARTICULARS OF DIRECTORS

NAME OF DIRECTOR	TAXPAYER REGISTRATION NUMBER	EMAIL
1.		
2.		
3.		
4.		

15. ADDITIONAL PARTICULARS OF COMPANY SECRETARY

NAME OF SECRETARY	TAXPAYER REGISTRATION NUMBER	EMAIL

FOR OFFICIAL USE ONLY	COMPANY #:

THE COMPANIES ACT

ARTICLES OF INCORPORATION: COMPANY LIMITED BY GUARANTEE AND NOT HAVING A SHARE CAPITAL

(Pursuant to sections 8 & 20 of the Companies Act)

FORM 1B – continuation page

PARTICULARS OF INDIVIDUAL SUBSCRIBERS

7. PARTICULARS OF INDIVIDUAL SUBSCRIBERS

SUBSCRIBER PARTICULARS	SUBSCRIBER 1	SUBSCRIBER 2	SUBSCRIBER 3	SUBSCRIBER 4
NAME				
ADDRESS				
OCCUPATION				
SIGNATURE				
DATE				
WITNESS PARTICULARS	**WITNESS FOR SUBSCRIBER 1**	**WITNESS FOR SUBSCRIBER 2**	**WITNESS FOR SUBSCRIBER 3**	**WITNESS FOR SUBSCRIBER 4**
WITNESSED BY (NAME OF WITNESS)				
AT (LOCATION/ADDRESS)				
SIGNATURE				
DATE				
	☐ While on Visit	☐ While on Visit	☐ While on Visit	☐ While on Visit

FOR OFFICIAL USE ONLY COMPANY #:

FORM 1B – continuation page
PARTICULARS OF COMPANY SUBSCRIBERS

THE COMPANIES ACT

ARTICLES OF INCORPORATION: COMPANY LIMITED BY GUARANTEE AND NOT HAVING A SHARE CAPITAL

(Pursuant to sections [illegible] of the Companies Act)

COMPLETE THIS FORM IN BLOCK CAPITALS ONLY WITHIN THE PRESCRIBED FIELDS. PUT "N/A" IN FIELDS THAT DO NOT APPLY.

8 PARTICULARS OF COMPANY SUBSCRIBERS

COMPANY PARTICULARS		
COMPANY NAME		
COMPANY REGISTERED OFFICE ADDRESS /OTHER ADDRESS		
OFFICER PARTICULARS	**OFFICER 1**	**OFFICER 2**
OFFICER NAME		
OFFICE HELD IN COMPANY		
SIGNATURE		
DATE		
WITNESS PARTICULARS	**WITNESS FOR OFFICER 1**	**WITNESS FOR OFFICER 2**
WITNESSED BY (NAME OF WITNESS)		
AT (LOCATION/ ADDRESS)		
SIGNATURE		
DATE		
	☐ While on Visit	☐ While on Visit

SEAL

If an officer and a witness are located in different countries, 'While on visit' must be selected

FOR OFFICIAL USE ONLY COMPANY #:

FORM 1B – continuation page

PARTICULARS OF DIRECTORS

THE COMPANIES ACT

ARTICLES OF INCORPORATION: COMPANY LIMITED BY GUARANTEE AND NOT HAVING A SHARE CAPITAL

(Pursuant to sections 6 & 20 of the Companies Act)

COMPLETE THIS FORM IN BLOCK CAPITALS ONLY WITHIN THE PRESCRIBED FIELDS. PUT "N/A" IN FIELDS THAT DO NOT APPLY.

10. PARTICULARS OF DIRECTORS

DIRECTOR #____ (Where the director is an individual the name must be represented as FIRST MIDDLE LAST)

FULL NAME			
FULL RESIDENTIAL ADDRESS or REGISTERED OFFICE ADDRESS	STREET/DISTRICT		
	TOWN	POST OFFICE	
	PARISH	COUNTRY	
OCCUPATION		CONTACT	

DIRECTOR #____ (Where the director is an individual the name must be represented as FIRST MIDDLE LAST)

FULL NAME			
FULL RESIDENTIAL ADDRESS or REGISTERED OFFICE ADDRESS	STREET/DISTRICT		
	TOWN	POST OFFICE	
	PARISH	COUNTRY	
OCCUPATION		CONTACT	

DIRECTOR #____ (Where the director is an individual the name must be represented as FIRST MIDDLE LAST)

FULL NAME			
FULL RESIDENTIAL ADDRESS or REGISTERED OFFICE ADDRESS	STREET/DISTRICT		
	TOWN	POST OFFICE	
	PARISH	COUNTRY	
OCCUPATION		CONTACT	

DIRECTOR #____ (Where the director is an individual the name must be represented as FIRST MIDDLE LAST)

FULL NAME			
FULL RESIDENTIAL ADDRESS or REGISTERED OFFICE ADDRESS	STREET/DISTRICT		
	TOWN	POST OFFICE	
	PARISH	COUNTRY	
OCCUPATION		CONTACT	

FOR OFFICIAL USE ONLY COMPANY #:

☐ **New Incorporation**
(Requires Stamp Duty)

☐ **Amended Articles**

☐ **Re-registration**
(Changing from one type of a company to another)

FORM 1C
READ INSTRUCTIONS BEFORE COMPLETING

THE COMPANIES ACT

ARTICLES OF INCORPORATION: COMPANY LIMITED BY GUARANTEE WITH SHARE CAPITAL

(Pursuant to sections 8 & 20(2) of the Companies Act)

COMPLETE THIS FORM IN BLOCK CAPITALS ONLY WITHIN THE PRESCRIBED FIELDS. PUT "N/A" IN FIELDS THAT DO NOT APPLY.

1A. NAME OF COMPANY

____

____

> The name here must be completely consistent with the name reserved in pursuance of this registration

1B. JUSTIFICATION FOR PROPOSED NAME (if applicable)

____

____

> The use of words such as 'Caribbean', 'Global' and 'International' must be explained.

1C. CORE BUSINESS OF THE COMPANY
(The activities of the business are not restricted to the area(s) stated below unless indicated at item 1D)

____

____

1D. RESTRICTION ON THE BUSINESS OF THE COMPANY (if applicable)

____

____

> It is not required that you restrict the activities of your company. If there are no restrictions insert 'N/A'.

1E. COMPANY TELEPHONE NUMBER __________

1F. COMPANY EMAIL ADDRESS __________

1G. TYPE OF COMPANY
☐ Private ☐ Public

2. THE REGISTERED OFFICE IS LOCATED IN JAMAICA AND THE LIABILITY OF THE MEMBERS IS LIMITED

3. COMPANY'S ARTICLES (RULES) **Please check the appropriate box below (ONLY ONE BOX MUST BE CHECKED)**

3a. ☐ Standard Articles **Articles 1–78, 80–136** with **Varied Article 79** and **Additional Articles 137–143** SEE SCHEDULE(S) __________

3b. ☐ Standard Articles **Articles 1–78, 80–136** with **Varied Article 79** only SEE SCHEDULE __________

3c. ☐ Standard Articles **Articles 1–136** with **Additional Articles 137–143** only SEE SCHEDULE(S) __________

3d. ☐ Standard Articles in their entirety **Articles 1–136**

3e. ☐ Other
*(If "Other" is checked, please list the numbers of the articles from **Table A** and/or **Table B** that are to apply (if any) and/ or state the name(s) of the schedule(s) which contain the additional/varied articles which are to apply below)*

____

____

> Table A and Table B of the First Schedule of the Companies Act 2004 provide standard articles (rules) for the internal management of a company limited by guarantee with share capital.
>
> At this section you may select any combination of articles from these two tables. If you do not choose to accept them at all, you must attach your own articles (rules) for the internal management of the company to this form and select the 'Other' option. You are also required to attach schedules containing the varied or additional articles which you wish to include.

NOTES FOR PRIVATE COMPANIES

- The right to transfer shares is restricted;
- Subject to **section 28(1)(b)** of the **Companies Act 2004**, the number of members of the company is limited to twenty
  (This is exclusive of persons who having been formerly in the employment of the company were, while in that employment, and have continued after the determination of such employment to be members of the company)
- Provided that where two or more persons hold one or more shares in the company jointly they shall for the purpose of this regulation be treated as a single member; Any invitation to the public to subscribe for any shares or debentures of the company is prohibited
- Any invitation to the public to deposit money for fixed periods or payable on call whether bearing or not interest is prohibited;
- Subject to the exceptions provided for the in Twelfth Schedule to the Act, any person other than a shareholder is prohibited from having any interest in any of the company's shares;
- The company shall not have to the power to issue share warrants to bearer.

FOR OFFICIAL USE ONLY COMPANY #:

4. AUTHORIZED NUMBER OF SHARES This is the maximum number of shares that your company is authorized to issue

The total number of shares in all classes should not exceed the total number of shares, if any, indicated at item 4

4A. CLASSES OF SHARES (Indicate by ticking the class or classes of shares that the company issue on incorporation)	4B. TOTAL NUMBER OF SHARES IN EACH CLASS
☐ ORDINARY	
☐ PREFERENCE	
☐ OTHER Specify ______________	

Shares may be issued with different rights, privileges and conditions. Shares with the same rights, privileges and conditions are grouped into classes.

All companies limited by shares must issue at least one class of shares (e.g. ordinary shares) and may issue two or more classes of shares. Where different classes of shares are issued at incorporation, a Form 3 should be completed and attached to this form.

5. RESTRICTIONS ON SHARE TRANSFER (eg Directors must give consent to the transfer of shares)

____

____

____

All private companies must restrict the right to transfer shares (e.g. shares must be first offered to existing shareholders)

A public company may only restrict the right to transfer shares which have not been fully paid up

6. NON-CASH CONSIDERATION

Were any shares issued for non-cash consideration (that is, as a payment for goods, services, property, good will, shares in other companies etc.) based on a contract that existed before incorporation? (ONLY ONE BOX MUST BE CHECKED)

☐ Yes – Complete item 6A

☐ No – Continue to item 7

6A. PLEASE INDICATE THE NATURE AND VALUE OF THE NON-CASH CONSIDERATION BELOW

____

____

7. PROPOSED NUMBER OF MEMBERS AT THE TIME OF INCORPORATION ☐

8. THE TERMS OF UNDERTAKING AND THE EXTENT OF GUARANTEE

____

____

____

Every member of the association undertakes to contribute to the assets of the association in the event of the same being wound up or closed. Ordinarily, members will be liable to the extent of the guarantee as well as the amount unpaid on the shares received.

9. MINIMUM NUMBER OF DIRECTORS ☐

AND/OR

9A. MAXIMUM NUMBER OF DIRECTORS ☐

A private company must have at least one director; he/she cannot also be the company secretary. A public company must have a minimum of three (3) directors, two of them however should not be employed by the company or any of its affiliates.

10. PARTICULARS OF DIRECTORS

DIRECTOR 1 (Where the director is an individual the name must be represented as FIRST MIDDLE LAST)

FULL NAME			
FULL RESIDENTIAL ADDRESS or REGISTERED OFFICE ADDRESS	STREET/DISTRICT		
	TOWN	POST OFFICE	
	PARISH	COUNTRY	
OCCUPATION		CONTACT	

FOR OFFICIAL USE ONLY COMPANY #:

DIRECTOR 2 (Where the director is an individual the name must be represented as FIRST MIDDLE LAST)

FULL NAME			
FULL RESIDENTIAL ADDRESS or REGISTERED OFFICE ADDRESS	STREET/DISTRICT		
	TOWN	POST OFFICE	
	PARISH	COUNTRY	
OCCUPATION		CONTACT	

DIRECTOR 3 (Where the director is an individual the name must be represented as FIRST MIDDLE LAST)

FULL NAME			
FULL RESIDENTIAL ADDRESS or REGISTERED OFFICE ADDRESS	STREET/DISTRICT		
	TOWN	POST OFFICE	
	PARISH	COUNTRY	
OCCUPATION		CONTACT	

DIRECTOR 4 (Where the director is an individual the name must be represented as FIRST MIDDLE LAST)

FULL NAME			
FULL RESIDENTIAL ADDRESS or REGISTERED OFFICE ADDRESS	STREET/DISTRICT		
	TOWN	POST OFFICE	
	PARISH	COUNTRY	
OCCUPATION		CONTACT	

DIRECTOR 5 (Where the director is an individual the name must be represented as FIRST MIDDLE LAST)

FULL NAME			
FULL RESIDENTIAL ADDRESS or REGISTERED OFFICE ADDRESS	STREET/DISTRICT		
	TOWN	POST OFFICE	
	PARISH	COUNTRY	
OCCUPATION		CONTACT	

11. PARTICULARS OF COMPANY SECRETARY (Where the secretary is an individual the name must be represented as FIRST MIDDLE LAST)

FULL NAME			
FULL RESIDENTIAL ADDRESS or REGISTERED OFFICE ADDRESS	STREET/DISTRICT		
	TOWN	POST OFFICE	
	PARISH	COUNTRY	
OCCUPATION		CONTACT	

FOR OFFICIAL USE ONLY	COMPANY #:

12. PARTICULARS OF INDIVIDUAL SUBSCRIBERS (shareholders who are individuals)

SUBSCRIBER PARTICULARS	SUBSCRIBER 1	SUBSCRIBER 2	SUBSCRIBER 3	SUBSCRIBER 4
NAME				
ADDRESS				
OCCUPATION				
SHARES TAKEN UP	The total of the number of shares subscribed to by all subscribers may not exceed the authorised number of shares stated at item 4.			
CLASS OF SHARES 1. ORDINARY ______ 2. PREFERENCE ______ OTHER 3. ______	AMOUNT OF SHARES 1. ______ 2. ______ 3. ______	AMOUNT OF SHARES 1. ______ 2. ______ 3. ______	AMOUNT OF SHARES 1. ______ 2. ______ 3. ______	AMOUNT OF SHARES 1. ______ 2. ______ 3. ______
SIGNATURE				
DATE				
WITNESS PARTICULARS	WITNESS FOR SUBSCRIBER 1	WITNESS FOR SUBSCRIBER 2	WITNESS FOR SUBSCRIBER 3	WITNESS FOR SUBSCRIBER 4
WITNESSED BY (NAME OF WITNESS)				
AT (LOCATION/ADDRESS)				
SIGNATURE				
DATE				
If a subscriber and a witness are located in different countries "While on Visit" must be selected	☐ While on Visit	☐ While on Visit	☐ While on Visit	☐ While on Visit

FOR OFFICIAL USE ONLY COMPANY #:

13. PARTICULARS OF COMPANY SUBSCRIBERS (**shareholders who are companies**)

COMPANY PARTICULARS	
COMPANY NAME	
COMPANY REGISTERED OFFICE ADDRESS /OTHER ADDRESS	

SHARES TAKEN UP The total of the number of shares subscribed to by all subscribers may not exceed the authorized number of shares stated at item 4

CLASS OF SHARES		AMOUNT OF SHARES
	1. ORDINARY SHARES	1.
	2. PREFERENCE SHARES	2.
	OTHER 3. Specify	3.

SEAL

OFFICER PARTICULARS	OFFICER 1	OFFICER 2
OFFICER NAME		
OFFICE HELD IN COMPANY		
SIGNATURE		
DATE		

WITNESSS PARTICULARS	WITNESS FOR OFFICER 1	WITNESS FOR OFFICER 2
BY (NAME OF WITNESS)		
AT (LOCATION/ADDRESS)		
SIGNATURE		
DATE		
If an officer and witness are located in different countries 'while on visit' must be selected	☐ While on Visit	☐ While on Visit

14 SUBSCRIBER(S) HOLD(S) SHARES ON BEHALF OF BENEFICIAL OWNER(S): ☐ No ☐ Yes, and schedule(s) detailing beneficial owners is/are attached

Beneficial owners are persons who enjoy and have a right to the benefits of ownership of the shares eg the right to dividends without being registered on the company's books/records as the owner.

15. DECLARATION OF ACCURACY OF PRESENTED INFORMATION

NAME OF DECLARANT		SIGNATURE OF DECLARANT	
CAPACITY	☐ Director ☐ Secretary ☐ Authorized Official	DATE	

FOR OFFICIAL USE ONLY COMPANY #:

F1C

16. FILED BY
PARTICULARS OF INDIVIDUAL/COMPANY FILING THE FORM WITH THE COMPANIES OFFICE OF JAMAICA

NAME: ....

COMPLETE ADDRESS: ....

....

EMAIL ADDRESS: ....

CONTACT NUMBER: ....

FAX NUMBER ....

17. ADDITIONAL PARTICULARS OF DIRECTORS

NAME OF DIRECTOR	TAXPAYER REGISTRATION NUMBER	EMAIL
1.		
2.		
3.		
4.		
5.		

18. ADDITIONAL PARTICULARS OF COMPANY SECRETARY

NAME OF SECRETARY	TAXPAYER REGISTRATION NUMBER	EMAIL

FOR OFFICIAL USE ONLY	COMPANY #:

FORM 1C – continuation page
PARTICULARS OF DIRECTORS

THE COMPANIES ACT

ARTICLES OF INCORPORATION: COMPANY LIMITED BY GUARANTEE WITH SHARE CAPITAL

(Pursuant to sections 8 & 20(2) of the Companies Act)

COMPLETE THIS FORM IN BLOCK CAPITALS ONLY WITHIN THE PRESCRIBED FIELDS. PUT "N/A" IN FIELDS THAT DO NOT APPLY.

10. PARTICULARS OF DIRECTORS

DIRECTOR # (Where the director is an individual the name must be represented as FIRST MIDDLE LAST)

FULL NAME			
FULL RESIDENTIAL ADDRESS or REGISTERED OFFICE ADDRESS	STREET/DISTRICT		
	TOWN	POST OFFICE	
	PARISH	COUNTRY	
OCCUPATION		CONTACT	

DIRECTOR # (Where the director is an individual the name must be represented as FIRST MIDDLE LAST)

FULL NAME			
FULL RESIDENTIAL ADDRESS or REGISTERED OFFICE ADDRESS	STREET/DISTRICT		
	TOWN	POST OFFICE	
	PARISH	COUNTRY	
OCCUPATION		CONTACT	

DIRECTOR # (Where the director is an individual the name must be represented as FIRST MIDDLE LAST)

FULL NAME			
FULL RESIDENTIAL ADDRESS or REGISTERED OFFICE ADDRESS	STREET/DISTRICT		
	TOWN	POST OFFICE	
	PARISH	COUNTRY	
OCCUPATION		CONTACT	

DIRECTOR # (Where the director is an individual the name must be represented as FIRST MIDDLE LAST)

FULL NAME			
FULL RESIDENTIAL ADDRESS or REGISTERED OFFICE ADDRESS	STREET/DISTRICT		
	TOWN	POST OFFICE	
	PARISH	COUNTRY	
OCCUPATION		CONTACT	

FOR OFFICIAL USE ONLY	COMPANY #:

THE COMPANIES ACT

ARTICLES OF INCORPORATION: COMPANY LIMITED BY GUARANTEE WITH SHARE CAPITAL

(Pursuant to sections 8 & 20(2) of the Companies Act)

FORM 1C – continuation page

PARTICULARS OF INDIVIDUAL SUBSCRIBERS

12 PARTICULARS OF INDIVIDUAL SUBSCRIBERS (shareholders who are individuals)

SUBSCRIBER PARTICULARS	SUBSCRIBER 1	SUBSCRIBER 2	SUBSCRIBER 3	SUBSCRIBER 4
NAME				
ADDRESS				
OCCUPATION				
SHARES TAKEN UP	The total of the number of shares subscribed to by all subscribers may not exceed the **authorized number of shares** stated at **Item 4.**			
CLASS OF SHARES 1. ORDINARY ____ 2. PREFERENCE ____ OTHER 3. ____	AMOUNT OF SHARES 1. ____ 2. ____ 3. ____	AMOUNT OF SHARES 1. ____ 2. ____ 3. ____	AMOUNT OF SHARES 1. ____ 2. ____ 3. ____	AMOUNT OF SHARES 1. ____ 2. ____ 3. ____
SIGNATURE				
DATE				
WITNESS PARTICULARS	**WITNESS FOR SUBSCRIBER 1**	**WITNESS FOR SUBSCRIBER 2**	**WITNESS FOR SUBSCRIBER 3**	**WITNESS FOR SUBSCRIBER 4**
WITNESSED BY (NAME OF WITNESS)				
AT (LOCATION/ADDRESS)				
SIGNATURE				
DATE				
If a subscriber and a witness are located in different countries 'while on visit' must be selected	☐ While on Visit	☐ While on Visit	☐ While on Visit	☐ While on Visit

FOR OFFICIAL USE ONLY COMPANY #:

THE COMPANIES ACT

ARTICLES OF INCORPORATION: COMPANY LIMITED BY GUARANTEE WITH SHARE CAPITAL

(Pursuant to sections 8 & 20(2) of the Companies Act)

FORM 1C – continuation page

PARTICULARS OF COMPANY SUBSCRIBERS

13. PARTICULARS OF COMPANY SUBSCRIBERS **(shareholders who are companies)**

COMPANY PARTICULARS	
COMPANY NAME	
COMPANY REGISTERED OFFICE ADDRESS /OTHER ADDRESS	

SHARES TAKEN UP The total of the number of shares subscribed to by all subscribers may not exceed the **authorized number of shares** stated at **Item** Error! Reference source not found.

CLASS OF SHARES		AMOUNT OF SHARES	
	1. ORDINARY SHARES		1. ______
	2. PREFERENCE SHARES OTHER		2. ______
	3. Specify ______		3. ______

SEAL

OFFICER PARTICULARS	OFFICER 1	OFFICER 2
OFFICER NAME		
OFFICE HELD IN COMPANY		
SIGNATURE		
DATE		
WITNESSS PARTICULARS	**WITNESS FOR OFFICER 1**	**WITNESS FOR OFFICER 2**
BY (NAME OF WITNESS)		
AT (LOCATION/ADDRESS)		
SIGNATURE		
DATE		
If an officer and witness are located in different countries "while on visit" must be selected.	☐ While on Visit	☐ While on Visit

FOR OFFICIAL USE ONLY COMPANY #:

THE COMPANIES ACT

ARTICLES OF INCORPORATION: COMPANY LIMITED BY GUARANTEE WITH SHARE CAPITAL

(Pursuant to sections 6 & 20(2) of the Companies Act)

FORM 1C – SCHEDULE

PARTICULARS OF BENEFICIAL OWNERS

14. PARTICULARS OF BENEFICIAL OWNERS

BENEFICIAL OWNER PARTICULARS	BENEFICIAL OWNER ___	BENEFICIAL OWNER ___	BENEFICIAL OWNER ___	BENEFICIAL OWNER ___
NAME				
ADDRESS				
NATIONALITY				
SHARES HELD ON BEHALF OF BENEFICIARY	[illegible] on behalf of beneficiaries may not exceed the total number of shares held by the subscriber			
CLASS OF SHARES: 1. ORDINARY ___ 2. PREFERENCE ___ OTHER 3. ___	AMOUNT OF SHARES: 1. ___ 2. ___ 3. ___	AMOUNT OF SHARES: 1. ___ 2. ___ 3. ___	AMOUNT OF SHARES: 1. ___ 2. ___ 3. ___	AMOUNT OF SHARES: 1. ___ 2. ___ 3. ___

SUBSCRIBER PARTICULARS	SUBSCRIBER HOLDING SHARES ON BEHALF OF BENEFICIARY ABOVE	SUBSCRIBER HOLDING SHARES ON BEHALF OF BENEFICIARY ABOVE	SUBSCRIBER HOLDING SHARES ON BEHALF OF BENEFICIARY ABOVE	SUBSCRIBER HOLDING SHARES ON BEHALF OF BENEFICIARY ABOVE
NAME				

FOR OFFICIAL USE ONLY COMPANY #:

☐ **New Incorporation**
(Attracts Stamp Duty)

☐ **Amended Articles**

☐ **Re-registration**
(Changing from one type of a company to another)

FORM 1D
READ INSTRUCTIONS BEFORE COMPLETING

THE COMPANIES ACT

ARTICLES OF INCORPORATION: UNLIMITED COMPANY WITH SHARE CAPITAL

(Pursuant to section 6)

COMPLETE THIS FORM IN BLOCK CAPITALS ONLY WITHIN THE PRESCRIBED FIELDS. PUT "N/A" IN FIELDS THAT DO NOT APPLY.

1A. NAME OF COMPANY

____

____

The name here must be completely consistent with the name reserved in pursuance of this registration.

1B. JUSTIFICATION FOR PROPOSED NAME (if applicable)

____

____

The use of words such as "Caribbean", "Global" and "International" must be explained.

1C. CORE BUSINESS OF THE COMPANY
(The activities of the business are not restricted to the area(s) stated below unless indicated at item 1D)

____

____

1D. RESTRICTION ON THE BUSINESS OF THE COMPANY (if applicable)

____

____

It is not required that you restrict the activities of your company. If there are no restrictions insert "N/A".

1E. COMPANY TELEPHONE NUMBER

____

1F. COMPANY EMAIL ADDRESS

____

1G. TYPE OF COMPANY

☐ Private ☐ Public

2. THE REGISTERED OFFICE IS LOCATED IN JAMAICA AND THE LIABILITY OF THE MEMBERS IS UNLIMITED

3. COMPANY'S ARTICLES (RULES) Please check the appropriate box below (ONLY ONE BOX MUST BE CHECKED)

3a. ☐ Standard Articles **Articles 1–78, 80–136** with **Varied Article 79** and **Additional Articles 137–143 SEE SCHEDULE(S)** _______________

3b. ☐ Standard Articles **Articles 1–78, 80–136** with **Varied Article 79** only **SEE SCHEDULE** _______________

3c. ☐ Standard Articles **Articles 1–136** with **Additional Articles 137–143** only **SEE SCHEDULE(S)** _______________

3d. ☐ Standard Articles (Rules) in their entirety Articles 1–136

3e. ☐ Other
*(If "Other" is checked, please list the numbers of the articles from **Table A** that are to apply (if any) and/ or state the name(s) of the schedule(s) which contain the additional/varied articles which are to apply below)*

____

____

Table A of the First Schedule of the Companies Act 2004 provides standard articles (rules) for the internal management of an unlimited company with shares

In Table A

- Articles 1-78 detail share capital, share transfers, general meetings, votes of members, directors etc
- Varied Article 79 allows the company to borrow money
- Articles 80-136 detail the duties of directors, the seal, accounts, audit and indemnity etc
- Articles 137-143 detail that share transfers must be authorized by the directors etc

TO COMPLETE THIS SECTION
You may choose from Table A

- Most of the Rules in their entirety with common varied and additional articles
- Most of the Rules in their entirety with a common varied article
- All of the rules in their entirety with common additional articles.
- All of the rules in their entirety
- Your custom combination of articles

If you do not choose to accept them at all, you must attach your own articles (rules) for the internal management of the company to this form and select the "Other" option. You are also required to attach schedules containing the varied or additional articles which you wish to include

NOTES FOR PRIVATE COMPANIES

- The right to transfer shares is restricted
- Subject to **section 25(1)(b)** of the **Companies Act 2004**, the number of members of the company is limited to twenty
(This is exclusive of persons who having been formerly in the employment of the company were, while in that employment, and have continued after the determination of such employment to be members of the company)
- Provided that where two or more persons hold one or more shares in the company jointly they shall for the purpose of this regulation be treated as a single member. Any invitation to the public to subscribe for any shares or debentures of the company is prohibited
- Any invitation to the public to deposit money for fixed periods or payable on call whether bearing or not interest is prohibited;
- Subject to the exceptions provided for the in Twelfth Schedule to the Act, any person other than a shareholder is prohibited from having any interest in any of the company's shares.
- The company shall not have to the power to issue share warrants to bearer.

FOR OFFICIAL USE ONLY COMPANY #:

4. AUTHORIZED NUMBER OF SHARES This is the maximum number of shares that your company is authorized to issue.

	The total number of shares in all classes should not exceed the total number of shares, if any, indicated at item 4.

4A. CLASSES OF SHARES (Indicate by ticking the class or classes of shares that the company issue on incorporation)	4B. TOTAL NUMBER OF SHARES IN EACH CLASS
☐ ORDINARY	
☐ PREFERENCE	
☐ OTHER Specify ________________	

Shares may be issued with different rights, privileges and conditions. Shares with the same rights, privileges and conditions are grouped into classes.

All companies limited by shares must issue at least one class of shares which are non-redeemable (e.g. ordinary shares) and may issue two or more classes of shares. Where different classes of shares are issued, at incorporation a Form 3 should be completed and attached to this form.

5. RESTRICTIONS ON SHARE TRANSFER (eg Directors must give consent to the transfer of shares)

____

____

____

All private companies must restrict the right to transfer shares (e.g. shares must be first offered to existing shareholders).

A public company may only restrict the right to transfer shares which have not been fully paid up.

6. NON-CASH CONSIDERATION

Were any shares issued for non-cash consideration (that is, as a payment for goods, services, property, good will, shares in other companies etc.) based on a contract that existed before incorporation? **(ONLY ONE BOX MUST BE CHECKED)**

☐ Yes = Complete **Item 6A**

☐ No = Continue to **Item 7**

6A. PLEASE INDICATE THE NATURE AND VALUE OF THE NON-CASH CONSIDERATION BELOW

____

____

7. **MINIMUM NUMBER OF DIRECTORS** ☐

AND/OR

7A. **MAXIMUM NUMBER OF DIRECTORS** ☐

A private company must have at least one director, he/she cannot also be the company secretary. A public company must have a minimum of three (3) directors; two of them however should not be employed by the company or any of its affiliates.

8. **PARTICULARS OF DIRECTORS**

DIRECTOR 1 (Where the director is an individual the name must be represented as FIRST MIDDLE LAST)

FULL NAME			
FULL RESIDENTIAL ADDRESS or REGISTERED OFFICE ADDRESS	STREET/DISTRICT		
	TOWN	POST OFFICE	
	PARISH	COUNTRY	
OCCUPATION		**CONTACT**	

DIRECTOR 2 (Where the director is an individual the name must be represented as FIRST MIDDLE LAST)

FULL NAME			
FULL RESIDENTIAL ADDRESS or REGISTERED OFFICE ADDRESS	STREET/DISTRICT		
	TOWN	POST OFFICE	
	PARISH	COUNTRY	
OCCUPATION		**CONTACT**	

FOR OFFICIAL USE ONLY COMPANY #:

DIRECTOR 3 (Where the director is an individual the name must be represented as FIRST MIDDLE LAST)

FULL NAME			
FULL RESIDENTIAL ADDRESS or REGISTERED OFFICE ADDRESS	STREET/DISTRICT		
	TOWN	POST OFFICE	
	PARISH	COUNTRY	
OCCUPATION		CONTACT	

DIRECTOR 4 (Where the director is an individual the name must be represented as FIRST MIDDLE LAST)

FULL NAME			
FULL RESIDENTIAL ADDRESS or REGISTERED OFFICE ADDRESS	STREET/DISTRICT		
	TOWN	POST OFFICE	
	PARISH	COUNTRY	
OCCUPATION		CONTACT	

DIRECTOR 5 (Where the director is an individual the name must be represented as FIRST MIDDLE LAST)

FULL NAME			
FULL RESIDENTIAL ADDRESS or REGISTERED OFFICE ADDRESS	STREET/DISTRICT		
	TOWN	POST OFFICE	
	PARISH	COUNTRY	
OCCUPATION		CONTACT	

9. PARTICULARS OF COMPANY SECRETARY (Where the secretary is an individual the name must be represented as FIRST MIDDLE LAST)

FULL NAME			
FULL RESIDENTIAL ADDRESS or REGISTERED OFFICE ADDRESS	STREET/DISTRICT		
	TOWN	POST OFFICE	
	PARISH	COUNTRY	
OCCUPATION		CONTACT	

10. PROPOSED NUMBER OF MEMBERS AT THE TIME OF INCORPORATION

FOR OFFICIAL USE ONLY	COMPANY #:

11. PARTICULARS OF INDIVIDUAL SUBSCRIBERS (shareholders who are individuals)

SUBSCRIBER PARTICULARS	SUBSCRIBER 1	SUBSCRIBER 2	SUBSCRIBER 3	SUBSCRIBER 4
NAME				
ADDRESS				
OCCUPATION				
SHARES TAKEN UP	The total of the number of shares subscribed to by all subscribers may not exceed the authorized number of shares stated at item 4			
CLASS OF SHARES 1. ORDINARY 2. PREFERENCE OTHER 3. ______	AMOUNT OF SHARES 1. ______ 2. ______ 3. ______	AMOUNT OF SHARES 1. ______ 2. ______ 3. ______	AMOUNT OF SHARES 1. ______ 2. ______ 3. ______	AMOUNT OF SHARES 1. ______ 2. ______ 3. ______
SIGNATURE				
DATE				
WITNESS PARTICULARS	WITNESS FOR SUBSCRIBER 1	WITNESS FOR SUBSCRIBER 2	WITNESS FOR SUBSCRIBER 3	WITNESS FOR SUBSCRIBER 4
WITNESSED BY (NAME OF WITNESS)				
AT (LOCATION/ADDRESS)				
SIGNATURE				
DATE				
[illegible]	☐ While on Visit	☐ While on Visit	☐ While on Visit	☐ While on Visit

FOR OFFICIAL USE ONLY COMPANY #:

12. PARTICULARS OF COMPANY SUBSCRIBERS (shareholders who are companies)

COMPANY PARTICULARS	
COMPANY NAME	
COMPANY REGISTERED OFFICE ADDRESS (OTHER ADDRESS)	

SHARES TAKEN UP The total of the number of share(s) subscribed to by all subscribers may not exceed the authorized number of shares stated at item 4

CLASS OF SHARES		AMOUNT OF SHARES	
	1. ORDINARY SHARES		1.
	2. PREFERENCE SHARES Other		2.
	3. Specify		3.

SEAL

OFFICER PARTICULARS	OFFICER 1	OFFICER 2
OFFICER NAME		
OFFICE HELD IN COMPANY		
SIGNATURE		
DATE		
WITNESS PARTICULARS	**WITNESS FOR OFFICER 1**	**WITNESS FOR OFFICER 2**
BY (NAME OF WITNESS)		
AT (LOCATION/ADDRESS)		
SIGNATURE		
DATE		

If an officer and a witness are located in different countries, which one must be selected.

☐ While in Visit ☐ While on Visit

13. SUBSCRIBER(S) HOLD(S) SHARES ON BEHALF OF BENEFICIAL OWNER(S): ☐ No ☐ Yes, and schedule(s) detailing beneficial owners is/are attached

Beneficial owners are persons who enjoy, and have a right to the benefits of ownership of the shares, eg the right to dividends, without being registered on the company's books/records as the owner.

14. DECLARATION OF ACCURACY OF PRESENTED INFORMATION

NAME OF DECLARANT		SIGNATURE OF DECLARANT	
CAPACITY	☐ Director ☐ Secretary ☐ Authorized Official	DATE	

FOR OFFICIAL USE ONLY COMPANY #:

F1D

15. FILED BY
PARTICULARS OF INDIVIDUAL/COMPANY FILING THE FORM WITH THE COMPANIES OFFICE OF JAMAICA

NAME
COMPLETE ADDRESS
EMAIL ADDRESS
CONTACT NUMBER
FAX NUMBER

16. ADDITIONAL PARTICULARS OF DIRECTORS

NAME OF DIRECTOR	TAXPAYER REGISTRATION NUMBER	EMAIL
1.		
2.		
3.		
4.		
5.		

17. ADDITIONAL PARTICULARS OF COMPANY SECRETARY

NAME OF SECRETARY	TAXPAYER REGISTRATION NUMBER	EMAIL

FOR OFFICIAL USE ONLY	COMPANY #

FORM 1D – continuation page
PARTICULARS OF DIRECTORS

THE COMPANIES ACT

ARTICLES OF INCORPORATION: UNLIMITED COMPANY WITH SHARE CAPITAL

(Pursuant to section 8 of the Companies Act)

COMPLETE THIS FORM IN BLOCK CAPITALS ONLY WITHIN THE PRESCRIBED FIELDS. PUT "N/A" IN FIELDS THAT DO NOT APPLY.

5. PARTICULARS OF DIRECTORS

DIRECTOR # (Where the director is an individual the name must be represented as FIRST MIDDLE LAST)

FULL NAME			
FULL RESIDENTIAL ADDRESS or REGISTERED OFFICE ADDRESS	STREET/DISTRICT		
	TOWN	POST OFFICE	
	PARISH	COUNTRY	
OCCUPATION		CONTACT	

DIRECTOR #___ (Where the director is an individual the name must be represented as FIRST MIDDLE LAST)

FULL NAME			
FULL RESIDENTIAL ADDRESS or REGISTERED OFFICE ADDRESS	STREET/DISTRICT		
	TOWN	POST OFFICE	
	PARISH	COUNTRY	
OCCUPATION		CONTACT	

DIRECTOR #___ (Where the director is an individual the name must be represented as FIRST MIDDLE LAST)

FULL NAME			
FULL RESIDENTIAL ADDRESS or REGISTERED OFFICE ADDRESS	STREET/DISTRICT		
	TOWN	POST OFFICE	
	PARISH	COUNTRY	
OCCUPATION		CONTACT	

DIRECTOR # (Where the director is an individual the name must be represented as FIRST MIDDLE LAST)

FULL NAME			
FULL RESIDENTIAL ADDRESS or REGISTERED OFFICE ADDRESS	STREET/DISTRICT		
	TOWN	POST OFFICE	
	PARISH	COUNTRY	
OCCUPATION		CONTACT	

FOR OFFICIAL USE ONLY COMPANY #:

THE COMPANIES ACT

ARTICLES OF INCORPORATION: UNLIMITED COMPANY WITH SHARE CAPITAL

(Pursuant to section 8 of the Companies Act)

FORM 1D – continuation page

PARTICULARS OF INDIVIDUAL SUBSCRIBERS

11. PARTICULARS OF INDIVIDUAL SUBSCRIBERS (shareholders who are individuals)

SUBSCRIBER PARTICULARS	SUBSCRIBER 1	SUBSCRIBER 2	SUBSCRIBER 3	SUBSCRIBER 4
NAME				
ADDRESS				
OCCUPATION				
SHARES TAKEN UP	The total of the number of shares subscribed to by all subscribers may not exceed the **authorized number of shares** stated at **item 4**			
CLASS OF SHARES 1. ORDINARY ______ 2. PREFERENCE ______ OTHER 3. ______	AMOUNT OF SHARES 1. ______ 2. ______ 3. ______	AMOUNT OF SHARES 1. ______ 2. ______ 3. ______	AMOUNT OF SHARES 1. ______ 2. ______ 3. ______	AMOUNT OF SHARES 1. ______ 2. ______ 3. ______
SIGNATURE				
DATE				
WITNESS PARTICULARS	**WITNESS FOR SUBSCRIBER 1**	**WITNESS FOR SUBSCRIBER 2**	**WITNESS FOR SUBSCRIBER 3**	**WITNESS FOR SUBSCRIBER 4**
WITNESSED BY (NAME OF WITNESS)				
AT (LOCATION/ADDRESS)				
SIGNATURE				
DATE				
If a subscriber and a witness are located in different countries, "while on visit" must be selected	☐ While on Visit	☐ While on Visit	☐ While on Visit	☐ While on Visit

FOR OFFICIAL USE ONLY COMPANY #:

THE COMPANIES ACT
ARTICLES OF INCORPORATION: UNLIMITED COMPANY WITH SHARE CAPITAL
(Pursuant to section 3 of the Companies Act)

FORM 1D – continuation page
PARTICULARS OF COMPANY SUBSCRIBERS

12. PARTICULARS OF COMPANY SUBSCRIBERS (shareholders who are companies)

COMPANY PARTICULARS	
COMPANY NAME	
COMPANY REGISTERED OFFICE ADDRESS /OTHER ADDRESS	

SHARES TAKEN UP The total of the number of shares subscribed to by all subscribers may not exceed the **authorized number of shares** stated at **item** Error! Reference source not found.

CLASS OF SHARES		AMOUNT OF SHARES	
	1. ORDINARY SHARES		1.
	2. PREFERENCE SHARES OTHER		2.
	3. Specify		3.

SEAL

OFFICER PARTICULARS	OFFICER 1	OFFICER 2
OFFICER NAME		
OFFICE HELD IN COMPANY		
SIGNATURE		
DATE		

WITNESSS PARTICULARS	WITNESS FOR OFFICER 1	WITNESS FOR OFFICER 2
BY (NAME OF WITNESS)		
AT (LOCATION/ADDRESS)		
SIGNATURE		
DATE		
If an officer and a witness are located in different countries 'while on visit' must be selected	☐ While on Visit	☐ While on Visit

FOR OFFICIAL USE ONLY COMPANY #:

THE COMPANIES ACT

ARTICLES OF INCORPORATION: UNLIMITED COMPANY WITH SHARE CAPITAL

(Pursuant to section 8 of the Companies Act)

FORM 1D – SCHEDULE

PARTICULARS OF BENEFICIAL OWNERS

13. PARTICULARS OF BENEFICIAL OWNERS

BENEFICIAL OWNER PARTICULARS	BENEFICIAL OWNER ___	BENEFICIAL OWNER ___	BENEFICIAL OWNER ___	BENEFICIAL OWNER ___
NAME				
ADDRESS				
NATIONALITY				
SHARES HELD ON BEHALF OF BENEFICIARY	[illegible]			
CLASS OF SHARES: 1. ORDINARY ___ 2. PREFERENCE ___ OTHER 3. ___	AMOUNT OF SHARES: 1. ___ 2. ___ 3. ___	AMOUNT OF SHARES: 1. ___ 2. ___ 3. ___	AMOUNT OF SHARES: 1. ___ 2. ___ 3. ___	AMOUNT OF SHARES: 1. ___ 2. ___ 3. ___

SUBSCRIBER PARTICULARS	SUBSCRIBER HOLDING SHARES ON BEHALF OF BENEFICIARY ABOVE	SUBSCRIBER HOLDING SHARES ON BEHALF OF BENEFICIARY ABOVE	SUBSCRIBER HOLDING SHARES ON BEHALF OF BENEFICIARY ABOVE	SUBSCRIBER HOLDING SHARES ON BEHALF OF BENEFICIARY ABOVE
NAME				

FOR OFFICIAL USE ONLY COMPANY #:

PRINTED BY JAMAICA PRINTING SERVICES (1992) LTD., (GOVERNMENT PRINTERS), DUKE STREET, KINGSTON,

www.ingramcontent.com/pod-product-compliance
Ingram Content Group UK Ltd.
Pitfield, Milton Keynes, MK11 3LW, UK
UKHW022229230426
12048UKWH00016BA/1152